Content Analysis
Second Edition

Second Edition

Content Analysis
An Introduction to Its Methodology

Klaus Krippendorff
University of Pennsylvania

WITHDRAW

SAGE Publications
International Educational and Professional Publisher
Thousand Oaks ■ London ■ New Delhi

For information:

 Sage Publications, Inc.
2455 Teller Road
Thousand Oaks, California 91320
E-mail: order@sagepub.com

Sage Publications Ltd.
6 Bonhill Street
London EC2A 4PU
United Kingdom

Sage Publications India Pvt. Ltd.
B-42, Panchsheel Enclave
Post Box 4109
New Delhi 110 017 India

Printed in the United States of America

Library of Congress Cataloging-in-Publication Data
Krippendorff, Klaus.
Content analysis : an introduction to its methodology / Klaus Krippendorff.— 2nd ed.
    p. cm.
Includes bibliographical references and index.
ISBN 0-7619-1544-3 — ISBN 0-7619-1545-1 (pbk.)
    1. Content analysis (Communication) I. Title.
P93.K74 2004
401'.41—dc21

                                    2003014200

Printed on acid-free paper.

05   06   07   08   09   10   9   8   7   6   5   4   3   2

Acquiring Editor:	Margaret H. Seawell
Editorial Assistant:	Jill Meyers
Production Editor:	Claudia A. Hoffman
Copy Editor:	Judy Selhorst
Typesetter:	C&M Digitals (P) Ltd.
Indexer:	Molly Hall
Cover Design:	Concept by Klaus Krippendorff
Execution by:	Michelle Lee Kenny

Contents

Preface to the Second Edition   xiii

Acknowledgments   xv

Introduction   xvii

Part I. Conceptualizing Content Analysis

1. **History**   3

   1.1   Some Precursors   3

   1.2   Quantitative Newspaper Analysis   5

   1.3   Early Content Analysis   6

   1.4   Propaganda Analysis   8

   1.5   Content Analysis Generalized   11

   1.6   Computer Text Analysis   12

   1.7   Qualitative Approaches   15

2. **Conceptual Foundation**   18

   2.1   Definition   18

   2.2   Epistemological Elaborations   21

   2.3   Examples   26

   2.4   Framework   29

     2.4.1   Texts   30

     2.4.2   Research Questions   31

     2.4.3   Context   33

     2.4.4   Analytical Constructs   34

     2.4.5   Inferences   36

     2.4.6   Validating Evidence   39

   2.5   Contrasts and Comparisons   40

3.   Uses and Inferences   **44**

   3.1   Traditional Overviews   44

   3.2   Extrapolations   47

      3.2.1 Trends   49

      3.2.2 Patterns   50

      3.2.3 Differences   51

   3.3   Standards   54

      3.3.1 Identifications   54

      3.3.2 Evaluations   55

      3.3.3 Judgments   57

   3.4   Indices and Symptoms   58

   3.5   Linguistic Re-Presentations   62

   3.6   Conversations   66

   3.7   Institutional Processes   68

   3.8   Areas of Likely Success   74

Part II. Components of Content Analysis

4.   The Logic of Content Analysis Designs   **81**

   4.1   Content Analysis Designs   81

      4.1.1 Components   83

      4.1.2 Quantitative and Qualitative
           Content Analysis   87

   4.2   Designs Preparatory to Content Analysis   89

      4.2.1 Operationalizing Knowledge   90

      4.2.2 Testing Analytical Constructs as Hypotheses   91

      4.2.3 Developing a Discriminant Function   91

   4.3   Designs Exceeding Content Analysis   93

      4.3.1 Comparing Similar Phenomena
           Inferred From Different Bodies of Texts   93

      4.3.2 Testing Relationships Among Phenomena
           Inferred From One Body of Texts   94

      4.3.3 Testing Hypotheses Concerning How
           Content Analysis Results Relate to
           Other Variables   95

5. **Unitizing** 或单位   **97**

   5.1   Units   97

   5.2   Types of Units   98

      5.2.1 Sampling Units   98

      5.2.2 Recording/Coding Units   99

      5.2.3 Context Units   101

   5.3   Ways of Defining Units   103

      5.3.1 Physical Distinctions   103

      5.3.2 Syntactical Distinctions   104

      5.3.3 Categorial Distinctions   105

      5.3.4 Propositional Distinctions   106

      5.3.5 Thematic Distinctions   107

   5.4   Productivity, Efficiency, and Reliability   109

6. **Sampling**   **111**

   6.1   Sampling in Theory   111

   6.2   Sampling Techniques Applicable to Texts   113

      6.2.1 Random Sampling   114

      6.2.2 Systematic Sampling   115

      6.2.3 Stratified Sampling   115

      6.2.4 Varying Probability Sampling   116

      6.2.5 Cluster Sampling   116

      6.2.6 Snowball Sampling   117

      6.2.7 Relevance Sampling   118

      6.2.8 Census   120

      6.2.9 Convenience Sampling   120

   6.3   Sample Size   121

      6.3.1 Statistical Sampling Theory   121

      6.3.2 Sampling Experiments   122

      6.3.3 The Split-Half Technique   124

7. **Recording/Coding**   **125**

   7.1   The Function of Recording and Coding   125

	7.2	Coder Qualifications	127
		7.2.1 Cognitive Abilities	127
		7.2.2 Background	128
		7.2.3 Frequency	128
	7.3	Coder Training	129
	7.4	Approaches to Defining the Semantics of Data	132
		7.4.1 Verbal Designations	132
		7.4.2 Extensional Lists	133
		7.4.3 Decision Schemes	135
		7.4.4 Magnitudes and Scales	136
		7.4.5 Simulation of Hypothesis Testing	137
		7.4.6 Simulation of Interviewing	139
		7.4.7 Constructs for Closure	141
	7.5	Records	143
		7.5.1 Administrative Information	144
		7.5.2 Information on the Organization of Records	145
		7.5.3 Substantive Information About the Phenomena of Interest	146

8. Data Languages — **150**

	8.1	The Place of Data Languages in Analysis	150
	8.2	Definitions	153
	8.3	Variables	155
	8.4	Nominal Variables	161
	8.5	Orderings	161
		8.5.1 Chains	162
		8.5.2 Recursions	163
		8.5.3 Cubes	163
		8.5.4 Trees	164
	8.6	Metrics	165
		8.6.1 Ordinal Metrics	166
		8.6.2 Interval Metrics	168
		8.6.3 Ratio Metrics	169
	8.7	Mathematical Operations	169

9.   Analytical Constructs   **171**

   9.1   The Role of Analytical Constructs   171

   9.2   Sources of Certainty   173

       9.2.1   Previous Successes and Failures   173

       9.2.2   Expert Knowledge and Experience   175

       9.2.3   Established Theories   176

       9.2.4   Embodied Practices   179

   9.3   Types of Constructs   179

       9.3.1   Extrapolations   180

       9.3.2   Applications of Standards   180

       9.3.3   Indices and Symptoms   180

       9.3.4   Re-Presentations   182

       9.3.5   Conversations/Interactions   183

       9.3.6   Institutional Processes   183

   9.4   Sources of Uncertainty   185

       9.4.1   Variance of the Target   185

       9.4.2   Confidence Levels   186

       9.4.3   Appropriateness of the Construct   186

Part III. Analytical Paths and Evaluative Techniques

10.   Analytical/Representational Techniques   **191**

   10.1   Tabulations   192

   10.2   Cross-Tabulations, Associations, and Correlations   194

   10.3   Multivariate Techniques   197

   10.4   Factor Analysis and Multidimensional Scaling   200

   10.5   Images, Portrayals, Semantic Nodes, and Profiles   202

   10.6   Contingencies and Contingency Analysis   205

   10.7   Clustering   208

11.   Reliability   **211**

   11.1   Why Reliability?   211

   11.2   Reliability Designs   214

	11.2.1 Types of Reliability	214
	11.2.2 Conditions for Generating Reliability Data	216
	11.2.3 Reliability Data	219
11.3	α-Agreement for Coding	221
	11.3.1 Two Observers, Binary Data	223
	11.3.2 Two Observers, Many Nominal Categories	227
	11.3.3 Many Observers, Many Nominal Categories, Missing Values	230
	11.3.4 Data With Different Metrics	232
11.4	Statistical Properties of α	236
	11.4.1 Insufficient Variation	236
	11.4.2 Statistical Significance	237
	11.4.3 Sampling Considerations	238
	11.4.4 Standards for Data Reliability	241
11.5	Other Coefficients and Correspondences	244
11.6	α-Agreement for Unitizing	251
12.	**Computer Aids**	**257**
12.1	What Computers Do	257
12.2	How Computers Can Aid Content Analyses	258
12.3	Accounts of Character Strings	262
12.4	Text Searches	272
12.5	Computational Content Analyses	281
	12.5.1 Coding/Dictionary Approaches	283
	12.5.2 Statistical Association Approaches	289
	12.5.3 Semantic Network Approaches	292
	12.5.4 Memetic Approaches	298
12.6	Interactive-Hermeneutic Explorations	303
12.7	Frontiers	307
	12.7.1 Intelligent Browsers	307
	12.7.2 Common Platforms	308
	12.7.3 Computational Theories of Meaning	309

12.7.4 Utilization of Intertextualities 309

12.7.5 Natural Interfaces 310

13. Validity **313**

13.1 Validity Defined 313

13.2 A Typology for Validating Evidence 318

13.2.1 Sampling Validity 321

13.2.2 Semantic Validity 323

13.2.3 Structural Validity 330

13.2.4 Functional Validity 332

13.2.5 Correlative Validity 333

13.2.6 Predictive Validity 336

14. A Practical Guide **339**

14.1 Designing an Analysis 340

14.1.1 Text-Driven Analyses 341

14.1.2 Problem-Driven Analyses 342

14.1.3 Method-Driven Analyses 355

14.2 Writing a Research Proposal 357

14.2.1 Rhetorical Function 358

14.2.2 Contractual Function 359

14.2.3 Outline for a Research Proposal 359

14.3 Applying the Research Design 361

14.4 Narrating the Results 362

14.4.1 Outline for a Research Report 363

References **365**
Index **391**
About the Author **413**

Preface to the Second Edition

Content analysis is potentially one of the most important research techniques in the social sciences. The content analyst views data as representations not of physical events but of texts, images, and expressions that are created to be seen, read, interpreted, and acted on for their meanings, and must therefore be analyzed with such uses in mind. Analyzing texts in the contexts of their uses distinguishes content analysis from other methods of inquiry.

Methods in the natural sciences are not concerned with meanings, contents, intentions, and references. These scientists hardly reflect on their own conceptions of nature, excluding their conceptions from their object of study by dismissing them as subjective in contrast to what can be determined through detached observation and objective measurement. Where social researchers adopt natural scientific methods of inquiry, the epistemology that is inscribed in such methods prevents them from addressing what matters most in everyday social life: human communication, how people coordinate their lives, the commitments they make to each other and to the conceptions of society they aspire to, what they know, and why they act. Certainly, content analysis is not the only research method that takes meanings seriously, but it is a method that is both powerful and unobtrusive. It makes sense of what is mediated between people—textual matter, symbols, messages, information, mass-media content, and technology-supported social interactions—without perturbing or affecting those who handle that textual matter.

In the first edition of *Content Analysis,* published in 1980, I suggested that content analysis was at a crossroads. Content analysts at that time had a choice: They could continue their shallow counting game, motivated by a journalistic fascination with numbers and a narrow conception of science in which quantitative measurement provides the only evidence that counts (Lasswell, 1949/1965b), or they could refocus content analysis methods on social phenomena that are both generated by and constituted in texts and images and, hence, need to be understood through their written and pictorial constituents. Although the logic and methods that I presented in the first edition of *Content Analysis* have survived their challenges, the textual fabric of contemporary society has undergone radical transformations, due in no small part to the ongoing information revolution. The increasingly widespread availability of electronic, and hence computer-readable, texts concerning virtually everything that matters to society and its members has moved content analysis, particularly computer-aided text analysis, into the center of how society examines itself.

In the 1980s, content analysis was a research method that had entered the psychological and social sciences, but was used mainly in journalism and communication research. At that time, the amount of human effort required to collect, transcribe, and code textual data made content analysis a time-consuming and labor-intensive effort. Today, content analysis has become an efficient alternative to public opinion research, a method of tracking markets, political leanings, and emerging ideas; it is used as a way to settle legal disputes and as an approach to the exploration of individual human minds—not to dwell on the many improvements that content analysts have made in traditional content analytic inquiries of the mass media. Despite remarkable progress, content analysts can hardly claim to have met the challenges of this new era. The imagined analytical potential is far ahead of what can be done today, fueling the work of many developers of new analytic tools.

Although the outline of this new edition remains essentially unchanged from that of the first, this volume clarifies numerous methodological issues in content analysis and responds to the technique's latest challenges. Accordingly, I have substantially rewritten all chapters, addressing developments that have taken place since 1980, especially Chapter 12, on computer-aided text analysis, and Chapter 14, a practical guide, which incorporates my experiences in teaching and consulting on academic and commercial research projects. I have also substantially revised my earlier discussions of the epistemology, logic, and methods of content analysis.

I thank my students at the University of Pennsylvania's Annenberg School for Communication for their open minds and my colleagues for presenting me with the challenging problems of their content analyses. I would also like to thank numerous readers of the first edition—both students and practicing content analysts—for sharing their comments and criticisms, and Sage Publications for giving me more space for this edition.

The first edition of *Content Analysis* has been translated into Italian, Japanese, Spanish, and Hungarian, and during the 23 years since its publication, it has reached an enormous audience. It has been widely adopted as a text in social science, humanities, and business curricula. It has served researchers as a guide to the design and execution of large and small content analyses, and it has provided a standard for justifying as well as critically evaluating content analysis findings. When I travel to national and international conferences, I continue to be amazed and pleased to meet researchers from all over the world who tell me how studying this text has helped them in their current inquiries. This new edition is written for the same wide audience of practicing researchers, social scientists, and students.

—Klaus Krippendorff
Gregory Bateson Term Professor for Cybernetics, Language, and Culture
The Annenberg School for Communication
University of Pennsylvania

Acknowledgments

This book is dedicated to scholars—beginning and established—who, while critical of any methodology as they should be, nevertheless are willing to add another perspective to their reading of especially voluminous textual matter.

I would like to thank my students at the University of Pennsylvania's Annenberg School for Communication for teaching me over the years what is important in a textbook on content analysis and for offering invaluable feedback on a draft of this new edition. I am grateful also for thoughtful reviews of the manuscript by William Benoit, Wayne Danielson, Gavan Duffy, William Evans, Kenneth Janda, and Mark West. In particular, I thank Kenneth Janda for his most thorough critique and William Benoit for not only making detailed recommendations but also giving the manuscript a test run in his course.

Introduction

The term *content analysis* is about 60 years old. *Webster's Dictionary of the English Language* included the term in its 1961 edition, defining it as "analysis of the manifest and latent content of a body of communicated material (as a book or film) through classification, tabulation, and evaluation of its key symbols and themes in order to ascertain its meaning and probable effect." The intellectual roots of content analysis, however, can be traced far back in human history, to the beginning of the conscious use of symbols and voice, especially writing. This conscious use, which replaced the magical use of language, has been shaped by the ancient disciplines of philosophy, rhetoric, and cryptography. It has also spawned religious inquisitions and political censorship on the part of ruling establishments. Today, symbolic phenomena are institutionalized in art, literature, education, and the mass media, including the Internet. Theoretical and analytical concerns are found in such academic disciplines as anthropology, linguistics, social psychology, sociology of knowledge, and the comparatively younger field of communication studies. Many practical pursuits have grown from these fields: psychotherapy, advertising, politics, the arts, and so on. Virtually all disciplines within the whole spectrum of the humanities and the social sciences, including those that seek to improve the political and social conditions of life, are concerned with the functions and effects of symbols, meanings, and messages. In recent years, the emergence of the information society has moved the minutiae of communication—texts, contexts, images, interfaces, and, above all, information—into the very center of researchers' attempts at self-understanding.

However ancient the roots of analyzing symbolic and textual matter might be, today's content analysis is significantly different, in aim and in method, from that of the past. Contemporary content analysis has three distinguishing characteristics.

First, content analysis is an *empirically grounded method,* exploratory in process, and predictive or inferential in intent. Many of our current concepts relating to language are of Greek origin; for example, the words *sign, significance, symbol,* and *logic* all have Greek roots. However, the ancient Greeks' interest in language was largely prescriptive and classificatory, not empirical. Aristotelian logic set the standards for clear expression, and much of rhetorical theory was directed toward a normative conception of persuasive argumentation. Science that explores rather than declares is a relatively recent accomplishment. Only a century ago, George Boole and his contemporaries believed that the brain works according to (Boolean) logic and that human conduct is entirely rational. However, computers built on this logic turned out to be rather disappointing thinking machines. Empirical research in psychology is replacing Aristotelian categories in favor of a "psycho-logic." And we no longer measure human communication against the ideal of transmitting information. Instead, we inquire into what happens to the relationships between people who converse with one another.

With new conceptualizations and an empirical orientation, contemporary content analysts join other researchers in seeking valid knowledge or practical support for actions and critique. However, unlike researchers who employ other empirical techniques, content analysts examine data, printed matter, images, or sounds—texts—in order to understand what they mean to people, what they enable or prevent, and what the information conveyed by them does. These are questions for which natural scientists have no answers and for which their methods are generally insensitive.

Second, contemporary content analysis *transcends traditional notions of symbols, contents, and intents.* This may be seen in the evolution of the concept of communication, in how the development of media technologies has shaped our attention to communication, and in the role of culture in assigning significance to what is being analyzed. I would argue that in recent years our awareness of communication has undergone four conceptual revolutions, as described below, and probably is in the midst of a fifth:

- The idea of *messages:* the early awareness not only that verbal discourse is movable when written, but that writing has predictable effects. This awareness emerged in ancient Greece when messengers were used as the carriers of significance, history became documented, laws of the land were laid down in writing, and written instructions built organizational structures, directed events, and influenced (and possibly deceived) their receivers or the public. The concept of a message was a precursor of the rhetorical exploration of language. Tropes, syllogisms, and meanings came to be thought of as inherent qualities of speeches, letters, or documents. But a message is the metaphorical container of all these, a "container of content," a vehicle for shipping meanings from one place to another—for example, when we now leave a message for someone on an answering machine or say that a message was meaningful (full of meanings) or meaningless (void of meanings).

- The idea of *channels:* the awareness of the constraints that every medium imposes on human communication. This awareness came with the increased reliance on different media of communication and served to explain their limitations: The alphabet limits what one can say in writing; the telephone confines communication to sound; and a television station can air no more than what is transmittable without interference from other stations, appealing to large audiences, and deemed profitable by its sponsors. The channel metaphor conjures images of canals and pipes with restricted capacities for shipping messages (with their contents) of certain forms and volumes.

■ The idea of *communication:* the awareness of the relational space between senders and receivers, of the processes through which interpersonal relations are negotiated, social structures are constituted, and members of large populations come to know about each other. This awareness developed as an offshoot of the growth in mass media. By producing and disseminating identical messages—news and entertainment—to everyone, the mass media promised to be an agent of sharing, of building community relationships, of democratization, ideally, worldwide. Modeling themselves on the idea of mass production, the mass media also made us aware of where this one-way model failed: in interpersonal conversation, point-to-point telephone communication, public debate, and dialogue. In U.S. culture, mass-media technology has become synonymous with progress, and communication is understood as the cure for most social problems—for example, we often blame lack of communication or miscommunication when interpersonal as well as national conflicts arise.

■ The idea of *systems:* the awareness of global, dynamic, and technologically supported interdependencies. This idea emerged with the growth of communication networks—telephone nets, wire services, mass-media systems, and most recently the Internet—transforming commerce, politics, and interpersonal relationships, creating networks whose properties have so far defied attempts to theorize them adequately. Unlike the one-way mass media, systems are marked by the interactivity and simultaneity of parallel communication on a massive scale and with the potential of nearly universal participation.

■ The idea of *computation:* the awareness of the algorithmic nature of certain routine cognitive and social processes and their implementation in increasingly powerful computers. The processing of digital data in place of cognitive and social practices, along with the ability to reproduce these data in visual and textual forms for reading, rearticulating, and disseminating by and to ideally everyone, is encouraging an entirely new literacy that undercuts traditional organizational structures, including national boundaries. The fluidity and enormous complexity that computation has introduced into almost all spheres of life amplify the possibilities for scientific exploration as well as present unprecedented challenges for collective understanding.

This rather sketchy history of communication suggests that researchers who are concerned with texts can no longer focus only on symbols or representations, nor can they limit themselves to questions about "who says what, through which channels, to whom, and with which effects" (Lasswell, 1960). The popular and simplistic notion of "content" has outlived its explanatory capabilities as well: *content,* the *what* of a communication, an entity that authors think they *enter* into messages and *ship* to remote receivers, who *remove* it for *what it is* and henceforth *share it* among others. This bizarre notion leads to authors as authorities of what they put into messages and to the conception of *content analysts* as experts who provide objective accounts of what messages were *intended to convey* or *actually contain.*

The virtuality of electronic media encourages short-lived access to messages that, without knowledge of their human authors, calls for a new technological basis for trust. It coordinates the lives of many people, overcoming old distinctions among channels of communication, obviating physical distances, and pushing capacities of the human participants to their limits. This erodes the validity of traditional communication theories, all the while enabling computer systems to thrive in this new environment. It is these computer systems that simulate and coordinate parts of the very social processes that researchers wish to understand. This is a radically changing world in which texts play distinctly new roles. Newspaper accounts, public opinion polls, corporate reports, files in government agencies, credit information, bank transactions, and, above all, huge textual data archives—all are now linked into networks that can be analyzed from numerous positions. In effect, the social systems that we conceived of as explaining society are now holographically retreating into our computers. This development calls for a redefinition of content analysis, one that aligns content—the target of the research—with how contemporary society operates and understands itself through its texts.

With the container metaphor rendered useless, perhaps the term *content analysis* no longer fits the realities of contemporary society. For better or for worse, I continue to use the term in this book, but I also plead with readers to oppose unflinchingly the naive and misleading entailments of the pervasive container metaphor.

Third, *contemporary content analysis has been forced to develop a methodology of its own,* one that enables researchers to plan, execute, communicate, reproduce, and critically evaluate their analyses whatever the particular results. Content analysts have had to develop such a methodology for three reasons:

- *Content analysts now face larger contexts.* The shift in interest from small collections of printed messages to systems and then to electronic texts and images circulating in the environment of content analysts is tied less to the nature of textual data than to the increasingly complex worlds that produce and are sustained by these data. This shift calls for theories and conceptions that earlier content analysts did not need. Although content analysts have frequently lamented the lack of general theories that could justify their work, progress in implementing more specific or micro-level theories is encouraging. This is especially true where content analysis has migrated through disciplines that were not previously concerned with textual data, such as the cognitive sciences and artificial intelligence.

- *Greater numbers of researchers need to collaborate in the pursuit of large-scale content analyses.* This observation is a correlate of the growing sample sizes of relevant texts, the analysis of which easily exceeds what individual analysts can handle. It implies that content analysts must work together, in parallel, and as research teams. Teamwork, however, needs to be organized reliably. Both the social problem of coordinating researchers and the methodological problem of assuring replicability tend to be solved through the adoption of a language whose vocabulary enables researchers to clarify the analytical procedures they use, negotiate the individual responsibilities of the participants, assure agreement on the analytical categories, and evaluate the performance of team members.

■ *The large volumes of electronically available data call for qualitatively different research techniques,* for computer aids. Such aids convert large bodies of electronic text into representations if not answers to research questions that content analysts need to understand. However, exactly what sophisticated text analysis software does—aside from promising to carry out the more labor-intensive clerical parts of processing textual data—is often difficult to retrace and inaccessible to the average content analyst. These computer aids participate in content analysis much as human analysts do. They become part of its methodology, with transparency being a major issue.

To be clear, *methodology* is not a value in itself. The purpose of methodology is to enable researchers to plan and examine critically the logic, composition, and protocols of research methods; to evaluate the performance of individual techniques; and to estimate the likelihood of particular research designs to contribute to knowledge. Every researcher must become proficient in defining the terms of an analysis and justifying the analytical steps taken to a skeptical friend or questioning colleague. Methodology provides a language for talking about the process of research, not about subject matter. In the history of scientific pursuits, the development of methodology has always been a major accomplishment. For example, for thousands of years humans preserved history by retelling or chanting stories, since the *Iliad* in writing, before the historian Leopold von Ranke, only a century ago, gave the "document" the methodological status it now has in the academic study of history. Similarly, scholars practiced "content analysis" well before Berelson and Lazarsfeld (1948) undertook the first codification of this method. Although many observers have argued that each content analysis is unique, possibly focusing largely on its subject matter, I would argue that all content analyses share a procedural logic and need to be justified through the use of socially acceptable criteria. These commonalities form the substance of this book.

I disagree with the frequent contention that content analysis is "nothing more than what everyone does when reading a newspaper, except on a larger scale." Content analysis may have been that way, in its early, journalistic stage, and its methodology does not rule out such readings, but this narrow definition is no longer sufficient today. As newspaper readers, we are perfectly justified in applying our individual worldviews to texts and enacting our interest in what those texts mean to us; in fact, we cannot do otherwise. But as content analysis researchers, we must do our best to explicate what we are doing and describe how we derive our judgments, so that others—especially our critics—can replicate our results.

This book, then, introduces readers to ways of analyzing meaningful matter, texts, images, and voices—that is, data whose physical manifestations are secondary to what they mean to particular populations of people. The chapters are grouped into three main parts. Part I, "Conceptualizing Content Analysis," begins with a brief chapter on the history of content analysis. In Chapter 2, I develop a definition of content analysis that distinguishes this technique from other methods of inquiry, and in Chapter 3, I present a discussion of some of the ways in which content analysis has been applied. The chapters in Part II, "Components of Content Analysis," outline the procedures used in content analyses, beginning with their procedural logic and moving naturally from unitizing to sampling, recording/coding, data languages, and analytical constructs. The chapters in Part III, "Analytical Paths and Evaluative Techniques," trace several paths through content analysis protocols. In this part of the book, I discuss analytical constructs that enable researchers to draw inferences from data, the use of computers and computational techniques, and the two principal criteria used in evaluating content analyses: reliability and validity. In the final chapter, I provide a practical guide that summarizes the foregoing discussion from a practitioner's perspective.

Readers who have never done a content analysis may want to begin by reading Chapter 1, on the history of content analysis, and Chapter 3, on the uses of this technique, to get a sense for whether or not it suits their research interests. If it does, they should familiarize themselves with the conceptual foundations of content analysis by reading Chapter 2. Beginners in content analysis are advised to start with a small pilot project, to get a feel for what is involved in conducting a larger study. Methodology without some practice is empty. The guidelines in Chapter 14, although written as a summary, could also serve as a start. In this chapter, readers will find many helpful references to pertinent chapters in this volume, which may answer emerging questions and place these answers within the context of larger methodological issues. Beginning researchers will soon realize that analyzing text is not a mechanical task, and neither is designing a content analysis. Both undertakings require creativity and competence.

Readers who have had some experience with coding will acquire a larger perspective on what they had been doing. As the table of contents suggests, coding is only a small part of content analysis—despite popular misconceptions. In fact, only Chapter 7 is devoted to issues of coding or recording, something researchers need do only when their data or texts are unwieldy. By coding/recording textual matter, one learns to appreciate both the conceptual problems involved in imposing analytical categories on ordinary readings of text and the ways in which competent researchers have managed to solve such problems. Designing a content analysis is something different, however. I recommend that readers who have had experience with coding expand on that experience by examining the chapters offered here about all the other components of content analysis, adding these to their conceptual frameworks. Such readers might well look into Chapter 12, on computer aids, to gain an alternative perspective on coding.

Readers who have already undertaken content analyses or similar text-based research will discover in this book alternative paths for such inquiries and a vocabulary that they can use in deliberating about what is involved in analyzing texts—not as observations of naturalistic phenomena, but as data whose significance stems from the meanings that others bring to their readings. Those who think they know what content analysis is are advised to start with Chapter 2, on the conceptual foundations of content analysis. This chapter discusses the ways that researchers talk about content and exposes readers to the larger perspective they will need in order to conceive a content analysis or critically evaluate the content analyses of others. As a condition for publication, scholarly journals increasingly demand some demonstration of why a content analysis should be taken seriously. In the past, content analysts relied heavily on conceptions of content as "contained" in messages, as discussed above, or "inherent" to texts. This settled the thorny issue of multiple text interpretations by fiat and consequently disabled explicitness about the researchers' procedures. Several research traditions—such as interpretive research, discourse analysis, literary scholarship, and rhetoric—tend to be plagued by similar conceptions. Researchers from these traditions would greatly benefit from explicating their approaches, checking their results against the work of others, and evaluating the social consequences of their findings outside their own schools of thought—as I am suggesting.

For experts in content analysis, this book raises several epistemological questions that practitioners rarely ask, transforms them into methodological ones, and provides new solutions to practical problems.

Readers who must make decisions concerning whether or not to trust the findings of content analyses and other text-based research—for instance, judges in courts of law, practitioners in the fields of public relations and advertising, and reviewers of research submitted for funding or publication in scientific journals—will find the vocabulary of this book useful as they need to weigh the quality of findings and make informed recommendations for improvements. Such readers will find the discussions in Chapters 2, 11, and 13 (on conceptual foundations, reliability, and validity, respectively) especially applicable to their evaluative endeavors.

While this book may serve as a handbook for various practitioners, it grew out of my experiences in teaching courses and seminars in content analysis, and I conceive of it foremost as a textbook for advanced undergraduate and beginning graduate students. Teachers and their students may not want to work through all the chapters in their numerical order; for instance, those intending to use computers will find Chapter 12 more important than Chapter 7, on recording/coding, and may omit Chapter 11, on reliability issues. Students with specific projects in mind may pass over sections that may not be useful to their projects. However, readers should not rule out chapters as irrelevant before knowing the possibilities they offer.

Finally, for me, the book will have achieved its purpose if it helps to make the newly acquired wealth of textual data accessible to systematic analysis, if it improves the social significance of research in the humanities and the social sciences, and if it furthers the development of methods of inquiry into the realities that human communication constructs.

Part I

Conceptualizing Content Analysis

CHAPTER 1

History

Empirical inquiries into the meanings of communications date back to theological studies in the late 1600s, when the Church found the printing of nonreligious materials to be a threat to its authority. Such inquiries have since mushroomed, moving into numerous areas and becoming the backbone of communication research. This chapter discusses several stages in the history of content analysis: quantitative studies of the press; propaganda analysis during World War II; social scientific uses of the technique in studies of political symbols, historical documents, anthropological data, and psychotherapeutic exchanges; computer text analysis and the new media; and qualitative challenges to content analysis.

SOME PRECURSORS   1.1

Content analysis entails a systematic reading of a body of texts, images, and symbolic matter, not necessary from an author's or user's perspective. Although the term *content analysis* did not appear in English until 1941 (Waples & Berelson, 1941, p. 2; cited in Berelson & Lazarsfeld, 1948), the systematic analysis of text can be traced back to inquisitorial pursuits by the Church in the 17th century. Religions have always been captivated by the written word, so it is not surprising that the first known dissertations about newspapers were defended in 1690, 1695, and 1699 by individuals pursuing academic degrees in theology. After the advent of the printing press, the Church became worried about the spread of printed matter of a nonreligious nature, and so it dealt with newspaper content in moralizing terms (Groth, 1948, p. 26). Surprisingly, in spite of the rhetorical tradition of ancient Greece, which was normative and oral in orientation, the 17th century contributed very little to the methodology of content analysis.

Probably the first well-documented quantitative analyses of printed matter occurred in 18th-century Sweden. According to Dovring's (1954–1955) account, these analyses were undertaken as the result of the publication of the *Songs of Zion,* a collection of 90 hymns of unknown authorship. The collection had passed the Royal Swedish censor, but soon after its publication it was blamed for undermining the orthodox clergy of the Swedish state church. When the collection became popular, it was said to be "contagious" and was accused of aiding a dissenting group. Outstanding in this case is the fact that literary scholars of good reputation participated in the controversy, which crystallized around the question of whether the songs harbored dangerous ideas and, if so, how. Scholars on one side made a list of the religious symbols in the songs and became alarmed. Those on the other side, however, found the very same symbols in established songbooks and so discounted the claimed difference. Then some scholars noted that the symbols in the songs occurred in different contexts and had acquired meanings that were different from those taught in the official church. A debate arose about whether the meanings should be interpreted literally or metaphorically. The interpretations came to be compared with the results of a German study of the outlawed Moravian Brethren, a religious sect whose members later emigrated to the United States. This process—of revising a method in response to criticism—continued until it became clear to both sides in the debate how the symbols in the *Songs of Zion* differed from the symbols used in the official songbooks and how this (in the end political) phenomenon could be explained. The controversy generated many ideas that are now part of content analysis and stimulated debates about methodology that continue today.

In 1903, Eugen Löbl published in German an elaborate classification scheme for analyzing the "inner structure of content" according to the social functions that newspapers perform. His book, which became well-known in journalistic circles, contributed to the idea of *Publizistik,* or newspaper science, and foreshadowed functionalism, but it did not stimulate empirical investigations.

At the first meeting of the German Sociological Society in 1910, Max Weber (1911) proposed a large-scale content analysis of the press, but for a variety of reasons the research never got off the ground. During the same period, Andrei Markov (1913), who was working on a theory of chains of symbols, published a statistical analysis of a sample of Pushkin's novel in verse, *Eugene Onegin.* These inquiries were discovered only recently or influenced the content analysis literature only indirectly. For example, Weber is celebrated as one of the great sociologists, but his advocacy of the use of content analysis as a method for understanding the mass media is relatively unknown. And Markov's probability theories entered the content analysis literature only through Shannon's mathematical theory of communication (see Shannon & Weaver, 1949), which influenced Osgood's (1959) contingency analysis and cloze procedure.

QUANTITATIVE NEWSPAPER ANALYSIS 1.2

The beginning of the 20th century saw a visible increase in the mass production of newsprint. In the United States, the boom in newspapers created mass markets and interest in public opinion. Journalism schools emerged, leading to demands for ethical standards and for empirical inquiries into the phenomenon of the newspaper. These demands, plus a somewhat simplistic notion of scientific objectivity, were met by what was then called *quantitative newspaper analysis*.

Probably the first quantitative newspaper analysis, published in 1893, asked the rhetorical question, "Do newspapers now give the news?" (Speed, 1893). Its author showed how, between 1881 and 1893, New York newspapers had dropped their coverage of religious, scientific, and literary matters in favor of gossip, sports, and scandals. In a similar but far more simplistic study published in 1910, Mathews attempted to reveal the overwhelming space that one New York daily newspaper devoted to "demoralizing," "unwholesome," and "trivial" matters as opposed to "worthwhile" news items. By simply measuring the column inches that newspapers devoted to particular subject matters, journalists in the early 20th century attempted to reveal "the truth about newspapers" (Street, 1909). Some believed that they had found a way of showing that the profit motive was the cause of "cheap yellow journalism" (Wilcox, 1900); others became convinced that they had established "the influence of newspaper presentations on the growth of crime and other antisocial activity" (Fenton, 1910). At least one concluded that a "quarter century survey of the press content shows demand for facts" (White, 1924).

Quantitative newspaper analysis seemingly provided the needed scientific ground for journalistic arguments. The respect for numbers has a long history, and facts that could be quantified were considered irrefutable. In a footnote, Berelson and Lazarsfeld (1948) quote from a source published more than 200 years ago:

> Perhaps the spirit of the battle over ratification is best reflected in the creed ironically attributed to each of the contending parties by its opponents. The recipe for an Anti-Federalist essay which indicates in a very concise way the class-bias that actuated the opponents of the Constitution, ran in this manner: "wellborn, nine times—Aristocracy, eighteen times—Liberty of the Press, thirteen times repeated—Liberty of Conscience, once—Negro Slavery, once mentioned—Trial by Jury, seven times—Great men, six times repeated—Mr. Wilson, forty times . . . —put them together and dish them up at pleasure. (p. 9; quoted from *New Hampshire Spy*, November 30, 1787)

Quantitative newspaper analysis led to the development of many valuable ideas, however. In 1912, Tenney made a far-reaching proposal for a large-scale and continuous survey of press content to establish a system of bookkeeping of the "social weather" "comparable in accuracy to the statistics of the U.S.

Weather Bureau" (p. 896). He demonstrated what he had in mind with an analysis of a few New York newspapers for different ethnic groups, but his proposal exceeded the scope of what was then feasible. Quantitative newspaper analysis culminated in sociologist Malcolm M. Willey's 1926 book *The Country Newspaper*. In this model study, Willey traced the emergence of Connecticut country weeklies, examining circulation figures, changes in subject matter, and the social role these papers acquired in competition with large city dailies.

When other mass media became prominent, researchers extended the approach first used in newspaper analysis—measuring volumes of coverage in various subject matter categories—initially to radio (Albig, 1938) and later to movies and television. Content analysis in subject matter categories continues today and is applied to a wide variety of printed matter, such as textbooks, comic strips, speeches, and print advertising.

1.3   EARLY CONTENT ANALYSIS

The second phase in the intellectual growth of content analysis, which took place in the 1930s and 1940s, involved at least four factors:

■ During the period following the 1929 economic crisis, numerous social and political problems emerged in the United States. Many Americans believed that the mass media were at least partially to blame for such problems as yellow journalism, rising crime rates, and the breakdown of cultural values.

■ New and increasingly powerful electronic media of communication, first radio and later television, challenged the cultural hegemony of the newspapers. Researchers could not continue to treat these new media as extensions of newspapers, because they differed from the print media in important ways. For example, users of radio and television did not have to be able to read.

■ Major political challenges to democracy were linked to the new mass media. For example, the rise of fascism was seen as nourished by the as-yet little-known properties of radio.

■ Perhaps most important, this period saw the emergence of the behavioral and social sciences as well as increasing public acceptance of the theoretical propositions and empirical methods of inquiry associated with them.

In the 1930s, sociologists started to make extensive use of survey research and polling. The experience they gained in analyzing public opinion gave rise to the first serious consideration of methodological problems of content analysis, published by Woodward in a 1934 article titled "Quantitative Newspaper Analysis as a Technique of Opinion Research." From writings about public opinion, interest in social stereotypes (Lippmann, 1922) entered the analysis of communications in various forms. Questions of representations were raised, with researchers examining topics such as how Negroes were presented in the Philadelphia press (Simpson, 1934); how U.S. textbooks described wars in which the United States had taken part, compared with textbooks published in countries that were former U.S. enemies (Walworth, 1938); and how nationalism was expressed in children's books published in the United States, Great Britain, and other European countries (Martin, 1936).

One of the most important concepts that emerged in psychology during this time was the concept of "attitude." It added evaluative dimensions to content analysis, such as "pro-con" or "favorable-unfavorable," that had escaped the rough subject matter categories of quantitative newspaper analysis. Attitude measures redefined journalistic standards of fairness and balance and opened the door to the systematic assessment of bias. Among the explicit standards developed, Janis and Fadner's (1943/1965) "coefficient of imbalance" deserves mention. Psychological experiments in rumor transmission led Allport and Faden to study newspaper content from an entirely new perspective. In their 1940 article "The Psychology of Newspapers: Five Tentative Laws," they attempted to account for the changes that information undergoes as it travels through an institution and finally appears on the printed page.

The interest in political symbols added another feature to the analysis of public messages. McDiarmid (1937), for example, examined 30 U.S. presidential inaugural addresses for symbols of national identity, of historical significance, of government, and of fact and expectations. Most important, Lasswell (1938), viewing public communications within his psychoanalytical theory of politics, classified symbols into such categories as "self" and "others" and forms of "indulgence" and "deprivation." His symbol analysis led to his "World Attention Survey," in which he compared trends in the frequencies with which prestige newspapers in several countries used national symbols (Lasswell, 1941).

Researchers in several disciplines examined the trends in scholarship, as reflected in the topics that representative journals published. Rainoff's (1929) Russian study regarding physics was probably the first of this kind, but the most thorough analyses were conducted in the field of sociology (Becker, 1930, 1932; Shanas, 1945) and later in journalism (Tannenbaum & Greenberg, 1961).

Several factors influenced the transition from quantitative newspaper analysis, which was largely journalism driven, to content analysis:

- Eminent social scientists became involved in these debates and asked new kinds of questions.

- The concepts these social scientists developed were theoretically motivated, operationally defined, and fairly specific, and interest in stereotypes, styles, symbols, values, and propaganda devices began to replace interest in subject matter categories.

- Analysts began to employ new statistical tools borrowed from other disciplines, especially from survey research but also from experimental psychology.

■ Content analysis data became part of larger research efforts (e.g., Lazarsfeld, Berelson, & Gaudet, 1948), and so content analysis no longer stood apart from other methods of inquiry.

The first concise presentation of these conceptual and methodological developments under the new umbrella term *content analysis* appeared in a 1948 mimeographed text titled *The Analysis of Communication Content,* authored by Berelson and Lazarsfeld, which was later published as Berelson's *Content Analysis in Communications Research* (1952). This first systematic presentation codified the field for years to come.

1.4   PROPAGANDA ANALYSIS

Berelson described content analysis as the use of mass communications as data for testing scientific hypotheses and for evaluating journalistic practices. Yet the most important and large-scale challenge that content analysis faced came during World War II, when it was employed in efforts to extract information from propaganda. Before the war, researchers analyzed texts in order to identify "propagandists," to point fingers at individuals who were attempting to influence others through devious means. Fears concerning such influence had several origins. Propaganda was used extensively during World War I (Lasswell, 1927), and the years between the two world wars witnessed the effective use of propaganda by antidemocratic demagogues in Europe. In addition, Americans tend to have deep-seated negative attitudes toward religious fanatics, and the lack of knowledge concerning what the extensive use of the new mass media (radio, film, and television) could do to people raised concerns as well. According to the Institute for Propaganda Analysis (1937), propagandists reveal themselves through their use of tricks such as "name-calling," employing "glittering generalities," "plain folks" identifications, "card stacking," "bandwagon" devices, and so on. Such devices could be identified easily in many religious and political speeches, even in academic lectures, and this approach to propaganda analysis led to a kind of witch-hunt for propagandists in the United States. Theories concerning subliminal messages, especially in advertising, raised widespread suspicion as well.

In the 1940s, as U.S. attention became increasingly devoted to the war effort, the identification of propagandists was no longer an issue. Nor were researchers particularly interested in revealing the power of the mass media of communication to mold public opinion; rather, military and political intelligence were needed. In this climate, two centers devoted to propaganda analysis emerged. Harold D. Lasswell and his associates, having written on political symbolism, worked with the Experimental Division for the Study of Wartime Communications at the U.S. Library of Congress, and Hans Speier, who had organized a research project on totalitarian communication at the New School for Social Research in New York, assembled a research team at the Foreign

Broadcast Intelligence Service of the U.S. Federal Communications Commission (FCC). The Library of Congress group focused on analyzing newspapers and wire services from abroad and addressed basic issues of sampling, measurement problems, and the reliability and validity of content categories, continuing the tradition of early quantitative analysis of mass communications (Lasswell, Leites, & Associates, 1965).

The FCC group analyzed primarily domestic enemy broadcasts and surrounding conditions to understand and predict events within Nazi Germany and the other Axis countries, and to estimate the effects of Allied military actions on the war mood of enemy populations. The pressures of day-to-day reporting left the analysts little time to formalize their methods, and Berelson (1952) thus had little to say about the accomplishments of the FCC group. After the war, however, Alexander L. George worked through the volumes of reports that resulted from these wartime efforts to describe methods that had evolved in the process and to validate the inferences the researchers had made by comparing them with documentary evidence now available from Nazi archives. These efforts resulted in his book *Propaganda Analysis* (1959a), which made major contributions to the conceptualization of the aims and processes of content analysis.

The assumptions that propagandists are rational, in the sense that they follow their own propaganda theories in their choice of communications, and that the meanings of propagandists' communications may differ for different people reoriented the FCC analysts from a concept of "content as shared" (Berelson would later say "manifest") to conditions that could explain the motivations of particular communicators and the interests they might serve. The notion of "preparatory propaganda" became an especially useful key for the analysts in their effort to infer the intents of broadcasts with political content. In order to ensure popular support for planned military actions, the Axis leaders had to inform, emotionally arouse, and otherwise prepare their countrymen and women to accept those actions; the FCC analysts discovered that they could learn a great deal about the enemy's intended actions by recognizing such preparatory efforts in the domestic press and broadcasts. They were able to predict several major military and political campaigns and to assess Nazi elites' perceptions of their situation, political changes within the Nazi governing group, and shifts in relations among Axis countries. Among the more outstanding predictions that British analysts were able to make was the date of deployment of German V weapons against Great Britain. The analysts monitored the speeches delivered by Nazi propagandist Joseph Goebbels and inferred from the content of those speeches what had interfered with the weapons' production and when. They then used this information to predict the launch date of the weapons, and their prediction was accurate within a few weeks.

Several lessons were learned from these applications of content analysis, including the following:

- ■ Content is not inherent to communications. People typically differ in how they read texts. The intentions of the senders of broadcast messages may have little to do with how audience members hear those messages. Temporal orderings, individuals' needs and expectations, individuals' preferred discourses, and the social situations into which messages enter are all important in explaining what communications come to mean. Interpretations on which all communicators readily agree are rare, and such interpretations are usually relatively insignificant.

■ Content analysts must predict or infer phenomena that they cannot observe directly. The inability to observe phenomena of interest tends to be the primary motivation for using content analysis. Whether the analyzed source has reasons to hide what the analyst desires to know (as in the case of an enemy during wartime or the case of someone needing to impress) or the phenomena of interest are inaccessible in principle (e.g., an individual's attitudes or state of mind, or historical events) or just plain difficult to assess otherwise (such as what certain mass-media audiences could learn from watching TV), the analyst seeks answers to questions that go outside a text. To be sure, the questions that a content analyst seeks to answer are the analyst's questions, and as such they are potentially at odds with whether others could answer them and how. Quantitative newspaper analysts made inferences without acknowledging their own conceptual contributions to what they thought they found but actually inferred. Content is not the whole issue; rather, the issue is what can be legitimately inferred from available texts.

■ In order to interpret given texts or make sense of the messages intercepted or gathered, content analysts need elaborate models of the systems in which those communications occur (or occurred). The propaganda analysts working during World War II constructed such models more or less explicitly. Whereas earlier content analysts had viewed mass-produced messages as inherently meaningful and analyzable unit by unit, the propaganda analysts succeeded only when they viewed the messages they analyzed in the context of the lives of the diverse people presumed to use those messages.

■ For analysts seeking specific political information, quantitative indicators are extremely insensitive and shallow. Even where large amounts of quantitative data are available, as required for statistical analyses, these tend not to lead to the "most obvious" conclusions that political experts would draw from qualitative interpretations of textual data. Qualitative analyses can be systematic, reliable, and valid as well.

Convinced that content analysis does not need to be inferior to unsystematic explorations of communications, numerous writers in the postwar years, such as Kracauer (1947, 1952–1953) and George (1959a), challenged content analysts' simplistic reliance on counting qualitative data. Smythe (1954) called this reliance on counting an "immaturity of science" in which objectivity is confused with quantification. However, the proponents of the quantitative approach largely ignored the criticism. In his 1949 essay "Why Be Quantitative?" Lasswell (1949/1965b) continued to insist on the quantification of symbols as the sole basis of scientific insights. His approach to propaganda analysis produced several working papers but very few tangible results compared with the work of the FCC group of scholars. Today, quantification continues, although perhaps no longer exclusively.

CONTENT ANALYSIS GENERALIZED   1.5

After World War II, and perhaps as the result of the first integrated picture of content analysis provided by Berelson (1952), the use of content analysis spread to numerous disciplines. This is not to say that content analysis emigrated from mass communication. In fact, the very "massiveness" of available communications continued to attract scholars who looked at the mass media from new perspectives. For example, Lasswell (1941) realized his earlier idea of a "world attention survey" in a large-scale study of political symbols in French, German, British, Russian, and U.S. elite press editorials and key policy speeches. He wanted to test the hypothesis that a "world revolution" had been in steady progress for some time (Lasswell, Lerner, & Pool, 1952). Gerbner and his colleagues pursued Gerbner's (1969) proposal to develop "cultural indicators" by analyzing, for almost two decades, one week of fictional television programming per year, mainly to establish "violence profiles" for different networks, to trace trends, and to see how various groups (such as women, children, and the aged) were portrayed on U.S. television (see, e.g., Gerbner, Gross, Signorielli, Morgan, & Jackson-Beeck, 1979).

Psychologists began to use content analysis in four primary areas. The first was the inference of motivational, mental, or personality characteristics through the analysis of verbal records. This application started with Allport's (1942) treatise on the use of personal documents, Baldwin's (1942) application of "personal structure analysis" to cognitive structure, and White's (1947) value studies. These studies legitimated the use of written material, personal documents, and individual accounts of observed phenomena as an addition to the then-dominant experimental methods. A second application was the use of verbal data gathered in the form of answers to open-ended interview questions, focus group conversations, and verbal responses to various tests, including the construction of Thematic Apperception Test (TAT) stories. In the context of TAT stories, content analysis acquired the status of a supplementary technique. As such, it allowed researchers to utilize data that they could gather without imposing too much structure on subjects and to validate findings they had obtained through different techniques. Psychological researchers' third application of content analysis concerned processes of communication in which content is an integral part. For example, in his "interaction process analysis" of small group behavior, Bales (1950) used verbal exchanges as data through which to examine group processes. The fourth application took the form of the generalization of measures of meaning over a wide range of situations and cultures (which derived from individualist notions of meaning or content). Osgood (1974a, 1974b) and his students found numerous applications for Osgood, Suci, and Tannenbaum's (1957) semantic differential scales and conducted worldwide comparisons of cultural commonalities and differences.

Anthropologists, who started using content analysis techniques in their studies of myths, folktales, and riddles, have made many contributions to content analysis, including the componential analysis of kinship terminology (Goodenough, 1972). Ethnography emerged in anthropology, and although ethnographers often interact with their informants in ways that content analysts cannot interact with authors or readers, after ethnographers gather their field notes they start to rely heavily on methods that are similar to those that content analysts use.

Historians are naturally inclined to look for systematic ways to analyze historical documents, and they soon embraced content analysis as a suitable technique, especially where data are numerous and statistical accounts seem helpful. Social scientists also recognized the usefulness of educational materials, which had long been the focus of research. Such materials are a rich source of data on processes of reading (Flesch, 1948, 1951) as well as on a society's larger political, attitudinal, and value trends. In addition, literary scholars began to apply the newly available techniques of content analysis to the problem of identifying the authors of unsigned documents.

On the one hand, this proliferation of the use of content analysis across disciplines resulted in a loss of focus: Everything seemed to be content analyzable, and every analysis of symbolic phenomena became a content analysis. On the other hand, this trend also broadened the scope of the technique to embrace what may well be the essence of human behavior: talk, conversation, and mediated communication.

In 1955, responding to increasing interest in the subject, the Social Science Research Council's Committee on Linguistics and Psychology sponsored a conference on content analysis. The participants came from such disciplines as psychology, political science, literature, history, anthropology, and linguistics. Their contributions to the conference were published in a volume titled *Trends in Content Analysis*, edited by Ithiel de Sola Pool (1959a). Despite obvious divergence among the contributors in their interests and approaches, Pool (1959a, p. 2) observed, there was considerable and often surprising convergence among them in two areas: They exhibited (a) a shift from analyzing the "content" of communications to drawing inferences about the antecedent conditions of communications and (b) an accompanying shift from measuring volumes of subject matter to counting simple frequencies of symbols, and then to relying on contingencies (co-occurrences).

1.6   COMPUTER TEXT ANALYSIS

The late 1950s witnessed considerable interest among researchers in mechanical translation, mechanical abstracting, and information retrieval systems. Computer languages suitable for literal data processing emerged, and scholarly journals started to devote attention to computer applications in psychology, the humanities, and the social sciences. The large volumes of written documents to be processed in content analysis and the repetitiveness of the coding involved made the computer a natural but also a difficult ally of the content analyst.

The development of software for literal (as opposed to numerical) data processing stimulated new areas of exploration, such as information retrieval, information systems, computational stylistics (Sedelow & Sedelow, 1966), computational linguistics, word processing technology, and computational content analysis. New software also revolutionized tedious literary work, such as indexing and the creation of concordances. Probably the first computer-aided content analysis was reported by Sebeok and Zeps (1958), who made use of simple information retrieval routines to analyze some 4,000 Cheremis folktales. In a Rand Corporation paper titled *Automatic Content Analysis,* Hays (1960) explored the possibility of designing a computer system for analyzing political documents. Unaware of both these developments, Stone and Bales, who were engaged in a study of themes in face-to-face interacting groups, designed and programmed the initial version of the General Inquirer system. This culminated in a groundbreaking book by Stone, Dunphy, Smith, and Ogilvie (1966) in which they presented an advanced version of this system and demonstrated its application in numerous areas, ranging from political science to advertising and from psychotherapy to literary analysis.

The use of computers in content analysis was also stimulated by developments in other fields. Scholars in psychology became interested in simulating human cognition (Abelson, 1963; Schank & Abelson, 1977). Newell and Simon (1963) developed a computer approach to (human) problem solving. Linguistics researchers developed numerous approaches to syntactic analysis and semantic interpretation of linguistic expressions. Researchers in the field of artificial intelligence focused on designing machines that could understand natural language (with very little success).

In 1967, the Annenberg School of Communications (which later became the Annenberg School for Communication) sponsored a major conference on content analysis. Discussions there focused on many areas—the difficulties of recording nonverbal (visual, vocal, and musical) communications, the need for standardized categories, the problems involved in drawing inferences, the roles of theories and analytical constructs, what developments content analysts could expect in the near future—but the subject of the use of computers in content analysis permeated much of the conference. Stone et al.'s (1966) book on the General Inquirer had just been published, and it had created considerable hope among content analysts. The contributions to the 1967 conference are summarized in a 1969 volume edited by Gerbner, Holsti, Krippendorff, Paisley, and Stone, the publication of which coincided with Holsti's (1969) survey of the field.

In 1974, participants in the Workshop on Content Analysis in the Social Sciences, held in Pisa, Italy, saw the development of suitable algorithms for computer content analysis as the only obstacle to better content analyses (Stone, 1975). Since that time, computational approaches have moved in numerous directions. One has been the development of customizable content analysis packages, of which the General Inquirer was the most important precursor. Attempts to apply the General Inquirer system to German texts revealed that software's English-language biases and led to more general versions of General Inquirers, such as TextPack. The basic ingredient of the General Inquirer and TextPack is a dictionary of relevant words. In the 1980s, Sedelow (1989) proposed the idea of using a thesaurus instead, as a thesaurus might be more accurate than a dictionary in reflecting "society's collective associative memory" (p. 4; see also Sedelow & Sedelow, 1986). In the 1990s, George Miller initiated a major research effort to chart the meanings of words using a computer-traceable network called WordNet (see Miller et al., 1993). In the 1980s, some authors observed that the enthusiasm associated with large systems that had appeared in the 1960s was fading (see Namenwirth & Weber, 1987), but today the development of text analysis software is proliferating, fueled largely by the historically unprecedented volumes of electronic and digital texts available for content analysis. Diefenbach (2001) recently reviewed the history of content analysis by focusing on four specific areas: mass communication research, political science, psychology, and literature.

Naturally, many researchers have compared computer-based content analyses with human-based content analyses. For example, Schnurr, Rosenberg, and Ozman (1992, 1993) compared the Thematic Apperception Test (Murray, 1943) with a computer content analysis of open-ended free speech and found the low agreement between the two to be discouraging. Zeldow and McAdams (1993) challenged Schnurr et al.'s conclusion, however. Nacos et al. (1991) compared humans' coding of political news coverage with data from Fan's (1988) computer-coded approach to the same coverage and found satisfactory correlations between the two. Nacos et al. came to the conclusion that content analysts can best use computers in their research by thinking of them as aids, not as replacements for the highly developed human capabilities of reading, transcribing, and translating written matter. As one might expect, today scholars hold many different opinions regarding the future of the use of computer-based content analysis.

Another development that has influenced how content analysts employ computers in their work is the increasingly common use of word processing software, which provides users with such features as spell-checkers, word- or phrase-finding and -replacing operations, and even readability indices. Although not intended for this purpose, ordinary word processing software makes it possible for a researcher to perform basic word counts and KWIC (keyword in context) analyses, albeit laboriously.

Word processing software is inherently interactive; it is driven by the user's reading of the textual material, not fixed. In the absence of computational theories of text interpretation, content analysts have found the symbiosis of the human ability to understand and interpret written documents and the computer's ability to scan large volumes of text systematically and reliably increasingly attractive. In such collaborations, human coders are no longer used as text-level content analysts; rather, they serve as translators of text or sections of text into categories that emerge during reading and then into a data language (that preserves relevant meanings), which enables various computational algorithms (that cannot respond to meanings) to do housekeeping and summarizing chores. This has given rise to a new class of software designed for computer-aided qualitative text analysis, of which NVivo and ATLAS.ti are two examples. Such interactive-hermeneutic text analysis software is becoming increasingly accessible, especially to students.

The most important stimulus in the development of computational content analysis, however, has been the growing availability of text in digital form. It is very costly to enter written documents, such as transcripts of audio recordings of interviews, focus group protocols, transcripts of business meetings, and political speeches, into a computer. Scanners have vastly improved in recent years, but they are still too unreliable to be used without additional manual editing. In the 1970s, data consortia emerged through which social scientists could share costly data, but the operations of these consortia were marred by a lack of standards and the usually highly specialized nature of the data. Then, in 1977, DeWeese proposed and took the remarkable step of bypassing the costly transcription process by feeding the typesetting tapes of a Detroit newspaper directly into a computer to conduct an analysis of the paper's content the day after it was published. Since that time, word processing software has come to be an integral part of the internal operations of virtually all social organizations; personnel create texts digitally before they appear on paper, use electronic mail systems, and surf the Internet to download materials relevant to their work.

Today, a fantastic amount of raw textual data is being generated daily in digital form, representing almost every topic of interest to social scientists. Electronic full-text databases, to which all major U.S. newspapers, many social science and legal journals, and many corporations contribute all of the materials they publish, are growing exponentially and have become easily available and inexpensive to use online. Add to this the volume of electronic publications, the research potential of the Internet, data available from online multiuser discussions (MUDs) and news groups, which may well replace focus groups and surveys in certain empirical domains, and it is clear that the landscape of how society presents itself has been altered drastically. With more and more people interested in this wealth of digital data, there is a corresponding demand for increasingly powerful search engines, suitable computational tools, text base managing software, encryption systems, devices for monitoring electronic data flows, and translation software, all of which will eventually benefit the development of computer-aided content analysis. The current culture of computation is moving content analysis toward a promising future.

QUALITATIVE APPROACHES · 1.7

Perhaps in response to the now dated "quantitative newspaper analysis" of a century ago or as a form of compensation for the sometimes shallow results reported by the content analysts of 50 years ago, a variety of research approaches have begun to emerge that call themselves *qualitative.* I question the validity and usefulness of the distinction between quantitative and qualitative content analyses. Ultimately, all reading of texts is qualitative, even when certain characteristics of a text are later converted into numbers. The fact that computers process great volumes of text in a very short time does not take away from the qualitative nature of their algorithms: On the most basic level, they recognize zeros and ones and change them, proceeding one step at a time. Nevertheless, what their proponents call qualitative approaches to content analysis offer some alternative protocols for exploring texts systematically.

Discourse analysis is one such approach. Generally, *discourse* is defined as text above the level of sentences. Discourse analysts tend to focus on how particular phenomena are represented. For example, Van Dijk (1991) studied manifestations of racism in the press: how minorities appear, how ethnic conflicts are described, and how stereotypes permeate given accounts. Other discourse analysts have examined how television news programs and other TV shows in the United States manifest a particular ideological vision of the U.S. economy (Wonsek, 1992), the components of "age markers" in the humorous context of the TV series *The Golden Girls* (Harwood & Giles, 1992), and the portrayal of the peace movement in news editorials during the Gulf War (Hackett & Zhao, 1994).

Researchers who conduct *social constructivist analyses* focus on discourse as well, but less to criticize (mis)representations than to understand how reality comes to be constituted in human interactions and in language, including written text (Gergen, 1985). Such analysts may address how emotions are conceptualized (Averill, 1985) or how facts are constructed (Fleck, 1935/1979; Latour & Woolgar, 1986), or they may explore changing notions of self (Gergen, 1991) or of sexuality (Katz, 1995).

Rhetorical analysis, in contrast, focuses on how messages are delivered, and with what (intended or actual) effects. Researchers who take this approach rely on the identification of structural elements, tropes, styles of argumentation, speech acts, and the like; Kathleen Hall Jamieson's book *Packaging the Presidency* (1984) is an example of such an analysis. Efforts to study negotiations (Harris, 1996), what works and what doesn't, might be described as rhetorical analyses as well.

Ethnographic content analysis, an approach advocated by Altheide (1987), does not avoid quantification but encourages content analysis accounts to emerge from readings of texts. This approach works with categories as well as with narrative descriptions but focuses on situations, settings, styles, images, meanings, and nuances presumed to be recognizable by the human actors/speakers involved.

Conversation analysis is another approach that is considered to be qualitative. The researcher performing such an analysis tends to start with the recording of verbal interactions in natural settings and aims at analyzing the transcripts as records of conversational moves toward a collaborative construction of conversations. This tradition is indebted to the work of Harvey Sacks, who studied numerous interactive phenomena, including the collaboration among communicators in the telling of jokes (Sacks, 1974). Goodwin (1977, 1981) extended conversation analysis by incorporating video data in his groundbreaking study of turn taking.

Qualitative approaches to content analysis have their roots in literary theory, the social sciences (symbolic interactionism, ethnomethodology), and critical scholarship (Marxist approaches, British cultural studies, feminist theory). Sometimes they are given the label *interpretive*. They share the following characteristics:

- They require a close reading of relatively small amounts of textual matter.

- They involve the rearticulation (interpretation) of given texts into new (analytical, deconstructive, emancipatory, or critical) narratives that are accepted within particular scholarly communities that are sometimes opposed to positivist traditions of inquiry.

- The analysts acknowledge working within hermeneutic circles in which their own socially or culturally conditioned understandings constitutively participate. (For this reason, I refer to these approaches as interactive-hermeneutic, a description that speaks to the process of engaging in interpretations of text.)

To summarize: One could say that content analysis has evolved into a repertoire of methods of research that promise to yield inferences from all kinds of verbal, pictorial, symbolic, and communication data. Beyond the technique's initially journalistic roots, the past century has witnessed the migration of content analysis into various fields and the clarification of many methodological issues. After a short period of stagnation in the 1970s, content analysis is today growing exponentially, largely due to the widespread use of computers for all kinds of text processing. As of August 2003, an Internet search for *"content analysis"* using the Google search engine found 4,230,000 documents. In comparison, *"survey research"* turned up 3,990,000 hits and *"psychological test,"* 1,050,000. Since the term's casual introduction in 1941—that is, with a frequency of one—the body of research that content analysis has produced has clearly grown to an astonishing volume.

CHAPTER 2

Conceptual Foundation

Content analysis has its own approach to analyzing data that stems largely from how the object of analysis, content, is conceived. This chapter defines content analysis, develops a conceptual framework through which the purposes and processes of content analysis may be understood in general terms, outlines the essential concepts of content analysis, and contrasts content analysis with other social science methods of inquiry.

2.1   DEFINITION

Content analysis is a research technique for making replicable and valid inferences from texts (or other meaningful matter) to the contexts of their use.

As a *technique,* content analysis involves specialized procedures. It is learnable and divorceable from the personal authority of the researcher. As a research technique, content analysis provides new insights, increases a researcher's understanding of particular phenomena, or informs practical actions. Content analysis is a scientific tool.

Techniques are expected to be *reliable.* More specifically, research techniques should result in findings that are *replicable.* That is, researchers working at different points in time and perhaps under different circumstances should get the same results when applying the same technique to the same data. Replicability is the most important form of reliability.

Scientific research must also yield *valid* results, in the sense that the research effort is open for careful scrutiny and the resulting claims can be upheld in the face of independently available evidence. The methodological requirements of reliability and validity are not unique to but make particular demands on content analysis.

The reference to *text* in the above definition is not intended to restrict content analysis to written material. The phrase "or other meaningful matter" is included in parentheses to indicate that in content analysis works of art, images, maps, sounds, signs, symbols, and even numerical records may be included as data— that is, they may be considered as texts—provided they speak to someone about phenomena outside of what can be sensed or observed. The crucial distinction between text and what other research methods take as their starting point is that a text means something to someone, it is produced by someone to have meanings for someone else, and these meanings therefore must not be ignored and must not violate why the text exists in the first place. Text—the reading of text, the use of text within a social context, and the analysis of text—serves as a convenient metaphor in content analysis.

In the content analysis literature, scholars have provided essentially three kinds of definitions of this research method:

1. Definitions that take content to be *inherent* in a text

2. Definitions that take content to be *a property of the source* of a text

3. Definitions that take content to *emerge in the process of a researcher analyzing a text* relative to a particular context

Each of these kinds of definitions leads to a particular way of conceptualizing content and, consequently, of proceeding with an analysis.

Berelson's original definition of content analysis is an example of the first kind. Berelson (1952) defined content analysis as "a research technique for the objective, systematic and quantitative description of the manifest content of communication" (p. 18). His requirement that content analysis be "objective" and "systematic" is subsumed under the dual requirements of replicability and validity in our definition. For a process to be replicable, it must be governed by rules that are explicitly stated and applied equally to all units of analysis. Berelson argued for "systematicity" in order to combat the human tendency to read textual material selectively, in support of expectations rather than against them. Our requirement of validity goes further, demanding that the researcher's processes of sampling, reading, and analyzing messages ultimately satisfy external criteria. Replicability is measurable and validity is testable, but objectivity is neither.

Our definition of content analysis omits three of Berelson's further requirements. One is his insistence that content analysis be "quantitative." Although quantification is important in many scientific endeavors, qualitative methods have proven successful as well, particularly in political analyses of foreign propaganda, in psychotherapeutic assessments, in ethnographic research, in discourse analysis, and, oddly enough, in computer text analysis. The ability of computers to crunch words as well as numbers is well-known. When a computer program is used to analyze words, the algorithms that determine the program's operation must embody some kind of theory of how humans read texts, rearticulate texts, or justify actions informed by the reading of texts. Reading is fundamentally a qualitative process, even when it results in numerical accounts. By including the attribute "manifest" in his definition, Berelson intended to ensure that the coding of content analysis data be reliable; this requirement literally excludes "reading between the lines," which is what experts do, often with remarkable intersubjective agreement (I will have more to say on this topic later in this chapter).

My chief objection to Berelson's definition, and numerous derivatives of that definition, is related to his phrase "description of the manifest content of communication." It implies that content is *contained* in messages, waiting to be separated from its form and described. Berelson felt no need to elaborate on the crucial concept of "content" in his definition because for him and his contemporaries, at the time he was writing, there seemed to be no doubt about the nature of content—it was believed to reside *inside* a text.

Berelson's operationalization of the attribute "manifest" is telling. If sources, receivers, and content analysts have different interpretations of the same message, which is quite natural, Berelson's definition restricts content to what is *common to all of these accounts,* what everyone can agree to. Gerbner (1985) starts from a similar assumption when he insists that mass-media messages carry the *imprint* of their industrial producers. For him, too, content is right there to be described for what it is. However, Gerbner goes beyond Berelson's notion by suggesting that the messages of the mass media are revealed in statistical accounts of their contents. Mass-media audiences, he suggests, are affected by certain statistical properties of mass-produced messages of which neither mass producers nor mass audiences are conscious. This privileges content analysts' accounts over the readings by audience members. Shapiro and Markoff's (1997) definition equates content analysis with scientific measurement as well, specifically, with "any systematic reduction . . . of text (or other symbols) to a standard set of statistically manipulable symbols representing the presence, the intensity, or the frequency of some characteristics relevant to social science" (p. 14). Its implicit representationalism is common in several definitions of content analysis. For example, in a recent textbook, Riffe, Lacy, and Fico (1998) start with the proposition that content is central to communication research but then assert that the purpose of content analysis is to describe "it" so as to make "it" amenable to correlations with other (noncontent) variables—as if content were a variable or thing inherent to mass-media messages. These examples demonstrate that the container metaphor for meaning still abounds in much of the communication research literature (Krippendorff, 1993). The use of this metaphor entails the belief that messages are containers of meaning, usually one meaning per message, and justifies calling any analysis of any conventionally meaningful matter a content analysis, regardless of whether it counts words or offers in-depth interpretations. Clearly, this is an insufficient way to define content analysis.

Definitions of the second kind distinguished above tie the content analysis of texts to *inferences about the states or properties of the sources of the analyzed texts* (Krippendorff, 1969a, p. 70; Osgood 1959, p. 35). Shapiro and Markoff (1997), among others, have criticized such definitions as too limiting. Holsti

(1969, p. 25) elaborates on this idea by committing content analysis to an encoding/decoding paradigm in which message sources are causally linked to recipients through encoding processes, channels, messages, and decoding processes. Holsti wants the content analyst to describe the characteristics of communications in terms of "what," "how," and "to whom" in order to infer their antecedents in terms of "who" and "why" and their consequences in terms of "with what effects." The last of these could be determined more directly if sources and recipients were accessible to observation or were able to inform the analyst honestly. When antecedents and consequences are not accessible to direct observation, the analyst must make inferences. I am sympathetic to Holsti's logic, but putting sources—senders and/or receivers—in charge of the validity of the inferences may not be the best way for the content analyst to capture all of the communicators' intents. Moreover, describing message characteristics in terms of "what," "how," and "to whom" fails to acknowledge the analyst's own conceptual contributions to what constitutes the appropriate reading of the analyzed texts and the relevance of this reading to a given research question.

The analyst's conceptual contributions to the reading of a text are specifically recognized in an approach called *ethnographic content analysis* (Altheide, 1987); unfortunately, however, this approach has not been clearly defined. Proponents of ethnographic content analysis oppose the sequential nature of traditional content analysis, suggesting instead that analysts be flexible in taking into account new concepts that emerge during their involvement with texts. This approach acknowledges the theory-driven nature of content analysis but also demands that the analytical process be closely linked to the communicators studied. Ethnographic content analysis is emic rather than etic in intent; that is, it attempts to rely on indigenous conceptions rather than on analysts' theory-imposed conceptions. Although the preference for communicators' conceptions would appear to tie ethnographic content analysis to the second kind of definition noted above, by urging researchers to reflect on their involvement in the process, the approach acknowledges the possibility that researchers' theories can play a role in how analysis proceeds. The latter ties it more closely to the third kind of definition of content analysis, which we now explore.

EPISTEMOLOGICAL ELABORATIONS   2.2

The definition of content analysis offered at the opening of this chapter is of the third kind. It focuses attention on the process of content analysis and does not ignore the contributions that analysts make to what counts as content. The key to the definition lies in the operations that define the nature of content analysis data. Most content analysts probably realize that the starting points of their analyses, *texts* (printed matter, recorded speech, visual communications, works of art, artifacts), are quite unlike physical events in that they are meaningful to others, not just to the analysts. Recognizing meanings is the reason that researchers engage in content analysis rather than in some other kind of investigative method. A content analyst must acknowledge that all texts are produced and read by others and are expected to be significant to them, not just to the analyst. Inasmuch as linguistically competent communicators are able to transcend the physical manifestations of their messages and respond instead to what those messages mean to them, content analysts cannot remain stuck in analyzing the physicality of text—its medium, characters, pixels, or shapes. Rather, they must look outside these characteristics to examine how individuals use various texts. It would follow that the popular measurement model for conceptualizing content analysis, borrowed from mechanical engineering and widely used in the natural sciences and behavioral research, is misleading; it implies that there is something inherent to text that is measurable without any interpretation by competent authors, readers, users, and—we need to include—culturally competent analysts. Below, I elaborate on six features of texts that are relevant to our definition of content analysis.

1. *Texts have no objective*—that is, *no reader-independent*—*qualities.* Seeing something as a text entails an invitation, if not a commitment, to read it. Regarding something as a message implies that someone is trying to make sense of it. Accepting particular markers as data entails taking them as an unquestionable ground for subsequent conceptualizations. Thus texts, messages, and data arise in the process of *someone* engaging with them conceptually. A text does not exist without a reader, a message does not exist without an interpreter, and data do not exist without an observer. In a content analysis, it is methodologically trained researchers who, being familiar with their texts, design the analysis, instruct their coders to describe textual elements, and end up interpreting the results—always in the expectation of others' understanding. There is nothing inherent in a text; the meanings of a text are always brought to it by someone. Ordinary readers and content analysts merely read differently.

2. *Texts do not have single meanings* that could be "found," "identified," and "described" for what they are. Just as texts can be read from numerous perspectives, so signs can have several designations and data can be subjected to various analyses. One can count the characters, words, or sentences of a text. One can categorize its phrases, analyze its metaphors, describe the logical structure of its constituent expressions, and ascertain its associations, connotations, denotations, and commands. One can also offer psychiatric, sociological, political, or poetic interpretations of that text. All of these accounts may be valid but different. Untrained analysts may be overwhelmed by these choices. Researchers who pursue content analysis according to the first of the above definitions are led to believe that a message has but one content, all other meanings being deviant, wrong, or subjective, and hence excluded. This naive belief is an entailment of the unreflecting use of the container metaphor. Perhaps the term *content analysis* was ill chosen for this reason. The possibility that any text may have multiple readings renders the frequently published claims by some researchers that they

have analyzed *the* content of particular bodies of text untenable by our (third kind of) definition.

3. *The meanings invoked by texts need not be shared.* Although intersubjective agreement as to what an author meant to say or what a given text means would simplify a content analysis tremendously, such consensus rarely exists in fact. Demanding that analysts find a "common ground" would restrict the empirical domain of content analysis to the most trivial or "manifest aspects of communications," on which Berelson's definition relies, or it would restrict the use of content analysis to a small community of message producers, recipients, and analysts who happen to see the world from the same perspective. If content analysts were not allowed to read texts in ways that are different from the ways other readers do, content analysis would be pointless. In fact, psychiatrists are expected to interpret the stories they hear from their patients in ways that differ from the patients' interpretations. Anthropologists' analyses of cultural artifacts need not conform to what informants say about those artifacts, and conversation analysts have good reasons to see verbal interactions in ways conversants might not. As Gerbner and his colleagues have shown through content analyses, mass-media audiences are not aware of the statistical trends in the qualities of popular heroes, the kinds of violence depicted, and the representations of minorities in television programming. Critical scholarship would be stifled if it could not go outside of what everyone accepts as true. Content analysis is in trouble only when expert interpretations fail to acknowledge the uses of texts by designated populations of readers or actors, particularly when content analysts fail to spell out the criteria for validating their results.

4. *Meanings (contents) speak to something other than the given texts,* even where convention suggests that messages "contain" them or texts "have" them. Probably the most distinctive feature of communications is that they inform their recipients, invoke feelings, or cause behavioral changes. Texts can provide information about events at distant locations, about objects that no longer exist, about ideas in people's minds, about available actions—just as symbols represent things in their absence and stories walk their listeners through imagined worlds. Texts can also lead to responses of various kinds. All of these phenomena link the reading of present texts to something else. Whether these other phenomena concern purely mental constructions, past or future experiences, or hidden causes, the analyst must be able to conceive of them and verbalize them. It follows that content analysts must look outside the physicality of texts—for example, to how people other than the analysts use these texts, what the texts tell them, the conceptions and actions the texts encourage. This requirement is a key to understanding the limitations inherent in computer text analysis. Computers can be programmed to manipulate character strings in amazingly complex ways, but their operations remain confined to the conceptions of their programmers. Without human intelligence and the human ability to read and draw inferences from texts, computer text analysis cannot point to anything outside of what it processes. Computers have no environment of their own making; they operate in the contexts of their users' worlds without understanding those contexts.

5. *Texts have meanings relative to particular contexts, discourses, or purposes.* Although diverse readings of a text are typical, the task of content analysts is far from hopeless. Messages always occur in particular situations, texts are read with particular intents, and data are informative relative to particular problems. Statisticians, linguists, anthropologists, psychiatrists, and political analysts all have their own discipline-based reasons for interpreting given assertions differently. A therapist and a conversation analyst will view the same conversation differently. A speech on economics may be analyzed for its political implications, for how well it presents certain arguments, for what the speechwriter knows about economics, or for the emotions it arouses. We explain these differences by the *contexts* within which analysts choose to listen to that speech. Differences in interpretations do not preclude the possibility of agreements within particular contexts, however. In fact, once content analysts have chosen the context within which they intend to make sense of a given text, the diversity of interpretations may well be reduced to a manageable number, sometimes to one.

Every content analysis requires a context within which the available texts are examined. The analyst must, in effect, construct a world in which the texts make sense and can answer the analyst's research questions. A context renders perceptual data into readable texts and serves as the conceptual justification for reasonable interpretations, including for the results of content analysis. Often, analysts presuppose particular contexts based on their own disciplinary commitments, as in the above example about a speech on economics. Analysts working within particular disciplines, such as political science, rhetoric, economics, and psychology, hold particular theories concerning how texts are to be handled; that is, they are willing to accept only a certain context. Holsti's encoding/decoding paradigm, mentioned above, functions as a prominent analytical context in communication research, but it is by no means the only one. The contexts that psychiatrists are willing to construct are very different from those that political scientists are likely to accept or within which literary scholars prefer to work. Once an analyst has chosen a context for a particular body of text and clearly understands that context, certain kinds of questions become answerable and others make no sense.

Just as the analytical contexts that content analysts must adopt may vary from one analysis to another, these contexts may also differ from the interpretive schemes that unaided listeners, viewers, or readers employ in reading their sensory data, the characters of their texts, and the messages they receive. The same body of texts can therefore yield very different findings when examined by different analysts and with reference to different groups of readers. For a content analysis to be replicable, the analysts must explicate the context that guides their inferences. Without such explicitness, anything would go.

6. *The nature of text demands that content analysts draw specific inferences from a body of texts to their chosen context*—from print to what that printed matter means to particular users, from how analysts regard a body of texts to how selected audiences are affected by those texts, from available data to unobserved phenómena.

Texts, messages, and symbols never speak for themselves. They inform someone. Information allows a reader to select among alternatives. It narrows the range of interpretations otherwise available. For the content analyst, the systematic reading of a body of texts narrows the range of possible inferences concerning unobserved facts, intentions, mental states, effects, prejudices, planned actions, and antecedent or consequent conditions. Content analysts infer answers to particular research questions from their texts. Their inferences are merely more systematic, explicitly informed, and (ideally) verifiable than what ordinary readers do with texts. Recognizing this apparent generality, our definition of content analysis makes the drawing of inferences the centerpiece of this research technique.

The element of "making inferences" is not entirely absent from other definitions of content analysis. For example, Stone, Dunphy, Smith, and Ogilvie (1966) define content analysis as "a research technique for making inferences by systematically and objectively identifying specified characteristics within a text" (p. 5). Although their inclusion of "within a text" here would suggest a commitment to "inherentist" conceptions of meaning, Stone et al. nevertheless recognize the inferential character of the processes of coding and categorizing textual material, in their case by computer. Their dictionary of fixed linguistic classifications of word meanings leads to semantically simplified representations of a text's conventional readings. Other authors have equated inferences with statistical generalizations (e.g., Roberts, 1997), which do not, however, move into the context of textual matter. As early as 1943, Janis (1943/1965) pointed to the need for researchers to validate the results of content analyses of mass communications by relating research findings to audience perceptions and to behavioral effects. Our definition requires that content analysts be able to validate their results as well, whether those results are used to predict something, to inform decisions, or to help conceptualize the realities of certain individuals or groups. But validation becomes an issue only where inferences are specific and thus have the potential for failing.

Regarding the drawing of inferences, Merten (1991) paraphrases the essential elements of my definition of content analysis (Krippendorff, 1980b) when he writes, "Content analysis is a method for inquiring into social reality that consists of inferring features of a nonmanifest context from features of a manifest text" (p. 15; my translation). All theories of reading (hermeneutics) and theories of symbolic forms (semiotics), including theories of message meanings (communication/conversation theory), can be operationalized as processes of moving from texts to the contexts of the texts' use. I would also suggest that a context is always constructed by someone, here the content analysts, no matter how hard they may try to objectify it. This is true even for ethnographers who believe that they can delegate the definition of the context to their informants' world conceptions. It is the ethnographers who are held responsible for what they end up reporting. One cannot deny content analysts' interest and conceptual participation in what their analysis reveals. Whether the analysts' context coincides with the many worlds of others is a difficult question to answer. Whether the analysts' world makes sense to their scientific peers depends on how compellingly the analysts present that world.

2.3   EXAMPLES

In this section, I offer some examples to illustrate how our definition of content analysis applies to practical situations.

Example 1. Consider the situation of wartime analysts of enemy broadcasts who want to gauge, among other phenomena, the popular support that enemy elites enjoy in their country. In peacetime, researchers could obtain such information directly, through public opinion surveys, for example, or by on-site observations. In wartime, however, information of this nature is difficult to get, if not deliberately concealed, and analysts are forced to use indirect means of obtaining it. The inability to use direct observation is an invitation to apply content analysis. Here, analysts are typically not interested in the literal meanings of enemy broadcasts, in the rhetorical devices political leaders use, or in judging whether individual citizens are being deliberately misled. In fact, wartime propaganda analysts have good reasons to overlook manifest contents and ignore their truths. To infer from enemy domestic broadcasts the extent of popular support for elite policies, the analysts must understand that the broadcasts are part of a complex communication network in which the mass-media system and political system interact with a population to make news acceptable. The propaganda analysts have to know something about the actors involved in the governing elite and in the military, about the media these actors have access to, and about other institutions that have a stake in current affairs. They must also have some knowledge of the political-economic processes that keep a country together and how the public tends to respond to mass-mediated messages. The picture they construct of what they are dealing with amounts to the context of their analysis. It connects the intercepted broadcasts to the phenomena of interest, whether they concern popular support of the governing elite's policies, planned military actions, or evidence of war weariness.

Example 2. Historians are never mere collectors of documents. They offer reconstructions of past events that they deem consistent with current readings of all available documentary evidence. Historians are far removed from the worlds they wish to articulate. They cannot interview Julius Caesar, ask Homer about his sources for the *Iliad,* participate in the experiences of African slaves entering colonial America, or listen to conversations between Pablo Picasso and Henri Matisse. Historical figures reside in our readings of available documents, not in facts. And although some have left their writings to us, it is unlikely that they anticipated contemporary historians' readings. Past happenings become comprehensible to us only by inferences from documents that have survived to the present (Dibble, 1963). Historians who infer past events from available texts are, by our definition, involved in content analysis. It is not surprising, therefore, that historians are keenly aware of the need to place the documents they analyze within the context of other relevant documents. Without the appropriate context, a document means very little; a document placed in the wrong context acquires incorrect meanings, or at least meanings that may not make much sense. Historiographical methods organize available documents into webs of inferential relationships that may ultimately answer a historian's questions.

Example 3. Psychological researchers have a long tradition of developing theories whose generalizability is established by repeated experiments. The subjects of psychological research must be present, however, making it difficult for researchers to study developmental issues and individuals who are available only through their writings. Expanding psychological research methods, Allport (1942) added personal documents, witness accounts, and letters to the repertoire of data amenable to psychological inquiries. The research he proposed amounts to content analysis by our definition: There are texts in the form of personal documents, diaries, letters, and recorded speeches, and researchers construct the contexts for analyzing these texts with the help of available theories concerning the correlations between what people say and a variety of psychological variables (e.g., cognitive processes, attitudes, emotional arousal, personality traits, worldviews, or psychopathologies). Different schools of psychology direct their researchers to different questions, but they all are interested in inferring psychological variables of authors from the texts they left behind. In the course of analyzing personal documents, psychologically oriented content analysts have developed a variety of inferential techniques (e.g., type/token ratios of key concepts, the discomfort/relief quotient, graphological interpretations, readability yardsticks, thematic apperception tests, and personal structure analysis). In individual psychology, content analysis has become an established method of inquiry since Allport's (1965) pioneering work.

Example 4. For good reasons, interview and focus group data are frequently subjected to content analysis. Structured interviews generate predefined question-answer pairs, and the researcher then analyzes their distribution. The researcher's conceptions are imposed on the interviewees, who cannot express the reasons for their choices among predefined answers and whose individual conceptions are ignored. In open-ended interviews and focus groups, in contrast, participants are allowed to speak freely and in their own terms. To explore the conceptions that are manifest in such conversations, researchers need to perform what amounts to content analysis on the transcripts of these conversations. In a breast cancer study, for example, patients were asked about their lives after they had received treatment (Samarel et al., 1998). The answers were naturally freewheeling, as expected, enabling the researchers to adapt their theory of "coping" to the transcripts at hand. The researchers' reformulated theory then provided the context for a subsequent content analysis. Armed with questions derived from the researchers' theory, coders looked for and identified answers within the transcripts, and by tabulating these, the researchers provided frequencies and statistical accounts that the funders of the research required. In this study, the qualitative inferences were made during the process of coding, not based on the resulting frequencies, which merely summarized these inferences.

Example 5. Mass communication is the archetypal domain of content analysis. Communication researchers tend to be interested in communicator conceptions, media biases and effects, institutional constraints, implications of new technologies, audience perceptions, public opinion, and how certain values, prejudices, cultural distinctions, and reality constructions are distributed in society—relying on mass-media messages as their causes or expressions. Typically, mass-media material calls for more reading than any single person can handle. Its analysis thus requires a framework, a theory, a vocabulary, and an analytical focus in terms of which the researcher can construct a suitable context for analysis and collaborate with other researchers on the same project. Different contexts answer different research questions, of course.

A stereotypical aim of mass-media content analysis is to describe how a controversial issue is "depicted" in a chosen genre. Efforts to describe how something is "covered" by, "portrayed" in, or "represented" in the media invoke a picture theory of content. This approach to content analysis decontextualizes the analyzed text and thus reverts to the first kind of definition of content analysis distinguished above. It conceals the researchers' interest in the analysis, hides their inferences behind the naive belief that they are able to describe meanings objectively while rendering the results immune to invalidating evidence. Consider common findings of political biases, racial prejudices, and the silencing of minorities on television as such issues. Although counts of evident incidences of such phenomena can give the impression of objectivity, they make sense only in the context of accepting certain social norms, such as the value of giving equal voice to both sides of a controversy, neutrality of reporting, or affirmative representations. Implying such norms hides the context that analysts need to specify. Unless analysts spell out whose norms are applied, whose attitudes are being inferred, who is exposed to which mass media, and, most important, where the supposed phenomena could be observed, their findings cannot be validated. Berelson and Lazarsfeld (1948, p. 6) noted long ago that there is no point in counting unless the frequencies lead to inferences about the conditions surrounding what is counted. For example, counting the numbers of mentions of *Microsoft* or *AIDS* or the term *road rage* over time in, say, the *New York Times* would be totally meaningless if the observed frequencies could not be related to something else, such as political, cultural, or economic trends. That something else is the context that lends significance to quantitative findings.

Example 6. Content analysis has many commercial uses. For example, word-association databases (which collect huge numbers of pairs of words that consumers associate in their minds, as determined through word-association experiments) can serve as the context within which advertising researchers can infer chains of associations for new products, services, or brand names. In another, very different application, Michael Eleey and I studied how publicity generated by the Public Broadcasting Service about its programming ended up in newspaper articles (Krippendorff & Eleey, 1986). The purpose of the study was to enable PBS analysts to infer how the Public Broadcasting Service is perceived by newspaper editors in different regions of the United States and to assess the effectiveness of PBS's publicity efforts. Here the context was very simple. It included what we knew about newspaper editors' access to wire services and press releases, their newspapers' coverage of PBS programming, and certain theories and assumptions about the difference between the two, which led us to infer the (controllable) persuasive force of PBS publicity and the (uncontrollable) attitudes and competencies of the journalists, further differentiated by region and size of the newspaper.

The foregoing suggests that purely descriptive intents, manifest in claims to have analyzed "*the content* of a newspaper," to have quantified "*the* media *coverage* of an event," or to have "*found* how an ethnic group is *depicted*," fail to make explicit the very contexts within which researchers choose to analyze their texts. Content analysts have to know the conditions under which they obtain their texts, but, more important, they also have to be explicit about *whose* readings they are speaking about, *which processes or norms* they are applying to come to their conclusions, and *what the world looks like* in which their analyses, their own readings, and their readings of others' readings make sense to other content analysts. Explicitly identifying the contexts for their analytical efforts is also a way of inviting other analysts to bring validating evidence to bear on the inferences published and thus advance content analysis as a research technique. The framework presented in the next section is intended to help content analysts to conceptualize the analytical process so that their results are arguably acceptable.

FRAMEWORK   2.4

The definition of content analysis offered at the opening of this chapter and illustrated in the above examples emphasizes the drawing of inferences of a certain kind. It also assigns content analysts a particular role vis-à-vis their objects of inquiry. Following from the above and previous work (Krippendorff, 1969b, pp. 7–13; 1980b), I offer a conceptual framework for content analysis within which that role becomes clear. This framework is intended to serve three purposes: Its *prescriptive* purpose is to guide the conceptualization and design of practical content analytic research; its *analytical* purpose is to facilitate the critical examination and comparison of the published content analyses; and its *methodological* purpose is to point to performance criteria and precautionary standards that researchers can apply in evaluating ongoing content analyses. Thus the use of the framework will lead to long-term systematic improvements of the method.

The framework, which is depicted in Figure 2.1, is simple and general, employing only a few conceptual components:

■ A body of text, the data that a content analyst has available to begin an analytical effort

■ A research question that the analyst seeks to answer by examining the body of text

■ A context of the analyst's choice within which to make sense of the body of text

■ An analytical construct that operationalizes what the analyst knows about the context

■ Inferences that are intended to answer the research question, which constitute the basic accomplishment of the content analysis

■ Validating evidence, which is the ultimate justification of the content analysis

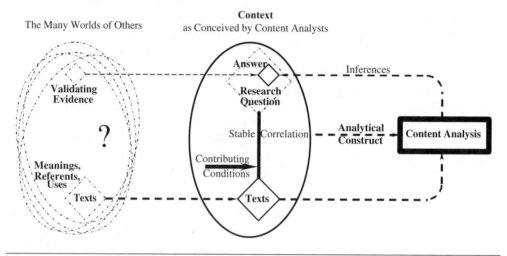

Figure 2.1   A Framework for Content Analysis

2.4.1   **Texts**

Data are the starting point of any empirical research. Data are *taken as givens*—that is, the researcher is not in doubt as to what they are. In surveys, focus groups, and psychological experiments, researchers attempt to control the generation of their data, thereby assuring that they know what the data mean, largely, if not exclusively, in the researchers' terms. Most content analyses start with data that are not intended to be analyzed to answer specific research questions. They are *texts* in the sense that they are meant to be *read, interpreted, and understood by people other than the analysts.* Readers may decompose what they read into meaningful units, recognize compelling structures, rearticulate their understandings sequentially or holistically, and act on them sensibly. When we are capable of this kind of rearticulation, we attribute textuality to what we see as writing, pictorial images, gestures, Web pages, musical compositions, even behavioral sequences. Text results from reading and rearticulation.

One could speak of symbolic qualities instead of text, but it is preferable not to assume such qualities to exist without reference to who regards them as such. An analyst's reading—the units, syntax, and narrative structures that constitute the texts for the analyst—naturally differs from the readings that initiate the interpretations of ordinary readers, including the texts' authors. It follows that an analyst's reading must never be taken as the only legitimate one, nor should content analysts assume the sole power to determine the form of the texts they analyze. They would then be examining only themselves. We presume that all authors write in the expectation of being understood by self and by others, and it is the implication of others that renders a text socially significant. Although content analysts are not bound to analyze their data with reference to the conceptions or intended audiences of their texts' authors, they must at least consider that texts may have been intended for someone like them. We know that interviewees answer questions differently when they know how the research findings could affect them, and so we need to read interview results in the context of possible self-interests. We know that when politicians speak, they anticipate being scrutinized by the public, and so we cannot take their speeches at face value, as natural objects. Content analysts have to acknowledge that the textuality they rely on is not the only one that counts.

Content analysts' best guarantee against the contamination of texts by the stakes their sources have in how their texts are analyzed is to focus on textual features of which their sources are unconscious, or to apply categories the sources of their texts are unable to control. This is most obviously possible when the sources of texts are of the past (historical), when they are unaware of how their texts are being analyzed, or when communication to the analysts is one-way, without feedback. However, given that the results of most content analyses are published, and that the categories that analysts use have the potential of becoming known to the text sources as well, content analysts are justified in applying unconventional categories, that is, in looking at textuality in ways others may not. As Figure 2.1 illustrates, texts occur in the analyst's world but acknowledge their origins in the worlds of others.

Research Questions   2.4.2

Research questions are the targets of the analyst's inferences from available texts. Generally, such questions delineate several possible and initially uncertain answers. In this respect, a research question is analogous to a set of hypotheses. However, in contrast to scientific hypotheses, which are pitted against direct observational evidence, the research questions of content analysis must be answered through inferences drawn from texts. The difference between testing scientific hypotheses and selecting an answer to a research question is crucial. Whereas observations are registered or measured for what they are and hypotheses about observational phenomena amount to generalizations from observations, texts inform an analyst about extratextual phenomena, about meanings, consequences, or particular uses. Thus, whereas scientific hypotheses are accepted on account of a preponderance of evidence in favor of one at the expense of other hypotheses, an ideally large number of observations that support one and rule out others, inferences from texts (although large numbers may play a role here as well) pertain to phenomena that are not observed during a content analysis, phenomena that are outside the texts and thus retain their hypothetical character until confirmed by validating incidences.

There are two reasons for content analysts to start with research questions, ideally in advance of undertaking any inquiries: *efficiency* and *empirical grounding*. One can surely explore the meanings that come to mind while reading a text, following the threads of the inferences to wherever they may lead, or engaging in so-called fishing expeditions. Hermeneutical, interpretive, and ethnographic approaches to reading cherish such open-endedness. However, when research is motivated by specific questions, analysts can proceed more expeditiously from sampling relevant texts to answering given questions. Content analysts who start with a research question read texts for a purpose, not for what an author may lead them to think or what they say in the abstract.

The pursuit of answers to research questions also grounds content analysis empirically. All answers to research questions entail truth claims that could be supported, if not by direct observation then at least by plausible argumentation from related observations. Our framework suggests that content analysis compensates for analysts' inability to observe phenomena in which they are interested, whether these phenomena pertain to the characteristics of writers or readers, to happenings hidden behind intentional information barriers, or to events in a distant past or future.

Formulating research questions so that the answers could be validated in principle protects content analysts from getting lost in mere abstractions or self-serving categorizations. For example, the question of how frequently a particular word occurs in a text can be answered by counting. Counting is what analysts do. Counts cannot be validated by independent evidence; to assure that counts are correct, analysts must repeat them, perhaps employing different persons as counters. The same is true for questions concerning whether one can categorize, measure, or analyze something. Their answer lies in a researcher's ability to execute these processes reliably. These questions cannot be answered by research. Questions concerning the statistical generalizability of textual attributes or "contents" (in the sense of the first kind of definition of content analysis discussed above) from a sample to a population from which this sample was drawn are not suitable content analysis research questions either, but for a different reason. Although their answers do rely on empirical evidence, without abductive inferences to phenomena outside the texts being analyzed, generalizations are inductive and cannot answer content analysis research questions. Thus, in content analysis, research questions have the following characteristics:

- They are believed to be answerable (abductively inferable) by examinations of a body of texts. (In Figure 2.1, this is indicated by the bold dashed arrows.)

- They delineate a set of possible (hypothetical) answers among which analysts select. (In Figure 2.1, an answer is indicated by the unlabeled diamond.)

- They concern currently inaccessible phenomena.

- They allow for (in)validation—at least in principle—by acknowledging another way to observe or substantiate the occurrence of the inferred phenomena. (In Figure 2.1, this is indicated by the thin dashed arrow from the worlds of others to the answer to the research question.)

Context 2.4.3

I have argued above that texts acquire significance (meanings, contents, symbolic qualities, and interpretations) in the contexts of their use. Although data enter a content analysis from outside, they become texts to the analyst within the context that the analyst has chosen to read them—that is, from within the analysis. A context is always someone's construction, the conceptual environment of a text, the situation in which it plays a role. In a content analysis, the context explains what the analyst does with the texts; it could be considered the analyst's best hypothesis for how the texts came to be, what they mean, what they can tell or do. In the course of a content analysis, the context embraces all the knowledge that the analyst applies to given texts, whether in the form of scientific theories, plausibly argued propositions, empirical evidence, grounded intuitions, or knowledge of reading habits.

The context specifies the world in which texts can be related to the analyst's research questions. This world is always one of many. Political analysts construct worlds that differ from those of politicians, often embracing additional perspectives, but those worlds also differ from the worlds of psychologists, journalists, historians, psychotherapists, scholars of literature, and—naturally—communication researchers, who pursue their own research agenda and approach texts with their own questions, concepts, models, and analytical tools. Scholars in different disciplines tend to place the same texts in different contexts but rarely without acknowledging that there are other readings, other contexts, other worlds, within which given texts function as well—authors, audiences, users, and beneficiaries, for example. In Figure 2.1, these worlds are shown in the ovals embracing texts and their multiple meanings.

Knowledge of the context for content analyzing given texts can be separated into two kinds:

- The network of stable correlations, which are believed to connect available texts to the possible answers to given research questions, whether these correlations are established empirically, derived from applicable theory, or merely assumed for the purpose of an analysis

■ Contributing conditions, which consist of all the factors that are known to affect that network of stable correlations in foreseeable ways

In Figure 2.1, these relationships are shown by a bold line and a bold arrow.

To use an example that is far from simple: In an ordinary conversation, what is observed and heard as being said at any one moment (the data) is understandable only in the context of what has been said before, by whom and to whom, the responses it elicited from the participants, and how it directed the conversation. This is an observer's account of a conversation, from outside of it. To participants, their version of what is going on (the contexts that include the other participants) is not necessarily shared. In fact, there would be no point in conversing if all participants saw their worlds, thought, and spoke alike. A conversation analyst contextualizes the transcript of a conversation (the text) in yet another way, by constructing a world (the analyst's context) within which the participants appear to "speak" in the analytical terms that the conversation analyst is familiar with and brings to the analyzed transcript. Whether a conversation analyst wants to infer the intentions of the participants to initiate certain moves (turn taking, for example) or how addressees will respond to a string of "he said–she said" (the evolution of a topic), the analyst draws on knowledge of the empirical relationship between these speech acts (the correlations that connect one to another) and the strengths (perlocutionary forces) of particular utterances, the network of connections that leads, hopefully, from texts to answers to the research question.

A conversation is not a mechanical system. Participants alter the rules of their engagement as it unfolds. This leaves outside observers uncertain as to what the participants mean, how they understand what is going on, and which rules govern the conversation at any one moment. Because conversation analysts tend not to participate in the conversations they analyze, and therefore have no way of asking the interlocutors how they see their situation, the analysts have to acknowledge other determining variables (the contributing conditions) and find ways to ascertain how they affect the correlations relied upon to lead to the intended inferences.

Inasmuch as a context stands in place of what is momentarily inaccessible to direct observation, there is no limit to the number of contexts that may be applicable in a given analysis. Unless told, readers of the conclusions of a content analysis may not know the context that the analyst was using and may come to seriously misleading interpretations. In view of this possibility, *content analysts need to make their chosen contexts explicit, so that the results of their analyses will be clear to their scientific peers and to the beneficiaries of the research results.* Without explication of the context, the steps that a content analyst takes may not be comprehensible to careful readers, and the results to which they lead may not be validatable by other means.

2.4.4   Analytical Constructs

Analytical constructs operationalize what the content analyst knows about the context, specifically the network of correlations that are assumed to explain how available texts are connected to the possible answers to the analyst's questions and the conditions under which these correlations could change. Analytical constructs represent this network in computable forms. Extracted from the known or assumed context and entered into the research process, analytical constructs *ensure that an analysis of given texts models the texts' context of use,* which means that the analysis does not proceed in violation of what is known of the conditions surrounding the texts. Procedurally, analytical constructs take the form of more or less complex "if-then" statements, much like those used in computer programs. These "if-then" statements amount to *rules of inference* that guide the analyst, in steps, from the texts to the answers to the research questions. They also render knowledge of the context *portable to other content analyses* of similar contexts and make it possible for students and critics to examine the procedures that a content analyst has been using. In this respect, analytical constructs function much like testable mini-theories of a context, with the provision that they are computable on the coded features of available texts.

For example, a computer-aided content analysis might employ a dictionary of tags that mimics how competent speakers of a language categorize words into classes with similar meanings. Such a dictionary assumes linguistic stability, which may not be warranted, but it at least models a standard competence of language use. Another approach that an analyst might take is to adopt a computational theory of a context—a neuronal network model, for instance— that promises to explain how people form categories from words that occur in proximity to each other. Of course, labeling an analytical construct a "model" does not guarantee that it accurately represents the network of relationships that are relevant to readers and writers. More often, content analysts draw on empirically obtained correlations between observed and currently unobserved variables. Correlations measure the extent of a linear relationship between variables—for example, between the rate of recorded speech disturbances and anxiety—which, if sufficiently general, could in turn be applied to individual cases, here yielding a prediction of a speaker's anxiety. However, as linguistic variables are rarely describable in intervals and linear regression equations tend to hold only under restricted conditions, the use of such constructs typically requires that the analyst have additional information about the conditions under which the construct is predictive of that behavior. Similarly, knowing that public agendas are influenced by the mass-media coverage of pertinent events may give a content analyst the idea of an analytical construct for analyzing media coverage in place of public opinion surveys. Such research, which has been done, requires a fairly detailed operationalization of the conditions under which verbal or pictorial elements influence particular public conversations.

Analytical constructs need not be perfect, of course, but unfortunately, many text analysts employ computational procedures that have no obvious relationship to any context in which given texts would arguably make sense. Counting units of text or applying sophisticated statistical techniques will always yield something, but this does not guarantee that the results will refer to anything. Content analysts must make sure that their analytical constructions model the contexts they have chosen. The purpose of all analytical constructs is *to ensure that texts are processed in reference to what is known about their use.*

2.4.5   Inferences

The inferential nature of content analysis should by now be obvious. Content analytic inferences may be hidden in the human process of coding. They may be built into analytical procedures, such as the dictionaries in computer-aided text analyses or well-established indices. Sometimes, especially after complex statistical procedures have been applied, inferences appear in the analyst's interpretations of the statistical findings. Figure 2.1 depicts the path that an inference takes with bold and broken lines, with the inference motivated or explained by an analytical construct that enters the analysis as a representation of the chosen context.

Because the word *inference* has several meanings, it is important to distinguish the meaning that is relevant to this discussion from others that are perhaps more familiar to readers. In logic, at least three types of inferences are distinguished:

- Deductive inferences are implied in their premises. For example, if all humans speak a language, then John, being human, must speak one as well. Deductive inferences are logically conclusive. They proceed from generalizations to particulars.

- Inductive inferences are generalizations to similar kinds. For example, I might infer from the fact that all of my neighbors speak English that all humans do. This inference is not logically conclusive, but it has a certain probability of being correct. Statistical generalizations from smaller samples to larger populations (typical of social research) and the idea of measuring the statistical significance of scientific hypotheses involve inferences of this kind. They proceed from particulars to generalizations.

- Abductive inferences proceed across logically distinct domains, from particulars of one kind to particulars of another kind. (These are the kinds of inferences of interest to content analysis, where they proceed from texts to the answers to the analyst's questions.) Consider linguistic competence and age. Logically, neither implies the other. However, if one has practical experience with infants' language acquisition, one might be able to infer children's ages from the sounds they make or from the vocabulary they use. Of course, one can make such inferences only with a certain probability, but the probability may be strengthened if one is able to take other variables (contributing conditions) into account.

Deductive and inductive inferences are not central to content analysis. The following examples of inferences employed in content analysis are all abductive in nature:

- One might date a document from the vocabulary used within it.

- One might infer the religious affiliations of political leaders from the metaphors used in their speeches.

- One might infer the readability of an essay from a measure of the complexity of its composition.

- One might infer whether someone is lying from his or her nonverbal (facial) behavior.

- One might infer the problems of a city from the concerns expressed in letters written to the city's mayor's office.

- One might infer the prevailing conceptualizations of writers and readers from the proximities of words in frequently used texts.

- One might infer editorial biases from a comparison of the editorial pages of different newspapers.

- One might infer a writer's psychopathology from the images used in her prose.

- One might infer the identity of the author of an unsigned document from the document's statistical similarities to texts whose authors are known.

- One might infer the political affiliations of citizens from the TV shows they choose to watch.

- One might infer an individual's propensity to engage in a hate crime from the ethnic categories he uses in ordinary speech.

- One might infer the likelihood of war from the coverage of international affairs in the elite newspapers of neighboring countries.

According to Eco (1994):

> The logic of interpretation is the Peircean logic of abduction. To explain a conjecture means to figure out a law that can explain a Result. The "secret code" of a text is such a Law. . . . in the natural sciences the conjecture has to try only the law, since the Result is under the eyes of everybody, while in textual interpretation only the discovery of a "good" Law makes the Result acceptable. (p. 59)

For Josephson and Josephson (1994, p. 5), abduction starts with a body of data (facts, observations, givens)—our text. A hypothesis—our analytical construct—if true, would explain these data. No other hypothesis can explain the data as well as the chosen one does. Therefore, the hypothesis is probably true and can be used to deduce other entailments—that is, answer our research questions.

Abductive inference is Sherlock Holmes's logic of reasoning as well (Bonfantini & Proni, 1988; Truzzi, 1988). Holmes's creator, Sir Arthur Conan Doyle, always lets him find empirical connections and apply bits of common knowledge in the context of established facts that he is then able to weave ingeniously into an inferential network containing the initially unrecognizable chain of logical steps from known facts to the perpetrator of an unobserved crime. Content analysts are in a similar position of having to draw inferences about phenomena that are not directly observable, and they are often equally resourceful in using a mixture of statistical knowledge, theory, experience, and intuition to answer their research questions from available texts.

In this respect, the whole enterprise of content analysis may well be regarded as an argument in support of an analyst's abductive claims. In Toulmin's (1958) theory of argumentation, which applies not just to abductions, the move from data (D) to conclusions or claims (C) must be justified by a suitable warrant (W). In his example, learning that "X is a Swede," the inference that "X most likely is a Protestant" is warranted by the knowledge that "most Swedes are Protestants." Because this inference is not without exceptions, it includes a qualification (Q) of the conclusion (C) (i.e., "most likely"). The warrant provides the logical bridge between the data and the conclusion. Toulmin also introduces another element: the ground on which the warrant may be justified, or the backing (B). In Figure 2.1 we may recognize the diagram that Toulmin (p. 104) uses to show the relationships among the above-mentioned parts of arguments:

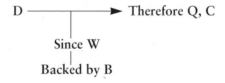

In moving from texts to the answer to a research question, as illustrated in Figure 2.1, it is the assumptive analytical construct plus the assurance that the analysis has been performed reliably that warrants that inference, which in turn is backed by the analyst's knowledge of the context in which the texts occur or are interpreted:

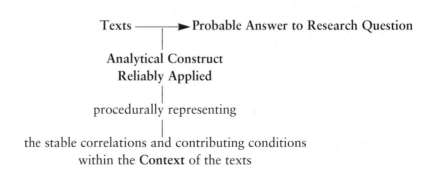

Validating Evidence   2.4.6

Any content analysis should be validatable in principle. Because the raison d'être of content analysis is the absence of direct observational evidence, validation may be difficult or infeasible, if not impossible, in practice. It is infeasible when a content analysis is to be acted upon in the absence of direct observational evidence—for example, in wartime analysis of planned military activities from domestic propaganda or in assessments of whether a politician is lying. It is impossible when research questions concern past or future happenings, such as inferences from surviving documents to historical facts, inferences from the works of deceased authors to their intentions, or inferences from psychological tests to an individual's aptitude for a particular job. The point of requiring that content analyses be "validatable in principle" is to prevent analysts from pursuing research questions that allow no empirical validation or that yield results with no backing except by the authority of the researcher. For example, a conclusion from an analysis of television fiction that hedonism is on the rise in the United States means nothing unless those who claim such findings can show that this conclusion is not merely their abstraction from fictional programming, but also has some independently observable reality—that is, unless they can show that a rise in hedonism is manifest in something other than television fiction.

Ex post facto validation of content analysis is not merely a matter of curiosity. It can increase confidence in the results of future content analyses of similar texts and in similar contexts, but only if the categories of analysis and the analytical constructs are used repeatedly, so that successes and failures can be weighted against each other and used to advance the technique in the long run. Much too often, researchers design content analysis studies ad hoc and conduct them without any thought of validation; such research contributes little to the literature on content analysis.

A good example of ex post facto validation is George's (1959a) effort (mentioned in Chapter 1) to examine documents captured after World War II to see whether they matched what the Federal Communications Commission propaganda analysts had inferred during the war and to evaluate the FCC researchers' techniques for use by future analysts. In 1943, Janis (1943/1965) proposed an indirect method of validation, suggesting that the results of mass-media content analyses should at least correlate with audience verbal reports or observed behaviors (e.g., public opinion polls, voting, consumption, or aggression). Thus Gerbner and his colleagues sought to correlate the amount of violence seen on television with survey data on audience members' perceptions of how violent their world "really" is (see, e.g., Gerbner, Gross, Signorielli, Morgan, & Jackson-Beeck, 1979; Gerbner, Gross, Morgan, & Signorielli, 1994).

As noted above, our framework demands merely that a content analysis be validatable *in principle*. For example, if a content analyst infers what a particular group of voters learned from TV campaign ads about a candidate for political office, then, potentially, a survey of those exposed to the ads could validate or invalidate this inference. However, if a content analyst insists that such TV campaign ads have certain contents, there is no way for others to validate this "finding." Repeating this particular content analysis would merely indicate the degree to which the original analysis was reliable. Similarly, finding that a certain word occurs with a certain frequency does not constitute an abductive inference. Recounting cannot validate what a frequency is inferred to mean.

2.5 CONTRASTS AND COMPARISONS

Every research technique has its powers and its limitations, and content analysis is no exception. A researcher can misapply a technique or use a technique that is ill suited for a particular purpose, in ignorance of better ones. In this section, I contrast content analysis with other techniques used in social research, paying special attention to the four distinguishing features of content analysis.

Content analysis is an unobtrusive technique. As Heisenberg's uncertainty principle tells us, acts of measurement interfere with the phenomena being assessed and create contaminated observations; the deeper the observer probes, the greater the severity of the contamination. For the social sciences, Webb, Campbell, Schwartz, and Sechrest (1966) have enumerated several ways in which subjects react to being involved in scientific inquiries and how these can introduce errors into the data that are analyzed:

- Through the subjects' awareness of being observed or tested

- Through the artificiality of the task or the subjects' lack of experience with the task

- Through the expectations that subjects bring to the role of interviewee or respondent

- Through the influence of the measurement process on the subjects

- Through stereotypes held by subjects and the subjects' preferences for casting certain responses

- Through experimenter/interviewer interaction effects on the subjects

Controlled experiments, interviews, focus groups, surveys, and projective tests are especially vulnerable to such errors. By contrast, content analyses, computer simulations, research using already available statistics, and interpretive research (in cultural studies, for example) are nonreactive or unobtrusive. Researchers using ethnographic methods subscribe to the unobtrusive ideal as well, but while conducting fieldwork even the most careful ethnographers cannot escape influencing their informers.

Social researchers may want to avoid reactive situations for two primary reasons. The first is that *undue influence on the situation that gives rise to the data may distort the data, jeopardizing the validity of the research*. For this reason, ethnomethodologists prefer to obtain data in natural settings, psychiatrists avoid asking their patients questions that might induce false memories, and economists investigate mathematical models rather than experiment with the real economy. The second reason is that *researchers need to conceal their interest in the data for fear of being manipulated by their sources*. Instrumental assertions are difficult to analyze (Mahl, 1959). Had Goebbels, the Nazi-era minister of propaganda in Germany, known how, by what methods, and for what purposes American analysts were examining his broadcasts during World War II, he would have found ways to deceive the analysts. Individuals can be taught how to achieve high scores on aptitude tests, and those who believe that success in their chosen career paths depends on their scoring well on these tests eagerly seek appropriate education. The extent to which preparatory instruction improves students' scores on a given test is also the extent of that test's invalidity. As an unobtrusive technique, content analysis can avoid such biases altogether.

Content analysis can handle unstructured matter as data. For efficiency's sake, researchers gain a considerable advantage if they can impose a structure on the data-making process so that the results are readily analyzable. Surveys, mail questionnaires, and structured interviews typically offer respondents predefined choices that are easily tabulated, coded, or processed by computer. But they thereby also prevent the respondents' individual voices from being heard. Subjects in laboratory experiments are often taught what amounts to a highly artificial data language: pushing buttons, scaling their opinions numerically, identifying shapes or forms they may never have seen before, or administering electric shocks to fellow subjects in place of less clearly measurable expressions of violence. These techniques are successful because they allow researchers to suppress unwieldy variations, which are due largely to the fact that ordinary human subjects see, talk, and behave in many different ways.

Typically, content analysts become interested in data only after the data have been generated. They have to cope with texts in a diversity of formats associated with different purposes, do not always find what they are looking for, and cannot fully anticipate the terms and categories used by the sources of their texts. This puts content analysts in an analytical position that is less than advantageous, a condition they share with ethnomethodologists, anthropologists doing fieldwork, historiographical researchers, and researchers using hermeneutical or interpretive approaches (such as those used in studies of politics, psychotherapy, feminist scholarship, and social constructionism). The chief advantage of the unstructuredness of content analysis data is that *it preserves the conceptions of the data's sources*, which structured methods largely ignore.

Content analysis is context sensitive and therefore allows the researcher to process as data texts that are significant, meaningful, informative, and even representational to others. Context-insensitive methods, such as controlled laboratory experiments, surveys, structured interviews, and statistical analyses, generate data without reference to their original contexts, thus disembodying observations, unitizing complex and contiguous events, and taking single words out of their contexts of use and representing them as data points in the analysts' theoretical spaces. In such methods, it no longer matters what gave rise to the data, how various elements in the data relate to each other, how others understand the data, or what the data mean to their sources. Context-sensitive methods, in contrast, acknowledge the textuality of the data—that is, they recognize that the data are read by and make sense to others, and they proceed by reference to contexts of their own. Inferences drawn through the use of such methods have a better chance of being relevant to the users of the analyzed texts.

Content analysts may not always be as qualitative as are political analysts, who live in the very process they analyze. Nor are they quite as free as cultural studies researchers and conversation analysts, who contextualize their texts in a vocabulary that may appear alien to the people they speak for or of. Finally, content analysts may not be quite as limited in scope as the users of projective tests, who confine themselves to inferences concerning individuals' psychological characteristics (much as in content analyses of the second kind of definition discussed above).

Content analysis can cope with large volumes of data. Much of ethnomethodology as well as case study approaches, historiographical methods, and interpretive research rely on small samples of text; the volume of data is limited largely by what a researcher can read reliably and without losing track of relevant details. Although content analysis can be used to analyze small samples of texts (in fact, this is quite common, especially in the academic world, where funds are few and stakes are not as high as in politics, commerce, or medicine), such uses do not realize the technique's full potential. The ability to process large volumes of text in content analysis is paid for by the explicitness of the method's procedures, which, if clearly stated, can be applied repeatedly, by many coders or by computer software. As noted above, Berelson and Lazarsfeld (1948) stated long ago that content analysts must be systematic in their reading of texts and suggested that category schemes be devised that could be applied to every unit of text equally and without exception. Explicit vocabularies enable content analysts to employ many coders and pool their readings, which allows them to process quantities of text that far exceed what single individuals can analyze reliably. Consider the following numbers of units of analysis processed in early content analyses, largely without the aid of computers:

- 481 personal conversations (Landis & Burtt, 1924)

- 427 school textbooks (Pierce, 1930)

- 4,022 advertising slogans (Shuman, 1937; cited in Berelson, 1952)

- 8,039 newspaper editorials (Foster, 1938)

- 800 news of foreign language radio programs (Arnheim & Bayne, 1941)

- 19,553 editorials (Pool, 1952a)

- 15,000 characters in 1,000 hours of television fiction (Gerbner et al., 1979)

Of course, these numbers, which were considered impressive in 1980, when the first edition of *Content Analysis* was published, are now dwarfed by the size of the electronic full-text databases that have emerged since. At the time of this writing, ERIC, a clearinghouse for educational and social science writing, has more than 750,000 articles in its database. In Britain, FT Profile holds a large array of different file types, including newspapers, news wire stories, magazines and journals, company and industry reports, lists of references, and research publications (Hansen, 1995). In the United States, LexisNexis provides online access to the full texts of all major legal publications, newspapers, scientific journals, and corporate materials—about 50,000 publications, some accumulating since the late 1980s and early 1990s, each containing numerous articles or news items. Dialog is an even more eclectic online source of texts. The exponentially growing Internet is an unimaginably large but for the most part unmined source of content analysis data. The availability of electronic texts is fast expanding to other kinds of materials, such as survey questions and responses, scientific findings, film scripts, transcripts of television news programs, image archives, sound recordings, and graphical representations in Web pages, making content analysis an increasingly important research technique. These explosive developments have had the effect of bringing content analysis closer to large population surveys, but without such surveys' undesirable qualities (i.e., without being obtrusive, meaning obliterating, and context insensitive). They are also shifting the bottleneck of content analysis from the costs of access and tedious human coding to needs for good theory, sound methodology, and software that is capable of coping with such volumes. Here, pioneering work is progressing.

CHAPTER 3

Uses and Inferences

This chapter reviews the breadth of applications of content analysis, not in terms of subject matter or the disciplines that engage the technique but in terms of the kinds of inferences that enable content analysts to accomplish their tasks. Several types of logic capable of relating data to their contexts are distinguished here: systems, standards, indices, representations, conversations, and institutions. These could be regarded as possible theories that content analyses need.

<table>
<tr><td>3.1</td><td></td><td>**TRADITIONAL OVERVIEWS**</td></tr>
</table>

Content analysis has an important place in the wide range of investigative tools available to researchers. As noted in Chapter 2, content analysis is an unobtrusive technique that allows researchers to analyze relatively unstructured data in view of the meanings, symbolic qualities, and expressive contents they have and of the communicative roles they play in the lives of the data's sources. The combination of these features is unique among research methods. Because virtually all social processes can be seen as transacted through matter that is meaningful to the participants—symbols, messages, images, performances, and organizational phenomena, even nondiscursive practices—the widest use of content analysis is found in the social sciences and humanities, although legal, political, and commercial applications are rising in number as well. Scholars who have surveyed content analysis research have used a variety of categories to describe the growing diversity of research techniques used under the umbrella of content analysis. Janis (1943/1965) offers the following classification:

(1) *Pragmatical content analysis*—procedures which classify signs according to their probable causes or effects (e.g., counting the number of times

44

that something is said which is likely to have the effect of producing favorable attitudes toward Germany in a given audience).

(2) *Semantical content analysis*—procedures which classify signs according to their meanings (e.g., counting the number of times that Germany is referred to, irrespective of the particular words that may be used to make the reference).

  (a) *designations analysis* provides the frequency with which certain objects (persons, things, groups, or concepts) are referred to, that is, roughly speaking, subject-matter analysis (e.g., references to German foreign policy).

  (b) *attribution analysis* provides the frequency with which certain characterizations are referred to (e.g., references to dishonesty).

  (c) *assertions analysis* provides the frequency with which certain objects are characterized in a particular way, that is, roughly speaking, thematic analysis (e.g., references to German foreign policy as dishonest).

(3) *Sign-vehicle analysis*—procedures which classify content according to the psychophysical properties of the signs (e.g., counting the number of times the word "Germany" appears). (p. 57)

Leites and Pool (1942; cited in Berelson & Lazarsfeld, 1948) describe four functions of content analysis:

■ To confirm what is already believed

■ To correct the "optical illusions" of specialists

■ To settle disagreements among specialists

■ To formulate and test hypotheses about symbols

Berelson (1952) lists 17 uses:

■ To describe trends in communication content

■ To trace the development of scholarship

■ To disclose international differences in communication content

■ To compare media or levels of communication

 ■ To audit communication content against objectives

■ To construct and apply communication standards

■ To aid in technical research operations (to code open-ended questions in survey interviews)

■ To expose propaganda techniques

- To measure the readability of communication materials

- To discover stylistic features

- To identify the intentions and other characteristics of the communicators

- To determine the psychological state of persons or groups

- To detect the existence of propaganda (primarily for legal purposes)

- To secure political and military intelligence

- To reflect attitudes, interests, and values (cultural patterns) of population groups

- To reveal the focus of attention

- To describe attitudinal and behavioral responses to communications

Stone, Dunphy, Smith, and Ogilvie (1966) note that although the historical origins of content analysis lie in journalism and mass communication, they found applications of the technique in the following empirical domains:

- Psychiatry

- Psychology

- History

- Anthropology

- Education

- Philology and literary analysis

- Linguistics

I have already mentioned Holsti's (1969) commitment to an encoding/decoding paradigm, which, much like Janis's approach, places message content in the context of communication between senders and receivers. Consequently, Holsti surveys content analyses in terms of three principal purposes:

- To describe *manifest characteristics* of communication—that is, asking what, how, and to whom something is said

- To make inferences as to the *antecedents* of communication—that is, asking *why* something is said

- To make inferences as to the *consequences* of communication—that is, asking *with what effects* something is said

The way in which I categorize the content analyses discussed in this chapter deviates from the ways used by the authors cited above in that it focuses on how researchers *use* content analytic techniques and on how researchers then justify the *inferences* they draw in their analyses. The categories addressed are as follows:

- Extrapolations

- Standards

- Indices and symptoms

- Linguistic re-presentations

- Conversations

- Institutional processes

Not all of the content analysts whose work is reviewed here have explicated the logic of their inferences as we would hope they would. In some cases, this logic is embedded in the notions of meaning that the analysts have subscribed to. In others, the logic can be found in the more or less explicit assumptions that the researchers have made regarding the contexts of their data. Often, this logic remains hidden because researchers take it for granted, presuming that their own tacit knowledge should be obvious to everyone. I have already noted that Berelson (1952) did not even feel the need to define content. Analysts need to render their assumptions, the logic they employ, examinable. The appropriateness of particular forms of reasoning is an empirical question, of course, not a logical one, and analysts need to judge the appropriateness of their inferences on a case-by-case basis. I have chosen to review content analyses in these terms because such a review will lead most naturally to an understanding of the notion of analytical constructs—but that is another chapter.

EXTRAPOLATIONS 3.2

Extrapolations are inferences of unobserved instances in the intervals between or beyond the observations (data points). Some well-known kinds of extrapolations are interpolations, predictions, extensions, derivations of theorems from other theorems, and systems. Let's take the notion of a system as a general case. A system is a conceptual device, a "complex variable," one might say. The reality that may be described in a system's terms is not part of the definition of a system, although its construction may well be so motivated. Mathematics supplies systems. Its axioms are mathematical, not empirical. Minimally, a system consists of the following:

- *A set of components* whose states are variable

- *Relations* that are manifest in constraints on the co-occurrence of the components' states

- *Transformations* according to which some relations imply other relations in time or in space

One example of a system is our solar system, in which celestial bodies move in relation to each other. The configurations of planets follow a temporal sequence. For someone who knows the system's transformation rules, data on one configuration imply all succeeding configurations. This is a classical Newtonian system. Kinship terminology also constitutes a system, although it is far from deterministic, not as dynamic as the solar system is conceived to be. It defines kin in terms of certain relations between individuals—in English, according to gender, descent, and marriage—and prescribes rights, obligations, modes of address, and so on among kinfolk toward each other. The system allows "extrapolations" in the sense of extending this terminology to individuals entering the system, whether as spouses, children, or adoptees, and it transforms the roles of these individuals relative to each other throughout their lifetimes within the system. Another example of a system is found in the treatment of language as a system of signs, as in the work of Ferdinand de Saussure. The components of language (words and sounds) are thought to be combinable into larger units (sentences and utterances), following grammatical rules. Knowledge of the system enables the knower to generate novel strings of words that are all considered well formed, such as English sentences. Grammar, it should be noted, is not a "natural" kind of system. It is constructed by academic linguists under the assumption that language is a system in its own right.

Some kinds of systems, especially social systems, can be quite complex. The inferences of interest to sociological content analysts are grounded in knowledge of a society's transformations, which enables analysts to extrapolate features of the system beyond the time and space of available texts—but always within the domain of the system's description. As in the case of grammar, the "rules" by which a social system works are not natural. They are sociological constructions. Although systems can be elaborate, in comparison with other kinds of inferences, extrapolations are relatively simple.

In content analysis, the idea of studying systems goes back to Tenney (1912), who asked:

> Why should not society study its own methods of producing its various varieties of thinking by establishing [a] . . . careful system of bookkeeping? . . . What is needed . . . is the continuous analysis of a large number of journals. . . . The records in themselves would constitute a series of observations of the "social weather," comparable in accuracy to the statistics of the United States Weather Bureau. (p. 896)

Tenney described systematic relations between subject matter categories within the newspapers he analyzed, noted changes in their distribution over time, and explored, especially, the ethnic characteristics of these publications. He equated the dynamics of press coverage in an entire country with the thinking processes of that country's population, but he lacked methods that were adequate to process the great volume of data that the construction of such a system would require. Tenney made his proposal not only before computers existed, but also before systems theory had been developed.

Rapoport (1969) prepared the ground for a systems theory of "verbal corpuses" as he sought answers to questions such as what it means to describe a large body of verbal data as behaving, changing, and evolving, and what the suitable components, relationships, and laws of interaction within such corpuses might be. Although he was aware that our symbolic world both mirrors and constitutes human existence, and that it can be both enriched in talk and polluted by institutional policies, he suggested that researchers could most fruitfully pursue the large-scale study of verbal corpuses, at least to start out with. This study would be done without reference to speakers, symbol users, and meanings—that is, as a system with its own autonomous regularities. From this perspective, content analysis could be said to probe selectively into what Boulding (1978) has called a "noosphere," a sphere of human knowledge distinct from the "biosphere" in which humans live qua organisms.

Trends   3.2.1

The prototype of a systems approach in content analysis is the extrapolation of trends. In one of the earliest content analyses ever conducted, Speed (1893) compared several New York dailies published in 1881 with the same newspapers published 12 years later and observed changes in the frequencies of subject matter categories. Of course, data on only two points in time hardly lend themselves to solid predictions, but Speed's lamenting the continuing decline of newspaper coverage of literary matters and the increase in gossip, sports, and fiction, raising the question of where this trend would lead, is a clear indication of his desire to predict how newspaper publishing was changing. Lasswell (1941) proposed a study and presented preliminary findings on trends in the frequencies with which references to various countries occurred in different national presses. Loeventhal (1944) studied the changing definition of heroes in popular magazines and found a drift (still ongoing today) away from working professionals and businessmen as heroes and toward entertainers.

Other trend studies have concerned values in inspirational literature, advertising themes, and political slogans, as well as the frequency of the use of the word *mainstreaming* in several subcategories of educational research (Miller, Fullmer, & Walls, 1996). Researchers have also undertaken numerous analyses of trends in scholarly literature, from sociology (Shanas, 1945) to content analysis (Barcus, 1959), to ascertain the directions in which particular fields seem to be moving. Shanas (1945), for example, analyzed emerging interests in the field of sociology in the United States by examining the distribution of articles in the *American Journal of Sociology* over a 50-year period. Scholars in many academic disciplines have, from time to time, made efforts to review their literature to assess the directions in which their fields were moving and to identify new frontiers. One of the more extensive content analyses conducted to date using a time-series analysis approach is Namenwirth's (1973) analysis of value changes in U.S. political party platforms over a 120-year period. Namenwirth and Weber (1987) also applied time-series analysis to a study of all speeches made by British monarchs between 1689 and 1972. Both studies revealed two independent cycles of value changes in the data, a short-term cycle and a long-term cycle—such findings amount to descriptions of the dynamics of autonomous systems. Thome and Rahlf (1996) analyzed these same data using a "filtering" methodology instead of time-series analysis, but both methods operate within the notion of a system that enables the analyst to interpolate between data points and extrapolate its ups and downs into the future.

Political party platforms, policy positions, and campaign materials are natural candidates for this kind of content analysis because they are recurrent and there is an interest in knowing what comes next. The European Consortium for Political Research, constituted in 1979, has undertaken numerous trend studies of how different political systems behave over time, in various dimensions, and concerning a variety of emerging issues (see, e.g., Budge, Robertson, & Hearl, 1987). For more than two decades, consortium researchers have coded nearly 2,000 party manifestos using a single coding scheme based on 56 categories and performed numerous trend analyses; they are now experimenting with computerizing this approach (Pennings & Keman, 2002).

3.2.2   Patterns

Another kind of content analysis involves the extrapolative use of patterns. In folklore, for example, researchers have conducted structural analyses of riddles, proverbs, folktales, and narratives with the aim of identifying patterns that have a high degree of commonality within genres, regardless of particular contents (Armstrong, 1959), and can therefore be regarded as generative of those genres. Such analysts begin by identifying the constituent elements within a body of literature and then seek to describe the logic that relates these elements. Thus Sebeok and Orzack (1953), analyzing Cheremis charms, found that in such charms a "purely factual statement" about the world is followed by a "motif of an extremely improbable eventuality." Labov (1972) found a set of components that accounted for the narratives he had elicited and considered these the building blocks for the construction of narratives generally.

Another example of the extrapolation of patterns is the analysis of genealogies within a body of literature through patterns of citation. Scholarly works tend to cite previously published scholarly works, which in turn cite earlier such works, and so on. Tracing such citations from the present into the past or from a designated origin into the present reveals networks that show how the various contributions to the literature are interconnected—for example, what happens to an idea as it moves through various scholars' publications. Garfield (1979) relied on this simple idea when he developed his "citation index" as an alternative to information retrieval by keywords. Communication researchers have charted communication channels among members of organizations as senders and receivers and have analyzed those connections in terms of typical network features that organizations tend to reproduce. Research concerning word co-occurrences within sentences or paragraphs has also revealed networklike "association" patterns that can permeate a genre.

Combined interest in trends and patterns has led to many interesting content analyses. Bales's (1950) "interaction process analysis" yielded patterns of communication, evaluation, control, decision making, tension reduction, and reintegration, all of which were identified within 12 basic categories of verbal exchanges in small groups. Holsti, Brody, and North (1965) studied public statements made by major decision makers in the United States and the Soviet Union during the 1962 Cuban missile crisis and distinguished perceptions and expressions within these successive statements that they described in terms of Osgood's semantic differential dimensions: evaluative, strength, and potency. With the help of a dynamic interdependency model, Holsti et al. found that these data proved moderately predictive of the pattern of emotional responses each group of decision makers made to the other.

Differences   3.2.3

Differences are central to all systems approaches. The differences of interest here stem from comparisons among the variable components of a system and may be extrapolated to differences among similar components elsewhere. For example, analysts may examine differences in the message content generated by two kinds of communicators or differences within one source in different social situations, when the source is addressing different audiences, or when the source is operating with different expectations or with different information. Differences in the news coverage of political campaigns have been correlated with editorial endorsements (Klein & Maccoby, 1954). Differences in the news coverage of civil rights issues have been explained in terms of various newspaper characteristics, such as geographic location, ownership, and political orientation (Broom & Reece, 1955). Differences in newspaper content have been correlated with whether or not newspapers face competition within their regions (Nixon & Jones, 1956).

Gerbner (1964) demonstrated how different ideological and class orientations are reproduced in the stream of French news media messages in the reporting of an apolitical crime. Researchers have also shown how messages from one source covary with the audiences they are intended to address by comparing, for example, the political speeches that John Foster Dulles made before different kinds of groups (Cohen, 1957; Holsti, 1962). Research has linked differences in television sports reporting of men's and women's athletics to prevailing cultural values (Tuggle,

1997) and has shown differences in works of fiction written for upper-, middle-, and lower-class readers (Albrecht, 1956) as well as in advertisements in magazines with predominantly black and predominantly white readerships (Berkman, 1963). Studies of differences between input and output in communication are exemplified by Allport and Faden's (1940) examination of the relationship between the number of sources of information available to a newspaper and what finally appears in print, by Asheim's (1950) analysis of what happens to a book when it is adapted into a movie script, and by studies that compare scientific findings with the information on such findings disseminated in the popular media.

The Hoover Institution's study titled Revolution and the Development of International Relations (RADIR) combined the analysis of differences between media and the analysis of trends. The RADIR researchers identified so-called key symbols such as *democracy, equality, rights,* and *freedom* in 19,553 editorials that appeared in American, British, French, German, and Russian prestige newspapers during the period 1890–1949. Analyses of these data led Pool (1951) to correlations that he felt able to generalize. He observed, for example, that proletarian doctrines replace liberal traditions, that an increasing threat of war is correlated with growth in militarism and nationalism, and that hostility toward other nations is related to perceived insecurity. Although these symbols refer to aspects of a political reality, and the researchers were no doubt keenly aware of the contexts from which they were taken, the researchers did not need these references to conduct their analyses. The analysts tried to establish which differences were maintained over time, which differences increased or decreased relative to each other, and how they compensated for or amplified each other. For example, Pool (1952b) observed that symbols of democracy become less frequent when a representative form of government is accepted rather than in dispute. It should be noted that the knowledge of whether a government is generally accepted or in dispute comes from outside the system of selected symbols the RADIR researchers were studying. To the extent that external variables explain a system's behavior, in the form of the contributing conditions illustrated in Figure 2.1, the system is not entirely autonomous. However, nobody can prevent content analysts who study such systems from including symbols of dissent, defiance, and struggle to render the systems self-explanatory.

In a very different approach, Gerbner and his colleagues accumulated a very large database on television violence in fictional programming that enabled them to make extrapolations (recommendations) of interest to policy makers (see, e.g., Gerbner, Gross, Morgan, & Signorielli, 1994; Gerbner, Gross, Signorielli, & Jackson-Beeck, 1979). Gerbner's (1969) "message systems analysis" proposes to trace the movement of mass-media culture through time by means of a system consisting of four kinds of measures of any category of content (component):

- The frequencies with which a system's components occur, or "what is"

- The order of priorities assigned to those components, or "what is important"

- The affective qualities associated with the components, or "what is right"

■ The proximal or logical associations between particular components, or "what is related to what"

One might question Gerbner's equation of frequencies with "what is," how stable these quantitative measures really are, and whether the system is sufficiently autonomous. The point, however, is that any system of measurements, when observed long enough, will allow analysts to make predictions in the system's own terms, whatever they mean.

Simonton (1994) has made an interesting and rather unusual use of the content analysis of systems of differences in his analysis of musical transitions in melodies. He analyzed 15,618 melodic themes in the works of 479 classical composers working in different time periods. Simonton was interested in the relationship between originality and success, and he inferred originality from the unusualness of the transitions in particular works and for particular composers relative to the pool of all melodic themes. For example, he found that Haydn's Symphony no. 94 employs transitions found in 4% of the theme inventory, whereas Mozart's "Introduction to the Dissonant Quartet" uses transitions that occur in less than 1% of this inventory.

Unfortunately, most practical uses of systems notions in content analysis are marred by simplistic formulations. Systems of verbal corpuses tend to require far more complex analytical constructions than simple sets of variables such as those most researchers take as the starting points of their analyses. Studies of trends, the most typical extrapolations, often focus on just one variable at a time, which denies analysts the opportunity of tracing the interactions among several variables longitudinally. The patterns that are studied often concern only one kind of relationship, such as word associations. This generates graphically neat patterns, but at the expense of the ability to relate these to different kinds of patterns that might be operating simultaneously. For example, it is not too difficult to graph networks from multiple reports on "who talks to whom about what" within an organization. Such networks are made of simple binary relationships and are unable to represent more complex patterns of friendship, power, age, or goal-oriented collaborations in terms of which individuals may well think when talking with each other. Organizational communication researchers hope that, given a sufficient amount of text from what transpired within an organization, they will be able to understand or predict the workings of that organization. However, extrapolating social systems into the future presents seemingly insurmountable challenges.

One problem is the sheer volume of data that researchers would need to identify sufficiently invariant transformations. For this reason, most content analyses involving patterns tend to be qualitative and based on small data sets. As larger volumes of text are becoming available in electronic form, the slow development of theories and algorithms for handling large bodies of text as systems is emerging as the bottleneck of content analysis. It is unlikely that the needed theories and algorithms are derivable from Newtonian mechanics or from biological systems notions; rather, they must reflect the richly interactive and ecological nature of textual dynamics (Krippendorff, 1999).

3.3   STANDARDS

Humans measure observed phenomena against standards to establish (a) the kinds of phenomena they are (identifications), (b) how good or bad the phenomena are (evaluations), and (c) how close the phenomena come to expectations (judgments). I discuss each of these three uses of standards below. The facts that identities do not reveal themselves (they require someone to identify them as such), that evaluations are not objective or natural (they are the products of someone's values), and that audits by themselves are inconsequential (unless someone can invoke institutional consequences) reveal that standards facilitate inferences of a certain kind. In content analysis, standards are often implicit. People are quick to be for or against something without any clear idea of why. As suggested in Chapter 2, content analysts should take care to make explicit why they infer what they do, and this includes defining the standards they apply in their studies.

3.3.1   Identifications

Identification concerns *what something is,* what it is to be called, or to what class it belongs. Identifications are "either/or" inferences—that is, something either is or is not of a certain kind. Most basically, all computer text analyses start with the identification of character strings, not meanings. Any two strings are either the same as or different from each other. In his above-cited typology of content analyses, Janis (1943/1965) calls one type "sign-vehicle analysis." In this type of analysis, researchers use procedures that classify content according to the psychophysical properties of the signs (e.g., by identifying the word *Germany* and then counting how often it appears). Dibble (1963), who analyzes the kinds of inferences that historians habitually make in their work, includes "documents as direct indicators" as one kind of inference. For example, suppose a historian wants to know whether the British ambassador to Berlin communicated with England's foreign ministry the day before World War I began; a letter from the ambassador in the file of that ministry would provide direct evidence of its having been sent and received. Because identifications are often obvious, it is easy to overlook their inferential nature. In content analysis, the simplest task requires that a decision be made concerning whether something has occurred, was said, or has been printed. For example, when officials of the Federal Communications Commission are alerted that certain four-letter words have been broadcast over the public airwaves, they need definite proof that those words have been aired before they can consider suspending the offending station's broadcasting license. Identifications are rarely so simple, however.

The legal system's use of content analysis as an evidentiary technique provides us with many examples of identifications (see "Content Analysis," 1948;

Lashner, 1990). Tests aimed at establishing whether a particular publication is defamatory, whether a given political advertisement is based on facts, whether a certain signature is real, and whether a given painting is the work of a particular artist all involve either/or-type inferences about identities or class memberships, but not all of them are simple and obvious. For example, to identify a statement as defamatory in the context of a legal proceeding, an analyst must show that all components of the applicable legal definition of defamation are satisfied.

Evaluations 3.3.2

Well before the term *content analysis* appeared, at a time when media research was equated with the journalism-inspired premises of quantitative newspaper analysis, the evaluation of press performance was an important issue, as it still is. Early concerns about changes in newspaper publishing (Speed, 1893), which surfaced in public criticisms of increases in the coverage of "trivial, demoralizing, and unwholesome" subject matter at the expense of "worthwhile" information (Mathews, 1910), were certainly motivated by largely unquestioned ideals, evaluative standards, and norms couched in seemingly objective frequency measures. Some cultural critics today may share the concerns expressed by the authors of these early studies, but journalism has changed in the intervening years and has shown itself to be responsive to the evolving cultural climate and to shifting political and economic conditions.

Evaluative studies of newspaper reporting have focused largely on two kinds of bias: the bias in accuracy (truth) of reporting and the bias in favoring one side of a controversy over the other. For example, Ash (1948) attempted to determine whether the U.S. public was given a fair opportunity to learn about both sides of the controversy that accompanied the passage of the Taft-Hartley Labor Act. Accuracy in reporting and favoritism in reporting can be difficult to separate, however. During election campaigns, for instance, most politicians allege that some segments of the media display bias in their election coverage. The more popular candidates, who enjoy frequent attention from the press, tend to complain about inaccuracies in reporting, whereas the less popular candidates, struggling for publicity, are more likely to complain about inattention. Because journalists are committed to being fair to all sides in their reporting, many are defensive when the press is accused of taking sides and take the measurement of bias quite seriously.

In practice, evaluative studies of journalistic practices have not solved the now century-old problem of the lack of unquestionable criteria. Janis and Fadner (1943/1965) sought to put this deficiency to rest with their publication of a coefficient of imbalance, in which

f = the number of favorable units,

u = the number of unfavorable units,

r = the number of relevant units = $f + u$ + the number of neutral units, and

t = the total number of units = r + the number of irrelevant units.

The "coefficient of imbalance C," which Janis and Fadner derived from 10 propositions intended to capture the prevailing intuitions regarding (im)balance in reporting, measures the degree to which favorable statements, f, outnumber unfavorable statements, u, relative to the two ways of assessing the volume of a text, r and f:

$$C = \begin{cases} \dfrac{f^2 - fu}{rt} & \text{when } f \geq u \\ \dfrac{fu - u^2}{rt} & \text{when } f < u \end{cases}$$

This coefficient ranges in value from −1 to +1. It is a good example of an evaluative standard that enables the kind of inferences we often make without much thinking: It defines an ideal (here a balance between positive and negative evaluations), and it measures deviations from that ideal in degrees (here in either the positive or the negative direction). The reality of evaluative standards is far from clear, however. For example, whether journalists can always be impartial is an unsettled issue; some would argue that there are circumstances under which they may not have to be, or under which impartiality may not be possible. In the last days of Nixon's presidency, for example, it was difficult for journalists not to take the side of the public. And so it is in situations of war, where loyalty tends to outweigh fairness to both sides. To give one's nation's enemies a fair hearing might be an intellectual challenge, but in practice it is utterly unpopular. In the early 1960s, Merrill (1962) tried to differentiate dimensions of evaluative standards for journalistic practices. He proposed a battery of evaluative criteria to be applied to journalistic presentations (attribution bias, adjective bias, adverbial bias, contextual bias, photographic bias, and outright opinion), but his catalog is far from complete.

To assess accuracy in reporting, one must have standards against which to judge representations. Insofar as the reality we know is always already described, accuracy amounts to correspondence with sources that are deemed authentic. In a landmark study, Berelson and Salter (1946) compared the racial composition of the population of fictional characters in magazines with that of the U.S. population. The statistical operationalization of "representativeness" that they used has also been employed in many subsequent evaluative studies (Berkman, 1963). But whether the population of fictional characters in magazines, in plays, or in television programs should be statistically representative of the audience in characteristics such as ethnicity, age, occupation, and artistic capability remains debatable. The community television projects of the 1970s died precisely because audience members did not find it particularly entertaining to look into the lives of their ordinary neighbors. The "reality" TV shows of today may give the impression of being representative of real life, but they actually amount to contrived games played by carefully selected people. A bit less controversial are comparisons of the contents of narratives with those of other narratives. The Council on Interracial Books for Children (1977) has proposed and demonstrated a method for evaluating history texts in the United States by comparing the information in them with known historical facts. Here too, however, matters are not as simple as they seem. In the presentation of history, some selectivity is unavoidable; such evaluative efforts should aim to discover systematic exclusions and overstatements, not variations around an ultimately arbitrary standard. In journalism, the standard of truthful reporting is almost universally subscribed to, but it often conflicts with journalists' responsibility for the consequences of their reporting—for example, preventing fair trials, stimulating public fears, hyping people into action, and creating scandals.

Judgments   3.3.3

Like identifications and evaluations, judgments are based on standards, but with the additional provision that they are *prescribed or legitimated by institutions,* and research using such standards tends to have institutional implications. For example, when the FCC grants licenses to television stations, the stations are obligated to maintain certain proportions of news, community, and public service programming; that is, the FCC sets explicit criteria with which broadcasters must comply. Content analysts have measured the proportions of different kinds of programming aired on some stations and, in effect, have influenced FCC decisions regarding the status of the stations' broadcasting licenses.

Social scientists have long been fascinated with social deviance, and many have theorized about crime, pornography, obscenity, and the like. In doing so, they have influenced the community of their peers and undoubtedly affected public opinion. However, for content analyses to have institutional implications, their results must be presented in the target institutions' terms; otherwise, they do not have any effect. Content analysts may study such social problems as plagiarism, discriminatory communication practices, and the effects of fictional programming on particular kinds of crimes, but their findings are not likely to support judgments with consequences unless the researchers use the concepts, categories, and language of laws, enforceable agreements, or other institutional standards that are applicable to the institutions concerned with these problems. For example, organizational communication researchers are often asked to perform so-called communication audits of industrial or business organizations, in which they ask what is being said, how, and to whom, and what function it serves. Such an audit is usually driven not by scientific curiosity or public concerns, but by expectations from within the organization that the results will be useful, solve problems, or inform effective actions. Early communication audits often failed because they were conducted by academics who measured their findings against communication theories that had little to do with how organizations have to function. If the results of organizational communication research are to lead to consequences, they must be couched in the studied organization's terms and be measured against the standard of communication structures known to be successful.

3.4   INDICES AND SYMPTOMS

An index is a variable whose significance rests on its correlation with other phenomena. According to the semiotician C. S. Peirce, an index must be causally connected to the event it signifies, as smoke indicates fire. This presumes an underlying mechanism such that the relation between an index and what it signifies is a matter of necessity rather than convention (symbol) or similarity (icon). Indices are so conceived in medicine, where they are called *symptoms.* To diagnose, a physician looks for visible or measurable manifestations of an illness. However, even in medicine, symptoms have their histories, and medical practitioners must be educated to recognize them for what they are, which makes symptoms a property of the institution of medicine as much as of the phenomena the symptoms are supposed to indicate. In the social domain, where physical mechanisms (causalities) tend to be absent, the observer-dependent nature of indices is even more prominent. As Rapoport (1969) has noted, "An index . . . does not depend on (or should not be confused with) the physical entities or events from which it is derived" (p. 21).

In content analysis, indices of unobservable or only indirectly accessible phenomena are most common. Typically, analysts use measures of textual (verbal and paralinguistic), visual (gestural and pictorial), and communicational characteristics to address extratextual phenomena. For example, the ratio of disturbed speech to normal speech (speech-disturbance ratio) may serve as an index of a patient's anxiety during psychiatric interviews (Mahl, 1959); the frequency of a category of assertions or images related to action, goals, and progress is understood to indicate their producer's achievement motive (McClelland, 1958); and the frequencies of expressed concerns for an issue and the typographical positions of its expressions in a medium (e.g., in newspapers: size of headlines, front or inside pages, lead paragraphs of stories or mere mentions) are seen as indices of the amount of public attention to that issue (e.g., Budd, 1964). Gerbner et al. (1979) created a television violence index based on the numbers of violent scenes in fictional TV programs. Krendel (1970) developed an index of citizen dissatisfaction based on letters of complaint to city halls. Flesch's (1948, 1951, 1974) "readability yardstick" is derived through a formula that, after several incarnations, responds to two factors: average sentence length (in number of words) and average number of syllables per word. Danielson, Lasorsa, and Im (1992) used Flesch's criteria in their comparison of the readability of newspapers and novels. Government contractors are required to apply a version of Flesch's yardstick before finalizing instructions to military personnel, and insurance companies use it to evaluate contracts. Hawk (1997) extended Flesch's criteria for readability to evaluate the "listenability" of television news. Jamieson (1998) has constructed a campaign conduct index that takes into account Americans' expressed concerns about how much money politicians spend on campaigns, what candidates say to get elected, candidates' ethics and morals, and the proportion of negative ads used in political campaigns. Broder's (1940) adjective-verb ratio has been employed as an index of schizophrenia (Mann, 1944), and above-chance co-occurrences of nouns have been interpreted as indicators of associations in speakers' and receivers' minds (Osgood, 1959).

In mass communication research, five indices have had a long history of use:

- The *presence* or *absence* of a reference or concept is taken to indicate the source's *awareness* or *knowledge* of the object referred to or conceptualized.

- The *frequency* with which a symbol, idea, reference, or topic occurs in a stream of messages is taken to indicate the *importance of, attention to,* or *emphasis on* that symbol, idea, reference, or topic in the messages.

- The *numbers of favorable* and *unfavorable characteristics* attributed to a symbol, idea, or reference are taken to indicate the *attitudes* held by the writers, the readers, or their common culture toward the object named or indicated.

- The kinds of *qualifications*—adjectives or hedges—used in statements about a symbol, idea, or reference are taken to indicate the *intensity, strength,* or *uncertainty* associated with the *beliefs, convictions,* and *motivations* that the symbol, idea, or reference signifies.

- The frequency of co-occurrence of two concepts (excluding those that have grammatical or collocational explanations) is taken to indicate the *strength of associations* between those concepts in the minds of the members of a population of authors, readers, or audiences.

The use of such easily computable quantities as indices is not without its problems. Chomsky (1959) took Skinner to task for suggesting that promptness of response, repetition, and voice volume are natural indices of the intensity of motivation and that meanings can be discerned from the co-occurrence of words with the objects they refer to. He observed that most words are uttered in the absence of what they mean. Rapoport (1969) compares two hypothetical women, each of whom has just received a luxurious bouquet of flowers. The first woman, upon seeing the flowers, shouts, "Beautiful! Beautiful! Beautiful! Beautiful!" at the top of her lungs, thus giving evidence, according to Skinner's criteria, of a strong motivation to produce the response. The second woman says nothing for 10 seconds after she first sees the flowers, then whispers, barely audibly, "Beautiful." Frequency and voice volume would not be good indications of the importance of these flowers or, in Skinner's terms, the motivation to respond.

In content analysis, as in many social scientific inquiries, researchers often simply *declare* indices without demonstrating their empirical validity, especially when the phenomena to be indicated are abstract and far removed from validating data. Obviously, a researcher would not declare a measure to be an index if his or her claim is unlikely to be convincing (i.e., to have face validity) to scientific peers. Simple declarations, however, do not constitute an index as defined above. A declaration is discursive in nature and should not be confused with a correlation between an index and what it claims to indicate. A correlation needs to be demonstrated or at least hypothesized, so that it is testable in principle. Take, for example, a researcher's declaration that the frequency of violence in TV fictional programming is a measure of attention to violence (in real life). To make this claim, the researcher must first clarify whose attention this frequency is supposed to indicate. The author's or editor's? The audience members actually exposed to the violence so measured, or the audiences that producers had in mind attracting, the public at large, or the culture in which these kinds of mass communications are circulating? Given the target of the intended inferences, the researcher must also describe how the attention to be indicated will manifest itself—directly (by observation of TV-related violence) or indirectly (by correlation with other observable phenomena, such as [in]tolerance for otherness, domestic/disciplinary violence, or crime rate). Counting, emphasizing, paying attention to, and expressing concerns about something are four wholly different things. Their correlation is an empirical question.

Quantification is not an end in itself. Researchers must distinguish between quantifications that lead to the testing of a statistical hypothesis and quantifications that indicate something other than what is counted. These two uses are often confused in the early content analysis literature. For example, in his famous essay "Why Be Quantitative?" Lasswell (1949/1965b) celebrates quantification as the only path to scientific knowledge, by which he means the testing of statistical hypotheses; however, in most of his content analyses Lasswell used frequency measures as declared indices of extracommunicational phenomena.

In a study of the indicative power of frequencies of mentions, a student of mine used a book on U.S. presidents that was written by a scholar who was available on our university's campus. The student examined the book thoroughly, counting the numbers of mentions of the different presidents; the numbers of chapters, pages, and paragraphs in which each president is mentioned; and the numbers of sentences devoted to each president. He then asked the author to rank the U.S. presidents according to their importance and according to their contributions to U.S. history. He also asked the author how other scholars might rank the presidents and how the public might rank them. Finally, the student even asked the author how much attention he thought he had paid to each of the presidents in his book. Surprisingly, all correlations were very low, to the point that probably none of the measures could serve as a valid index of the author's attention or emphasis. The tentative insight we may derive from this exploratory study is that frequencies may not be good indicators of conceptual variables, such as importance or favoring one side over the other in a complex political controversy. Frequency measures are more likely to succeed as indicators of frequency-related phenomena—for example, the number of mentions of crime and the number of people believing crime to be an issue (not to be confused with actual crime statistics, which can be very detailed and may not correlate with public concerns), or the number of favorable references to a political candidate and the number of votes that the candidate is likely to attract (not to be confused with how much the candidate has done for his or her constituency), or the proportion of unfavorable letters written to city hall (Krendel, 1970) and the likelihood that the mayor will not be reelected.

The use of Dollard and Mowrer's (1947) discomfort-relief quotient demonstrates some of the difficulties involved in establishing an index. Dollard and Mowrer applied learning theory in deriving this very simple quotient as an index of the anxiety of speakers. The quotient is computed as the proportion of the number of "discomfort" or "drive" words and the sum of this number and the number of "comfort" or "relief" words. Despite Dollard and Mowrer's sound theoretical arguments and careful definitions of the two kinds of words, tests of the indicative power of this quotient have led to mixed results. Significant correlations with palmar sweating have been reported, but correlations with other measures of anxiety seem to be demonstrable only in very restricted circumstances. Murray, Auld, and White (1954) compared the discomfort-relief quotient with several other motivational and conflict measures applied during therapy and found that the quotient was not sensitive to changes in therapeutic progress. What the quotient indicates is therefore far from clear and simple.

The empirical evidence in favor of the above-mentioned indices for readability is more convincing. Clearly, sentences that include foreign expressions, long and compound words, complex grammatical constructions, and many punctuation marks are more difficult to read than simpler sentences. The success of Flesch's readability formula may well lie in two of its features: (a) Overall judgments concerning the readability of a piece of writing are formed cumulatively, with each encountered difficulty reducing the readability score; and (b) the indices are validated by the judgments of a population of readers. Both of these features are frequency related. Many word processing programs now are capable of providing not only counts of the numbers of characters, words, paragraphs, and pages in a document but also a readability score. Such scores might lend themselves to interesting correlational studies.

Researchers have also used indices successfully to settle disputes about authorship. In the 1940s, Yule (1944), an insurance statistician, reconsidered whether Thomas à Kempis, Jean Gerson, or one of several others wrote *The Imitation of Christ*. He correlated frequencies of nouns in works known to have been written by each prospective author and thereby developed discriminating indices to their identities, which he then applied to the disputed work (the inference was in favor of à Kempis). Mosteller and Wallace (1964), arguing that the choices of nouns are more specific to content than to author identity, found function words to be far more distinctive in their effort to settle the disputed authorship of 12 of the *Federalist Papers*. Evidence from their analysis favored Madison as the author, a finding that historians increasingly believe to be correct.

Again, declarative definitions are not sufficient. Calling frequencies a measure of attention does not make them an index of attention as measured by any other means. Even where correlations are found between an index and what it is said to indicate, there remains the problem of generalizability. For example, Morton and Levinson (1966) analyzed Greek texts by known authors and extracted seven discriminators of style that, according to the researchers, tap the unique elements of any person's writing: sentence length, frequency of the definite article, frequency of third-person pronouns, the aggregate of all forms of the verb *to be*, and the frequencies of the words *and, but,* and *in*. Morton's (1963) analysis of the 14 Epistles attributed to Paul in the Bible led him to conclude that 6 different authors wrote these works and that Paul himself wrote only 4 of them. Ellison (1965) then applied the constructs that Morton used to texts by known authors, which led to the inference that James Joyce's novel *Ulysses* was written by five different authors, none of whom wrote *A Portrait of the Artist as a Young Man*. Ellison found in addition that Morton's own article was written in several distinct styles. This research casts serious doubt on the generalizability of Morton's stylistic indices of an author's identity.

The inability to demonstrate high correlations should not prevent analysts from using quantitative measures, however. Researchers may be able to strengthen the indicative capabilities of such measures by adding independent variables, or they may observe these measures for long periods of time and then construct regularities that can be extrapolated into yet-unobserved domains. In addition, researchers may vindicate their construction of such measures by successfully correlating them with other phenomena not initially anticipated (correlative validity). In any case, it is always advisable to use indices cautiously.

In a self-reflective moment, Berelson (1952) wondered what Martians might infer from the high frequencies of love and sex found in modern Earth's mass-media recordings: Would they infer a promiscuous society or a repressive one? As noted above, Pool (1952b) has observed that symbols of democracy occur less frequently where democratic processes govern than where they are in question; thus they represent something other than the degree to which democracy is accepted. Although most learning theories suggest that repetition strengthens beliefs, repetition is also known to lead to semantic satiation—not only a loss of interest but also a loss of meaning. Thus it is not a simple matter to determine what it is that frequency measures indicate, and it is certainly not an issue that can be settled by proclamation.

3.5   LINGUISTIC RE-PRESENTATIONS

In language, the analogue of indicating is *naming*. Both establish one-to-one relationships—in the case of indices, relationships between two kinds of variables, and in the case of naming, relationships between words and particular persons, things, concepts, or experiences. A name recalls the named. Although narratives use names, naming is not sufficient to allow us to understand what narratives do. Narratives conjure, bring forth, and make present (re-present as they are reread, hence *re-presentation*, with a hyphen) rich worlds consisting of people in relationships with each other, objects that do things, and ideas, morals, and perspectives that guide observations. Narratives are imaginable and, under favorable circumstances, realizable through actions. Thus texts do not merely map, speak about, or indicate features of an existing world, they can *construct worlds* for competent speakers of a language to see, enact, and live within. To analyze *texts as re-presentations*—not to be confused with picturelike representations—*is to analyze the conceptual structure that a text invokes in particular readers,* the worlds they can imagine, make into their own, and consider real.

Written text is not just a collection of words; rather, it is sequenced discourse, a network of narratives that can be read variously. Hays (1969) provides the following examples of some typical streams of text that social or political scientists may be interested in understanding:

- ■ *A sequence of editorials:* The staff of a newspaper, experiencing an epoch, produces a series of essays that recapitulate some of the day's events, placing them in context with respect to historical trends, theory, and dogma. The essays express opinions about the true nature of situations that are necessarily not fully comprehended and about the responses called for.

- ■ *International exchanges of an official character:* This kind of correspondence is comparable to a sequence of newspaper editorials as described above, except that there are two or more parties involved, each pursuing its own policy.

- ■ *Personal documents:* These may be letters, diaries, or written materials of other kinds. Such materials differ from newspaper editorials or official governmental exchanges in the particularity of their content.

- ■ *Interview transcripts:* Usually in an interview situation there are two parties, one naive and the other sophisticated. The purpose of the interview may be, for example, therapeutic or diagnostic.

- ■ *Social interaction:* Two or more persons participate, discussing a fixed task or whatever other topic they deem suitable.

Such streams of texts, which could be extended to include types of literature, folktales, reports of scientific findings, and corporate reports, have several characteristics in common. For instance, they are all sequential in nature. Narratives respond to each other and are no longer individual accomplishments. The structures of interest are not manifest in vocabularies of words or in sentential constructions, but in larger textual units, in intertextualities. An analysis of texts as re-presentations has to acknowledge the connectedness of these larger textual units. The container metaphor that informed early conceptions of content analysis continues to influence many content analysts, making them most comfortable with classifications of content and indices that tend to ignore linguistic or narrative structures. Because such textual data tend to stem from several narrators, not one, analysts cannot presume consistency from narrator to narrator.

Nevertheless, inconsistencies make sense as motivators of interactions and as causes of evolution. Re-presentations essentially provide *conceivable worlds*, spaces in which people can conceptualize reality, themselves, and others. An analysis of these re-presentations proceeds with reference to designated readers, the imaginability of actors and actions, and how each datum contributes to the unfolding of the data stream.

A simple yet generic example of such content analysis is the development of maps. Maps are not just descriptive. The user of a map needs to understand that map in order to participate in the alleged reality that the map depicts. A road map aids a driver in seeing the possibilities for realizing self-chosen goals. Without a map, the probability of the driver's reaching his or her destination would be no better than chance. But maps not only enable, they also constrain thought and enforce coordination of their users relative to each other. Inferences drawn from maps should concern what their users do or could do with them. Lynch (1965), an architect, placed verbal statements of what informants recalled seeing when moving within a city onto a composite map of that city as seen by its residents. He wanted to infer what city planners should do to provide citizens with needed orientations, but found also how and where people would go when they had particular goals in mind. In his book *Letters From Jenny*, Allport (1965) reported on an analysis of personal correspondence, showing what the world of the letter writer looked like and what kind of psychological insights one could derive from her reality constructions. Gerbner and Marvanyi (1977) developed maps of the world based on their analysis of news coverage in U.S., East European, West European, Soviet, and some Third World newspapers; they distorted the sizes of the regions in the maps to correlate with the volume of news devoted to the regions. So (1995) developed maps of the field of communication research based on the titles of papers presented at several of the International Communication Association's annual conferences and on the sources cited in the papers in order to infer the "health" of the discipline. Although all the studies I have mentioned here as examples lacked good ways of tapping into complex linguistic structures, the researchers who conduct such studies tend to compensate for this shortcoming by providing rich interpretations of their findings.

Qualitative content analysts clearly recognize the need to respond to texts as connected discourse. Such researchers have examined the social construction of emotions in everyday speech (Averill, 1985), the metaphorical notion of facts in scientific discourse (Salmond, 1982), the prejudicial path toward an institutionally acceptable understanding of the causes of AIDS in medical writing (Treichler, 1988), the role of psychotherapists as depicted in fictional literature featuring psychotherapists (Szykiersky & Raviv, 1995), the portrayal of African Americans in children's picture books in the United States (Pescosolido, Grauerholz, & Milkie, 1996), the construction of natural disasters in U.S. print media (Ploughman, 1995), and the depiction of women in the media, to name a few recent topics. To be clear, many of these qualitative studies have lacked formalization, and so the findings are difficult to replicate or validate. Many of these studies have also had avowedly descriptive aims; in some cases, the researchers have stated their intent to reveal biases in representations. For example, Gerbner and Marvanyi (1977) created the maps mentioned above with the intention of appealing to a fairness standard of equal attention. The use of content analysis to describe how particular media depict members of certain professions, people from certain nations, or certain social problems or political figures usually amounts to the development of maps in which the concepts of interest occupy certain places.

Analysts of re-presentations seek to rearticulate relevant portions of texts to make the readers of their analyses aware of alternative readings or readings by particular others. For example, critical discourse analysts offer accounts of the roles of language, language use, and (in)coherences and of the communicative uses of texts in the (re)production of dominance and inequalities in society (see Van Dijk, 1993). Critical discourse analysis also includes an element of self-reflexivity in that it may be applied to its own text—asking what critical analysis is, what its practitioners do to a text, and so on. Such analyses have been characterized as explorations of social cognition and the public mind. However, in the absence of the reality that re-presentations bring forth, the only criteria applicable to the analyses of re-presentations are whether they *answer* informed readers' *questions,* whether they can *withstand critical examination* from the per-spective of individuals who are familiar with the context of the data, and whether *the worlds they rearticulate resemble or add to the worlds of specified readers* of the analyzed texts or of other content analysts.

Examples of analyses of re-presentations that start from the other end of this spectrum of complexity are found in simulations of cognitive processes (Abelson, 1968) and in applications of such simulations to aid political campaigns (Pool, Abelson, & Popkin, 1964). In such research, analysts use a large number of gram-matically simple propositions, goals, and scripts that people know how to follow—for example, how to order a meal from a menu, how to drive a car, or how a kinship system works (Wallace, 1961)—and compute entailments from the way they hang together semantically. Without the use of computers, but certainly with that in mind, Allen (1963) proposed a logical content analysis of legal docu-ments that demonstrated, by means of a formal procedure, which options (loop-holes) existed for the signatories of an arms limitation agreement. This led Allen to infer the directions in which the parties to this agreement could, and probably would, move, given appropriate incentives, and the conflicts that could be expected to emerge. Emphasizing constraints rather than options, Newell and Simon (1956) proposed a "logic theory machine" that shows how a sequence of logical implica-tions (a proof) from available evidence (premises, axioms) may lead to decisions within an unknown problem area (the validity of a theorem). Danowski (1993) used the data obtained from a semantic network analysis to arrive at recommen-dations concerning how persuasive messages ought to be constructed. Semantic network analysis is the content analysts' version of expert systems that artificial intelligence researchers aim to build in various empirical domains.

Hays (1969) developed a vision for this kind of content analysis, calling it *con-versationalist.* It would accept a stream of linguistic data—dialogue, diplomatic exchanges, treaty negotiations, and the like. It would recognize that an understanding of any linguistic form presumes a great deal of background knowledge, including knowledge about beliefs and assumptions, and it would allow for such knowledge to be added to the linguistic data. If several interlocutors populate the context of an analysis, which is typical, the analysis must acknowledge differences in their background knowledge as well. The analysis would also recognize that meanings change over time and would place every assertion in the context of previous assertions. A content analysis of re-presentations, Hays's conversationalist, would *answer questions of interest to the analyst that are not literally found in the text*. The conversationalist is an engine that computes a text's implications that answer the questions given to it.

In the terms employed in our framework, as described in Chapter 2, the context of such content analyses is the reality that available texts make present to a specified community of readers. The stable relations are manifest in the reasons that the community of readers would accept for answering specific questions from specific texts, for pursuing the logical implications of these data to a chosen target. Although many content analyses of re-presentations are not so clear about their aims and rarely care to go as far, this idea is being realized, at least in part, in fifth-generation computers, so-called expert systems. The discussion of expert systems has been overshadowed by interest in search engines for the Internet, computer networking, and collaborative systems, to name just a few, but the fact that we now have large volumes of textual data available in computer-readable form makes the content analysis of re-presentations increasingly possible and a challenge.

Sherlock Holmes's detective work provides a literary example of the analysis of linguistic re-presentations. For dramatic reasons, Arthur Conan Doyle constructed each Holmes story so that the logical links between the physical evidence of a crime and the crime's perpetrator are neither straight nor simple. Much of the reader's fascination with these stories derives from the pleasure of following Holmes's dazzling ingenuity as he weaves factual observations and propositions of common sense that typically are overlooked into chains of logical links from the known to the unknown, often in very many small steps. A content analysis of linguistic re-presentations does the same thing, but more systematically and for other purposes.

3.6   CONVERSATIONS

When children in well-to-do families say they are hungry, they may well want to have something to eat, but they could also want to avoid going to bed, to gain attention, to prevent their parents from doing something, and so on. In the context of a lived history of interacting with their children (knowing when they last ate, for example), parents tend to know how to respond when their children claim to be hungry. In such a situation, the propositional content of an utterance is secondary to the role that utterance plays in an ongoing interaction. In an attempt to infer anxiety from speech, Mahl (1959) addressed the difficulties of analyzing this kind of instrumental use of language, but he ended up bypassing the problem in favor of developing nonverbal indicators of anxiety instead. The path he took demonstrates the limitation of content analyses that are guided by a representational concept of content. Already in the 1950s, Bateson (1972; Ruesch & Bateson, 1951) had suggested that all messages convey content *and* relational information (a concept addressed by many researchers since, from Watzlawick, Beavin, & Jackson, 1967, to Baxter & Montgomery, 1996). When we view utterances as only representations, we ignore their relational or conversational functions. The essential feature of *conversational interactions* is that they *take place in and create interpersonal relations* and *define their own conditions for continuing the process.* When we blame someone for lying, we invoke the standard of representational truths, which is only one of many possible conversational frames interlocutors can adopt and one that makes continuing a conversation less important than being right. In content analyses of conversations, *inferences concern the continuation of the process.* Indexical and representational aspects (content in the sense of what is conveyed in processes of communication) are at best a means to that end.

Conversation analysis has emerged as one approach to the study of talk in natural settings (Atkinson & Heritage, 1984; Goodwin, 1981; Hopper, Koch, & Mandelbaum, 1986; Jefferson, 1978; Sacks, 1974; ten Have, 1999). Unlike discourse analysts, who start with written texts (Van Dijk, 1977, 1993), regard a discourse as a string of sentences, and aim to account for what the discourse (re)presents, as well as how and why it (re)presents what it does, conversation analysts tend to start with voice or video recordings of naturally occurring speech. They then proceed by transcribing conversational interactions, using highly specialized transcription conventions that enable them to capture not only words and who uttered them but also intonations, overlaps, and incompletions, as well as nonverbal behaviors such as gaze and especially silences and turns at talk. Broadly speaking, conversation analysts aim to understand the structure of naturally occurring speech, which necessarily includes two or more of its participants. Their methods of study are intended to preserve as much of the richness of human communication as possible. One typical analytical strategy is to differentiate among speech acts, or utterances that do something, such as questions, requests, promises, declarations, and expressions of feelings that are constitutive of relationships between the conversants.

Although conversation analysts are beginning to address reliability issues in their studies (e.g., Carletta et al., 1997; Patterson, Neupauer, Burant, Koehn, & Reed, 1996), efforts to establish the validity of conversation analyses have been marred by a lack of consensus concerning what constitutes supporting evidence. Most published reports of conversation analysis research can be characterized as "show and tell." In these reports, researchers reproduce exemplary fractions of transcribed dialogue to demonstrate their explanations of "what is 'really' going on." It is generally futile to ask the conversants to confirm conversation analysts' claims, as ordinary speakers engage each other "on the fly" and without access to or understanding of the analytical tools that conversation analysts have developed to transcribe and examine verbal interactions in great detail. However, inasmuch as conversations involve several participants whose utterances are made in response to previous utterances and in anticipation of future responses (thus the process is directed from within a conversation), researchers have the opportunity to understand conversations as cooperatively emerging structures that are, at each point in the process, responsive to past interactions and anticipatory of moves to come. A content analysis of data as conversation could involve (a) *inferring from any one moment of a recorded history of interactions the range of moves that could follow,* (b) *reinterpreting that history from the moves that actually did follow,* and (c) *systematically applying this explanatory strategy to all moments of naturally occurring conversations.*

This form of analysis is applicable not just to everyday conversations but also to exchanges between actors in organizational roles or as representatives of national governments. In exchanges between managers and employees, just as between therapists and their clients or between professors and their students, power issues enter through the speech acts the interlocutors choose, accept, or deny each other. Power relationships have become a favorite topic of critical scholarship among conversation analysts. Social organizations can be seen as reproducing their members' commitment to the preservation of the organizations' form. Commitments need to be asserted, heard, believed, and enforced. Thus organizations reside in certain speech acts, in how members respond to each other's talk. This makes organizations analyzable as networks of conversations of a certain kind. Analyses of exchanges between representatives of nations are not new, but conversation analyses of the unfolding dynamics in such exchanges offer a new approach to international relations. Content analyses of negotiations have advanced an understanding of the process (Harris, 1996). Pathologies of communication gain new currency when analyses reveal restrictions or constraints on conversation. Some scholars have called for the quantification of interactions (e.g., Hopper et al., 1986). This has been demonstrated, for example, regarding doctor-patient interactions (Ford, Fallowfield, & Lewis, 1996; Katz, Gurevitch, Peled, & Danet, 1969).

3.7   INSTITUTIONAL PROCESSES

The foregoing discussion has moved beyond the traditional notion of content in two senses: in the assertion that content analysis may be applied to any kind of data—texts, images, sounds, music, artifacts, anything that humans vary, for effect or unconsciously—and in the assertion that analysts may draw inferences from the data to features of any specifiable context. In this section, I discuss expanding the scope of content analysis to include inferences about institutional phenomena of which the institutions' constituents may be only dimly aware.

Much communication that takes place within institutions is routine, relational, and coordinative, and it is valued as such, even enforced, without apparent reason. Moreover, institutions reside in particular qualities of communication. Because communication in institutions tends to go beyond unaided readers' scope of comprehension, content analyses that probe into institutional properties call for *analytical instruments and theories* that, like microscopes, telescopes, and computer intelligence, *provide inferential access to social realities that are too complex to be accessible otherwise.*

Berger and Luckmann (1966) outline the context of this kind of content analysis. To start, they suggest that *habitualization* is an important prerequisite of institutionalization:

> Any action that is repeated frequently becomes cast into a pattern, which can then be reproduced with an economy of effort and which, *ipso facto,* is apprehended by its performer *as* that pattern. Habitualization further implies that the action in question may be performed again . . . with the same (or reduced) economical effort. . . . Habitualization carries with it the important psychological gain that choices are narrowed. (p. 53)

An example is the pattern of grammar, which directs our thoughts and actions in ways we rarely notice. For instance, the English language recognizes just two genders. Consequently, native English speakers tend to find the distinction between males and females natural and obvious. In turn, many institutions in English-speaking societies are built on this distinction. Because this is an artifact of grammar and vocabulary, which change only slowly, and not a fact, numerous problems arise from the lack of space for in-between identities, such as gay bashing, the shunning of transvestites, and the difficulties that androgynous people face in their lives. That members of other cultures draw different distinctions demonstrates the institutional nature of such grammatical categories.

The ways in which we greet each other every day, the repetitive and utterly predictable categories of television programming and news coverage that we have come to take for granted, the ceremonial nature of the political process, the pervasiveness of climates of power in everyday life—all such patterns, weathered in the process of apparent successes, are the backbone of the institutionalization of human behavior. However, the comfortable certainties that this kind of habitualization offers also suppress our ability to see untested alternatives. Content analysts who study institutions can infer habitualization from repetition and the narrowing of choices from the absence of mention of alternative ways of being or doing things. Surprisingly, Shannon's information theoretical notions of redundancy (a quantification of the nonuse of otherwise available alternatives) and information (a measure of surprise in the context of available messages) can be seen to have institutional interpretations (see Shannon & Weaver, 1949).

Regarding habitual *patterns,* to the extent that people are concerned, they talk of them in a language that *categorizes* (typifies) not only the *actions* that constitute these patterns but also the *actors/participants* involved. Teaching is what teachers do in front of students. Entertaining is what entertainers do for their audiences. Such obvious and semantically tautological propositions involve categories that furnish people with spaces they may occupy or grow into, not only to fit the categories but also *to see each other* in terms of those categories. Berger and Luckmann (1966, p. 54) identify institutions in terms of such *reciprocal categorizations*. For instance, knowing what a bank is enables the individuals in the context of a bank to interact with each other as certain categories of people—customers, tellers, guards, bank presidents, even bank robbers—regardless of who they are as individuals and regardless of whether the bank is in Philadelphia or Hong Kong. The same applies to understanding what is being said as proper. Reciprocal categorizations provide a key to how institutions are constituted, and such categorizations are easily identified in the texts that institutions generate—employee handbooks, memos on hiring practices, minutes of meetings, reports to shareholders—especially those generated by mass-media entertainment, which is highly institutionalized.

Berger and Luckmann note that *we grow into a world already constructed by others,* without knowing why things have become the way they are. This lack of knowledge of the histories of institutions leads to the belief that "things are good this way because this is the way they have 'always' been." This belief discourages, if not punishes, deviations from established patterns. Thus our lack of knowledge of history fuels institutional controls. Moreover, playing down human participation, without which institutions cannot exist, we tend to transfer agency to institutions, as when we say, "Science says . . . ," "The media show . . . ," or "The military discriminates against . . ." We consider institutions to be capable of preserving themselves, as when we speak of the "interests of government." Institutions do not really control deviance from institutional patterns, nor do they assign powers to the roles people play in them. Individual participants do these things to each other. Talk that prevents people from realizing the roles they play in maintaining institutional practices is one target of content analyses of institutions.

Institutions tend to remain hidden behind habitual practices until flaws emerge and certainties break down. Families, bureaucracies, and nations are unthinkable without routine forms of communication. The existence of family therapists suggests that the routine enactment of the institution of family can get living families into trouble. The emergence of international conflicts, which are rarely ever intended and in which nobody really likes to participate, especially when they may die as a result, is evidence of the fact that people can get involved in such events without knowing how. It thus appears that institutional structures have their own powerful lives. We seem to witness institutions only occasionally and at moments of breakdowns, such as when participants see that something is wrong and needs fixing, or when someone tries to escape an institution and is prevented from doing so. Content analyses of institutions often focus on communications at moments of such breakdowns. For instance, Berelson's (1949) study of "what 'missing the newspaper' means," conducted during a newspaper publishing strike in New York, revealed numerous previously unrecognized uses of newspapers and how their absence made people aware of these institutionalizations.

It is at moments of emerging difficulty or fear of the consequences of deviation from normalcy that the human constituents of institutions invent, appeal to, and apply institutional rules of conduct. Often such rules grow into systems of institutionalized explanations that become accessible through the very communications that invoke them. Mass communications researchers who have examined institutional processes have focused on legal, economic, political, and technical-structural explanations for those processes.

Legal explanations emphasize that communicators operate under certain legal conditions; for example, they may have to be licensed or must comply with or avoid violating contractual arrangements. Communicators may speak in an official capacity for particular social organizations, or they may question the legitimacy of certain practices. Texts obtained in legally regulated contexts reflect the legal constraints under which the institutional communicators who are being studied operate.

Economic explanations emphasize that when communication (production, transmission, and consumption) incurs costs, someone must pay them in some form, which creates networks of stakeholders with economic interests in what is being communicated. For example, in the United States, the traditional mass media are paid for largely by advertising; thus what is aired must be profitable in some way and cannot offend its sponsor. The effects of media ownership—in particular, the effects of monopolies and certain commercial interests—on communications have been a frequent target of content analyses.

Political explanations emerge when communications are disseminated widely and become of concern to competing public interests. The institution of ethical standards may result from debates about apparent problems, such as the violation of individuals' privacy by photographers (paparazzi) or reporters in the competitive pursuit of sensationalist material. Intentional misrepresentations by journalists and campaign advertisements perceived as "dirty," "slanderous," or "unfair" may lead to legal actions. Newspaper publishers, television stations, and other kinds of organizations cannot afford to displease vocal publics if they expect to have some longevity, whether the publics that concern them are made up of governing elites or masses of audience members. Thus communications reflect as well as enact the prevailing configurations of rhetorical power. In conducting content analyses aimed at examining power relationships, researchers have to be careful not to fall into the trap of believing that everyone perceives power as they do. Instead, they may want to look at how power is enacted, received, or undone (Krippendorff, 1995b).

Technical-structural explanations of institutional processes emphasize that all communications must be producible, recordable, disseminable, and accessible through various technologies, and that communications not only become shaped in that process but shape the institutions in whose terms they are processed. The film and television industries employ techniques of mass production that are vastly different from those employed by the newspaper industry. This is a matter not of intention but of the nexus between technology and the institutions that thrive on it. An even greater difference exists between newspapers and what computer-mediated communication—the Internet, for example—can make available. Content analyses have shed light on the systematic changes in content that take place when a book is made into a film (Asheim, 1950), on the role of gatekeepers in news flow (e.g., what happens to controversial content; White, 1964), on how news is made as opposed to reported (Gieber, 1964), on the social role of the magazine cover girl as a function of channels of distribution (Gerbner, 1958), and on how expectations about institutions shape the forms of petitions directed to those institutions (Katz, Gurevitch, Danet, & Peled, 1969). In addition, based on an examination of mass communication from a technical-structural perspective, Adorno (1960) has contended that the institutionalized repetitiveness of the mass production of messages preserves and strengthens social stereotypes, prejudices, and ideologies rather than corrects them.

There are a few fundamental generalizations from which content analyses of institutionalized texts may start. One is that *everything said, written, listened to, or read—every communication—not only says something to its receiver but also institutes the very pattern of which it is a part.* For example, a person who cashes a check at a bank is not merely taking part in a mutually beneficial transaction; his or her action also manifests trust in money and supports banking as an institution. If people did not bank regularly, the banking industry could not exist. Banks are instituted in our trust in money, in our belief in the safety of banks, in the belief that one should earn interest on savings, and so on. When people turn on their television sets to see certain shows, they are not only gaining entertainment, they are supporting the shows they watch by increasing the programs' ratings. Their actions also legitimate the mass media as an institution to provide such entertainment. If nobody were to watch television for a while, the mass media could not exist as usual. The use of racial categories—whether on television, in everyday talk, or in survey questions—demonstrates that they are important, of public or interpersonal concern, and the very use of these categories invariably strengthens ethnic prejudices and makes them real. People's participation in a pattern of reciprocal categorization is an essential requirement for institutions to persist, and this applies also to issues of race. Therefore, analyses of such communication phenomena cannot stop at what is being said or heard. What matters is that the very act of communication strengthens that act, allows for repetition, and keeps people in attendance. Researchers conducting content analyses of institutionalized texts—which most mass communications are—have to observe whether communications constitute new patterns, strengthen what has been said before through repetition, or weaken a pattern by omission or attention to alternatives.

The properties of the medium of communication in which an institution is constituted have profound effects on the development of that institution. Innis (1951) compared oral communications with written communications and concluded that writing has the effect of freezing traditions, rendering institutions more permanent and reliable; thus written communications can support empires that extend control over larger geographic areas. Radio and television, with their virtually instantaneous transmission over vast distances, tend to support the development of geographically widely dispersed organizational forms, but because such media do not leave many records behind, these forms are far less stable than those supported by written media. Oral and audiovisual media are also less controllable than written ones. The revolution against the shah of Iran succeeded largely because of the support generated among the people of Iran through the distribution of audiotapes that escaped the control of the state, unlike all other media in that country. The short-lived pro-democracy movement in China was organized largely through fax communication, which recognized no national boundaries. The Internet now provides vast numbers of geographically dispersed users with almost instantaneous access to computer-mediated communications; moreover, it is capable not just of disseminating data, but of facilitating discussion among parties to negotiations and commitments as well as the rise of commercial enterprises and virtual communities that can undermine more traditional institutions. These diverse spatial, memory-related, and coordinative properties of communications media have profound effects on institutional dynamics, and research that focuses on single messages or on readings of individual users cannot possibly reveal those effects. Content analyses in institutional contexts can lead to inferences regarding the weakening or strengthening of certain institutions, and frequencies play important roles in such inferences.

Finally, *communications tend to reinforce the very institutional explanations and rules by which they are created and disseminated.* For one example, the traditional mass media, which operate in conformity with the one-way theory of communication, produce communications that demonstrate the workings of this theory and are likely to encourage the widespread use of this theory at the expense of alternative ways of thinking about human communication. It is therefore not surprising that from its inception the field of communication research has been fundamentally committed to a model of communication that consists of a sender, messages, and receivers—as if no others were conceivable or worthy of attention. One-way communication technology has given rise to totalitarian regimes but also to disciplines such as advertising and concepts such as persuasion theory. The emergence of interactive media has challenged this paradigm somewhat, but even today many researchers who seek to understand computer-mediated communication, which is well instituted, start with mass communication models. To infer institutional controls, content analysts have to observe what is not said, what happens when institutions are challenged or break down, and what is done to those who dare to deviate from institutionalized practices. Content analyses of textual data in view of such phenomena can add to our understanding of the workings of institutionalized patterns of thinking and acting. All of these phenomena become evident through analyses of the use of language.

Lasswell (1960) sought to clarify the institutional roles of communication by distinguishing among three functions:

- Surveillance of the environment

- Correlation (coordination) of a society's parts in response to the environment

■ Transmission of social heritage from one generation to the next (culture)

To these, Wright (1964) added one more function:

■ Entertainment

Echoing Parsons's (1951) sociological systems theory, both Lasswell and Wright argue that any society has to develop institutions that specialize in performing these functions. In the United States, journalism could be seen as serving the surveillance function in that journalists report publicly on events that take place, and politics could be regarded as serving the correlation function by mobilizing individuals to behave in ways that serve society as a whole and coordinating the distribution of resources (Lasswell, 1963). Functionalist accounts of institutions, to which this classification is indebted, are not the only accounts, however. Nor can they be accepted without question, for they preserve sociological theorists' vision of what society is. Instead of imposing theoretical categories from outside or from a position of authority, content analysts attempt to understand institutions through how the participants in them talk with each other and about their own institutional involvements, how they participate in maintaining these institutions through talk and writing, and how they judge the legitimacy and appropriateness of institutions' actions. Institutions are constituted, constructed, and reconstructed in language use and in the distribution of narratives of that use through particular media of communication; hence the need for content analyses of this kind. Lasswell's classification at least acknowledges that institutions are manifest in all communicative practices and serve as the glue that holds a society together.

3.8   AREAS OF LIKELY SUCCESS

Having completed the above survey of areas in which content analysis may be applied, I conclude this chapter by offering a brief answer to the question of where content analysis might be used most fruitfully. To this end, I draw on the conceptual issues discussed in Chapter 2, including my argument against the use of the container metaphor, which entails the conception of content as a tangible entity, contained in messages and shipped from one place to another, that researchers presume to be able to analyze through the use of objective (i.e., observer-independent) techniques. I have argued instead for the metaphor of reading, which shifts attention from what content is to what readers do with texts, how they relate texts to the contexts of their use—individually, politically, socially, and culturally—and what this means for various social phenomena. In this shift readers and their communities become central, whether the readers are authors, users, bystanders, or content analysts. Content analysts cannot exclude themselves from the population of readers, albeit their reading is aided by systematic methods of careful inquiry.

To determine what use of content analysis is likely to be most fruitful, we must consider texts as the by-products of ongoing conversations. We must acknowledge that people learn to read and write a language only after they have learned to speak it. Texts build on the experience of speech. They can substitute for speech, as when people write letters. They can extend the range of speech, as in the use of communication technology—mass and computer-mediated communication—and they usually revert back to speech, by being read, interpreted, talked about, accepted, dismissed, or selectively enacted. Texts are more durable than speech; they may be reread and analyzed repeatedly and by several analysts. This is why conversation analysts, for example, record and transcribe speech before they analyze it or talk about it. Written texts are also monological, because the reasons for their being what they are and how they are responded to or used are not evident within them. The metaphor of reading leads us to literacy, or the competence to handle text, which is embodied in and shared by the members of a speech community. In this sense, texts are always rooted in the dialogical context of conversations.

Scholars have studied the effects of reading and writing, and the uses of the mass media, for some time, although this research has always lagged behind technological developments (information technology, for example). As noted above, typical topics of research have included deception, attitude change, message effects, uses and gratifications, technological biases, rational decision making, institutionalization, and causal connections between textual and nontextual phenomena.

Regarding assessments of crime, unemployment, and the economy, for example, studies have repeatedly demonstrated that correlations between what the mass media present—text in our generalized sense—and what public opinion polls find or individuals express as concerns are higher than the correlations between either of these and actual statistics on crime, unemployment, and the economy. This suggests that content analyses are generally more successful when they stay close to the uses of language—after all, public and individual opinions involve talk, not physical measurement. Another example is the well-studied phenomenon of agenda setting by the mass media (McCombs & Shaw, 1972; McCombs, Shaw, & Weaver, 1997)—that is, the fact that themes and issues distributed by the mass media in the form of print, speech, and images have a good chance of becoming topics of public conversations and, in turn, affecting civic actions, informing political decisions, and stimulating artistic rearticulations. The simple reason for this phenomenon is that widely distributed texts enter, are adopted into, and come alive in conversations, not only conversations between interviewers and interviewees, but also conversations in public places ranging from side-street cafés to political demonstrations. If new words and expressions resonate with readers' or listeners' previously acquired language habits, they may take hold in the public imagination and become part of many people's vocabularies.

Content analyses are most successful when they focus on facts that are constituted in language, in the uses of the very texts that the content analysts are analyzing. Such linguistically constituted facts can be broken down into four classes:

■ *Attributions:* Concepts, attitudes, beliefs, intentions, emotions, mental states, and cognitive processes ultimately manifest themselves in the verbal attributes of behavior. They are not observable as such. The words that make them real are acquired, largely in conversations but also through reading and attending to various media of communication. The attribution of competence, character, morality, success, and belongingness to particular categories of people enables or discourages actions, makes or breaks politicians, creates heroes and demonizes villains, identifies leaders and marginalizes minorities. These facts cannot exist without language, and to the extent that texts are instrumental in disseminating and creating such attributions, they are natural targets of successful content analyses.

■ *Social relationships:* Noting that statements or questions can be uttered either subserviently or authoritatively, Bateson introduced the distinction between the content and the relationship aspect of all human communication (Ruesch & Bateson, 1951, pp. 179–181). Relationships may be established implicitly or taken for granted in how communication takes place. For example, by offering third-person plural accounts of observed "Others," scientific observers set themselves apart from their subjects and assume a position of superiority. This is manifest in the grammar of talk or writing. But relationships may also be negotiated, unilaterally imposed, and explicitly accepted or rejected. Authority, power (Hillman, 1995; Krippendorff, 1995b), contractual agreements, and inequalities are all constituted primarily in *how* language is used and only secondarily in *what* is said. Content analyses tend to be more successful when they focus on how language is used, relying on social grammars of recorded speech or written communication of which speakers or writers may not be fully aware.

■ *Public behaviors:* Individuals' values, dispositions, conceptions of the world, and commitments to their way of being surface in conversations that involve repeated confirmations. Without such repetition, individuals drift apart; their behaviors become no longer coordinated, and they experience difficulties in understanding each other. To the extent behavior is public, and hence observed and judged by others, it is brought into the domain of language. Narratives too, are essentially public. They may inspire individuals to act, but they are always told by someone and listened to by others, rendering inspiration a social experience. Reading a newspaper may be an individual act, but not only do newspapers print what editors consider to be of public interest, newspaper readers also talk to others about what they read, and so make newspaper reading a public activity. The vocabularies we use are all acquired from others who have used the words before us. Inasmuch as a vocabulary suggests the range of what a person can talk about and conceive, the conceivable is transmitted from parents to children, from speakers to listeners, and from writers to readers. All uses of language ultimately are public—not shared, but in the open. Content analyses are more likely to succeed when they address phenomena that are of a public, social, or political nature or concern phenomena of individuals' participation in public, social, or political affairs. Cognition, for example, the supposed crown of individualism, is never an exclusively individual phenomenon. It always reflects the contexts of others, much as texts do.

■ *Institutional realities:* We often overlook the institutional nature of social realities—of marriage, money, government, history, illness, and even scientific pursuits. Public opinion, for example, is a construction that relies heavily on the language of social science, on statistics in particular, but it also depends crucially on being taken as a political reality and acted upon. Without the institution of free speech, the authority of journalism, and constitutional democracy, public opinion research would not make much sense. Mental illness has an institutional reality as well. It is projected onto identified patients in terms of categories that mental health professionals and insurance companies have developed for their convenience. The factuality of these phenomena derives from certain institutionalized texts, such as the *Diagnostic and Statistical Manual of Mental Disorders (DSM-IV-R)*, which is published by the professional authority on mental illness, the American Psychiatric Association (2000). These texts legitimate numerous therapeutic interventions. For still another example, consider how a social organization such as a family or a corporation constitutes itself. Members of an organization coordinate their activities through communication and continually affirm their membership, often shielding from outsiders vital stories about inside practices. When exchanges within organizations take place in written form, they stabilize organizational memories, identities, and practices. Disrupting an organization's network of communication can cause the organization to collapse. Organizational communication research has successfully inquired into how organizations arise in the communications among members and develop nourishing organizational cultures. Content analysis of what is said and written within an organization provides the key to understanding that organization's reality, but it is most likely to succeed if it considers the more stable categories in which the organization constitutes itself.

In sum, content analyses are most likely to succeed when analysts address linguistically constituted social realities that are rooted in the kinds of conversations that produced the texts being analyzed. Repetitive, routine, public, and institutionalized phenomena are easier to infer than are rare and unconventional ones. Moreover, because content analysis presupposes familiarity with, if not literacy in, the language of the analyzed texts, the more cognizant content analysts are of vocabulary and subtle discursive conventions, including their own, the more successful they are likely to be.

Part II

Components of Content Analysis

CHAPTER 4

The Logic of Content Analysis Designs

As a technique, content analysis relies on several specialized procedures for handling texts. These can be thought of as tools for designing suitable analyses. This chapter outlines the key components of content analysis and distinguishes among several research designs, especially designs used in the preparation of content analyses and designs for content analyses that contribute to larger research efforts.

CONTENT ANALYSIS DESIGNS 4.1

The very idea of *research*—a *re*peated *search* within data for apparent patterns—presupposes explicitness about methodology. Unless researchers explain clearly what they have done, how can they expect to be able to replicate their analyses or to process more texts than an individual can read? Beyond that, how can they convince others that their research was sound and thus their results should be accepted?

A *datum* is a unit of information that is recorded in a durable medium, distinguishable from and comparable with other data, analyzable through the use of clearly delineated techniques, and relevant to a particular problem. Data are commonly thought of as representing observations or readings, but they are always the products of chosen procedures and are always geared toward particular ends—in content analysis, data result from the procedures the researcher has chosen to answer specific questions concerning phenomena in the context of given texts. Hence data are made, not found, and researchers are obligated to say how they made their data.

The network of steps a researcher takes to conduct a research project is called the *research design*, and what knits the procedural steps into the fabric of a coherent research design is the design's *logic*. Generally, this logic concerns two qualities: the efficiency of the procedural steps (avoiding structural redundancies while preventing "noise" from entering an analysis) and the evenhandedness of data processing (preventing the favoring of one outcome over another). This logic enables analysts to account to their scientific community for how the research was conducted. For a research design to be replicable, not merely understandable, the researcher's descriptive account of the analysis must be complete enough to serve as a set of *instructions* to coders, fellow researchers, and critics—much as a computer program determines what a machine is to do. Although the thoroughness of a computer program may serve as a scientific ideal, in social research the best one can hope for is an approximation of that ideal. Content analysts in particular must cope with a good deal of implicitness in their instructions. (I will return to this topic in subsequent chapters.)

Traditional guides to research methods tend to insist that all scientific research tests hypotheses concerning whether or not patterns are evident in the data. Content analysis, however, has to address prior questions concerning why available texts came into being, what they mean and to whom, how they mediate between antecedent and consequent conditions, and, ultimately, whether they enable the analysts to select valid answers to questions concerning their contexts. Hence the logic of content analysis designs is justifiable not only according to accepted standards of scientific data processing (efficiency and evenhandedness), but also by reference to the context in relation to which texts must be analyzed.

Figure 2.1 represents an attempt to conceptualize the situation that the content analyst has to observe. It may be seen to contain Figure 4.1, which represents the simplest content analysis design. Here, the analyst relies solely on available texts to answer a research question. Although this figure locates texts and

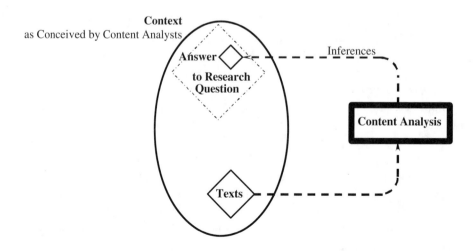

Figure 4.1   Content Analysis: Answering Questions Concerning a Context of Texts

results—inputs and outputs of the analysis—in a chosen context, it suggests nothing about the nature of the context that justifies the analysis (discussed in Chapter 3) or about the network of needed analytical steps, which I address below.

Components   4.1.1

Here we open the "content analysis" box in Figure 4.1 and examine the components the analyst needs to proceed from texts to results. Listing these components is merely a convenient ways to partition, conceptualize, talk about, and evaluate content analysis designs step by step. As accounts of what the components do must also serve as instructions for replicating them elsewhere, each component has a descriptive and an operational state:

- *Unitizing:* relying on unitizing schemes
- *Sampling:* relying on sampling plans
- *Recording/coding:* relying on coding instructions
- *Reducing* data to manageable representations: relying on established statistical techniques or other methods for summarizing or simplifying data
- Abductively *inferring* contextual phenomena: relying on analytical constructs or models of the chosen context as warrants
- *Narrating* the answer to the research question: relying on narrative traditions or discursive conventions established within the discipline of the content analyst

Together, the first four components constitute what may be summarily called *data making*—creating computable data from raw or unedited texts. In the natural sciences, these four are embodied in physical measuring instruments. In the social sciences, the use of mechanical devices is less common—often impossible—and data making tends to start with observations. The fifth component, abductively inferring contextual phenomena, is unique to content analysis and goes beyond the representational attributes of data. I describe each of the components in turn below.

Unitizing is the systematic distinguishing of segments of text—images, voices, and other observables—that are of interest to an analysis. In Chapter 5, I discuss different units of analysis—sampling units, recording units, context units, units of measurement, units of enumeration—and the different analytical purposes they serve. Given these differences, unitizing may occur at various places in a content analysis design. Content analysts must justify their methods of unitizing, and to do so, they must show that the information they need for their analyses is represented in the collection of units, not in the relationships between the units, which unitizing discards.

Sampling allows the analyst to economize on research efforts by limiting observations to a manageable subset of units that is statistically or conceptually representative of the set of all possible units, the population or universe of interest. Ideally, an analysis of a whole population and an analysis of a representative sample of that population should come to the same conclusion. This is possible only if the population manifests redundant properties that do not need to be repeated in the sample drawn for analysis. But samples of text do not relate to the issues that interest content analysts in the same way that samples of individuals relate to populations of individuals of interest in surveys of public opinion, for example. Texts can be read on several levels—at the level of words, sentences, paragraphs, chapters, or whole publications; as literary works or discourses; or as concepts, frames, issues, plots, genres—and may have to be sampled accordingly. Hence creating representative samples for content analyses is far more complex than creating samples for, say, psychological experiments or consumer research, in which the focus tends to be on one level of units, typically individual respondents with certain attributes (I discuss the issues involved in sampling for content analysis in depth in Chapter 6). In qualitative research, samples may not be drawn according to statistical guidelines, but the quotes and examples that qualitative researchers present to their readers have the same function as the use of samples. Quoting typical examples in support of a general point implies the claim that they represent similar if not absent cases.

Recording/coding bridges the gap between unitized texts and someone's reading of them, between distinct images and what people see in them, or between separate observations and their situational interpretations. One reason for this analytical component is researchers' need to create durable records of otherwise transient phenomena, such as spoken words or passing images. Once such phenomena are recorded, analysts can compare them across time, apply different methods to them, and replicate the analyses of other different researchers. Written text is always already recorded in this sense, and, as such, it is rereadable. It has a material base—much like an audiotape, which can be replayed repeatedly—without being in an analyzable form, however. The second reason for recording/coding is, therefore, content analysts' need to transform unedited texts, original images, and/or unstructured sounds into analyzable representations. The recording of text is mostly accomplished through human intelligence. I discuss the processes involved in recording and coding in Chapter 7, and then, in Chapter 8, I discuss the data languages used to represent the outcomes of these processes. In content analysis, the scientific preference for mechanical measurements over human intelligence is evident in the increasing use of computer-aided text analysis (discussed in Chapter 12); the key hurdle of such text analysis, not surprisingly, is the difficulty of programming computers to respond to the meanings of texts.

Reducing data serves analysts' need for efficient representations, especially of large volumes of data. A type/token statistic (a list of types and the frequencies of tokens associated with each), for example, is a more efficient representation than a tabulation of all occurrences. It merely replaces duplications by a frequency. Because one representation can be created from the other, nothing is lost. However, in many statistical techniques for aggregating units of analysis—correlation coefficients, parameters of distributions, indices, and tested hypotheses—information is lost. In qualitative pursuits, rearticulations and summaries have similar effects: They reduce the diversity of text to what matters.

Abductively *inferring* contextual phenomena from texts moves an analysis outside the data. It bridges the gap between descriptive accounts of texts and what they mean, refer to, entail, provoke, or cause. It points to unobserved phenomena in the context of interest to an analyst. As I have noted in Chapter 2, abductive inferences—unlike deductive or inductive ones—require warrants, which in turn may be backed by evidence. In content analysis, such warrants are provided by analytical constructs (discussed in Chapter 9) that are backed by everything known about the context. Abductive inferences distinguish content analysis from other modes of inquiry.

Narrating the answers to content analysts' questions amounts to the researchers' making their results comprehensible to others. Sometimes, this means explaining the practical significance of the findings or the contributions they make to the available literature. At other times, it means arguing the appropriateness of the use of content analysis rather than direct observational techniques. It could also entail making recommendations for actions—legal, practical, or for further research. Narrating the results of a content analysis is a process informed by traditions that analysts believe they share with their audiences or the beneficiaries of their research (clients, for example). Naturally, most of these traditions are implicit in how social scientists conduct themselves. Academic journals may publish formal guidelines for researchers to follow in narrating their results and let peer reviewers decide whether a given content analysis is sound, interesting, and worthwhile.

The six components of content analysis do not need to be organized as linearly as suggested by Figure 4.2. A content analysis design may include iterative loops—the repetition of particular processes until a certain quality is achieved. Or components may recur in various guises. For example, unitizing may precede the sampling of whole documents, but it may also be needed to describe the details of their contents. Thus coding instructions may well include unitizing schemes. Moreover, a content analysis could use components that are not specifically highlighted in Figure 4.2. Decisions, to mention just one analytical action, typically direct the content analysts along an inferential path with many forks and turns toward one or another answer to the research question. Here, decisions are part of the inference component. Finally, it is important to note that there is no single "objective" way of flowcharting research designs.

The analyst's written instructions (represented in boldface type in Figure 4.2), which specify the components in as much detail as feasible, include all the information the analyst can communicate to other analysts so that they can replicate the design or evaluate it critically. The traditions of the analyst's discipline (in medium type in Figure 4.2) are an exception to the demand for explicitness. Most scientific research takes such traditions for granted.

Any set of instructions, it must be noted, imposes a structure on the available texts. Ideally, this structure feels natural, but it may feel inappropriate or forced,

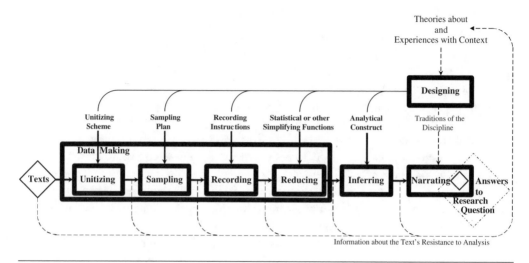

Figure 4.2   Components of Content Analysis

if not alien, relative to the analyst's familiarity with the texts' context. Take unitizing, for example. Texts may be cut into any kind of units, from single alphabetical characters to whole publications. Unitizing is arbitrary, but not for a particular content analysis. For example, if an analyst wants to infer public opinion from newspaper accounts, stories may be more natural for an examination of what readers think and talk about than, say, value-laden words that occur in these accounts. The use of inappropriate units leads analysts to experience conceptual trouble. Or an analyst may apply a particular sampling plan and then discover, perhaps too late, not only that the sampled documents are unevenly relevant but that the sampling plan has excluded the most significant ones. Finally, in reading given texts, an analyst may encounter important concepts for which the coding instructions fail to provide suitable categories; such a discovery would render the recording/coding task arbitrary or uncertain. During the development phase of content analysis design, a sensible analyst "resists the violence" that poor instructions can inflict on the texts and attempts to reformulate instructions as needed so that they are appropriate to the texts at hand. This sensible approach is illustrated in Figure 4.2 by the dashed lines, which show another flow of information that is motivated by the analyst's resistance to inappropriate analytical steps. The instructions in good content analysis designs always take such information into account.

A final point regarding Figure 4.2: As noted in Chapter 2, texts are always the observable parts of a chosen context. The context directs the analysis of a text, and the results of the analysis contribute to a (re)conceptualization of the context, redirecting the analysis, and so forth. This reveals the essentially recursive nature of the process of designing content analyses. This recursion contrasts sharply with the application of a content analysis design, which is essentially a one-way transformation of available texts into the answers to the analyst's research questions. We must therefore distinguish between the *development* of a content analysis, during which a design emerges that possesses context-sensitive specificity, and the *execution* of a content analysis, during which the design is relatively fixed and ideally replicable, regardless of what the texts could teach the analyst. Interestingly, the context-sensitive path that the content analyst takes while developing the design is no longer recognizable when the finished design is applied to large volumes of text and/or replicated elsewhere.

Quantitative and Qualitative Content Analysis   4.1.2

In Chapter 2, I noted that quantification is not a defining criterion for content analysis. Text is always qualitative to begin with, categorizing textual units is considered the most elementary form of measurement (Stevens, 1946), and a content analysis may well result in verbal answers to a research question. Using numbers instead of verbal categories or counting instead of listing quotes is merely convenient; it is not a requirement for obtaining valid answers to a research question. In Chapter 1, I suggested that the quantitative/qualitative distinction is a mistaken dichotomy between the two kinds of justifications of content analysis designs: the explicitness and objectivity of scientific data processing on the one side and the appropriateness of the procedures used relative to a chosen context on the other. For the analysis of texts, both are indispensable. Proponents of quantification—Lasswell (1949/1965b), for example—have been rightly criticized for restricting content analysis to numerical counting exercises (George, 1959b) and for uncritically buying into the measurement theories of the natural sciences. Proponents of qualitative approaches, who have come largely from the traditions of political analysis, literary scholarship, ethnography, and cultural studies (Bernard & Ryan, 1998), have been criticized for being unsystematic in their uses of texts and impressionistic in their interpretations. Although qualitative researchers compellingly argue that each body of text is unique, affords multiple interpretations, and needs to be treated accordingly, there is no doubt that the proponents of both approaches sample text, in the sense of selecting what is relevant; unitize text, in the sense of distinguishing words or propositions and using quotes or examples; contextualize what they are reading in light of what they know about the circumstances surrounding the texts; and have specific research questions in mind. Thus the components of content analysis in Figure 4.2 are undoubtedly present in qualitative research as well, albeit less explicitly so. I think it is fair to say that:

■ Avowedly qualitative scholars tend to find themselves in a hermeneutic circle, using known literature to contextualize their readings of given texts, rearticulating the meanings of those texts in view of the assumed contexts, and allowing research questions and answers to arise together in the course of their involvement with the given texts. The process of recontextualizing, reinterpreting, and redefining the research question continues until some kind of satisfactory interpretation is reached (see Figure 4.3). Scholars in this interpretive research tradition acknowledge the open-ended and always tentative nature of text interpretation. Taking a less extreme position, content analysts are more inclined to limit such hermeneutic explorations to the development phase of research design.

■ Qualitative scholars resist being forced into a particular sequence of analytical steps, such as those illustrated in Figure 4.2. Acknowledging the holistic qualities of texts, these scholars feel justified in going back and revising earlier interpretations in light of later readings; they settle for nothing less than interpretations that do justice to a whole body of texts. As such readings cannot easily be standardized, this process severely limits the volume of texts that a single researcher can analyze consistently and according to uniform standards. Because this process is difficult to describe and to communicate, qualitative studies tend to be carried out by analysts working alone, and replicability is generally of little concern. By contrast, faced with larger volumes of text and working in research teams, content analysts have to divide a body of texts into convenient units, distribute analytical tasks among team members, and work to ensure the consistent application of analytical procedures and standards. For these reasons, content analysts have to be more explicit about the steps they follow than qualitative scholars need to be.

■ Qualitative researchers search for multiple interpretations by considering diverse voices (readers), alternative perspectives (from different ideological positions), oppositional readings (critiques), or varied uses of the texts examined (by different groups). This conflicts with the measurement model of the natural sciences—the assignment of unique measures, typically numbers, to distinct objects—but not with content analysts' ability to use more than one context for justifying multiple inferences from texts.

■ Qualitative researchers support their interpretations by weaving quotes from the analyzed texts and literature about the contexts of these texts into their conclusions, by constructing parallelisms, by engaging in triangulations, and by elaborating on any metaphors they can identify. Such research results tend to be compelling for readers who are interested in the contexts of the analyzed texts. Content analysts, too, argue for the context sensitivity of their designs (or take this as understood), but they compel readers to accept their conclusions by assuring them of the careful application of their design.

■ Qualitative researchers tend to apply criteria other than reliability and validity in accepting research results. It is not clear, however, whether they take this position because intersubjective verification of such interpretations is extraordinarily difficult to accomplish or whether the criteria they propose are truly incompatible with the making of abductive inferences from texts. Among the many alternative criteria qualitative scholars have advanced, Denzin and Lincoln (2000, p. 13) note, are trustworthiness, credibility, transferability, embohdiment, accountability, reflexivity, and emancipatory aims.

Given the above, qualitative approaches to text interpretation should not be considered incompatible with content analysis. The recursion (hermeneutic circle) shown in Figure 4.2 is visible in Figure 4.3 as well, although the former figure provides more details and is limited to the design phase of a content analysis. Multiple interpretations are not limited to qualitative scholarship either. Content analysts can adopt multiple contexts and pursue multiple research questions. The researchers' reflexive involvement—systematically ignored in naturalist inquiries, often acknowledged in qualitative scholarship—manifests itself in the awareness that it is content analysts who construct contexts for their analysis, acknowledging the worlds of others, in the pursuit of their own research questions and in the adoption of analytical constructs based on available literature or prior knowledge about the contexts of given texts. Whether a close but uncertain reading of small volumes of text is superior to a systematic content analysis of large bodies of text is undecidable in the abstract.

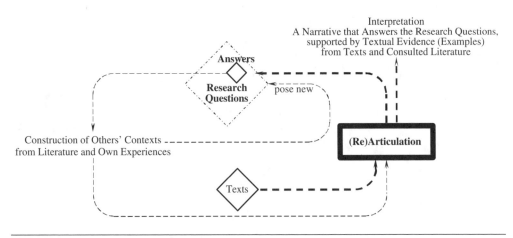

Figure 4.3   Qualitative Content Analysis

DESIGNS PREPARATORY TO CONTENT ANALYSIS   4.2

Making data—describing what was seen, heard, or read—is relatively easy. Content analyses succeed or fail, however, based on the validity (or invalidity) of the analytical constructs that inform their inferences. Once established, analytical constructs may become applicable to a variety of texts and may be passed on from one analyst to another, much like a computational theory concerning the stable features of a context. Below, I discuss three ways of establishing analytical constructs.

4.2.1   Operationalizing Knowledge

Content analysts, by their very ability to read and have an interest in given texts, acknowledge at least cursory knowledge of their sources: who writes, reads, appreciates, or uses the texts; what the texts typically mean and to whom; what institutionalized responses are possible and likely; and what makes the texts hang together. Knowledge of this kind, unclear as it may seem in the beginning, concerns the stable features surrounding texts. Figure 4.4 suggests that such knowledge needs to be rearticulated into an inference mechanism. Without a clear conception, that procedure may not qualify as a "design." I provide more specific discussion of this process in Chapter 9, but because the three preparatory designs all yield the same result, an analytical construct, I present them here for comparison.

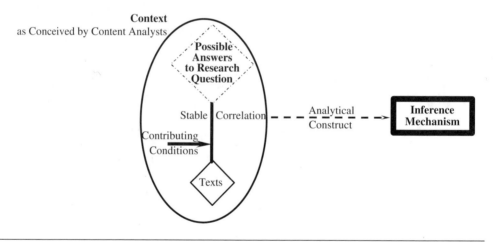

Figure 4.4   Operationalizing Expert Knowledge

Operationalizing available knowledge may be as simple as equating the frequency with which two concepts co-occur and the strength of the association between the two concepts in an author's mind. Other examples are building linguistic knowledge into the dictionary of a computer program, formulating an algorithm that accounts for propositions found in the message effects literature, and writing a computer program for tracing the linguistic entailments through a body of texts. Such operationalizations must be justified, of course, and available theory, literature, or acknowledged experts may suffice.

Testing Analytical Constructs as Hypotheses   4.2.2

The most traditional way to come to a valid analytical construct is to test several mutually exclusive hypotheses (conceivable constructs) of text-extratextual relations and let empirical evidence select the most suitable one. This is how researchers establish psychological tests, validate behavioral indices, and develop predictive models of message effects. Once the correlations between textual and extratextual features are known, content analysts can use these correlations to infer extratextual correlates from given texts—provided the correlations are sufficiently determinate and generalizable to the current context. This is why we speak of stable or relatively enduring relations operating in the chosen context. Osgood (1959), for example, conducted word-association experiments with subjects before building the correlation he found between word co-occurrences in text and patterns of recall into his contingency analysis. In a carefully executed study, Phillips (1978) established a correlation between reports of suicides of important celebrities and the fatality rate due to private airplane crashes. He found that the circulation of such suicide reports did predict an increase in airplane crashes. Whether such an index has practical consequences is another matter.

To test such statistical hypotheses, one must have large enough sample sizes available and make sure that the resulting generalization holds in the current content analytical context as well. This design therefore applies only to situations in which the research questions are asked frequently and the relations between texts and the answers to these questions are stable, not unique (see Figure 4.5).

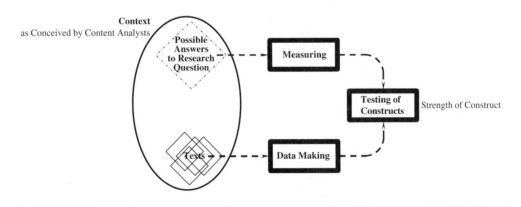

Figure 4.5   Testing Analytical Constructs as Hypotheses

Developing a Discriminant Function   4.2.3

This design proceeds iteratively: The analyst compares inferences from a content analysis of text with relevant observations of the context and uses any discrepancies found to alter incrementally the relevant parts of the analysis, typically its analytical construct. Through this process, the design converges toward a "best fit." This is how intelligent content analysts learn from their failures, as did the Federal Communications Commission propaganda analysts during World War II, who simply became better analysts with time (George, 1959a).

More interesting, however, are the procedures involved in this process. For example, to help teachers who must grade large numbers of essay exams, software has been developed that can be taught to distinguish, in students' written answers to exam questions, particular words and phrases that correlate with grades assigned by the instructor on a subset of exams; eventually, the software can assign grades without further human involvement. Houle (2002) describes artificial intelligence experiments with so-called support vector machines (SVMs), which can be trained within a few seconds on 30,000 documents to develop easily comprehensible rules that distinguish whether similar documents have or do not have a given property. He reports accuracy rates as high as 90% in the SVMs' distinguishing Associated Press news wire stories in about 30 categories and as low as 60% in their distinguishing medical papers in more than 1,000 categories. In current content analyses, paths to discriminant functions are provided by neuronal networks that "learn" the most successful connections between texts and selected contextual variables (see Chapter 12, section 12.5.2) and by traditional discriminant analyses that improve the accuracy of answers to questions by combining features of text best suited to distinguish among them. Even regression analyses that attempt to predict extratextual (and dependent) variables by identifying their textual (and independent) predictors may be mentioned here as a one-step process (see the discussion of LIWC in Chapter 12, section 12.5.1). Processes that converge to a discriminant function are iterative and circular, as shown in Figure 4.6. Measured discrepancies between proposed

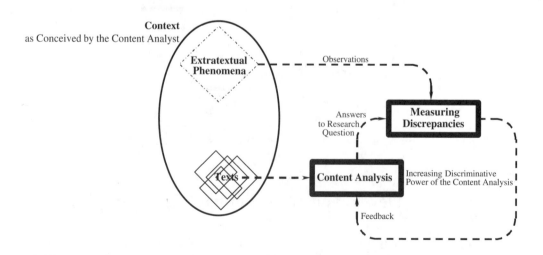

Figure 4.6   Developing a Discriminant Function

answers and validating evidence (observations) cause the discriminant function (the analytical construct in a content analysis) to reduce these discrepancies the next time around.

DESIGNS EXCEEDING CONTENT ANALYSIS   4.3

Unfortunately, starting with Berelson's (1952) account, the content analysis literature is full of insinuations that content analyses are aimed at testing scientific hypotheses, which brings us back to the notion of content as something inherent in or indistinguishable from text, a conception we have abandoned (see Chapter 2). According to the definition of content analysis employed in this volume, content analysts rely on hypothetical generalizations in the form of analytical constructs. But the test of these generalizations lies in their effects. It comes after content analysts have answered their research questions, made their abductive inferences, or interpreted their texts systematically. For example, to test a hypothesis concerning the behavioral correlates of anxiety, one must know the level of anxiety and separately observe the behavioral correlates of interest. By inferring the level of anxiety from an individual's talk—from accounts of feelings, distress vocabulary, or speech disturbances (Mahl, 1959)—the content analysis becomes a necessary part of a larger research effort. Despite what Figure 4.1 might suggest, content analyses do not need to stand alone, and they rarely do. Below, I briefly discuss three research designs in which content analysis is instrumental.

Comparing Similar Phenomena   4.3.1
Inferred From Different Bodies of Texts

In this design, researchers have reasons to draw distinctions within a body of text and apply the same content analysis to each part (see Figure 4.7). For example, to study speeches made before, during, and after a given event—or trends—analysts must distinguish texts according to time periods. To compare the treatment of one event in different media, analysts would have to distinguish texts by source. To examine how candidates for a political office tailor their promises to different audiences, analysts would want to distinguish texts according to audience demographics. And to test hypotheses regarding the impacts of competition between newspapers on the papers' journalistic qualities, analysts would distinguish texts by how their sources are situated. What content analysts compare—the hypotheses they test—in this design do not concern differences among textual properties, but differences among the inferences drawn from texts, which are a function of the assumed context, not directly observed.

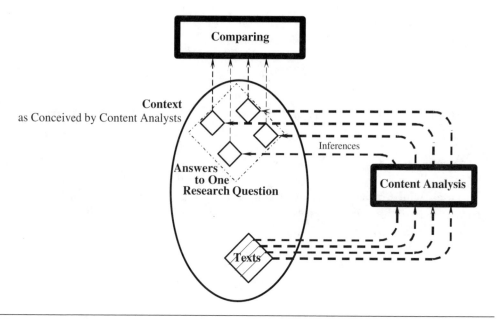

Figure 4.7   Comparing Similar Phenomena Inferred From Different Texts

4.3.2   Testing Relationships Among Phenomena Inferred From One Body of Texts

In this design, the researcher analyzes one body of text from different perspectives, with reference to different contexts, through different analytical constructs, or addressing different dimensions of meaning, and then correlates the results (see Figure 4.8). In behavioral research, such separately inferred phenomena tend to appear as different variables, which can be compared, correlated, or subjected to hypothesis testing. On a micro level, examples of such designs are found in analyses of attributions (multiple adjectives that qualify nouns), co-occurrences of concepts (inferred from word co-occurrences), KWIC lists (keywords in their textual contexts), contingencies (Osgood, 1959), and conversational moves (adjacency pairs or triplets). On a macro level, examples include efforts to understand how public concerns—crime, environment, health, unemployment, and politics—compete with or stimulate each other in the mass media. Such designs also enable an analyst to compare readings of the same texts by readers of different genders or readers from divergent socioeconomic, educational, ethnic, or ideological backgrounds. Here, the content analyst would define diverse contexts in reference to which texts are being read and analyzed.

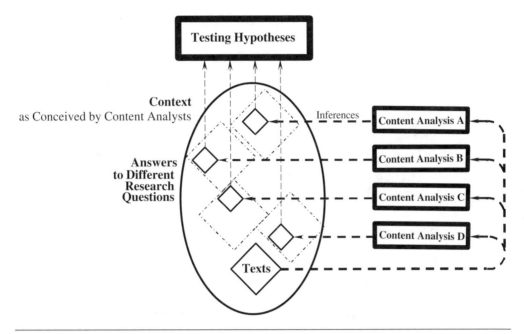

Figure 4.8   Testing Hypotheses Concerning Relations Among Various Inferences From One Body of Texts

Testing Hypotheses Concerning How   4.3.3
Content Analysis Results Relate to Other Variables

Typically, this kind of design brings communicational or symbolic and behavioral variables together. For example, the cultivation hypothesis, which asserts that there are correlations between media coverage and audience perceptions, calls for comparing the results of a content analysis of mass-media presentations with interview data on audience members' perceptions of everyday reality. Gerbner and his colleagues have explored the relationship between the "world of TV violence" and how TV audiences perceive the world outside of television (see, e.g., Gerbner, Gross, Morgan, & Signorielli, 1995). In comparing newspaper coverage of crime with crime statistics and public opinion, Zucker (1978) found that the frequency of crime reports in the media correlated more highly with public opinion than with official crime statistics. Conversation analysts usually are satisfied with their own accounts of what they see in the transcripts of naturally occurring conversations; thus their approach conforms to the design illustrated in Figure 4.8. However, if they were to relate their interpretations to participants' awareness of the phenomena being inferred, then they would compare inferences from texts with other accounts. Such designs have three primary aims:

- To provide variables about the nature of communications that enable the testing of hypotheses concerning the causes, correlates, and effects of such communications

- To enrich indicators of observed behavioral phenomena by adding measures that concern the meanings of these phenomena (multiple operationalism), especially concerning individuals' perceptions or interpretations of social phenomena, which cannot be observed as such

- To substitute more economical measures for measures that are cumbersome (for example, using content analysis of TV news instead of surveys of what the public knows)

This design is represented in Figure 4.9.

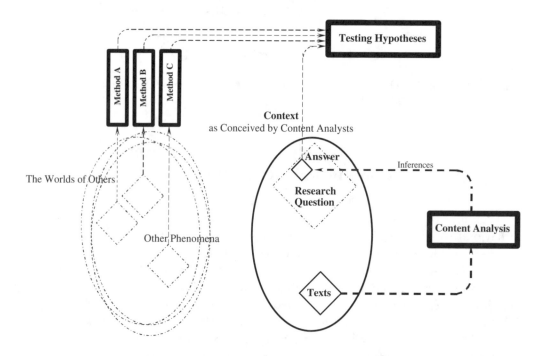

Figure 4.9   Testing Hypotheses Concerning Relations Between Observations and Inferences From Texts

I should emphasize here that actual research designs need not conform to any one distinguished above. Researchers can combine designs to obtain more complex forms that embrace many variables, and they can use any design in tandem with other techniques. There is no methodological limit to the use of content analysis in large social research projects.

CHAPTER 5

Unitizing

This chapter discusses the units of analysis used in content analysis: sampling units, recording units, and context units. It also addresses the purposes of unitizing and discusses five ways of defining units so as to increase the productivity, efficiency, and reliability of content analysis research.

UNITS 5.1

The first task in any empirical study is to decide what is to be observed as well as how observations are to be recorded and thereafter considered data. Empirical research needs to rely on a multitude of observational instances that collectively support an often statistical hypothesis or conclusion, or that exhibit patterns that single cases cannot reveal. In unitizing, the researcher draws relevant distinctions within an observational field. This creates a multiplicity of observations, information-bearing instances, or units for short, and readies that multiplicity for subsequent analysis.

Generally, units are wholes that analysts distinguish and treat as independent elements. For example, in the operation of counting, the objects that are counted must be distinct—conceptually or logically, if not physically—otherwise the numerical outcome would not make sense. Thus we can count pennies but not water; we can count words or sentences, but not text. The counting of meanings is problematic unless it is possible to distinguish among meanings and ensure that one does not depend on another. The wholeness of a unit of analysis suggests that it is not further divided in the course of an analysis or at a particular stage of an analysis. Physical definitions of units demand that their boundaries not overlap. Statistical definitions of units stress that "there is very little freedom for variation within [a unit] but much freedom at its boundaries" (Pool, 1959b, p. 203). However, in content analysis, units need not be motivated physically or statistically—these are mere options.

A political speech may serve as an example. Whereas ordinary listeners may well respond to the speech as a whole experience, being inspired or bored by it, or find the speaker impressive or unconvincing, political analysts may see the speech as addressing several distinct public issues. They may thus divide the speech into different parts and, ignoring the connections between the parts, probe, one at a time, how these issues are defined, what solutions the politician offers, and whether the discussions of the issues in the speech are used to attack, acclaim, or defend (Benoit, Blaney, & Pier, 1998). Linguists, in contrast, are likely to break the speech into sentences. Because there are no grammatical rules that would make one sentence construction dependent on another, there would seem to be no need to consider units larger than that. Computer text analysis software that identifies character strings as words, on the other hand, would produce units of a vastly different size and kind. Linguists would have little interest in a list of words, just as political analysts would find a collection of sentences insufficient to help them understand what is important about a speech. Content analysts might collect not one speech but many speeches delivered during a particular political campaign and identify different kinds of units in them so as to compare them with one another or relate them to other data.

Although text, being ultimately composed of characters, would seem to be unitizable naturally, the unitizing of text poses many epistemological questions that I cannot attempt to address here. For purposes of this discussion, suffice it to say that units should not be considered givens. They emerge in processes of reading and thus implicate the experiences of the analyst as a competent reader. Units are often regarded as a function of the empirical tenacity of what is observed, but it is the act of unitizing that creates them and recognizes them as such. This act crucially depends on the analyst's ability to see meaningful conceptual breaks in the continuity of his or her reading experiences, on the purposes of the chosen research project, and on the demands made by the analytical techniques available to date.

5.2   TYPES OF UNITS

In content analysis, three kinds of units deserve distinction: sampling units, recording/coding units, and context units. I elaborate the analytical purposes and uses of each kind below, after which I discuss five different ways of defining such units.

5.2.1   Sampling Units

Sampling units are *units that are distinguished for selective inclusion in an analysis*. Someone who claims to have analyzed a certain number of issues of a newspaper talks of sampling units. These units may have been drawn from a larger population of issues of that newspaper, or they may include every issue ever published. I present a full discussion of sampling in Chapter 6; here, I want merely to address the purpose of sampling units relative to the others units. In survey research, where units tend to be individuals who are capable of answering questions, sampling from a population is straightforward, the difference between sampling units and recording units disappears, and context units are irrelevant. In content analysis, these three kinds of units have different functions.

The use of inferential statistics (*inductive* inferences from data, not abductive ones) to test statistical hypotheses, for example, is predicated on the mutual independence of sampling units. Frequencies, probabilities, and the computed likelihood that a sample represents a population would be meaningless without that mutual independence. Thus survey researchers take great pains to ensure that their interviewees are not aware of each other's answers, experimenters make sure that the stimuli they manipulate are unrelated, and sociologists conducting research into causes make certain that their dependent and independent variables are clearly distinct. Without such precautions, the statistical correlations that result could be spurious and difficult to interpret.

The kinds of data of interest to content analysts are not so controllable. It is quite natural for people to create meaningful connections among almost any variety of things, including among the units that a content analyst has sampled. When analysts sample issues of newspapers, for example, it could be argued that such issues are not truly independent because most news events unfold in time and over several issues, building on what was published previously, and thus issues of newspapers are not strictly independent of each other. Indeed, reading just one newspaper issue out of context—say, an issue from 50 years ago—makes one realize how little one can understand without knowing what happened before. Similarly, during an election campaign, the speeches delivered by candidates for political office tend to refer or respond to other speeches, and some may even result from strategic alliances among speakers. If such connections are relevant to an analysis, sampling separate speeches would not only prevent the researcher from recognizing the connections in the data, it would also confound the findings. Content analysts must define sampling units so that (a) connections across sampling units, if they exist, do not bias the analysis; and (b) all relevant information is contained in individual sampling units, or, if it is not, the omissions do not impoverish the analysis. It is not easy to break a highly interconnected stream of messages into separate sampling units.

Recording/Coding Units   5.2.2

Recording/coding units are *units that are distinguished for separate description, transcription, recording, or coding.* Whereas sampling units are distinguished for inclusion in or exclusion from an analysis, ideally in a way that acknowledges natural boundaries, recording units are distinguished to be separately described or categorized. Thus recording units are typically contained in sampling units, at most coinciding with them, but never exceeding them. Holsti (1969), relying on the image of categorization, defines a recording unit as "the specific segment of content that is characterized by placing it in a given category" (p. 116).

The text included in any one recording unit need not be contiguous. Suppose an analyst samples fictional narratives with the aim of studying the populations of characters occurring in them. Narratives have definite beginnings and definite endings; thus they constitute natural sampling units among which the analyst can easily make decisions regarding inclusion or exclusion in a sample, even without much reading. In a typical narrative, however, the characters are rarely dealt with one at a time, or one per paragraph, for example. They tend to interact and evolve over the course of the narrative, and information about them emerges in bits and pieces, often becoming clear only toward the end. To be fair to the nature of narratives, the analyst cannot possibly identify one unit of text with each character. Thus information about a recording unit may be distributed throughout a text. Once the analyst has described the recording units, it is these descriptions, the categories to which they are assigned, that are later compared, analyzed, summarized, and used as the basis for intended inferences.

A good reason for choosing recording units that are significantly smaller than the sampling units is that sampling units are often too rich or too complex to be described reliably. For example, whole movies are conventionally labeled "documentary," "fiction," "comedy," "tragedy," "popular," "class A (or B or C)," "R-rated," and so on. Such categories are very superficial and say little about what movies of each type mean in the lives of viewers and other stakeholders. To capture meaningful variations among movies, analysts would surely need to have a rich vocabulary of descriptive terms at their disposal. But so do film critics, who claim to be able to describe movies without ever expecting to agree among themselves on all details. To obtain reliable accounts of larger units of text, content analysts have found it convenient to describe smaller units on which they can more easily agree and then use analytic procedures to obtain descriptions of larger units. To ensure agreement among different analysts in describing the coding/recording units of a content analysis, it is desirable to define these units of description as the smallest units that bear all the information needed in the analysis, words being perhaps the smallest meaningful units of text.

Recording units may also be distinguished and described on several *levels of inclusion*. In recording newspaper data, for example, an analyst may have one set of categories for describing the newspapers included in the sample, such as cosmopolitan versus local, or having a certain circulation; a second set of categories for addressing the actual newspaper issue being included in the sample, weekday or Sunday edition, or consisting of a certain number of pages; a third set of categories concerned with a particular article printed in that issue, its writer or source, its placement in the issue (front, middle, or last page), and its length; and a fourth that is concerned with the individual propositions in that article. These multilevel recording units form inclusion hierarchies. Newspapers publish many issues. Each issue contains many articles. Each article is made up of a number of sentences or propositions. Ingenious definitions of recording units can open the door to many interesting content analyses.

Context Units 5.2.3

Context units are *units of textual matter that set limits on the information to be considered in the description of recording units*. In the above example of describing the characters in a narrative, a natural choice for the context unit might be the whole narrative in which the characters play the roles they do. However, when analysts are trying to ascertain particular characters' development—where the characters emerge, what they do, and what happens to them—maybe chapters would be a better choice as context units, as this choice would allow characters to vary in the course of the narrative. More generally, the meaning of a word typically depends on its syntactical role within a sentence. To identify which meaning applies to a word from a list of dictionary entries, one must examine the sentence in which the word occurs. How else would one know, for example, whether the word *go* is meant to denote a game, an action, or a command? Here, the sentence is the context unit and the word is the recording unit. Sentences are the minimal context units for individual words, but sentences may not be enough. To identify the referent of a personal pronoun, for instance, an analyst may need to examine a few sentences preceding that pronoun. To judge whether a political commentary is positive or negative for a candidate, an analyst might need to examine even larger context units, such as a paragraph or a whole speech.

Unlike sampling units and recording units, context units are not counted, need not be independent of each other, can overlap, and may be consulted in the description of several recording units. Although context units generally surround the recording units they help to identify, they may precede the occurrence of a recording unit (as in the example concerning personal pronouns) or be located elsewhere, such as in footnotes, indices, glossaries, headlines, or introductions. There is no logical limit to the size of context units. Generally, larger context units yield more specific and semantically more adequate accounts of recording units than do smaller context units, but they also require more effort on the part of analysts.

Geller, Kaplan, and Lasswell (1942) have demonstrated how the characterization of a recording unit (and ultimately the research results) depends on the size of the context unit. They had their subjects judge how positively or negatively "democracy" was presented in an article, using a sentence, a paragraph, three sentences, and the entire article as context units. Although the results from the four methods were generally in agreement as to the direction of the bias (favorable, neutral, unfavorable), they differed in extent. As the size of the context increased, the number of neutral evaluations decreased significantly.

Evidently, the context of a symbol contains a great deal of information, especially concerning affect.

The size of context units also affects the reliability and efficiency of the descriptive effort. To describe the treatment of fictional characters in the context of a whole novel, an analyst would need to read the entire book first and then assign each character to the appropriate categories. Not only would this process be time-consuming, it would also invite unreliability, because different individuals approach a novel differently, and the analyst would have to keep the whole in mind when making judgments. Going through a document sentence by sentence, or watching one scene of fictional programming at a time (perhaps even in slow motion), or recording dramatic encounters within their immediate setting, or looking for the characterization of a concept within a context no larger than a paragraph might be more reliable and more efficient, provided what is lost is not too significant. The best content analyses define their context units as large as is meaningful (adding to their validity) and as small as is feasible (adding to their reliability).

Conceivably, context units could be defined so that the original text can be reconstructed without loss. This would require that all relevant information about the organization of the text be retained in the description of each recording unit, much as in a hologram. A complete concordance that retains the positions of all the words it lists, including function words and punctuation marks (which most concordances omit), would exemplify this possibility. Some computer text analysis software stores texts in this manner. However, as soon as fewer and more conceptual recording units are applied to a text and an analyst's conception of the context of the analysis enters their description, this goal becomes less likely to be achievable. Reconstructibility, even when not perfect, preserves the possibility of analyzing data in several ways and on several levels.

Some authors who write on content analysis (e.g., Holsti, 1969) also mention *units of enumeration*. The importance given to these units derives largely from the early definitional requirement of content analysis that it be quantitative (Berelson, 1952; Lasswell, 1949/1965b), which simply meant that textual units had to end up being categorized or measured in numerical terms. In content analysis, quantities may be of three different kinds and uses:

- Quantities that are extraneous to but associated with sampling units, such as a newspaper's circulation figures, a television show's Nielsen ratings, or a movie's box-office figures. These numbers are *descriptive*, here of *recording units* that happen to coincide with sampling units. The difference of describing units in numbers or in categories is not important methodologically.

- Quantities that measure a recording unit, such as the size of a photograph, the column inches of an article, or the length of a speech, or enumerate something contained in a recording unit, such as number of speech disturbances encountered within a period of time. These measures or counts are also *descriptive*, here explicitly of *recording units,* and do not need any special attention either.

■ Quantities that result from the counting of recording units, especially within the categories to which they are assigned. These express the *sizes or magnitudes of classes of units,* whether they are expressed relative to a sample, within a hierarchy of recording units, or within cross-tabulations of coincidences. These numbers refer to classes that are formed in the process of analysis. They do not describe units of text.

In early content analyses, these rather different kinds of quantities were often confused. Researchers tried to satisfy Berelson's (1952) and Lasswell's (1949/1965b) quantification requirement without considering the functions the rather different quantities served. Quantities of the first kind tend to come into play, for example, when analysts are deciding on which newspapers to sample or how to weigh the importance of TV shows. I discuss these in Chapter 6. Quantities of the second kind are measures that are no different from coding recording units in numerical categories, using a yardstick instead of qualitative judgments, or recording a count rather than a category. Coders need to be instructed, and these measures are parts of a data language. I discuss these issues in Chapters 7 and 8. In contrast, quantities of the third kind are of no concern to coders. They emerge after the analyst has put recording units into categories or measured them, as a matter of convenience for summarizing data or applying suitable statistical techniques: cross-tabulations of frequencies, correlations, variance analyses, factor analyses, and so forth. These numbers are useful computational artifacts, and I discuss some of the statistical techniques for which they are useful in Chapter 10.

The three principal kinds of units distinguished above all serve different analytical functions. Sampling units are units of selection and may provide an analyst with a basis for judging the statistical representativeness of data. Recording units are units of description that collectively bear the information that content analysts process and provide the basis for statistical accounts. Context units are units that delineate the scope of information that coders need to consult in characterizing the recording units.

WAYS OF DEFINING UNITS 5.3

Content analysts identify units according to one or more of five kinds of distinctions: physical, syntactical, categorial, propositional, and thematic. I discuss each of these in turn below.

Physical Distinctions 5.3.1

Physical distinctions arise in *the use of mechanisms to sever a physical medium.* Being incapable of understanding and insensitive to meanings, yet repetitive and systematic, mechanisms unitize by imposing their own structure onto the material being unitized. The units resulting from such a process coincide only accidentally with the discontinuities that humans typically recognize in a medium. An everyday example is the digitization of photographic images. If the resolution of a digitized photo is very fine, a viewer can distinguish between background and foreground and make out objects, people, or shapes. Newspaper images are of a quality barely above where a grid is noticeable but not too distracting. However, if a photo's resolution is very low, showing a grid of uniformly colored squares, the viewer is aware of the fact that the grid has nothing to do with the nature of the original image. Diagonal lines appear jagged, colors are averaged, and details that do not coincide with the grid disappear. Digitization is the result of a mechanism that recognizes neither wholes nor shapes, but imposes its own distinctions.

In content analysis, physical distinctions partition a medium by time, length, size, or volume but not by the information it would provide analysts. Osgood (1959) sampled pages of Goebbels's diary. Ekman and Friesen (1968) used frames of film as their smallest recording unit. Dale (1937) analyzed newsreel film foot by foot, and Albig (1938) provided his observers with a clock and requested that they summarize each minute of broadcasting. Recently, Cappella, Turow, and Jamieson (1996) coded public radio broadcasts in 30-second intervals. Time units are also common in studies of interpersonal behavior (Weick, 1968). Similarly, in my own work I have applied a grid to photographs of crowds to count how many people appeared in each cell.

5.3.2   Syntactical Distinctions

Syntactical distinctions are *"natural" relative to the grammar of the medium of the data.* They do not require judgments on meaning. Being "natural," they seem hardly questionable: books, issues of a newspaper, letters, poems, posters, theatrical performances, television shows. Their naturalness stems from the content analyst's familiarity with the data source's grammar, often because both share the same culture and find multiple ways to distinguish the same. For example, TV shows are listed in the *TV Guide,* separately produced, selectively watched, individually named, and so on. Such distinctions are reproduced in so many contexts that the analyst can hardly ignore them.

Words are the smallest and, as far as reliability is concerned, the safest recording unit for written documents. Lasswell's (1941; Lasswell, Lerner, & Pool, 1952) World Attention Survey, many literary detection efforts (e.g., Mosteller & Wallace, 1964; Yule, 1944), the analysis of style (Herdan, 1960; Miles, 1951), the analysis of psychodiagnostic inferences (Dollard & Mowrer, 1947), and research on readability (Flesch, 1948, 1951; Taylor, 1953) all rely on words or symbols. For computers, words are easily recognizable, so they often serve as a first step in computer-aided analyses (see Chapter 12). However, there are other easily recognizable syntactically defined units in text: sentences, quotations, paragraphs, chapters, journal articles, monographs or books, series, collections, and so on. In the nonverbal media, we have such units as the acts in theatrical performances, news items in television broadcasts, and editing shots in films. In conversation analysis, we have utterances between turns of talk.

The so-called proximity operators of queries in text searches (see Chapter 12) define "natural" units as well, relying on typographical conventions. Thus words may be identified as character strings that are bracketed by blank spaces or punctuation marks, sentences may be identified as strings of words that begin with a capital letter and end with a period, paragraphs may be identified as text fragments bracketed by carriage controls (¶), and chapters may be identified as text bracketed by headings or the end of a written work. These typographical definitions may not always coincide with the distinctions that knowledgeable readers make in text, but they clearly rely on the conventions of the medium under consideration.

Categorial Distinctions   5.3.3

Categorial distinctions define units by their *membership in a class or category—by their having something in common*. A common reference is typical: any character string that refers to a particular object, event, person, act, country, or idea. So "the 37th president of the United States" may also be referred to as "he" or "him" (where the context makes the referent unambiguous), as "the first U.S. president to visit China," as "Richard M. Nixon," as "Tricky Dick," or as "the occupant of the White House between 1969 and 1974." All of these character strings designate the same person. If a person is the target of an analysis, units may be defined in terms of their common reference. Whether this reference is direct or indirect, the grammatical form that is used, or the perspective it entails then becomes secondary to the definition of the unit. Aside from synonyms, categorial distinctions tend to rely on taxonomies. Coders ignore any subdivisions when they are asked to identify a politician, a nation, a hero, or an animal.

Categorial distinctions can also result from a theory that has been adopted for an analysis. For the psychiatric profession, mental illnesses are defined in the *Diagnostic and Statistical Manual of Mental Disorders* (American Psychiatric Association, 2000), which provides the official recording units for psychiatrists to use in making insurance claims and justifying appropriate treatment. Sociologists may define a family as a group in which members are related through marriage or descendancy. This definition may be at variance with how the members of a family define their family, but it may serve analysts well when they are recording how families appear in texts. Early content analysts defined symbols (usually single words) by their denotations but categorized them according to the values, attributes, and qualifications associated with them (e.g., Pool, 1959a). For them, categorial distinctions required not only a theory-driven reference but also the presence of adjectives (or else one could not describe them in the proper terms). A content analysis of how doctors are portrayed in non-medical literature (Posen, 1997; Turow, 1989) has to rely on recording units that contain information about doctors and may not apply institutional definitions but popular versions of "doctor." When an Internet search engine retrieves articles according to a query, it effectively identifies units that meet one or more search criteria, which presumably embody the relevant criteria for a category of meaning.

5.3.4 Propositional Distinctions

Propositional distinctions delineate units according to *particular constructions,* such as those that have a particular *propositional form* or exhibit certain *semantic relations* between conceptual components. For example, in his proposal for a linguistic content analysis, Roberts (1989) suggests using clauses as units. He defines clauses as sentences that include an inflected verb and, optionally, a subject, object, and related modifiers. The coder would have four types of clauses from which to select: perception, recognition, justification, and evaluation. A perception clause describes an activity (e.g., "Businesspeople vote predominantly Republican"). A recognition clause classifies a phenomenon as belonging (or not belonging) in a category (e.g., "He is a politician," or "This is not a scientific statement"). A justification clause claims that an action is reasonable or unreasonable, and an evaluation clause asserts how well a phenomenon fits a particular category.

Another example comes from Osgood, Saporta, and Nunnally's (1956) evaluative assertion analysis, which I describe further in Chapter 9. All verbal material that enters this form of analysis must be reduced to a set of propositions of two kinds:

Attitude Object / Verbal Connector / Common (Evaluative) Meaning Term

Attitude Object$_1$ / Verbal Connector / Attitude Object$_2$

Because natural discourse rarely comes this way, Osgood et al. felt the need to develop and publish explicit rules by which analysts could decompose compound sentences into these basic kernels. According to these rules, the sentence "He had AIDS and lived in fear of not being able to finish his only novel" would become four units:

he / has / AIDS

he / is writing / (his only) novel

(the) novel / is / desirable

(the) novel / may not be / completed

One may note that the word *fear* is omitted from this kernelization, but the concept of fear is represented in the last two forms. Conventions vary regarding how many liberties analysts can take in this process, including whether or not they may add implicit propositions. What the personal pronoun *he* represents in the sentence above would have to be obtained from the linguistic environment of the sentence. *He, AIDS,* and *novel* are attitude objects. *Has, is writing, is,* and *may not be* are verbal connectors, the first three associative, the last one dissociative. *Desirable* and *completable* are common meaning terms of a favorable nature.

Similarly, in analyses of human interactions, including conversation analysis, it is common for researchers to decompose long sequences of verbal exchanges into collections of so-called interaction triplets. In an interaction between A and B, for instance, an interaction triplet would consist of the following:

A's utterance

B's response to A's utterance

A's acceptance or rejection of B's response to A's utterance

It is presumed that any interaction sequence between two people, A and B, can be analyzed into a series of such triplets, from which the original sequence can be reconstructed without loss. Although reconstructibility is neither a goal nor a requirement of content analysis, it is worth noting that a mere collection of the statements made by A or B would lose information on the interaction and prevent a reconstruction of the interaction sequence.

Propositions are elementary statements—basic sentences, complete claims, whole assertions, not yet analyzed—that can be strung together with the logical connectors *and* or *or*, much as a text can be constructed through the sequencing of separate sentences. Conversely, a compound statement can be thought of as decomposable or analyzable into basic propositions or kernels.

Thematic Distinctions   5.3.5

According to Smith (1992a), "The term *thematic* connotes the analysis of storylike verbal material, and the use of relatively comprehensive units of analysis such as *themas* (Murray, 1943), *themes* (Holsti, 1969), . . . combinations of categories (Aron, 1950)," motifs (Thompson, 1932), imagery, and thoughts (p. 4). Through their work on thematic apperception tests, Smith and his colleagues realized the virtue of unitizing freely generated narratives thematically and analyzing them toward ends that are comparable to the ends of such tests.

For example, in their attempts to infer the achievement motives of subjects, McClelland, Atkinson, Clark, and Lowell (1992) start by searching stories for statements of goals, assertions of individuals' being or failing to be successful in competing with other individuals according to their own standards of excellence.

These researchers then characterize the individuals in the stories as having *needs* or *motives,* as anticipating the accomplishment of *goals* or the frustration of failing to reach their objectives, and as engaging in *instrumental activities* in attempts to reach their goals, which may be either *blocked* by obstacles or *helped* by circumstances or other people, resulting in negative or positive feelings. The rearticulation of any part of a story in these terms constitutes a thematic unit. McClelland et al. then score the thematic units to infer the achievement motive of the subject—but recording/coding them is another matter.

Another example of the use of thematic units is Katz, Gurevitch, Danet, and Peled's (1969) analysis of letters of appeal to shed light on how emigrants use Israel's administrative services. These researchers defined their thematic units as requests to authorities for favors or exemptions that included as constituent elements descriptions of the writers' personal qualifications and the reasons their requests should be granted.

Thematic unitizing of folkloristic material goes back to Thompson (1932), who listed and described motifs that fill six large volumes and aimed at an exhaustive coding scheme. Armstrong (1959) reviewed some of the problems with using thematic units in folkloristics. More recently, treating historical writing as a kind of folklore, the Council on Interracial Books for Children (1977) published a list of sexist and racist themes—themes in which recurring stereotypes, distortions, and omissions are manifest—that the council's researchers applied to U.S. history texts.

Holsti (in North, Holsti, Zaninovich, & Zinnes, 1963, p. 137) instructed coders to edit and rephrase political documents in terms of an action framework containing the following components:

The perceiver and incorporated modifiers

The perceiver other than author of the document and incorporated modifiers

The perceived and incorporated modifiers

The action and incorporated modifiers

The object acted upon (other than an actor-target) and incorporated modifiers

The auxiliary verb modifier

The target and incorporated modifiers

Accordingly, his actor-action-target theme has up to seven components, and the textual material that specified these units could be distributed over several sentences. Readers of political accounts seem to have no difficulty thinking in these terms. (For other operationalizations of actor-action-target units, see Heise, 1995; Kleinnijenhuis, 1990; Kleinnijenhuis, De Ridder, & Rietberg, 1997. See also Chapter 12, section 12.5.3.)

Although the choice of units is always dictated by the purpose of an analysis, because of the descriptive richness of thematic units and their link to readers' understanding, many content analysts with representational aims find thematic definitions of units attractive. However, because thematic units may have to rely on textual features that are distributed throughout a text, even carefully trained coders can easily be led in different directions, making reliability difficult to achieve. Themes, even when they are relatively formalized or limited in scope, are not as easily analyzed as simpler units.

PRODUCTIVITY, EFFICIENCY, AND RELIABILITY   5.4

The five ways of defining units just discussed differ mainly in the kinds of cognitive operations coders must go through to identify units within a text. Generally, the simpler and more "natural" these operations are, the more efficient and reliable unitizing is, and the easier it is for the analyst to formulate reliable instructions and program computers to aid in the task. But simple units may not be the analytically most productive ones. Content analysis researchers have to optimize productivity without losing too much in efficiency and reliability.

Physical distinctions emerge from strictly mechanical operations, as noted above. Mechanical devices are reliable by nature, so when humans identify units in physical terms, errors arise mainly from the careless application of formal rules. However, physically distinguished units are totally oblivious to meanings. When the material to be unitized requires a complex reading and relevant meanings span several units, physical distinctions can discard relevant information and invite unreliability into subsequent coding. For example, coders of 30-second intervals of talk on talk radio shows may end up coding incomplete utterances or finding the answer to a question in different 30-second intervals that, because they are separate units, may no longer be seen as connected. Seconds of talk are unnatural units, much as are lines of printed text or the individual frames of a movie. Physically distinguished units may be better suited to definitions of sampling units: time periods in years, articles containing keywords, sampling every fifth issue of a daily newspaper, for example. Such uses may not interfere much with how meanings are read.

Syntactical distinctions tend to be efficient and reliable, but they are not always productive in subsequent analyses. This is especially so when the source employs units on various levels of inclusion, whereas the analyst operates on only one level. For example, if an analysis proceeds sentence by sentence, as is customary in linguistics, hierarchies of syntactical units are ignored: paragraphs making a point, chapters elaborating a topic, and a book addressing a theme. It may be unproductive to define sentences as units of text, at least by standards of the source's or other readers' conceptions. The use of context units that are larger than the recording units eases this problem by allowing at least two levels of information to enter the units' subsequent descriptions: information from the recording unit and information from its surroundings, both encoded in the recording unit. But the distinction between recording and context units may not capture how a source organizes its contents and how ordinary readers understand the text. Whether reference to a text's source or to specific readers is relevant to an analysis depends on how the analytical context of the content analysis is defined.

To make *categorial distinctions,* one must be familiar with the meanings of character strings, references of names, connotations of symbols, contents of short expressions, and the like. Because the definitions of such units depend on inter-pretations, the identification of units becomes unreliable when multiple interpre-tations are possible. A stretch of text may not be simultaneously a unit and not a unit. Context units can improve the reliability of unitization. (I should note that multiple descriptions of recording units are not excluded; however, my concern here is with distinguishing units, with deciding what is to be sampled, the size of the context to be consulted, and the recording units to be described.) In content analysis, categorial distinctions among units are most commonly used for defining sampling—but especially for defining recording units.

Propositional distinctions require considerable clarity about the formal require-ments of an analysis, as illustrated by the examples given above concerning the extraction of rather specific propositional forms from complex or compound sen-tences. They call for familiarity with the logical syntax and semantics of source lan-guage expressions and require mastery of the rules for kernelizing and rearticulating these expressions. Unless the latter are commensurate with the verbal production or thought processes of a source, propositional units often seem artificial and contrived although clearly focused on the analysts' purpose. Although propositional distinc-tions lead to very rich and interesting content analyses, the process of using such dis-tinctions can be quite inefficient, largely because the identification of such units can be tedious, even when coders have well-formulated rules to guide them.

Thematic distinctions are rich in information and potentially very productive, and they would therefore be preferable to all other kinds of distinctions if their use did not make it so difficult to achieve reasonable levels of reliability. Research communities whose members have worked together and refined their methodology for a long time often report remarkable reliability in using thematic distinctions. This is the case with one group of scholars that has analyzed achievement motives for years, starting with McClelland's work in the 1940s (see Smith, 1992b). Beginners are often attracted to thematic content analysis because it seems to preserve the richness of textual interpretations, but they often fail to satisfy the reliability requirements and give up.

In unitizing, analysts aim to select the empirically most meaningful and informa-tive units that are not only efficiently and reliably identifiable but also well suited to the requirements of available analytical techniques. To achieve these often-conflicting objectives, analysts must be prepared to make compromises. Most often, this means letting unreliable information go, unitizing by propositional distinctions instead of by thematic ones, unitizing by categorial distinctions instead of by propositional ones, or redefining the target of inferences so as to be able to make sense of the data.

Calculating the reliability of unitizing is not a simple matter. Several scholars have proposed methods for assessing the reliability of cutting a large text or a sequence of images into units of analysis (see Chapter 11).

CHAPTER 6

Sampling

The universe of available texts is too large to be examined as a whole, so content analysts need to limit their research to a manageable body of texts. Although attempting to answer research questions from a limited set of data introduces the specter of sampling bias, it is possible to collect data by means of sampling plans that minimize such bias. This chapter extends the theory of sampling from populations of individuals to the sampling of texts. It discusses available sampling techniques and makes suggestions concerning how analysts can determine adequate sample sizes.

SAMPLING IN THEORY 6.1

Printing, sound and video recording, photocopying, word and image processing, digital storage media—from floppy disks to whole libraries—and the worldwide dissemination of texts in electronic form have exploded the availability of content-analyzable matter. Thus when communication researchers ask questions that available texts could answer, they can easily become overwhelmed by volumes of relevant data. This situation creates a challenging problem for researchers: how to answer their research questions from a small body of texts. Even when researchers generate their own data—say, by videotaping speeches or verbal interactions—transcribing and analyzing such data in sufficient detail can consume 10 to 100 times the hours spent taping these situations. Researchers who are unfamiliar with the theory and techniques of sampling might realize at some point during data analysis that their task exceeds available resources and may be forced to terminate data analysis prematurely, leaving their results incomplete or biased by the researchers' own limitations.

Statistical sampling theory gained prominence when researchers began to address the problems associated with measuring public opinion through survey research. Survey researchers attempt to estimate the properties of an entire population by observing or asking questions of only a select subset of individuals drawn from that population. At one extreme, if all individuals in a given population were identical, a sample of one would be sufficient. This assumption guides much of engineering and consumer research, where the qualities of one product from an assembly line are tested and the results are assumed to be true of all the products coming from the same assembly line. At the other extreme, if each individual in a population were unique, no sample would be able to represent the whole population. A researcher would have to study every member of the population. The challenges of sampling arise between these extremes. Usually, there are similarities *and* differences within any population, and research findings need to be perfect only within certain limits. A sample is said to be representative of a population if studying it leads to conclusions that are approximately the same as those that one would reach by studying the entire population. Thus, fundamentally, sampling theory is concerned with the ability to generalize the properties found in a sample to the population from which the sample is drawn. It relies on the law of large numbers to estimate the bias introduced by generalizations from inadequate sample sizes, and it provides justifications for several sampling techniques aimed at minimizing such biases.

Sampling theory, as outlined above, does not, however, fully map onto the sampling problems that content analysts face. Four of its assumptions prevent its wholesale application to the *sampling of texts:*

- In the above-outlined sampling theory, *sampling units are individuals—* actual or, when applied elsewhere, metaphorical—that is, they are indivisible unities, independent of each other, and hence individually countable by their properties, opinions, or behaviors. Texts, in contrast, may be variously conceptualized and unitized. For example, textual units could be conceived of in terms of hierarchies in which one level includes the next (film genre, movie, scene, episode, encounter, shot, assertion/action, frame, and so on; see Chapter 5). They could be read as sequentially ordered events, jointly constituting narratives whose integrity would be lost if the components were permuted, or as networks of intertextualities (co-occurring, making reference to, building on, or erasing each other). There is no single "natural" way of counting texts.

- In the above sampling theory, *the units sampled are the units counted.* In content analysis, this is rarely the case. Content analysts may sample letters, issues of newspapers, or time periods of movie production, but they find answers to their research questions by enumerating sentences, categorizing references, or interpreting the details of visual images. In Chapter 5, I distinguished between sampling units and coding/recording units. The sampling of sampling units constrains the sampling of recording units, which tend to be the ones counted.

■ *Survey researchers control the questions* asked of their interviewees and *decide on the legitimacy of the interviewees' answers.* By virtue of their membership in a population of interest, all sampled individuals are considered *equally informative* about the survey researchers' questions. In contrast, the texts that content analysts utilize typically are generated for purposes other than being analyzed, and it is rare for different textual units to have equal relevance for a content analyst's research question.

■ Traditional sampling theory is a theory of representation, in the sense that the sample drawn from a population has the same distributional properties as the population. It offers all members of *that (single) population an equal chance of being included in the sample.* Content analysts, in contrast, have to consider at least two populations at once: the population of answers to a research question and the population of texts that contains or leads to the answers to that question. Therefore, content analysts are rarely interested in accurate representations of the textual universe; rather, their concern is that the texts of interest are relevant to the research question and help to answer it fairly. Texts must be sampled in view of what they mean, the interpretations they enable, and the information they contain. Thus content analysts *have to sample their texts to give their research questions a fair chance of being answered correctly.* Sampling from one population in view of another is a problem that differs radically from the problems addressed by statistical sampling theory.

SAMPLING TECHNIQUES APPLICABLE TO TEXTS   6.2

All content analyses are (or should be) guided by research questions. Sampling problems do not arise when analysts can answer their research questions by examining all texts of a particular population of texts, such as all of a given writer's works, all issues of a newspaper within a chosen period, all documents generated by a legal proceeding, the complete medical record of a patient, or all e-mails received and answered by a certain office, on a certain issue, and during a certain period in time. When researchers analyze a sample of texts in place of a larger population of texts, however, they need a *sampling plan* to ensure that the textual units sampled do not bias the answers to the research question.

Only when all sampling units are *equally informative* concerning a research question is sampling in content analysis the same as sampling in survey research. For such situations, statistical sampling theory offers three sampling techniques, summarily called *probability sampling* because they are designed to ensure that all sampling units have the same chance to be included in the sample. In the following subsections, I describe these sampling techniques first.

When sampling units are *unequally informative,* which is far more typical in content analysis than in survey research, the sampling of texts becomes a function of what is known about the distribution of information (content) within a textual universe. I describe below four sampling techniques that respond to this condition.

In addition to the distinction between equal and unequal informativeness of sampling units, there are situations in which researchers *know their populations of texts* well enough to *enumerate* (assign numbers to) or comprehensively *list* the members of those populations. Regular publications, for example, have sequential dates of publication that are known before sampling. Many institutions keep accounts of texts in various forms, including library catalogs; *Books in Print;* professional guides to scholarly journals; records of legal transactions; variously kept logs, diaries, chronicles, histories, and almanacs; reference works such as dictionaries and encyclopedias; and alphabetical directories. Among the many existing and widely used systems for enumerating texts are the ISBNs (International Standard Book Numbers) of books, URLs of Web pages on the Internet, telephone numbers, product numbers in catalogs—all the way to the page numbers of books. The first four sampling techniques reviewed below rely on systems of this kind. (Enumeration systems may not be of uniform quality; for example, most URLs do not name active Web pages, and for some daily newspapers there may be publication gaps.)

A more challenging situation is one in which a population of text has a conceptual boundary but no enumerable members, for example, when a researcher is interested in information on a certain issue that could appear in a rather diverse population of texts. Cluster sampling, the fifth technique described below, is useful in situations where sampling units can be listed in larger chunks, or clusters. Cluster sampling also may be used in situations in which sampling units and recording units differ in kind and/or in number. Following the discussion of cluster sampling, I address three sampling techniques that deviate even further from the idea of selecting a representative subsample from a population. And the final technique discussed, convenience sampling, contradicts the most important features of statistical sampling theory.

6.2.1   Random Sampling

To draw a simple random sample, a researcher must enumerate (or list) all sampling units to be included in or excluded from the analysis (issues of journals, authors, Web pages, speeches, turns at talk, sentences). The researcher then applies a randomization device—a device that grants each unit the same probability of being included in the sample—to the enumerated units to determine which will be analyzed. Throwing dice is one way of selecting units at random, but a random number table is more versatile.

Systematic Sampling   6.2.2

In systematic sampling, the researcher selects every kth unit from a list after determining the starting point of the procedure at random. In content analysis, systematic samples are favored when texts stem from regularly appearing publications, newspapers, television series, interpersonal interaction sequences, or other repetitive or continuous events. The interval k is a constant, so it will create a biased sample when it correlates with a natural "rhythm" in a list of units, such as seasonal variations or other cyclic regularities. For example, if a researcher examining issues of newspapers were to select every seventh day of the week, the *New York Times* science section, which is published every Tuesday, would be overrepresented if sampling commenced on a Tuesday and never included otherwise. For this reason, researchers should take care not to select every seventh issue of a daily publication or every even (as opposed to odd) turn at talk in two-person conversations. Hatch and Hatch's (1947) study of marriage announcements in Sunday editions of the *New York Times* unwittingly demonstrated this kind of bias. The researchers systematically sampled all June issues between 1932 and 1942 and found an absence of announcements concerning marriages performed in Jewish synagogues; however, they failed to realize that all the issues sampled coincided with a period during which Jewish tradition prohibits marriages (Cahnman, 1948).

Systematic sampling can be applied to any kind of list; the units need not necessarily be consecutive events.

Stratified Sampling   6.2.3

Stratified sampling recognizes distinct subpopulations (strata) within a population. Each sampling unit belongs to only one stratum, and the researcher carries out random or systematic sampling for each stratum separately. Thus stratified samples represent all strata either in equal numbers (i.e., in proportion to their actual size) or according to any other a priori definition, whereas the properties within individual strata are sampled without a priori knowledge. Newspapers, for example, may be stratified by geographic area of distribution, by frequency of publication, by size of readership, or by audience composition as obtained from readership surveys.

For many years, Gerbner and his colleagues analyzed a "typical week of U.S. television programming" each year, constructing that typical week through stratified sampling from the entire year's programming by the three major TV networks (see, e.g., Gerbner, Gross, Morgan, & Signorielli, 1995). The strata were the networks' programming slots, much as they are listed in *TV Guide*. For each year, the researchers obtained a "typical week" by randomly selecting 1 out of the 52 programs aired over the year for each programming slot of each weekday. This "week" had no empty periods or duplications, and the sampling method granted each program aired on the networks the same probability of inclusion.

6.2.4   Varying Probability Sampling

Varying probability sampling recognizes that textual units are unequally informative about the answers to analysts' research questions and so assigns to each sampling unit an individual probability of contributing to any one answer. In pursuit of answers to research questions about public opinion, for example, analysts may sample newspapers according to their circulation figures. In such a sample, large-circulation newspapers, which presumably affect more people, would have to be overrepresented relative to low-circulation newspapers in order for their contents to relate to public opinion variables. Thus when Maccoby, Sabghir, and Cushing (1950) were interested in the information that newspaper readers were exposed to, they listed all dailies within each of nine census districts (strata) in descending order of their circulation figures and assigned a probability to each newspaper according to its share in total circulation. Here, readership determined the likelihood that any given newspaper would be included in the sample.

Analysts may not find it easy to assign probabilities to sources of text in terms of their importance, influence, or informativeness. One strategy that has been used in such cases is to have experts rank the sources. In surveying psychological literature, for instance, Bruner and Allport (1940) enlisted professional psychologists to rank publications in order of their importance to the field. In studying newspaper coverage, Stempel (1961) relied on journalists. Some other kinds of evaluative sources that analysts might consult when sampling with unequal probabilities include best-seller lists, reviews (of books, plays, films) in prestige journals, book awards, and lists showing frequencies of citations.

Researchers may also use varying probability sampling to reverse certain known statistical biases in representations of reality. For example, the mass media are likely to air the voices of celebrities and to suppress unaffiliated voices that may not fit the media's own conceptions of the stories being reported. To infer what might exist outside of such selective reporting, an analyst might need to give the rare occasion of normally silenced views more weight than uninformed reiterations of mainstream ideas.

6.2.5   Cluster Sampling

Cluster sampling is the technique of choice when analysts cannot enumerate all units of analysis but find lists of larger groups of such units, or clusters. Analysts start by listing available clusters, then select among them randomly, systematically, or stratificationally and bring all units of analysis contained in those chosen into the analysis. In fact, wherever sampling units and recording units (see Chapter 5) differ, cluster sampling is taking place. Because the units that are contained in the sampled clusters are unknown, not only in kind but also in number, the probability that a particular unit will be included in an analysis depends on the size of the chosen cluster. In content analysis, cluster sampling is used far more often than many realize.

Since the early days of quantitative newspaper analysis, communication researchers have sampled among issues of newspapers but then measured, coded, and analyzed every article, paragraph, or proposition contained in the chosen issues. If such sampling is done correctly, every issue will have the same chance of being included in the sample. And if the sample is large enough, it should also accurately represent the population of newspapers from which the sample was drawn, but it will not represent the population of units contained in the newspapers, because the probability of particular units' inclusion in the analysis depends on such factors as where the newspaper is printed, which newspapers publish which kinds of articles, and which tend to reflect which kinds of perspectives, discourses, or attitudes. In content analysis, cluster sampling is convenient because text tends to be organized in relatively large units—journals containing articles, television shows featuring casts of characters, news broadcasts presenting issues, conversations occurring among participants—that address different topics. Analysts handle these large units (each of which consists of material that was printed, recorded, or aired in one piece) as wholes; they give the units names or label them by dates, keywords, headlines, author names, or genres and catalog them for easy retrieval. The text's constitutive elements, usually the primary focus of an analysis, thereby become secondary or implied by the way the large textual units, the clusters, are handled.

From the perspective of statistical sampling theory, the variance within cluster samples is likely to be exaggerated and sampling error remains uncontrolled. In content analysis, where researchers choose texts according to the texts' likely ability to contribute to decisions on rather specific research questions, sampling by clusters is more economical than sampling from a list of all available recording units. If the recording units are very unevenly distributed across the sampled clusters, the researcher will find it difficult to justify statistical generalizations about these units. However, because generalization is not a very important issue in content analysis, it is usually sufficient for a researcher to take precautions to prevent the uneven distribution of recording units.

Snowball Sampling   6.2.6

Snowball sampling is a multistage technique. Analysts start with an initial sample of units to which they repeatedly apply a given set of sampling criteria. This recursion produces a sequence of additions of sampling units that cause the sample to grow in size until a termination criterion is reached. A good example is the sampling of the literature on a particular subject. Researchers may start with a recent text, note its references, examine the cited works for their references, and so on. If the field examined is a close-knit one, the researchers will find themselves in a dense network of duplicate citations. Snowball sampling naturally terminates when the process generates no new references. In the case of a study of the content analysis literature, the trail stops with an obscure 1690 dissertation referred to by a historian of *Publizistic* (German for *newspaper science*) named Otto Groth (1948). One could complement this snowball sampling criterion by adding the requirement that the term *content analysis* be used and thus get up to 1941 (Waples & Berelson, 1941) as probably the earliest use of the term. This example illustrates snowball sampling that relies on citations of one work in another. The *Science Citation Index* (Garfield, 1979) has expanded snowball sampling of scholarly literature into the other direction, by iteratively generating lists of published articles in which particular works are cited.

Underlying all snowball sampling is the idea of intertextuality, the notion that units of text are connected, that they form actual or virtual networks within natural boundaries. The network of scientific references is just one example. The unfolding in time of a story in the news, which makes one news item dependent on a preceding one; the reproduction of information from news wire services to public conversations; networks of literary relationships within which ideas but also plagiarisms travel; hypertext links connecting one text to another and one Internet site to another—all of these may be used as bases for snowball sampling. Sociologists have studied the effects of social networks, such as how the buddy system in an organization influences promotions, how a subject is able to get a message to a famous person via a chain of acquaintances, and how rumors spread. Analysts could use all such intertextualities to sample relevant texts naturally.

Snowball sampling starts with an initial set of sampling units, as I have noted—and it is important that researchers choose these units wisely. Snowball sampling ends when it reaches natural boundaries, such as the complete literature on a subject. When it reaches its boundaries, the importance of the starting sample diminishes in favor of the sampling criteria that recursively create the boundaries. (All rumors, for example, have origins, but their transmission quickly renders those origins unimportant. The limits that rumors reach have much to do with the networks through which they travel and the needs they serve in a population.) But snowball sampling can also explode growing sample sizes exponentially, like an avalanche, in which case the researchers need to accept some constraints (e.g., requiring that chosen samples conform to more stringent inclusion criteria—that citations be multiple, for instance, not casual—or that the sample not exceed a manageable size).

6.2.7   Relevance Sampling

In the sampling techniques reviewed above, texts are sampled according to their sources, situations, time periods, genres, and intertextualities—all of these can be used without significant reading or analysis of the sampled texts. Relevance sampling, in contrast, aims at selecting all textual units that contribute to answering given research questions. Because the resulting sample is defined by the analytical problem at hand, relevance sampling is also called *purposive sampling* (see, e.g., Riffe, Lacy, & Fico, 1998, p. 86).

It is important to remember that the use of random samples always entails the admission that one does not have a clue regarding what the population of interest looks like or where to find the needed information. In content analysis, this is rarely the case. Cluster sampling already acknowledges that the universe of texts is partitioned onto large clusters and makes use of this knowledge. Snowball sampling presumes knowledge of the networklike organization of this universe of texts. When using relevance sampling, analysts proceed by actually examining the texts to be analyzed, even if only superficially, often in a multistage process. Suppose researchers are interested in alcoholism in the United States; more specifically, they want to find out what conceptions drive the use of alcohol on college campuses, what makes this a problem, and for whom. A random sample drawn from all that people read, write, and talk about would certainly contain answers to these research questions, but the task of sorting through the mostly irrelevant records in the sample would be a hopeless undertaking. Perhaps the researchers' first step in reducing the task would be to think about where they might find relevant documents and what those documents are likely to contain. When searching the Internet for *alcohol*, using the Google search engine, the researchers may find, say, 7,230,000 mentions of the word. They then narrow the search to find documents relevant to alcohol consumption, say, on campuses: "*alcohol + students*" yields 1,140,000 hits; *alcoholism,* 658,000; "*alcoholism + students,*" 131,000; "*alcoholism + students + academic,*" 40,000; "*alcoholism + students + academic + rehabilitation,*" 10,500; and so on. Thus the size of a universe of possible texts is reduced to a sample containing, ideally, a manageable number of relevant texts. Of course, relevance sampling is not limited to Internet searches, nor does it require electronic texts and their containing keywords as criteria for relevance. In the case of research into alcoholism on college campuses, possibly the most relevant data are recorded interviews of students by students, reports by student counselors, accounts of fraternity parties, and medical and police reports.

Relevance sampling is not probabilistic. In using this form of sampling, an analyst proceeds by following a conceptual hierarchy, systematically lowering the number of units that need to be considered for an analysis. The resulting units of text are not meant to be representative of a population of texts; rather, they are the population of relevant texts, excluding the textual units that do not possess relevant information. Only when the exclusion criteria have exhausted their ability to shrink the population of relevant texts to a manageable size may the analyst apply other sampling techniques. Issues of accurate representation may arise at that point, but only relative to the relevant units from which the sample was drawn, not relative to the whole population of possible texts.

Relevance sampling is so natural that it is rarely discussed as a category of its own. It has motivated political scientists since Lasswell's (1941) World Attention Survey, which compared the political climates of several countries; Lasswell restricted his analysis to the "prestige" newspapers in these countries (ignoring the "less influential" local papers). In a study of the coverage of foreign affairs during the 1990 U.S. congressional campaign, Wells and King (1994) used the same logic to limit their content analysis to the *New York Times,* the *Washington Post,* the *Los Angeles Times,* and the *Chicago Tribune.* They reasoned that these newspapers include extensive international coverage, have their own news-gathering abilities, and serve as the main channels of knowledge about other countries for U.S. political elites as well as other newspapers. Most researchers adopt some kind of relevance criteria for defining the populations from which they sample.

The problems associated with relevance sampling have gained in importance with the increasing use of very large electronic text databases and the Internet, where irrelevant texts are vast in number. Relevance sampling selects relevant data in ways that statistical sampling theory has not yet addressed.

6.2.8   Census

A body of texts that includes all of its kind is called a *census.* Studying the collected works of a particular author requires no sampling. The analysts may have to exert some effort to get ahold of these works, but that is a clerical task; the analysts do not make any choices concerning what to include or exclude. For another example, if content analysts want to know something about the press coverage of a given event and collect all newspaper articles pertaining to the event, that complete set of texts constitutes a census. Because it is complete, the analysts have no need to expand the number of texts by snowballing, and if the set of texts is manageable in size, they have no need to reduce it by using relevance or random sampling.

6.2.9   Convenience Sampling

A convenience sample is motivated by analytical interest in an available body of texts that is known not to include all texts of the population that the analysts are concerned with. Such a sample is convenient in the sense that the analysts do not care to make an effort or find it too difficult to sample from that population. By proceeding from available texts without any sampling effort, analysts leave the matter of how and why the data—and which data—get into the sample to circumstances out of their control, to the interests of the texts' channels or sources, whether or not the latter are aware of how their texts will be analyzed.

The idea of sampling entails choosing to include or exclude data, with the intent of being fair to all possible data. Convenience samples do not involve such choices and leave uncertain whether the texts that are being analyzed are representative of the phenomena that the analysts intend to infer. Convenience samples may contain biases, or, worse, the analysts may be deceived or used by others in ways they may not understand. For example, personal diaries are written for many reasons, such as to preserve the writer's ideas for posterity, to impress a particular community, or to revise history in the writer's favor. Without the benefit of other corroborating texts and without knowledge of why the diaries were written, analysts of diaries may be unwittingly drawn into the project of the writer—which may be, for example, to assure the writer's place in history.

Examples of convenience samples are many: enemy broadcasts, which are produced for propaganda purposes; psychotherapeutic conversations, which contain only features that therapists and patients consider relevant to the therapy; and election campaign speeches, which are unlikely to mention issues, intentions, and knowledge that the candidates believe will cost them the election. Historical accounts rarely are fair representations of what happened (Dibble, 1963). All documents from which we might infer past events are those that have survived for particular physical, personal, political, and institutional reasons. Consider how few witness accounts are available from the victims of the Holocaust, the Napoleonic campaign in Russia, or the enslavement of Africans in America.

Convenience samples present content analysts with the potential problem of having to undo or compensate for the biases in such data, taking into account the intentions that brought these texts into being and into the analysts' hands.

SAMPLE SIZE 6.3

After an analyst decides on a sampling plan, the question that naturally follows concerns how large the sample must be to answer the research question with sufficient confidence. There is no set answer to this question, but the analyst can arrive at an appropriate sample size through one of three approaches: by reducing the research question so that it can be answered, given statistical sampling theory; by experimenting with the accuracy of different sampling techniques and sample sizes; or by applying the split-half technique.

Statistical Sampling Theory 6.3.1

As noted above, the sampling of texts may not conform to the assumptions of statistical sampling theory. Sampling units and recording units tend to differ. Texts have their own connectivity, and recording units may not be as independent

Table 6.1   Sample Size: Least Likely Units and Significance Level (all sampling units equally informative)

| | | **Probability of Least Likely Units in the Population** | | | | |
		.1	**.01**	**.001**	**.0001**	**.00001**
	.5	7	69	693	6,931	69,307
	.2	16	161	1,609	16,094	160,942
	.1	22	230	2,302	23,025	230,256
Desired Level of Significance	**.05**	29	299	2,995	29,955	299,563
	.02	37	390	3,911	39,118	391,198
	.01	44	459	4,603	46,049	460,512
	.005	51	528	5,296	52,980	529,823
	.002	59	619	6,212	62,143	612,453
	.001	66	689	6,905	60,074	690,767

as the theory requires. Textual units tend to be unequally informative, and the researcher must sample them so as to give the research question a fair chance of being answered correctly. Nevertheless, there is one solid generalization that can be carried from statistical sampling theory into content analysis concerns: *When the units of text that would make a difference in answering the research question are rare, the sample size must be larger than is the case when such units are common.*

This is illustrated by the figures in Table 6.1, which lists the sizes of samples required to "catch" rare units on different levels of significance. For example, assuming the probability of the rarest relevant instances to be 1 in 1,000, or .001, and the desired significance level of the answers to research questions to be .05, a sample of 2,995 would give the analyst 95% certainty that it includes at least one of these instances. This logic is applicable not only to the sampling of rare incidences but also to critical decisions. When an election is close and its outcome depends on very few voters, political pollsters need larger sample sizes in order to predict the results accurately than they do when candidates' levels of popularity are wide apart. Although this generalization is sound, researchers who rely on the actual numbers in this table should understand that they derive from statistical sampling theory, from the binominal distribution in particular. Thus an analyst should use these figures only if the assumptions on which they are based do not violate the research situation in major ways.

6.3.2   Sampling Experiments

Analysts may elect to experiment with various sample sizes and sampling techniques in order to find the combination best suited to answering their research questions. Stempel (1952), for example, compared samples of 6, 12, 18, 24, and

48 issues of a newspaper with issues from an entire year and found, when he measured the average proportion of subject matter in each sample, that increasing the sample size beyond 12 did not produce significantly more accurate results. Riffe et al. (1998, pp. 97–103) have reported replications of these early studies as well as the results of experiments designed to determine how the use of different sampling techniques affects how well a sample represents a population. In one study, Riffe at al. used local stories printed in a 39,000-circulation daily over a 6-month period as the closest practical approximation to the population. They then drew 20 samples for each of three methods, selecting issues at random (random sampling), in fixed intervals (systematic sampling), and by constructing artificial weeks (stratified sampling) "with 7-, 14-, 21-, and 28-day samples." The researchers defined sufficiency of a technique as follows:

> A sampling technique was sufficient when the percentage of accurate sample means fell within the percentage for one and two standard errors found in a normal curve. In other words, if 68% of the 20 sample means fell within plus or minus one standard error of the population mean and 95% of the sample means fell within plus or minus two standard errors of the mean, a sampling technique was adequate. (p. 98)

Riffe et al. found remarkable differences among the methods:

> It took 28 days of editions for simple random sampling to be adequate, and consecutive-day sampling never adequately represented the population mean. One constructed week adequately predicted the population mean, and two constructed weeks worked even better. . . . one constructed week was as efficient as four, and its estimates exceeded what would be expected based on probability theory. (p. 98)

It follows that different sampling techniques yield samples of different degrees of efficiency. It is wise, however, to be wary of unchecked generalizations. Different media may have different properties, and results like Stempel's and Riffe et al.'s actually reflect measuring frequencies of content categories and may be generalizable only within a genre. If newspapers were to change their reporting style and feature, say, more pictures, many more sections, and shorter stories (as is typical among today's tabloid papers), or if content analyses were to use measures other than proportions of subject matter or frequencies, the findings noted above may no longer be generalizable.

What is common to experimental generalizations regarding adequate sample sizes is the researchers' approach, which involves these steps:

- Establish a benchmark against which the accuracy of samples can be assessed, usually by analyzing a very large sample of textual units, thereafter taken as the population of texts. Obtain the standard error of this large sample for the adopted benchmark.

- Draw samples of increasing sizes and, if appropriate, by different sampling techniques, and test their accuracy by comparing the measures obtained for them with the confidence interval of the benchmark.

- Stop with the combination of sample size and sampling technique that consistently falls within the standard interval of the method (see Riffe et al.'s criteria above).

Such experiments require a benchmark—that is, the results from an analysis of a reasonably large sample of data against which smaller sample sizes can be measured. Researchers can conduct experiments like these only when they have a reasonable idea of the population proportions and they intend to generalize statements about the minimal sample sizes needed. The former is rarely available, hence the following recommendation.

6.3.3   The Split-Half Technique

The split-half technique is similar to the experimental method described above, except that it does not require a population measure against which the adequacy of samples is assessed and does not allow generalizations to other samples drawn within the same genre. It does not even require knowledge of the size of the population from which samples are drawn. The split-half technique calls for analysts to divide a sample randomly into two parts of equal size. If both parts independently lead to the same conclusions within a desired confidence level, then the whole sample can be accepted as being of adequate size. Analysts should repeat this test for several equal splits of the sample, as it is expected to yield the same results for as many splits as are demanded by the confidence limit. If such tests fail, the content analysts must continue sampling until the condition for an adequate sample size is met.

CHAPTER 7

Recording/Coding

In making data—from recording or describing observations to transcribing or coding texts—human intelligence is required. This chapter addresses the cultural competencies that observers, interpreters, judges, or coders need to have; how training and instruction can help to channel these to satisfy the reliability requirements of an analysis; and ways in which the syntax and semantics of data languages can be implemented cognitively. It also suggests designs for creating records of texts in a medium suitable for subsequent data processing.

THE FUNCTION OF RECORDING AND CODING 7.1

Research is *re-search*, a repeated search for patterns. Thus research must be recorded in a medium that is durable enough to withstand recurrent examinations. Human speech vanishes unless it is audio-recorded (taped) or written down (transcribed). Social situations are lost unless witness accounts of them are preserved. And even written texts and photographic images will defy content analytic techniques that cannot recognize at least some of their features. Transcribing speech, describing observations, creating field notes, interpreting messages, judging performances, categorizing television presentations—all of these are ways of recording or coding transient, unstructured, or fuzzy but otherwise perfectly meaningful phenomena into the terms of a data language that can be analyzed through the use of appropriate techniques.

As Figure 4.2 indicates, recording/coding is one among several procedural components of content analysis. In practice, however, it represents a major problem for analysts, who must formulate recording instructions that they and other researchers can reliably execute. The recognition of the rather unique role that coding plays in content analysis explains why older definitions of content analysis virtually equate the technique with coding. For example, Janis (1943/1965) provides this definition:

> "Content Analysis" may be defined as referring to any technique (a) for the classification of *the sign-vehicles* (b) which relies solely upon the *judgments* (which theoretically may range from perceptual discrimination to sheer guesses) of an analyst or group of analysts as to which sign-vehicles fall into which categories, (c) provided that the analyst's judgments are regarded as the report of a scientific observer. (p. 55)

Another early characterization of content analysis comes from Miller (1951):

> In order to handle larger blocks of verbal material in a statistical way, it seems necessary to reduce the variety of alternatives that must be tabulated. This can be accomplished by putting a wide variety of different word patterns in a single category. (p. 95)

Although Janis's conception of recording—categorizing sign-vehicles—is severely limited by the semiotic terminology of his time, he nevertheless acknowledges the role of specially trained analysts (as noted in Chapter 3) and different levels of what I refer to in this volume as *data languages* (see Chapter 8). Miller's assertion invokes measurement theory, the simplest form of which is categorization (Stevens, 1946).

Recording takes place when observers, readers, or analysts interpret what they see, read, or find and then state their experiences in the formal terms of an analysis; *coding* is the term content analysts use when this process is carried out according to observer-independent rules. The preference in the natural sciences for data making by mechanical instruments privileges the latter; thus researchers attempt to formulate recording instructions that contain explicit and detailed rules that coders can apply reliably, just as mechanical devices would.

However, where texts and images are involved, or, more generally, where the phenomena of interest to analysts are social in nature, mechanical measurements have serious shortcomings that only culturally competent humans can overcome. Notwithstanding the many advances that have been made in computer-aided text analysis in recent years (see Chapter 12), in most content analyses the researchers at some point find they need to fall back on human interpretive abilities (Shapiro, 1997). This said, I use the term *coder* in this volume merely as a convenient generic designation for a person employed in the process of recording observations, perceptions, and readings of texts—coders may be readers, interpreters, transcribers, observers, or analysts. By using the term *coder,* I acknowledge that the recording instructions that content analysts create are intended to explicate rules that minimize the use of subjective judgments in the recording process, without denying the participation of human abilities. Even very strict instructions need to be read, understood, and followed by humans, and coders are humans even when they are asked to act like computers.

The recording instructions for a content analysis must contain everything needed to replicate the analysis elsewhere. In the following pages, I recommend that such instructions include specific information in four major areas:

■ The qualifications that coders need to have

■ The training that coders must undergo in preparation for the task of recording

■ The syntax and semantics of the data language, preferably including the cognitive procedures that coders must apply in order to record texts and images efficiently and reliably

■ The nature and administration of the records to be produced

Specifying the recording process is only one function of the instructions that content analysts need to develop. Another is assuring that the meanings of the resulting records are available to others, which provides for the interpretability of the research findings. The check marks on a data sheet, the numbers entered into boxes, the annotations written in the margins of a text, the transcription symbols used by conversation analysts, the scales used to indicate extents—all provide information as long as their connections to the original recording units are clear. If a study's instructions, codebook, or scale definitions are lost—which does sometimes happen—the data language is left without a semantics, and the records that a study has generated are reduced to nothing more than a collection of meaningless marks or numbers—computable, but no longer interpretable.

CODER QUALIFICATIONS   7.2

The coders involved in a content analysis must have the necessary cognitive abilities, but what is perhaps more important is that they have appropriate backgrounds. In addition, the qualifications they bring to the content analysis must be shared by a sufficiently large population of potential coders.

Cognitive Abilities   7.2.1

Even where recording is reduced to coding—that is, to the seemingly mechanical application of stated rules for mapping textual units into the terms of a data language—coders must be capable of *understanding these rules and applying them consistently* throughout an analysis. Recording is a highly repetitive analytical task that requires strenuous attention to details. Not everyone is capable of maintaining consistency under these conditions.

7.2.2   Background

In selecting coders, content analysts should not underestimate the importance of coders' familiarity with the phenomena under consideration. In order to read and interpret texts, or even observe visual images, coders need a level of familiarity with what they are looking at that usually cannot be made explicit by any instruction. Literacy, for example, is a social ability. It is acquired through a lifetime of using texts in a certain community. It would be impossible to convey all that is involved in reading, observing, and understanding in a document or instruction. When it comes to interpreting what local folks are saying to each other, coders who lack familiarity with the local vernacular may feel that they are able to understand what is being said, yet they may not be able to agree with those who do understand the vernacular about what the speakers mean. Although we cannot not understand, we cannot know what we do not know and are generally unable to articulate how our understanding differs from that of others. *Familiarity* denotes a sense of understanding that coders must bring to a content analysis. But the sharing of similar *backgrounds*—similar histories of involvement with texts, similar education, and similar social sensitivities—is what aids reliability.

Even the most detailed recording/coding instructions take for granted that coders and content analysts have similar backgrounds and so will interpret the written instructions alike. To ensure high reliability of coding, moreover, it makes sense for content analysts to employ coders from the same cultural/educational/professional background (Peter & Lauf, 2002). In analyses of therapeutic discourse, licensed therapists are an obvious choice. In literary applications, English majors are likely to do well, whereas in analyses of intricate visual images, graphic artists or connoisseurs of film might do better. The challenge for content analysts is to find *clear and communicable descriptions of coders' backgrounds* so that other analysts can select coders with backgrounds similar to those in the original research.

7.2.3   Frequency

Scientific research demands an intersubjective understanding of the process as well as of its results. Thus content analysts must allow other scholars to replicate their analyses. Adequate instructions are easy enough to communicate, but coders are not. Analysts attempting to replicate previous research need to choose coders from the same population that provided the coders for the original research. To ensure the availability of potential coders, content analysts must make sure that the above-noted coder qualifications (suitable cognitive abilities and appropriate backgrounds) are common—that is, that they *occur with sufficient frequency* within the population of potential coders. If they do not, the recording process may not be replicable, and the research results become questionable. Any researcher who claims to be the only one who is capable of reading a text correctly in fact denies the possibility of replicating the research elsewhere. The requirement of frequency might be disheartening to those who consider themselves outstanding experts, but even experts need to be able to communicate, and the requirement that particular coder qualifications occur with the necessary frequency ensures that they will.

CODER TRAINING   7.3

Recording/coding is not a natural or everyday activity. It may be motivated by abstract theory about the context of available texts or by the necessities of a complex research design. Coders may be asked to interpret texts in terms that are unfamiliar or difficult, even seemingly contrived or meaningless to persons without knowledge of the research questions. Although instructions ideally should be understood as written, it is typical for content analysts to provide coders with additional training in using the recording instructions.

Content analysts have reported spending months in training sessions with coders, during which time they refined categories, altered instructions, and revised data sheets until the coders felt comfortable with what was expected of them and the analysts were convinced they were getting the data they needed. It is typical for analysts to perform reliability tests during the development of the coding instructions until the reliability requirement is met as well. Singer's (1964) report on his study of Soviet-American attitudes provides a good example of how definitions of a data language emerge during the training of coders:

> The purpose of the study was to generate an accurate picture of Soviet and American foreign policy goals and strategies as far as they might be reflected in elite articulations regarding (A) the international environment, (B) the distribution of power, (C) the other's operational code, and (D) their own operational code.
>
> The procedure followed two main phases: designing and refining our coding procedure and applying it. The first phase followed six more or less distinct steps:
>
> (1) The questions that seemed most germane to the study at hand were compiled. These were, of course, based on a multiplicity of sources: The author's general knowledge of the subject, the parameters of his own social science conceptual schemes, and those dimensions of foreign policy suggested by the writings and research of others in the field.
>
> (2) Once a tentative set of essentially a priori dimensions was set up and arranged, these dimensions were discussed, criticized, and modified by the author, his assistants, some consultants, and several professional colleagues.

(3) This set of dimensions was then applied by the coders to a sample of the material to be coded, resulting in the deletion of some dimensions, the rephrasing of others, and the addition of a few new dimensions.

(4) The author then re-appraised the dimensions and further tightened up the three categories under each dimension, in order to maximize mutual exclusiveness as well as exhaustiveness of the categories under each dimension.

(5) The dimensions and their categories were then pre-tested by the coders themselves to ensure that:

    a. The literature to be coded made frequent enough reference to the dimensions to be worth coding,

    b. The dimensions themselves did not overlap one another (except in a few cases where some subtle shadings of attitude were being sought),

    c. The dimensions themselves were clear and unambiguous enough to assure that independent coders would have a high agreement that a specific article should or should not be coded along that dimension,

    d. The three category alternatives under each dimension were as mutually exclusive as possible, yet exhaustive of the possible ranges of relevant response.

(6) When the pretests had demonstrated (by agreement between two or more independent coders) that the dimensions and categories were adequately refined and clarified, they were settled upon as final. (pp. 432–433)

In this example, the analyst achieved closure. However, a methodological problem lies in the implicitness of the process. During the negotiations that Singer describes, the boundaries of categories shifted until their meanings could accommodate what Singer wanted and what the coders were able to code with reliability and ease. When coders participate in such conceptual development, it becomes difficult to determine whether they have merely become more careful or have instead developed a new, group-specific unwritten consensus concerning what is expected of them. Summarizing the use of content analysis in psychotherapy, Lorr and McNair (1966) observe the effects of such implicit adjustments on replicability:

Even though most investigators publish respectable indices of inter-rater agreement in categorizing the responses, these are open to serious questions. Usually the published inter-rater agreement is based on two people who have worked together intimately in the development of a coding scheme, and who have engaged in much discussion of definitions and disagreements. Inter-rater agreement for a new set of judges given a reasonable but practical period of training with a system would represent a more realistic index of reliability. Trials with some existing systems for content analysis suggested that reliabilities obtained by a new set of judges, using only the formal coding rules, definitions, and examples, are much lower than usually reported. Often they do not meet minimum standards for scientific work. (p. 583)

Ideally, the individuals who take part in the development of recording instructions should not be the ones who apply them, for they will have acquired an implicit consensus that new coders cannot have and that other scholars who may wish to use the instructions cannot replicate. Ideally, the recording instructions themselves should incorporate everything that transpired during their development, and the finalized instructions should be tested for reliability with a fresh set of coders.

Coders need to learn to work with the recording instructions as their sole guide. They should not rely on extraneous sources of information (e.g., the evolution of the instructions, the intentions of the researchers, emerging yet hidden conventions, and gentlemen's agreements), nor should they confer among themselves as to why they do what they do. Extraneous information undermines the governance of the recording instructions, and communication among coders challenges the independence of individual coders; both make replicability unlikely. If analysts decide that they need to amend or correct any of their recording instructions, they must do so in writing.

If analysts need to provide coders with any additional training material, they should report on what they gave to coders so that the calibration of coders can be replicated elsewhere. My colleagues and I once devised a detailed self-teaching program for the coders we employed to record incidents of television violence: Initially, the trainees were briefed about the nature of the task. Thereafter they worked by themselves, applying the written coding instructions to a preselected set of television shows. After trainees had identified units and recorded them on one data sheet, we provided them with the ostensibly correct scores (established by a panel of experts). The comparison provided immediate feedback on the trainees' own performance and enabled them to adapt to a standard interpretation of the instructions. This method not only allowed us to plot the increasing reliability of individual trainees but also helped us to decide at the end of the training period which individuals were suited to the task. Such a self-teaching program is easily communicated and replicable, and it yields similar results across studies almost by necessity.

Content analysts may be tempted to apply the recording instructions they have formulated by themselves. This is a questionable practice, however, for it is not possible to distinguish whether the data generated under these conditions are the products of the written instructions or of the analysts' conceptual expertise, especially when the analysts have certain conclusions in mind. Self-applied recording instructions are notoriously unreliable. Content analysts should be able to find other coders who are able to understand and reliably apply the recording instructions before they assert that the instructions account for their data.

| 7.4 | **APPROACHES TO DEFINING THE SEMANTICS OF DATA** |

The reliability of recording is greatly enhanced if the task that an instruction delineates is natural, relies on familiar conceptual models, and remains close to how the texts to be recorded would be read ordinarily.

The two requirements that categories be mutually exclusive and exhaustive (see Chapter 8) are not only important because of the syntactical requirements of subsequent computation; they are of semantic concern as well. Coders must be able to conceptualize clearly what they read. *Exhaustive* refers to the ability of a data language to represent all recording units, without exception. No unit must be excluded because of a lack of descriptive terms. *Mutually exclusive* refers to the ability of a data language to make clear distinctions among the phenomena to be recorded. No recording unit may fall between two categories or be represented by two distinct data points. These two requirements assure that the resulting records represent texts completely and unambiguously.

A set of categories that lacks exhaustiveness may be rendered exhaustive through the addition of a new category that represents all units not describable by the existing ones. Such fail-safe categories typically are labeled "not applicable," "none of the above," or simply "other." Because categories like these are defined by their negation of all informative categories, they tend to contribute little, if anything, to answering the research questions.

It is more difficult to resolve a situation in which two or more categories lack mutual exclusivity. The well-intended practice of adding categories such as "undecidable," "ambiguous," or "applicable to two or more categories" to sets of categories with overlapping meanings does not alter the categories' fundamental indistinctiveness; it invites indecision on the part of coders and rarely renders a variable sufficiently reliable. When content analysts use such categories, they reveal more about their own unclear conceptions than about the properties of texts, and they bias their research results in the direction of easily describable phenomena. There is no real remedy for ambiguous conceptions.

Little has been written about how coders actually read texts or perceive visual phenomena in order to record them. Instead of outlining a theory of purposeful reading, or coding, here, I shall approach this problem from the other end, by distinguishing a few cognitive devices that analysts have utilized to delineate meanings within texts: verbal designations, extensional lists, decision schemes, magnitudes and scales, simulation of hypothesis testing, simulation of interviewing, and constructs for closure and inferences. Analysts may use these devices in their written instructions for coders with some degree of confidence that adherence to the instructions will yield reliable records.

7.4.1   Verbal Designations

It is most typical for content analysts simply to name their categories, using verbal designations that are common and widely understandable—ideally dictionary definitions, perhaps with some additional technical terms. For example, in English, gender is either *male* or *female*. Although we may therefore easily put living beings in either category, actual texts may not do us the favor of revealing what we wish to know about gender. Missing information on gender may call for the addition of a third gender category, such as "gender neutral" or "unspecified." In recording the actions of TV characters, my colleagues and I have found many instances of roles unmarked by gender: babies, mummies, robots, cartoon characters, and abstract persons referred to by their dramatic functions, such as murderers, mayors, managers, and doctors. Ordinary language tends to discriminate against rare categories, but given that fiction privileges the unusual, for purposes of coding an analyst may need to expand the conventional gender binary.

Single-word designations for categories—proper nouns—are easy to understand, but they are often inadequate for recording more complex meanings. By using longer definitions of concepts, content analysts gain more freedom in asking coders to make theoretically motivated distinctions rather than common ones. Mahl (1959) developed the following set of eight categories to identify indicators of psychiatric patients' anxiety levels. Note the absence of abstractions in these definitions:

1. *"Ah"*: A definite "ah" sound occurs in speech.

2. *Sentence correction* (SC): Any correction in the form or content of an expression within the word-word progression. Such a correction must be sensed by the listener as an interruption in the word-to-word sequence.

3. *Sentence incompletion* (Inc): An expression is interrupted, clearly left incomplete, and the communication proceeds without correction.

4. *Repetition* (R): The serial superfluous repetition of one or more words, usually of one or two words.

5. *Stutter* (St).

6. *Intruding incoherent sound* (IS): A sound that is absolutely incoherent as a word to the listener. It merely intrudes without itself altering the form of the expression and cannot be clearly conceived of as a stutter, omission, or tongue-slip (although some may be such in reality).

7. *Tongue-slip* (T-S): Includes neologisms, transpositions of words from their correct serial position, and substitutions of unintended words for intended words.

8. *Omission* (O): Parts of words or, rarely, entire words are omitted (contractions are exempted). Most omissions are terminal syllables of words.

Extensional Lists   7.4.2

Extensional lists become important when the analyst's conceptions are difficult to communicate to coders. In such lists, the analyst enumerates all the instances that define each category. Extensional lists are essential to computer-aided text analysis, in the construction of computer dictionaries (see Chapter 12, section 12.7.1) in particular. Coders tend to find extensional lists awkward to use, and content analysts often find it difficult to anticipate in advance of an analysis all occurrences of the desired kinds. For conceptually difficult tasks, however, the use of extensional lists may be a technique of last resort.

An interesting example is provided by O'Sullivan (1961), who attempted to quantify the strength of relationships reported to hold between variables in theoretical writings on international relations. Prior commitments to factor analysis required him to conceptualize "strength of relation" as a "correlation coefficient" between two conceptual variables. The conceptual variables were easily identifiable, but early on, during coder training (the coders were all well-informed graduate students), O'Sullivan realized that the idea of the strength of a relationship, expressed in words, was incompatible with the formal requirements of the statistical definition of a correlation. Mapping the former onto the latter was totally unreliable. After much experimentation, O'Sullivan came up with the following extensional lists for each of six correlation coefficients:

0.2 is less likely to; in certain situations induces; may lend some; may be due to; may be, to the extent that; can be used without; possible consequences seem to follow

0.3 has introduced additional; not merely a function of, but of the; is a factor of; will depend not only on but upon; depends in part on; possibility of

0.4 leads; is likely to be; tends to produce; would tend to; will tend to induce; tends to; tends toward; tends to introduce

0.5 makes it improbable that; strongly affects; is most likely to result from; is most likely to occur; creates essentially; depends primarily on; depend primarily on; is a major source of; creates a problem of

0.6 will heighten; requires at least; will enhance; necessitates; will determine; produces; depends on; is inevitable; produces; depends; is the result of; will reflect; will impose; prevents; will override; weakens; strengthens; offers maximum; will be less; will add to

0.7 will; any must first; are least when; as will be; puts a; has; is a; is less when there has been; if it is this is; there is; there has been, and is; is directly related to; will be enhanced in direct relation to; is inversely related to; will influence in direct proportion to; is directly related to; there is a direct relationship between; stand in marked contrast to; to the extent that; the longer the more; the greater; the greater the greater the more; the greater the less the greater; the greater the greater the greater; the greater the more; the wider the less; the more the less; the more the more; the more the larger the more; the more the greater; the more the less likely; more than; the wider the greater; the wider the more;

the higher the greater; the longer the less; the shorter the greater must be; the fewer the greater; becomes more as the; is more likely to be the more; the less the fewer; the less the less; will be more the larger; the larger the more

Decision Schemes   7.4.3

In a decision scheme, each recorded datum is regarded as the outcome of a predefined sequence of decisions. Decision schemes are uniformly reliable for four reasons.

First, it comes naturally to most people to organize complex judgments in terms of what has to be decided first, second, third, and so on. When coders take each of these steps with separate criteria in mind, criteria confusion is minimized.

Second, it is always difficult for coders to consider fairly large numbers of categories. As a rule of thumb, humans cannot keep the meanings of more than seven (plus or minus two) alternatives in mind simultaneously. Larger numbers encourage coding habits to form and allow preferences to develop. Decision schemes can drastically reduce large numbers of alternatives to numbers that coders can conceptualize simultaneously.

Third, decision schemes can prevent unreliabilities due to categories that are defined on different levels of generality or that overlap in meaning. Schutz (1958) has demonstrated how the drawing of a decision tree can clarify the meanings of seemingly confusing categories used in a content analysis of comic strips: "United States," "Foreign," "Rural," "Urban," "Historical," and "Interstellar" (Spiegelman, Terwilliger, & Fearing, 1953a). He organized the categories in terms of dichotomous decisions (and added two logically helpful verbal designations, "Contemporary" and "Earth," to preserve the logic of these distinctions), which eliminated the confusion of logical levels:

Interstellar   Earth
    Foreign   United States
        Historical   Contemporary
            Rural   Urban

Fourth, and finally, when recording involves several dimensions of judgments, decision schemes offer coders the opportunity to decide each separately.

Figure 7.1, which comes from Carletta et al.'s (1997) analysis of conversational moves, illustrates several of these advantages. As one can see, this decision tree has 12 terminal categories. If the analysts had attempted to write a definition for each—similar to, say, the above example from Mahl (1959)—the results would have been lengthy, confusing, and probably unreliable.

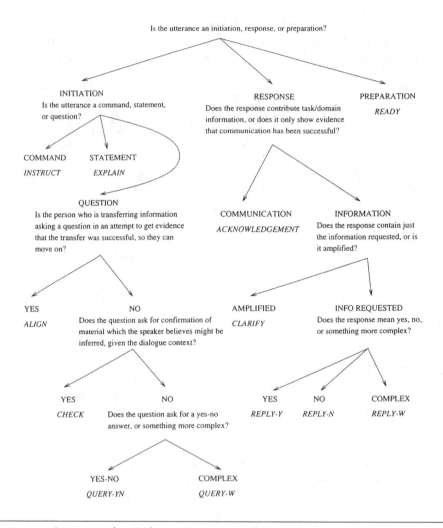

Figure 7.1   Categories for Coding Conversational Moves
SOURCE: Carletta et al. (1997, p. 15).

7.4.4   Magnitudes and Scales

When magnitudes and scales are used as recording devices, coders are expected to conceptualize the meanings of texts as continua, as having more or less of something, as possessing a metric. Osgood, Suci, and Tannenbaum's (1957) widely used semantic differential scales serve as an example:

Good   :_____:_____:_____:_____:_____:_____:_____:_____: Bad
Active :_____:_____:_____:_____:_____:_____:_____:_____: Passive
Strong :_____:_____:_____:_____:_____:_____:_____:_____: Weak

Semantically, each scale is anchored by the common meanings of two opposing adjectives. The intermediate scale points remain undefined except for the suggestion of equal intervals between the named extremes. Coders are asked to conceptualize a recording unit according to the semantic dimension that these opposites share and to judge its proper place along this presupposed continuum.

Seven-point semantic differential scales are widely used in psychological research, where experimenters can control their subjects' responses. In this research, the above three scales—potency, activity, and evaluative—explain much of the variation in what scholars in psychology refer to as human affective cognition (Osgood, 1974a, 1974b; Osgood et al., 1957). In content analysis, however, such scales are somewhat problematic. Text is not always scalable. Legal procedures distinguish between *legal* and *illegal,* and between these there are no intermediate points. The polarity of *news* and *fiction* may not be unidimensional, as a scale with these two words as endpoints would imply. And if coders are instructed to mark the midpoint of a scale whenever they encounter something that is not codable along such semantic dimensions, uncodability comes to be confused with perfect balance.

Furthermore, enforcing a scale that does not seem to work causes unreliabilities. In content analyses, semantic differential scales turn out to be unreliable mainly when information about the attributes to be recorded is absent or unclear. For example, in fictional narratives, characters become known only in the dimensions that are relevant to their roles in that narrative. Fictional characters may not have all the attributes of real people. Naturally, the less that is known about a character, and the more coders need to guess, the greater the unreliability of a scale that requires coders to make choices among polar attributes. In 1964, Zillmann introduced a scale that avoids this difficulty, his "semantic aspect scale." It is a 7-point unipolar scale that ranges from zero, the absence of an attribute, to 6, the pervasive presence of that attribute. The use of such a scale is appropriate when attributes, qualities, or phenomena can be more or less, including absent—more or less significant to a character, more or less present in an assertion, or more or less frequent. For example:

	absent						very much present
Honesty:	: 0	: 1	: 2	: 3	: 4	: 5	: 6 :

Simulation of Hypothesis Testing   7.4.5

The recording devices discussed above rely on cognitive models of labeling, categorizing, deciding, and interpreting what is read within a framework of established natural language definitions. Simulation of hypothesis testing addresses a text's presuppositions, implications, and omissions over and above its explicit meanings. For example, if someone is presented as a Swede, we might assume several things about that person: There is a good chance that he or she is

Protestant, understands other Scandinavian languages, has not fought in or experienced war, is blond, enjoys nature, and so on. These characteristics may not be mentioned, can be presupposed, and would not be surprising if found true. A subscriber to the *New York Times* most likely knows English, is old enough to be interested in what happens in society, has some political sophistication and cosmopolitan interests (the newspaper has no comics page!), and so on. These are presuppositions, things that "go without saying."

Television commentators on the speeches of political leaders, for example, are adept at revealing the speeches' implications, which might escape ordinary audience members' attention otherwise. The implications of a political speech are not only more interesting than what was said, they usually are the point of the speech. Of particular interest are omissions, what a politician should have said but did not, what was conveniently left out—for example, about contested issues such as abortion, women's rights, gay marriage, religious commitment, or the candidate's own less desirable history—that could cost the candidate reelection. Such omissions say a lot about the climate of political expectations and about how the candidate perceives the might of his or her community. One cannot count what is not there, but one can ask content analysts to address such implications of language use.

In pursuit of such implications, it would be impossible for content analysts to list all conceivable interpretations or omissions reliably, but it is quite feasible for them to ask coders the more limited question of whether a textual unit can be read as supporting or opposing a stated set of alternative propositions. These propositions function similarly to a set of hypotheses about what a text tells the coder, who records his or her judgment of *each* textual unit in categories such as these:

a. Affirmed

b. Implicitly affirmed by not denying the proposition when it would have been easy to do so (e.g., by not arguing against it or opposing alternative propositions)

c. Neither affirmed nor denied—irrelevant

d. Implicitly denied by not affirming the proposition when it would have been easy to do so (e.g., by not arguing in favor of it or talking about alternative propositions)

e. Denied

In fact, answering such questions is the qualitative analogue of testing statistical hypotheses. It proceeds by verbal logic—the truth of each proposition is rejected by counterexample, by disproof, or by evidence in favor of the opposite—not by the frequency of confirming cases. Such a testing of mutually exclusive propositions (hypotheses) is nothing but a disciplined way of recording what ordinary readers do when reading, say, a detective story, weighing the evidence against each of a set of suspects. Back to the point, this cognitive device calls on coders to look for any evidence, within a specified context unit, for whether a recording unit speaks in favor of or against either of the stated hypotheses—for example, when scanning the literature for statements about the connection between smoking and lung cancer, the connection between oil consumption and global warming, the connection between hate talk and ethnic violence, the connection between the curbing of civil liberties and homeland security, or the attribution of guilt and innocence following a human-made disaster.

A classic example of the simulation of hypothesis testing is found as early as in Lasswell's (1965a) effort to detect foreign propaganda in domestic German broadcasts during World War II. Lasswell presumed that the Nazi elites pursued four basic propaganda aims, stated them in his terms, and asked his coders to judge whether radio news items, public pronouncements, and commentaries about events implicitly supported or undermined any one or more of these aims. Coders could thus record what was not explicit, insinuated, or implied, as long as it was relevant to the propositions. A hypothetical example of a beneficial use of this recording device would be an analysis aimed at inferring ethnic prejudices from writings by authors on entirely unrelated topics. For the past 50 years, authors have rarely expressed ethnic prejudices explicitly—in fact, hate talk is a crime in many U.S. states, so those who hold such prejudices are forced to express them indirectly or to hide them deliberately in their constructions.

Given the implicitness of much of ordinary writing, this underutilized recording strategy should appeal to psychotherapists, who must attempt to diagnose their patients' mental illnesses; to political analysts, who look for the public implications of campaign speeches; to public opinion researchers, who seek to understand the public perceptions of particular events; and to medical discourse analysts, who attempt to ascertain the cognitive models that underlie patients' accounts of their illnesses.

Simulation of Interviewing   7.4.6

Interviewing is a way to come to know other persons—their beliefs, attitudes, and expectations—and to understand the cognitive models that shape their worldviews. It is a common device used by journalists and public opinion researchers for information gathering. In practice, interviewing is limited to people who actually are available to answer questions, which excludes historical figures, people who do not have time to answer detailed questions, and people who prefer to hide behind their writing.

The simulation of interviews from available texts offers content analysts a means of obtaining answers to questions that they could conceivably have asked the authors of these texts, had the authors been accessible. When using this device, content analysts have coders start by familiarizing themselves with a particular author's writing, a book or article, which, having been written by one individual, would be the recording unit. Then coders go through the author's text a second time, this time looking for evidence from anywhere within it that would indicate how the author might feel about certain issues and how that author would be likely to answer the content analysts' questions.

A good example of the use of such a simulation is found in Klausner's (1968) content analysis of a stratified sample of 199 out of 666 child-rearing manuals published in the United States over a period of two centuries. The attitudes toward child rearing and conceptions of child-rearing practices of each of the manuals' authors were recorded in terms of sets of predefined answers to 80 questions. One of these questions and its possible answers was as follows:

Question 32:   **How does the book legitimate the authority of the parent in the parent's eyes? (the basis on which the author appeals to parent to attend the child)**

Answers: 1 Not discussed
            2 Legitimation assumed, but no specific basis given
            3 The parent has knowledge superior to the child
            4 The parent is morally superior to the child (appeal to sense of personal responsibility)
            5 The parent is a moral representative of the community
            6 The parent influences the child morally, intellectually whether or not he wills it and so has the responsibility for the consequences of his own acts
            7 Parent influences the child psychologically whether or not he wills it
            8 Other
            0 NA (question not applicable and does not deal with question)

Note that in this case, the recording unit is a whole manual. Each question amounts to one variable of the data language, and Question 32 has nine numerical values with the above-stated meanings.

Like the simulation of hypothesis testing, the simulation of interviews relies on the coder's logical and interpretive abilities, but the simulation of interviews relies additionally on the coder's ability to assume an author's role and answer as the author would, given what that author wrote. Assuming the author's position is a cognitive device that literary scholars commonly use in their efforts to infer authors' intentions—what they had in mind—as well as what authors stood for, valued, justified, and hoped to accomplish.

Typically, the simulation of interviewing becomes unreliable when the writing is voluminous and the informative passages are scarce and therefore easily overlooked. In such a situation, content analysts would be wise to use context units of sizes smaller than the whole work.

Interview simulations can be used in analyses of texts that were written long ago or by authors currently unavailable, ranging from foreign dignitaries to indicted criminals. Unlike real-life interviews, they can be repeated as often as needed. For the latter reason, content analysts may use such simulations because simulated "interviewees" are unaware of how they are being questioned and thus unable to speak into the analysts' intentions. Because content analysts can define the context of the analysis, they can place simulated interviewees in situations where they can answer embarrassing questions (Barton, 1968) with ease and without moral qualms.

Constructs for Closure   7.4.7

Experienced therapists often advise their students to discount what their patients say and to listen instead to what they omit. We have many metaphors for this epistemologically questionable but common practice: "reading between the lines," "detecting latent meanings," "hearing silences," "discovering hidden motivations." Conspiracy theorists thrive on such metaphors, and the above-noted advice legitimates therapists' denial of their patients' stories. The well-studied phenomenon of "induced memories"—"filling gaps" in recollections—and the public demonization of slightly deviant groups both result from undisciplined interpretations of what is not said. Such practices may result in public consensus, but that consensus is usually highly unreliable. Under certain conditions, however, it is quite possible to "complete the picture" from what is said (to use still another metaphor) and specify in advance, and without devious intentions, the abstract organization of the whole that would enable content analysts to infer the missing parts, to obtain closure and accomplish this quite reliably.

One, perhaps procedurally less specific, example is found in George's (1959a) account of the FCC's inferences from domestic enemy broadcasts during World War II. In the course of their work, in fact during several war years, the analysts developed elaborate constructs that they believed explained why these broadcasts came into being and what perceptions and antecedent conditions had caused them. I discuss their approach in more detail in Chapter 10; here, it suffices to say that the analysts developed and utilized highly specific constructs of the network of the political and military players in Germany and generalizations regarding the Nazi elite's political and propaganda behavior that allowed the analysts to obtain military intelligence and to predict political changes in the Axis countries. George provides a good description of the analytical constructs that were developed in this situation and the cognitive processes the analysts employed to make rather specific recommendations that were not obvious in the domestic broadcasts. He suggests:

> The analyst's reasoning takes the form of filling in, or assigning a value to, each of the major unstable variables, which are not already known, and supporting this reconstruction both by generalizations and by logic-of-the-situation assessments. This type of inferential reasoning may be likened to

an effort to reconstruct the missing pieces in a mosaic. Certain parts of the mosaic are given or readily assumed. Other pieces in the mosaic, however (including the conditions which the analyst particularly wants to clarify), are missing. In effect, therefore, the analyst rehearses in his mind the different possible versions of each particular missing variable which he wants to infer, trying to decide which version is the most plausible, given the known value of the content variable and the known or postulated values of other antecedent conditions. (p. 61)

Another example of recording absences comes from Shneidman's (1966, 1969) effort to analyze suicide notes collected by a suicide prevention center in San Francisco. Shneidman started with the fair assumption that each individual is logically coherent relative to his or her own world constructions. Readers as well as the analysts know only the asserted premises and the conclusions that the writer draws from them. Shneidman calls the particular logic by which a person thinks and argues that person's *idio-logic*. Accordingly, writers are assumed to accept their own idio-logical conclusions, even when they are fallacious relative to standard textbook logic. Adopting this textbook logic as a construct, Shneidman asked his coders to focus on a suicide letter's manifest fallacies of reasoning and then identify all the unwritten propositions that the writer must have taken for granted in order for his or her conclusions to be coherent in terms of that textbook logic. In a second step, Shneidman inferred from the coders' list of hidden assumptions how someone would be able to communicate (reason) with the writer and enter his or her world—a *pedago-logic*, in Shneidman's terms.

Incidentally, the examples of logical fallacies, the idio-logical propositions that would seem to make these fallacies acceptable to the writer, as well as the pedago-logical recommendations in Shneidman's (1966) codebook are mostly drawn from political speeches. This is due to Shneidman's (1963) parallel interest in studying political communication, especially the worldviews inferable from the logical fallacies that national leaders find acceptable, to explain why leaders are prone to misunderstanding each other and what one could recommend to either side. Here, too, content analysts record and infer what omissions entail under the assumption of a very detailed framework that assures some reliability.

The foregoing discussion of strategies for operationalizing the semantics of a data language is by no means complete—I have presented only the major approaches here. Nor is it my intention to create the impression that the tools discussed are mutually exclusive alternatives. Content analysts can draw on any of these as well as others—as long as they rely on cognitive models that coders are familiar with and can learn to use. Familiarity and specificity have a chance to ensure the efficiency and reliability of recording.

RECORDS 7.5

The computational part of content analysis starts where recording stops, with the records it produces. Records are the most basic and explicit representations of the phenomena being analyzed. Records may come in many forms, from notations in the margins of written documents to tags entered into electronic text (Stone, Dunphy, Smith, & Ogilvie, 1966), binary data stored on optically readable microfilm (Janda, 1969), codes added to searchable images (Ekman & Friesen, 1968), and coding sheets modeled after interview schedules. Figure 7.2 shows the most general form of a collection of records imaginable (but only imaginable); it depicts a huge spreadsheet of all recording units of the analyzed body of text by all the variables of the applicable data language, containing transcriptions, categories, or numbers in its cells.

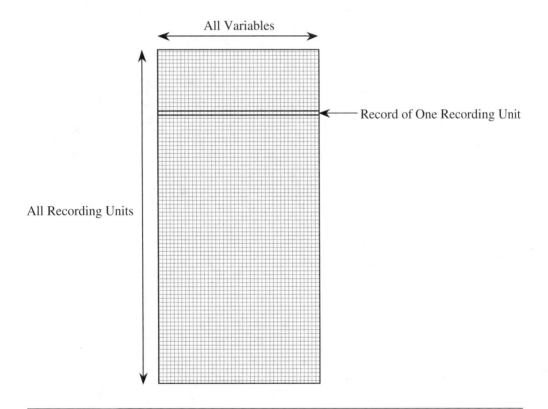

Figure 7.2   Most General Structure of Data

Designing records for a suitable storage medium—data sheets, coding forms, questionnaires, or computer screens—requires much ingenuity on the part of the content analyst. Because the demands made on recording texts are so varied, it is impossible for anyone to suggest a standard or optimal form they should take. A few recommendations may be made, however. The most general derives from the common practice of tabulating and enumerating recording units. To be countable, units must be described separately and in comparable terms, the categories of the same set of variables. It makes sense, therefore, for analysts to create records, one for each recording unit, that have the same organization of variables, into which coders enter the appropriate values. This is analogous to answering all applicable questions on an interview form. When records are organized in this way, a content analysis needs as many forms as there are units to be recorded, which may be many—hence the need for simplification.

The records of a content analysis—an array of descriptions in the form of alphabetical characters, check marks, or numbers—should contain three kinds of information: administrative information, information on the organization of the records, and information on the phenomena represented in the records. The last of these is obvious; the first two are often overlooked.

7.5.1 Administrative Information

Administrative information guides the handling of data. It is impossible to overstate its importance in most research efforts. For example, data sheets can get out of order, and unless analysts can find out how those sheets were generated, they have no way to know what the data mean. Coders make clerical mistakes, do not record all required variables, and unless the records include information about who coded them and where to locate the recording unit that was coded, there may be no simple way to correct even simple oversights. Much too often, analysts lose valuable time when they find sets of completed forms in their possession and are unable to determine whether they came from a pretest, whether the data have been verified, entered into a computer, when, by whom, and so on.

Typically, administrative information includes the following:

- The name of the content analysis *project* to which the data belong

- The *version of the recording instructions* (e.g., the first or second version) used to generate the record

- The *kind of texts* the record represents (e.g., a test sample or the main body of text)

- The *state of the record* (e.g., whether it has been completed, verified, entered into a computer, or otherwise processed), including information on what is still to be done with it

- The *identities of the coder* who created the record and *others* who checked or processed it

- The serial number of the recording unit or any way to get to it

- If multiple units are used, the names or numbers of the *recording units* the coded one *contains*

The first three pieces of information on this list are common to a larger set of recording units, and these may be preprinted on all data-entry forms used in a particular recording effort. I discuss the final item on the list below. Complete administrative information is essential to efficient data management. When records are computerized, analysts may have fewer opportunities to mess them up, but they must ensure that their programmers make provisions for recording all of the kinds of information listed above.

Information on the Organization of Records   7.5.2

One of the features of content analysis that is rarely found in other kinds of research is the use of several levels of recording units that reflect the organization of the texts being analyzed. Many content analyses employ nested recording units, such as the following:

The newspapers sampled

The issues of a newspaper sampled

The articles in an issue of a newspaper sampled

The paragraphs in an article in an issue of a newspaper sampled

The propositions constituting a paragraph in an article in an issue of a newspaper sampled

Similar hierarchies can be found in the organization of discourse, the world of theater, decision making in social organizations, and social interaction. On each level, a different set of categories applies, and following the nesting, categories applied to higher-level units apply also to all the units they contain. In the above newspaper example, newspapers may be characterized by circulation figures, prestige, access to news services, and ownership. Issues may be coded by publication date, day of the week, and size. Articles may be distinguished in terms of kind, placement, length, and so forth, until one comes to, say, propositions. Where multilevel units are used, each largest unit consists of all units it contains, and each smallest unit is specified by all higher-order units of which it is a part.

Not all multiple-unit content analyses produce such neat hierarchies of inclusion. Web page links and hypertext documents operationalize relationships of inclusion as well but allow recursions—that is, the possibility that one unit of text contains references to another, and another, and so forth, but also back to the text where one started from. Such organizations are not hierarchical but heterarchical, or networklike. When working with such multilevel data, analysts must keep track of whether and how the categories that are applied on one level of units relate to the categories applied to subordinate units or to units that can be reached from the former, directly or indirectly. There are essentially three ways to accomplish this:

■ The analysts might keep a *master file,* a separate file that preserves *all connections among separately coded recording units,* whether these connections form hierarchies or heterarchies. The above newspaper example involves a hierarchy of inclusions, and the appropriate master file would tell the analysts where each recording unit belongs in relation to all others.

■ The analysts might code *each recording unit* separately but include *references to all units in which each occurs* (where it can be reached from) and *references to all the units each contains* (the units that can be reached from it).

■ The analysts might keep a *complete but redundant record* of all variables by all smallest recording units identified in the body of texts, similar to the data structure in Figure 7.2. Here, the category assignments of any one unit are duplicated for each unit it contains and hence redundant in parts.

To cross-tabulate or correlate categories on different levels of description, such as the circulation figures of newspapers and favorable or unfavorable mentions of a public personality, content analysts working with multilevel recording units need to connect the categories of (large in total number of recorded details and numerically few) newspapers included in the study and the (small and numerous) recording units asserting the evaluations of interest. Analysts using the first method above must consult the master file, those using the second must trace the connections from one recording unit to the next, and those using the third may have to be observant about the exaggerated frequencies resulting from duplication of categories for recording units that include many smaller ones. I must point out that the use of redundant records is suitable only to hierarchies of inclusion of recording units.

7.5.3   Substantive Information About the Phenomena of Interest

Generating analyzable data is, of course, the raison d'être of the recording process. Whatever the device, coders must be able to record information with ease, verify instantaneously what they have entered, and correct their mistakes. Each medium for recording data has its own properties and makes special demands on human coders. Optical scanners call for the use of pencils of a particular kind, otherwise some uncertainty can be created about how marks are read. The accuracy of punch cards is difficult to verify without mechanical readers. Spreadsheets offer convenient overviews of whole data arrays, but they often make it difficult for analysts to connect cell contents to recording units and available categories. Although computer aids are available that allow coders to generate electronic data files on the fly—during telephone interviews or while watching television, for example—such tools must be carefully designed so that they interface easily with coders, minimize mistakes, and provide ample feedback for verification, much as traditional paper data sheets do.

Most Americans are familiar with the conventions of filling out questionnaires, and many are also comfortable with using a mouse to point and click on a computer screen. Analysts should rely on coders' competencies where possible. Most people know how to write, how to copy texts, how to fill in blanks, how to circle options in a list, and how to enter a check mark to select an item. The more natural a recording medium is to the coders, the fewer errors they will make.

Above, I outlined several proven approaches to defining the semantics of a data language. Here, I focus on some easily avoidable errors that content analysts make when designing the instruments that coders use to record what they have observed, categorized, judged, or scaled. One frequent source of errors is the overuse of numbers. Numbers are short and concise, but when they are used for everything they can become confusing. Content analysts tend to number their categories, their variables, their coders, the units to be recorded, the pages of instructions where the numbered values of numbered variables are defined, and so on. Many times, the designers of content analysis instructions could specify the required organization of data by using descriptive words instead of numbers whose meanings must be learned, by using typographical or spatial arrangements instead of paragraphs of prose, or even by using icons, which may cause less confusion than numbers.

A second source of errors is the inconsistent use of category names or numbers across different variables. For example, when the default category of "not applicable" or "other" is coded "0" for one variable and "9" or "99" for another, confusion is bound to arise. The same is true when analysts use the same words but with different intended meanings in different variables. Explicitly defined differences are easily forgotten.

A third source of errors is the hand copying of uncommon text into a record. This is one reason various qualitative software packages allow users to highlight text, assign codes, and cut and paste text. These features significantly reduce the chance of spelling errors, which are bound to introduce unintended differences.

A fourth source of errors is poor design of the presentation of options on the recording medium. In unwritten but widely used graphic computer interface conventions, users are asked either to check "boxes" on or off or to click on alternative "radio buttons," which selects among options. These are logically different operations. And whereas a computer interface can be designed to force users to comply with a designer's intentions—for example, by disabling unavailable options—paper instruments are not so intelligent. Nevertheless, the designer of a recording medium can do much to discourage coders from recording data incorrectly and thus avoid unreliability and polluting the data with illegitimate values. Consider the following three ways of recording the outcome of an interpersonal interaction:

Enter the appropriate number	Encircle one only	Check ☑ as many as applicable
☐ 0 - favorable to neither 1 - favorable to recipient 2 - favorable to initiator 3 - favorable to both	*favorable to* **neither** **recipient only** **initiator only** **both**	☐ *favorable to initiator* ☐ *favorable to recipient*

Although these three alternatives are effectively equivalent, they differ in the kinds of errors they invite. In the version on the left, the coder is asked to enter a number in a box. There is nothing to prevent a coder from writing a number larger than 3 in the box. Any number larger than 3 would be undefined, regardless of what the coder had in mind, and hence illegitimate. Leaving the box blank is not a legitimate option either, although it might make sense to a coder who found nothing favorable to record. This version is also sensitive to bad handwriting. In addition, it is not uncommon for coders to confuse category numbers with, for example, coder ID numbers, unit numbers, variable numbers, or scale points, as mentioned above. The middle version does nothing to discourage or prevent the coder from circling more than one option, circling something between two equally imperfect alternatives, or failing to circle the category "neither" when none is evident. The version on the right resists illegitimate entries altogether, but this solution is limited to binary values—to being checked or not checked, present or absent. Checking or not checking a box is a simple, unambiguous alternative. Analysts can reduce recording errors by phrasing the recording options so that they require a minimum of writing; the best way to do this is to provide a list of appropriate alternatives and instruct coders to "check all that apply"—not burdening the coders with the information that each then becomes a binary variable on its own (see Chapter 8).

Errors can also occur if the recording instructions are not well spelled out and coders must exert too much effort to consult instructions when they need to. One extreme solution for this kind of problem is to merge the recording instructions with the recording medium, so that the recording medium is similar to a questionnaire in survey research. The high level of consistency this ensures, however, is counterbalanced by the fact that using such a medium is tedious and producing it is costly. Having a coder use one recording instruction and/or data sheet for each recording unit can be excessive when recording units are small and numerous (e.g., words, frames of videotape, seconds of verbal interaction). At the other extreme, the analyst presents the coder with a spreadsheet—a large grid of recording units by variables, as in Figure 7.2—that the coder completes according to separately formulated instructions. This method invites a host of confusions; for instance, while consulting the instruction manual to resolve indecision, coders may lose track of which row they are coding, or may enter the categories (numbers) for one variable into the cells of another. In addition, most of these kinds of errors are difficult to detect. The following recommendations chart a middle course between these two extremes:

■ At each data entry point, the analyst should present the coders with some verbal description of the variable and, where feasible, a list of options and what each means (abbreviations of the terms used in the more elaborate recording instructions are better than numbers that say nothing about the category). The analyst should also provide instructions just where they are needed.

■ The analyst should supply the coders with alternatives to be selected from a well-defined list—in computer applications, from pull-down menus, for example, or a row of bull's-eyes. Ideally, coders should not need to do much writing. Asking coders to enter numerical or alphabetical characters into boxes is problematic, especially when these characters have no intrinsic relation to the phenomena to be recorded, because the coders then need to learn to correlate the numbers or letters with what they mean and can easily forget the meanings, especially of rare categories, which tend to be the ones that matter most.

■ The analyst should create visual analogues (mappings) showing the relationship between the way the analyzed text is organized and the way the recording medium is designed. This is relatively easy when coders are recording the geometric relations of text (locations of newspaper articles on the front page, above the center fold, inside) with visual devices (depicting a few *pages* from which *the locations* of interest may be selected) that can be reproduced in the recording medium, temporal sequences (with *before* on the left and *after* on the right), or such conceptual distinctions as between sender, message, and receiver (which may be represented to coders diagrammatically or according to linguistic conventions).

The availability of computer software that allows users to enter choices and select among alternatives enables content analysis designers to take advantage of coders' increasing familiarity with reliable interface conventions. It has also opened up the possibility of using computers to enter content analysis data directly, allowing for validation and tests of reliability.

CHAPTER **8**

Data Languages

Categories and measurements are the entry points to empirical research. We treat their particular organization as a data language, which is conceived to have a syntax and a semantics. The semantics of a data language ties data to the phenomena of the observed world, to coders' readings of texts, and the syntax of a data language links the data to the computational processes of an analysis. This chapter is concerned with the forms that satisfy the syntactical requirements of data languages for content analyses. It provides definitions of terms related to the construction of such languages, illustrates the essential features of data languages, and distinguishes variables—categories, measurement scales, and the like—according to the orderings and metrics they exhibit.

 THE PLACE OF DATA LANGUAGES IN ANALYSIS

A data language is the descriptive device in which terms analysts cast their data. For natural scientists, a data language is a system of physical measurements and records of basic observations. For content analysts, who start with textual matter, images, verbal exchanges, transmissions, and records of observed phenomena, a data language describes how all the categories, variables, notations, formal transcripts, and computer-readable accounts hang together to form one system. For both kinds of researchers, data languages mediate between otherwise unstructured phenomena and the scientific discourse about them, and in the case of content analysis, they mediate between the experiences of reading text, interpreting images, and observing transient social phenomena of interest on the one hand and the formal demands made by available analytical or computational procedures on the other.

Treating a system of categories and measurements as a data language allows analysts to separate syntactical considerations from semantic ones. The semantics of a data language delineates the meanings of its terms, operationalized in the process of coding or recording, whereas the syntax of a data language satisfies the formal operations required in the scientific handling of data. When the semantics of a data language is ill defined, one cannot know how to interpret the marks or numbers that observers or coders have left behind, and when the syntax of a data language is incompatible with the demands made by the analytical technique employed, computational results are unintelligible.

I have discussed the problem of operationalizing the semantics of a data language in Chapter 7, will address at least some of the demands that analytical techniques make in the data they accept in Chapter 10, and will consider the consequences of ambiguities in the semantics of a data language in Chapter 11. This chapter concerns mainly the *syntax* of the data languages that are of interest to content analysts. Regarding their syntax, data languages must meet three criteria:

- They must *be free of syntactical ambiguities* and inconsistencies.

- They must *satisfy the requirements of the analytical techniques* to be used.

- They must *transmit enough information* about the phenomena of interest.

In order to meet the first of these three requirements, data languages should be formal or formalized. Formal languages are computable in principle. Humans, being naturally sensitive to contexts and bringing their own experiences to any readings of texts, are well equipped to cope with syntactical ambiguities. Explicit analytical techniques are not. For example, an ordinary reader with access to the context of the sentence "They are flying planes" rarely encounters difficulty in deciding whether *they* refers to a group of pilots or to several objects seen in the sky. In fact, when reading the sentence in context, an ordinary reader would rarely notice its syntactical ambiguity. In a content analysis, such syntactical ambiguities have to be removed through human editorial interventions—for example, for the sentence above, analysts need to specify whether *flying* is a verb or an adjective. Similarly, "Jim or Joe and Mary are coming" can be read either as "(Jim or Joe) and Mary are coming" or as "Jim or (Joe and Mary) are coming." Naturally occurring texts are full of such ambiguities, which are rarely problematic for ordinary readers. Content analysts are well-advised to design coding sheets, checklists, and rules for transcribing text or kernelizing sentences in ways that will prevent syntactical inconsistencies and ambiguities from entering the analysis.

The second demand on data languages stems from the formal requirements imposed by the analytical techniques that analysts intend to use. Although this may seem obvious, it is amazing how often researchers generate data on a very interesting phenomenon only to discover, usually too late, that the formal characteristics of the data make it impossible to process them. A few examples should suffice: Factor analysis requires multiple correlations, which in turn presupposes interval data on several dimensions; multidimensional scaling techniques start with distances between pairs of data points; causal connections can be shown only in time-series data that allow the analyst to check for spurious correlations. Although most analytical techniques accept numbers as inputs, the mere fact that data are in numerical form is no guarantee that the analysis will make sense. Applying a variance analysis on ranks, which do not live up to the requirements of such analysis, produces results that are difficult to interpret (for an opposing view, see Tukey, 1980). Researchers make more drastic mistakes when they analyze nominal data as if they were ordered: Analyzing people according to their social security numbers or using the numbers that football players wear as interval data is bound to produce garbage.

Researchers have attempted to design computer software for text analysis (see Chapter 12) in order to circumvent the problems addressed by the first two criteria above. Computational efforts assume a data language that recognizes a text as a finite string of characters, recording words, for example, or pairs of words occurring within a window of a finite number of characters that slides over a text. This is an easily computable data language that bypasses, however, the meanings of text that reading would reveal.

The third requirement that data languages must meet derives from the target of content analysis, selecting among appropriate inferences from text. Lasswell (1960), paralleling similar questions for political science (Lasswell, 1963), once characterized communication research as asking, "Who says what, in which channel, to whom, and with what effect?" He then suggested that content analysis answers the "says what" part of the question, audience research answers the "to whom" part, and effects research answers the "with what effects" part. In so distinguishing among analytical approaches, Lasswell failed to see that separate answers to the questions of "who," "what," "to whom," and "what effects" cannot provide the information that analysts need to say anything meaningful about processes of communication, the influence asserted, the relationships established, the coordination accomplished, and so on (Krippendorff, 1970d). A data language may fail to provide enough information by assuming a perspective from which the whole cannot be comprehended—as in Lasswell's separation of content analysis from analyses of other facets of communication—by leaving out important variables, ignoring the correlations between them, or making too few distinctions. The information flow through an analysis can be traced and measured (see Krippendorff, 1991). The amount of information that analysts need to ultimately select a defensible answer to a given research question can often be spelled out in advance. An appropriate data language must provide at least as much to answer a research question. Redundant information (distinctions, correlations, and variables) is better than insufficient amounts.

Given the requirements discussed above, we can define a data language in terms general enough to cover most content analysts' concerns.

DEFINITIONS 8.2

The data language used in an analysis prescribes the form in which the data are recorded. The syntax of a data language consists of the following:

- *Variables* whose *values* represent the variability within one conceptual dimension

- The *values* within variables, which may be *ordered* and/or exhibit a *metric*

- *Constants* whose operational meanings are fixed within the data language and specify how the values of different variables are related to each other

- A *grammar* whose rules govern the construction of well-formed expressions (data records or descriptions)

- A *logic* that determines how the expressions of the data language imply each other or are equivalent, specifying logical (a priori) dependencies among these expressions

For example, in the algebraic formula

$$A \cdot X + B = C,$$

A, B, C, and *X* are *variables,* each of which is a placeholder for a numerical *value*. The symbols + and · have the operational meanings of addition and multiplication, respectively, and are invariant to the values in the variables. In the process of recording data, and in order to apply analytical procedures to a data language, analysts have to enter values into the places that the variables provide.

The *grammar* of a data language makes certain combinations of values within variables illegitimate or ill formed. According to the rules of algebra, for example, both sides of the above equation are well formed, whereas the string "*ABXC* = + ·" would not be and must therefore not occur.

The symbol = is a logical sign that defines the two sides of the formula as numerically equivalent and as mutually substitutable. The *logic* of a data language defines the relationships between combinations of values from different expressions: equality, entailment, or orderings.

In many content analyses, the syntax and logic of data languages are so simple that they may not be recognizable as such. The most basic form of a data language consists of the product of a finite set of, say, *n* variables, such as:

$$A \cdot B \cdot C \cdot D \cdot E. \ldots$$

The product sign between these variables allows the values of different variables to co-occur freely. In effect, for *n* logically independent variables, this defines an n-dimensional space. Raw data then take the form of a collection of "n-tuples" of values a, b, c, d, e, . . . , one value for each variable, $a \in A$, $b \in B$, and so on. A collection of r such n-tuples could be listed as an r-by-n matrix:

$$<a_1, b_1, c_1, d_1, e_1, . . .>$$
$$<a_2, b_2, c_2, d_2, e_2, . . .>$$
$$<a_3, b_3, c_3, d_3, e_3, . . .>$$
$$<a_r, b_r, c_r, d_r, e_r, . . .>$$

They could also be seen as listed in a spreadsheet similar to Figure 7.2. This basic data language can be thought of as defining an n-dimensional space in which each unit, described as an n-tuple, finds a unique cell to occupy and the data as a whole define a particular distribution in this n-dimensional space. In this basic data language, the values from different variables can co-occur without constraint. There is no particular logic by the above definition.

I mention the grammar and logic of a data language here mainly because exciting developments are taking place in fields related to communication research, notably in linguistics and cultural anthropology, that content analysts need to consider. For example, transformational grammars, whose syntax includes rewrite rules that are aimed at characterizing natural language expressions, cannot be represented spatially and without logic. But even relatively unambitious content analyses may include recursions that violate the idea of multidimensional representations of data. For instance, in a content analysis of native-foreigner attitudes in Africa, Piault (1965) recorded answers to open-ended questions in terms of the following:

a. An ordered set of variables concerning social characteristics of the individuals X and Y
b. The origin of a judgment, using statements of the following form:

X judges Y to be [   ]
X talks about Y judging X to be [   ]
X talks about Y talking about X. . . .

c. Relations between X and Y, relative to the origin of the judgment
d. Three kinds of *themes* (i.e., arguments) associated with each judgment
e. A lexicon consisting of 675 terms, variables (that note presences or absences), and constants (in the form of Boolean operators AND and OR and qualifiers) in terms of which arguments are entered in the places provided by [   ]

Here, item a associates a set of social variables with the individuals who are speaking or being talked about. Item b describes who judges whom, allowing for recursive judgments, . . . , and item e preserves the original attributes used by the respondents as an open-ended variable that can be searched with Boolean operators. This data language met the syntactical demands of the information retrieval routines that Piault used in the course of her analysis.

Research may be viewed as a series of systematic transformations of one data language into another. For example, counting the recorded *n*-tuples eliminates redundant listings and adds an additional (*n* + 1st) variable to the array, their observed frequency. Developing an index maps a set of variables into one, the index, whose variability is a function of the various original data it represents. Applying a replacement dictionary to text reduces the great diversity of expressions to fewer and more relevant kinds. Data languages do not need to be confined to traditional statistical distributions in multidimensional geometric spaces. With linguistically sensitive analytical techniques increasingly available, sophisticated grammatical rules and forms of logic have become increasingly important, especially in analyses of themes. I will not develop this topic here, however; instead, I focus on what is common to all data languages: variables.

VARIABLES   8.3

A variable is a concept that allows for variations of its instances. In the above, we took a variable as a placeholder for any one of several mutually exclusive values. In *Merriam-Webster's Collegiate Dictionary* (11th edition), the adjective *variable* is defined as "able or apt to vary," and the noun *variable* is defined as "something that is variable" and as "a quantity that may assume any one of a set of values." Variation is what enables data to be "informative." Indeed, the variable sex has no descriptive significance unless one can distinguish between males and females, and the notion of bias in journalism is meaningless unless journalists have the option of leaning toward one or the other side of a controversy. In other words, if the units of a content analysis do not exhibit variation in their description, analysis of the units cannot inform anything.

The individual values of a variable must be *mutually exclusive* relative to each other. This satisfies the requirement that a data language be unambiguous and in effect *partitions the set of recording units* (the sample) *into mutually exclusive classes*. Jointly, the values of a variable must provide an *exhaustive* account of all units, which means that the partition of the sample should leave nothing unaccounted for. In content analysis, the requirement of exhaustiveness is sometimes relaxed when it comes to irrelevant matter. In this respect, the social sciences deviate from physics, for example, which assumes that all physical objects have the same dimensions.

The idea of a variable of mutually exclusive and descriptively exhaustive values is so general that it occurs in numerous intellectual endeavors, albeit with different names. Some correspondences are presented below. The set theoretical expression "$a \in A$" probably is the most general one; it simply states that the element a is a member of the set A of elements.

Values of a *Variable*

a	$\in$	A
Categories		Set of categories
Points		Scale
Members		Family or class
Position		Dimension
Locations		Space
Measures		Gauge
States		System
Tokens		Type
Elements		Set
Sets		Possible sets

The concept of a variable with mutually exclusive values does not mean that content analysts are limited to single-valued descriptions, to assigning one and only one value to each recording unit. Text typically affords multiple interpretations, whether because readers with different backgrounds and interests come up with unique but, in the aggregate, divergent interpretations or because ambiguity leads a single reader to alternative and equally valid interpretations. A variable that records possible sets (the last on the above list), possible patterns, or possible connections affords multi-valued descriptions. Multiple interpretations of text may present problems for coding—for the semantics of a data language and for reliability—and for the analytical techniques available for handling such data, but they are not incompatible with the notion of variables.

Variables may be *open-ended* or *limited*. At least in principle, numerical variables are open-ended—there is no largest or smallest number. Open-ended variables require conceptual clarity on the part of coders or, in the natural sciences, knowledge of the construction of the measuring instrument. For instance, when coding instructions call for the rephrasing of a text into the form

$$[\qquad] \text{ says } [\qquad] \text{ to } [\qquad],$$

such as "[Jim] says [hi] to [Mary]," coders are guided by concepts of what would fit in the empty places. In context, one could easily rephrase this as "who" says "what" to "whom"—much as Piault had no doubt as to which words attributed personal qualities, but no idea of which would show up. The values in open-ended variables are outside the control of the research designer.

When variables are limited, analysts may define them *implicitly*, by *specifying their range*, or *explicitly*, by *listing all alternative values*. Many social variables are defined by concepts that imply definite ranges. For example, the concepts of gender, marital status, and kin offer limited vocabularies to describe all possible kinds. Sometimes institutions limit the ranges of variables (e.g., kinds of criminal offenses in a legal code or kinds of mental illnesses in the *DSM-IV-R*) and sometimes particular theories do (e.g., dramaturgical roles in fiction or types of personalities). Somewhat more tailored for quantification are verbally anchored scales of measurement, such as 7-point semantic differential scales. A semantic differential scale shows a pair of words representing polar opposites separated by a quantified continuum. For example:

Prosocial  Antisocial

When using such a scale, coders presumably create in their minds a continuum of meanings between the designated extremes and then judge where an observed phenomenon or verbal expression would belong. The endpoints of the scale are defined by the conceptions that readers have of these adjectives; the remainder is semantically implicit in the use of the continuum, which pertains to the syntax of the data language using this variable.

Finally, analysts may define variables *explicitly,* in terms of complete *lists of values.* For example, Searle (1969) claimed to have identified a mutually exclusive and exhaustive set of five values for the variable "speech acts":

Representatives

Directives

Commissives

Expressives

Declaratives

The three ways of defining variables noted above may also be recognized in the design of coding sheets, recording devices, and computer interfaces. Coders typically handwrite or type the values of open-ended variables into prepared openings; indicate variables defined implicitly by turning knobs, arranging objects to indicate how different they are, or marking or clicking on the points of scales; and indicate those defined by explicit lists by checking one of several alternatives.

Usually, analysts can choose among alternative data languages for recording the same kind of information. For example, one could ask coders to identify which of 20 logically possible communication networks are operating within a five-person group or which of 10 possible communication channels between pairs of members of that group are being used. These two ways provide the same information. The choice of one data language over another may be informed by differences in the coding effort required, perhaps by issues of reliability, but certainly by differences in the amount of information the data languages provide. In general, content analysts should construct data languages that are as detailed and basic as they can possibly be and leave as much to computation as possible. For example, Budd's (1964) attention measure, Gerbner, Gross, Signorielli, Morgan, and Jackson-Beeck's (1979) violence index, and Hawk's (1997) listenability scores for TV programming, modeled after Flesch's (1974) readability yardstick, are all computed on the results of numerous simple coding judgments.

An analyst could, of course, define a far simpler higher-level data language—a ratio scale for recording attention, violence, and listenability as an overall coder judgment, for example—but it has been shown that such measures do not achieve reliability, and they cannot provide the fine distinctions that aggregate measures produce.

Unfortunately, content analysts often publish their results without making their "conceptual schemes" or "systems of categories" explicit, perhaps because they are not clear themselves as to the nature of the data languages they employed. Consider the following scheme, reported in the literature by Herma, Kriss, and Shor (1943):

Standards for rejecting Freud's dream theory:

A. Depreciation through value judgment
   1. Ridicule and mockery
   2. Rejection on moral grounds
   3. Denial of validity

B. Denial of scientific character of theory
   1. Questioning analyst's sincerity
   2. Questioning verification of theory
   3. Questioning methodology

C. Exposure of social status of theory
   1. Disagreement among experts
   2. Fashionableness
   3. Lack of originality

This scheme looks more like the outline for a paper than a coding scheme. But given that it has been published as a system of categories, one interpretation could be that it defines but one variable consisting of nine values, A1, A2, . . . , through C3, with a merely convenient grouping of these values into A, B, and C kinds that could aid conceptualizing these nine values, without having any other descriptive significance. A second interpretation is that there are three variables (A, B, and C) with three values (1, 2, and 3) each, defined differently for each variable. This interpretation would suggest that the researchers regarded the arguments against Freud's dream theory as having a valuational, scientific, and social dimension. A third interpretation is that there are nine variables whose values are *present* and *absent*, with the breakdown into A, B, and C providing three convenient conceptual contexts for their definitions.

Readers of content analysis research may find important clues to the data language in use by examining how data are treated. An invariant organization of the data suggests constants. Variables, by contrast, vary, allowing coders to express different kinds of observations or readings. Separate judgments suggest separate variables. Inasmuch as the mutually exclusive values of a coding instrument partition a sample into mutually exclusive sets of units, the summing of frequencies to a total always points to the mutual exclusivity of values or combinations of values. Several ways of summing frequencies suggest independent variables—in cross-tabulations, for example. In the example of coding for Freud's dream theory, a careful reading of Herma et al.'s report of their study reveals the first of the three interpretations offered above to be correct, only because the frequencies reported for the nine values sum up to 100%. The grouping into *A, B,* and *C,* defined within the same variable, allowed the researchers to lump findings into simpler categories later. This, however, is not evident from their published conceptual scheme.

There have been unfortunate misunderstandings among content analysts and sometimes even resistance to being clear about the data language employed. For example, in interactive-hermeneutic explorations of texts, specifically when the researchers are using computer-aided text analysis software (see Chapter 12, section 12.6), coders are given considerable freedom to highlight any relevant portions of a document and to assign any number of codes to them (see Figure 8.1).

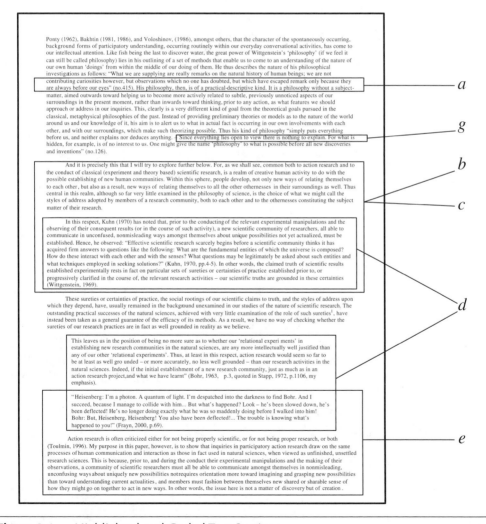

Figure 8.1   Highlighted and Coded Text Sections

Subsequent to the coders' work, the qualitative researchers can retrieve, reorganize, and tabulate the coded sections for further examination. Note that in the example in Figure 8.1, the first and second textual units are assigned one code each, *a* and *g,* respectively. The third unit is assigned two codes, *b* and *c.* That third unit also contains a fourth unit that is assigned the code *d.* If all the highlighted text segments were as separate as the first two units, their codes could be treated as the values of a variable. In this case, *a, b, c,* and *d* are all binary variables, not categories in the technical sense.

Because overlapping units cannot be enumerated, quantitative researchers shy away from double coding. In contrast, qualitative researchers find uniform unitizations irresponsive to the nature of the texts they study, and so they shy away from more formal analyses. Both attitudes limit the analysis of textual matter, which often is complex in structure. However, when an analyst treats each code as a binary variable (i.e., either present or absent) and keeps references to the beginnings and ends of the highlighted text (on the reliability of unitizing, see Chapter 11, section 11.6), this constitutes a data language that would enable the analyst to correlate these codes and apply more complex analyses. In Figure 8.1, the third highlighted text segment would contribute to a correlation between *b* and *c,* and the overlapping text segments would count toward correlations between *b* and *d,* between *c* and *d,* and between *d* and *e.* As the highlighting and coding of text is implemented in a computer, there are no ambiguities or inconsistencies. By being clear about the data languages by which data are created from raw text, researchers can enrich content analysis research and encourage the development of suitable analytical techniques.

The values of variables may be unordered or ordered, and, in the latter case, they may exhibit one of several metrics. *Ordering* refers to a system of relationships between the values of a variable, determining which pairs of values are neighbors. For example, in a hierarchy, one value neighbors several other values that are not neighbors of each other, and each of the latter may neighbor other values that are not neighbors of each other either, and so forth, until all values are so ordered. In a chain, each value has two neighbors, except for the values at the beginning and end of the chain, which have one neighbor each.

Metrics define quantitative differences between all pairs of values in a variable. We distinguish several kinds of metrics according to the *mathematical operations applicable to these differences.* Thus two dollar amounts may be added or subtracted, representing the experience of earning or spending, but addition and subtraction would not make sense when the values to be compared are qualitative attributes such as individuals' emotional states, citizenship, or occupation. When qualitative attributes are expressed numerically—telephone numbers, Social Security numbers, the numbers on the jerseys of basketball players—addition and subtraction are mathematically possible but do not make sense semantically. Being concerned here only with the syntax of data languages, I distinguish among the possible metrics of variables by the operations that are applicable to their values. The metric of money differs from the metric of telephone numbers, for example. I will start with the simplest of all variables whose values are unordered and do not have a metric—nominal variables—and then introduce several orderings and several metrics.

NOMINAL VARIABLES   8.4

Nominal variables, the most basic kinds of variables, are defined by the absence of both ordering and metric. Their values are merely distinct from each other, and hence unordered. The mathematics for nominal variables is set theory, a calculus concerned with unordered entities. The adjective *nominal* suggests the "by name only" nature of these variables. Calling nominal variables "nominal *scales*" is a misnomer, because a "scale" conjures images of a linear ordering of values, which is precisely what the values of nominal variables do not possess. They may be arranged in any way conceivable without making a difference. Data recorded in nominal categories are also called *qualitative* because the difference between any two values of a nominal variable is the same for all possible pairs of values.

The nine standards for rejecting Freud's dream theory listed above constitute one nominal variable. Other examples are alphabetical characters, speech acts, forms of government, ethnic identities, and social security numbers. Analysts must take care not to be misled by the use of numbers as names for nominal categories. Numerical listings of bank customers' PINs or of the numbers on the jerseys of athletes have no operational significance. A more technical way of stating this property is to say that *the distinctions within a nominal variable are preserved under all permutations of its values.*

All variables reduce to nominal variables when their orderings and their metrics are removed from them. In the following sections, I discuss what distinguishes other variables from nominal variables. Table 8.1 shows, orderings by metrics, the types of variables to be discussed and useful in content analysis.

Table 8.1   Types of Variables by Orderings and Metrics

Order: Metric	None	Chains	Recursions	Cubes	Trees
None	Nominal variable				
Ordinal	Grouping	Ordinal scale	Loop	Cross-tab of ord. variables	Typology
Interval	Network of distances	Interval scale	Circle π	Geometric space	Interval tree
Ratio		Ratio scale		Vector space	Ratio tree

ORDERINGS   8.5

For a variable to make sense, any ordering of its values must somehow be appropriate to the phenomena the variable is to record. Something that varies along one dimension, such as length, audience size, or positive or negative evaluation, is very different from daily time, which repeats over and over again and is circular, or individual names, which are either this or that but nothing in between.

Networks of concepts extracted from a writer's work (Baldwin, 1942), the semantic connections within a text as stored in a computer (Klir & Valach, 1965), and the hierarchy of organizing a piece of writing (from the work as a whole to its chapters, down to individual sentences)—these exhibit other orderings. Below, I discuss four common orderings of values: chains, recursions, cubes, and trees. These are not intended to constitute an exhaustive classification; I have chosen them merely to expand the conventional limitation to linear scales of measurement, so-called measuring scales, which are favored by statisticians but rarely capture the meanings of text.

8.5.1   Chains

Chains are linearly ordered sets of values, as in scales of measurement. The values of a chain are transitive in the sense that $a{\rightarrow}b$ and $b{\rightarrow}c$ implies $a{\rightarrow}c$ for any three values of a chain. In speaking of body temperature, for instance, we have a conception of what is normal and we conceive of temperature as going up or down in degrees. Temperature is a unidimensional variable. It can move through all of its values between extremely high and extremely low, never moving sidewise, never bypassing or jumping over any one temperature. The actual unit of measurement (degrees Fahrenheit, degrees Celsius, or degrees Kelvin) is secondary to the conception that it moves to one or the other of two neighbors. When we talk of more or less, before or after, or changes, we tend to imply chains, even when we use relative terms such as *wealthy, intelligent, successful,* or *progressive.* Chains may be open-ended or bounded. Polar adjective scales, introduced in Chapter 7 and mentioned above, have defined beginnings and ends. Chains may also be conceived of as emanating from one outstanding value in one direction, as in the size, readership, or frequency of a newspaper or Zillmann's (1964) semantic aspect scale, or in two directions, as in the positive or negative bias of reporting. Figure 8.2 adds a train schedule and a ladder conception to the examples of chains.

The familiar ordinal scales, interval scales, and ratio scales are all chains to begin with; the difference between these scales and chains is one of metrics. As noted above, the term *nominal scale* is a misnomer, as nominal variables exhibit no ordering at all.

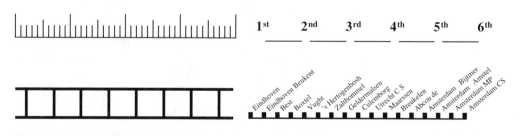

Figure 8.2   Chains

Recursions   8.5.2

Recursions are circular connections between values. Recursions can be conceived of as chains whose ends are seamlessly joined. Each value has exactly two immediate neighbors; there is no end and no outstanding value. Moving from any given value in one direction eventually brings one back to where one began—which was arbitrary to begin with. Transitivity applies locally but not to all values. Figure 8.3 shows this graphically. Examples of recursively ordered phenomena include seasonal fluctuations, ecological cycles, and human-computer interactions. Namenwirth and Weber (1987) demonstrated cyclicity in the use of political values and adopted a recursive notion of time (see Figure 10.5). Biologists describe biological phenomena in terms of life cycles, and cyberneticians have identified the stabilizing efforts of complex systems in terms of circular causal feedback loops. In accounts of how social prejudices take hold in a population, how political candidates get elected, and how the "spiral of silence" affects public opinion, recursive variables are indispensable.

The practice of cutting recursions into more easily analyzable linear continua usually destroys their circular essence. For example, some social psychology researchers have cut speech acts out of the ongoing circularity of human interactions that realize their meanings, and this may account for the rather artificial causal conceptions that dominate social psychological explanations of language use. In the same way, when one describes a computer interface in terms of the graphics involved, one hides the dynamic nature of the interface. Many so-called inconsistent preferences, such as $a \rightarrow b$, $b \rightarrow c$, and $c \rightarrow a$, in fact define recursions. These are far from irrational or abnormal; rather, they belong to a nonlinear ordering.

Figure 8.3   Loops and Circles

Cubes   8.5.3

Cubes depict variations multidimensionally. The values in cubes are ordered so that neighboring values differ in only one of a cube's dimensions. Cubes often arise by default. Consider Lasswell and Kaplan's (1950) eight value categories:

Power

Rectitude

Respect

Affection

Wealth

Well-being

Enlightenment

Skill

Superficially, these eight values have no apparent order and so resemble a nominal variable. However, Lasswell and Kaplan allowed their recording units—persons, symbols, and statements—to score high on more than one of these values. If the eight kinds of values are taken as a nominal variable, the permission to record combinations of such values would violate the mutual exclusivity requirement of variables and render the data so recorded no longer analyzable as a nominal variable. In fact, any instruction to coders to "check as many as applicable" signals a data structure other than a scale. When any of the eight values could be present or absent independent of all of the others, the values define an eight-dimensional cube consisting of eight binary variables. Figure 8.4 shows cubes of increasing dimensionality created by the presence or absence of independent qualities.

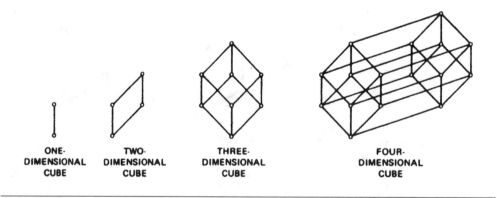

ONE-DIMENSIONAL CUBE   TWO-DIMENSIONAL CUBE   THREE-DIMENSIONAL CUBE   FOUR-DIMENSIONAL CUBE

Figure 8.4   Cubes

8.5.4   Trees

Trees have one origin and two kinds of values, terminal and branching. All of them are available for coding. Trees show no recursions, as Figure 8.5 illustrates.

Each value in a tree can be reached from its one origin by a separate path that passes through a number of branching values. Trees are basic to the recording of linguistic representations and conform to one of the earliest theories of meaning. Aristotle's notion of a *definition,* for example, requires naming the *genus* (the general class) to which the *definiens* (the word to be defined) belongs and distinguishing the latter from all other species of that genus. Moving from genus to genus describes moving through the branching points of a tree. The system of categories in the Linnean classification in biology—not the organisms it classifies—constitutes a tree. Closer to content analysis, a reference to Europe is implicitly a reference to France, Italy, Germany, and so on. A reference to France is implicitly a reference to the regions of that country. The relation connecting "Europe," "France," and "Provence" is one of inclusion and defines a path or chain through a tree. France and England are on different paths, as neither includes the other.

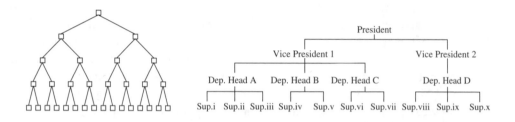

Figure 8.5   Trees

Most content analyses fix the level of abstraction on which countries, populations, products, or mass-media programs are coded. Trees offer a richer alternative. Other examples include family trees, decision trees, telephone trees, the trees that the rules of a transformational grammar generate, and social hierarchies in business organizations, in the military, and in government. (I discuss the possible confusion of trees with groupings below, in section 8.6.1. Note here only that each branching point can be occupied by a value.)

METRICS   8.6

Any two values may differ quantitatively—whether they are neighbors or not. In a semantic network, singular concepts (its nodes) are linked to each other by relational concepts (for example, *[Joe]* <runs for> *[Governor]; [Joe]* <was> *[an accountant]*). A metric defines how closely any two concepts are associated, how similar they are, or how much they have to do with each other, not whether they are neighbors or where their ordering locates them. A metric recognizes various kinds of differences and specifies what an analyst can do with them. The literature on metrics developed largely on chainlike variables and in the context of a measurement theory that distinguishes among nominal, ordinal, interval, and ratio scales (Stevens, 1946). These four metrics (listed here in the order of their increasing power) differ in the information they can represent and are therefore often called levels of measurement. I describe the three principal metrics below and define their mathematical properties in Table 8.2.

8.6.1   Ordinal Metrics

Ordinal metrics describe recording units in such relational terms as "larger than," "more than," "precedes," "causes," "is a condition of," "is a refinement of," "is contained in," "supervises"—in short, in terms of *ranks*. Ordinal scales (chains with ordinal metrics) are probably most common in the social sciences, largely because relationships between people and objects tend to occur in language, spoken or written, and are then also more easily recorded in words. When the stock market is said to "gain," an ordinal metric is implied. When it is said to "gain 5 points," an interval metric is invoked. Ordinal scales using 3, 5, and 7 points are most closely associated with language and hence natural in content analysis. Polar opposites lend themselves to 3-point scales (e.g., a scale from *good* to *bad*, with *neutral* as its midpoint); the addition of simple adjectives, such as *more* or *less*, results in 5-point scales, and the addition of superlatives (e.g., *most* and *least*) leads to 7-point scales.

In content analysis, ranks may be variously operationalized. Newspaper editors, for example, employ several typographical devices to express the importance they assign to the news items they publish. Suppose, after interviewing a sample of newspaper editors, a researcher found the following rank order to correlate highly with the editors' judgment of how important news items were— of course always relative to what happened that day:

1st: Largest multicolumn headline above the center fold of the front page

2nd: Any other headline above the center fold of the front page

3rd: Any headline below the center fold of the front page

4th: Any multicolumn headline on the second, third, or last page

5th: Any other headline above the center fold of any other inside page

6th: Any headline below the center fold of any other inside page

7th: Any other news item

Assuming that the editors' judgments are those of a somewhat stable journalistic culture, are used quite consistently, and have little variation, content analysts can use this construct to infer the importance of news items by ranking them with this 7-point ordinal scale.

As Table 8.2 suggests, ordinal metrics are not limited to chains. Grouping an unordered set of values into conceptual categories introduces inequalities between the otherwise pairwise equal differences. Groupings suppose that the values within one group have more in common with each other than with the values in different groups. The above-mentioned standards for analyzing Freud's dream theory represent a grouping: The difference between *A1* and *A2* is smaller than the difference between *A1* and *B1,* but nothing indicates by how much. Graham and Witschge (2003) introduced such differences in ranks by categorizing messages, the posts to online discussion groups, in four convenient phases, effectively grouping 21 categories on four levels. Figure 8.6 shows the researchers' process. In Phase 1, messages were distinguished into three groups, two of which were final categories. In Phase 2, messages that responded to previous messages were grouped into two kinds, depending on whether they manifested reasons. In Phase 3, the nonreasoned claims led to three final categories. The reasoned claims were divided into four types of responses and, in Phase 4, each led to four groups indicating the kind of evidence used in the arguments. Frequencies were obtained for each final category, which could be summed in the reverse order of the distinctions that led to them. Although the data are qualitative, showing no ordering, the grouping imposed a metric that assumes that categories of messages in the same group are more similar to each other than to categories of messages in different groups. Figure 8.6 suggests that messages that manifest reasons and those that do not are more different than messages that differ in whether they contain counterarguments, rebuttals, refusals to rebut, or rational affirmations.

Groupings reflect conceptual hierarchies that are defined on top of an original set of values. When used repeatedly, any decision tree—for example, that depicted in Figure 8.6, but also the one in Figure 7.1—creates groupings. Decision trees proceed from rougher to finer distinctions and from larger and less differentiated sets of units of analysis to smaller and more specialized sets. One analytical implication of grouping is that it suggests the order in which frequencies of values may be summed, undoing decisions one by one. Hierarchical clustering procedures, for instance, proceed that way as well. They capitalize on unequal differences between elementary qualities to develop a hierarchy, represented by a dendrogram, that could explain the collection of these qualities as groupings (for instance, see Figure 10.10).

Groupings and trees are easily confused, and as both are important in content analysis, I want to highlight their distinction. As I have said, groupings provide convenient conceptualizations of a given set of values, the terminal points of a decision tree, like the outline of a book in chapters and sections. Groups do not constitute values in a grouping, however. An outline is not the text it organizes. In contrast, the values of a tree are not limited to the terminal values of the tree; they include its branches as well. Thus their values are not merely different; they may include each other, enabling the coding of different levels of inclusion, abstraction, or entailments. Take the above-mentioned Linnean classification system as an example. It groups organisms into classes and subclasses and provides concepts that label these groups on different levels.

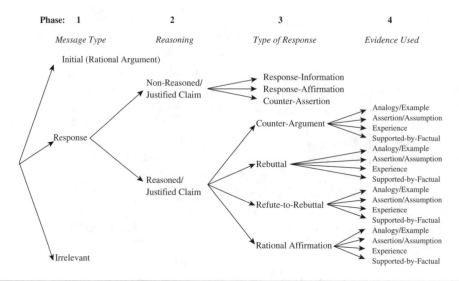

Figure 8.6   A Grouping of Messages From Online Deliberations

SOURCE: Adapted from Graham and Witschge (2003, p. 181, fig. 1).

For instance, *mammal* is not an organism but the name of a group that includes humans, whales, and mice. The Linnean system *groups organisms* but it defines a *tree for the names of groups* of organisms that describe organisms on different levels of commonalities.

8.6.2   Interval Metrics

Interval metrics represent quantitative differences between recording units. Measures of time, distance, and volume as well as changes in quantities and movement in space all assume meaningful intervals. When applied to chains, an interval metric creates interval scales and enables the addition or subtraction of differences between scale points. In psychological tests, subjects are often asked to use rating scales with equal intervals to answer questions. In content analysis, the semantic differential scales that are used to record judgments of biases, personality traits of characters, and so on are often conceptualized as equal-interval scales. Intervals do not need to be equal, however.

Interval data are the preferred kind in empirical social research, largely because of the wealth of statistical techniques that are available and accessible for them, especially techniques that require the calculation of differences, as in variance calculations, correlational methods, factor analyses, multidimensional scaling, and clustering. Interval metrics might well be an artifact of these techniques. In the natural sciences most measures, except for time, have ratio metric properties, and in content analysis interval scales tend not to be as reliable as data with a less powerful metric. For example, in research on the personality characteristics of fictional characters on television, semantic differential scales, which are treated as interval scales, have been notoriously unreliable. This has been so not only because language is rarely as precise as would be necessary for differences to be calculable, but mainly because personality characteristics that are irrelevant to a plot may not be present at all, causing coders to guess when they are forced to choose among interval values. Nevertheless, many secondary measures that content analysts provide—quantitative indices of phenomena, geometric depictions of findings—have valid interval qualities.

Ratio Metrics 8.6.3

Ratio metrics are defined from absolute zero points relative to which all differences between values are expressed. Lengths, weights, speeds, masses, and absolute temperatures in degrees Kelvin (but not in degrees Fahrenheit or Celsius) exemplify ratio scales in the physical sciences, none of which can go below its absolute zero point. There are also many examples of ratio-level measurements of text, such as column inches of newsprint, sizes of photographs, frequencies of publication, audience sizes, and Nielsen ratings, as well as amounts of information and costs. These have no negative values either. In content analysis, these measures may have less to do with what a text says or the role it plays in a particular context than with how prominent recording units are or how much they say to the analyst.

The list of metrics is far from settled, and far more orderings are available than are relevant for content analysis. Regarding data languages—of which variables, orderings, and metrics are the most prominent features—it is probably most important to keep their Janus-faced character in mind. The data language must be appropriate to the phenomenon being recorded—and from this perspective, the best data language is the raw text itself. The data language must also render the data amenable to analysis. Given the currently available analytical techniques, the gap between the form in which texts are easily available and the forms these techniques require often seems large. For content analysts, the challenge is to develop computational techniques whose requirements are easily satisfied by naturally occurring texts and images.

MATHEMATICAL OPERATIONS 8.7

As noted above, a metric is defined by the mathematical operations under which the relations between the recorded units remain invariant. Adding 4 to the values of a semantic differential scale transforms a –3-to-+3 scale into a 1-to-7 scale, yet the algebraic differences between the scale's values remain exactly the same. However, when these values are multiplied by 4, the numerical differences between neighboring values become very uneven; only their ordering remains unchanged (i.e., it remains a chain). Thus I distinguish two kinds of operations on the values of a variable, one preserving the original numerical relationships between the values of a variable and the other preserving their orderings. Table 8.2 lists these functions. The table amounts to permission for analysts to apply analytical techniques that employ these transformations and suggests the kinds of relationships in texts that various operations preserve or omit.

Table 8.2 lists metrics in the increasing order of their *power*. Ratio metric data, which are most powerful and potentially most informative, may be computed as interval data at the expense of all information about the location of values relative to their absolute zero point. Using the more readily available variance-type statistics on ratio-level data, for example, discards this information. Ratio and interval data may be computed with ordinal techniques, which treat them as ordinal data, but only at the additional expense of all information about the numerical differences between values. Finally, ratio, interval, and ordinal data may be computed as nominal data, at which point all information about their orderings and metric qualities are lost. Losses of relational information are irreversible.

Going in reverse through these metrics, applying an ordinal technique on nominal data produces uninterpretable results. Applying an interval technique on ordinal data yields spurious findings. The lesson to be learned from the above is that *the power of a data language must match or exceed the power of the analytical procedures to be employed.*

Table 8.2   Operational Properties of Metrics

Metric	Relations R_{xy}	Relation-Preserving $f(\ )$s $R_{xy} = R_{f(x)f(y)}$	Order-Preserving $f(\ )$s $f(R_{xy}) > f(R_{wz}) \Leftrightarrow R_{f(x)f(y)} > R_{f(w)f(z)}$
None	Distinctions $x \neq y$	1:1 Permutations	1:1 Permutations
Ordinal	Ranks $x \geq y$	Monotonically increasing fs	Monotonically increasing fs
Interval	Differences $x - y$	$x' = x + b$	Linear functions $f(\ )$: $x' = ax + b$
Ratio	Proportions x/y	$x' = ax$	Expotential functions $f(\ )$: $x' = bx^a$

CHAPTER 9

Analytical Constructs

Following the discussions in previous chapters of different uses of content analysis and the kinds of inferences they make, this chapter illustrates several ways of operationalizing analytical constructs from various ways of knowing the contexts of given texts. It also presents examples of the forms that such constructs might take.

THE ROLE OF ANALYTICAL CONSTRUCTS 9.1

An analytical construct operationalizes what the content analyst knows, suspects, or assumes about the context of the text and procedurally accounts for the drawing of inferences from that text. Figure 4.2 shows the role of the analytical construct among other analytical components of content analysis. In its simplest form, an analytical construct is a function, a collection of "if-then" statements, or a computer program that defines at least one path from available text to the answers sought.

In Chapter 2, I identified the inferential step from text to the answer to a research question *abductive* because the two domains—texts (along with their descriptions or transcriptions) and what these texts imply—are logically independent of each other, and bridging this logical gap requires justification. So conceived, an analytical construct functions as a hypothesis, the best hypothesis or explanation that the analyst can imagine and defend, of how a body of text is read, what it does, or to what use it may be put in a context of the analyst's choice. Appropriating Toulmin's (1958) terms, I suggested in Chapter 2 that analytical constructs, if reliably executed, *warrant* the intended inferences (guide the analyst along a logical path), but they must in turn be *backed* by knowledge of the context of the analyzed texts (assure the analyst that the path leads to valid conclusions). I discuss the justifications for analytical constructs that underlie

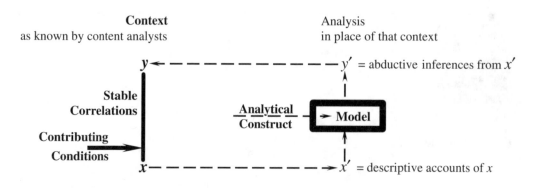

Figure 9.1 Analytical Construct as Specifying the Model of a Context

content analyses in Chapter 13; here, my focus is on how content analysts can derive these constructs.

In the processes of operationalizing an analysis, ideas (which may well emerge during the analyst's reading of some of the texts), hypotheses, or theories about the context are formalized, "tamed," or structured so that they meet the researcher's need to go from here to there in an analysis—much as a computer is programmed to accept certain inputs and produce usable outputs. For a content analysis to proceed relative to a context, its analytical construct must also be *a model of the relationships between the texts and the target of intended inferences,* what the analyst wants to know about that context. What warrants these inferences is the computational nature of the model—that it can be executed repeatedly and reliably, as is expected of all scientific research. What backs these inferences is a demonstration, or at least an arguable assumption, that they are empirically rooted in the context of the given body of text, that the analytical construct represents the stable correlations within a context (as in Figure 2.1), leaving two main uncertainties or variables: (a) the contributing conditions under which these correlations are presumed stable (and the analytical construct applicable) and (b) the available texts by means of which the research questions are to be answered. Either of these two uncertainties may require qualifications (in Toulmin's sense) of the research results.

To be specific, Figure 9.1 extracts the analytical construct from Figure 2.1 and presents it as a model of the relevant features of the context. In Figure 9.1, x is the sampled texts. The arrow from x to x' defines a mapping that summarizes the processes of unitizing, sampling, recording, and reducing, described as data making in Chapter 4. The analytical construct computes y', which remains indeterminable or open until x' is known (much as in algebra, where a function, such as squaring, has no answer unless the number to which it is applied is known). If there is a mapping from y to y' on which grounds y' can be said to point to, represent, or at least correlate with specific features of the context to which y belongs as well, then y' is valid. The abduction is justified by the assumption that the analytical construct is a true or heuristic model of the context. In taking the analytical construct as invariant, at least during an analysis, a researcher is led to distinguish, according to George (1959a), between the stable or unchanging conditions, which are the ones modeled, and the unstable or variable conditions, which may become fixed if the analyst obtains a body of relevant text, x, analyzes it, and infers y' from it. The point of a content analysis, y, always remains more or less uncertain, y' being its best approximation.

Below, I address some ways in which content analysts can develop analytical constructs, operationalizing x' y'' relationships, that, when implemented, have a good chance of selecting valid answers, y', to the content analysts' questions concerning y.

SOURCES OF CERTAINTY   9.2

Analysts need to justify their analytical procedures, not only in their final form, but also at each step taken during their development. In constructing an analysis, the analyst needs to preserve the modeling relationship to the chosen context. The structure of the texts themselves, significant as it is, shows up in the analyst's appropriate choices of a data language and suitable recording instructions, which I have addressed in Chapters 7 and 8; here, the focus is on analytical constructs only.

Content analysts rely on one or more sources of certainty in developing analytical constructs:

- *Previous successes and failures* of content analyses to argue for functional correspondences between the construct and a chosen context

- *Expert knowledge and experience* of/with a context to argue for structural correspondences between the construct and the context

- *Established theories* about a context to argue for structural correspondences between the construct and that context

- *Embodied practices,* sampled from a context, to argue for the representative nature of the inferences obtained from these practices

I discuss each of these sources in turn below.

Previous Successes and Failures   9.2.1

Previous successes and failures provide an analyst with very practical reasons for developing and adopting a particular analytical construct. The contention is obvious: What succeeded in the past must have had something to do with the context in which it worked, and, unless that context has changed, one might as well continue to use what worked—until it runs into failures. Typically, there is no theory for the success of an analysis, no justification for the structure of its construct except for its having worked before.

Recall that in Chapter 4, I mentioned one design (development of a discriminant function) that increases the success of a content analysis incrementally. Stone and Hunt's (1963) computer analysis of real versus simulated suicide notes provides an example of this atheoretical way of proceeding. The real notes in their study came from court records in Los Angeles. The simulated notes were written by a panel made up of individuals who matched the authors of the real notes in population characteristics (sex, age, race, occupation, and so on). The researchers' decision to analyze these notes was motivated by a suicide prevention center's interest in knowing whether the center's personnel should take particular suicide notes seriously. Stone and Hunt analyzed 15 pairs of notes with known identity (real or simulated) for what differentiated them and reached three conclusions:

1. The frequency of references to concrete things, persons, and places is higher in real notes.

2. The frequency of the actual word *love* is higher in real notes.

3. The total number of references to thought and decision processes is higher for simulated notes.

From these findings, the researchers developed an index by simply subtracting the total number of references to thought and decision processes (finding 3) from the sum of the frequency of references to concrete things, persons, and places (finding 1) and the frequency of the word *love* (finding 2). This discriminant function enabled them to infer the alleged authenticity of the notes. In fact, it correctly differentiated 13 of the 15 pairs of notes used in this preparatory analysis.

Having succeeded thus far, albeit with some uncertainty remaining in the results, Stone and Hunt then applied the discriminant function to 18 more pairs of notes whose identity, real or simulated, was not revealed to the two researchers, and they were able to determine correctly the authenticity of 17 out of 18 notes. In addition to being statistically significant, the performance of the discriminant function developed solely on past successes and failures also turned out to be significantly better than human judgments obtained in separate experiments.

Obviously, Stone and Hunt reached the three conclusions listed above without having any particular theory in mind. It would indeed be a challenge for researchers to find a rationale for how these three variables of suicide notes are connected to feeling suicidal. The adding and subtracting of scores, for example, would make sense if there were hidden quantities that cooperated (measured by variables 1 and 2) or competed for each other (measured by variable 3 versus variables 1 and 2). However, such quantities are difficult to imagine as the cause for a writer's suicidal versus nonsuicidal inclinations. Nevertheless, the analytical construct in the form of this discriminant function succeeded statistically, and this demonstration would be a sufficient argument for its use.

Ultimately, all content analyses must demonstrate success to a degree better than chance. Unfortunately, opportunities for repeated analyses are rare—which brings us to the next path to analytical constructs.

Expert Knowledge and Experience   9.2.2

Familiarity concerning the chosen context is a valuable asset to all content analysts, of course. It can provide analysts with important face validity checks on the decisions they are making, but familiarity may not be sufficient. Even hard-nosed researchers occasionally get carried away by conceptions that make sense to them but, in reality, have little to do with the contexts they are analyzing. Yet when content analysts are faced with a novel situation, with having to design a content analysis without precedents to rely on, or without history of research and theorizing about the context they are working with, personal knowledge, perhaps of known experts, may be all the analysts have to start with.

Leites, Bernaut, and Garthoff (1951) provide a fascinating example of the development of an analytical construct out of researchers' experiences with the context of given texts. These analysts, all experts on the politics of the Soviet Union, were interested in the distribution of power within the Kremlin and particularly in predicting the succession in Soviet leadership. In governments in which succession is not regulated politically, such as in the Soviet Union of the 1950s, succession remains largely hidden to outside observers. Predicting the succession of leadership in such governments is both a favorite game of political analysts and important to foreign policy decision makers, for example, in the United States. Leites et al. obtained the public speeches made by politburo members on the occasion of Stalin's 70th birthday in 1949, all of which expressed adulation of Stalin, as would be expected. Initially, political scientists attributed differences among the speeches to the individual speakers' styles and therefore found them of no interest.

The key to finding politically relevant differences among these speeches, Leites et al. surmised, might lie in linguistic modes of expressing nearness, for which Soviet political discourse seemed to offer two distinct approaches. The analysts noted that one set of "symbols of nearness and intimacy (father, solicitude, and so on) appears most frequently in the popular image of Stalin and [is] stressed for that audience which is far removed from him." The other set of symbols derived from the prevailing "depreciation of such nearness in political relationships. The ideal party member does not stress any gratification he may derive from intimacy for political ends. . . . Those closer to Stalin politically are permitted to speak of him in terms of lesser personal intimacy ('leader of the party,' etc.)" and are thus privileged to refrain from the crudest form of adulation. Leites et al. conclude their argument for the inferential strategy they adopted by suggesting that the relative emphasis on the "Bolshevik image" as opposed to the "popular image" of Stalin "not only reflects the Bolshevik evaluation of the party as distinguished from and superior to the masses at large, but also indicates the relative distance of the speaker from Stalin" (pp. 338–339).

Leites et al. tabulated the numbers of both kinds of references and ranked the speakers according to their relative emphasis on one kind versus the other. They found the speeches of Molotov, Malenkov, and Beria (in that order) to have the highest numbers of references to Stalin's Bolshevik image, and from this they inferred that these three politburo members were probably closest to Stalin. The power struggle that ensued immediately after Stalin's death clearly confirmed the validity of their inferences. Just out of curiosity, I translated the logic of Leites et al.'s arguments into a simple construct in the form of a distance function (Krippendorff, 1967, pp. 118–119):

$$D_{toStalin} = \frac{N_{popular} + \dfrac{N_{ambiguous}}{2}}{N_{popular} + N_{ambiguous} + N_{Bolshevik}},$$

where Ns are the frequencies of a politburo member mentioning popular, ambiguous, and Bolshevik images in their speeches. The ranking obtained by this construct replicated the inferences on the top of Leites et al.'s list but ended differently. It suggested that Khrushchev was the furthest removed from Stalin, immediately preceded by Bulganin and Kosygin. As we now know, those furthest removed from Stalin ended up playing major roles in the fight to overcome Stalinism in the Soviet Union. The content analysis did not foretell the actual political events, but it led to the correct inference of a variable, the politically significant players.

The preceding example is intended to suggest that the experts of a context for content analysis can often provide a wealth of disconnected propositions that content analysts may be able to sort out and assemble into constructs for analyzing available texts. Unless researchers put such expert knowledge into the formal terms of an analytical construct, texts may remain silent about the questions that analysts are asking.

Without adding another example, I will merely note here that fifth-generation computers, so-called expert systems, contain huge collections of propositions that represent what experts know about particular subjects. They are designed to answer knowledge questions by finding inferential links (not only abductive ones) between factual givens and the possible answers to users' questions. Such computers could be used for content analysis as well.

In moving from incomplete, perhaps even contradictory, expert knowledge to a construct that is suitable for a content analysis, analysts need to preserve the structural correspondence between what they do and that context at each analytical step they take. Analysts using expert knowledge proceed from the bottom up, so to speak, whereas those using established theories proceed from the top down.

9.2.3   Established Theories

If a context is well researched and theorized, especially including the role that available texts play in it and the research questions the analyst seeks to answer, then the analyst may derive analytical constructs from available generalizations about that context. In Chapter 4, I outlined how a researcher might test analytical constructs as theories about a context. Here I address the development of analytical constructs from available theories and from the results of related research.

Theories come in diverse forms, of course. Sometimes theories are fairly specific propositions that have been tested in a variety of situations—for example, concerning correlations between speech disturbances and the anxiety levels of speakers, between the frequency of reported crimes and public concerns with law-and-order issues, or between the number of arguments people advance for or against a public issue and the level of their political competence and knowledge. Berelson and Steiner (1964) have published an inventory of 1,025 scientific findings in the social and behavioral sciences that content analysts might consult. Inventories specializing in content analysis are not available, but propositions of a comparable nature can be found in handbooks on psychiatry, social psychology, sociology, and sociolinguistics. Sometimes such propositions derive from more general theories, such as theories regarding the expression of emotions, linguistic manifestations of psychopathologies, or how and according to which criteria the mass media select and their audiences receive or make use of news. The "uses and gratifications" approach to media research exemplifies the latter. Perhaps for good reasons, a general theory of communication that includes interpretations of texts and perceptions of images has not been formulated. Content analysts have lamented this deficit for years.

An example of how a particular theory became an analytical construct is found in Osgood, Saporta, and Nunnally's (1956) "evaluative assertion analysis." I present only the result of this development here. The technique is derived from a version of dissonance theory, which assumes the following:

1. Concepts (attitude objects) are valued, "liked" or "disliked," in degrees, ranging from positive through neutral to negative.

2. All linguistic assertions can be decomposed into one or more pairs of concepts (attitude objects) whose connections are accounted for by relations of association or dissociation, expressed in degrees. *Is, has, likes, supports, belongs,* and *cooperates* are strongly associative, whereas *is not, dislikes, opposes, fights,* and *denies* are strongly dissociative, with several shades of strengths in between.

3. Some concepts, called *common meaning terms,* are unalterable in value. These consist mostly of adjectives such as *good, bad, dishonest, ugly,* and *mean.* Others are valuationally variable, for example, *United States, vine, psychotherapy, teacher,* and *Richard Nixon.* Their valuations depend on how they are used, which is the point of the analysis.

4. Individuals accept concept pairs that are balanced—that is, assertions containing associations between two similarly valued concepts ("I like my friend") and dissociations between two dissimilarly valued concepts ("I hate my enemy"). Individuals reject concept pairs that are imbalanced or modify them so as to achieve balance. These are assertions containing

dissociations between two similarly valued concepts ("I hate my friend") and associations between two dissimilarly valued concepts ("I love my enemy"). Graphically, let the evaluation of attitude objects be represented in parentheses, (+) and (−), and let associations be represented as positive links, — + —, and dissociations as negative links, — − —.

$$(+) — + — (+),$$
$$(+) — − — (−), \text{ and}$$
$$(−) — − — (+) \text{ are balanced,}$$
$$\text{whereas } (+) — − — (+),$$
$$(+) — + — (−), \text{ and}$$
$$(−) — + — (+) \text{ are imbalanced.}$$

From the psycho-logic sketched above, and under the assumption that individuals seek to avoid imbalance and move to achieve balance, it would follow that concepts with open valuation are valued implicitly, and analysts can therefore infer their value from suitably recorded texts:

$$\text{From } (+) — + — (?) \text{ one can infer } (?) = (+),$$
$$\text{from } (+) — − — (?) \text{ one can infer } (?) = (−), \text{ and}$$
$$\text{from } (−) — − — (?) \text{ one can infer } (?) = (+).$$

Evidently, this is made possible by the assumption that balance is the usual way of speaking and thinking, effectively ruling out the three imbalance triplets.

Osgood et al. moreover stipulate a quantitative relationship between the degrees of positive/negative valuation of the concepts involved and the degree of association/dissociation between them. This motivates a calculus of valuation, which enabled Osgood et al. to infer not only the direction of a concept's (implicit) valuations but also its extent. It also leads to a statistic of these valuations, conceived of as describing the attitude structures of individual writers or readers. This may be a long story, but content analysts who work in well-researched contexts may have to develop similar constructs in support of their intended inferences. Osgood et al.'s calculus is derived from a psycholinguistic theory. Theories surely must exist in other empirical domains that could be so adopted in content analysis.

Deriving analytical constructs from established theories does not guarantee that the constructs will be flawless. Some theories have not been formulated with large bodies of text in mind. An analyst may close gaps in a theory with assumptions that send the construct astray. A theory might not be as general as the analyst assumes. In the case of evaluative assertion analysis, irony has no place, asserted changes in evaluation (e.g., I am starting to like my opponent) are difficult to deal with, reflections on a connection (e.g., Why should I love him?) cannot be handled, and other forms of resolving imbalances, including tolerating them (e.g., agree to disagree), mess up the inferences. Some scholars have raised doubts as to whether it makes sense to decompose a whole text into pairs of concepts and whether the notion of an attitude structure predicts anything. Be that as it may, analytical constructs that conform to a valid theory are valid on account of their structural correspondence with that context. Although evaluative assertion analysis is far from perfect, it has passed several tests.

Embodied Practices   9.2.4

Without history of other content analyses to rely on and no theory or expert knowledge about the selected analytical context, content analysts may be tempted to sample individuals who are known to embody the needed analytical constructs, who are competent readers, interpreters, and users of the texts in the chosen context. Researchers use this strategy far more often than is noticed. For example, when researchers employ coders because of their familiarity with the language or subject matter of the texts to be analyzed, this amounts to importing their knowledge without having to theorize or translate it into coding instructions or analytical constructs. It is assumed that other readers of the texts, not involved in coding, share the background and familiarity that the sampled coders bring to the research.

The key to the methodological problem with this strategy is found in the difference between content analysis and direct observational techniques. If the questions that content analysts are asking could be answered through direct observation or interviewing subjects, content analysis would be superfluous. The point of content analysis is not to study observable behavior or common interpretations, but to answer questions concerning events that are not accessible at the time, actions that have not yet been taken, large-scale social phenomena that escape individuals' unaided perceptions, or evidence in court for something otherwise difficult to ascertain. Although most content analyses do draw on embodied experiences and the qualifications of coders, for example, may be justified by induction, the objective of content analysis goes beyond individuals' interpretive competencies. Coding is not the same as interpreting texts by a multitude of readers. Content analysis is fundamentally abductive. It must not be confused with psychological experiments that attempt to generalize responses to stimuli, including to texts, from a sample to a population of individual readers or interpreters.

TYPES OF CONSTRUCTS   9.3

In Chapter 4, I discussed the following kinds of inferences:

- Extrapolations
- Applications of standards
- Indices and symptoms

- Re-presentations

- Conversations/interactions

- Institutional processes

Analytical constructs can be grouped into these types as well. Below, I offer a few comments on each, with the bulk of the discussion reserved for indices and symptoms on which content analyses most commonly depend.

9.3.1   Extrapolations

Extrapolations of trends, patterns, and differences call for analytical constructs that take the form of *recursive* or *autocorrelative functions*. Underlying extrapolations is the idea of *systems* that determine their own behavior within self-maintained boundaries. The behavior of a system—or, if time is not a factor, the entailments of a system—can be inferred from recurrent interactions or stable relations *within* the system, hence *auto*correlatively.

9.3.2   Applications of Standards

The application of standards for identifying, evaluating, or auditing involves two steps: (a) comparing a variable, a representation of texts, with a given or assumed standard; and (b) judging what this entails. I have mentioned, as examples, the diagnosis of psychopathology according to manuals of professional standards; the evaluation of press performance, journalistic bias, and codes of conduct in the mass-media industry against established ideals or in reference to tolerable limits; and the audit of communication or accounting practices within an organization. Generally, the analytical constructs for the use of standards are embodied in institutional practices. They are invariant to the extent that institutions manage to enforce them.

9.3.3   Indices and Symptoms

Indices and symptoms are variables that are claimed to correlate with other variables of interest to analysts. The most basic form of an analytical construct for what George (1959b) called *direct* indicators is a one-to-one relationship, a mapping or mathematical function from a variable (often numerical), the supposed index, to the phenomenon it is supposed to indicate. Such simple relationships are found when anthropologists date artifacts by measuring the potency of radiocarbon; they are also present when physicians link medical symptoms to diagnoses and treatments. In content analysis, indicative functions are often tied to frequencies: the proportion of discomfort words as an index of anxiety, the relative frequency and space devoted to a topic as an index of an author's knowledge or interest or the importance that the mass media attached to that topic, the change in frequency of value words in party platforms as an indicator of changes in a country's political climate. Analysts can establish these simple analytical constructs, for example, through the use of regression equations or even agreement coefficients.

In addition to needing to correlate with the phenomena they claim to represent, indices must satisfy two additional conditions. First, indices should *not* correlate with phenomena that are considered to be independent of indicated phenomena. In other words, indices must not only point to but also distinguish among phenomena: A chosen answer to a research question must exclude other answers. For example, a therapist cannot identify a patient's mental illness from the way the patient talks unless there is enough variation in the ways different people talk to allow the therapist to draw distinctions and exclude some illnesses from the list. If all textbooks had identical readability scores, the readability measure for a particular text would not mean anything. Even drawing inferences regarding who may be the author of an anonymously written book means making informed choices. Paisley (1964), who reviewed the literature on research efforts to infer the authors of unsigned documents, found the following conditions necessary for indices to distinguish among alternative authors:

- Indices should exhibit low variance within a communicator's known work.

- Indices should exhibit high variance among the works of all communicators being compared.

- The frequencies contributing to the value of an index should be high relative to the sampling error.

I shall continue this thread in Chapter 13.

Second, indices should not be affected by variables that are accidental or irrelevant to the phenomenon indicated. For example, in their attempt to infer the authorship of the *Federalist Papers,* Mosteller and Wallace (1963) argued against using Yule's (1944) method of counting of nouns, because individuals may write on different subjects, and the choice of content words may hence contaminate what could otherwise reveal an author's identity: "The words we want to use are non-contextual ones, words whose rate of use is nearly invariant under change of topic. For this reason, the little filler words, called function words, are especially attractive" (Mosteller & Wallace, 1963, p. 280).

The shift from counting frequencies of words, symbols, references, or subject matter to counting frequencies of pairs of words, co-occurrences of symbols, patterns of references, or relationships within texts does not affect how indices are developed, but it took 50 years for content analysts to develop an interest in co-occurrences and patterns. Baldwin (1942) had explored such ideas in his analysis of personality structures from autobiographies. Pool (1952b) observed that symbols tend to occur together or to come in clusters, but he was unable to realize this observation analytically. Osgood (1959) built the co-occurrences of words into his contingency analysis, demonstrating its power in his study of Goebbels's diary, and conducted experiments to determine what co-occurrences indicate. Now, computing indices from co-occurrences has become a standard option in several computer aids to content analysis. What these indices indicate, however, often remains an open question.

It is important that I warn against a conceptual confusion here. In content analysis, frequencies are used in two ways: as indices for magnitudes and as bases for testing the significance of hypotheses. For example, Berelson (1952) justifies his insistence on quantification largely in terms of the need to test statistical hypotheses, but all of his examples concern frequency indicators of other phenomena—attention, emphasis, and bias, to name but three.

In opposing the use of frequencies as *direct* indicators, George (1959a, 1959b) considered analytical constructs for *indirect* forms of inferences. These recognize variable institutional conditions under which the use of correlations might be warranted; I take up this thread in section 9.3.6, below.

9.3.4   Re-Presentations

Re-presentations, the kinds of contents usually intended or seen as the purpose of communications, demand analytical constructs that are discourse specific. Analyses of texts as re-presentations involve knowledge of how readers or users understand the language of texts and, most important, how they conceptualize their subject matter, which the preceding constructs hardly need. Such analyses usually employ several components: (a) an operationalization of the linguistic structure of the texts, yielding syntactical accounts of the units of text (usually sequences of sentences or propositions) being analyzed; (b) a listing of the possible meanings of words (which one might obtain from a discourse-specific dictionary), sentences (as analyzed by semantic parsers), and their semantic entailments on interpretations; (c) a mapping of these semantic interpretations onto a world model or territory of the larger discourse, whose logic allows the analyst (d) to obtain answers to questions that could be inferred from the information entered into this model (Hays, 1969; Krippendorff, 1969b).

The expert systems mentioned above can construct these very components for linguistic representations computationally. So far, such systems have been successful only in relatively small and well-structured worlds (medical diagnosis, mathematics, chemistry, and event analysis) and in cases where the vocabulary of the analyzed texts is not too rich or fuzzy. An interesting commercial application is the automatic generation of answers to frequently asked questions posed by clients of software companies, who describe their problems in their own everyday language. Although the syntactical analysis component may be minimal here, there surely is a dictionary-like component that looks for words and phrases with relevant meanings, which are then entered into a map of the software from which help can be made available. The world model of a particular software usually is far smaller and more structured than the world model of, say, a particular international situation with treaties in force, deception possible, and threats responded to.

Conversations/Interactions   9.3.5

Analytical constructs for verbal exchanges recognize the interactive meanings of assertions. Texts are partitioned into turns at talk or similar units of text, such as e-mail messages, public performances, or even political events. These are sequenced so that each unit of text is seen as someone's response to another's unit of text. In conversations, inferences from texts stay within a conversation and concern the possible responses that the units of text entail. Most important, each such unit is seen as expanding or constraining the space of possible continuations of the participants of that conversation. Holsti, Brody, and North (1965) developed a crude interaction model into which they mapped measures of affect and actions obtained from messages exchanged internationally during the Cuban missile crisis. Conversation analysis (see Chapter 3) has made major strides in suggesting concepts that might well be operationalized for content analyses of such verbal interactions, whether they are between individuals or between institutional communicators, such as during political campaigns or negotiations of international treaties.

Institutional Processes   9.3.6

Institutional processes do not follow easily generalizable formats. Analytical constructs for such processes are highly specific to the institutions involved and tend to have the following characteristics:

- They are qualitative, using institutionalized modes of reasoning as well as statistical ones.

- They rely on multiple methods for interpreting texts, as texts are generated and responded to by diverse participants, not one or a few.

- They consider known laws, operating rules, and regulations, each entailing constraints on vocabulary use, strategic moves, and instrumental actions, thus accounting for spaces of possibilities before locating any one move (text) in them.

- They recognize that any text at one point in time can have the effect of changing the context for analyzing future texts.

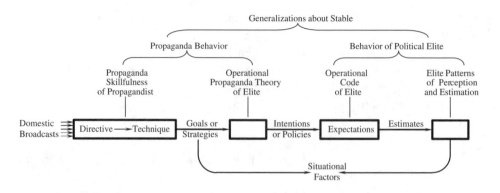

Figure 9.2   Analytical Construct for Political Elites' Stable Behavior Patterns
SOURCE: Adapted from George (1959a, p. 53).

Although the seeming lack of formal rigor might discourage some content analysts from facing the uncertainties apparent in such constructs, researchers have reported considerable success with them, especially when analyses are made over time, allowing partial validations to take place as institutional interactions are unfolding.

A good example of such an analytical construct is found in George's (1959a) account of the inferences made by the Federal Communications Commission regarding domestic enemy broadcasts during World War II. It is sketched in Figure 9.2. In the course of their regular inferences, the FCC analysts developed elaborate constructs that were intended to explain why certain broadcasts came into being and what, therefore, the antecedent conditions, perceptions of their producers, and possible military plans were. In this particular situation, the constructs were built on generalizations about the following:

- The propaganda skillfulness of the major propagandist

- The operational propaganda theory of the elites—that is, the role they assigned to the mass media in pursuing their policies

- The elites' operational code—that is, how the elites translated their estimates of the situation and their capabilities into policies

- The elites' pattern of perceiving and estimating themselves and their environment

Figure 9.2 illustrates how the analysts assembled these generalizations (about the stable features of the source) into a model, linking the major (unstable) variables of the context, especially the broadcasts, to the research questions. In this diagram, horizontal arrows indicate the order in which inferences were made, which is the inverse direction of the causalities that were presumed to work in this context. The model that these propaganda analysts used was evident in the justifications of the inferences they were asked to make in regular intervals, which George analyzed after the war (an institutional content analysis in its own right). He points out that these justifications were far more complex and not quite as linear as the model suggests. Moreover, as the analysts monitored these broadcasts and correlated them with known events, the analytical construct evolved as the war unfolded. Institutions are not carved in stone, and their analysts need to keep up with how they develop.

SOURCES OF UNCERTAINTY   9.4

The inferences that a content analysis yields might give the impression of precision, but contexts rarely cooperate with their analyst. As early as the development phase of a content analysis, the researcher may want to consider three particular issues, because problems in these areas can weaken the eventual findings: variance of the target of these inferences, confidence levels, and the appropriateness of the construct. Analysts might not always be able to solve all of these problems simultaneously.

Variance of the Target   9.4.1

Content analysts may underestimate the variance of the targets of their research questions, for several reasons:

■ Content analysts rarely have the imagination to list all relevant categories. Coders usually have difficulty thinking of all possible interpretations of a text, and analysts often discourage them from doing so. Consequently, content analysts may be surprised to find that they have not captured voices that turn out to be significant.

■ Theories are always simplifications. Analytical constructs that are derived from theories tend to be skeletal as well, accounting for far smaller amounts of variation than may be evident in the context. In the propaganda analysis effort sketched above, for example, an evaluation of this war effort revealed that the analysts assumed far more rigidity and determinism than were present.

■ Computations are deterministic and everywhere defined. Ideally, they are mathematical functions with multiple inputs but one output. To the extent that analytical constructs specify computations, analysts have a tendency to make inferences that are too precise and more single valued than may be warranted.

■ Content analysts with behaviorist orientations are inclined to predict the means of a distribution at the expense of its variance. Researchers with qualitative orientations tend to talk of "average readers," "typical phenomena," or "dominant forces," and this discounts existing diversity. Both kinds of analysts thus ignore actual variations in their targets, in the first case because of methodological commitments and in the second because of linguistic simplifications, not valid arguments.

Content analysts may be able to solve the problem of underestimating variance in the target of the research question by matching the variance in the target with the variance in the analytical procedure. Analysts may consider the analytical procedure as a communication channel that has enough capacity to allow them to select fairly among the possible answers to the research question.

9.4.2   Confidence Levels

Here, *confidence* refers to the inductive probability that the analytical construct is not an accidental product of the circumstances of its construction, that it is the best one available.

■ For a statistical interpretation of this uncertainty, the analyst may apply the procedure (described in Chapter 4) of testing analytical constructs as hypotheses. The smaller the sample size, the lower the confidence in the construct that is selected.

■ For qualitative interpretations of this uncertainty, the analyst may increase confidence levels by finding that the arguments for a structural or functional correspondence of a construct are more compelling than those against, that the number of theories that lead to the same construct is larger than the number leading to another, or that research has brought forth more evidence in favor of the construct than against it.

The classic solution to low confidence levels is larger sample size, a luxury that most content analysts may not be able to afford.

9.4.3   Appropriateness of the Construct

The correlations that an analytical construct is to describe may not be as stable as the analyst assumes. In Figures 2.1 and 9.1, the possibility that contributing conditions could alter the text/target relationships is acknowledged. This may happen in several ways:

■ Analytical constructs developed under laboratory conditions or with samples made up of undergraduate subjects, for example, may not be generalizable to the circumstances in which the actual content analysis is conducted.

- A context in which a content analysis proved successful at one time may have changed. Analytical constructs of institutional processes typically embrace such changes, whereas analytical constructs for indices and symptoms are likely to be at a loss when this occurs.

- Content analysts whose work concerns historical documents often make the mistake of ignoring the fact that linguistic conventions are unstable over long periods of time, that past readings could dramatically differ from contemporary ones, and that the institutions that accounted for the documents' creation are not comparable to the ones with which the analyst is familiar.

- Content analysts may simply be mistaken in their choice of analytical constructs. For example, the first three types of constructs described above assume that the context exhibits no intelligence. Suppose a source has a sense of how it is being analyzed and tailors the texts it makes available so as to achieve favorable results. Content analysts who employ constructs that cannot cope with such intelligence are blinded by their own methodological commitments and become unwitting instruments of their text sources' intentions.

- The publication of especially large-scale content analyses of social significance may affect the analyses' own contexts and weaken subsequent findings. For example, once the television violence indicators that Gerbner and his colleagues developed were published (see, e.g., Gerbner, Gross, Signorielli, Morgan, & Jackson-Beeck, 1979), the three major television networks had the opportunity to respond to the way the researchers measured violence in TV programming. If violence indicators had then declined over time, it would not have been clear whether there was actually less violence on television or whether the networks had found ways to circumvent Gerbner et al.'s measures.

Without invalidating evidence, content analysts may never know whether any of their choices were inappropriate. When invalidating evidence emerges, even only in small hints, analysts may be able to solve some of the problems noted above by altering their analytical constructions.

Part III

Analytical Paths and Evaluative Techniques

CHAPTER 10

Analytical/ Representational Techniques

Methods in content analysis largely address the making and processing of data and the application of analytical constructs that preserve some of the data's meanings, leading to valid inferences. This chapter discusses ways in which researchers can represent the results of content analyses such that they may recognize patterns and discover new ways of exploring their findings. Such representations are informative relative to often-implicit standards, several of which are reviewed in this chapter.

After texts have been recorded and analytical constructs have been applied, the content analyst needs to do the following:

- Summarize the inferences from text so that they are easily understood, interpreted, or related to intended decisions

- Discover patterns and relationships within findings that an unaided observer would otherwise easily overlook, to test hypotheses concerning various relationships

- Compare the findings with data obtained by other means or from other situations to support conclusions drawn from other research (multiple operationalism), to gain confidence in the validity of the content analysis at hand, to add another dimension to the intended inferences, or to provide missing information

In practice, these three tasks are not entirely distinct. They are not entirely unique to content analysis either. Much scholarly work, especially in statistics, is concerned with summarizing large bodies of data, making various comparisons, and testing statistical hypotheses. I cannot possibly review all techniques that content analysts might use, so I focus in this chapter on a few that benefit content analysts especially. Moreover, I will not attempt to discuss these techniques in such detail that readers can replicate them—some require expertise found in common textbooks on research methods, and others are built into readily available statistical packages. Rather, my aim in this chapter is to suggest ways of analyzing and representing results tied to texts.

10.1   TABULATIONS

Owing to the large volumes of text that content analysts typically consider, tabulation is by far the most common technique used to render data comprehensible. *Tabulation* refers to collecting same or similar recording units in categories and presenting counts of how many instances are found in each. Tabulations produce tables of *absolute frequencies,* such as the number of words in each category occurring in a body of text, or of *relative frequencies,* such as percentages expressed relative to the sample size, proportions of a total, or probabilities. Measures of volume, column inches, time, space, or other quantitative indices have the same origin. They enumerate standard units of measurement of certain qualities of text and need not be treated differently here. Frequencies and related measures are convenient shortcuts to long lists and provide entry to statistical considerations. Although frequencies are often celebrated for their precision and simplicity, they should not be granted any special scientific significance. In comparing the results of tabulations, readers of frequency data typically apply several interpretive standards, often without being explicit about them. Content analysts should recognize and note them explicitly.

Content analysts refer to the standard of a *uniform distribution* when reporting that the frequency in one category is larger or smaller than the average frequency for all categories. The idea of bias in reporting, such as a newspaper's attending to one candidate for political office more than to another, exemplifies the implicit use of this standard. If coverage, both favorable and unfavorable, were the same for both candidates, analysts would not call this bias and probably would not bother to write about it—except perhaps in surprise, because this rarely happens. Figure 10.1, which is taken from Gerbner, Gross, Signorielli, Morgan, and Jackson-Beeck's (1979) work on television violence, invites questions about such issues as why weekend children's programs are so much more violent than other programs and which networks increased or decreased the violence in their programming from 1977 to 1978. When content analysts find observed frequencies noteworthy enough to report, this implies their deviation from what would not be noteworthy, and that is usually when differences among them are absent, which is true for a distribution in which frequencies are uniform

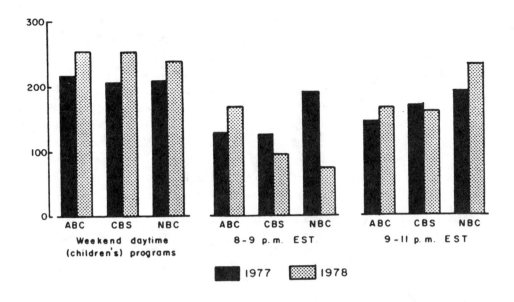

Figure 10.1   Bar Graph Representation of Frequencies
SOURCE: Gerbner et al. (1979).

for all categories. The bar graph in Figure 10.3, which comes from Freeman's (2001) study of letters to auto industry shareholders, does not even show frequencies, displaying only deviations from their average, just what is significant.

When analysts observe changes in frequencies over time, they are likely to ask why some changes are irregular and deviate from what would be expected if changes were regular and predictable. They then refer to a *stable pattern* as an interpretive standard; deviations from that pattern are noticed and considered important. Figure 10.2, which comes from an analysis conducted by Strodthoff, Hawkins, and Schoenfeld (1985), shows trend lines for environmental content, environmentalism, and substantive content of special-interest and general-audience channels, largely magazines. The researchers also list four kinds of events in hopes that these might explain the deviations from the otherwise smooth increase over time.

Equally important and perhaps more typical in the content analysis literature is the standard of *accurate representation*, which is implied when an analyst notes that the relative frequencies differ from what would be expected if the data were a statistically correct representation of a population. This standard was introduced by Berelson and Salter (1946), who compared the population of characters featured in magazine fiction with the known demographics of the U.S. population; they found that minorities and poor people were all but absent in magazine fiction, and that popular heroes were overrepresented. Many critics of the mass media have noted that the population of television characters is not representative of the U.S. population or of the members of the mass-media audience. In early television research, analysts demonstrated this especially for ethnic groups but also for people in particular occupations, people with low socioeconomic status, women in positions of leadership, and elderly people, and these studies were used to infer social prejudices, economic interests, and technological biases.

Whether a population of audience members is the appropriate standard against which the population of television characters should be judged is debatable. Many popular figures, from film stars to television commentators, exist only in the media, not in any unmediated population, and there are good reasons popular talents are more likely to be shown on the screen than on the street. In any case, application of the standard of accurate representation can have political consequences. For example, content analysis research in the late 1950s demonstrated the systematic underrepresentation of African Americans on U.S. television, and these research findings contributed to the eventual achievement of at least some racial balance on TV.

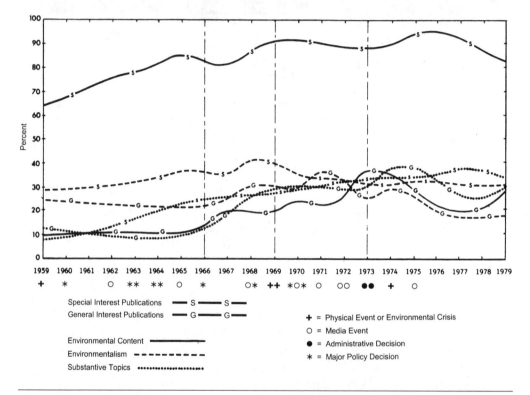

Figure 10.2   Trend Lines for Environmental Content, Environmentalism, and Substantive Content of Special-Interest and General-Audience Channels Juxtaposed With "Real World" Events

SOURCE: Strodthoff et al. (1985, fig. 4).

 ## CROSS-TABULATIONS, ASSOCIATIONS, AND CORRELATIONS

The standard of *chance* is probably most common in statistical accounts of content analysis findings. It arises from analysts' efforts to cross-tabulate the

frequencies of several variables and to observe the frequencies of co-occurrences of values or categories rather than of simple categories. For example, a content analysis of 2,430 acts performed by television characters yielded the observed/expected frequencies of co-occurrences shown in Table 10.1 (Brouwer, Clark, Gerbner, & Krippendorff, 1969). Simple frequencies say nothing about relationships between content variables. Table 10.1, for example, shows that good characters are the origin of most acts, a total of 1,125, followed by 935 acts by bad characters and 370 by neutral ones. Out of the 1,125 acts by good characters, most (751) are unrelated to the law. Although these are large frequencies, and far from uniformly distributed, by themselves they say little about the relationship between the favorable-unfavorable evaluation of television characters and their association with the law. If one is interested in the statistical relationship between two variables, one must compare the observed frequencies of co-occurrences with those obtained by chance. In cross-tabulations, frequencies are at the level of chance when all columns and all rows are proportional to their respective margins, which means that the marginal frequencies explain the distribution of frequencies within the table. In Table 10.1, the frequencies obtainable by chance are shown in italics directly below the observed frequencies, which are shown in bold-face type.

Table 10.1   Cross-Tabulation of Frequencies of Acts Engaged in by Characters in Fictional Television Programming

Acts Initiated by Fictional Characters who are:

	Good	Neutral	Bad	
Associated with Law Enforcement	**369**	**27**	**23**	419
	194	*64*	*161*	
Unrelated to Law	**751**	**328**	**454**	1533
	710	*233*	*590*	
Criminals	**5**	**15**	**458**	478
	221	*73*	*184*	
Totals of	1125	370	935	2430 Acts

SOURCE: Brouwer et al. (1969).

What is noteworthy in such a table are co-occurrences of categories whose observed frequencies deviate significantly from what would be expected when variables were independent and co-occurrences were chance events. In Table 10.1, the largest frequency of 751 is also nearly as expected (710 is the expected frequency) and thus does not contribute to the significance of the relationship between the two variables. In fact, when one uses a χ^2 test to establish this significance, the cells that make the largest contribution to this relationship are the four corner cells, which indicate the extremes of good and bad and of upholding and breaking the law. The differences between the observed and the expected frequencies in these cells tested statistically significant, and thus can be interpreted as supporting the statistical hypothesis that the *good guys* are more likely acting on the side of the law, whereas the bad guys are acting in opposition to it. I say "statistical hypothesis" here because the table shows that there are exceptions, although significantly fewer than chance.

Cross-tabulations are not limited to two or three variables, but they are more easily visualized and interpreted when the number of variables is small. Multivariate techniques are available for testing complex structures within multidimensional data (Reynolds, 1977).

When variables are nominal (an unordered set of categories), we speak of associations, as shown above, but when they consist of numerically ordered values, we speak of correlations. The standard of chance is common to both, but the use of correlation coefficients adds another standard to that of chance, the standard of *linearity*. Correlation coefficients are zero if data are as expected by chance, and they are unity when all data fall on a straight line, a regression line (see also Chapter 11, section 11.5). Otherwise, correlation measures the degree to which data resemble a regression line as opposed to chance. Above-chance statistical relations—associations and correlations—may be of two kinds:

- Within the results of a content analysis, as in Table 10.1

- Between the results of a content analysis and data obtained independently, as in Figure 10.3

Because content analysts control the definitions of their variables, there is always the danger that the statistical relations within content analysis results are artifacts of the recording instrument. In Table 10.1, the positive association (good cops, bad criminals) is notable because the underlying relation could have gone in the other direction (bad cops, good criminals). But a positive association between, say, feminine-masculine personality traits (gender) and sex (its biological manifestation) is expected in our culture precisely because these two variables are semantically related. Association and correlation coefficients do not respond to semantic relationships between variables, and if such relationships do exist, these correlation measures are partly spurious and uninformative by themselves.

Correlations between the results of a content analysis and data obtained by other means are less likely so affected because the two kinds of variables differ in how the data are generated. Figure 10.3 comes from Freeman's (2001) study of U.S. auto industry letters to shareholders. Freeman compared the attention paid to a set of categories functional to a corporation in Chrysler's letters to shareholders with the company's return on assets and found a strong negative correlation between these variables.

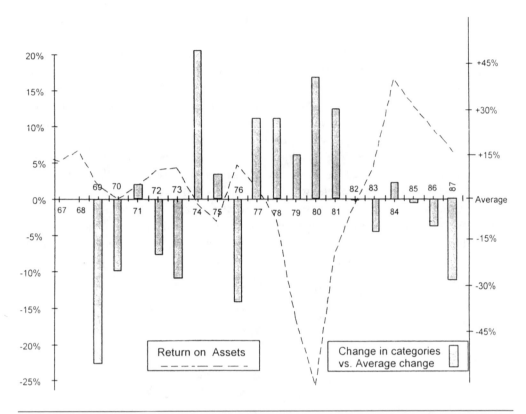

Figure 10.3   Correlation Between Chrysler's Return on Assets and Year-to-Year Attention to Functional Categories in Chrysler's Letters to Shareholders

SOURCE: Freeman (2001, fig. 5).

MULTIVARIATE TECHNIQUES   10.3

The standard of chance underlies most multivariate techniques of data analysis and representation. Correlations are worth reporting only when the data deviate significantly from chance, ideally approximating linearity. One prominent technique is multiple regression analysis. It presupposes that the variables being analyzed are of two kinds: independent and dependent. The variation in the dependent variables is to be explained, and the variation in the independent variables serves as the explanation. Indeed, many questions that content analysts pursue are reducible to problems of regression. For example, which characteristics of novels predict their popularity? A clear answer to that question would please authors and publishers alike. Or which factors explain media content—government actions, interest groups, economics (advertising), technology, or artistic talent? Or which features of messages are effective in encouraging members of a target population to change their health care habits? The most common kind of regression analysis orders a number of independent variables according to how much they contribute to predicting the values of one chosen dependent variable.

Another multivariate technique entails the use of structural equations. Each variable is considered a dependent variable of all other variables. Only under certain conditions can such a network of multivariate correlations be interpreted in causal terms. Constraints of space prevent me from discussing these conditions here, but I must note that it is extremely difficult to establish causality from exclusively textual data. One important ingredient of the use of causal explanations is time. Figure 10.4 shows the results of a path analysis conducted by Weaver, Buddenbaum, and Fair (1985) that features regression correlation (beta) coefficients above .20 between variables whose relationship to the development of the media in Third World countries was suspected. Weaver et al. compared this path analysis with one that used the same variables but also included data concerning all countries and concluded that in most Third World countries, the media tend to be used to facilitate the functioning of the economy and to perpetuate the power of the rulers.

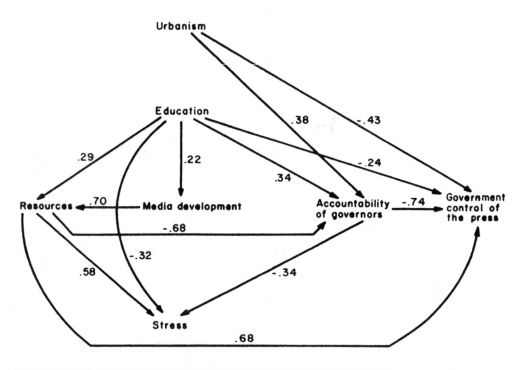

Figure 10.4 Paths for Predicting Governmental Control of the Press for Third World Countries, 1950–1979

SOURCE: Weaver et al. (1985, fig. 2).

Correlational techniques are not limited to linear relationships, however. A good illustration of this is found in the work of Namenwirth (1973; Namenwirth & Weber, 1987), who analyzed the Lasswellian values (see Chapter 8, section 8.5.3) in speeches from the British throne between 1689 and 1972, covering the British mercantilist and capitalist periods. Over such a long period, fluctuations in the frequencies of values are to be expected, but instead of correlating these with external events that the British Empire had to face, Namenwirth considered values as expressing the workings of an autonomous cultural/political system in which the frequencies of one kind decline as others rise, in endless cycles. To test this hypothesis, he applied a kind of Fourier analysis to these fluctuations. A Fourier analysis decomposes the complex fluctuations of a measure—whether of waves of light or of economic activity—over time into a series of additive sinus curves. Namenwirth identified at least three concurring cycles that turned out to explain much of the variance in the data: a 146-year cycle, a 52-year cycle, and a 32-year cycle.

Figure 10.5 depicts the internal structure of the 52-year cycle. Categories of values that peak are listed at the rim of the circle. Accordingly, the

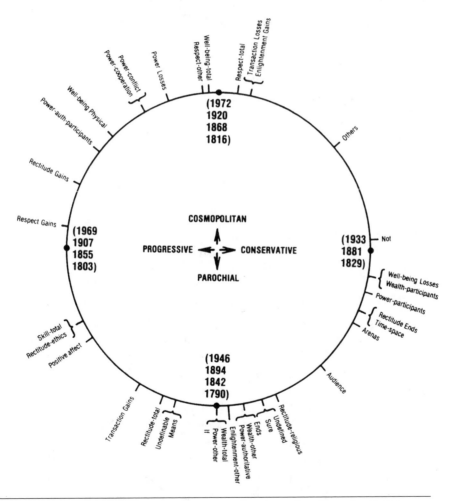

Figure 10.5   A 52-Year Cycle of Values Found in Speeches from the British Throne, 1689–1972

SOURCE: Namenwirth and Weber (1987, p. 139, fig. 5.5; also in Namenwirth, 1973).

"6 o'clock" position, corresponding to the years 1790, 1842, 1894, and 1946, witnesses concern about the poor performance of the economy, prevailing (un)certainties, and search for knowledge (enlightenment). In the "9 o'clock" position, rectitude and respect gain and concerns for social welfare and conflict grow. In the "12 o'clock" position, welfare and respect reach their peaks, and enlightenment co-occurs with an international orientation. At the "3 o'clock" position, wealth, trade, and conflict become issues, and well-being is feared to degenerate. In the center of this figure, Namenwirth summarizes this dynamic as a thematic progression from parochial to progressive, to cosmopolitan, to conservative, and back to the beginning. This interpretation loosely follows Parsons and Bales's (1953) theory suggesting that every society, facing four functional requirements, cycles from an expressive phase to an adaptive phase, then to an instrumental phase, then to an integrative phase, and then back to an expressive phase, and so on. One could describe this technique as one of curve fitting. Here the usual linearity assumptions of correlation coefficients are replaced by sinus curves.

10.4   FACTOR ANALYSIS AND MULTIDIMENSIONAL SCALING

Factor analysis, a favorite method of behavioral scientists in the 1960s and 1970s, is a way to summarize the correlations among many variables by constructing a space with fewer dimensions in which these data might be represented with a minimum of loss in explanatory power. It computes a set of hypothetical and ideally orthogonal dimensions or variables and offers measures of how closely the original variables are correlated with these. These correlations (of the original variables with the virtual dimensions) provide clues that help analysts to make sense of the virtual dimensions. This is the path that Osgood (1974a, 1974b) took to obtain what he called the "basic dimensions" of affective meaning. He used data in the form of numerous semantic differential scales and found three basic dimensions that explain between 50% and 75% of the variance. After examining which of the original scales correlated highly with these, he called them the "evaluative" (good-bad), "activity" (active-passive), and "potency" (strong-weak) dimensions of affective meaning (see also Chapter 7, section 7.4.4).

Whereas factor analysis reduces the dimensionality of the original data while trying to preserve their variance, multidimensional scaling (MDS) reduces the dimensionality of the original (geometric) distances between data points, trying to preserve their positions relative to each other. It requires data on how far apart pairs of elements, concepts, and even variables are. The analyst can fulfill this condition in various ways, such as by measuring differences, dissimilarities, disagreements, dissociations, or lack of co-occurrences between all pairs, whether using objective measurements or subjective judgments. Even correlation coefficients can be and have been converted into distances and subjected to MDS techniques.

MDS starts out with a space of as many dimensions as there are data points, which usually escapes human comprehension. It then attempts to remove one dimension at a time, so as to represent the data in fewer dimensions with a minimum of adjustments to the distances between the data points—much as when one attempts to represent a three-dimensional distribution of points in two dimensions. Figure 10.6 displays the MDS results of a content analysis conducted by Andsager and Powers (1999), a three-dimensional representation of a set of frames used by four women's magazines in discussing breast cancer. The point of this presentation is to suggest which concepts, ideas, and media sources—here called "frames"—are similar, which cluster in small areas, and which are far apart. If all data points were equidistant from one another to begin with, there would be no point in scaling down the dimensionality of these data. Apparently, the standard against which MDS results become noteworthy is that of equal differences.

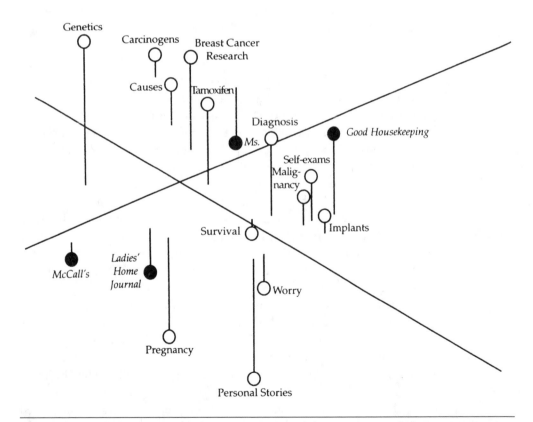

Figure 10.6   Three-Dimensional Representation of the Frames Used by Four Women's Magazines to Discuss Breast Cancer

SOURCE: Andsager and Powers (1999, p. 541, fig. 1).

10.5	**IMAGES, PORTRAYALS, SEMANTIC NODES, AND PROFILES**

Content analysts often focus on one or a few concepts, persons, or events and seek to ascertain how they are depicted or portrayed in text and what symbolic qualities readers might find associated with them. In the content analysis literature, titles like "Medicine in Medieval Literature," "The Rôle of Scientists in Popular Media," "The Human Body in Women's and Men's Magazines," "How the Portrayal of the United States Has Shifted in Arab Dailies," and "The Public Image of AT&T" abound. Researchers seek to answer questions of this kind by analyzing the linguistic or textual contexts in which references to the selected ideas occur.

In attribution analysis, the researcher tabulates the adjectives used to describe a chosen concept. A single list of attributes is quite uninformative, however, unless it is compared with some other list that provides a standard against which deviations may be noted. In a comparative attribution analysis, at least two lists are contrasted—for example, the image of one candidate for political office may be compared with the image of his or her opponent; or the portrayals of a country in textbooks before a war may be compared with those after that war; or the way one medium depicts a political scandal may be compared with how another medium covers that scandal. The analyst compares the lists to finds out what attributes they share and what attributes distinguish among them. If all the attributes are shared among all the lists, there is little for the analyst to say. This reveals the standard that is common to this kind of analysis, the *sharing of attributions* against which differences in portrayals become noteworthy. Some researchers who conduct attribution analyses use expectations as a basis for comparison, reporting on how and how much a given image deviates from the typical or usual. Unless a researcher has data on such expectations, formal tests may not be applicable. However, verbal highlights of what is unexpected or abnormal are common to many interpretations of images, portrayals, and the like (see the discussion of interactive-hermeneutic explorations in Chapter 12, section 12.6).

Another standard, common largely in linguistics, appears in the comparison of the linguistic context of one word or expression with the set of all grammatically and semantically acceptable contexts in which that word or expression can occur. The subset of actually used linguistic contexts is then equated with the meaning of the word or expression. This idea can easily be expanded to the meanings of politicians, professionals, academic disciplines, and countries.

Thus the notion of "attribute" should not be construed too narrowly. The image of a U.S. president that spin doctors and advertisers are so worried about can hardly be reduced to a list of adjectives. This would be a convenient but limited operationalization. It may have to include a president's speeches, editorials discussing what the president does, opinion polls, even cartoons presenting that president's public or private life. What is particular about the image of U.S. presidents is how what is said about them differs from what is said about comparable other personalities. Similarly, the image of, say, human genetics in science fiction makes sense only in comparison with how other scientific theories enter this genre.

Computer-aided text analysis (CATA), which I discuss in depth in Chapter 12, has provided us with several useful devices for the analysis of images and portrayals. One is the KWIC (keyword in context) list, a tabulation of sentences or text fractions that contain a particular word or phrase. Figure 12.1 shows such a tabulation for the word *play*. Weber (1984, p. 131) compared the KWIC lists for the word *rights* as used by Republicans and Democrats and found significant differences in how the two groups employed the word; these differences are what make Weber's findings interesting. (See Chapter 12 for a fuller discussion of Weber's study.) Researchers can examine the contexts of keywords or key phrases by using the "find" function of ordinary word processing programs, although this is a cumbersome method. Qualitative text analysis software moves from listing the contexts of single words to listing the contexts of categories of textual units (see Chapter 12, section 12.6).

Analyzing the nodes of semantic networks in terms of how one node is connected to others follows the same logic. For example, Figure 12.5 depicts the concept "hacker" as it appears in the narratives of students describing each other. In such networks, nodes are typically characterized in one of two ways:

- They may be characterized in terms of measures that describe their position within a network—for example, with how many other nodes they are connected, their centrality or peripherality, or how often they occur. Carley (1997) has measured the positional properties of nodes in terms of density, conductivity, and intensity.

- They may be characterized in terms of the semantic connections between them and any other nodes. Figure 10.7, for example, depicts the semantic connections among nodes found by researchers who examined the characteristics attributed to robots in post-1960s texts (Palmquist, Carley, & Dale, 1997). This figure also displays the percentages of texts in which the connections occur.

Comparison of the linguistic environments in which a concept occurs gives rise to a variety of analytical possibilities. Two concepts that occur (or can occur) in the same linguistic environment are interchangeable, have the same meanings, and are considered synonymous. Concepts that mediate between many other concepts are the central concepts of a belief system, a story, or a discourse, which a network represents. An analysis of the environments that two concepts do not share elucidates differences in their meanings. "True" opposites share the environments of their genus but differ in everything else.

Figure 10.7 is one of several "maps" that Palmquist et al. (1997) compared in their examination of texts involving robots written before, during, and after 1960. What they found supported their hypotheses about changes in emotions associated with the robot image—over time, the texts showed emerging trust, loyalty, and friendship that increasingly counterbalanced persistent fears.

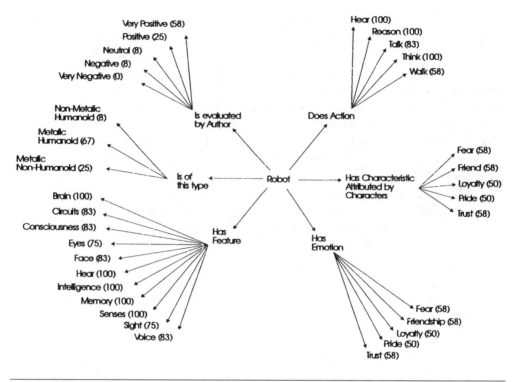

Figure 10.7   The Robot Image: Robot Types, Features, and Actions From Post-1960s Texts

SOURCE: Palmquist et al. (1997, p. 178, fig. 10.4).

When analysts use profiles—whether of potential authors of unsigned documents, applicants for a certain job, or persons with mental illnesses—they apply the same interpretive standard, but with the addition that the attributes, correlates, or linguistic environments must be predictive of something. That is, they must answer a question, such as, Who wrote the unsigned document? Who is most likely to succeed in a given job? How should a therapist treat a patient who has a particular manner of talking?

Take the analysis of plagiarism as an example. Suppose that there are two literary works by different authors, A and B, and B is alleged to have plagiarized A's work. Suspicions that one author has plagiarized the work of another are usually grounded in the recognition of surprising similarities between the two works in word choices, grammatical constructions, plot structure, outline, and so on. Even if the similarities are compelling, they do not constitute sufficient evidence of plagiarism. Before content analysts can enter a plagiarism dispute, it must be established that B had access to A's work before or while writing the disputed work. This is the easy part, to be addressed by a court of law. Once the accessibility of A's work to B has been established, analysts can focus their attention on how the similarities between the two works can be explained. Figure 10.8 diagrams the relationships that content analysts may have to consider. The similarity or agreement

α_1 could be due to B's shameless copying of A's work, B's creativity (chance), or A's and B's common literary and/or cultural background. If the similarity α_1 can be shown to exceed α_2 substantially, this would add weight in favor of plagiarism on B's part. If α_3 exceeds α_1 to a degree better than chance, then A may actually be the plagiarist of B's previous work, rather than B having plagiarized A.

Authors, by definition, create new literature, and A and B could have come to these similarities on separate paths, especially if they are acquainted with each other's previously published work. Previous works may not be available for comparison or may not be considered relevant when the similarities being examined concern content, subject matter, or unusual personal experiences. But even the most imaginative writers rely on a background of literature, education, cultural practices, media exposure, and common sense that they share widely with others—otherwise their works would be unintelligible. This common background provides authors with a vocabulary of metaphors, sayings, myths, and themes that they weave into their writing. Most similarities between different authors' works are due to the background they share without realizing it. In a famous plagiarism case concerning a book about teaching in New York, the similarity turned out to be explained by the fact that, unknown to plaintiff and defendant, they had both taught in the same classroom in different years. If one subtracts the vocabulary and background that A and B share from the profiles of the two works, one is left with two profiles whose similarity or difference can be explained by creativity (or chance) or plagiarism. If the remaining similarities are well above chance, this finding might support a charge of plagiarism. The analysis of images, portrayals, semantic nodes, or profiles can lead in numerous directions.

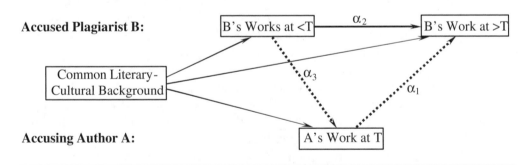

Figure 10.8   Comparisons of Works Needed to Establish or Dispel Accusations of Plagiarism

CONTINGENCIES AND CONTINGENCY ANALYSIS

10.6

Contingency analysis is a technique that enables researchers to infer networks of associations from patterns of co-occurrences in texts, whether they are generated by a source or attended to by readers. Contingency analysis started with the observation that symbols often occur in pairs of opposites, that concepts or ideas form clusters. Contingency analysis is based on the assumption (analytical construct) that concepts that are closely associated cognitively will also be closely related proximally. Content analysts have successfully applied this assumption to individual authors, to social groups with common prejudices or ideological commitments, and to whole cultures permeated by cultural stereotypes or conventions. Experiments have shown that exposure to statistical contingencies in messages can cause corresponding association in their receivers as well, followed by the reproduction of these contingencies in speech, so that contingency analysis can be used to infer associations not only in the sources of texts but also in the audiences that are exposed to such statistical contingencies (Osgood, 1959, pp. 55–61). Regardless of these correlational validations, contingency analysis is an analytical technique in its own right.

Contingency analysis starts with a set of recording units, each of which is characterized by a set of attributes, concepts, or features that are either present or absent. The choice of recording units is important insofar as such units must contain sufficient numbers of co-occurrences. A word is too small a unit. A sentence usually contains several concepts, but units larger than sentences tend to be more productive. Osgood (1959), who first outlined this analysis, illustrated the steps involved in his analysis of 38 talks given by W. J. Cameron on the *Ford Sunday Evening Hour* radio program. First, Osgood regarded each talk as one recording unit and recorded the presence or absence of 27 conceptual categories in each unit. In the second step, he counted the co-occurrences of these categories and entered them in a square matrix of all pairs of categories (attributes, concepts, or features). In the third step, he tested the statistical significance of these co-occurrences. Co-occurrences that are significantly above chance suggest the presence of associations, whereas co-occurrences that are significantly below chance suggest the presence of dissociations.

The interpretive standard implicit in this technique is that of co-occurrences by chance, of course, a complete disconnection of the categories in question. Osgood plausibly argues that both directions of deviation from chance are of psychological importance. The association pattern that Osgood inferred from this rather small data set is depicted in Figure 10.9. Here, mentions of factories, industry, machines, production, and so on (FAC) tended to be associated with mentions of progress (PRO); Ford and Ford cars (FD); free enterprise and initiative (ENT); laymen, farmers, shopkeepers, and the like (LAY); and business, selling, and the like (BUS). But when Cameron talked about these things, he tended *not* to talk about (to dissociate them from) such categories as youth (YTH), intellectuals, lily-livered bookmen, and so on (INT), and disease (DIS), which form another cluster of associations, dissociated from the former cluster. The figure shows also associations among violence and destruction (DES); assorted "isms," such as communism, fascism, and totalitarianism (ISM); fear and bewilderment (FEAR); and sundry evils (RVL) (Osgood, 1959, pp. 67–68). Even without having heard these speeches, one can get a sense of the mentality of the speaker and of the times in which these speeches were broadcast.

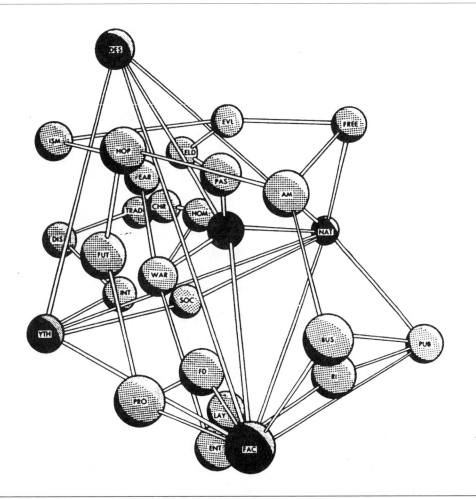

Figure 10.9   Spatial Representation of an Association Structure

SOURCE: Osgood (1959, p. 68, fig. 4).

The fundamental assumption underlying the analysis of contingencies is that co-occurrences in texts indicate associations in someone's mind or underlying cultural practices. This assumption, along with the idea of neuronal networks, has motivated Woelfel (1993, 1997) to develop software that allows a researcher to tabulate all co-occurrences of words within a sliding window of a specified length (e.g., 100 characters) and then compute clusters of contingencies. (I discuss this software, CatPac, in more detail in Chapter 12, section 12.5.2.) Incidentally, this idea underlies computational procedures that have recently been given the fancy name of "data mining." Text searches can identify contingencies as well within other kinds of windows, sentences, paragraphs, and documents. Thus several computer-aided approaches to text attend to contingencies within linguistic contexts. What distinguishes the latter from what Osgood had proposed is the absence of human readers, coders, or transcribers of the categories that are subjected to contingency analysis. Woelfel's aim is to bypass human readers or coders altogether, but the results that such software produces are bound to be shallow compared with analyses in which intelligent human readers are involved.

When tables of possible co-occurrences become very large, analysts may find it difficult to conceptualize the results. Examining a matrix of something like 200×200 associations between concepts, which is not unusual in content analysis, is a formidable task, and analysts trying to discover patterns in such a flood of numerical data are likely to overlook important relationships. Then clustering becomes important.

10.7   CLUSTERING

Clustering operationalizes something humans do most naturally: forming perceptual wholes from things that are connected, belong together, or have common meanings, while separating them from things whose relationships seem accidental or meaningless. Clustering is closely allied with the conception of content as a representation, inviting abstraction, producing a hierarchy of representations that, on any one level, preserve what matters and omit only insignificant details from the original data. Procedurally, clustering either works from the bottom up, by lumping together objects, attributes, concepts, or people according to what they share, or proceeds from the top down, by dividing sets of such entities into classes whose boundaries reflect the more important differences between them. The direction that clustering takes results from the analyst's choices of the similarity measure and the clustering criterion. Clustering techniques differ widely regarding these. Contingency is but one similarity measure; others are agreement, correlation, proximity, the number of shared attributes, and common meanings, either by semantic definition or by relations within a thesaurus.

The choice of a clustering criterion is decisive for the kind of clusters a particular analysis provides. Some clustering criteria create long and snakelike clusters, whereas others produce compact and circular clusters. Some are sensitive to how much diversity accumulates within a cluster, others are not, assuring only the largest dissimilarities between the forming clusters. Under ideal circumstances, a clustering criterion reflects the way clusters are formed in the reality of the data source and relies on semantic similarities rather than purely syntactical ones. Content analysts must bear in mind that different clustering procedures may yield vastly different results; thus, to avoid ending up relying on arbitrary findings, they must always justify their use of particular clustering techniques in relation to the contexts of their analyses.

The most common of the available clustering procedures consists of the following iterative steps:

1. Within a matrix of similarity measures, search for two clusters (initially of two unclustered objects) that are, by the chosen criterion, most similar and the merger of which will least affect the overall measure of the differences in the data.

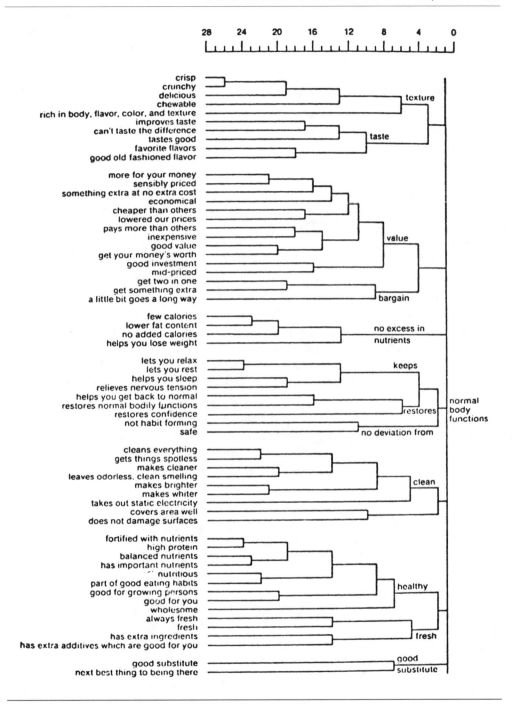

Figure 10.10 Part of a Large Dendrogram Resulting From Clustering Advertising Appeals

SOURCE: Adapted from Dziurzynski (1977, pp. 25, 39, 40, 41, 50, figs. 3, 6, 11, 12, 13, 14, 53).

2. Lump these, taking into account the losses incurred within the newly formed cluster.

3. Recompute all measures of similarity with the newly formed cluster, thereby creating a new matrix of similarity measures within which the next two candidates for lumping are to be found.

4. Record the clustering step taken and the losses incurred for the user to retrace.

5. Repeat steps 1 through 4 until there is nothing left to merge (see Krippendorff, 1980a).

For a small amount of data and simple criteria, an analyst may even do clustering by hand.

Clustering steps are typically recorded in the form of so-called dendrograms, which are treelike diagrams that indicate when and which objects are merged and the losses the clustering incurred. Figure 10.10 shows a fraction of Dziurzynski's (1977) analysis of some 300 television advertising appeals. The resulting classification of appeals into those referring to texture, taste, value, and bargain appears to have considerable face validity.

As suggested above, clustering is popular in content analysis because, unlike factor analysis and multidimensional scaling, it is based on intuitively meaningful similarities among units of analysis, and its resulting hierarchies resemble the conceptualization of text on various levels of abstraction. This is why so many clustering algorithms are available. Often, however, the creators of these algorithms do not reveal how the algorithms work, and that puts the burden of proving their structural validity on the content analysts who use them (see Chapter 13, section 13.2.3).

CHAPTER 11

Reliability

This chapter discusses two general purposes of reliability in scientific research. It distinguishes among three designs for generating data to measure reliability, which leads to three manifestations of reliability: stability, reproducibility, and accuracy. All turn out to be functions of the agreement achieved among observers, coders, judges, or measuring instruments. Krippendorff's agreement coefficient alpha is presented as a tool to assess such agreement, and its computation is demonstrated, starting with the simplest kind of data and moving to embrace the most common forms, nominal data, several metrics, multiple observers, and incomplete data. The chapter also discusses the statistical issues of sample sizes, alpha's distribution, and reliability standards.

WHY RELIABILITY? | 11.1

Data, by definition, are the trusted ground for reasoning, discussion, or calculation. To stand on indisputable ground, content analysts must be confident that their data (a) have been generated with all conceivable precautions in place against known pollutants, distortions, and biases, intentional or accidental, and (b) mean the same thing for everyone who uses them. Reliability grounds this confidence empirically. There are two ways of operationalizing this confidence. In Kaplan and Goldsen's (1965) words: "The importance of reliability rests on the assurance it provides that data are obtained independent of the measuring event, instrument or person. Reliable data, by definition, are data that remain constant throughout variations in the measuring process" (pp. 83–84). Accordingly, a research procedure is reliable when it responds to the same phenomena in the same way regardless of the circumstances of its implementation. This is the measurement theory conception of reliability.

The other operationalization acknowledges that the phenomena of interest, which are encoded or inscribed in analyzable data, usually disappear right after they have been observed and recorded—human voices, historical events, radio transmissions, and even physical experiments. The analyst's ability to examine these phenomena in their absence, compare them with other phenomena, and, particularly, discuss them with members of a community of stakeholders relies heavily on a consensual reading and use of the data that represent, point to, or invoke experiences with the phenomena of interest. Empirical inquiries into bygone phenomena have no choice other than to presume that their data can be trusted to mean the same to all of their users. In content analysis, this means that the reading of textual data as well as of the research results is replicable elsewhere, that researchers demonstrably agree on what they are talking about. Here, then, reliability is the degree to which members of a designated community agree on the readings, interpretations, responses to, or uses of given texts or data. This is an interpretivist conception of reliability.

In either case, researchers need to demonstrate the trustworthiness of their data by measuring their reliability. If the results of reliability testing are compelling, researchers may proceed with the analysis of their data. If not, doubts as to what these data mean prevail, and their analysis is hard to justify.

To perform *reliability tests*, analysts require data in addition to the data whose reliability is in question. These are called *reliability data*, and analysts obtain them by duplicating their research efforts under various conditions—for example, by using several researchers with diverse personalities, by working in differing environments, or by relying on different but functionally equal measuring devices. Reliability is indicated by substantial agreement of results among these duplications.

In contrast to reliability, *validity* concerns truths. Researchers cannot ascertain validity through duplications. *Validity tests* pit the claims resulting from a research effort against evidence obtained independent of that effort. Thus, whereas reliability provides assurances that particular research results can be duplicated, that no (or only a negligible amount) of extraneous "noise" has entered the process and polluted the data or perturbed the research results, validity provides assurances that the claims emerging from the research are borne out in fact. Reliability is not concerned with the world outside of the research process. All it can do is assure researchers that their procedures can be trusted to have responded to real phenomena, without claiming knowledge of what these phenomena "really" are.

In content analysis, reliability and validity can be related by two propositions and a conjecture:

- *Unreliability limits the chance of validity.* In everyday life, disagreements among eyewitness accounts make it difficult for third parties to know what actually happened or whether the witnesses are reporting on the same event. For such accounts to be considered reliable, witnesses must concur well above chance. If the coding of textual matter is the product of chance, it may well include a valid account of what was observed or read, but researchers would not be able to identify that account to a degree better than chance. Thus, the more unreliable a procedure, the less likely it is to result in data that lead to valid conclusions.

- *Reliability does not guarantee validity.* Two observers of the same event who hold the same conceptual system, prejudice, or interest may well agree on what they see but still be objectively wrong. Content analysts are not exempt from such concurrences. Because they have acquired a language and concepts that make them see the world from the unique perspective of their academic discipline, their observations and readings are based in a consensus that is not likely shared by many people outside of their scholarly community. Content analysts' shared worldview may deviate radically from the worldviews of those whose intentions, perceptions, and actions are at issue and could validate the intended inferences. A highly reliable research process may well be artificial and thus have little chance of being substantiated by evidence on the intentions, perceptions, actions, or events that were inferred. Even perfectly dependable mechanical instruments, such as computers, can be wrong—reliably. Thus a reliable process may or may not lead to valid outcomes.

This relationship is illustrated in Figure 11.1, which depicts reliability as repeating the same score and validity as being on-target. The top part of the figure suggests that with diminishing reliability, validity increasingly becomes a chance event. The bottom part suggests that reliability does not guarantee being on-target.

Thus reliability is a necessary, but not a sufficient, condition for validity. The following conjecture does not have the logical force of the preceding propositions, but it is born out of the experiences by numerous content analysts:

- *In the pursuit of high reliability, validity tends to get lost.* This statement describes the analyst's common dilemma of having to choose between interesting but nonreproducible interpretations that intelligent readers of texts may offer each other in conversations and oversimplified or superficial but reliable text analyses generated through the use of computers or carefully instructed human coders. Merritt's (1966) study of the rising national consciousness among the 13 original American colonies on the basis of newspaper accounts provides an example of a case in which complexity of interpretation was sacrificed for reliability. Because national sentiments are difficult to define and identify, Merritt elected to enumerate the mentions of American place-names instead. A shift in the use of the names of places in colonial England to the names of places in America may well be an attractive index, and counting words instead of themes causes fewer reliability problems, however, the use of place-names surely is only one manifestation of "national consciousness," and a richer account of this phenomenon could well have led to more interesting inferences. Merritt's index is attractive, as I have suggested, but its validity remains thin.

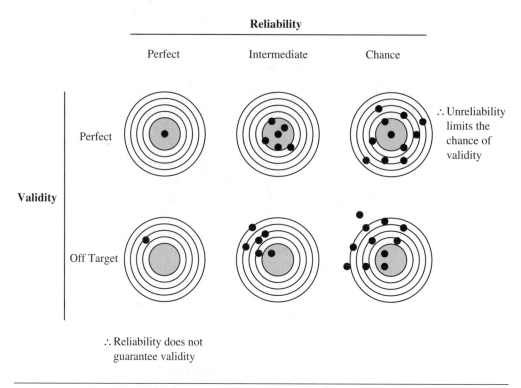

Figure 11.1   The Relationship Between Reliability and Validity

The use of computers in content analysis, praised for increasing reliability, has highlighted this dilemma even more clearly. Computers process character strings, not meanings. They sort volumes of words without making sense of them. Although it is possible to program computers to perform amazing functions, when analysts rely on them rather than on intelligent readers they run the risk of trivializing the meanings of texts (see Chapter 12, section 12.1). In content analysis, researchers should approach highly reliable procedures with as much caution as they approach fascinating interpretations that nobody can replicate.

11.2   RELIABILITY DESIGNS

11.2.1   Types of Reliability

There are three types of reliability: stability, reproducibility, and accuracy (see Table 11.1). These are distinguished not by how agreement is measured but by the way the reliability data are obtained. Without information about the

Table 11.1 Typese of Reliability

Reliability	Designs	Causes of Disagreements	Strength
Stability	test-retest	intraobserver inconsistencies	weakest
Reproducibility	test-test	intraobserver inconsistencies + interobserver disagreements	medium
Accuracy	test-standard	intraobserver inconsistencies, + interobserver disagreements, + deviations from a standard	strongest

circumstances under which the data for reliability assessments have been generated, agreement measures remain uninterpretable.

Stability is the degree to which a process is unchanging over time. It is measured as the extent to which a measuring or coding procedure yields the same results on repeated trials. The data for such assessments are created under *test-retest* conditions; that is, one observer rereads, recategorizes, or reanalyzes the same text, usually after some time has elapsed, or the same measuring device is repeatedly applied to one set of objects. Under test-retest conditions, unreliability is manifest in variations in the performance of an observer or measuring device. With reference to humans, such variations, also called *intraobserver disagreement* or *individual inconsistencies,* may be due to insecurity, carelessness, openness to distractions, difficulties in comprehending written instructions, or the tendency to relax performance standards when tired. Even the inherently human characteristic of learning through practice, creatively improving one's performance over time, shows up in disagreements over time. Stability, the weakest form of reliability, is insufficient as the sole criterion for accepting data as reliable. But because test-retest data are the easiest reliability data to obtain, and internal inconsistencies limit other reliabilities as well, measuring stability may be an analyst's first step in establishing the reliability of data.

Reproducibility is the degree to which a process can be replicated by different analysts working under varying conditions, at different locations, or using different but functionally equivalent measuring instruments. Demonstrating reproducibility requires reliability data that are obtained under *test-test* conditions; for example, two or more individuals, working independent of each other, apply the same recording instructions to the same units of analysis. Disagreements between these observers' performances are due to both intraobserver inconsistencies and *interobserver differences* in the interpretation and application of given recording instructions. Compared with stability, reproducibility, which is also variously called *intercoder reliability, intersubjective agreement,* and *parallel-forms reliability,* is a far stronger measure of reliability.

Accuracy is the degree to which a process conforms to its specifications and yields what it is designed to yield. To establish accuracy, analysts must obtain data under *test-standard* conditions; that is, they must compare the performance of one or more data-making procedures with the performance of a procedure that is taken to be correct. Observed disagreements between the two kinds of performances are due to intraobserver inconsistencies, interobserver differences, and *deviations from a given standard*. Because it responds to all three sources of variation, accuracy is the strongest reliability test available. It is surpassed in strength only by validity measures that appear to conform to the test-standard design, but the standard is truth, or at least what is known to be true, a requirement that lies outside reliability considerations (and that I take up in Chapter 13).

When data making is merely clerical or computational, the meaning of accuracy is clear. Typos, for instance, are errors by comparison to existing spelling standards. In linguistics, conversation analysis, and therapeutic contexts, analysts perform accuracy checks by comparing novices' uses of transcription conventions, for example, with those of acknowledged experts. In content analysis, accuracy measurements often include testing the work of trainee coders against standards that have been established by panels of experienced content analysts. In the more problematic parts of content analysis, such as the interpretation and transcription of complex textual matter, suitable accuracy standards are not easy to find. Because interpretations can be compared only with other interpretations, attempts to measure accuracy presuppose the privileging of some interpretations over others, and this puts any claims regarding precision or accuracy on epistemologically shaky grounds. Thus the use of accuracy is limited to coder training and other areas where objective standards are readily available.

Stability, on the other end of the spectrum, is too weak to serve as a reliability measure in content analysis. It cannot respond to individually stable idiosyncrasies, prejudices, ideological commitments, closed-mindedness, or consistent misinterpretations of given coding instructions and texts.

One method that some scholars have mentioned as a reliability test is the split-half technique. This technique would call on content analysts to divide a sample of recording units into two approximately equal parts and have the two parts coded by different observers, one unit at a time. The analysts would then compare the frequency distributions obtained for the two parts. If the difference between the two distributions is statistically insignificant, the data would be considered reliable; otherwise, they would be considered unreliable. However, this measure merely assesses the degree to which two subsamples resemble each other or whether the larger data set can be considered homogeneous. (The test can also be used to determine whether a sample is large enough to represent a population; see Chapter 6, section 6.3.3.) However, as there may be good reasons why two subsamples are different, or no reasons why they should be the same, homogeneity says nothing about whether data can be trusted. In content analysis—or, more generally, when the reliability of categorizing or describing units is at issue—the split-half technique is not a suitable reliability test, and its use must be discouraged as uninformative and misleading.

11.2.2   Conditions for Generating Reliability Data

As noted in Chapter 2 (section 2.1), content analysis must be *reproducible,* at least in principle. To check on this possibility, analysts must generate reliability data at least under test-test conditions and account not only for individual instabilities but also for disagreements among observers, coders, or analysts. Any analysis using observed agreement as a measure of reproducibility must meet the following requirements:

- It must employ communicable coding instructions—that is, an exhaustively formulated, clear, and workable data language plus step-by-step instructions on how to use it. This widely accepted requirement may need to be extended to include rarely mentioned training programs that coders typically undergo before qualifying for the task—otherwise, one may not know what the data mean and how to reproduce them.

- It must employ communicable criteria for the selection of individual observers, coders, or analysts from a population of equally capable individuals who are potentially available for training, instruction, and coding elsewhere.

- It must ensure that the observers who generate the reliability data work independent of each other. Only if such independence is assured can covert consensus be ruled out and the observed agreement be explained in terms of the given instructions and the phenomena observed or the texts interpreted.

Inasmuch as reliability serves as a condition for research to proceed with the data in hand, the content analysis literature is full of evidence of researchers' well-intended but often misguided attempts to manipulate the process of data generation so as to increase the appearance of high levels of agreement. Most of these involve violations of one or more of the above conditions, as the following examples illustrate.

In the belief that consensus is better than individual judgment, some researchers have asked observers to discuss what they read or see and reach their decisions by compromise or majority vote. This practice may indeed moderate the effects of individual idiosyncrasies and take advantage of the possibility that two observers can notice more than one, but data generated in this way neither ensure reproducibility nor reveal its extent. In groups like these, observers are known to negotiate and to yield to each other in tit-for-tat exchanges, with prestigious group members dominating the outcome. Here, observing and coding come to reflect the social structure of the group, which is nearly impossible to communicate to other researchers and replicate. Moreover, subjective feelings of accomplishment notwithstanding, the data that are generated by such consensual coding afford no reliability test. They are akin to data generated by a single observer. Reproducibility requires at least two independent observers. To substantiate the contention that coding by groups is superior to coding by separate individuals, a researcher would have to compare the data generated by at least two such groups and two individuals, each working independently.

It is not uncommon for researchers to ask observers to work separately, but to consult each other whenever unanticipated problems arise. Such consultation is a response to a common problem: The writers of the coding instructions have not been able to anticipate all possible ways of expressing relevant matter. Ideally, these instructions should include every applicable rule on which agreement is being measured. However, the very act of observers' discussing emerging problems creates interpretations of the existing coding instructions to cope with the newly discovered problems that are typical of the group and not communicable to others. In addition, as the instructions become reinterpreted, the process loses some of its stability over time: Data generated early in the process use instructions that differ from those that evolve. The higher measure of reliability in the end is partly illusory.

Because content analysts may not be able to anticipate all of the possible complications in their texts, it is a common practice to expand the written coding instructions by adopting new and written rules as the process unfolds. The idea is that the coding instructions evolve, eventually requiring no new rules. To avoid being misled by unwritten consensus among coders engaged in the dual task of interpreting text and expanding the common instructions to do so, content analysts should put the final instructions to a reliability test, using different coders, and reexamine the data generated before these final instructions have been reached.

Content analysts are sometimes tempted to assume, and act on the assumption, that data making is served best by experts, exceptionally acute observers, or individuals who have long histories of involvement with the subject of the research. They should be reminded, however, that the requirement of reproducibility means that any individual with specifiable qualifications could perform the same coding tasks as well and know exactly what is meant by the categories, scales, and descriptive devices used in the research. If there are no other experts against whom the performance of the available expert observers can be checked, the observers' interpretations may be insightful and fascinating, but the analyst cannot claim that they are reliable. This is the basis of arguments against a content analyst's doing his or her own coding (as a principal investigator may sometimes do, for instance) unless the analyst's performance is compared with that of at least one other coder. To satisfy this requirement, the analyst may be tempted to find that other coder among friends or close associates with whom the analyst has worked for a long time. Two such coders are likely to agree—not, however, because they carefully follow the written instructions, but because they know each other and the purpose of the research; they are likely to react similarly without being able to convey the source of their convenient commonalities to others. Analysts should choose observers from a specifiable population of potential observers from which other researchers can select as well.

Sometimes content analysts accept as data only those units of analysis on which observers achieve perfect agreement. This is a particularly problematic practice, because it gives researchers the illusion of perfect reliability without affording them the possibility of separating agreement due to chance from agreement based on the sameness of reading or observation. For binary or dichotomous data, agreement by chance is at least 50%. Omitting units on which coders happen to disagree cannot change the chance nature of those on which they do agree. There is no escape from true chance events. This is true also when agreement is well above chance but not perfect. Units that are coded by chance populate both agreement and disagreement cells of a coincidence table, and in the agreement cells there is no way of separating units according to whether observers agreed by chance or by following the instructions. Most important, when analysts rely on data that are easily coded, the data become an artifact of the analytical procedure—they are no longer representative of the phenomena the researchers hope to analyze.

Content analysts who employ the following two-step procedure can achieve both data whose reliability is measurable and an improvement in their confidence in the data beyond the measured reliability. First, they have to employ three or more observers working independent of one another. This yields reliability data whose reliability can be measured. Second, they reconcile discrepancies in these data either by relying on a formal decision rule—majority judgments or average scores—or by reaching consensus in postcoding deliberations. The data *before* such reconciliation are reliability data proper and do yield reportable reliabilities. Although it is reasonable to assume that postcoding reconciliation improves the reliability of the data beyond the reliability of data generated by any one individual observer, this is an assumption without measurable evidence. The only publishable reliability is the one measured before the reconciliation of disagreements. The reliability of the data after this reconciliation effort is merely arguable.

Reliability Data   11.2.3

As noted above, the data that enable researchers to assess reliability, called *reliability data*, duplicate the very data-making process whose reliability is in question. Reliability data make no reference to what the data are about. Only the assignment of units to the terms of a data language matters.

In their most basic or *canonical* form, reliability data consist of records generated by two or more observers or measuring devices and concern the same set of phenomena. In content analysis, two data-making processes are distinguishable: unitizing and coding. In the practice of research, unitizing and coding may occur together, but the mathematical processes used in evaluating their reliability are different, and so are their reliability data.

Unitizing is identifying within a medium—within an initially undifferentiated continuum—contiguous sections containing information relevant to a research question. These sections become the units of analysis or recording units, and sections between the identified units are left unattended. Examples of unitizing include clipping relevant articles from a newspaper, earmarking pertinent sections in a video recording for subsequent analysis, isolating conversational moves within a conversation, and identifying historically significant events in time. Reliability calculations for unitizing are not as transparent as those for coding and, unfortunately, are still uncommon. Later in this chapter (in section 11.6), I will state, but not develop, reliability measures for unitizing and refer interested readers to work published elsewhere (Krippendorff, 1995a, in press-a). The reliability data for unitizing may be depicted as a three-dimensional cube of observers-by-continuum-by-categories of identified units, as in Figure 11.2.

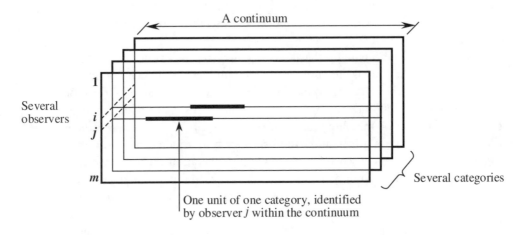

Figure 11.2   Reliability Data for Unitizing

Coding is the transcribing, recording, categorizing, or interpreting of given units of analysis into the terms of a data language so that they can be compared and analyzed. A distinction can be drawn between single-valued and multi-valued data. In single-valued data, each unit of analysis receives a unique description, one value from each variable. In multi-valued data, multiple descriptions or interpretations are allowed. As not too many statistics can handle the latter, I present reliability calculations of single-valued data only in this chapter. The data structure for coding single-valued data may be visualized as in Figure 11.3.

A comment on terminology: In discussing the generation of reliability data, I use the word *observers* in a general sense. They could be called coders, scorers, interpreters, unitizers, analysts, or judges. Outside of content analysis, they might be referred to as raters, interviewers, or acknowledged experts. Moreover, reliability data are not limited to those recorded by individual human beings. Business accounts, medical records, and court ledgers, for example, can be interpreted as the work of institutionalized observers. And mechanical measuring instruments—which convert phenomena into numbers—are included here as well.

In the process of unitizing a given continuum, observers characterize *units* by their length, duration, or size, and by their location in the continuum, using appropriate instructions. In coding, recording units are given or predefined, and the observers' efforts are directed toward their transcription, interpretation, or coding. In public opinion research, individuals often are the units of analysis; in educational research, units are often called (test) items, and elsewhere they may be known as cases. In content analysis, units may be single words or longer text segments, photographic images, minutes of video recordings, scenes in fictional television programs, Web pages, utterances, distinct experiences—anything that could have distinct meanings to an analyst.

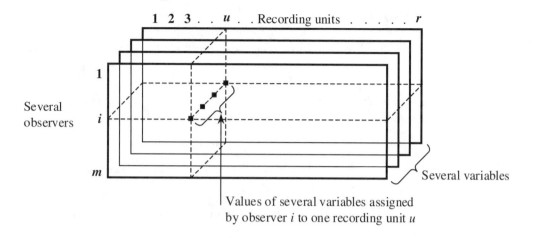

1 2 3 . . *u* . . Recording units . . . . . *r*

Several
observers

1

i

m

Several variables

Values of several variables assigned
by observer *i* to one recording unit *u*

Figure 11.3   Reliability Data for Coding

In the context of coding, I use *values* as the generic term for names, categories, ranks, scores, scale points, measurements, answers to questions, even written text that describes itself and may be entered in the cells of a spreadsheet and located in the coordinates of rows and columns of reliability data. Values vary along dimensions called *variables*. As discussed in Chapter 8, a variable has mutually exclusive values.

Given these preliminaries, how can analysts assess agreement within reliability data as defined above?

α-AGREEMENT FOR CODING   11.3

Analysts always aim for the highest reliability achievable, of course. As perfect reliability may be difficult to achieve, especially when coding tasks are complex and so require elaborate cognitive processes, analysts need to know by how much the data deviate from the ideal of perfect reliability and whether this deviation is above or below accepted reliability standards. These are the two main questions that any agreement measure should answer.

Several coefficients for measuring agreement are available, specialized for particular kinds of data. Popping (1988) identifies 39 for nominal data, and his list is blatantly incomplete. In section 11.5, I will review a few popular ones regarding how they measure what their proponents claim they measure and explore their suitability for reliability assessments. Here, I am relying on Krippendorff's α, not because I invented it, but because it is the most general agreement measure with appropriate reliability interpretations in content analysis, as shall become clear (see Krippendorff, 1970a, 1970b, 1978, 1980b, 1987,

1992). α-agreement should not be confused with Cronbach's (1951) alpha, which is widely used in biometric and educational research for an entirely different purpose and is unsuitable for evaluating reliability in content analysis. Krippendorff's α allows uniform reliability standards to be applied to a great diversity of data:

- It is applicable to any number of values per variable. Its correction for chance makes α independent of this number.

- It is applicable to any number of observers, not just the traditional two.

- It is applicable to small and large sample sizes alike. It corrects itself for varying amounts of reliability data.

- It is applicable to several metrics (scales of measurements)—nominal, ordinal, interval, ratio, and more.

- It is applicable to data with missing values in which some observers do not attend to all recording units.

In its most general form, α is defined by

$$\alpha = 1 - \frac{D_o}{D_e},$$

where D_o is a measure of the observed disagreement and D_e is a measure of the disagreement that can be expected when chance prevails.

This definition reveals two reference points that are essential for any reliability measure: When agreement is observed to be perfect and disagreement is, therefore, absent, $D_o = 0$ and $\alpha = 1$, indicating perfect reliability. When agreement and disagreement are matters of chance and observed and expected disagreements are equal, $D_e = D_o$, $\alpha = 0$, indicating the absence of reliability. α could become negative, in fact, –1. However, as the aim is the highest reliability possible, negative values are too far removed from where differences in reliability matter. Negative values result from two kinds of errors: sampling errors and systematic disagreements. For reliability considerations, α's limits are

$$1 \geq \alpha \geq 0 \begin{cases} \pm \text{ sampling error} \\ - \text{ systematic disagreement} \end{cases}$$

- *Sampling errors* happen for a variety of reasons; in this inequality, when sample sizes are too small. They manifest themselves when observations are few, each having large effects on α. These deviations from the true value of α occur when it turns out to be impossible for observed disagreements to equal the expected disagreements, causing α values to dance above and below zero.

- *Systematic disagreements* occur when observers agree to disagree or pursue opposing interpretations of the instructions given to them. All observed disagreements distract from perfect reliability, but systematic disagreements can cause α values to drop below what would be expected by chance.

Foreshadowing the development of α, which I undertake in small steps, I offer a *first interpretation* of α, one of four I am proposing, in the form of this equation:

$$\alpha = 1 - \frac{D_o}{D_e} = 1 - \frac{\text{Average }_{\text{metric}}\ \delta_{ck}^2 \text{ within all units}}{\text{Average }_{\text{metric}}\ \delta_{ck}^2 \text{ within all data}},$$

where D_o is the average difference between values within units, regardless of who assigned them; D_e is the average difference between all values, regardless of who assigned them and to which units; and δ^2 is the squared difference between any two values c and k, a function of the applicable *metric*.

Inasmuch as differences within units count toward unreliability (are in error), and differences within all values include both the justified or true differences between units and the error differences within units, *α is the extent to which the proportion of the differences that are in error deviates from perfect agreement, α = 1 always being its largest value.*

Before I get to the details of the agreement coefficient α, I should mention that I do assume that content analysts will use computer programs to analyze the reliabilities they need to know. However, to understand how α indicates agreement, it is important that content analysts be able to construct coincidence matrices by hand, calculate at least elementary α-measures, and thereby understand how observed disagreements affect reliability. In what follows, I introduce α, beginning with a simple example, and slowly add complications. Readers may find the next two sections to be a straightforward presentation of basic ideas, covering the kinds of data that are most common in content analysis. If these explanations suffice, they may want to skip to the discussion of standards in section 11.4.4 and, if still curious, the discussion of other coefficients in section 11.5.

Two Observers, Binary Data   11.3.1

The conceivably simplest reliability data are generated by two observers who assign one of two available values to each of a common set of units of analysis. For example, suppose a political scientist is interested in references to the United States in the Chinese press and, unable to read Chinese, hires two individuals (Jon and Han) who claim to be competent readers of Chinese to identify the presence or absence of such references. They mark each newspaper article "0" for absent or "1" for present. Their results may be tabulated as follows:

Article:	1	2	3	4	5	6	7	8	9	10
Jon's values:	1	1	0	0	0	0	0	0	0	0
Han's values:	0	1	1	0	0	1	0	1	0	0

This is called a reliability data matrix. It tells us that Jon and Han agree regarding 6 out of the 10 articles. Although 60% agreement sounds good, this figure does not tell us anything about the condition under which the assignment of values is the product of chance. In fact, 0% agreement is about as unlikely to achieve by chance as is 100%. Because 0% has no meaningful reliability interpretation, the %-agreement measure has no second reference point and does not constitute a reliability scale. When agreement deviates from 100%, as in this example, %-agreement is uninterpretable and can say nothing about the extent to which the data can be relied upon.

To gain a clearer view of these reliability data, one can create a matrix of the observed coincidences. Such a matrix accounts for all the values that the two observers used—20 in our example. Here, each unit contains two pairs of values, a Jon-Han pair and a Han-Jon pair. In the first unit, we find two pairs of values, 1-0 and 0-1. They do not match. In the second unit, the two pairs of values, 1-1 and 1-1, match perfectly and are in fact indistinguishable. Given that there are 10 units with two pairs of values in each, we need to tabulate 20 pairs, which equals the number of values in the above reliability data matrix. Let o_{ck} be the number of observed coincidences of the two values c and k. In our reliability data matrix we count ten 0-0 pairs, so, $o_{00} = 10$; four 0-1 pairs, $o_{01} = 4$; four 1-0 pairs, $o_{10} = 4$; and two 1-1 pairs, $o_{11} = 2$. A tabulation of these pairs yields the following matrix of observed coincidences:

	Values:	0	1			0	1	
Matrix of observed coincidences	0	o_{00}	o_{01}	n_0	0	10	4	14
	1	o_{10}	o_{11}	n_1	1	4	2	6
Number of values:		n_0	n_1	n		14	6	20

Coincidence matrices should not be confused with the better-known *contingency matrices*, which are familiar in the tradition of assessing statistical associations or correlations, not agreements. Contingency matrices retain the identities of the two observers and treat them as independent variables. They tabulate the number of *units* being coded, not the number of *values* that participate in pair comparisons. There is a simple relationship between coincidence matrices and contingency matrices, however: Coincidences sum contingencies and their inverses, thereby omitting the references to the individual observers, considering them interchangeable. If x_{ck} is the number of times a particular observer uses c while the other uses k, then the number of coincidences $o_{ck} = x_{ck} + x_{kc}$. Accordingly, our 2-by-2-coincidence matrix can be seen as the sum of the contingencies in the Jon-Han matrix and in its inverse, the Han-Jon matrix:

Coincidence matrix   =   Contingency matrix + Inverse contingency matrix

$$
\begin{array}{c}
\\
\text{Values:} \\
\\
\\
\text{Number of:}
\end{array}
\quad
\begin{array}{cc|c}
0 & 1 & \\
\hline
10 & 4 & 14 \\
4 & 2 & 6 \\
\hline
14 & 6 & 20 \text{ values}
\end{array}
\quad = \quad \text{Han's}
\begin{array}{c}
\text{Jon's values} \\
\begin{array}{c}
\;\; 0 \quad 1 \\
\end{array} \\
\begin{array}{c|cc|c}
0 & 5 & 1 & 6 \\
1 & 3 & 1 & 4 \\
\hline
& 8 & 2 & 10 \text{ units}
\end{array}
\end{array}
\quad + \quad \text{Jon's}
\begin{array}{c}
\text{Han's values} \\
\begin{array}{c}
\;\; 0 \quad 1 \\
\end{array} \\
\begin{array}{c|cc|c}
0 & 5 & 3 & 8 \\
1 & 1 & 1 & 2 \\
\hline
& 6 & 4 & 10 \text{ units}
\end{array}
\end{array}
$$

Both kinds of matrices show mismatched pairs in their off-diagonal cells. However, coincidence matrices are symmetrical around the diagonal, whereas contingency matrices are not. The margins of coincidence matrices enumerate the *values* actually used by all observers. The margins of contingency matrices enumerate the *units* being recorded by each observer. The two margins of coincidence matrices are the same. The two margins of contingency matrices typically differ.

Disagreements in the matrix of observed coincidences determine the quantity of observed disagreement D_o, the numerator of α. We now need to consider what goes into the denominator of α, the expected disagreements D_e, which averages all differences between values that are pairable within the whole reliability data matrix, ignoring who assigned them to which units. The disagreements that determine the quantity of expected disagreement D_e are found in the matrix of the expected coincidences, which represents what could happen by chance. Ideally, and in our example, we would base such expectations on knowledge of the proportion of references to the United States that actually occur in the Chinese press. However, we cannot know this proportion without completing the very analysis whose reliability is in question. Lacking knowledge of this kind, we estimate the population of references in the Chinese press from what we do know, the proportion of references that all available observers jointly identify. With Jon finding U.S. references in 2 out of 10 articles and Han finding them in 4 out of 10, the two observers have jointly identified 6 out of 20, or 30%. This is our population estimate. It also happens to be, as it should, the proportion of ones in the original reliability data regardless of who contributed them.

Given these proportions, we now calculate how often one can expect Jon and Han to agree under conditions that they do not read anything at all and draw zeros and ones randomly out of a hat. Suppose we place 20 balls in that hat, 6 balls labeled "1" and 14 balls labeled "0," mix them thoroughly, and let two individuals draw balls out of the hat blindly. To draw two 1s in a row, the first individual can be expected to draw a 1 in 6 out of 20 cases. Having removed a 1 from the hat and thereby reduced the remaining number of 1s and the total by one, the second individual will draw a 1 in 5 out of 19 balls. To get to expected frequencies, just as in the matrix of observed coincidences, we multiply these two probabilities by the total number $n = 20$ and obtain the expected frequencies of 1-1 pairs as $(6/20)(5/19) \cdot 20 = 1.5789$. By contrast, if the first individual drew a 1 from the hat, the number of 0s stayed the same and the second individual would be expected to draw a 0 in 14 out of 19 cases. This gives us the following matrix of expected coincidences (the computational formulas are reproduced on the right of these matrices):

Where:

Values:		0	1			0	1	
Matrix of expected	0	e_{00}	e_{01}	n_0	0	9.6	4.4	14
coincidences	1	e_{10}	e_{11}	n_1	1	4.4	1.6	6
Number of values:		n_0	n_1	n		14	6	20

$e_{00} = n_0 \cdot (n_0 - 1)/(n - 1)$

$e_{01} = e_{10} = n_0 \cdot n_1/(n - 1)$

$e_{11} = n_1 \cdot (n_1 - 1)/(n - 1)$

We now have everything we need to calculate the agreement for binary reliability data. What counts as disagreement are the off-diagonal entries of the two matrices. Because coincidence matrices are symmetrical, $o_{01} = o_{10} = 4$ and $e_{01} = e_{10} = 4.4211$, we do not need to add the contents of both off-diagonal cells and can express α for binary data by

$$_{binary}\alpha = 1 - \frac{D_o}{D_e} = 1 - \frac{o_{01}}{e_{01}} = 1 - \frac{4}{4.4211} = 0.095.$$

Bypassing the construction of the matrix of expected coincidences, which is informative but can be cumbersome, a computationally more direct form for this α is

$$_{binary}\alpha = 1 - \frac{D_o}{D_e} = 1 - (n - 1)\frac{o_{01}}{n_0 \cdot n_1} = 1 - (20 - 1)\frac{4}{14.6} = 0.095.$$

By whichever form, in this numerical example, the reliability turns out to be barely 10% above what can be expected by chance. As the agreement that can be expected by chance is already $(9.6 + 1.6)/20 = 56\%$, the 60% agreement that had been noted before looks far less impressive. Our data suggest that the two observers' performances are statistically equal to their having actually read (and reliably recorded) only about 10% of all newspaper articles, which is 1 article in our sample of 10, and assigned 0s or 1s to the remaining 90% by throwing dice. In light of the first of the three propositions in section 11.1, it is important to realize that we cannot know which the one correctly identified unit is, hence unreliability limits the chance of valid results.

Upon inspection of the circumstances of this devastating result, our political scientist may discover that the instructions to the two observers were incomprehensible or inappropriate to the coding task. Perhaps one or both observers failed to read the instructions carefully or did not know Chinese well enough to undertake the coding task. Whatever the reason, these data are far from being reliable, and content analysts would have to reject them without hesitation. Evidently, measuring 60% agreement means little by itself—a fact that should be a clear warning against the use of a reliability measure that does not account for chance, such as %-agreement.

For nominal data, I offer a *second interpretation*. It follows from the decomposition of the observed coincidences into two parts, α times the coincidences in a matrix of the ideal or perfect agreements, with all n values in the diagonal, plus $(1 - \alpha)$ times the coincidences in a matrix of what would be expected by chance:

$$
\begin{bmatrix} o_{00} & o_{01} \\ o_{10} & o_{11} \end{bmatrix} = \alpha \begin{bmatrix} n_0 & \\ & n_1 \end{bmatrix} + (1-\alpha) \begin{bmatrix} e_{00} & e_{01} \\ e_{10} & e_{11} \end{bmatrix}
$$

With reference to these three coincidence matrices: *α is the degree to which agreement exceeds expectations.* Specifically, *α is the proportion of the perfectly matching coincidences that, when added to the complementary proportion of chance coincidences, accounts for the coincidences that were observed.* This algebraic relationship can be demonstrated by means of the frequencies from our example:

$$
\alpha \text{ times } \textit{perfectly agreeing } \text{coincidences:} \quad .095 \begin{bmatrix} 14 & \\ & 6 \end{bmatrix} = \begin{bmatrix} 1.33 & \\ & .57 \end{bmatrix}
$$

$$
+
$$

$$
(1-\alpha) \text{ times } \textit{expected } \text{coincidences:} \quad (1-.095) \begin{bmatrix} 9.6 & 4.4 \\ 4.4 & 1.6 \end{bmatrix} = \begin{bmatrix} 8.67 & 4 \\ 4 & 1.43 \end{bmatrix}
$$

$$
\text{Total} = \textit{observed } \text{coincidences:} \quad \begin{bmatrix} 10 & 4 \\ 4 & 2 \end{bmatrix}
$$

Two Observers, Many Nominal Categories   11.3.2

I state this extension in three easily executable steps, first in general terms and then with a simple numerical example.

First step. Tabulate the values c and k that m observers, here the $m = 2$ observers A and B, respectively assign to each of r units, generically labeled u. This tabulation creates a *2-by-r reliability data matrix:*

Units u:	1	2	...	u	...	r
Observer A:	c_1	c_2	...	c_u	...	c_r
Observer B:	k_1	k_2	...	k_u	...	k_r

The following 2-by-12 reliability data matrix will serve as our example:

Units:	1	2	3	4	5	6	7	8	9	10	11	12
Mary:	a	a	b	b	b	b	b	c	c	c	c	c
Dave:	a	b	b	b	b	b	c	c	c	c	c	c

Second step. Construct the *matrix of observed coincidences*. With v different values in the reliability data, this matrix is a v-by-v matrix with v^2 cells containing all pairs of values assigned to units, or found in the columns of the reliability data matrix. Each value used in the reliability data matrix contributes one to the coincidence matrix, and each unit contributes two, one c-k pair of values and one k-c pair of values:

$$
\begin{array}{c|cccc|c}
\textbf{Values:} & \textbf{1} & . \; \textbf{k} & . \; . & \textbf{v} & \\
\hline
\textbf{1} & o_{11} & . \; o_{1k} & . \; . & o_{1v} & n_1 \\
. & . & . & & . & . \\
. & . & . & & . & . \\
\textbf{c} & o_{c1} & . \; o_{ck} & . \; . & o_{cv} & n_c = \Sigma_k \, o_{ck} \\
. & . & . & & . & . \\
\textbf{v} & o_{v1} & . \; o_{vk} & . \; . & o_{vv} & n_v \\
\hline
 & n_1 & . \; n_k & . \; . & n_v & n = \Sigma_c \Sigma_k \, o_{ck}
\end{array}
$$

Sum the contents of the rows and columns in this matrix to their respective margins n_c and n_k and sum these margins to the total n. For this coincidence matrix to be accurate, its cells should be symmetrical around the diagonal, $o_{ck} = o_{kc}$. The total n should be $2r$, which is the number of values in the reliability data matrix. The vertical margin should equal the horizontal margin, and each n_c must equal the number of values c found in the reliability data matrix.

In our example, there are $v = 3$ values: a, b, and c. The observed coincidence matrix has 3-by-3 = 9 cells. As each unit is represented by two pairs of values, it will have to contain a total of $n = 24$ values. For example, the first unit contributes 2 entries in the a-a cell, the second contributes 1 to the a-b cell and 1 to the b-a cell, the next four units together contribute 8 to the b-b cell, and so on:

$$
\begin{array}{c|ccc|c}
 & a & b & c & \\
\hline
a & 2 & 1 & 0 & 3 \\
b & 1 & 8 & 1 & 10 \\
c & 0 & 1 & 10 & 11 \\
\hline
 & 3 & 10 & 11 & 24
\end{array}
$$

Third step. Compute the *agreement coefficient* α as follows:

$$
_{\text{nominal}}\alpha = 1 - \frac{D_o}{D_e} = 1 - (n-1)\frac{n - \sum_c o_{cc}}{n^2 - \sum_c n_c^2}
$$

$$
= 1 - (24 - 1)\frac{24 - (2 + 8 + 10)}{24^2 - (3^2 + 10^2 + 11^2)} = .734.
$$

We can also construct the *matrix of expected coincidences*. It can serve as a convenient aid to interpreting reliability data, but, as demonstrated above, it is not necessary for computing α:

Values c: 1 . k . . v

$$
\begin{array}{c|ccccc|c}
 & 1 & . & k & . & . & v & \\
\hline
1 & e_{11} & . & e_{1k} & . & . & e_{1v} & n_1 \\
. & . & & . & & & . & . \\
. & . & & . & & & . & . \\
c & e_{c1} & . & e_{ck} & . & . & e_{cv} & n_c = \Sigma_k e_{ck} \\
. & . & & . & & & . & . \\
. & . & & . & & & . & . \\
v & e_{v1} & . & e_{vk} & . & . & e_{vv} & n_v \\
\hline
 & n_1 & . & n_k & . & . & n_v & n = \Sigma_c \Sigma_k o_{ck}
\end{array}
$$

where:

$$
e_{ck} = \begin{cases} n_c(n_k - 1)/(n-1) & \text{iff } c = k \\ n_c \cdot n_k/(n-1) & \text{iff } c \neq k \end{cases}
$$

This matrix has the same margins as the matrix of the observed coincidences. The reason for treating the expectations in cells of matching values, $c = k$, differently from those of mismatching cells, $c \neq k$, follows from the discussion in section 11.3.1. In our example, expectations are computed as follows:

$$
\begin{aligned}
e_{aa} &= n_a(n_a - 1)/(n - 1) = 3(3 - 1)/(24 - 1) = 0.2609, \\
e_{ab} &= n_a \cdot n_b/(n - 1) = 3 \cdot 10/(24 - 1) = 1.3043, \\
e_{bc} &= n_b \cdot n_c/(n - 1) = 10 \cdot 11/(24 - 1) = 4.7826,
\end{aligned}
$$

and so on.

The expected coincidences are tabulated as follows:

$$
\begin{array}{c|ccc|c}
 & a & b & c & \\
\hline
a & .26 & 1.30 & 1.44 & 3 \\
b & 1.30 & 3.91 & 4.78 & 10 \\
c & 1.44 & 4.78 & 4.78 & 11 \\
\hline
 & 3 & 10 & 11 & 24
\end{array}
$$

By comparing the expected with the observed coincidences, one can locate sources of disagreement in the coincidences that fail to deviate from expectations. Comparisons of this kind give rise to several algebraic expressions within which we can recognize a *third interpretation* of α—restricted to nominal data, however:

$$
_{nominal}\alpha = 1 - \frac{D_o}{D_e} = \frac{A_o - A_e}{A_{max} - A_e} = \frac{\sum_c o_{cc} - \sum_c e_{cc}}{n - \sum_c e_{cc}} = \frac{\sum_c (o_{cc} - e_{cc})}{\sum_c (n_c - e_{cc})}.
$$

In the second version of α, A_o is the observed agreement, A_e is the expected agreement, and A_{max} is the largest possible agreement. Agreements, A, can be proportions, percentages, or frequencies. In the third version, agreements A appear as the sum of the diagonal entries in the observed and expected coincidence matrices, respectively, where $A_{max} = n$ is the total number of values. In the forth version we see the same differences but now expressed as the sum of the differences between the observed and expected coincidences in the diagonal cells. Thus α *is the proportion of the observed to expected above-chance agreement.*

Entering the numbers from our example into each version yields the following—excepting rounding errors:

$$_{\text{nominal}}\alpha = 1 - \frac{.1667}{.6268} = \frac{83\% - 37\%}{100\% - 37\%} = \frac{(2 + 8 + 10) - (.26 + 3.91 + 4.78)}{24 - (.26 + 3.91 + 4.78)}$$

$$= \frac{(2 - .26) + (8 - 3.91) + (10 - 4.78)}{(3 - .26) + (10 - 3.91) + (11 - 4.78)} = 0.734$$

As one may recognize, the proportions are the same whether of the difference between %-agreements (second version), the difference between the frequencies in the diagonals of the two coincidence matrices (third version), or the sum of the differences between agreements in each of the diagonal cells in the two coincidence matrices (fourth version).

11.3.3   Many Observers, Many Nominal Categories, Missing Values

Applying the *first step* in section 11.3.2 now to any number m of observers, we start with an m-by-r reliability data matrix of these observers' values. For example:

Recording units u:	1	2	3	4	5	6	7	8	9	10	11	12
Observer A:	📖	✉	☎	☎	✉	📖	💻	📖	✉			
Observer B:	📖	✉	☎	☎	✉	✉	💻	📖	✉	📁		
Observer C:		☎	☎	☎	✉	☎	💻	✉	✉	📁	📖	☎
Observer D:	📖	✉	☎	☎	✉	💻	💻	📖	✉	📁	📖	
Number of values m_u:	3	4	4	4	4	4	4	4	4	3	2	1

Here, $m = 4$ observers categorized $r = 12$ messages, which are the units of analysis, by their sources, which are represented by icons. Note that 7 out of the 4-by-12 = 48 cells are empty. These are missing values. Observer C failed to consider unit 1. Observer A stopped coding after unit 9, B after unit 10, and D after unit 11. To account for these irregularities, we add one row to this reliability data matrix, which lists the number m_u of values assigned to unit u. Note the lone ☎ in unit 12, $m_{12} = 1$. It cannot be compared with anything in that unit.

Let us now focus on the *second step*, the construction of the *matrix of observed coincidences*. This step generalizes the second step in section 11.3.2. For two observers and 2-by-r reliability data matrices without missing values, the pairing of values and their tabulation was obvious. We now extend the idea of counting mismatches to more than two observers, to multiple pair comparisons among any number m_u of values in units or columns. To start, note that from m_u values, we can form $m_u(m_u - 1)$ pairs of values. In unit 1 there are

$m_1(m_1 - 1) = 3(3 - 1) = 6$ matching 📖–📖 pairs. In unit 2, containing 3 ✉s and 1 ☎, we can form a total of $m_2(m_2 - 1) = 4(4 - 1) = 12$ pairs, $3(3 - 1) = 6$ matching ✉–✉ pairs, $3 \cdot 1 = 3$ ✉–☎ pairs, and $1 \cdot 3 = 3$ ☎–✉ pairs. One of the extremes can be seen in unit 6. Here all 4 values are different and so are the 12 pairs of values that can be formed from them. The other extreme can be seen in unit 12. The lone ☎ does not participate in any pair, which is indicated by $m_{12}(m_{12} - 1) = 1(1 - 1) = 0$ pairs of values. To be pairable, $m_u > 1$.

By our earlier definition, a matrix of observed coincidences accounts for the number of values that are pairable within units of analysis—not for the numbers of *units* being coded and not for the number of *pairs* that can be formed from these values. In order for each value to contribute exactly one entry to a coincidence matrix, each of the $m_u(m_u - 1)$ possible pairs of values contained in unit u must contribute $1/(m_u - 1)$ to the coincidence matrix. Except for now proportioning the contribution of each pair of values to the matrix of observed coincidences, everything else is exactly as in section 11.3.2.

Values:

$$
\begin{array}{c|ccccc|c}
 & 1 & . & k & . & . & v \\
\hline
1 & o_{11} & . & o_{1k} & . & . & o_{1v} & n_1 \\
. & . & & . & & & . & . \\
. & . & & . & & & . & . \\
c & o_{c1} & . & o_{ck} & . & . & o_{cv} & n_c = \Sigma_k\, o_{ck} \\
. & . & & . & & & . & . \\
v & o_{v1} & . & o_{vk} & . & . & o_{vv} & n_v \\
\hline
 & n_1 & . & n_k & . & . & n_v & n = \Sigma_c \Sigma_k\, n_{ck}
\end{array}
$$

where:

$$o_{ck} = \sum_u \frac{\text{Number of } c\text{-}k \text{ pairs in } u}{m_u - 1}$$

Accordingly, the 6 matching 📖–📖 pairs in unit 1 contribute $6/(3 - 1) = 3$ to the 📖–📖 cell of that matrix. The three kinds of pairs in unit 2 add $6/(4 - 1) = 2$ to the ✉–✉ cell, $3/(4 - 1) = 1$ to the ✉–☎ cell, and 1 to the ☎–✉ cell of that matrix. The 12 pairs of values in unit 6 add $1/(4 - 1) = 1/3$ each to 1 of 12 cells of that matrix. The contributions of these three units are seen in the first three matrices below. The fourth matrix sums the contributions of all 12 units, whereby it is important to realize that the lone ☎ in unit 12 makes no contribution to this matrix as it does not have anything with which to compare that ☎.

	📖	✉	☎	💻	📁		📖	✉	☎	💻	📁		📖	✉	☎	💻	📁		📖	✉	☎	💻	📁	
📖	3												1/3	1/3	1/3				7	4/3	1/3	1/3		$9 = n_{📖}$
✉							2	1					1/3		1/3	1/3			4/3	10	4/3	1/3		$13 = n_{✉}$
☎							1						1/3	1/3		1/3			1/3	4/3	8	1/3		$10 = n_{☎}$
💻													1/3	1/3	1/3				1/3	1/3	1/3	4		$5 = n_{💻}$
📁																							3	$3 = n_{📁}$
																			9	13	10	5	3	$40 = n$

Unit 1 · Unit 2 · Unit 6 · Sum over all 12 units

The construction of the rightmost of these four coincidence matrices completes the second step. For the *third step,* the computation of the agreement coefficient α, we follow the definition in section 11.3.2:

$$_{\text{nominal}}\alpha = 1 - \frac{D_o}{D_e} = 1 - (n-1)\frac{n - \sum_c o_{cc}}{n^2 - \sum_c n_c^2}$$

$$= 1 - (40-1)\frac{40 - (7 + 10 + 8 + 4 + 3)}{40^2 - (9^2 + 13^2 + 10^2 + 5^2 + 3^2)} = .743$$

11.3.4   Data With Different Metrics

Calculations of such data follow the first and second steps from section 11.3.2 when there are two observers and the first and second steps from section 11.3.3 when there are more than two observers, but they differ in the *third step,* the *computation of the agreement coefficient α,* which we will now generalize to any metric.

In nominal data, values either match or they do not. This had simplified the calculations of α in the previous situations. We now recognize other and more quantitative relationships between values, and they depend on the metric underlying a variable. As noted in Chapter 8 (section 8.4), a metric is defined by the operations that are applicable to the values of a variable. Although researchers generally can choose the metrics with which they want to analyze their data, they also need to acknowledge the nature of their data, whether the operations that define a metric make sense. For example, one cannot add two names or multiply ranks. The values of a ratio metric cannot be negative. Thus, in choosing an appropriate metric for α, researchers must take into account what a variable represents, which mathematical operations it can afford. Equally important is that they keep in mind the demands made by the data analysis methods they anticipate using. An analysis of variance requires interval data, contingencies are computed from nominal data, and so forth.

The way α accounts for diverse metrics is by using metric-specific difference functions δ_{ck}^2 to weigh the observed and expected coincidences of *c-k* pairs of values. To make the role of these differences transparent, we restate the first interpretation of α in section 11.3 as

$$\alpha = 1 - \frac{D_o}{D_e} = 1 - \frac{\text{Average }_{\text{metric}}\,\delta_{ck}^2 \text{ within all units}}{\text{Average }_{\text{metric}}\,\delta_{ck}^2 \text{ within all data}}$$

$$= 1 - \frac{\sum_c \sum_k o_{ck\,\text{metric}}\delta_{ck}^2}{\sum_c \sum_k e_{ck\,\text{metric}}\delta_{ck}^2} = 1 - \frac{\sum \boxed{o_{ck}} \times \boxed{\delta_{ck}^2}}{\sum \boxed{e_{ck}} \times \boxed{\delta_{ck}^2}}.$$

The last of these four versions of α depicts coincidences and differences as square matrices whose entries are multiplied and summed as indicated in the third version. We now attend to the difference functions for the most common metrics—nominal, ordinal, interval, and ratio metrics—which we will state in two ways, in mathematical terms, which are general, and in terms of difference matrices, here exemplified with six typical values.

Nominal metric. For the nominal data used so far, reference to a metric was not needed, as they entail no quantitative differences. Values are merely distinct and freely permutable. When nominal values are represented numerically—area codes, banking PINs, the numbers on the jerseys of football players—adding or subtracting them from one another makes no sense. Two values are either the same or different—they match or they do not match. For generality's sake, we define and tabulate this property as a difference function, albeit of a primitive kind:

$$_{\text{nominal}}\delta_{ck}^2 = \begin{cases} 0 \text{ iff } c = k \\ 1 \text{ iff } c \neq k \end{cases}$$

	📖	✉	☎	🖥	💾	🗁
📖	0	1	1	1	1	1
✉	1	0	1	1	1	1
☎	1	1	0	1	1	1
🖥	1	1	1	0	1	1
💾	1	1	1	1	0	1
🗁	1	1	1	1	1	0

Naturally, all differences δ_{cc}^2 between matching values are zero, which can be seen in the diagonal entries of their tabular forms. Off-diagonal differences are metric specific. It is a property of nominal data that all differences between mismatching values are identical, here 1.

Ordinal metric. In data, values are ranks. They have the meaning of 1st, 2nd, 3rd, 4th, and so forth. Ordinal differences are a function of how many ranks there are between any two ranks. The numerals used to label these ranks merely indicate their ordering.

We demonstrate the idea of ordinal differences with the example from section 11.3.3 whose marginal frequencies n_c are now interpreted as of rank c: $n_{1st} = 9$, $n_{2nd} = 13$, $n_{3rd} = 10$, $n_{4th} = 5$, $n_{5th} = 0$, $n_{6th} = 3$. We add an unused rank, the 5th rank, for illustrative purposes.

$$_{\text{ordinal}}\delta_{ck}^2 = \left(\frac{n_c}{2} + \sum_{g>c}^{g<k} n_g + \frac{n_k}{2} \right)^2 \text{ where } c < k$$

	1st	2nd	3rd	4th	5th	6th	
1st	0	11^2	22.5^2	30^2	32.5^2	34^2	$n_{1st} = 9$
2nd	121	0	11.5^2	19^2	21.5^2	23^2	$n_{2nd} = 13$
3rd	506	132	0	7.5^2	10^2	11.5^2	$n_{3rd} = 10$
4th	900	361	56	0	2.5^2	4^2	$n_{4th} = 5$
5th	992	462	100	6.3	0	1.5^2	$n_{5th} = 0$
6th	1,156	529	132	16	2.3	0	$n_{6th} = 3$

$\delta_{1st,3rd} = 22.5$

$\delta_{4th,6th} = 4$

How ordinal differences are defined may be seen on the right of this difference matrix. The marginal frequencies of the ranks used by all observers are depicted as bar graphs, and shaded areas illustrate what goes into the differences between two ranks. That ordinal differences are not affected by the numerical values assigned to them may be seen in the example of the 5th rank. It is not used and does not make a difference in how far apart the 4th and 6th ranks are. Only a rank's ordering matters.

Note that the mathematical expressions state what the difference matrices exemplify. All difference matrices are symmetrical, $\delta_{ck} = \delta_{kc}$, and all of their diagonal entries are zero, $\delta_{cc} = \delta_{kk} = 0$.

Interval metric. One cannot add and subtract ranks, but the more familiar interval scales do afford these mathematical operations. In interval data, it is the simple algebraic differences that specify how far apart any two values are:

$$_{interval}\delta_{ck}^2 = (c - k)^2$$

	−1	0	1	2	3	4
−1	0	1^2	2^2	3^2	4^2	5^2
0	1	0	1^2	2^2	3^2	4^2
1	4	1	0	1^2	2^2	3^2
2	9	4	1	0	1^2	2^2
3	16	9	4	1	0	1^2
4	25	16	9	4	1	0

Imagine drawing lines of equal differences in this matrix. These lines would parallel the diagonal, and their intervals would rapidly narrow with increasing distance from that diagonal.

Note that when all ranks are of equal frequency, $_{interval}\delta_{ck}$s and $_{ordinal}\delta_{ck}$s are proportional, and their agreement coefficients are equal: $_{ordinal}\alpha = {}_{interval}\alpha$.

Ratio metric. In ratio scales, algebraic differences between two values matter only in relation to how remote they are from zero, which is their reference point. Guessing the age of an older person within a year of accuracy may be remarkable, whereas guessing the age of a baby within a year is not. Losing a dollar may not be noticeable to a millionaire, but would mean losing everything for somebody who has only one. Age and income are ratio scales, as are frequencies. Algebraic differences between small values weigh more than the same differences between large values. The following difference function reflects these intuitions:

$$_{ratio}\delta_{ck}^2 = \left(\frac{c - k}{c + k}\right)^2$$

	0	1	2	3	4	5
0	0	$(\frac{1}{1})^2$	$(\frac{2}{2})^2$	$(\frac{3}{3})^2$	$(\frac{4}{4})^2$	$(\frac{5}{5})^2$
1	1	0	$(\frac{1}{3})^2$	$(\frac{2}{4})^2$	$(\frac{3}{5})^2$	$(\frac{4}{6})^2$
2	1	.11	0	$(\frac{1}{5})^2$	$(\frac{2}{6})^2$	$(\frac{3}{7})^2$
3	1	.25	.04	0	$(\frac{1}{7})^2$	$(\frac{2}{8})^2$
4	1	.36	.11	.02	0	$(\frac{1}{9})^2$
5	1	.44	.18	.06	.01	0

Whereas in interval metrics the lines of equal differences are parallel to the diagonal, in ratio metrics they all join in the zero-point and extend, fanlike, into infinity, with ratio differences being the tangent of the angular deviation from the 45-degree diagonal line.

By acknowledging the above metrics, our third computational step generalizes the way the nominal α was calculated in sections 11.3.2 and 11.3.3:

$$D_o = \frac{1}{n} \sum_c \sum_k o_{ck \text{ metric}} \delta_{ck}^2,$$

$$D_e = \frac{1}{n} \sum_c \sum_k e_{ck \text{ metric}} \delta_{ck}^2 = \frac{1}{n(n-1)} \sum_c n_c \sum_k n_{k \text{ metric}} \delta_{ck}^2.$$

In the form recommended for computational convenience, we bypass references to the matrix of expected coincidences by computing these expectations indirectly, from the margins of the matrix of observed coincidences. And because coincidence and difference matrices are symmetrical, we can reduce the number of algebraic operations by half when summing only one of the two triangles with off-diagonal coincidences:

$$_{\text{metric}}\alpha = 1 - \frac{D_o}{D_e} = 1 - (n-1) \frac{\sum_c \sum_{k>c} o_{ck \text{ metric}} \delta_{ck}^2}{\sum_c n_c \sum_{k>c} n_{k \text{ metric}} \delta_{ck}^2}.$$

To demonstrate this now generalized third step in the calculation of α, we continue to make use of the coincidences we already know from the example in section 11.3.3, for which purpose we recode their values by 📖 = 1, 📖 = 2, ☎ = 3, 💻 = 4, and 🗀 = 5. According to the above, we need the observed coincidences, their marginal frequencies, and differences for each coincidence:

Observed coincidences o_{ck}

	1	2	3	4	5	
1	7	4/3	1/3	1/3		9
2	4/3	10	4/3	1/3		13
3	1/3	4/3	8	1/3		10
4	1/3	1/3	1/3	4		5
5					3	3
	9	13	10	5	3	40

Interval differences $_{\text{interval}}\delta_{ck}^2$

	1	2	3	4	5
1	0	1^2	2^2	3^2	4^2
2	1^2	0	1^2	2^2	3^2
3	2^2	1^2	0	1^2	2^2
4	3^2	2^2	1^2	0	1^2
5	4^2	3^2	2^2	1^2	0

$$_{\text{interval}}\alpha = 1 - \frac{D_o}{D_e} = 1 - (n-1) \frac{\sum_c \sum_{k>c} o_{ck} (c-k)^2}{\sum_c n_c \sum_{k>c} n_k (c-k)^2} = 1 - (40-1)$$

$$\frac{4/3 \cdot 1^2 + 1/3 \cdot 2^2 + 1/3 \cdot 3^2 + 4/3 \cdot 1^2 + 1/3 \cdot 2^2 + 1/3 \cdot 1^2}{9(13 \cdot 1^2 + 10 \cdot 2^2 + 5 \cdot 3^2 + 3 \cdot 4^2) + 13(10 \cdot 1^2 + 5 \cdot 2^2 + 3 \cdot 3^2) + 10(5 \cdot 1^2 + 3 \cdot 2^2) + 5 \cdot 3 \cdot 1^2} = .849$$

For interval α coefficients, we offer this computational simplification:

$$_{interval}\alpha = 1 - (n-1)\ \frac{\sum_c \sum_{k>c} o_{ck}\,(c-k)^2}{\sum_c n_c \sum_{k>c} n_k\,(c-k)^2}$$

$$= 1 - (n-1)\ \frac{\sum_c n_c c^2 - \sum_c \sum_k o_{ck}\, ck}{n\sum_c n_c c^2 - \left(\sum_c n_c c\right)^2}\ .$$

Referring to previous findings regarding our example, one may ask why the $_{interval}\alpha$, just calculated as .849, is larger than the $_{nominal}\alpha$, earlier calculated to be .743. Although this difference is small and our example has far too few units to allow us to draw interesting conclusions, if neither were the case, one might notice that observed mismatches are more frequent near the diagonal than away from it, which would be typical of interval data, and one may then be tempted to conclude that coders were using these values as if they had some kind of ordering, as if the intervals between them mattered.

11.4   STATISTICAL PROPERTIES OF α

The agreement coefficient α is a statistical measure. Below, I briefly discuss four conditions and precautions for accepting or rejecting measured reliabilities: insufficient variation, sampling considerations, statistical significance, and standards for the reliability of data.

11.4.1   Insufficient Variation

A frequently puzzling condition arises when reliability data show insufficient variation. Consider this rather extreme example:

									Observed coincidences			Expected coincidences		
Reliability Data									0	1		0	1	
Units:	1	2	3	4	5	6	7	8						
Observer A:	0	0	0	0	0	0	0	0	0 14	1	15	0 14	1	15
Observer B:	0	0	0	0	0	0	0	1	1 1	0	1	1 1	0	1
									15	1	16	15	1	16

Here, the matrices of observed and expected coincidences are identical, $D_o = D_e = 0$ and $\alpha = 0$ by definition. Technically, α would be indeterminate, as $1 - 0/0$ can be either 0 or $-\infty$. I use zero not only because extreme negative values have no meanings here but because such data could not be relied upon, although here for lack of variation. Time and time again, statistical novices have found this condition difficult to accept. They have argued that there evidently is considerable agreement on the value "0," in fact in 7 out of 8 units or 88%. How could α suggest reliability to be absent? This argument overlooks the requirement that reliability data must exhibit variation. Perhaps the material coded was mostly of the same kind, perhaps the observers found their task boring and settled on scoring habitually—we do not know. However, in the 8th unit, in which one observer noticed something out of line, in the only unit that seems to be at variance with all the others, the two observers fail to agree, and $\alpha = 0$, as it should. When one wants to report on the overwhelming frequency of one value, exceptions are particularly important.

Now, suppose observer B had assigned a "0" to unit 8 as well. Then we would have even less evidence that the observers did their job. They could have been too tired to notice unusual variations, or they could have been lazy—assurances to the contrary aside—and agreed in advance simply to label everything "0" without reading. In effect, they functioned just as two measuring instruments with frozen numerals would, just as a broken clock does, showing the same time all the time. Variability is a prerequisite of any measuring instrument's responsiveness to phenomena external to it.

Suppose further that the two observers agree on a "1" for unit 8, then observer A's change of heart concerning this value would cause α to jump from 0 to +1. This might seem surprising. Although the two 1s are still rare values, by chance alone, they could show up either in one unit and yield $\alpha = 1.00$, as suggested, or in two different units and yield $\alpha = -.071$. There is at least some variation to which α does respond.

Statistical Significance   11.4.2

A common mistake that researchers make is to accept or reject data as reliable when the null hypothesis that agreement occurs by chance can be rejected with statistical confidence. However, the whole reason for measuring the reliability of data is to ensure that they do not deviate too much from perfect agreement, not that they deviate from chance. In the definition of α, chance agreement merely serves as one of two anchors for the agreement scale to be interpretable, the more important reference point being perfect agreement. As the distribution of α is unknown, approximating a χ^2 distribution only in appearance, we have resorted to generating distributions of α by bootstrapping—that is, by drawing several thousand subsamples from the available reliability data, computing α for each, and thereby generating a probability distribution of hypothetical α values that could occur within the constraints of the observed coincidences. Figure 11.4 depicts a typical distribution of bootstrapped α values. It gives us two statistical qualifications of the observed α:

■ α's *confidence interval* for the chosen level of significance p (two-tailed):

$$\alpha_{largest} \geq \alpha_{observed} \geq \alpha_{smallest}$$

■ The probability q of failing to reach the smallest acceptable reliability α_{min}:

$$q \mid \alpha < \alpha_{min}$$

The confidence interval spells out the range within which the observed α can be expected to vary with $(1 - p)\%$ certainty. The probability q of failing to reach the required reliability is the probability of making the wrong decision of accepting data as reliable when they could well be below the accepted standard.

For the numerical example in section 11.3.3, we measured $_{nominal}\alpha = .743$. After drawing 20,000 samples from these data, the 99% confidence interval is between $\alpha_{smallest} = .615$ and $\alpha_{largest} = .860$, and the probability of failure to exceed $\alpha_{min} = .667$ is $q = .198$.

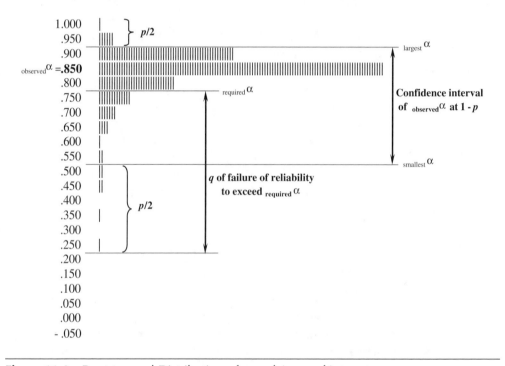

Figure 11.4   Bootstrapped Distribution of α and Areas of Interest

11.4.3   Sampling Considerations

A frequent question concerns how large the sample of units should be for α to be meaningful. There is no simple answer to this question. I consider two distinct issues of sampling reliability data below and then make a practical recommendation.

To establish the *reliability of data*, reliability data need to be representative of the population of data whose reliability is in question. The size of adequate samples is inversely related to the proportion of units in different categories. Rare but important categories must occur in sufficient numbers so as to make the same difference in the reliability calculations as subsequent analyses. As a rule of thumb, each category of units should occur often enough to yield at least five agreements by chance (I will be more specific below, however). Where the research results are particularly important or data are not very numerous, content analysts have resorted to coding all data at least twice. This can be time-consuming and costly, but it bypasses sampling problems altogether, and the measured α is the α of the population of data.

To establish the *reliability of instructions*—data languages, systems of categories, or the measuring instruments that are to be applicable to all possible data—the diversity of the reliability data is more important than their representativeness of the data in hand. When the reliability of data is at issue, the unreliability of categories that do not occur in the data does not need to enter the agreement measures, as it will not affect the trustworthiness of the given data. Moreover, in assessing the reliability of data, there may be good reasons for disagreements on rare categories to be compensated by agreements on frequently used ones. In contrast, when the reliability of coding instructions is in question—reliable coding instructions should generate reliable data regardless of which categories are used and whatever their frequencies may be—reliability data need to contain all the categories of units or values that the instrument lists as possible. Ideally, reliability data here contain each category of units that the instrument distinguishes with equal and sufficiently large frequency. This would justify the oversampling of rare kinds of units and the undersampling of frequently occurring ones.

To obtain *required sample sizes* for either situation, we rely on Bloch and Kraemer's (1989, p. 276) Formula 3.7, which estimates α's variance for binary data (2-by-2 matrices). The minimum number of units,

$$N_c = z^2 \left(\frac{(1 + \alpha_{min})\,(3 - \alpha_{min})}{4(1 - \alpha_{min})\,p_c(1 - p_c)} = \alpha_{min} \right),$$

turns out to be a function of the smallest estimated proportion p_c of values c in the population, the smallest acceptable reliability α_{min} below which data would have to be rejected as unreliable, and the desired level of statistical significance, represented by the corresponding z value for one-tailed tests.

For convenience, Table 11.2 lists the sample sizes for the three smallest acceptable reliabilities α_{min}, four levels of statistical significance, and 10 probabilities p_c. The latter are expressed here as the probabilities of the number of equally likely values. For example, suppose the least frequent of all categories is expected to occur with $p_c = 0.125$. If α is to exceed the smallest acceptable reliability of, say, $\alpha_{min} = .667$, to be sure that 95% of all αs (at the .05 level of statistical significance) satisfy this condition, the table suggests a minimum reliability sample size of 71 units. If one has no clue of the expected probabilities, one may start sampling assuming that all categories are equally likely but then add units to the sample to compensate for the unequal proportions found in the data.

Table 11.2 Required Sample Sizes

Significance level	Smallest acceptable α .667				.800				.900			
	.100	.050	.010	.005	.100	.050	.010	.005	.100	.050	.010	.005
10 values or p_c = .100	53	86	172	211	90	147	294	360	181	298	595	730
9 values or p_c = .111	48	79	157	192	82	134	267	328	165	271	542	665
8 values or p_c = .125	43	71	141	173	74	121	241	295	149	245	489	600
7 values or p_c = .143	39	63	126	154	66	108	215	263	133	218	437	535
6 values or p_c = .167	34	56	111	136	58	95	189	232	117	192	384	471
5 values or p_c = .200	29	48	96	117	50	82	164	200	101	167	333	408
4 values or p_c = .250	25	41	81	99	43	70	139	170	86	142	284	348
3 values or p_c = .333	21	34	68	83	36	59	117	143	73	120	239	292
2 values or p_c = .500	19	30	60	74	32	52	103	127	65	106	212	259

Bloch and Kraemer's Formula 3.7 assumes that α is normally distributed, which is not quite so, as suggested by Figure 11.4. Moreover, the formula for N_c and Table 11.2 do not take into account the number of observers involved in the data-making process. To understand how this number affects the confidence in the required sample sizes, it is important to keep the purpose of reliability evaluations in mind. Reproducibility amounts to predicting from a measured agreement among actual observers the agreement that potential observers working elsewhere would achieve as well. The ability to generalize the reliabilities from a sample to a population of data is only half of the problem—the representativeness of the observers is the other half. If observers with similar qualifications are unavailable elsewhere, the measured agreement may not be interpretable as reproducibility. An increase in the number m of observers grants added assurances that the process is replicable elsewhere. Our estimated sample sizes do not address this experience. However, they err merely by being conservative.

Standards for Data Reliability   11.4.4

The ultimate aim of testing reliability is to ensure that unreliabilities are negligible so as to justify continuing the coding or starting an analysis of the data toward answering research questions. Below, I answer three commonly asked questions regarding reasonable standards.

What is an acceptable level of reliability? Facing the real difficulties of obtaining perfect agreement, can one require that α be at least .95, .90, or .80? Unfortunately, although every content analyst faces this question, there is no set answer. To shed light on how different levels of reliability can be interpreted, Marten Brouwer, a colleague of mine from the Netherlands, designed an experiment. He gave coders who spoke only English a set of complicated Dutch words and asked them to describe U.S. television characters using those words. The Dutch words had no resemblance to any words in English, and the English speakers could hardly pronounce them, but the words must have invoked some consistent associations with perceived personality characteristics because the agreement was $\alpha = .44$. Knowing the observers' unfamiliarity with these words, nobody in their right mind would draw conclusions from the records these subjects created to what they had observed or read. The agreement was well above chance, but on account of entirely unknown associations in the observers' minds, associations that the researcher and the users of findings based on them can hardly imagine. This finding gives us another reference point on the scale of α's values, one that one should not approach. After further explorations of the relationship between achieved agreement and understanding of the categories involved, we adopted the following policies:

■ Rely only on variables with reliabilities above $\alpha = .800$.

■ Consider variables with reliabilities between $\alpha = .667$ and $\alpha = .800$ only for drawing tentative conclusions.

These standards have been adopted in numerous content analyses in the social sciences and they might continue to serve as guidelines. Similar guidelines have been proposed for other coefficients—for example, Fleiss (1981) has proposed guidelines for Cohen's κ (kappa). However, relying on α's distribution gives us criteria that are more justifiable, as a distribution responds to the sample size as well. In these terms, the recommendations could be rephrased:

- Do not accept data with reliabilities whose confidence interval reaches below the smallest acceptable reliability α_{min}, for example, of .800, but no less than .667.

- Ensure that the probability q of the failure to exceed the smallest acceptable reliability α_{min} is reasonably small, for example, .050, or the tolerable risk of drawing wrong conclusions.

I recommend such levels with considerable hesitation. The choice of reliability standards should always be related to the validity requirements imposed on the research results, specifically to the costs of drawing wrong conclusions. If the outcome of a content analysis will affect someone's life—such as in court proceedings—the analyst should not rely on data whose probability of leading to a wrong decision is less than what is commonly accepted (for example, the probability of being killed in a car accident). The results of most content analyses do not have drastic consequences, however, and so the researchers can adopt far lower standards. Even a cutoff point of $\alpha = .800$—meaning only 80% of the data are coded or transcribed to a degree better than chance—is a pretty low standard by comparison to standards used in engineering, architecture, and medical research.

Whether a content analysis is exploratory or intended to be decisive, no researcher should ignore reliability, set reliability standards so low that findings cannot be taken seriously, use deceitful ways of generating reliability data, or apply deceptive agreement measures to prop up the appearance of reliability. In content analysis, the famous phrase "beyond reasonable doubt" has an operationalizable meaning.

Given the α values of separate variables, how reliable are the data as a whole? α is defined for separate variables, and most content analyses involve many. Ideally, the variables of a data language are logically independent, free of conceptual redundancies, and observed disagreements affect the research results equally. Under these conditions, every variable counts and every variable must also be reliable.

It is a serious mistake to average the reliabilities of the variables of a complex instrument and take this average as a measure of overall data reliability. Computing averages assumes that higher values compensate for lower ones. Typical content analyses include clerical variables, publication, date, length, and mechanically obtained measures that tend to be perfectly reliable, whereas the variables that matter are most typically more difficult to code and end up being less reliable.

Researchers who average such reliabilities will have an unwarranted sense of trust that may lead them astray in their conclusions. A condition in which averaging may make sense arises when the values of several variables are subsequently summed or averaged to form a composite index. Averaging their reliabilities is justifiable only if this index is such that scoring on one account is as good as scoring on another and omissions in one variable compensate for commissions in another, so that agreements in one variable balance disagreements in another. These rather stringent conditions are not easy to meet.

Generally, when variables are equally important to the research effort, any unreliable variable can become a bottleneck for confidence in the data as a whole. Thus, *for multivariate data, the lowest α among the variables is the joint reliability of the data as a whole.* This might appear a harsh criterion, but it is entirely consistent with the common practice of dropping unreliable variables from further analysis. Trading the information that one hoped unreliable variables would provide for the reliability of the data as a whole is the only valid strategy for improving joint reliability once data have been gathered.

How does unreliability affect the quality of findings? Part of this question has already been answered in section 11.1: Unreliability limits the chance that results will be valid. Here we are concerned with where reliability should be measured. Because data generation—the reading, coding, or transcribing of texts—typically is the most uncertain part of a study, content analysts routinely assess the reliability of their data at the *front end* of the research effort. Indeed, when the data can be shown to be reliable, the remainder of the work is generally unproblematic. Yet some content analyses are robust in that the unreliabilities that enter the data-making process are barely noticeable in the results. In others, small differences may tip the scale in important decisions, turning affirmative answers into negatives. To appreciate this sensitivity, analysts would have to know how disagreement in the data is transmitted through the analytical process to its outcome. Ideally, this would entail analyzing not just one set of data but as many as the researchers can obtain by permuting the values among which disagreements were encountered. This would generate a distribution of possible results. If this distribution is too wide to allow the analysts to draw conclusions from these data, the reliability standard for front-end coding would need to be set higher. If the distribution does not limit the drawing of conclusions, front-end reliability standards may be relaxed. Analysts can achieve a simple but not quite sufficient approximation of this distribution by performing separate analyses on each observer's data and ascertaining how the results would differ. At the very minimum, content analysts need to trace observed disagreements through the analysis to the results. Generally, data reduction techniques—creating frequency accounts, for example, or combining several variables into an index—tend to reduce the effects that front-end disagreements have on the results. If disagreements are amplified, customary standards for front-end reliabilities may not suffice. Although the reliability of data is surely critical to the success of a content analysis, this is not the only reliability measure that counts.

11.5   OTHER COEFFICIENTS AND CORRESPONDENCES

In a survey of content analyses published in the journal *Journalism & Mass Communication Research* from 1971 through 1995, Riffe and Freitag (1996; cited in Riffe, Lacy, & Fico, 1998) found that only 56% reported assessments of reliability. In their review of the consumer research literature from 1981 through 1990, Kolbe and Burnett (1991) noted similar deficiencies: 31% of the published content analyses showed no concerns for reliabilities; 19% mentioned reliability without revealing any method of calculation; 35% reported %-agreement, including Holsti's; 8% used one of several less well-known measures (each mentioned only once or twice in the sample); and 7% used Krippendorff's α. Lombard, Snyder-Duch, and Bracken (2002) found reliability discussed in 69% of 200 content analyses indexed in *Communication Abstracts* from 1994 through 1998. These are discouraging findings. In this section, I review the most popular agreement indices found in the literature and discuss their shortcomings and relationships to the α coefficient.

Some content analysts make the common but serious mistake of considering the performances of individual observers as variables; applying readily available association, correlation, or consistency measures to them; and interpreting these as measures of reliability. Correlation coefficients—Pearson's product-moment r_{ij}, for example—measure the extent to which two logically separate interval variables, say X and Y, covary in a linear relationship of the form $Y = a + bX$. They indicate the degree to which the values of one variable predict the values of the other. Agreement coefficients, in contrast, must measure the extent to which $Y = X$. High correlation means that data approximate *any* regression line, whereas high agreement means that they approximate the 45-degree line. If one observer is consistently, say, two points behind the other, or they follow a regression line as suggested by the gray dots in the right of the following two contingency matrices, correlation is perfect, but agreement is not. The same holds for cross-tabulations of nominal data. In the contingency matrix on the left, ● signifies a nonzero frequency of co-occurring categories. There is a 1-to-1 relationship between the two sets of categories, association is perfect, and the use of categories by one observer is perfectly predictable from that by the other. But as categories do not match, there is no agreement whatsoever.

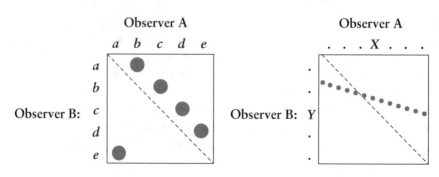

Although correlation coefficients have been used as reliability measures, even recommended (Potter & Levine-Donnerstein, 1999, p. 277), especially in the literature on psychological testing (see the otherwise informative exposition of reliability and validity issues by Carmines & Zeller, 1979; and a review by Salgado & Moscoso, 1996), the above should make clear that in content analysis their use is seriously misleading.

Regarding agreement indices, I have already noted criticism of %-agreement— or "crude" agreement, as this measure is sometimes called—in section 11.3.1. Yet its relatives creep into the literature in different guises. Holsti (1969, p. 140), for example, describes Osgood's (1959, p. 44) reliability index as $2M/(N_1 + N_2)$, wherein M is the number of units on whose categorizations two readers agree, N_1 is the number of units identified by one reader, and N_2 is that number identified by another. Although Holsti presents pertinent criticism of %-like agreement indices, citing Bennett, Alpert, and Goldstein's (1954) arguments and building up to his recommendation of Scott's (1955) π (pi), it is amazing how many content analysts still overlook the by now widely published objections to this uninterpretable agreement measure. For example, Neuendorf (2002) and Lombard et al. (2002), instead of discouraging %-agreement and its relatives, discuss it as a (perhaps too) liberal alternative.

Bennett et al. (1954) were probably the first to realize that %-agreement A_o was the more difficult to achieve the more categories were available for coding. They proposed a coefficient $S = (A_o - 1/K)/(1 - 1/K)$ that corrects for this effect, where K is the number of categories available for coding. It is remarkable that this coefficient has been reinvented at least five times since it was originally proposed: as Guilford's G (Holley & Guilford, 1964), as the RE (random error) coefficient (Maxwell, 1970), as Janson and Vegelius's (1979) C, as κ_n (Brennan & Prediger, 1981), and, most recently, as intercoder reliability coefficient I_r (Perreault & Leigh, 1989). Perreault and Leigh (1989) were at least aware of S. Proponents of this coefficient cite reasons ranging from fairness to each category and consistency with the research traditions of their disciplines to the absence of hard knowledge about the true distribution of categories in the population from which reliability data were sampled. In treating all categories as equally likely, S inflates agreement when used unevenly, especially when some are not used at all. The latter enables researchers to manipulate reliability in their favor by adding unused or rarely used categories to the set. Perreault and Leigh (1989) argue that chance-corrected agreement coefficients, such as κ, are too conservative, whereas S (or their I_r), they say, is not. For arguments against this assessment, see Krippendorff (in press-b).

In response to S's shortcomings, Scott (1955) proposed his reliability index π (pi), which is of the aforementioned form $_{nominal}\alpha = (A_o - A_e)/(A_{max} - A_e)$:

$$\pi = \frac{A_o - P_e}{1 - P_e},$$

where A_o is the proportion of units with matching categories (%-agreement), $P_e = \Sigma_k\, p_k^2$ is the proportion of pairs of values that are expected to match by chance, and p_k is the proportion of values k in the reliability data jointly identified by two observers.

In effect, p_k estimates the proportion of values k in the *population of units* that the observers are facing. P_e treats observers as interchangeable and considers their collective judgment as the best estimates of the population proportions, assuming (as is customary) that differences among observers wash out in their average. Thus P_e becomes the agreement that can be expected to occur in the population when chance prevails.

Subsequently, Cohen (1960) introduced an unfortunate modification of Scott's π into the literature, trying to bring agreement measurement closer to conventional contingency approaches, as he said, and calling it κ (kappa). This coefficient is popular in biomedical and educational research, where most of its proponents work, but inappropriate in assessing reliability in content analysis, as we shall see. Cohen merely replaced Scott's expected agreement P_e with a proportion that conforms to the tradition of association statistics, which I call P_c. κ is defined by

$$\kappa = \frac{A_o - P_c}{1 - P_c},$$

where A_o is the proportion of units with matching categories (%-agreement) (as in Scott's π), $P_c = \Sigma_k \, p_{Ak} \cdot p_{Bk}$ (unlike the P_e in π), p_{Ak} is the proportion of the value k used by observer A, and p_{Bk} is the proportion of value k used by the other observer, B. Here, P_c is the agreement that can be expected when the two observers' proclivity to use their categories differently is assumed and taken for granted.

A numerical example may demonstrate how π and κ differ in their results. Consider two contingency tables containing the frequencies of units recorded by two observers:

	Observer A			
Categories:	a	b	c	
a	12	9	9	30
Observer B b	9	14	9	32
c	9	9	20	38
	30	32	38	100

$A_o = .460$
$\pi = .186$
$\kappa = .186$

	Observer A			
Categories:	a	b	c	
a	12	18	18	48
Observer B b	0	14	18	32
c	0	0	20	20
	12	32	56	100

$A_o = .460$
$\pi = .186$
$\kappa = .258$

Both tables show reliability data to have the same %-agreement A_o, 46 out of 100, as can be seen in their identical diagonal entries. But they differ in how disagreements are distributed, which is also manifest in the two observers' marginal frequencies. In the left-hand table, observers agree on these frequencies and Scott's π and Cohen's κ are the same, as they should be. But when they disagree on these frequencies, as is apparent in the table on the right, κ exceeds π, suggesting that there is more agreement. Evidently, this is far from so. There are still only 46 units in the diagonal cells. How can κ be so mistaken? Note that the 54 mismatches, initially populating both off-diagonal triangles, have now become unevenly distributed, occupying only one. What has increased thereby is not agreement but the predictability of the categories used by one coder from the categories used by the other. Unlike κ, π is not affected by where the mismatching values occur. In content analysis, it indeed should not matter who contributed which disagreements and, when data are nominal, which categories are confused. Moreover, predictability has nothing to do with reliability. Thus, when mismatches in a contingency table are unequally distributed, κ adds a measure of the uneven distribution of mismatching categories to the coefficient, π does not. κ overestimates reliability and cannot serve as a reliability index in content analysis and similar coding tasks.

It should be pointed out that Cohen (1960), in his original proposal of κ, falsely criticized π for ignoring "one source of disagreement between a pair of judges [due to] their proclivity to distribute their judgments differently over the categories" (p. 41). His proposal to modify π achieved just the opposite. κ counts disagreements among observer preferences for available categories as agreements, not as disagreements, as Cohen claimed it would. This is a major conceptual flaw. Brennan and Prediger (1981) describe this property of κ by pointing out that "two judges who independently, and without prior knowledge, produce similar marginal distributions must obtain a much higher agreement rate to obtain a given value of kappa, than two judges who produce radically different marginals." The first two judges "are in a sense penalized" for agreeing on marginal frequencies (p. 692). Many proponents of κ reproduce Cohen's false claim without verification. Zwick (1988), citing others, mentions this flaw as well and suggests testing for marginal homogeneity before computing κ, but this merely patches up κ's obvious inadequacies.

The structural differences between the most popular agreement coefficients (Kolbe & Burnett, 1991; Lombard et al., 2002; Neuendorf, 2002) can be seen most clearly when reduced to their simplest binary or dichotomous forms. We will state these in terms of a 2-by-2 contingency matrix, containing proportions a, b, c, and d of the $n = 2r$ values contributed by the two observers.

	Observer A's Values:	0	1		**Population Estimates**
Observer B's Values:	0	a	b	p_B	from $n = 2r$ = the number of values used
	1	c	d	q_B	jointly by both observers
		p_A	q_A	1	$\bar{p} = (p_A + p_B)/2$
					$\bar{q} = (q_A + q_B)/2 = 1 - \bar{p}$

Agreement = 1 −   Observed / Expected Disagreement

%-agreement	$A_o = 1 −$	$(b + c)$ /
Bennett et al. (1954)	$S = 1 −$	$(b + c) / 2 \cdot \tfrac{1}{2} \cdot \tfrac{1}{2},$
Scott (1955)	$\pi = 1 −$	$(b + c) / 2 \bar{p} \, \bar{q},$
Krippendorff (1970a)	$\alpha = 1 − \dfrac{n-1}{n}$	$(b + c) / 2 \bar{p} \, \bar{q},$
Cohen (1960)	$\kappa = 1 −$	$(b + c) / p_A q_B + p_B q_A.$

where ½ is the logical probability of 0 or 1; $\bar{p}$ and $\bar{q} = (1−\bar{p})$ are population estimates; $n = 2r$ = the total number of values used jointly by both observers; and $(n − 1)/n$ corrects α for small sample sizes.

Evidently, all of these measures contain the proportion of mismatches $(b + c)$. The measure of %-agreement A_o stops there, making no allowances for expected disagreements and saying nothing about the categories that are available for coding and about the population of data being categorized.

S acknowledges expectations but states them relative to the number of categories in the coding instrument. In its binary form, with the two categories being equally likely, the expected disagreement is $2 \cdot \tfrac{1}{2} \cdot \tfrac{1}{2} = \tfrac{1}{2}$, or 50%. S is sensitive to the number of categories available but says nothing about the population of data whose reliability is at stake.

In both π and α, the expected disagreement in the two cells b and c is $2 \bar{p} \, \bar{q}$, which is obtained from the population estimates $\bar{p}$ for 0s and its complement $\bar{q}$ for 1s. π and α are alike except for the factor $(n − 1)/n$, which corrects α for small sample sizes. With rising sample sizes, π and the nominal α become asymptotically indistinguishable.

Cohen's κ, by contrast, reveals itself as a hybrid coefficient (Krippendorff, 1978). Its observed disagreement $(b + c)$, conforms to all the other agreement coefficients, but its expected disagreement, $p_A q_B + p_B q_A$, resembles that of correlation and association measures. In fact, it calculates expected disagreements in the off-diagonal cells just as the familiar χ^2 statistic does. Yet in assessments of agreements, association and predictability are not at issue, as already suggested. Evidently, κ is concerned with the two individual observers, not with the population of data they are observing, which ultimately is the focus of reliability concerns.

To relate the structure of these agreement coefficients to our conception of reliability, I want to be clear: Reliability concerns arise when the trustworthiness of data is unknown and there are doubts about how reliably the phenomena of interest have been observed and are described by these data. It is the population of phenomena that is of ultimate interest to researchers and that interchangeable observers face in the form of samples and record, hopefully without disagreement.

Having no privileged access to the whole population of phenomena, researchers must estimate its composition from whatever they can reasonably trust. It is a fundamental assumption of reliability concerns that the perceptions of many are trusted more than the perception of any one. Consequently, we must estimate the distribution of categories in the population of phenomena from the judgments of as many observers as possible (at least two), making the common assumption that observer differences wash out in their average. Evidently, by estimating the proportions of categories in a population of phenomena, π and α refer to this population and build the above reliability conception into their definitions; κ does not.

This brings us to the *fourth interpretation*. According to the above, α's reliability scale is anchored at two hypothetical points: the condition of all observers applying the same conceptualizations to the same set of phenomena, one at a time and without disagreement, yielding—sampling considerations aside— individually identical and collectively accurate accounts of the distribution of phenomena in the population; and the condition of observers applying the same conceptualizations to the same set of phenomena, but without coordination as to what they are recording, yielding individually randomized but still collectively accurate accounts of this distribution. The latter is the best estimate of the categories in the population of phenomena. On this scale, α *is the degree to which independent observers, using the categories of a population of phenomena, respond identically to each individual phenomenon.* Thus α can be interpreted as measuring the reliability of data relative to an estimated population of the very phenomena that these data are to represent. κ does not estimate such a population and cannot speak about the reliability of data in their capacity to represent the phenomena of interest.

Probably because the aforementioned Cronbach's (1951) alpha has also been called a measure of reliability, it has found its way into the content analysis literature as well. However, this coefficient was never intended to assess coding efforts and in fact it cannot. In its binary form, it is Kuder and Richardson's (1937, p. 158) KR-20 and measures what in our context could be called the consistency of individual coders' judgments. It takes the variances of individual observers ($\Sigma_i p_i q_i$) as the variance of the "true" scores and expresses this as a proportion of the total variances (σ_T^2), which is the sum of the true score and the measurement error (Carmines & Zeller, 1979). In its familiar terms, and in the above terms, it is defined as follows:

$$\text{Cronbach's alpha} = \frac{m}{m-1}\left(1 - \frac{\Sigma_i p_i q_i}{\sigma_T^2}\right)$$

$$= 2\left(1 - \frac{p_A q_A + p_B q_B}{a(p_A + p_B)^2 + (b+c)(p_A - p_B)^2 + d(q_A + q_B)^2}\right).$$

It belongs to the family of correlation coefficients and must not be construed as an agreement measure. Their popularity and use in other empirical domains notwithstanding, %-agreement, Cohen's κ, and Cronbach's alpha are simply not appropriate for assessing the reliability of coding.

With the exception of Krippendorff's α, the above-listed coefficients were all conceived for nominal data generated by just two observers. α is appropriate to all common metrics, not just the nominal metric, and applicable to any number of observers, not just two. Moreover, α copes with missing data and is corrected for small sample sizes. As sample sizes become large, the nominal α approaches Scott's π, as noted above. The ordinal α then becomes identical to Spearman's rank correlation coefficient ρ (rho) without ties in ranks, and the interval α turns out to equal Pearson et al.'s (1901) intraclass correlation coefficient R_I, which is the correlation coefficient r_{ij} applied to coincidence rather than contingency matrices (Krippendorff, 1970a). These correspondences attest to α's generality, demonstrate its connections to well-established statistics, and enable researchers to apply uniform reliability standards to a variety of data.

There have been other proposals to extend agreement coefficients to several observers (Fleiss, 1971; Krippendorff, 1970b, 1971). Because these issues can become very complex, most researchers consider special cases. Landis and Koch (1977) have considered κ-type agreements in terms of majority opinion. Hubert (1977) has taken the approach of accepting only perfect consensus. Craig (1981) has proposed a modification of Scott's π to account for majorities among observer judgments. My extension of α to many observers was initially guided by Spiegelman, Terwilliger, and Fearing's (1953b) effort to rank patterns of disagreement in nominal data by subjective judgments. The pairwise sum of differences $\Sigma_i\Sigma_j\delta_{ij}^2$ in D_o and in D_e approximates their subjective ranks nearly perfectly, which gave me the confidence to apply this function to any number of observers. α demands neither majority judgments nor consensus and privileges no particular number of observers. For multiple observers, the interval α is compatible with variance analysis (Krippendorff, 1970b). Its handling of multiple observers is consistent with Siegel and Castellan's (1988, p. 286) recent extension of Scott's π to many observers (although reluctantly named κ there, causing much confusion). The ability to cope with missing data is a natural by-product of α's extension to many interchangeable observers (Krippendorff, 1992).

In the first edition of *Content Analysis,* I sketched several diagnostic devices—devices for computing the reliability of individual units, for identifying unreliable observers within a group of observers, for determining the metric in use by observers, for tracing the flow of disagreement through coding decision hierarchies—and ways to trade information for increased reliability, for example, by lumping unreliable categories or using variables conditionally (Krippendorff, 1980b, pp. 148–154). Recent advances include the ability to evaluate the reliability of multiple interpretations (the above is limited to assigning at most one value to units of analysis; see section 11.2.3), the use of standards to determine accuracy, and the bootstrapping of α's distribution. A presentation of these analytical capabilities must await another publication. A recent breakthrough was α's extension to calculating the reliability of unitizing (Krippendorff, 1995a). As this is a frequent problem, including in computer-aided qualitative text analysis, I outline its steps in the following section, being aware that developing it further would go beyond the needs of most readers.

α-AGREEMENT FOR UNITIZING   11.6

In most content analyses, units are not given or natural. They must be identified within an otherwise undifferentiated continuum, for example, of linearly ordered text, time records, tape recordings, or flows—within any continuous and quantifiable dimension. I have already mentioned the example of clipping newspaper articles, to which can be added highlighting and coding text segments (as in qualitative text analysis software) pertaining to a research question, identifying episodes of a certain kind in video recordings of social interactions, and generating data by having subjects push buttons to mark periods of interest, disinterest, or emotional arousal while watching TV shows. Analysis of the reliability of unitizing has been largely ignored, mostly because the development of adequate reliability measures has lagged far behind the development of coding methods. Guetzkow (1956) was the first to address the reliability of unitizing. Unfortunately, his coefficient measures the extent to which two observers agree on the *number of identified units,* not on the actual units counted, leaving totally open the question of what, if anything, the observers had in fact agreed on. Osgood's (1959, p. 44) and Holsti's (1969, p. 140) %-like indices have the same problem but moreover fail to consider chance. α_U (Krippendorff, 1995a) overcomes these deficiencies while taking its place in the family of α coefficients, sharing its essential properties. Below, I sketch the basic idea and offer a simple computational example (I do not expect that readers will perform calculations on larger data sets by hand).

Units of length. Unitizing starts with an initially undifferentiated *continuum,* about which we need to know only its beginning, B, and length, L. The unit for measuring these lengths is *the smallest distinguishable length, duration, or number*—for example, the characters in text, the frames of a video, the smallest measurable length on a ruler, or the smallest time interval one can distinguish. Lengths are expressed in full integers, not in decimal points, and not in units of varying size (such as fractions of inches for small lengths and feet or miles for larger ones).

Reliability data. Unitizing means partitioning a given continuum into sections. Reliability data for unitizing (see Figure 11.2) require that at least two observers or methods unitize the same continuum. These sections are numbered consecutively for each individual observer or unitizer. Each section is characterized by the following:

- Its consecutive number g or $h,$ separately for each observer
- The observer i or j who identified it
- The category c or k to which units are assigned

- Its beginning b, subscripted by $<cig>$, $<cjh>$, $<kig>$, $<kjh>$, and so on, locating it on the continuum

- Its length ℓ, also subscripted by $<cig>$, $<cjh>$, $<kig>$, $<kjh>$, and so on, expressing its extent

- A binary value w, also subscripted by $<cig>$, $<cjh>$, $<kig>$, $<kjh>$, and so on, indicating whether it is an identified unit or an empty stretch between two units:

$$w_{cig} = \begin{cases} 0 \text{ iff section } <cig> \text{ is not a unit} \\ 1 \text{ iff section } <cig> \text{ is a unit} \end{cases}$$

These terms enable us to specify each observer's unitization of the same continuum as diagrammed in Figure 11.5.

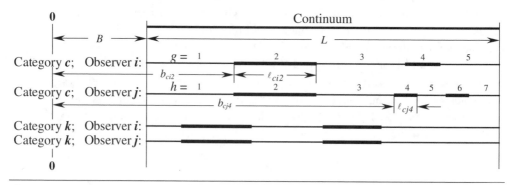

Figure 11.5   Unitizing Terms

Difference function δ^2_{cigjh}. For reliability to be perfect, units must be of the same category and occupy the same stretch of the continuum. Deviations from this ideal give rise to differences. The difference δ^2_{cigjh} between any two sections $<cig>$ and $<cjh>$ of the same category c and identified by two observers, i and j, is a function of their failure to overlap perfectly. In the above terms, this function is

$$\delta^2_{cigjh} = \begin{cases} (b_{cig} - b_{cjh})^2 + (b_{cig} + \ell_{cig} - b_{cjh} - \ell_{cjh})^2 & \text{iff } w_{cig} = w_{cjh} = 1 \text{ and } + \ell_{cjg} < b_{cig} - b_{cjh} < \ell_{cjh}, \\ \ell^2_{cig} & \text{iff } w_{cig} = 1, w_{cjh} = 0 \text{ and } \ell_{cjh} - \ell_{cig} \geq b_{cig} - b_{cjh} \geq 0. \\ \ell^2_{cjh} & \text{iff } w_{cig} = 0, w_{cjh} = 1 \text{ and } \ell_{cjh} - \ell_{cig} \leq b_{cig} - b_{cjh} \leq 0. \\ 0 & \text{Otherwise.} \end{cases}$$

The first condition pertains to pairs of overlapping units. Here δ^2 is the sum of the squares of the two nonoverlapping lengths. The second condition applies when observer i's unit g is fully contained in observer j's gap h. The third condition is the converse of the second and applies when observer i's gap g fully contains observer j's unit h. The fourth condition applies when two sections of the continuum overlap perfectly, are both gaps (not units), or have nothing in common in the continuum. To see how this function behaves in response to different degrees of overlap between two observers' unitizations, consider the examples in Figure 11.6.

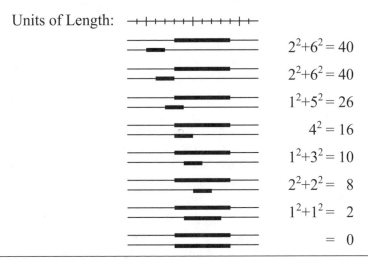

Figure 11.6   Examples of Differences for Unitizing

Observed disagreement D_{oc}. The observed disagreement D_{oc} for unitizing a continuum and assigning its units to category c is obtained—much as the observed disagreement D_o of the α-measures for coding is obtained—through comparison of each observer's sections with all other observers' sections on the continuum. Summing the observed differences and dividing the sum by its maximum yields the measure of the observed disagreement D_{oc}:

$$D_{oc} = \frac{\sum_{i=1}^{m} \sum_g \sum_{j \neq i}^{m} \sum_h \delta^2_{cigjh}}{m(m-1)L^2},$$

where m is the number of observers that unitize the continuum, $m(m-1)$ is the number of pairs of observers whose units are being compared, L is the length of the continuum, and δ^2_{cigjh} is the difference between two sections $<cig>$ and $<cjh>$. Incidentally, $\delta^2_{cigjh} = \delta^2_{cjhig}$. Note that the four sums pair all observers, i and j, with each other but not with themselves and run through all pairs of sections of any one category c.

Expected disagreement D_{ec}. The expected disagreement measures the differences between $mL(mL-1)$ virtual comparisons of all possible unitizations, combining the actually identified units and gaps between them in all possible ways, and applying the above disagreement measure D_{oc} to each pair. Actually making these comparisons would be a transcomputational task, hence the need for a simpler formula for D_{ec}. With $N_c = \sum_{i=1}^{m} \sum_g w_{cig}$ = the total number of units of category c identified by all m observers, the expected disagreement for units in category c is

$$D_{ec} = \frac{\frac{2}{L}\sum_{i=1}^{m}\sum_g w_{cig}\left[\frac{N_c-1}{3}\left(2\ell_{cig}^3 - 3\ell_{cig}^2 + \ell_{cig}\right) + \ell_{cig}^2 \sum_{j=1}^{m}\sum_h \left(1-w_{cjh}\right)\left(\ell_{cjh} - \ell_{cig} +1\right) \;\; \text{iff} \;\; \ell_{cjh} \ge \ell_{cig}\right]}{mL(mL-1) - \sum_{i=1}^{m}\sum_g w_{cig}\ell_{cig}(\ell_{cig}-1)}.$$

Its proof is lengthy; I provide it elsewhere (see Krippendorff, 1995a). Note that, just as the expected disagreement for coding makes no reference to observers and recording units, the expected disagreement for unitizing makes no reference to the original location of the sections on the continuum or to who identified them.

Let me merely point out the principal components of the above equation. The first double summation in its numerator goes through all observers' segments, with w_{cig} separating these into units proper and the omitted gaps between two units. The first expression in the square brackets accounts for the differences between one unit and all other units overlapping with that unit in all possible ways. The double summation in the square brackets checks whether the one unit would fit into any of the gaps between units and adds the differences due to each. In the denominator, mL is the number of possible locations for a unit to occur in the continuum, and $mL(mL-1)$ is the number of pair comparisons of such units that the disagreement measure calculates virtually. The second expression in the denominator discounts the results of comparing sections with themselves.

α_U-*agreement for all categories.* Similar to coding,

$$\alpha_U = 1 - \frac{\sum_c D_{oc}}{\sum_c D_{ec}}.$$

For a computational example, we assign numerical values to the beginnings and lengths of the units in Figure 11.5

Continuum	B	L	
	150	300	
Sections	*b*	ℓ	*w*
$ci1$	150	75	0
$ci2$	225	70	1
$ci3$	295	75	0
$ci4$	370	30	1
$ci5$	400	50	0
$cj1$	150	70	0
$cj2$	220	80	1

*cj*3	300	55	0
*cj*4	355	20	1
*cj*5	375	25	0
*cj*6	400	20	1
*cj*7	420	30	0
*ki*1	150	30	0
*ki*2	180	60	1
*ki*3	240	60	0
*ki*4	300	50	1
*ki*5	350	100	0
*kj*1	150	30	0
*kj*2	180	60	1
*kj*3	240	60	0
*kj*4	300	50	1
*kj*5	350	100	0

The nonzero *differences* between the two observers' sections in category c are

$$\delta^2_{ci2j2} = (225 - 220)^2 + (225 + 70 - 220 - 80)^2 = 5^2 + 5^2 = 50 = \delta^2_{cj2i2},$$

$$\delta^2_{ci4j4} = (370 - 355)^2 + (370 + 30 - 355 - 20)^2 = 15^2 + 25^2 = 850 = \delta^2_{cj4i4}$$

$$\delta^2_{ci5j6} = 20^2 = 400 = \delta^2_{cj6i5}$$

Evidently, the first pair of units in category c, showing observer i as merely a bit more conservative than j is, contributes very little by comparison to the remaining three units, which appear more scattered on the continuum. In category k all differences are zero:

$$\delta^2_{ki2j2} = 0 = \delta^2_{ki4j4}.$$

With these differences in hand, the *observed disagreement* in category c becomes:

$$D_{oc} = \frac{\delta^2_{ci2j2} + \delta^2_{ci4j4} + \delta^2_{ci5j6} + \delta^2_{cj2i2} + \delta^2_{cj4i4} + \delta^2_{cj6i5}}{m(m-1)L^2} = \frac{2(50 + 850 + 400)}{2(2-1)\,300^2} = .0144.$$

In category k, the observed disagreement $D_{ok} = .0000$, of course.

Calculating the *expected disagreement* with the above formula requires a few more steps. In category c, with a total of $N_c = 2 + 3 = 5$ identified units, the expected disagreement is obtained as follows:

$$D_{ec} = \cfrac{\dfrac{2}{300}\left\{\begin{array}{l}\left[\dfrac{5-1}{3}(2\cdot70^3 - 3\cdot70^2 + 70) + 70^2 \begin{pmatrix}75-70+1\\+75-70+1\\+70-70+1\end{pmatrix}\right]\\[3em] + \left[\dfrac{5-1}{3}(2\cdot30^3 - 3\cdot30^2 + 30) + 30^2 \begin{pmatrix}75-30+1\\+75-30+1\\+50-30+1\\+70-30+1\\+55-30+1\\+30-30+1\end{pmatrix}\right]\\[5em] + \left[\dfrac{5-1}{3}(2\cdot80^3 - 3\cdot80^2 + 80)\right]\\[3em] + \left[\dfrac{5-1}{3}(2\cdot20^3 - 3\cdot20^2 + 20) + 20^2 \begin{pmatrix}75-20+1\\+75-20+1\\+50-20+1\\+70-20+1\\+55-20+1\\+25-20+1\\+30-20+1\end{pmatrix}\right]\\[6em] + \left[\dfrac{5-1}{3}(2\cdot20^3 - 3\cdot20^2 + 20) + 20^2 \begin{pmatrix}75-20+1\\+75-20+1\\+50-20+1\\+70-20+1\\+55-20+1\\+25-20+1\\+30-20+1\end{pmatrix}\right]\end{array}\right\}}{2\cdot300(2\cdot300-1) - \begin{pmatrix}70(70-1)\\+30(30-1)\\+80(80-1)\\+20(20-1)\\+20(20-1)\end{pmatrix}} = .0532.$$

And in category k, with a total of $N_k = 2 + 2 = 4$ identified units, the expected disagreement turns out to be $D_{ek} = .0490$.

Finally, the α_U-agreement for unitizing with the two categories is

$$\alpha_U = 1 - \frac{D_{oc} + D_{ok}}{D_{ec} + D_{ek}} = 1 - \frac{.0144 + .0000}{.0532 + .0490} = .8591,$$

which concludes this illustration.

CHAPTER 12

Computer Aids

This chapter describes how computers can support content analysis research. Computers have been hailed as reliable, fast, and increasingly inexpensive tools for processing large volumes of textual data, and a great deal of progress is being made in the development of computer software that can assist what content analysts need to do. This chapter reviews some of the procedures and approaches that are available today and likely to stay. Although the use of computers allows content analysts to circumvent the tedium involved in manual data handling and virtually eliminates the problem of unreliable coding, computer applications are approaching other kinds of limits, and these are discussed here as well.

WHAT COMPUTERS DO 12.1

Content analysis, done entirely "by hand," is often time-consuming, and unreliability is a persistent problem. Before the advent of digital computers, texts were exclusively written, typed, printed, and read. The widespread use of computers has revolutionized the manipulation of texts in ways that are attractive to content analysts. The following characteristics of computers deserve special attention here:

■ Computers are sequential machines.

■ Computers can process large volumes of numerical and textual data with astonishing speed.

■ Computers apply logical or algebraic operations to the internal representations of data, entered as inputs, and produce new representations, outputs, some of which are available for human inspection—for example, on a computer screen or in print.

257

■ Computers must be programmed. Software packages, mostly developed and sold separately from computer hardware, tend to provide bundles of computer programs whose details escape the comprehension of ordinary computer users. However, such software allows users to make choices concerning what a computer is to do with the data in hand, using a mouse to point and click on menu options or keying in character strings, for example. At any one point in time, the computer program in use is a theory of what that computer does.

■ Computers' operations are always deterministic and hence perfectly reliable. Within a computer, ambiguities and uncertainties do not exist.

Several compelling analogies can be made between the way computers work and what content analysts do. The sequential input of discrete characters into a computer resembles the lines of text that readers follow with their eyes. Computers perform logical operations much as rational human beings are thought to do in order to comprehend, draw conclusions, make decisions, and argue. The programs within a computer resemble the instructions (unitization schemes, sampling plans, recording instructions, analytical procedures—see Figure 4.2) that content analysts give to their assistants or hired coders with the expectation that they will be followed completely and reliably—that is, "mindlessly." In descriptions of how data enter a computer, the metaphor of "reading" is common, and terms like *coding, data processing, symbol manipulation,* and *computation* have migrated back to the domain of human intelligence. It is widely believed that if an adequate theory of how readers interpret text existed and could be formulated in a suitable computer language, computers could be made to read text just as intelligent readers would, only faster and more reliably. Although there are good reasons why adequate computational theories of literacy are unavailable to date, many developments of computer content analyses are fueled by the hope that such theories are possible and in sight. But there are less ambitious aims.

12.2 HOW COMPUTERS CAN AID CONTENT ANALYSES

The most important reason for using computers in content analysis is their ability to process large volumes of data at high speed. A pioneering example of research demonstrating this capacity is DeWeese's (1977) online analysis of newsprint. DeWeese developed a device that converted typesetting instructions for newsprint (which, at the time of his research, came in the form of a paper tape that created the templates for rotary printing presses) into a computer-readable form, which enabled him to analyze the text of a newspaper virtually while it was being printed. Today, only a little more than 25 years after DeWeese's innovation journalists and printing presses communicate with one another electronically, as do individuals in virtually all spheres of text production and communication, making text naturally available to computer analysis.

Another example of the ability of computers to process large amounts of data quickly is found in the creation of concordances for literary works. Before the advent of computers, the task of creating a list of all significant words in the works of a productive writer and keeping track of their locations in a body of writing could easily occupy the lifetime of a literary scholar plus numerous assistants. Now, for any computer-readable text, the creation of an alphabetical list of key words is a matter of hours at most. Every day, more and more books, journals, and research reports are available in electronic form, and more and more people are able to access ever-growing electronic full-text databases. In addition, extraordinary progress has been made in the reliability of optical scanning for converting written and printed materials into electronic form. In many practical situations, analysts can expect to make sense of the large volumes of text available everywhere, including online, by using fast and powerful computers.

A second reason computers are useful in content analysis is their ability to process textual material reliably. This is a blessing with a hitch, however. Mechanical computation virtually eliminates errors and nourishes the dreams of some content analysts to bypass human coders altogether. However, it is easy to overlook the fact that computers recognize only character strings. Literate humans are astonishingly proficient at intuiting the etymology of words or the syntactical rules that explain complex expressions, and they have little difficulty verbalizing the point that the author of a text seems to be making or knowing how other members of their community would read given texts. All texts are created to be read by someone. Humans cannot help but read meanings into texts, and they do not always do so reliably. The reliability that computer analysis offers, in contrast, lies in the processes of character string manipulation, which may be far removed from what humans do when reading.

Unlike humans, computers are deterministic machines. They cannot *not* process text reliably. Computers have no sense of what they do, who their users are, or what the character strings they are processing may mean to human readers, nor are they sensitive to the shifting cultural contexts relative to which we read and understand text. Computers do not even know the difference between randomly generated character strings and words or symbols that have meaning to humans unless someone tells them how they differ—for example, by entering a dictionary of legitimate words. Therefore, it is seriously misleading to characterize computers as being able to read texts or data. When we say that computers "read," we are simply using a metaphor drawn from what we humans think we do with texts. Ordinarily, the use of this metaphor may not matter much, but content analysts who are contemplating the use of computer aids in their research would be wise to consider the above and not let themselves be misled into believing that a computer could read text the way they do. Programming a machine to mimic how humans so effortlessly understand, interpret, and rearticulate text turns out to be an extraordinarily difficult, if not impossible, undertaking.

What, then, are the specific demands of computer-aided content analysis? Recall that we have defined content analysis in terms of the drawing of inferences from available text—abductive inferences, to be specific. A computer-aided content analysis should do the same. Content analysis results, it is important to recognize, are texts as well (see Chapter 14), texts that answer analysts' research questions about particular unobserved phenomena. Thus, in addition to being understandable to the analysts, their scientific peers, and the beneficiaries of the research results, the path that a content analysis takes must be related to how the analyzed body of text is, was, or will be used in the context relative to which that text is analyzed. Therefore, in the process of any content analysis, conducted with or without the aid of computers, relevant readings or uses of the original texts should be preserved.

To satisfy this criterion, a computer analysis of text should in effect represent, model, or embody at least some of the processes of a text's contextualization (see Figure 9.1). In the extreme, this condition would be satisfied when a computer responds to a body of text in the same way a selected community of readers would. But, as noted above, it is extremely difficult to program a computer to do what ordinary readers of text do naturally.

It follows that the use of computers in content analysis invokes a shift in methodological emphasis, from solving the human problem of achieving reliable coding for large volumes of text at a reasonable rate to solving the computational problem of preserving relevant readings of the texts. In traditional content analysis, semantically valid reading is intuitively satisfied. Coders do not easily violate their tacit understanding. The use of computers in content analysis is limited by the difficulty of achieving semantic validity (see Chapter 13, section 13.2.2).

There are two reasonable compromises that content analysts can make when using computers without jeopardizing the preservation of the relevant readings or meanings of the original texts:

■ Analysts may use computer applications that do preserve relevant readings, albeit in highly *specialized contexts*. Even traditional content analysts typically ask highly specific research questions—for example, in the context of a particular psychological theory, election campaign, or crime investigation. There is a place for the development of computer applications for content analyses in well-structured contexts and for simple variables. Diction (Hart, 1985), for example, is a content analysis software that is designed to infer something like the rhetorical tone of political speeches. For political rhetoricians who know the original texts, the results that Diction produces make sense, hence Diction satisfies the criterion. But this software would not be useful to analysts investigating charges of plagiarism, attempting to infer biases in reporting, or seeking to provide information about the psychological states of the sources of the analyzed texts. It is not designed to be general, but it is a plausible tool for political rhetoricians who are asking the very questions it can answer.

■ Analysts may use computational *tools* that preserve relevant readings, but only for *small intermediate steps*. Content analysis involves many analytical procedures (see Figure 4.2); some are clerical and relatively easy to accomplish, and others call for human intelligence that is difficult to specify in advance. The use of computers is most appropriate for recurrent and repetitive tasks that can be conceptualized without uncertainty. Searching, coding, sorting, listing, and counting are obvious candidates. Their steps are small, and their operation is transparent. Content analysts have no difficulty comprehending what they do and employing them where needed—without surrendering their judgment to their results. A search engine that can make a body of potentially relevant texts available for human analysts to do the rest is one such tool. When an analytical task is divided into what humans do best and what computers do best, computers do not perform the analysis but aid it; thus I refer to this approach as *computer-aided text analysis,* or CATA for short.

To justify the use of CATA software, content analysts must assure themselves, as well as the community of their peers, that the way a software package processes the data is compatible with what is known about the context of the texts, how texts are read, what they mean, and what role they play. For example, if the meanings of interest are tied to sentence constructions, a computer program that cuts a large body of text into words and accounts for that body of text in terms of word frequencies will not retain the sentential meanings (Krippendorff, 1969a). If the research question concerns political categories, an analysis of texts in psychological terms is irrelevant. If textual meanings are changing over time, by context, or for different readers, an analysis that treats all textual units alike will be misleading. If a diagnosis is wanted, a clustering program is irrelevant. In Chapter 13, I address these issues in terms of validity, semantic validity being most important to this discussion. There is no universal computer content analyzer.

Potential CATA users must be careful not to fall prey to fancy labels and abstract concepts claiming to describe what sophisticated software can do. Vendors of CATA software tend to market their products in terms of metaphors that suggest much but mean less in practice. For example, the claim that a software package can "extract content," with no explication of how it does what, leaves naive users thinking that it can do something they cannot. Similarly, without a specified context, the promise to perform a "concept analysis" is as empty as the assurance that the software does a content analysis (see Chapter 2, especially on the use of the content metaphor). Concepts are always someone's concepts and may have interesting implications, but only if embodied somewhere. Claims of "theme identification," "auto-categorization," "information mining," "knowledge discovery," and "relational text analysis" may leave the novice user of CATA software in awe but say little about what features of text the software responds to or preserves. Beginners may find themselves wondering what their computational results could possibly mean and, being human, undoubtedly find explanations. Responsible software developers provide explicit information about what their software does and/or enable researchers to trace samples of text through the analytical process to see for themselves what happens to them.

Because the CATA software market is evolving rapidly, I cannot possibly provide a comprehensive survey of the content analysis aids currently available, although I cannot help but mention some of the most widely used packages. For reviews of CATA software, see Tesch (1990), Weitzman and Miles (1995), Popping (1997, 2000), Alexa (1997), and Alexa and Züll (1999). In addition, the University of Alabama's Content Analysis Resources Web site (http://www.car.ua.edu) provides frequently updated links to literature, software, and people connected with content analysis. The Text Analysis Info Web site (http://textanalysis.info), maintained by one software developer, is another resource.

Although up-to-date information about available CATA software is more likely found on the Internet than in a book, researchers must bear in mind that the Web does not always include fair overviews of various software packages or methodological criteria for selection. In the remainder of this chapter, my focus is on helping potential CATA users to ask appropriate questions about various kinds of software, so that they do not invest their time in mastering one software only to find out that it cannot provide them with the answers they seek. I distinguish and discuss the following computer aids:

- *Accounts of character strings:* These partition a given body of text into convenient textual units (i.e., character strings) and list, sort, count, and cross-tabulate them as needed. The readings that these accounts preserve reside in the readings of these units.

- *Text searches:* These identify units of text (documents, for example, but also shorter expressions) according to whether they contain character strings with desired textual attributes. Their meanings are encoded in an analyst's query.

- *Computational content analyses:* These transform a body of text into representations that bring it closer to answering a researcher's question. Such analyses embody some theory of meaning or can be said to model how the given body of text is used in the context of the intended content analysis.

- *Interactive-hermeneutic approaches:* These enable a single analyst to manage text segments of different sizes systematically and to develop coding categories while reading.

I conclude this chapter with a discussion of the frontiers of CATA software in which I offer some suggestions to users concerning what they should look for and to developers concerning what would be desirable to work toward.

12.3 ACCOUNTS OF CHARACTER STRINGS

As noted above, this kind of software partitions a typically large body of text into mutually exclusive parts and gives the user various accounts of these partitions, usually in the form of lists of types and/or counts of tokens. These accounts are straightforward and simple because they use syntactical criteria, not meanings.

Most word processing programs make available to their users information about the numbers of characters, words, paragraphs, and pages in any given file. In fact, they enumerate certain designated characters: alphabetical, numerical, and typographical ones, including wingdings, spaces, punctuation marks, paragraph signs, line divisions, page divisions, and so on. Because these characters are purely typographical or syntactical, the frequencies computed from them cannot reveal anything about the role of a file, how it could be read, or what it is about. Most people would not call such an accounting a content analysis, but this is where accounts of character strings begin.

Accounts of otherwise meaningful character strings, such as lists of words, phrases, or sentences, do not require any theory of meaning—with reference to the source, the reader, or the analyst. The identification of such character strings is a mechanical task, and a list of them typically violates the reasons a text was written. For example, if one chops a large body of text into mutually exclusive text segments—say, into words—the segments' positions within the text (at the beginning, in the middle, or toward the end) are lost, their grammatical functions are no longer recognizable (is *bear* a verb or a noun?), the relations between segments are gone (is *health* affirmed or denied, as in *not healthy*?), personal pronouns become empty (who is *she*?), and dialogical distinctions, such as between questions and answers, are irrecoverably obliterated. For computers, character strings are either the same or different, nothing else. Computers treat grammatical variations of a word (e.g., *bear, bore, borne,* and *born*) or stylistic variations that express the same idea (e.g., *empty, unfilled, vacant,* and *void*) as different character strings.

How can such accounts aid content analysis? The answer is surprisingly simple: They can do so only when they preserve the analyst's ability to read and make sense of the character strings that are tabulated and counted. However, reading a list of words of which a text is composed is obviously not the same as reading a coherent narrative. The difference between the two unequivocally demonstrates what an account of character strings omits. A primary motivation for accounting for the parts instead of the whole is expediency. Frequencies simplify a text. Whether such accounts are justified depends on the questions the analyst needs to answer. Listing and counting have no virtue in the abstract.

In the preparation of accounts of character strings, even the establishment of the syntactical categories of what is to be distinguished and counted is not entirely unproblematic. Take the simple idea of a word, for example. In computer accounts, a word tends to be defined as a character string bracketed by blanks, punctuation marks, or paragraph signs. This definition relies on known typographical conventions, not meanings. Anyone who has seen computer-generated frequency lists of words so defined can attest that such lists tend to include rather odd entries that intelligent readers would never make. Numbers, typographical characters, and misspellings are on equal footing with legitimate words. Plural and singular forms and other kinds of grammatical variations of one word appear as distinct words. Hyphenated words such as *co-occurrence,* compound terms such as *high school* or *North Pole,* abbreviations such as *St. Paul* and *Ph.D.,* and numerical expressions such as *$2,578.30* would all be cut into nearly meaningless pieces, as would colloquial expressions such as *run of the mill*—which has nothing to do with running or with mills. Nevertheless, such word lists can offer content analysts a sense of the vocabulary they are facing.

Most CATA software packages provide accounts of words. Among the better-known systems capable of handling very large data sets are VBPro, a simple free-ware program; WordStat; ZyINDEX, now part of ZyLAB; dtSearch, used largely in the legal profession; and Concordance, widely used in literary research. For the above-mentioned reasons, the lists of word frequencies produced by any one such software are rarely exactly the same. For example, the General Inquirer (Stone, Dunphy, Smith, & Ogilvie, 1966), the pioneer content analysis software (which is now freely available as well), counts idioms and labels such as *United States* as single words and counts hyphenated words that are not in its dictionary, such as *response-seeking,* as two words. CATA software users need to understand how the software they are using distinguishes words or other character strings before they can make use of their results.

Among the most useful kinds of word lists an analyst can expect CATA software to provide are the following:

- Standard (left-to-right) alphabetical ordering

- Reverse (right-to-left) alphabetical ordering

- Ordering in ascending or descending frequencies

Standard alphabetical word lists have the advantage of being easily comparable with other alphabetical lists, including dictionary entries. Lists in reverse alpha-betical order (that is, in which the first word ends with an *a* and the last word ends with a *z*) enable analysts to examine redundant endings, plurals, tenses, and suffixes, which aids in the construction of dictionaries and search terms with wildcards, both to be discussed below. Lists of words in ascending or descend-ing order of frequencies typically conform to Zipf's (1935) law: Word frequen-cies decline exponentially with increasing word length. That is, the most frequent words are short words, typically function words, such as articles, prepositions, logical connectors, and pronouns. The least frequent words, unique in the extreme, are long and statistically unrepresentative words. Misspellings, being infrequent, do not conform to this law. Words that distinguish most clearly between different texts tend to be located somewhere between these extremes (Rijsbergen, 1979, fig. 2.1). Word lists ordered by frequencies can help identify these. Some CATA software allows users to set limits, so that the only words listed are those within frequencies that are likely to matter most.

Users of word processing software are familiar with spell-checkers. These devices compare all character strings with words on a list of proper words and highlight strings that do not match, such as nonwords, words with typographical errors, foreign names, and rare words. Spell-checkers incorporate the most rudimentary form of word meaning: membership in a particular language. Some CATA software packages employ word lists that are analogous to spell-checkers—not to identify and enable users to correct errors but to act as "filters" on relevant character strings, usually words. Such filters may take one of the following forms:

- A list of "go-words," or keywords to be included in the account (All words not on this list are ignored.)

- A list of "stop-words," or keywords to be excluded from the account (All words not on this list are counted.)

- A list of character strings (of alphabetical and other characters) to be regarded as single words or phrases, such as compound words, abbreviations, and colloquial expressions (A special case of this is the treatment of negations. A list can be provided of negative forms of adjectives or expressions—for example, *not good, no problem,* or *rarely accurate*—that do not separate the negator from the negated [Péladeau, 2003].)

- A list of prefixes, suffixes, and grammatical markers to be removed from character strings, appearing in the account without the omitted parts

All of these devices are intended to eliminate irrelevant words and phrases or irrelevant variations of keywords from the accounts. The first three devices are self-explanatory. The fourth facilitates a process called *stemming*—the removal of grammatical endings to get to the "stem" or core of a word. For example, stemming reduces *talking, talked, talker, talks,* and *talkative* to *talk* (something that could also be accomplished through queries using wildcards; see section 12.4). Stemming can create many oddities that analysts need to examine carefully. For example, when the grammatical endings *ed* and *ing* are removed from all words, the words *red* and *ring* both become *r*, which makes them indistinguishable. And removing *er* from *porter* makes it impossible for one to know if the remaining word refers to the job of guarding a door, a harbor for shipping, or a kind of wine. (A process similar to stemming but more powerful is lemmatization, which I discuss in section 12.5.1 as a dictionary application.)

Aside from comparing the word frequencies of different bodies of text, content analysts may find it useful to compare distributional indices computed on such frequencies. Clement So (1995) applied entropy measures, also called measures of text temperature (Krippendorff, 1986, pp. 15–20), to assess the diversity of vocabularies and to compare the coverage in different media regarding different issues and in different geographic regions (see So in Lee, Chan, Pan, & So, 2002). Several CATA software packages and even some word processors feature versions of Flesch's (1974) measure of readability. These programs assign readability scores to texts based on the frequencies of certain categories of words, certain forms of punctuation, sentence lengths, and so on—all of which are distributional characteristics of frequency accounts of character strings.

Whereas lists of words and frequencies take words out of their original linguistic environments and thereby prevent content analysts from recognizing differences in use, so-called KWIC (keyword in context) lists provide inventories of the linguistic environments of selected words. A KWIC list enables content analysts to examine different uses of the same word. Users may want to restrict such lists to keywords, the go-words on a list, because a complete KWIC listing of all words explodes a text in size. KWIC lists can facilitate analysts' development of categories, whether for subsequent manual coding or for the construction of computer dictionaries. They can also aid analysts in formulating rules for distinguishing among unanticipated kinds of meanings. In Figure 12.1, which reproduces a fraction of a KWIC list for the keyword *play,* several different meanings of the keyword are apparent:

To play something (an instrument)

To play with something (a ball)

To play with someone (with a friend or by oneself)

To play versus to be serious

A play (as in a theatrical performance)

Before he analyzed campaign speeches made during the 1980 U.S. election, Weber (1984, p. 131) examined a KWIC list of these speeches using the keyword *rights.* This enabled him to observe that when Republicans used the word, it was in the context of discussing law-abiding citizens, state and local authorities, parents, and would-be Soviet immigrants. In the context of women, most occurrences of the word *rights* in Republican speeches came within claims that the Equal Rights Amendment was not needed. In contrast, when Democrats used the word, it tended to be in contexts concerning the rights of working women, minority women, striking workers, pregnant women, industrial laborers, farm laborers, the disabled, the victims of civil rights violations, and black South Africans. A KWIC list can bring the diversity of word senses, especially of homonyms, to the analyst's attention and suggest further analytical steps.

As Figure 12.1 shows, KWIC lists also provide references to the locations of words within a body of text. Such references are essential for another well-known type of textual account, the *concordance.* As noted above, concordances link important words in a body of texts (for example, the complete works of a given author) to their locations in the works. Not all CATA systems provide KWIC lists that are as easily readable as the fragment shown in Figure 12.1. The software packages Concordance and WordStat are notable exceptions. In these programs, the user can select a word from an alphabetical list of words together with their frequencies and see displayed all of the contexts and references to the word's occurrence. Others show one linguistic context at a time, like the "find" command in word processing systems.

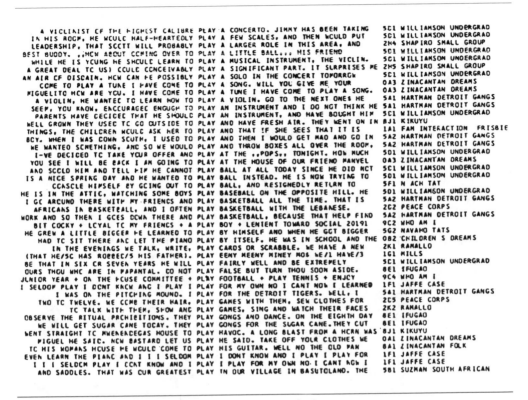

Figure 12.1   Partial KWIC Listing for the Keyword *Play*

SOURCE: Dunphy (1966, p. 159).

A somewhat forgotten but still useful account of character strings in text is the construction of a *map of a text* or body of texts. In such a map, relevant textual units—keywords, sentences, or paragraphs—are represented by outstanding characters and irrelevant units by visually less prominent ones. Such a map conveys a sense of where relevant textual matter is located in the texts being examined, how that matter is distributed, and which categories of words cluster, and thus directs analysts' attention to sections worthy of further examination. Sedelow (1967) pioneered the use of such maps. Figure 12.2 shows the geographic distribution of eight categories (three binary components) of informers for a huge lexical research project; this map was created using software called CodeMap (Montgomery, 1989; Pederson, McDaniel, Adams, & Liao, 1989). Although this map was created for a study that was not strictly a content analysis, it gives an idea of how a large textual database can be visualized in relevant categories. On his TextArc Web site (http://textarc.org), W. Bradley Paley provides an interesting demonstration of how to map a text visually; he describes his software as "a funny combination of an index, concordance, and summary; it uses the viewer's eye to help uncover meaning." Unfortunately, this experiment hides the sophistication of Paley's mapping technique behind an unfolding artistically

```
                        Code: Race/Sex/Age

          1 = W/F/13-65  92/152  A = B/F/13-65  16/51
          2 = W/M/13-65  90/163  B = B/M/13-65  14/40
          3 = W/F/66-99  80/166  C = B/F/66-99  10/53
          4 = W/M/66-99  95/236  D = B/M/66-99  10/53


        1         2         3         4         5         6         7
  1234567890123456789012345678901234567890123456789012345678901234567890

A                                          123143223141144.41332413        A
B                           4243241.4.  2C4141133222.A3D23431341.A.244.4    B
C                           31.314.2.   C4.11.2.3.2.3241331..4.22A1.4334    C
D                           122322..143.A1.442.3B241334.32.2.1.44414        D
E                           2342341C3A.4.22.B14.324344124C32C.3            E
F                           .3.A4...C2433.1.33..D.4D1A21.1B.4.3.43          F
G                           411AA144..4..BD1AB1D1.C21.21..13.3.3.11         G
H              4      2B     44.B21.......A.434.1...B..4.D..1B21.4.14        H
I           4               ..43131D4....2.3.44.1..2332B.3.D4.B.3...3       I
J         3        .      2  2...34.22....4..2...4..2.A.43.33131D.....      J
K      3 .A3                 .. 1....3......3.4D...4...43.2..1.....4.....    K
L        12.     .2         .2 21.1..2.....2.......2.B..241...132.1....     L
M      3         1           ....432...C.31.3....C..4..24121.......3..A     M
N       4                    ....1......23...1....2..3.............         N
O        4           .       .44....2..4...3..1..C43........2..........     O
P             .     2.1   .  44........4....3.1.................           P
Q     .3        .1     .4 .2..........3.2.1... ... .........1......         Q
R        .         ..        ..3........2.3..B........2      1.      .      R
S                           .1..2.............22...B1 .    ....    3.       S
T          4       1.2      ........2..A           .2.2 .    .. 2..         T
U     .. 1        ..     2   ..........                          ..         U
V       ..      .2.          ..........                    4.4 . .          V
W     12.    .    .1                                       .. . . .         W
X    4 1A1    ...                                          . . . .          X
Y            4.24                                          .. . .            Y
Z    4       ..1                                           1..2 1 1          Z
AA           ..                                            ... .             AA
AB  12       1.                                            2. ... 4          AB
AC  ..       2                                             . . . .           AC
AD    .4 1                                                 1 . . .           AD
AE    1.                                                   .22. AE
AF       .42                                              ... . AF
AG                                                          .   AG
AH                                                          .   AH


        1         2         3         4         5         6         7
  1234567890123456789012345678901234567890123456789012345678901234567890
```

Figure 12.2   An Eight-Category Map of a Lexical Item

SOURCE: Montgomery (1989).

NOTE: On LAGS, see Pederson et al. (1989).

motivated image. By visually mapping texts into simple categories, content analysts can get a good first view of what they are facing and then decide on the course of their analysis.

A useful kind of account that comes to content analysis from literary scholarship is the *table of co-occurrences* (usually of keywords). Such a table enables the analyst to compute associations but also serves as an entry to contingency analysis. Word co-occurrences are always counted within a larger stretch of text, which the user needs to define. Some applications register only immediate neighbors, whereas others allow the user to define a window of a certain width within which the co-occurrence of two or more words is recorded. Early implementations of such accounts defined a window of a fixed number of characters (Iker, 1975). As tables of word co-occurrences can become unmanageably large, it is essential that accounts be restricted to keywords on a go-word list. Current CATA software enables other definitions of windows, such as numbers of words, sentences, or paragraphs (see Woelfel, 1993, 1997). Proximity connectors, discussed below, further liberalize how the windows for identifying word co-occurrences are defined.

Finally, *Boolean accounts* sort the textual units of a given body of text into categories that are defined by user-supplied Boolean expressions. A Boolean expression specifies one category of textual units by the character strings that it must or must not contain. The textual units categorized thereby should be large enough to contain the character strings that identify them to be of a certain kind—whole documents, for example, but also individual paragraphs, even sentences. All textual units should be in the analyst's possession, or at least electronically accessible to be tabulated and/or counted.

One of the earliest content analyses to use Boolean accounts is attributed to Sebeok and Zeps (1958), who searched for patterns in a collection of Cheremis folktales. By contemporary standards this collection was small; today, the availability of CATA software has expanded Boolean accounts to much larger samples of text. One way in which analysts can account for larger collections of text is by applying Boolean operators not to the texts themselves but to indices of the texts. Scholars have been devising indices for large textual databases since the late 1960s, when Janda (1969) gained quick access to relevant political documents by sorting through indices of these documents stored on microfilm. Janda's system also allowed researchers to add indices as they examined the documents, thus expanding the scope of the accounts in the process of the analysis. Up until recently, computational accounts of visual representations were virtually unthinkable without manual indexing. In their research on facial expressions, Ekman, Friesen, and Taussig (1969) coded frames of film manually and tested their hypotheses on these codes. Today, advances in image processing and voice recognition have changed such research somewhat. One recently developed software system, Virage, is designed to automatically identify visual images and speech (see the company's Web site at http://www.virage.com). It searches audio-visual records, including records from television, for occurrences of logos, images, or sounds supplied by the user, even faces and verbal expressions, and creates accounts of where these occur within the records.

The simplest example of a Boolean account is a sorting of available texts according to whether they do or do not contain a chosen word or phrase. For example, a search for the words *alcohol* and *drugs* (which may appear singly, jointly, or not at all) in a collection of paragraphs defines two variables—mentioning alcohol or not and mentioning drugs or not—and in effect creates a cross-tabulation of these paragraphs. A Boolean account, once obtained, might be made more detailed; in this example, finer distinctions might be introduced among paragraphs mentioning the word *drugs* (e.g., illegal drugs, prescription drugs, over-the-counter drugs), thus expanding the variable *drugs*. One might also enlarge the cross-tabulation by adding other Boolean variables; in this example, such variables might include references to users, places, or treatments, which are logically independent from drugs and alcohol but most likely empirically related.

The Boolean operators are AND, the set theoretical intersection; OR, the set theoretical union; and NOT, the set theoretical complement. Boolean expressions can refer to many kinds of character strings, for example, those containing the word *drugs* AND *alcohol*. In so-called Venn diagrams, sets (of textual units with specific attributes) are depicted by their boundaries—by circles, for example. The effects of applying these operators to two textual attributes A and B are displayed in Figure 12.3. Not depicted in this figure is the use of parentheses, which enables the analyst to specify the order in which these operators are to be applied and thus gives rise to complex expressions. For example, one may verify in Figure 12.3 that (NOT A) AND B ≠ NOT(A AND B), which is the complement of A AND B. In the latter expression, NOT is applied to both A AND B; in the former, it is applied only to A, not to B. One may also verify that NOT(A AND B) = (NOT A) OR NOT B.

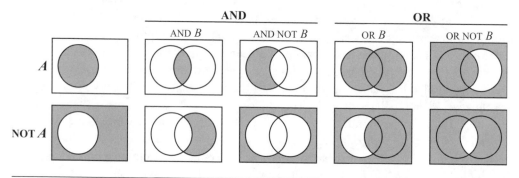

Figure 12.3   Effects of the Application of Boolean Operators

To obtain relevant Boolean counts, an analyst may want to take the following steps:

- Define the units of text to be individually examined, tabulated, and counted (as noted, these might be documents, paragraphs, even sentences).

- Specify relevant textual attributes, the character strings that a unit of text must contain or should not contain in order to be of the desired kind.

- Create a Boolean expression with as many textual attributes as needed, using the above Boolean operators and parentheses, and apply it to all units of text.

- Examine whether the units that the Boolean expression identifies as being of the specified kind include all and only the units of the desired kind. The result may not be satisfactory at first, violating intuition (see the discussion of semantic validity in Chapter 13, section 13.2.2), or may be too voluminous to handle. This calls for modifications of the Boolean expression until the identified textual units are of the desired kind, or at least approximately so.

As discussed in Chapter 8, the definition of a variable requires that its values be mutually exclusive relative to each other and that the whole set of values be exhaustive of all units of analysis. The distinction between A and NOT A is by definition a variable, albeit with just two categories. In Figure 12.3, this is depicted in the two Venn diagrams on the left-hand side. The number of mutually exclusive categories that Boolean expressions can distinguish grows exponentially with the number of textual attributes available. Boolean expressions defined on N textual attributes can distinguish up to 2^N mutually exclusive categories. For two attributes A and B, Figure 12.3 depicts these in the four Venn diagrams under the Boolean AND operator. The four Venn diagrams shown under the OR operator, by comparison, show categories that are not mutually exclusive. Following are four Boolean variables defined on one through four attributes (defined without the use of parentheses and the OR operator for transparency):

	N = 1	N = 2	N = 3	N = 4
1	A	A AND B	A AND B AND C	A AND B AND C AND D
2	NOT A	A AND NOT B	A AND B AND NOT C	A AND B AND C AND NOT D
3		NOT A AND B	A AND NOT B AND C	A AND B AND NOT C AND D
4		NOT A AND NOT B	NOT A AND B AND C	A AND NOT B AND C AND D
5			A AND NOT B AND NOT C	NOT A AND B AND C AND D
6			NOT A AND B AND NOT C	A AND B AND NOT C AND NOT D
7			NOT A AND NOT B AND C	A AND NOT B AND C AND NOT D
8			NOT A AND NOT B AND NOT C	NOT A AND B AND C AND NOT D
9				A AND NOT B AND NOT C AND D
...				...
16				NOT A AND NOT B AND NOT C AND NOT D

In these Boolean variables, each expression describes one category, the finest distinctions possible with the given number of textual attributes. Joining any of these expressions by OR, in effect lumping together the contents of the corresponding categories, creates other variables with fewer categories. One interesting variable can be created as follows: Take the presence of one attribute as the variable's first category, then, much as in stepwise regression analyses, consider what a second attribute adds to it, what a third attribute adds to both, and so on, until the leftover category, the absence of all attributes, is reached:

A

B AND NOT A

C AND NOT (A OR B)

D AND NOT (A OR B OR C)

E AND NOT (A OR B OR C OR D)

. . .

NOT (A OR B OR C OR . . . OR Z)

Many analytically appealing variables can be created through the algebraic combination of the Boolean expressions for mutually exclusive categories.

As long as they describe overlapping sets of textual units—not necessarily the exact same set—two or more Boolean variables yield Boolean cross-tabulations whose entries are the intersections of all categories in these variables. A two-way tabulation of one variable, say Z, with categories $\{z_a, z_b, z_c\}$, and a second variable, say V, with values $\{v_1, v_2, v_3, v_4, v_5\}$, would yield a table with the following cell contents:

	1	2	3	4	5	
a	z_a AND v_1	z_a AND v_2	z_a AND v_3	z_a AND v_4	z_a AND v_5	z_a AND V
b	z_b AND v_1	z_b AND v_2	z_b AND v_3	z_b AND v_4	z_b AND v_5	z_b AND V
c	z_c AND v_1	z_c AND v_2	z_c AND v_3	z_c AND v_4	z_c AND v_5	z_c AND V
	Z AND v_1	Z AND v_2	Z AND v_3	Z AND v_4	Z AND v_5	Z AND V

Like Boolean variables, Boolean cross-tabulations may list actual words or phrases—the units of text identified by the Boolean expressions—in a spreadsheet, for example. As in the steps suggested above, one may examine these in order to introduce finer distinctions, evaluate the semantic validity of the cells of the table, or interpret the relationships among the Boolean variables that emerge in the reading of the tabulated text. After counting the cell contents, one may also test the statistical significance of the relationships. In effect, a cross-tabulation such as this exemplifies the testing of hypotheses within a body of text as shown in Figure 4.7 and discussed in Chapter 4 (section 4.3.2). For other Boolean analyses, less related to content analysis, see Romme (1995).

Because these accounts are not concerned with meanings, computer aids, where available, can provide them with considerable efficiency. However, just as word frequencies mean little unless one is able to read the enumerated words, the results of Boolean analyses can easily escape comprehension unless one has a clear grasp of the Boolean expressions or, better still, can read what ends up in the rows, columns, and cells.

12.4   TEXT SEARCHES

Text searches involve the scanning of typically large textual databases, indexed for access by analysts, but not in their possession. Text searches are conducted to find, count, and/or retrieve texts that can be expected to contain information relevant to the analysts' research questions. I prefer the term *text search* to the older expression *information retrieval* because it describes more accurately what a computer does and separates from the search the concern for the semantic validity of its results. Character strings can become information only when read by someone and in the context of experiences with the use of similar text.

Text searches increase in importance with the size of the searchable universe of text and the scarcity of relevant text contained therein. Unlike complete accounts of the textual units that constitute a body of available text (discussed in the previous section), text searches operate in a largely unknown textual universe, most of which is of no interest to the analysts and will remain unknown to them. Analysts have no expectation that text searches will achieve complete accounts; rather, text searches have narrower aims that are guided by specific questions called *queries*.

Text searches are accomplished through the use of mechanisms called *search engines*. Users formulate their queries according to a search engine's requirements, and these queries serve to instruct the search engine to scan a textual universe for particular character strings, or *textual attributes*. Search engines incorporate three kinds of software: one for indexing character strings in the universes they search, one for identifying the indices that match user-specified queries, and one for identifying, retrieving, and displaying the units of text that contain these matches. Text searches can provide analysts with four levels of results:

- Counts of how often relevant textual attributes occur in the scanned textual universe (For example, in August 2003, an Internet search for "*text analysis software*" using the Google search engine yielded 3,239,000 hits—far too many to allow an individual to read through all of them.)

- References to the locations of textual units containing the desired textual attributes (Library catalogs, for example, provide book numbers and locations; Internet searches provide links to Web sites.)

- Abstracts, excerpts, or contexts in which the textual attributes occur

- Readable, downloadable, or printable texts for analysis by other means

Most Internet users are familiar with the concept of search engines, and many use search engines often to search online for material of interest to them. When a given query is entered into different Internet search engines, however, the results are rarely the same, in part because search engines differ in the sophistication of the queries they can handle, in part because search engines' indexing cannot keep up with the rate at which Web sites change and move, and in part because different search engines may search different universes (about which the user usually has no clue). Currently, Internet search engines are said to search (and thus retrieve from) only about 30% of what exists on the Internet. Statistically oriented social scientists may find that figure discouraging, but far more problematic is the uneven quality of the retrieved texts. Anyone can put anything on the Web, and it is often difficult to distinguish assertions made by experts from assertions made by lunatics. Moreover, the frequency counts produced by Internet search engines may not mean very much when URL owners can pay to have their Web sites appear on users' screens more readily, when the same documents are listed multiple times when they are accessible through different links, and so on. In spite of these drawbacks, the Internet represents an important inventory of texts that Internet users can access and may act on. Also, the use of the Internet cannot be studied without the Internet's texts.

Whereas Internet search engines are designed to pursue single questions and to yield (ideally) one but mostly (less ideally) several answers for users to choose from, content analysts pursue questions that can rarely be answered by a Web page or a document with a particular textual attribute. Although content analyses of Web sites are becoming increasingly common (e.g., Bauer & Scharl, 2000; Evans, 2002), most content analysts are interested in examining large bodies of text in order to discern patterns, distributions, trends, and answers to social or political questions. Moreover, content analysts are committed to demonstrating the reliability of their procedures and to addressing the validity of their results. Thus, both may use text searches, but they pursue different paths to answering questions.

A growing number of textual databases are available for content analysts to explore, including the following:

- LexisNexis is by far the most popular online searchable full-text archive of important newspapers and magazines, financial records, interview questions and results of opinion polls, legislative materials, and court decisions. I discuss this resource more fully below.

- The U.S. National Archives and Records Administration makes billions of documents (including motion pictures, sound and video recordings, and photographs) available from the three branches of the federal government, some online. The administration's Web site also provides links to presidential libraries.

- The Educational Resources Information Center (ERIC), established in 1966, is a national information system for education-related literature. It is supported by the U.S. Department of Education.

- The Oxford Text Archive is dedicated to the preservation of high-quality educational texts for research and teaching, largely in the humanities. It provides 2,500 resources in more than 25 languages.

- Corpus Linguistics, an online source with links to other depositories, collects literary corpora, transcripts, and samples of ordinary spoken language, including various dialects and from various eras.

- Project Gutenberg makes its large collection of books in electronic form freely available. To date, the collection includes more than 6,000 important works, ranging from light literature (Sherlock Holmes) to serious works (the Bible and classics), including reference works. The organization invites authors to share their books.

- The American Reference Library, a CD-ROM published by Western Standard Publishing Company, contains more than 55,000 documents.

Kenneth Janda calls this resource "the most important single source of political texts across U.S. history" (see Janda's personal Web site at http://www.janda.org).

- PoliTxts is a digital archive of political texts. It includes the inaugural addresses of all U.S. presidents, all of the presidents' State of the Union Addresses, transcripts of television debates between presidential candidates, U.S. political party platforms since 1840, and key historical documents.

As of this writing, Google searches for *"electronic text archives"* and *"digital libraries"* found thousands of text collections, national as well as university-based archives, with varying levels of accessibility. Skalski (2002) describes 21 "Message Archives," not necessarily electronic or online, including the Annenberg Television Script Archive and the UCLA Film and Television Archive.

For content analysts, LexisNexis is probably the most important source of textual data. Most universities, professional libraries, and institutions of law pay subscription fees for access to the archive, which includes the full texts of documents, not just headlines, abstracts, keywords, and indices. Users interact with LexisNexis via Internet connections, entering their queries and receiving information on the numbers of matches and lists of sources. They then have the option of viewing, printing, and/or saving full documents or relevant parts of documents. The LexisNexis database includes hundreds of sources of U.S. and international news and business information, plus state, federal, and international legal materials, statutes, codes, and patents. The news sources archived include newspapers, magazines, transcripts, and the full output of news wire services such as Reuters. The database also includes bibliographic data compiled from directories as well as election-related files. Information on public opinion polls is available that goes beyond the poll results, including the full text of questions and responses and the names of the polling agencies that conducted the research. Among the document sources included are U.S. congressional publications, U.S. Supreme Court reports, and the *Federal Register,* as well as some European Community publications. The full texts of numerous scholarly journals—scientific, medical, and educational—are available. Notwithstanding some limitations (Neuendorf, 2002, pp. 220–221), it is easy for a user to search LexisNexis for something that the *New York Times* printed in a particular period, to track the transmissions of the news wire services concerning a particular event (say, for a week from the day it occurred), to compare what various U.S. senators have said concerning a particular piece of legislation as printed in the *Congressional Record,* to locate legal precedents for a particular case, or to find out in what publications a particular cultural event has been reviewed or discussed.

Full-text online archives are especially attractive when they—as LexisNexis does—collect trustworthy (peer reviewed, authoritative, and authenticated) publications, systematically and over long periods in time, and when they maintain high indexing standards. The semantic validity of the search results of an archive depends on the quality of the archive's collections and systems of access.

Text searches are semantically valid (see Chapter 13, section 13.2.2) when they identify, count, and/or retrieve *all* and *only* relevant textual units or documents. Relevance is an attribute assigned by readers of a text after they have examined it from the perspective of a research question. Relevance embraces readers' trust in what they have read. "*All* and *only*" here means that the search should identify neither more nor fewer texts than are relevant. Semantic validity is reduced by two kinds of errors: errors of omission (the failure to retrieve relevant texts) and errors of commission (the retrieval of irrelevant texts).

In content analysis, researchers generally conduct text searches for three successive purposes:

- To identify a population of relevant texts within a universe of possible texts (documents, press releases, posts to newsgroups, books, Web pages, films) whose size is essentially unknown in advance of the search (Usually, the number of textual units that contain the textual attributes equals the size of that population. In Chapter 6, I referred to this use of a text search as relevance sampling; see section 6.2.7.)

- To sample from the identified population, selecting a number of texts that can be studied with the means available and that fairly represent the phenomena of interest (This calls for the use of any of the sampling techniques identified in Chapter 6.)

- To distinguish further, categorize, and cross-tabulate textual attributes within the retrieved texts (This amounts to using text searches as Boolean accounts of character strings.)

To these three uses of text searches, content analysts would be wise to add other analytical steps. An analysis that is limited to the identification of character strings is often unsatisfactory. The assessment of the semantic validity of text searches already requires that humans judge the relevance of the retrieved texts, and it is usually beneficial for analysts to employ human coders to continue processing the retrieved texts—provided the task is manageable. For example, in a study of negativity in political campaigns in national election years, Kenski (1999) searched for the phrases "*negative campaign*" and "*negative ads*" in newspapers and in the questions asked in national opinion polls during the past five U.S. presidential election years. She found frequencies that started low in 1980, peaked in 1988, and then dipped in 1996 to about half that peak. These frequencies characterized the population of texts, and Kenski obtained them without much effort, but, as she discovered, it was far from clear what these phrases actually meant. She therefore delved into polling results to gain greater clarity.

The second use of text searches noted above may bring forth variables that go beyond the search criterion. For example, an analyst may be able to judge the relevance of a text from the linguistic environment of the words matching the analyst's query. The message type, author, publication date, header, keywords, and length of the textual units with the desired textual attributes may enable the researcher to refine the query and get new ideas as to which variables are associated with the textual attributes. A Boolean account of this information might yield new variables, indicate trends, or reveal correlations or other systemic conceptions.

Formulating a semantically valid query is not always a simple matter. Take, for example, an Internet search for texts on the Gettysburg Address. If the user's query consists of the words *Gettysburg* and *Address,* entered separately, without quotation marks, an ordinary search engine will look for textual units that contain the two words, whether together or separately. In a *New York Times* article criticizing the treatment of history on the Internet, Robert Darnton (1999) reported getting 103,467,238 matches for the two words *Gettysburg* and *Address,* including a Gettysburg realtor's mailing address, personal Web pages that mentioned Gettysburg as well as addresses, and the policy of a fast-food restaurant that stated: "At Getty's Burgers, we promise. . . . When a member of our staff addresses a customer. . . ." A search with a query that used quotation marks around the full string of characters, "*Gettysburg Address,*" would have led to a different result. Most Internet search engines accept queries consisting of strings of words rather than individual words. This example illustrates errors of commission and how to reduce such errors. Apparently, errors of this kind are unanticipated. Reading does not work the way search engines do, and the results of text searches tend to surprise even experienced analysts. The relationship between a query and what makes a text relevant is rarely obvious.

When a concept can be represented by a single word or expression, the formulation of queries is straightforward. Bishop (1998), for instance, wanted to know when and where the concept of "road rage" emerged and how the meaning of the term has evolved. In this case, the compound term and the concept of interest define each other. Because this is a term of recent coinage (1988, as she found out), Bishop was able to obtain all relevant documents—probably without appreciable errors of omission—by searching the LexisNexis textual database. On the other extreme, Bermejo (1997) studied self-reference in the press—that is, occasions of a newspaper's reporting on its own practices, ethical issues, the politics and economics of newspaper publishing, and any other form of self-reflection. As this was a theoretical concept without any established set of words denoting self-reflexive practices, Bermejo found that the formulation of a suitable query proved extraordinarily difficult. He ended up using a Boolean expression consisting of more than 40 nested search words that identified not only relevant articles but also irrelevant texts such as obituaries of journalists, corrections of printing errors, reports on ownership changes of other newspapers, and references to sources that happened to be other newspapers. Because he used the text search only to identify a sample, he had no problems removing these errors of commission when coding the texts.

Formulating a query is like trying to "cover" the set of relevant texts, in Figure 12.4 represented by a triangle, with a Boolean expression of search words, represented by ovals in the figure. One of the generalizations immediately apparent in this figure and Figure 12.3 is that OR operators widen a search, whereas AND NOT operators limit it. In attempting to formulate suitable queries, analysts are

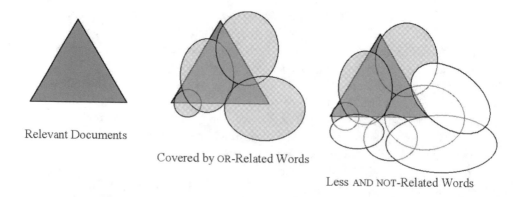

Relevant Documents

Covered by OR-Related Words

Less AND NOT-Related Words

Figure 12.4   Approximation of a Query to a Set of Relevant Documents

often led into a delicate dance, adding and subtracting textual attributes in an effort to approximate desired texts when they do not really know the relationships between textual attributes in the texts and the number of texts containing each. It helps if analysts have a good deal of intuition about language use, but query formulation rarely succeeds without practical explorations.

Researchers may want to develop their search queries by trying them out on small samples of texts they know well enough to learn from emerging errors of omission and commission. Here are a few practical suggestions for analysts to keep in mind when formulating queries:

- Words that are widely used (in a Venn diagram depicted as large circles) tend not to distinguish texts as well as do rarely used words (depicted as small circles in that diagram).

- Words with correlated meanings, which are likely to co-occur in the same texts (for example, logical opposites such as *liberals* and *conservatives*), are redundant search terms: They lengthen queries without making much difference in the results. (In a Venn diagram, the areas of correlated words would mostly overlap.)

- Synonyms (i.e., different words with the same meaning) have to be entered into queries one by one, as search engines cannot know their common meaning. The same applies to irregular verb forms and other mere grammatical variations, all of which need to be included as if grammar does not matter.

- Words for a general idea will not identify texts containing specific incidences of that idea. For example, the word *pets* in a query will not retrieve texts mentioning dogs or cats. Researchers interested in a general concept must include in their query all words and phrases signifying its specific instances.

- Homonyms (i.e., words that are spelled alike but have multiple meanings) in queries cause errors of commission. For example, a query using the word *play* would yield many irrelevant texts, because *play* has many different meanings (as illustrated in Figure 12.1). Researchers aware of homonyms in their text searches should include words in the vicinity of the homonyms that distinguish among their meanings.

- AND operators narrow a search and tend to reduce errors of commission while increasing errors of omission. OR operators expand a search and tend to increase errors of commission while reducing errors of omission. (One may verify this by examining Figure 12.3.)

Furthermore, researchers may find it helpful to consult one or more of the following kinds of sources as they formulate text search queries: lists of the vocabularies of the concepts in which they are interested, dictionaries of synonyms, thesauri, books of phrases and expressions, concept dictionaries such as the one developed by Laffal (1993), or, perhaps most important, lexical databases such as WordNet (Fellbaum, 1998; Miller et al., 1993). WordNet is an online lexical database maintained by Princeton University's Cognitive Science Laboratory (http://www.cogsci.princeton.edu); it contains more than 50,000 words and 40,000 phrases collected into more than 70,000 sense meanings. WordNet stores nouns, verbs, adjectives, adverbs, compound expressions, collocations, colloquialisms, and forms of speech in the form of synonym sets (about five words or phrases per set) connected by semantic relationships, such as super/subordination, lexical entailments, part of, made of, and contexts of use. (For an excellent online visualization of the relationships between words in WordNet, see the Plumb Design Visual Thesaurus at http://www.visualthesaurus.com/online/index.html.)

Text searches are not limited to traditional Boolean queries. Even some Internet search engines offer users the opportunity to formulate queries in advanced search languages. For content analysis, two expansions in search options have proven particularly important: the ability to search with a battery of queries simultaneously (see the discussion of Boolean variables above) and the ability to define search units within text by means of so-called proximity operators. Proximity operators allow analysts to search for noncontiguous character string (word) co-occurrences within stretches of text that are significantly smaller than whole documents, paragraphs, sentences, or a specified number of words.

The following summarizes the rules of the language that LexisNexis users employ in formulating their queries. This language, which features proximity operators, including Boolean operators as their special cases, is an example of one of the many kinds of specialized languages that different text search engines afford.

- *Phrases* are searched as character strings, just as are words.

- *Proximity connectors* enable defining the size of recording units surrounding a word, searching for co-occurrences of words or phrases and noncontiguous expressions for a single concept, and can limit the meanings of homonyms:

  pre/# Searches for words that occur within # words of each other in the specified order
  > *English pre/5 second language*

  w/# Searches for words that occur within # words of each other in any order
  > *Colorado river w/10 water rights*

  w/p Searches for words within the same paragraph

  w/s Searches for words within the same sentence

  w/seg Searches for words within the same segment of the article

- *Boolean operators,* now largely embraced by above proximity connectors:

  AND As in *A AND B,* retrieves articles containing both words

  OR As in *A OR B,* retrieves articles containing either or both words

  NOT As in NOT *A,* retrieves articles that do not contain that word

- *Nesting of multiple operators,* altering the sequence of applying operators from the normal left-to-right to one in which operations within parentheses are applied before those outside it
  > *(city w/3 center)* OR *(south w/5 Broad Street)*

- *Truncation*

  ! Searches all variations of a root. *Transport!* finds *transportation, transporting, . . .*

  * Searches without consideration of a character. *wom*n* finds *woman* and *women.*

- *Plurals* and *possessives* that are formed by adding *s* or *es* or by changing *y* to *ies* are automatically included in the search.

- *Date* qualifications:
  > *and date>1/93*
  > *and date<1995*
  > *and date=3/3/96*
  > *and date>8-21-93 and date<3-3-96*

- *Segments.* Documents are divided into segments and searches can be limited to the sections needed, for example, *headline, lead* (the first 50 words of a document), *publication, person, subject, type* (of material contained in an article, e.g., *analysis, letter), geographic* (location), *language, length* (of the article).

Search engines that identify textual attributes through exact matching of queries and character strings cannot identify expressions with typographical errors or misspellings, and this can cause omissions of potentially relevant texts. Search engine designers have begun to address this problem by offering fuzzy search options that can take a variety of similarities into account, such as the following:

- *Typographical similarities:* words in which characters have been omitted, duplicated, or transposed, or words resulting from other typical typing errors

- *Phonetic similarities:* words that are pronounced similarly but written differently (e.g., *Smith* and *Smyth*)

- *Stemming similarities:* words that have the same root meanings but differ in grammatical endings, suffixes, and prefixes

- *Thesaurus similarities:* words that are related in meanings, synonyms, associates, and members of word families (e.g., *go* used as a search word retrieves *going, goes, gone,* and *went;* or the search word *incendiary* brings up *arsonist, inflammatory, combustible,* and *bomb*) (See also the discussion of lemmatization in section 12.5.1.)

In addition to fuzzy search options, many search engines apply term weighting—that is, they assign differing weights to the terms retrieved according to the terms' degree of relevance to the search query. Such devices are intended to make text searches more efficient, but researchers should be aware that reducing errors of omission often results in increases in errors of commission. As noted above, the formulation of semantically valid text search queries is a dance between conflicting requirements.

COMPUTATIONAL CONTENT ANALYSES   12.5

Unlike accounts of character strings and text searches, which employ entirely syntactical operations, computational content analyses process text according to theories of meaning that are presumed to operate within the context of the analyzed text. Theories of this kind are usually rather rudimentary, as the discussion below will show, but their roots in the chosen context of available text carry their justification.

Before I present a review of some of these computational aids, I must point out that there are vast differences among them in the demands they make on the forms of data they can handle. In fact, many computational content analysis programs attain their high level of sophistication by demanding that users perform often elaborate preediting of raw text. The following are some of the most common tasks content analysts may have to accomplish to make ordinary texts available for computer processing:

Clerical text cleaning

- Correcting misspellings (When reading, we routinely overlook orthographical errors, especially our own. A computer may not know how to handle these. As noted above, a fuzzy search, when available, is one computational solution to this problem.)

- Replacing foreign characters with characters that a given CATA system recognizes, for example, with ASCII characters (Relatively recent systems may not be so limited.)

- Introducing special markers to indicate syntactical distinctions (for instance, by adding double periods after sentences, carriage controls after paragraphs, or certain markers to distinguish headlines, abstracts, or leads from the remainder of a document)

Adding information the computer does not have

- Replacing pronouns with proper names and indirect references with direct ones; adding speakers' names in transcripts at turns of talk

- Marking the syntactical functions of words (for example, marking *bear* as a verb or as a noun)

- Introducing analytical distinctions (for example, distinguishing among speakers, actors, actions, and targets or among explanations, justifications, and excuses for actions)

- Distinguishing the meanings of homonyms (for instance, Buffalo the city, buffalo the wild oxen, buffalo the sucker, *buffalo* the verb, *buffalo* the word)

Adapting the text to the theory underlying the computational content analysis

- Dropping vocabulary that does not matter for answering the research questions (for example, creating lists of stop-words and go-words)

- Decomposing (kernelizing) longer sentences into smaller units of text, such as propositions or clauses, which often means rewriting a whole text into a computable format to circumvent the need to compute complex grammatical constructions

- "Unwrapping" the needed text through manual editing or programming (Naturally occurring text is usually packaged and so is preceded by information on sources, channels, and dates as well as by headlines, abstracts, keywords, and so on, and succeeded by appendices, references, signatures, and more. Somewhere in between is the body of text that matters.)

Packaging the text

- Many computational content analysis programs require segmenting a text into computationally convenient records: lines of a certain number of characters in length, paragraphs of a certain length, documents not exceeding a limit in size (Diction, for example, limits document length to 500 words), or batches that users must assemble to be handled one by one. The different ways in which such programs define records have important implications for the kinds of questions they can answer.

Clearly, heavy preediting requirements can easily cancel out the advantages that CATA promises. To help alleviate this problem, several computational content analysis programs include computer-aided text entry features. For example, a software called CETA (Computer-aided Evaluative Text Analysis; Cuilenburg, Kleinnijenhuis, & De Ridder, 1988; Kleinnijenhuis, De Ridder, & Rietberg, 1997), which performs a version of contingency analysis (see Chapter 10, section 10.6), provides online support for human coders. This support takes the form of coder prompts during three preparatory stages of the analysis: while they are parsing texts, defining scoring options, and assigning numerical values to textual units. Cuilenburg (1991) has reported that in one month, 50 coders were able to code more than 400,000 textual units culled from 5,400 newspaper articles for use in CETA. In some software packages, such as Heise's (1995) Event Structure Analysis (ESA) and Schrodt, Davis, and Weddle's (1994) Kansas Events Data System (KEDS), by far the most elaborate features are dedicated to the preparation of text for analysis.

Having established these preliminaries, I review below four kinds of computational aids, which I categorize according to the theories of meaning they embody: coding/dictionary approaches, statistical association approaches, semantic network approaches, and memetic approaches.

Coding/Dictionary Approaches   12.5.1

The simplest theory of meaning, and the one that dominates coding/dictionary approaches, derives from taxonomy, the idea that texts can be represented on different levels of abstraction, that there are core meanings and insignificant variations of these cores, or that important meanings are thinly distributed in a body of text and need to be identified and extracted.

Early on, Sedelow (1967) provided a convincing demonstration that analysts need to compare texts not in terms of the character strings they contain but in terms of their categories of meanings. She analyzed two separate English translations of a Russian book, Sokolovsky's *Military Strategy,* and found that they differed in nearly 3,000 words: 1,599 words appeared only in the Rand translations, and 1,331 words appeared only in the translation published by Praeger. Given that these were both respectable translations, one could hardly conclude that they differed in content. The remarkable differences in vocabulary that Sedelow found demonstrate that text comparisons based on character strings can be rather shallow. Obviously, language provides for considerable stylistic variation and for many alternative forms of expressions. This observation led Sedelow to propose applying ordinary dictionary and thesaurus entries to the given texts and obtaining frequencies, not of actual character strings, but of word families that would account for texts on the basis of common meanings. This is the basic idea behind almost all coding/dictionary approaches.

One application of this idea involves the replacement of the words contained in texts with the entries in the dictionaries of a language, so-called lemmas. *Lemmatization* is "generally defined as the transformation of all inflected word forms contained in a text to their dictionary look-up form" (Boot, 1980, p. 175). It replaces, among others, the plurals and alternative spellings of nouns with their singular forms and the grammatical variations of verbs with their infinitive forms (for example, *is, was, will be, am, are, were, being,* and *been* are replaced by *be*). Evidently, lemmatization is more powerful than stemming. It embodies a theory of the very meaning found in the construction of ordinary dictionaries and reflects readers' use of such dictionaries. Although it operationally resembles a computer dictionary, lemmatization, where available, is often applied before other CATA dictionaries are applied.

Lemmatization and coding do not always require sophisticated CATA dictionaries. For example, Kim and Gamson (1999) used a word processing program (Microsoft Word) to scan a body of text for particular character sequences. They read each sequence they found in the linguistic context in which it occurred, replaced words with similar meanings with a word that stood for their class, and counted the replacements. Through this admittedly tedious procedure, Kim and Gamson eliminated stylistic and semantic variations that they judged to be unimportant for their research, using themselves as the embodiments of a theory of how given words and phrases are read and categorized. Underlying their procedure is the idea that texts are representative of other things and can themselves be represented in simpler and more general terms, terms that eliminate the idiosyncrasies of individual readers and favor instead what the majority of readers would take away from reading them—filtered, of course, through the analysts' research questions.

Manual coding or recording of textual units into abstract categories that embrace a diversity of more specific instances of text (see Chapter 7) is not that different from what a computer thesaurus and dictionary are designed to do, representing large bodies of text in fewer and simpler terms—except that the latter applies to character strings without anyone reading them. If done well, the construction of computer thesauri and dictionaries serves as a theory of how readers rearticulate given texts in simpler terms and categorize them according to the needs of their research.

CATA dictionaries list character strings as words in categories of what they have in common, much as thesauri group words with shared meanings on different levels of abstraction. Applied to a text, a CATA dictionary either tags original words with the names of categories or replaces words that have similar meanings with more general words that stand for what they share (doing automatically what Kim and Gamson did manually in the study mentioned above). The General Inquirer (Stone et al., 1966), which was the first fully operational computer content analysis program to use a dictionary, assigns tags to words according to a theory of meaning that reflects a research question or the vocabulary of an academic discipline. For example, Stone et al.'s psychosociological dictionary tags *I, me, my, mine,* and *myself* as *self,* and *we, us, our, ours,* and *ourselves* as *selves.* Analysts can obtain frequencies of tags on two levels of generalization—for example, *anxiety, guilt,* and *depression* are counted as *distress,* and *distress, anger, pleasure,* and *affection* are counted as *emotion.* Analysts can also examine the words in a text that are assigned to a given tag to get a sense of how well the tag represents the class of character strings that are tagged alike. In addition, analysts can inspect a list of "leftover" words that occur in the text but not in the dictionary, modify and extend the dictionary by creating new entries, and apply various statistics on the tags as well as on the tagged words. WordStat, a very versatile content analysis software package developed by Péladeau (1996), conceptualizes go-word lists and stop-word lists as dictionaries, with the former replacing listed words by their categories. This creates a text with fewer types but the same number of tokens, which an analyst can then examine using a variety of statistical tools provided by WordStat's parent program, SimStat. In the General Inquirer, one word may be tagged in various ways. In WordStat, analysts have the option of using mutually exclusive or overlapping categories. The General Inquirer uses stemming and incorporates a variety of disambiguation rules for homonyms. WordStat provides a spell-checker and an English thesaurus. Many CATA programs use dictionaries in various capacities.

One important difference among the various CATA software packages that take a coding/dictionary approach is whether or how easily users can tailor the dictionaries according to their own theories and context-specific research questions. The General Inquirer dictionary is customizable, as are the dictionaries in TextPack, TextQuest, VBPro, WordStat, and many others. In contrast, Minnesota Contextual Content Analysis (MCCA; McTavish, Litkowski, & Schrader, 1997; McTavish & Pirro, 1990), Diction (Hart, 1985), the Regressive Imagery Dictionary (RID; Martindale, 1990), and Linguistic Inquiry and Word Count (LIWC; Pennebaker, Francis, & Booth, 2001) are all somewhat limited in this regard; each of these packages embodies one theory of meaning or a medley of several.

MCCA assigns about 11,000 words to 116 predefined categories that reflect the developers' conception of a narrative. MCCA acknowledges that word meanings differ with their linguistic environments and defines four such environments (traditional, practical, emotional, and analytic), suggesting that these are sufficient to disambiguate most homonyms concerning social behavior. MCCA produces the frequencies with which these categories are used in a text, enables the comparison of two texts based on these frequencies, and assesses the over- or underrepresentation of these categories relative to a statistical norm that has emerged over years of research with this system, much as the Diction software does.

Diction attempts to infer what its developer, Hart (1985), calls "the tone of a verbal message." It is designed to search texts of 500 or fewer words in length—a barely adequate document size for political speeches (although analysts can process several 500-word batches)—for words that its dictionary maps into five rhetorical qualities:

Certainty: Language indicating resoluteness, inflexibility, completeness, and a tendency to speak ex cathedra

Activity: Language featuring movement, change, the implementation of ideas, and the avoidance of inertia

Optimism: Language endorsing or highlighting the positive entailments of some person, group, concept, or event

Realism: Language describing tangible, immediate, recognizable matters that affect people's everyday lives

Commonality: Language highlighting the agreed-upon values of a group and rejecting idiosyncratic modes of engagement

The frequencies in these categories lend themselves to comparisons of different texts and to the comparison of one text with a statistical norm obtained from a sample of some 20,000 public documents. Diction enables users to specify up to 10 additional categories, but Hart's conception of "tone" is the key to what it does.

RID is composed of about 3,200 words and word roots assigned to 29 categories of primary cognitive processes, 7 categories of secondary cognitive processes, and 7 categories of emotions. The dictionary focuses, as the name Regressive Imagery Dictionary implies, on such mental processes as the following:

Drive (oral, anal, sex)

Icarian imagery (ascend, descend, fire, water)

Regressive cognition (consciousness alter, timelessness)

Emotion (anxiety, sadness, anger, positive emotion)

Sensation words (touch, vision, cold, hard)

Martindale (1990) developed RID to test his psychoevolutionary theory of art history, and researchers interested in psychotherapy and in tracing cognitive development have since found it useful. RID can be inserted in WordStat and TextQuest.

LIWC's dictionary can be used in WordStat as well. LIWC is designed to provide researchers with an efficient and effective method for inferring the various emotional, cognitive, structural, and process components present in individuals' verbal and written speech samples. It analyzes written text on a word-by-word basis, calculates the percentages of words in a text that match each of up to 82 language dimensions, and generates output that can be analyzed by various statistical programs. The program's basic dictionary is composed of 2,290 words and word stems, and each is included in one or more word categories. For example, *cried* is part of four word categories: sadness, negative emotion, overall affect, and past-tense verb. With each occurrence of *cried* in text, each of these registers is increased.

There are many more CATA dictionaries in existence, although some are not widely accessible. For example, dictionaries exist for coding social (or functional) versus antisocial (or dysfunctional) behaviors (Potter & Vaughan, 1997), speakers' psychological states (anxiety, hostility, cognitive impairment, and so on; Gottschalk, 1995; Gottschalk & Bechtel, 1982), Lasswell's value categories (Namenwirth & Weber, 1987), and Osgood, Suci, and Tannenbaum's (1957) semantic differential scales (Holsti, Brody, & North, 1965). For older special-purpose dictionaries, see Stone et al. (1966, pp. 169–206) and Gerbner, Holsti, Krippendorff, Paisley, and Stone (1969).

The General Inquirer was conceived to accept any kind of dictionary, but the evolution of its Harvard Psychosociological Dictionary provides an important lesson for users of coding/dictionary software. The General Inquirer dictionary took off from Bales's (1950) interaction process analysis but then incorporated more and more systems of categories—Lasswell's values and Osgood's semantic differential, for example. This is possible because it allows one word to have more than one tag. (WordStat, as already mentioned, provides this facility as an option.) In 1965, it had 3,500 entries and 83 tags (Kelly & Stone, 1975, p. 47). Züll, Weber, and Mohler (1989) expanded version IV of this dictionary, and its Dartmouth adaptation now contains 8,500 entries (Rosenberg, Schnurr, & Oxman, 1990). These developments demonstrate a general trend for dictionaries to become bigger and more diversified, but also less changeable. Most content analyses would benefit from the construction of special-purpose dictionaries, but developing a dictionary from scratch can be a formidable task. It is not surprising, therefore, that content analysts usually try to build on available dictionaries before they attempt to develop their own. Researchers using the General Inquirer tend to add to its dictionary—if at all—rather than write their own.

How do analysts go about constructing new dictionaries? One early source of information on this subject is Stone et al.'s (1966, pp. 134–168) description of their work on the General Inquirer dictionary. Probably the best recent account is offered by Bengston and Xu (1995), who undertook a content analysis to examine changing values in the United States concerning national forests. To develop their dictionary, Bengston and Xu took the following steps:

1. They prepared a list of objects of value (both positive and negative) related to forests. Their choices of objects were of course informed by the kinds of inferences that interested them in this study.

2. They examined different size units of text regarding which would contain the needed descriptions of the objects on their list and decided on the basic unit of text that would contain the objects' valuation. They decided that a unit of text would have to contain the phrase *national forest* plus 50 words on either side.

3. They developed a list of words and expressions that could serve as indicators for text sources—writers, interviewees, or readers—to hold four basic kinds of values of interest to the researchers (these values had emerged from the first step). This amounted to four sets of words and expressions, one for each value.

4. They asked subject matter specialists to review these sets of value words and expressions (which formed the beginning of a value dictionary) and offer suggestions concerning refinement of the sets and additional words that might be included.

5. They examined the semantic validity (see Chapter 13, section 13.2.2) of the emerging dictionary entries with the help of KWIC lists applied to samples of text. In the course of this examination, they developed disambiguation rules and queries and then refined and tested these rules to see whether they correctly identified and distinguished among the four values. They then deleted any words and expressions that could not be disambiguated. (A disambiguation rule distinguishes among multiple readings. For instance, they found that economic words, by themselves, have no obvious value, but in the vicinity of words such as *devastating, ravaged,* and *misuse* they are clearly negative. A disambiguation rule combines two kinds of character strings to indicate a category, here of value.)

6. They sampled texts from three sources—the media, forestry professionals, and environmentalists, each over time—and applied the dictionary to them comparatively. The different sources had different relationships to forests and different ways of expressing values. The researchers continued this testing until at least 80% were correctly identified (on the semantic validity of text searches, see Chapter 13, section 13.2.2).

7. They conducted a final validity check on a representative random sample of data from these three sources.

These steps are easily replicable, and many content analysts create their own specialized dictionaries in similar ways. Others, however, rely on word databases such as the above-mentioned WordNet (Fellbaum, 1998; Miller et al., 1993), on conceptual dictionaries such as Laffal's (1993), on already available dictionaries or thesauri, on clustering techniques that reveal word co-occurrences, or on theories of the context in question.

To validate the semantics of a dictionary, analysts need to compare the dictionary's performance with categorizations obtained by other means—minimally, this means that the categorizations make sense to the researchers (face validity; see Chapter 13, section 13.1), but it would be better still if they can stand up against the judgments of human coders or the actual users of the texts, much as in the testing of a theory. The semantic validation of a dictionary ought to be a prerequisite of its use. Such an effort requires that the dictionary be open for detailed examination and that it can be applied to small texts that humans can read, tag, or categorize for comparison. The General Inquirer, for instance, aids in such examinations by offering lists of character strings that were stemmed, words with common tags, words not tagged, and more (Stone et al., 1966). WordStat produces lists of words not in the dictionary and lists of words to which the dictionary was applied. Software packages with fixed and hidden dictionaries do not offer the possibility of semantic validation.

A researcher may also determine a dictionary's functional validity (see Chapter 13, section 13.2.4) by measuring the success of the system that relies on it. Pennebaker et al.'s (2001) LIWC dictionary is a good example: It provides sufficient numbers of psychologically informed categories for analysts to define their own analytical constructs on top of the categories' frequencies of use. These analytical constructs resemble regression equations, which are selectively applied to the up to 85 dimensions that the LIWC dictionary produces and yield evidence for the presence of particular concepts. For example, Pennebaker et al. report that LIWC can identify an author's gender based on her or his word choices—a finding that is easy enough to validate against external evidence (predictive validity; see Chapter 13, section 13.2.6)—and various emotional states (Pennebaker, 1997). These researchers have developed equations for cognitive complexity, aging, depression or suicidality, lying, gender, and "talking presidential." In a demonstration of their system, Pennebaker and Stone (2001) applied a battery of similarly derived measures (cognitive complexity, talks like a woman, depression or suicidality, talks like an old person, talks like a liar, and talks presidential) to early contenders in the 2000 U.S. presidential election campaign; they found considerable face validity, although admittedly in retrospect.

Statistical Association Approaches   12.5.2

An unrealized dream of artificial intelligence researchers in the 1960s was the ability to generate abstracts of written documents automatically. Statistical abstracting assumed that the important words in a text are identifiable by their relative frequency; that their meanings are a function of their proximity to each other, which calls for the observance of co-occurrences; and that sentences that contain statistically prominent co-occurrences can then serve as representations of a text as a whole. These efforts did not quite succeed, owing to the aforementioned difficulties involved in formulating a computational theory of how the members of a literate community summarize the community's texts. The dream did not die, however. It stimulated the development of computational content analysis programs that do not require prior categorization of textual units or predefined dictionaries and that minimize human coding efforts. These statistical association approaches, as they are called, have become popular with the use of the mining metaphor, promising to "extract" concepts or "discover" relevant information from voluminous textual databases.

The theory of meaning underlying these ideas has two roots. One goes back to association psychology. In content analysis, it entered with Baldwin's (1942) personal structure analysis, which Osgood (1959) generalized into his contingency analysis (see Chapter 10). These early analyses started with the tabulation of co-occurrences of manually coded concepts into square matrices of word pairs to compare them against the baseline of statistical expectations. The theory assumes that associations of concepts in someone's mind manifest themselves in co-occurring words. Osgood (1959, pp. 56–78) generated validating evidence for this contention in the form of experiments with human subjects and demonstrated the use of the theory by analyzing a section of Goebbels's diary.

The other root suggests that meanings do not reside in words but rather in how words relate to their linguistic environments—that is, how words relate to other words. Accordingly, two words have the same meaning if they can occur in the same linguistic environment, if one can replace the other without violating the sense of the whole. For example, the words *apple* and *orange* are interchangeable in many sentences having to do with shapes, eating, and growing on trees. Their difference in meaning becomes evident in sentences in which they are no longer interchangeable—for example, in sentences concerning where they are respectively grown. If such a theory could account for how we read, it would make references to human coders and extralinguistic phenomena such as the social/institutional/political roles of texts unnecessary.

Implementing such notions, Iker (1974, 1975) and his associates (Iker & Harway, 1969) pioneered a program called WORDS, initially to identify patterns in psychotherapeutic interview transcripts. WORDS included many now-familiar features: the stemming of words to their roots, a dictionary of the most obvious synonyms, and a stop-word list that discarded function words and ruled out very frequent and very rare words for not contributing to the statistical significance of associations. Within analyst-specified textual units of various sizes—certain numbers of words, paragraphs, pages, uninterrupted stretches of talk, answers to interview questions—WORDS computed a contingency matrix of up to 215 word types. It then factor analyzed the intercorrelations in this matrix and rotated them against a varimax criterion to obtain simple structures. These structures were considered to be the themes underlying the analyzed text. Current software packages such as CatPac, TextAnalyst, TextSmart, and Semio create similar contingency matrices to draw statistical conclusions.

Woelfel's (1993, 1997; Woelfel & Fink, 1980) CatPac follows the initial steps of WORDS, but deviates from pursuing a co-occurrence statistic by adopting a neuronal network learning model. This model begins with the assumption that all the words that have been selected as keywords are linked with equal strength. As CatPac scans the text and encounters co-occurrences within specified units of text—a window of a certain width, the number of words, for example—it strengthens the links corresponding to the observed co-occurrences at the expense of the links corresponding to words that do not co-occur. If more than two keywords co-occur, CatPac strengthens all the binary links that join them. (This approach is based on the theory that when people repeatedly think certain thoughts, read particular texts, or enact specific sequences of behavior, the neuronal connections in their brains that represent those thoughts or actions are strengthened, and thereafter they can recall, conceptualize, and enact those thoughts and actions more readily than they can recall and enact thoughts and actions experienced rarely or a long time previously.) The analysis generates clusters of words that Woelfel describes as manifestations of more or less distinct ideas. An important attribute of these clusters is that they are nonhierarchical. Unlike in hierarchical clustering, nonhierarchical clustering allows a word to belong to more than one class. So, in a content analysis of communication research literature, *communication* might well end up with *mass* in one cluster and with *theory* and *research* in a different cluster—as *mass communication* is a concept different from *communication theory* and *communication research* (Barnett & Doerfel, 1997).

Tijssen and Van Raan (1994) provide a good review of the CatPac procedure and work done by researchers using this program. For example, in a recent study of student essays, CatPac yielded 55 sets of frequently used words that could be grouped into five categories (McKnight & Walberg, 1994). The results identified not only such obvious concepts as "street-crime," "gang-violence," and "school-problem," but also stereotypical associations such as "young-bad-Black" and conceptual correlates such as "money-city." Such results may be interpreted as some kind of common cognition, a generalization of a source characteristic, abducted by a theory of meaning—in CatPac's case, a theory of neuronal networks.

TextAnalyst, another software package that takes a neuronal network approach to text analysis, has been described as a business tool that can automatically abstract, index, store, and retrieve the volumes of documents that many businesses have to deal with. Sullivan (2001) describes this approach by using the aforementioned mining metaphors (see also the Megaputer Intelligence Web site, at http://www.megaputer.com).

The idea of neuronal learning nets is part of a more general effort on the part of researchers in artificial intelligence to develop algorithms that can simulate naturally occurring behavior, so that computers can learn to perform certain operations without being told how to do them—in the case of content analysis, the goal would be for computers to read text. One algorithm, called a support vector machine, can be trained on, say, 30 categories in 100,000 documents and then produce easily comprehensible rules for identifying these categories in other documents. Related algorithms go by the name of latent semantic analysis or latent semantic indexing (LSI). Another model is hyperdimensional analogue to language (HAL). For the latest elaborations of these ideas, interested readers should seek out sources on the Internet.

Danowski's (1982, 1993) program Wordlink uses word co-occurrences in still another way—it extracts all pairs of words within a window of specified width, except for those on a stop-word list, and records their distances from each other. With the help of NEGOPY (Richards & Rice, 1981), a software package designed for analyzing communication nets (among up to 6,000 nodes for the mainframe version and up to 3,000 for the PC version), Danowski used Wordlink to construct a very large word-distance matrix. He illustrates the information that this matrix can provide with data consisting of the answers car dealership sales and service personnel gave when asked, "When you think of 'customer satisfaction,' what comes to mind?" Danowski applied a "traveling salesman" algorithm to this huge distance matrix. This algorithm is designed to find the shortest path between any two nodes, passing through a number of intermediate nodes. For the most frequent words, the algorithm identified the following string: "Consumer satisfaction: good service on the new car done right the time first." Reversing the order of just the last two words in this string yields a grammatically correct sentence that probably expresses the gist of the beliefs shared by Danowski's respondents. In another study, he assigned values to different words and computed advertising slogans that might be worth disseminating.

Statistical association approaches differ in whether and how far analysts can supervise them to answer specific research questions. The issue of whether a neuronal network approach is superior to traditional clustering algorithms—which WordStat and several other CATA software packages enable—is undecided, and perhaps it is not too important for users, given that both rely on the same theories of meaning. The aim to substitute a general algorithm for human coding/reading has the effect of making statistical association approaches independent of particular contexts of analysis, and this raises conflicts for content analysts who are attempting to answer context-specific research questions.

12.5.3   Semantic Network Approaches

A network consists of several nodes linked by binary relations. It can be graphed from a collection of <node$_i$-connection$_j$-node$_k$> triplets. A network is called *semantic* when its nodes represent concepts or clauses and when these are linked to each other by more than one kind of binary relation. In the theory of meaning that underlies a semantic network approach, the meanings of nodes are a function of how they are connected with each other. The aim of semantic network approaches to content analysis is to find answers to questions that are not literally contained in a body of text but are implied by it. Hays's (1960, 1969) early content analyses of political documents are examples of such approaches, as are the current efforts of artificial intelligence researchers to design expert systems.

To be clear, the types of networks discussed above, in section 12.5.2, are not semantic by our definition because all of their links are of the same kind: co-occurrences or proximities within a textual unit. Networks are found everywhere: causal networks in physics, road networks on drivers' maps, citation networks in literary scholarship, networks of interactions in organisms. Communication networks, for example, can be both associative and semantic. When researchers count how often people talk with each other, communication networks are formally indistinguishable from transportation networks, cash-flow networks, or association networks. But when such networks include information about what is being said, or the kinds of social relationships within which individuals communicate with each other, their links mean different things and they therefore become semantic networks.

The idea of semantic networks probably originated in cultural-anthropological efforts to represent cognitive structures or mental models as relational graphs (D'Andrade, 1991, 1995; Quillian, 1968; Wallace, 1961). It has been facilitated by the psycho-logical theorizing of Abelson and Rosenberg (1958), by Schank and Abelson's (1977) inquiries into actionable knowledge structures, by causal inference modeling (Blalock, 1964; Simon, 1957), by graph theory (Harary, Norman, & Cartwright, 1965; Maruyama, 1963), by evaluative assertion analysis (Osgood, Saporta, & Nunnally, 1956), by studies of communication networks (Rice & Richards, 1985; Richards & Rice, 1981) and social networks (Wellman & Berkowitz, 1988), and by theories of communication networks (Rogers & Kincaid, 1981). Possibly the first mention of a computer analysis of texts using what we now call a semantic network is found in the work of Allen (1963), a lawyer and logician who proposed a system for studying the networks of propositions that constitute legal agreements, such as an arms limitation agreement, for loopholes that their signatories could utilize.

In artificial intelligence research, semantic networks are considered one approach to knowledge representation and natural language processing. Lindsay's (1963) demonstration of a system that "understands" natural language is an outstanding early example. His system features a relational memory, which creates what we now refer to as a semantic network. It keeps track of Basic English sentences (using 850 English words and a simplified grammar; Ogden, 1937) that mention kinship relations of the form "*a* is the *R* of *b*." As such sentences enter the system, it constructs a kinship network that the analyst can eventually question about kinship relationships not mentioned in the texts but implied by them. This is what makes semantic network approaches attractive to content analysts: the promise of finding answers that are not literally contained in a body of texts—in its readable character strings, in the abstractions that computer dictionaries can provide, or in the co-occurrences of words—by inferring what is semantically entailed by the given texts. Network conceptions of cognition and textual meanings are not entirely unproblematic, however (for a critique, see Johnson-Laird, Herrmann, & Chaffin, 1984).

As already stated, semantic networks are constructed from collections of birelational statements, two-valued predicates, or propositions containing two nodes with a particular link specified between them. The proposition "The candidate failed to clarify his position" links "the candidate" to his "position" by his "failure to clarify" it. The proposition "The U.S. women's soccer team won the 1999 World Cup" links "the U.S. women's soccer team" to the "1999 World Cup" by the team's having "won" it. And the proposition "Mary helps John" links "Mary" and "John" by her act of "helping." The first three components of Lasswell's (1960) famous formula "who says what to whom with which effect" define a connection in a semantic network of people or institutions sending and receiving particular messages, sharing "what" is being said. The <actor-action-target> triplets that some researchers employ to record interactions among individual actors and nations (Heise, 1995) constitute semantic networks, as people interact with each other in innumerable but conceptually distinguished ways.

In computing the implications of texts that constitute semantic networks, analysts need to acknowledge the relational properties of the connections between concepts. For example, "being married" is bidirectional and confined to two nodes. Being "the mother of" is unidirectional, and although it is confined to two nodes as well, it is recursively extendable (there are mothers of mothers, and so on). Subordination is unidirectional, transitive, and not confined to a pair of nodes: If C is subordinate to B, and B is subordinate to A, then C is subordinate to A. Reflexive connections turn back to the very nodes from which they originate. Moreover, there are key concepts that, if removed, would separate a network into smaller subnetworks, whereas others could drop out without making any appreciable difference. In content analysis, semantic networks are of particular interest because they preserve relationships between textual units, even when they occur in different parts of a text and thus form an interconnected web rather than separate categories of textual units.

An excellent but rather specialized example of a semantic network approach with online support for preediting is Heise's (1995) Event Structure Analysis, mentioned above. It facilitates the analysis of texts that describe a web of events involving actors, targets, outcomes, benefits, and the like. ESA is an online computational system that joins sociological conceptions of actions with narrative analyses and mathematical graph theory (Abell, 1987, 1993; Corsaro & Heise, 1990; Doreian, 1993; Durig, 1995). The process of using ESA essentially consists of two steps. In the first, the user identifies and orders the events being described within the text. To this end, the program guides the user with pertinent instructions. It produces a diagram that depicts how some events are necessary for other events to happen and how abstract events are represented in concrete happenings, and it facilitates decisions concerning whether the network is sufficient for analysis. In the second step, the user codes information on events into an "event frame." This frame has eight components: the agent, the action, the object (or target of the action), the instrument, the alignment (of the instrument), the setting (of other people, objects, and instruments in which the event takes place), the product, and the beneficiary. During this process, ESA makes the coding instructions for this dimensionalization of the events available to the user. After thus building the network of social events, the analyst can see how people, things, and actions are linked to what happened and can ask several analytical questions, even in quantitative terms, that would have been difficult to answer from the original text.

CETA, also mentioned above as a computer program that provides computational support for preediting of text, feeds into Kleinnijenhuis et al.'s (1997) extension of Osgood et al.'s (1956) evaluative assertion analysis. It distinguishes not two but five two-place predicate types:

- Predicates that evaluate something, implying an ideal or value (Osgood's common meaning term)

- Predicates that claim something to be real or true in the author's world

- Predicates that describe an actor's actions and targets

■ Predicates that claim a causal relationship between two variables, including "if-then" forms

■ Predicates that aver an affective relationship between two actors or between one actor and an object

These predicate types are displayed in Table 12.1. To distinguish several worlds (i.e., networks), Kleinnijenhuis et al. also attribute nuclear sentences to their authors, to speakers, to publications, and to sources quoted by authors. The positive and negative values of the ideal and the associative or dissociative properties of the link between any two concepts (e.g., "stimulates" is +, "inhibits" is –; "has" is +, "has not" is –) are expressed numerically between +1 and –1. Unlike other authors concerned with preediting efforts, Kleinnijenhuis et al. do attend to the reliability problems that such parsing necessarily poses.

Table 12.1 Predicate Types for Kleinnijenhuis et al.'s Semantic Network Analysis

Predicate Type	Author	Quoted Source	(IF) i	Predicate	(THEN) j
Evaluative	*A:*	*S:*	object	(dis)associated(+/–)	ideal(+/–)
Reality	*A:*	*S:*	A's or S's reality	predicate(+/–)	object
Action	*A:*	*S:*	actor	acts on(+/–)	object
Causal	*A:*	*S:*	object/variable	causes(+)/prevents(–)	object/variable
Affective	*A:*	*S:*	actor	(dis)affected(+/–)	actor/object

SOURCE: Kleinnijenhuis et al. (1997).

In Kleinnijenhuis et al.'s analysis of these triplets, the qualitative differences among predicates are dropped in favor of the magnitude of their expressed association or dissociation, and a mathematical calculus is employed that aggregates these to form a compound network of concepts (Cuilenburg, Kleinnijenhuis, & De Ridder, 1986, 1988; Kleinnijenhuis et al., 1997). The rules of inference provided by this calculus are based on a theory of affective meaning according to which the values of ideals flow through a network along associative links and reverse their valuation as they travel along dissociative links.

In a 1990 paper, Kleinnijenhuis analyzes the world of Israeli prime minister Shamir, compares Arafat and Goebbels, and discusses Israel's relations with Western governments as presented in the Dutch press. In a 1997 paper, Kleinnijenhuis et al. demonstrate semantic network analysis with data from public and parliamentary debates on economic issues in two leading Dutch newspapers during two periods of time, 1968–1976 and 1978–1984. They consider eight political actors (e.g., government, parties, and unions) and 29 economic variables (e.g., unemployment and interest rate) as well as "ideal" and "reality." Naturally, the directions of influence among several variables and the evaluation of several concepts changed during these periods, but Kleinnijenhuis et al. found that all changes moved away from the Keynesian policies of the first period to a neoorthodox view of the role of government in the Dutch economy during the second period. The way in which these authors derived inferences by tracing the flow of influence and affect through a semantic network amounts to a shift from the traditionally explicit coding of concepts to latent phenomena to a "systematic reading between the lines."

A third example of a semantic network approach is found in Carley's (1997) attempt to formalize social experts' knowledge. This research led Carley to the construction of semantic networks, which she calls "socio-conceptual" networks (mentioned in Chapter 10). The software she developed, MECA, aids coders in identifying any pair of concepts that occur in the same sentence, clause, or paragraph as subject or object, respectively, and the relationship pertaining between the two concepts. Carley distinguishes three levels of strength in the relationships between nodes, including the degree of agreement or consensus encountered among the contributors of the texts (hence the reference to a society in her name for these kinds of networks). Her definitions of the three levels are as follows:

Definitives are statements where one concept defines the other, such that in the society in question, if the first concept is used, the second is always implied.

Logicals are statements where the concepts are logically connected, such that in the society in question, if the first and second concept are used the speaker intends a specific relation among them.

Simple connectives are statements, such that in the society in question, if the two concepts are used and the speaker has not specified an alternative relation, then the socially accepted relation between them is assumed. (p. 87)

Unlike the researchers whose work provides the previous examples of semantic network approaches, Carley does not trace implications through her networks; rather, she attempts to characterize the meanings of each node (see Figure 10.7) by using five numerical indices of the role the focal concept plays within a network:

Imageability is the total number of nodes connected to the focal concept by arrows emanating from it.

Evokability is the total number of nodes connected to the focal concept by arrows reaching it.

Density is the sum of imageability and evokability.

Conductivity is the number of two-step paths through the focal concept, which amounts to the product of imageability and evokability.

Intensity is the fraction of all nuclear statements that contain the focal concept.

The three dimensions of density, conductivity, and intensity give rise to a taxonomy of concepts that reflects the concepts' positions within the network.

For example, ordinary concepts are low on all dimensions. Most concepts can be expected to be ordinary, and analysts use such concepts to define outstanding types. Symbols, for example, are high on all three dimensions. They represent highly embedded and multiply defined concepts on which there is often high consensus. Stereotypes are defined as concepts that are high in intensity and density but low in conductivity. Stereotypes are highly structured but change slowly due to their low level of conductivity. In addition to ordinary concepts, symbols, and stereotypes, Carley (1997, pp. 87–89) differentiates the network properties of prototypes, buzzwords, factoids, placeholders, and emblems.

In a study of MIT students' talk about tutors, Carley found that most concepts turned out to be factoids, which is not surprising, given that such talk often turns to decisions. The next-largest numbers of concepts were ordinary (e.g., "finishing thesis," "humorous comment") and stereotypes (e.g., "nerd," "hacker"). As these two concepts seem mutually distinct and opposite in evaluation, these labels would matter a great deal to tutors. Figure 12.5 illustrates the network position of the concept "hacker" in Carley's semantic network of tutor talk. I present only one such node here as an example of the analytical possibilities that semantic networks can provide for improving researchers' understanding of the relations among concepts.

Computationally, the less diverse the properties of the relationships among nodes, the easier semantic network analysis is to handle. This is why Kleinnijenhuis et al. (1997) restrict their list of predicates to five kinds, which is only slightly more than the two kinds of assertions of varying associative/dissociative strengths used in Osgood et al.'s (1956) evaluative assertion analysis. This is also why Carley (1997), who does not look for such simplifications, asks simpler questions to begin with, questions that can be answered through the comparison of only a few nodes at a time.

In an attempt to avoid the need for excessive preediting, Barnett and Doerfel (1997) have pursued still another interesting computational simplification. To infer scholarly groupings within the International Communication Association (ICA) from the titles of papers presented at the ICA's annual conferences from 1992 through 1996, they combined two research traditions: (a) bibliometric analyses of citations (Rice, 1990; Rice, Borman, & Reeves, 1988; So, 1988), which rely on the acknowledged use of one publication for ideas discussed in another; and (b) work in organizations conducted by Monge and Eisenberg (1987), who recommend measuring organizational networks through content analyses of members' key vocabulary, slogans, and stories. Assuming that intellectual groups sustain themselves through talk among peers, develop consensus on key concepts, and submit their papers to divisions they perceive to be sympathetic to their approaches, Barnett and Doerfel defined the connection between any two papers by the vocabulary the titles shared. Their triplets, <author$_i$-vocabulary in paper$_i$ and paper$_k$-author$_k$>, made coding unnecessary and led to a semantic network of these different kinds of connections. Their preferred type of analysis is clustering, and the groupings that emerged showed interesting correlations with the ICA divisions.

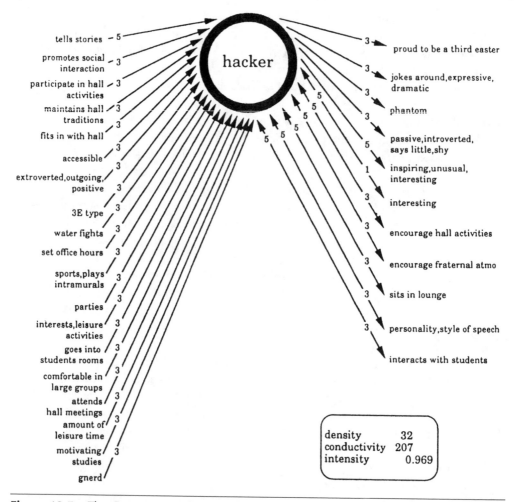

Figure 12.5 The Concept "Hacker" Within a Semantic Network of Tutor Talk
SOURCE: Carley (1997, p. 96, fig. 4.6).

12.5.4   Memetic Approaches

The CATA approaches discussed so far in this chapter all start from synchronic (i.e., atemporal) descriptions of texts and tend to provide inferences from single bodies of texts about common readings, shared categories, prevailing association structures, and semantic implications. They generally do not respond to interactions among texts over time. Yet we know that all texts are rooted in previous texts. Reading takes place in the present, but always against the backdrop of previous readings, including nonverbal responses of other readers, and with an eye toward future texts. Words not only have etymologies but their meanings change as they move through different texts, enter and leave conversations, and become reproduced, rearticulated, and used in novel texts.

Social realities, one can argue, manifest themselves within vast networks of rearticulations of texts that moreover organize themselves in the process of continuing rearticulations. The theory of meaning underlying memetic approaches attempts to relate currently available texts to the histories of their interpretations. This theory is enacted or embodied by other readers, other writers, and the media of communication disseminating the texts.

The word *meme* was coined by Dawkins (1976, 1982), a geneticist. Seeking to extend the theory of biological evolution to cultural phenomena, Dawkins conceived of the meme as a textual analogue to the biological gene. His starting point was that messages enter a brain as ideas and interact therein with other ideas, and the result of that interaction determines what the brain does. Because ideas are observable only in their consequences, if memes are to persist, they must be able to program a brain for their own replication. Memes that thus succeed can be passed on and enter other brains. Just as biological organisms can be thought of as a means for DNA replication, so the brains of a population of people can be viewed as temporary hosts where memes replicate themselves. Memes that do not reproduce eventually die out. A meme's replicability is enhanced when the meme manages either to prevent competing memes from entering its host, a brain, or to attract cooperative memes that increase the joint probability of one another's being replicated. For memes, brains are a scarce resource. The social networks that emerge as a consequence of memes' entering and programming the brains of members of a given population constitute additional ways for memes to create support for their own replication.

Dawkins's memetics surely is a mechanistic theory, but it has fueled the development of CATA methodology. Indeed, content analysts might do well to acknowledge meanings in the interactions between different texts. The idea of plagiarism (as discussed in Chapter 10, section 10.5) is based on comparisons of two authors' texts, written at different points in time, in the context of a shared literature. History consists of a network of texts that are read in the present but focus on an unobservable past, with historians mediating the interactions among these texts. Even such a common idea as public opinion is constructed on multiple text comparisons over time, as seen in the practices of those who measure it. Although pollsters may conceptualize the public as an object to be measured, this is far from reality. Public opinion is an institutional construction based on at least three kinds of texts: pollsters' questions, multiple interviewees' answers, and the published results of this construct as accepted by readers. The first two texts grow out of conversations between interviewers and respondents who happen to be asked their opinions about issues of interest to pollsters, not what they are concerned with in their lives. Conclusions derived from the comparison of these two texts say as much about the pollsters' interests as about the respondents' answers, and it is far from clear what either has to do with what people talk about in public. Significantly, the questions asked and the responses received are derived to a large extent from agendas set in the mass media, which also publish the results of opinion polls, all with the aim of establishing what is publicly acceptable, politically feasible, or true. Thus public opinion is embedded in texts that are both cause and consequence of an institutionalized network of textual rearticulations.

The naive view of public opinion held by many pollsters is not the only example of researchers' failure to recognize their discipline's memetic nature. Content analysts who believe they are able to analyze contents without contexts have fallen into the same trap. This is why I have argued against the conception of analyzing *the* content of texts and have advised analysts against reporting findings concerning "it" without making reference to readers, users, or the institutions that reproduce the texts being analyzed and without acknowledging the textual origins of the analytical constructs being used, albeit implicitly (see Chapter 2).

The study of the dynamics of very large bodies of text was envisioned by Tenney (1912), piloted by Lasswell (1941), and theorized by Rapoport (1969) and has been exemplified by Gerbner (1969, 1985) and his colleagues (Gerbner, Gross, Morgan, & Signorielli, 1994). However, all of these scholars lacked the requisite computational capabilities to process the interactions between large volumes of text and ended up making simple counts of frequencies or volumes. Confined to manual coding, Tenney could study only a few New York daily newspapers, Lasswell could study the elite newspapers of only a few countries, and Gerbner based his longitudinal studies on one week of television per year. These researchers also lacked adequate models or analytical constructs. Tenney relied on the metaphor of weather dynamics, Lasswell and Gerbner used symbol systems, and Rapoport applied systems theory. Below, I discuss two computational content analyses of a memetic nature, one informed by ecology and the other by epidemiology, much as memetics is indebted to genetics.

The first example is Best's (1997) study of newsgroups in the popular Usenet (or NetNews) discussion system on the Internet. Within Usenet, discussion groups evolve and continue along diverse lines of subject matter, ranging from science to politics, to literature, and to various hobbies. Participants in a newsgroup read each other's contributions (called *posts*), comment on them selectively, and bring new ideas into the discussion. Naturally, contributors have limited amounts of time available to spend on the Internet, and this has the effect of limiting the participation of most to one or a few newsgroups. Posts consist of the texts that individual participants contribute in response to other posts, thus defining a forward-moving network of linked texts, an ecology of evolving textual species. In this textual ecology, newsgroups function like islands on which certain memes reproduce themselves and evolve more readily than on other islands. Usenet has grown considerably since the late 1970s and early 1980s. Currently, newsgroups create about 100,000 new posts each day, making Usenet an excellent data source for the study of cultural microevolution.

Best's pilot study, which relied on 1,793 posts made over a 10-day period, is part of a larger effort (Best, 1998). The key to Best's approach is the marriage of two kinds of software, one designed to simulate artificial life (Alife) and one designed for information retrieval (LSI; Deerwester, Dumais, Furnas, Landauer, & Harshman, 1990; Dumais, 1992, 1993; Foltz, 1990; Furnas et al., 1988). LSI represents units of text (in Best's study, the posts) as vectors, which are a function of the frequencies of word co-occurrences within them. With a principal components analysis of these vectors, Best identifies frequently recurring vector subspaces, which represent word clusters that replicate together. For example, in a collection of posts from a military discussion group, *harbor, Japan,* and *pearl* turn out to replicate themselves in unison and can therefore be considered a meme. Best operationally defines a meme as the largest reliably replicating unit within a text corpus and considers it as a suitable cultural replicator (Pocklington & Best, 1997). Accordingly, a post is a collection of more or less successfully replicating memes. Best also addresses the issue of mutation, or the possibility that memes, especially larger ones, do not reproduce identically. One source of mutation is memes' traveling outside the electronic system as well, through their users' brains and real-life conversations, after which they may reenter the system in rearticulated forms. What actually happens to these memes outside the system is of course not accessible to this analysis. Best considers mutations of this kind by observing memotypes, which are paraphrasings, rephrasings, or different versions of the same story.

Alife calls for the identification of "quasi-species" (Eigen, McCaskill, & Schuster, 1988), which in Best's study are defined as collections of posts with threads to common ancestors that evolve while sharing a variety of memotypes. For example, *Japan* and *Pearl Harbor* are always embedded in stories that are related in some ways and can be said to be of a certain kind. Best then examines the pairwise interactions between these quasi-species as cross-correlations over time, much as such interactions are studied in ecology.

In ecology, one population can have either a positive effect (+) on another by increasing the other in numbers (i.e., increasing members' chances of replication and survival) or a negative effect (−) by decreasing the other's numbers. Best has tested four kinds of interactions—mutual (+, +), competitive (−, −), neutral (0, 0), and predator/prey (+, −) (see also Boulding, 1978)—and has found strong negative cross-time correlations that account for the interactions among quasi-species in Usenet. At first glance, Best thought these interactions to be of the predator/prey variety—that is, increases in one are obtained at the expense of the other, subject to the constraint that when the prey disappears, the predator will as well. However, the negative correlations could also be explained by competition for a limited resource—in this case, the attention of human participants. Competition was especially evident for quasi-species residing in relatively narrow ecological niches. The memetic hypothesis that memes compete for the scarce resource of participants' minds in order to replicate themselves seems to explain the speciation dynamics in Internet newsgroups.

The second example of the use of a memetic approach is the system that Fan (1988; Fan & Cook, 1997) developed for predicting public opinions and behaviors from mass-media data. Fan, a biologist by training, was not the first to see a parallel between the spread of diseases and the adoption of ideas and practices—the information diffusion literature had long thrived on this analogy (for one early example, see Rogers & Shoemaker, 1971; for one more recent, see Valente, 1993). To capture the dynamics of public opinion, Fan developed an analytical construct in the form of a complex recursive function and applied it to the day-by-day mass-media production of messages (containing memes).

Fan's assumptions include the following: At any one point in time, public opinion equals the distribution of ideas in a population—the memes that a survey could elicit. Much as a contagious disease is conceptualized in epidemiology, a meme enters someone's brain and either takes hold of it or does not. Memes that have entered a brain as ideas can be replicated and passed on. Fan deviates slightly from the epidemiological model by considering people not as mere passive receivers of "infectious" memes, but as holding one of two opposing ideas and as being able to change their ideas in either direction. The rate at which ideas change from one to another depends on memes' communicability.

To compute the rate of the adoption of ideas within a population of people, Fan relies on a fairly general mass-action law. If everyone reproduces memes at an equal rate, then the rate of their adoption is the product of two proportions: the proportion of people who hold the ideas in question and the proportion of people who do not. Mathematically, when these proportions are zero or one—in other words, when everyone is of the same mind—the adoption rate is zero. According to this law, the largest adoption rate can be expected when a population is evenly divided on an issue. However, when the two competing memes are equal in number, their persuasive forces cancel each other. It is only when they are unequal that opinions will shift.

Ordinarily, the distribution of memes circulating within a population reflects the distribution of public opinions. This correlation is significantly altered, however, when mass communication enters the picture, when the rate at which memes are reproduced or published is no longer equal for all but biased by the mass media, the great multiplier. This describes a memetic model of a dynamically shifting system of public opinion as it is recursively perturbed by the selective reproduction of memes by the mass media.

Mathematically, measuring public opinion at any one time and then adding the effects of mass-media coverage turns out to be equivalent to measuring a longer history of the daily mass-media coverage and acknowledging that media coverage loses its impact on public opinion over time. Fan assumes that the persuasiveness of media coverage has a half-life of one day. This mathematical equivalence enables Fan to bypass public opinion measurement (of ideas) altogether and take the history of mass-media coverage (meme dissemination) as data for predicting public opinion. One of Fan's motivations for making this choice is that conducting public opinion polls is costly and time-consuming, whereas the history of media coverage is easily available, and such an analysis can offer instant predictions.

This analysis starts with the identification of the pros and cons of a selected issue in the media coverage of the day. For simple issues, Fan generates such data with the aid of a computer; for more intricate ones, he employs human coders. With an initial estimate of the public opinion that the media coverage is likely to meet, which may be quite arbitrary, plus the textual data of the day, the system computes a first round of predicted opinions. These plus the following day's mass-media coverage of the issue yield a second round of predictions, and so forth. As the history of mass-media coverage unfolds, the predictions that emerge become increasingly independent from the initial public opinion estimate and increasingly correlated with the actual public opinion, measured independently. The recursive function of public opinion's dependence on mass communication, the analytical construct, develops over time, continuously adjusting itself to the emerging history of the coverage of an issue. It can learn from "mistakes" when the results of available opinion surveys occasionally enter the computations.

The recursive analytical construct, which is part of what Fan calls an "ideo-dynamic model," has been vindicated by numerous rather successful predictions in several areas of public opinion (see Fan, 1977).

INTERACTIVE-HERMENEUTIC EXPLORATIONS   12.6

The computer aids reviewed above support content analyses of typically large volumes of textual matter and tend to support various stages of the analytical process—identifying relevant texts, for example, or coding. Many require users to do preparatory work: preediting texts, formulating search terms, constructing or validating dictionaries and category systems, selecting among analysis options, and defining various statistical parameters. But once a procedure is set, usually after the analyst has developed it on a small sample, it is uniformly applied to all available texts. In this section, I review computer aids to another kind of content analysis, one whose tradition originated in ethnographic, cultural-anthropological, and interpretive scholarship, often labeled *qualitative research*. I have mentioned this research tradition briefly in Chapter 1 (section 1.7) and Chapter 4 (section 4.1.2).

I call computer aids in this research tradition interactive-hermeneutic—*interactive* because the categories of analysis and the choices of analytical constructs are not fixed, and content analysis categories become apparent to the analysts in the process of reading if not actively interrogating their texts; and *hermeneutic* because the process of analysis is directed by the analysts' growing understanding of the body of texts. This process enables content analysts to correct apparent errors in interpretation and allows for course corrections in midstream whenever interesting analytical avenues appear. In a hermeneutic circle, text is interpreted relative to an imagined context, and these interpretations in turn reconstruct that context for further examination of the same or subsequently available text. This iteration continues (see Figure 4.3) until some satisfactory understanding is achieved. Understanding is the point at which the reading of texts resonates with the analyst's background. Understanding is always a temporary state, and the analytical results of this approach to content analysis are always thought to be incomplete.

Computer aids expand the interactive-hermeneutic research tradition in at least three ways:

■ They offer their users text manipulation routines for handling, organizing, filing, and keeping track of texts that are more numerous than unaided analysts can handle.

■ They introduce some systematicity into users' reading, for example, by encouraging analysts to go through all available texts, by allowing analysts to highlight relevant sections, and by making analysts aware of the coding choices they made previously.

■ They record and make accessible for inspection some of the analytical distinctions within texts that analysts introduce during analyses, presenting these distinctions in several informative ways.

Below, I review the most typical functions that computer aids in this research tradition selectively support. No two systems enable the same functions, and no one system is best. The developers of qualitative text analysis software often compete with one another by inventing new features or making the features offered by other developers more user-friendly or efficient. As the software packages available change rather rapidly, this list is intended mainly to give potential users some idea about what features in a system they may want to look for as well as what features might render a system cumbersome for their purposes.

Text entering. Computer aids vary in the kinds of text formats they can accept, with most accepting text files with ASCII/ANSI characters. Some systems require their users to preedit text—for example, into lines (as in WinMAX Pro and AQUAD) or into paragraphs not exceeding a certain length (NUD*IST and NVivo recognize paragraphs by carriage returns). Others restrict the lengths of texts to a certain number of words, which may constrain an analysis. In addition, some systems store text files externally (e.g., HyperRESEARCH), whereas others process them after conversion into internal representations (e.g., AQUAD, ATLAS.ti, and NVivo). The ability to index raw text, a feature of most information retrieval software—ZyINDEX and dtSearch, for example—speeds up text searches but prevents text alterations; programs with this feature do not allow users to edit, correct typos, spell out abbreviations, eliminate headers, or create memos as they go on, all of which may be useful to analysts who are reading texts in depth. ATLAS.ti offers users the option of editing original text while the program is operating in read-only mode. Systems that operate on internal representations may have to reimport edited texts, which means users lose any work already done on those texts.

Display. All computer aids allow users to scroll through original texts on their computer screens, which enables selective and nonsequential reading of any portion of the texts. Some allow users to add permanent highlighting to relevant sections, whereas others facilitate the cutting and pasting of textual units into special files. Analysts often find frequency tabulations, KWIC listings, and concordances (see section 12.2) useful to have, and some systems provide these. Software packages vary in text window sizes and in the ways they allow users to manipulate texts. There are also considerable differences among programs in how they display the connections between original textual matter and the terms in which it is analyzed and in how they keep track of the structure of assigned categories or codes.

Manual coding. Virtually all interactive-hermeneutic computer aids allow users to assign sections of text to categories or codes manually. Categories or codes are not predefined, so users can invent them on the fly. Some systems impose restrictions on the kinds of textual units that can be categorized or coded. WinMAX Pro and AQUAD, for example, ask users to code lines of text one by one. In more recently developed systems, such as ATLAS.ti and NVivo, users can highlight any section of text and assign it to one or more categories. The coding of noncontiguous units of text poses problems for most systems.

Automatic coding. Older systems require users to read through whole texts to identify all relevant units on the screen and attach appropriate codes. Some newer systems, such as ATLAS.ti and NVivo, also support an automatic coding option. After users have created categories for particular character strings, they may either use the coded character strings as queries for coding all textual units with identical textual attributes or define coding categories in terms of queries that will find relevant units without the users' doing any further reading. NUD*IST and NVivo feature automatic categorization, which works similar to a dictionary. As automatic coding can fail the semantic validity criterion, analysts should look for automatic coding options that are supplemented by features that allow users to examine the actual text segments that end up in one category and to undo inappropriate assignments.

Hierarchical/nonhierarchical categorizing. When content analysts assign codes to any relevant section of text without restrictions, nonhierarchical representations of the original text may result. This aids the retrieval and examination of textual units with the same attributes but makes classical Cartesian analyses—cross-tabulations of textual attributes, for example—difficult if not meaningless. Analysts can prevent this difficulty by using units that are mutually exclusive and by assigning each unit to one code for each variable of classification. Most interactive-hermeneutic software packages do not accept this restriction, and thus limit the analytical possibilities of the emerging categorizations. NVivo, among others, allows users to categorize codes, assigning second-level codes to them (rather than to the original text), which gives the impression of a hierarchical category scheme. This hierarchy is not of mutually exclusive categories unless users restrict themselves to applying mutually exclusive categories. Nonhierarchical categories give rise to interesting measures of the strength of the categories' relationships—for example, in terms of the amount of text they jointly represent. ATLAS.ti provides users with easily intelligible diagrams of these relationships.

Systems also differ greatly in the ways they allow users to keep track of the codes used in analyses.

Memoing, commenting, and linking. An attractive feature of many computer aids used in interactive-hermeneutic explorations of texts is the ability for users to associate notes, memos, or other information with any segment of original text. Users can thus augment texts with accounts that are not explicit in the texts but are known to the analysts; these might include recollections that add to anthropological field notes, definitions of terms, names of speakers, information about nonverbal features available from video recordings or images, or the names of persons referred to by pronouns. ATLAS.ti, NUD*IST, NVivo, and WordStat include such options. Some systems allow users to add hyperlinks between files, which can accomplish similar text enrichments. It is important that any comments that users enter to become part of the text being analyzed can be easily distinguished from comments the users intend to remain private reminders of their thoughts while they were reading the text, and several text entry systems make this possible, including ESA, KEDS, CETA, and Carley's MECA.

Interoperability. Portability of CATA output across systems from different developers is rare. TextSmart and Verbastat are both SPSS products and so, naturally, they are compatible. LIWC output feeds into SPSS as well, and the LIWC dictionary can be used in WordStat and TextQuest. Files created using CATA software for interactive-hermeneutic explorations are rarely shareable, even among coworkers on the same project. The coding that emerges in interaction between one analyst and given texts stays essentially within the system, reflecting the conceptual repertoire of that one analyst. Alexa and Züll (1999) conclude their recent survey of CATA software—including interactive-hermeneutic computer aids—by saying, "There is no sufficient support for either exploiting already existing data, validating the analysis performed by other researchers or performing secondary analysis using the same text material but with a different text analysis package or with other software" (p. 144).

Despite the extremely valuable procedural and visual features the software packages described in this section offer for conceptualizing and analyzing medium-size texts, these systems also have two drawbacks that software makers tend to downplay or ignore. The first is that researchers using such software are unable to share among themselves the coding/conceptual schemes that emerge during their interactive explorations of text, or to apply those schemes to other texts or different situations. This inability effectively prevents researchers from testing the reliability of categorizations, which is an important precursor to assuring the validity of research findings (see Chapter 11, section 11.1). This is not a limitation of computing; rather, it reflects the premise of a research tradition that takes an individual analyst's understanding as the criterion for accepting analytical results, an understanding that is generalized to that analyst's scholarly community without evidence. Software packages that do not support the sharing of the systems of categories developed within them, coding schemes, and other intermediate results for reproduction elsewhere can easily become uncontestable tools for privileged experts.

To qualify the above worry, I must note that reliability checks for interactive-hermeneutic explorations of texts are not inconceivable. A research project could well instruct several analysts to apply a given set of codes to the same text. Reliability calculations for multiple interpretations of overlapping sections of text are available (see Chapter 11, section 11.6)—provided one could compare these analysts' codings. Hermetically closed computer systems preclude this possibility, however.

The second drawback of these computer aids is a product of the theories of meaning that are built into them. Coding textual units into categories, even if intended as a convenient tool for handling large texts and for talking about them in fewer categories, amounts to abstracting or redescribing a text in simpler, more relevant, and perhaps more general terms. This advantage is gained at the cost of buying into the classical representational theory of meaning. There are obviously other ways of reading texts and other ways of supporting the analysis of texts, some of which are reviewed above, such as computing association structures, developing semantic networks, and answering research questions by following the entailments of texts. One might add to these the rather different aims of critical scholarship, such as suggesting alternative readings or conceiving of less oppressive ways of interpretation (Krippendorff, 1995b). All computer aids carry the danger of blinding their users to alternative theories of meaning and epistemologies. To encourage analysts to retain their awareness of these alternatives, we conceptualize content analysis relative to a chosen context—any social reality, conceptual framework, or period in time worthy of analysts' explication. Such a conceptualization should apply to CATA software as well.

FRONTIERS 12.7

Technological breakthroughs are hard to predict, but it is not too difficult to outline some exciting possibilities for the extension of computer-aided content analysis. Below, I briefly discuss five particular areas that are in need of further attention.

Intelligent Browsers 12.7.1

Although there have been remarkable advances in the scope of text search engines, users of existing browsers overwhelmingly experience the shallowness of their results. This is true whether users are surfing the Web, consulting full-text databases online, or using search routines within current CATA software. The Internet is full of expectations that more powerful browsers will soon be available, and CATA software developers tend to claim that they offer all kinds of features: "concept searches," "content extractors," "meaning finders," "theory developers," and many more. Unfortunately, the operationalizations of these concepts, connoting essentially human abilities, often fall far short of what software descriptions promise.

If browsers are to find scarce information in large textual universes and content analysts are to answer intelligent questions from available texts, the aims of both are quite compatible, if not identical. In fact, content analysis could dissolve itself into intelligent browsers if browsers could learn to model their searches by what content analysts actually do with texts: search for or sample "truly" relevant texts, interpret these by means of one or more theories of the chosen contexts of these texts, and provide textual evidence for answers to the research questions that motivate the search. Such intelligent browsers may never substitute experts' readings of texts or replace well-trained content analysis designers, but they certainly could be modeled after the research strategies of content analysis and could apply these to large textual universes whose volumes generally exceed human comprehension.

12.7.2   Common Platforms

On the fertile ground of naturally occurring texts, the species of CATA software, including weeds, grow wild. Most systems work essentially on their own, competing for potential users' time and willingness to learn them. This competition is fueled by software companies' often-exaggerated claims that their products will relieve users of difficult cognitive tasks. Although all CATA software packages do process texts—a few can also handle images and sound—no widely accepted text file standards exist, and there are few ways to feed the results produced by one program into another. The software-specific preparation of raw text that most systems require is costly and discourages the use of alternative approaches. There are no interface standards that would allow software from different developers to work together. There is not even any common vocabulary for comparing various content analysis tools.

There have been a few notable, albeit small, steps toward the development of common platforms. TextSmart is distributed by SPSS and so is integrated in this statistical package. LIWC feeds into SPSS, and its dictionary also works in WordStat and TextQuest, as already mentioned. But these are very limited "collaborations." A common platform to run various CATA procedures in parallel (comparatively) and in sequence (cooperatively) would enable developers to concentrate on refining a few good tools that can compete for users' attention along the dimensions of mutual compatibility, computational efficiency, analytical power, and user-friendliness. It would give users a box of freely combinable analytical tools with which to design all kinds of text analyses, and it would accelerate analysts' ability to utilize available texts in ways currently unimagined.

Computational Theories of Meaning   12.7.3

Far too often, content analyses are conceptualized—naively, one might add—in terms of traditional behavioral science methods for analyzing nontextual data: as a measuring tool for generating data amenable to inferential statistics, hypothesis testing, and modeling of causes and effects. Although the content analysis literature recognizes that analyzing meaningful text differs quite radically from analyzing observational data, computational aids, which are so much simpler when formulated as context-insensitive procedures, tend to follow in the footsteps of behaviorist assumptions. This limits CATA to very superficial meanings. CATA is in dire need of computational theories of meaning that extend theorizing about the individual cognitive ability of a typical reader to whole communities' diverse uses of texts, embracing the public processes that make particular text attributes significant as well as the social processes in which institutions reside. Computational linguistics, with its current concern for parsing sentences and disambiguating words and phrases, has made only marginal contributions to computational theories of meaning, largely because it theorizes what is general to language, not what is specific to particular nonlinguistic contexts. Content analysis, in contrast, needs to answer specific questions that have not previously been answered about extratextual phenomena of analysts' concerns. Abstractions from what a text means generally may well be a start, but they are not a useful end. Computer dictionaries often end up claiming unwarranted generalizations tied to single words, one word at a time.

Content analysis advances with the availability of rather detailed theories that, to fuel CATA development, can be converted into analytical constructs and tailored to fit specific analytical contexts. These theories may learn from ideas developed in computer science or from efforts to shed light on psychological, sociological, or political problems. They do not need to be—and in fact are better when they are not—grand theories, as they have to cope with language use "on the ground," with processes of microevolution, as Best has suggested. The theories that are currently inscribed in CATA—categorizing text, identifying patterns of co-occurrences, tracing the entailments of semantic networks, and automatically extracting memes from textual interactions—barely describe the contours of what needs to be developed.

Utilization of Intertextualities   12.7.4

Many content analysts are content to summarize finely unitized text and measure the textual attributes that permeate these texts (Krippendorff, 1969a).

Reducing a text to a large set of independently analyzed textual units robs it of its narrative qualities, of what makes it coherent, informative, compelling, and predictive. *Coherence* refers to how well parts of text—not just words or phrases—hang together or support each other in telling a larger story. For instance, most narratives start by laying a foundation, then develop a point, and end with a conclusion or coda. Their beginnings are necessarily different from their ends. Histories find coherence in the chronological order of their narrative structure, which in turn constructs the histories we know. Political texts might have to be analyzed as parallel constructions that acknowledge each other where their media meet. Conversations are constituted in participants' responses to previous responses. Scholarly discourse hangs together as a network of acknowledgments and citations of prior scholarly work. The abundantly obvious point of these examples is that texts are more than collections of words, phrases, paragraphs, and documents. An important CATA frontier is the development of ways to account for relationships between larger textual units so that they are treated as dependent on each other, not as unordered entities permeating a text.

Small steps in this direction can be observed in existing systems for analyzing question-answer pairs from interview data. TextSmart and Verbastat specialize in this probably simplest coherence. They analyze questions and answers as two distinct but structurally related bodies of text, which they link largely by cross-tabulations. Code-A-Text is purportedly designed to analyze dialogue, acknowledging the interactive qualities of texts. A few years back, a system called the Coordinator came into vogue (Winograd & Flores, 1986, pp. 157–162). It did not analyze but used speech act theory to connect electronic communications to the networks of commitments that underlie social organizations. Garfield (1979) pioneered citation indexing, a system that traces chains of bibliographic citations, thus facilitating the exploration of connected bodies of scholarly discourse. Forensic agencies need to connect crime reports, media coverage of crime, telephone conversations, and other elements to the specific actions of individuals. Good scholarly work entails connecting literature from diverse sources, experiments, interviews, statistics, and theory. All of these are texts whose value lies in their connections, in their responding to each other, in their parallelisms. CATA software would advance greatly if it could explicate some of these intertextual coherences and use them to draw powerful inferences from multiple kinds of texts.

12.7.5 Natural Interfaces

Users can expect advances in the user-friendliness of CATA software in three areas:

- Ease of operating the software, in navigating an analysis through analytical options

■ Ease of handling text in various forms, including preediting

■ Ease of tracing text through its transformations to the answers to given research questions

CATA software packages are increasingly employing Windows-like formats. Using a mouse to point to, click on, and move text has become as conventional as making selections on menu-driven interfaces. Even so, there are still vast differences in user-friendliness among different text analysis programs. I will not discuss them here except to say that learning any system always amounts to a big investment of time, and users should be sure that the systems they choose are worth their efforts to learn how to use them.

Windows-like software is built on a metaphor of texts as movable objects, not as matter that needs to be read, rearticulated, compared, questioned, triangulated, and interpreted. Software that aids interactive-hermeneutic explorations is currently leading the search for new interface metaphors, although it has not grown much beyond supporting one or more readable windows (e.g., pages of text), fast text retrieval, highlighting, and coding facilities. Finding and implementing more natural interface metaphors for users to understand and handle large bodies of text constitutes a major challenge, especially when one acknowledges, as software developers should, that most texts arise out of and reenter conversations, that literacy is a social and responsive phenomenon, not reducible to individual reading, and that even text analysis takes place in the context of collaborators and stakeholders who may need to say something about how texts are interpreted. The absence of natural interface metaphors for what content analysts need to do is a major impediment to CATA use.

Users' understanding of what CATA software does is the most important yet least enabled aspect of true user-friendliness. I have already noted the tendency of CATA software developers to use fancy labels for describing the capabilities of their programs. Instead of using marketable labels that shortcut understanding, developers should provide, and users should demand, transparency of the analytical processes that the software follows. As I have already suggested, CATA software can be comprehended as a network of text transformations that maintains the readability of the original text relative to a chosen context. It would therefore be reasonable to expect that users be enabled to examine critically whether the theories of reading underlying these transformations make sense, modify them so that they do, and judge at least their face validity. Word frequencies are obvious—analysts can understand them as long as they can read the tabulated words. However, as soon as stemming and lemmatization take place, it is important that analysts have access to the words that end up in one or the other category, to KWIC lists of words that can provide a sense of what particular categories mean in a given body of text or different texts. Many of the companies that sell CATA software packages promise results without saying what produces those results. Without transparency, software users are asked to operate by faith. Perhaps developers might model user-friendly examinations of what their CATA software does on the debugging aids provided to computer programmers, which enable the tracing of computations through all their steps to find errors; such an aid could allow a user to trace an analysis back to the original text. Transparency of CATA software not only supports user understanding of what a program does with a given text, it is also a requirement for establishing semantic validity.

CHAPTER 13

Validity

Validation provides compelling reasons for taking the results of scientific research seriously. It can serve as the ground for developing theories and the basis of successful interventions. This chapter develops a typology of validation efforts that content analysts may utilize in justifying their research. It also shows ways in which analysts can quantitatively assess at least some of these efforts.

VALIDITY DEFINED   13.1

Validity is that quality of research results that leads us to accept them as true, as speaking about the real world of people, phenomena, events, experiences, and actions. A measuring instrument is considered valid if it measures what its user claims it measures. A content analysis is valid if the inferences drawn from the available texts withstand the test of independently available evidence, of new observations, of competing theories or interpretations, or of being able to inform successful actions.

Riffe, Lacy, and Fico (1998) suggest, "The essence of the validity problem in content analysis as well as in other research . . . is that research should speak as truthfully as possible to as many as possible" (p. 150). The meaning of *truthful* is the central focus of this chapter. The idea that research should speak "to as many people as possible" leads to useful distinctions among face validity, social validity, and empirical validity.

Face validity is "obvious" or "common truth." We appeal to face validity when we accept research findings because they "make sense"—that is, they are plausible and believable "on their face"—usually without having to give or expecting to hear detailed reasons. It makes sense, indeed, to measure public attention to an issue by the relative frequency with which the issue is mentioned

313

in mass media. It makes sense to measure the quality of political deliberations by the number of alternative reasons brought into a discussion. After subsequent empirical scrutiny, face validity may prove untenable, but it appears just right at the time the research is accepted. Face validity does not equal expectations. For example, it did not occur to anyone in the 1970s that members of minority groups were targets of jokes in U.S. television fiction more often than were members of the majority until content analysts thought to pursue this topic and found that correlation. Findings like these make sense in retrospect. Although face validity has its roots in common sense, in widely shared consensus, it is fundamentally an individual's judgment with the assumption that everyone else would agree with it.

The reason content analysts rely on face validity perhaps more than do researchers who use other methods of inquiry is that content analysis is fundamentally concerned with readings of texts, with what symbols mean, and with how images are seen, all of which are largely rooted in common sense, in the shared culture in which such interpretations are made, which is difficult to measure but often highly reliable at a particular time. This is not to say that the reliance on face validity is absent in other research endeavors. In fact, even the most rigorous researchers would not use methods or publish findings that violate their common sense. Face validity is the gatekeeper for all other kinds of validity. It is difficult to explain how face validity works, yet it is omnipresent.

Social validity is that quality of research findings that leads us to accept them on account of their contribution to the public discussion of important social concerns, such as violence on television, antisocial messages in rap music, racism in sermons, hate talk on radio talk shows, and lack of civility in political campaign advertisements. Research examining such public issues is socially validated by proponents and antagonists who worry about these issues and are eager to translate research findings into actions. In Riffe et al.'s (1998) terms, social validity is "the degree to which the content analysis categories created by the researchers have relevance and meaning beyond an academic audience" (p. 137). Unlike face validity, the social validity of content analysis studies is often debated, negotiated, and a matter of public concern. A content analysis that is socially valid can attract public attention, propose practical solutions, and generate funding. Publicly acknowledged authorities on the subject of research are key to the social validity of the findings. Arguing from the privileged position of scientists, content analysts may well inadvertently become such authorities, especially when they explain their findings in seemingly irrefutable quantitative terms at congressional hearings, for example, or to advocacy groups working in support of particular public agendas. The line between accepting research because of the reputation of the researcher and accepting it because of the evidence it brought forth is often blurred. Even empirically oriented test psychologists have started to take social issues increasingly seriously. A significant part of the latest edition of the *Standards for Educational and Psychological Testing* established by the American Educational Research Association, the American Psychological Association, and the National Council on Measurement in Education (1999) is concerned with fairness, with the responsibilities of the researcher for the test taker, and with testing and public policy. In these standards, social validity concerns appear as concerns about the possible social or psychological consequences of testing. Although most researchers enjoy this kind of validity, it is distinct from empirical validity, which is the focus of the remainder of this chapter.

Empirical validity is the degree to which available evidence and established theory support various stages of a research process, the degree to which specific inferences withstand the challenges of additional data, of the findings of other research efforts, of evidence encountered in the domain of the researcher's research question, or of criticism based on observations, experiments, or measurements as opposed to logic or process. Campbell (1957) calls the latter "internal validity." Empirical validity cannot deny intuition (face validity), nor can it divorce itself entirely from social, political, and cultural factors (social validity)—after all, scientific research is reviewed by the researchers' peers, who may have their own theoretical agendas and are hardly immune to social and political concerns. However, in the following I separate empirical validity from the face and social validities and consider it to be established largely within the scientific community and to be based on rational arguments that bring empirical evidence to bear on the research results, the research process, and the conditions under which data were acquired.

In discussing empirical validity, several content analysis textbooks follow the American Psychological Association's *Technical Recommendations for Psychological Tests and Diagnostic Techniques* (1954), a landmark publication that defined the kinds of validity concerns that psychologists face when they are developing tests of individual characteristics or abilities. In addition to face validity, the chief types of validities distinguished in the 1954 *Recommendations* were content validity, construct validity, criterion-related validity, and predictive validity. These *Recommendations* focused narrowly on evidence, and so did not mention social validity, which concerns questions regarding the larger context of psychological testing.

Content validity is the extent to which a psychological test captures all the features that define the concept that the test claims to measure. For example, measurement of an applicant's aptitude for a job would require a complete inventory of job requirements, not just IQ tests or motivational measures.

Construct validity acknowledges that many concepts in the social sciences—such as self-esteem, alienation, and ethnic prejudice—are abstract and cannot be observed directly. To validate a measure of self-esteem, for example, one would first have to spell out the observable behaviors and verbal responses that the self-esteem concept entails, then measure and correlate these with the proposed measure, and finally examine whether or not each correlation supports what a theory of self-esteem predicts.

Criterion-related validity, sometimes called *instrumental validity*, is the degree to which a measure correlates with or estimates something external to it; for example, IQ may be shown to correlate with grade point average. Customarily, criterion-related validity is divided into two kinds, concurrent and predictive.

Concurrent validity is demonstrated by correlations that concur with the test in question, and *predictive validity* concerns variables that estimate features that may become available sometime in the future.

These classical distinctions have undergone various transformations. The above-mentioned *Recommendations* gave way to the first version of the *Standards for Educational and Psychological Testing* in 1985, and these were followed by the 1999 *Standards,* which no longer support distinctions between validity types, referring instead to types of "validity evidence" (see American Educational Research Association et al., 1999, p. 11). They also recognize that theoretical constructs underlie all measurements, and this recognition led to a classification of validating evidence based on *test content, response process, internal structure, relations to other variables,* and, as mentioned above, the *consequences of testing* (pp. 11–17). The debate about these conceptions of validity is ongoing, but it is important to recognize that the above focuses narrowly on only one theory of scientific inquiry, measurement theory, and is informed mainly by one disciplinary orientation, the psychological testing of individuals. Measurements are only part of what content analyses can provide, and inferences about psychological characteristics of individuals or populations of individuals are rare in content analysis, although not excluded.

To understand the conceptions of validity that are useful in the conduct of content analysis, one must keep in mind that all empirical validation efforts enlist evidence and established theories to ensure that research results are taken seriously. When the goal is merely the construction of theory, a research project may matter only to a small scientific community. But when research is intended to have policy implications—when findings are to aid business decisions, provide evidence in court, categorize people, or affect the lives of individual human beings in other ways—wrong conclusions may have costly consequences. Validation reduces the risk of making decisions based on misleading research findings. Content analysts and psychologists concerned with testing have to cope with different risks.

Content analysts face at least three kinds of obstacles when they try to apply traditional methods of validation: substantive, conceptual, and methodological. We return to our conceptual framework of content analysis (as depicted in Figure 2.1) to understand all three.

Substantively, probably most important to content analysts is the acknowledgment that texts are used because of their meanings to people other than the analysts, starting with producing, reading, and interpreting text and proceeding to constructing, maintaining, or undoing social realities. The object of content analysis is far more complicated than analyzing how individuals respond to test questions with preformulated answers. Highlighting some of these differences, Potter and Levine-Donnerstein (1999) have introduced useful distinctions among three kinds of content analyses, liberally rephrased as content analyses that aim to describe manifest content, content analyses that provide inferences about latent patterns, and content analyses that provide interpretations (or "make projections," as they say; p. 261). The first kind conforms to a measurement conception of content analysis and is unproblematic as far as the application of the above kinds of validity is concerned, although it conflicts with the conclusions from Chapter 2. The second refers to a context—of experts, as Potter and Levine-Donnerstein suggest, and established theory in relation to which validity needs to be established. Figure 2.1 depicts just this, the scientific community or any chosen stakeholder group providing this context. The third kind of content analysis these scholars describe allows more freedom of imagination on the part of content analysts but is constrained by cognitive schemata and inferential rules that are embodied in a designated population of text users whose conceptions are both the focus of analysis and the source of validity. This ethnographic and interpretivist-sounding conception does not differ from that outlined in Chapter 2 as a definition of content analysis of the second kind, except for the authors' allowing research results to be more freewheeling. In this kind of content analysis, Potter and Levine-Donnerstein affirm, validity standards cannot be divorced from chosen contexts, but they limit analysis to the conceptions of individuals for whom the analyzed texts have the meanings they have. Sensitivity to a context distinguishes content analysis from other methods of inquiry and provides the criteria for acceptance of its results.

The *conceptual obstacle* to the validation of content analyses derives from an inadequate definition of *content as inherent in text* (see Chapter 2) and the attendant commitment merely to describe *it*. To be sure, all descriptions are abstract and as such arbitrary, and conceiving content as inherent to texts has enabled content analysts to apply any category schemes they please, provided the schemes are reliable. Content analysts with such a conception of content in mind confuse their descriptions of content with how others may read or use the same texts, seemingly needing no further validation. For example, suppose a content analysis of mass-media entertainment concludes that there has been a shift in the United States from material to spiritual values. There is no way to validate this finding unless the analysts are willing to take responsibility for their definitions and make clear where this claimed shift should be observable as well (other than in the analyzed media), in whose lives this shift is expected to make a difference, or which variables are expected to correlate with this abstraction in order for it to be considered as describing something real. As mentioned in Chapter 2, one reason for the popularity of the conceptions of content as inherent to text and of content analysis as merely descriptive of this content is the virtual impossibility of empirically (in)validating such findings. In the absence of specificity about what could validate or invalidate the findings of a content analysis, appeals to face and social validity, which researchers can more easily control through their own rhetoric, public testimony, and publication, seem to be the only recourse.

The *methodological obstacle* to validation is more difficult to overcome. Consider the following trilemma: (a) If content analysts happen to have no independent evidence about what they are inferring, then validity or invalidity cannot be established, at least not until pertinent data show up. Content analysis shares this epistemological constraint with all predictive efforts. (b) If these analysts had evidence about the context of their texts—that is, about phenomena related to the analyzed texts—but used it in the development of their analytical constructs, then this evidence would no longer be independent of the research results and hence cannot be used to validate the findings. And finally, (c) if these analysts had concurrent evidence that could validate their inferences but kept it away from their analysis, there would be no point in their conducting the content analysis. It would at best add one incident to vindicate the analysis. Content analysts can resolve this trilemma, at least in part, by relying on various forms of imperfect and indirect validating evidence about the phenomena of interest. I address how this could happen in the following section.

13.2 A TYPOLOGY FOR VALIDATING EVIDENCE

A fundamental difference between psychological testing and content analysis is that the latter is concerned with bodies of text that are meaningful in relation to a chosen context (see Chapter 2), whereas the former does not acknowledge that relationship and the inferential step it entails. It follows that content analysts must empirically demonstrate the context sensitivity of their research. In addition, it is important to bear in mind that content analysis data, texts, and findings, although unquestionably mediated by human individuals as language-using beings, readers/writers, conceptualizers, and actors, are not necessarily about individuals. This means that psychological measurement theoretical conceptions of validity have to be expanded by model theoretical conceptions, as graphically outlined in Figure 9.1. This epistemological shift calls for validating evidence that differs, albeit in only some categories, from the evidence defined by the above-mentioned *Standards*, whose conceptions content analysis can adopt only in parts. To start, three kinds of validating evidence may enter a content analysis:

- Evidence that justifies the treatment of text, what it is, what it means, and how it represents what (This is loosely related to what the *Standards* refer to as "evidence based on test content"; American Educational Research Association et al., 1999, p. 11.)

- Evidence that justifies the abductive inferences that a content analysis is making (Here, analysts are concerned with the validity of the analytical constructs on which they rely. This is loosely related to what the *Standards* call "evidence based on [the] internal structure" of a test; p. 13.)

- Evidence that justifies the results, whether a content analysis contributes answers to the research questions of other researchers or is borne out in fact (This is loosely related to the older "criterion-related validity," which the *Standards* discuss in terms of "evidence based on relations to other variables.")

These and the following distinctions are depicted in Figure 13.1.

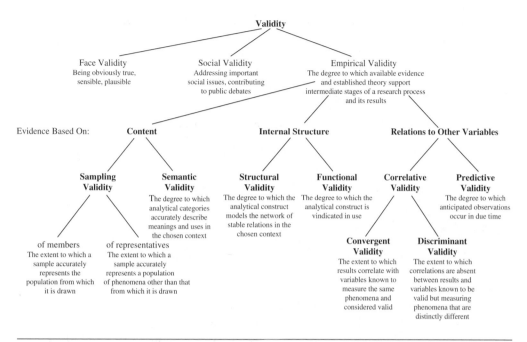

Figure 13.1   A Typology of Validation Efforts in Content Analysis

Evidence that justifies the treatment of texts concerns largely the sampling and recording phases of a content analysis. Such evidence may be divided into two kinds:

■ Evidence on *sampling validity* concerns the degree to which a sample of texts accurately represents the population of phenomena in whose place it is analyzed. Ideally, content analysts actively sample a population, using sampling plans that ensure representativeness. But in many practical situations, texts become available by their sources' choice and contain intentional biases in representing the phenomena of their interest. Content analysts may not be able to control such biases but want to know whether and how much such samples can be trusted.

■ Evidence on *semantic validity* ascertains the extent to which the categories of an analysis of texts correspond to the meanings these texts have within the chosen context. The anthropological preference for emic or indigenous rather than etic or imposed categories of analysis and ethnographers' efforts to verify their interpretations with their informers demonstrate concern for semantic validity, here with reference to the lives of populations of interviewees. In content analysis, other contexts are considered as well, but contexts they must be. Other kinds of research efforts (psychological testing for one, but also survey research) tend to avoid semantic validity by controlling the range of permissible answers to questions and not really exploring what these questions could mean to their subjects. Semantic validity is allied largely with content analysis.

Evidence that justifies the abductive inferences of a content analysis sheds light on how well the analytical construct in use actually does model what it claims to model. Again, two kinds of such evidence may be distinguished:

- Evidence on *structural validity* demonstrates the structural correspondence between available data or established theory and the modeled relationships or the rules of inference that a content analysis is using.

- Evidence on *functional validity* demonstrates a functional correspondence between what a content analysis does and what successful analyses have done, including how the chosen context is known to behave. If these behaviors covary repeatedly and over a variety of situations, one can suspect that they share an underlying construct.

This distinction between structural validity and functional validity is motivated by Feigl's (1952) distinction between

> two types of justification . . . validation and vindication. In this context, *validation* is a mode of justification according to which the acceptability of a particular analytical procedure is established by showing it to be derivable from general principles, . . . theories (or data) that are accepted quite independently of the procedure to be justified. On the other hand, *vindication* may render an analytical method acceptable on the grounds that it leads to accurate predictions (to a degree better than chance) regardless of the details of that method. The rules of induction and deduction are essential to (construct) validation while the relation between means and particular ends provide the basis for (construct) vindication. (Krippendorff, 1969b, p. 12)

In the 1980 edition of *Content Analysis,* I called these two kinds of validity *construct validation* and *construct vindication* (Krippendorff, 1980b). However, because construct validity has a slightly different definition in the psychological test literature, my use of this label caused some confusion, hence the current change in terms. Incidentally, Selltiz, Jahoda, Deutsch, and Cook (1964) call vindication *pragmatic validity,* as "the researcher then does not need to know *why* the test performance is an efficient indication of the characteristics in which he is interested" (p. 157).

Finally, one could be concerned with the validity of the results of a content analysis, criterion-based validity or instrumental validity, and consider two ways of supporting the results:

- Evidence on *correlative validity* ascertains the degree to which the findings obtained by one method correlate with findings obtained by other variables that are considered more valid than the method in question. To be correlated, all variables must be presently and simultaneously available. The result, therefore, is also called *concurrent validity.* Correlative validity requires a demonstration of both *convergent validity,* or high correlation with measures of the contextual characteristics it claims to indicate, and *discriminant validity,* or low correlation with measures of contextual characteristics it intends to exclude.

■ Evidence for *predictive validity* establishes the degree to which the answers of a content analysis accurately anticipate events, identify properties, or describe states of affairs, knowledge of which is absent or did not enter that analysis. Analogous to selecting among the possible answers to a research question, predictions spell out what can be anticipated and what is ruled out. Predictions may concern phenomena that precede, are concurrent to, or follow the texts used in making them.

Sampling Validity   13.2.1

Sampling validity becomes an issue whenever a sample of texts differs from the population of phenomena of interest, not just in size, which often is convenient, but also in composition, which can bias the content analysis of the sampled texts. As already stated, sampling validity is the degree to which a population is accurately represented in the sample. To begin with, two situations need to be distinguished:

(1) The sample consists of a *subset* of members of the population of interest.

(2) The sample consists of *representations* of phenomena that lie outside the sample and the population from which the sample is drawn.

Evidence in the first situation—drawing a sample from the very population of interest—is well understood by means of *statistical sampling theory,* as discussed in Chapter 6. Whether one is interested in a sample's medial, proportional, variational, or distributional accuracy, statistical theory provides measures of the sampling error. This error is a measure of a sample's *in*validity. For purposes of this discussion:

$$\text{Sampling Validity (1)} = 1 - \text{sampling error} = 1 - \frac{\sigma}{\sqrt{N}} \sqrt{\frac{n-N}{n-1}},$$

where σ is the standard deviation of the population, which is a measure of its diversity of categories; n is the size of the population; and N is the size of the sample.

In traditional sampling theory, sampling errors are a function of three factors. First and most important is the sample size, N. The larger the sample, the smaller the sampling error and the larger the sampling validity (1). Second is the diversity of categories within the population, represented by the standard deviation σ. Given two samples of equal size, the sample drawn from a more diverse population has larger sampling errors and is less likely to be valid than a sample drawn from a less diverse population. Third is the proportion of the population sampled. As samples become more inclusive, $(n - N) \to 0$, the sampling error shrinks and sampling validity (1) grows.

Evidence in the second situation—drawing samples of representations in view of what they represent—is not easy to obtain, yet it is a frequent concern for content analysts. To be clear, as I noted in Chapter 2, content analysts do not study texts, images, or distributional characteristics for their own sake or to generalize to other texts, images, or distributional characteristics; rather, they use texts as a means to get to what the texts' users have in mind, what the texts are about, what they mean or do and to whom. There rarely exists a one-to-one correspondence between meanings, references, uses, or contents and units of texts. Sampling theory offers no simple test to establish whether a sample of textual units fairly represents the phenomena that a content analyst intends to access through these texts. Additionally, the texts that reach the content analyst usually are *presampled* by others—by organizations following institutionalized rules; by individuals with particular intentions, who highlight some kinds of information and downplay others; or by media of communication that have their own built-in technological or economical filters. Communication researchers have long studied how reality is constructed, represented, and misrepresented in the mass media, but they have rarely used these findings in validation efforts. Concepts such as gatekeeping in news flows, ideological/racial/gender biases in writing, the positive spin that affected parties put on politically embarrassing stories, and the attention paid by institutions of journalism to particular stories (i.e., to whom journalistic institutions grant a voice and, by implication, what or whom they ignore) are well established and often quantified.

If the phenomena of interest need to be accurately represented in the texts that researchers are analyzing, then sampling must undo the biases that result from the selective ways texts are made available. Validating evidence for sampling validity (2) can be of two kinds:

- Knowledge of the population of phenomena with which one of its samples is to be compared

- Knowledge of the self-sampling practices of the source of the available texts

To measure the degree to which a population of phenomena is fairly represented in a sample of textual units, a simple percentage measure that derives from the well-known coefficient of contingency C is useful. In its incarnation as a validity measure, $1 - C^2$, it concerns proportions only and has two versions that correspond to the above two kinds of validating evidence:

$$\text{Sampling Validity (2)} = 1 - C^2 = \cfrac{1}{1 + \sum_i \cfrac{(P_i - p_i)^2}{p_i}} = \cfrac{1}{1 + \sum_i P_i \cfrac{b_i^2}{1 - b_i}}$$

where P_i is the proportion that is observed to represent phenomena of category i in the sample and p_i is the proportion representing phenomena of category i in the population from which the sample is drawn. When known or ascertainable, the proportions p_i serve as validating evidence in the first version of the formula for sampling validity (2). When the biases b_i of representing categories i are known, algebraically equivalent to $(1 - p_i/P_i)$, b_i serves as validating evidence in the second version of the formula for sampling validity (2). Studies of biases, assessing or estimating b_i, are more common, easier to conduct, and designed differently than those assessing the proportions p_i, hence the two versions.

The first version of the above-stated sampling validity (2) is a function of the observed proportion P_i in the sample and the proportion p_i in the population, which is the validating evidence and must be obtained independent of the sample. When $P_i = p_i$ for all categories i, sampling validity is unity. It declines with increasing differences between the two proportions.

The second version of sampling validity (2) is a function of the observed proportion P_i in the sample and the self-sampling bias b_i $(= 1 - p_i/P_i)$, which is the extent to which the source of the sampled text over- or underrepresents categories i. Here, the bias b_i serves as validating evidence, which must be obtained independent of the sample as well. If this bias $b_i = 0$ for all categories i, then sampling can proceed as usual. If this bias deviates from zero in either direction, then sampling validity (2) is reduced. If the source biases b_i are known, one can approximate a valid sample either by using the technique of varying probability sampling (Chapter 6, section 6.2.4), which compensates for the known biases, or by transforming the proportions P_i in a biased sample by $P_i' = (1 - b_i)P_i$, which corrects for the biases in representing the phenomena in question.

Semantic Validity 13.2.2

Semantic validity is the degree to which the analytical categories of texts correspond to the meanings these texts have for particular readers or the roles they play within a chosen context. Virtually all content analyses respond to texts according to their meanings: denotations, connotations, insinuations, implications, associations, metaphors, frames, uses, symbolic qualities, and so on. Users of the texts could serve as sources of validating evidence for the categories that a content analysis employs. In older definitions of content analysis, accurate descriptions of these meanings were the only aim mentioned, whether they referred to classifications of sign-vehicles (Janis, 1943/1965), descriptions of the "manifest content of communication" (Berelson, 1952, p. 16; Berelson & Lazarsfeld, 1948, p. 6), coding (Cartwright, 1953, p. 424), or "putting a variety of word patterns into [the categories] of a classification scheme" (Miller, 1951, p. 96). Although it is widely recognized that accurate descriptions of these meanings are the key to the success of content analyses, despite their ultimately inferential aims, what counts as accurate and particularly whose meanings are taken to be valid depend on the chosen context of an analysis.

In Chapter 2, I noted that even analysts involved in purely descriptive efforts must acknowledge a context that they or others could consult to validate those efforts. If content analysts claimed to describe meanings without reference to any context of specific uses and users—authors, readers, newspaper editors, professional experts, professionals with specialized perspectives, social institutions, standard thesauri or dictionaries, even analysts' own discourse communities— there would be no way to know what could validate or invalidate these descriptions, and analysts would be left to appeal to face validity or to play on their scientific (social or political) authority. Although semantic validity is an issue that most content analysts take seriously, it is rarely formally tested.

It is easy for researchers to take an objectivist stance and consider meanings as universal and as defined in general dictionaries, or to take an ethnographic stance and delegate decisions on meanings to the authors of given texts. However, both of these extremes deny the fact that all descriptions simplify or abstract, usually in the interest of the describer's questions. Categories are always more general than the objects they categorize. In fact, content analysts rarely take the unique meanings of the analyzed texts as the basis for their inferences; instead, they operate on a level of abstraction above that of ordinary talk. Concepts such as speech acts, monologue, self-esteem, ethnic prejudices, sexual harassment, and libel, as well as such distinctions as between pro- and antisocial behavior, are all fairly abstract and not necessarily shared with the sources of texts being analyzed. Distinctions among the functions of political campaign discourse in terms of acclaiming, attacking, and defending (Benoit, Blaney, & Pier, 1998) are analytically useful but may not help political candidates to organize their campaigns. It is the use of abstract categories that makes semantic validation the content analytic analogue to content validation of psychological tests. For example, the content validity of a test designed to determine the aptitude of a job candidate for a particular kind of employment is the extent to which the test includes all demands of that job, not just a few outstanding qualifications. Analogously, the semantic validity of the categories "acclaiming," "attacking," and "defending" should be the extent to which these categories embrace all functions of political campaign discourse and clearly distinguish among the three categories.

The preparations for an analysis of values in political documents may serve as an example of an iterative use of semantic validity criteria. In this study, we started with a collection of what a panel of political scientists could easily identify as "value-laden statements" of the kinds we would find in the documents to be examined for the values their authors expressed. To reproduce these experts' distinctions, we formulated explicit recording instructions. The coders varied greatly in their ability to make the same distinctions, and a computer program we had hoped to employ turned out to be virtually useless. The whole history of this effort is too long to relate, but we began by developing a list of political values the documents contained—democracy, freedom, progress, and the like—and allowed others to be added. This turned out to be far from satisfactory. A large number of value-laden statements contained none of the values on our list. We then looked into various modes of reasoning that led us to implicit goals, preferences for processes, criteria for decision making, and so on, added them to our emerging instructions, and reapplied them to our collection. Slowly, we narrowed the gap between the distinctions that our instructions suggested between value-laden and value-neutral statements and those that our panel of experts made (Krippendorff, 1970c). One might question our use of experts as providing the evidence for our semantic validation efforts. We could have used another population for reference, but because we were working under typical time constraints and our analysis was to make a contribution to the political science literature, the theoretical motivations seemed to justify the choice of this context, and we were satisfied that the instrument reasonably approximated the consensus reached by those we trusted to know what they were talking about.

Semantic validity arguments come in numerous guises. To validate the dictionary entries of the General Inquirer, a computer program for tagging texts and then analyzing the tags, Dunphy used a KWIC (keyword in context) list to explore the various meanings of tagged words. For example, the keyword *play* (see Figure 12.1) showed numerous senses that were not initially anticipated and that would have been confused by computer programs that tagged only single words (Dunphy, 1966, p. 159). To address such semantic problems, Stone, Dunphy, Smith, and Ogilvie (1966) developed so-called disambiguation procedures that looked into the linguistic environments of homonyms for clues to how their meanings could be identified more correctly. These rules improved the Inquirer's ability to distinguish between textual units according to how they would be read by ordinary English readers. In effect, these researchers' efforts were aimed at improving the semantic validity of the computer tagging of text.

Consider the distinction between *self* and *other* references made by a dictionary approach to computer text analysis (see Chapter 12, section 12.5.1). Suppose the words *self, I, my, myself, me, mine, we, our, ourselves,* and *us* are tagged *self,* and the words *other, you, your, yourself, he, his, him, himself, she, hers, her, herself, them,* and *themselves* are tagged *other.* Suppose sentences are the units of analysis. These two tags would identify two subsets of sentences within the set of all sentences in the sample. One could obtain evidence for the semantic validity of these dictionary entries by asking competent readers, working independently, to classify the sampled sentences into those that speak about the "self" of the authors and those that speak about what these authors consider "others." Figure 13.2 depicts two sets of tagged sentences surrounded by dashed lines and the sets that would serve as validating evidence within solid lines. The degree to which these two kinds of sets overlap is a qualitative indication of the semantic validity of the two tags that this dictionary is using. In computer-generated categorizations of text, the semantic validity is rarely as good as the figure suggests, but we are interested here only in what is meant by semantic validity: the complete overlap between a classification of uncertain validity with one we have reasons to trust.

A more traditional way for scholars to challenge the semantic validity of a content analysis is by creating counterexamples. This strategy is well established in linguistics, where as soon as one linguist makes a claim that a proposed grammar accounts for all grammatically correct sentences, another comes up with

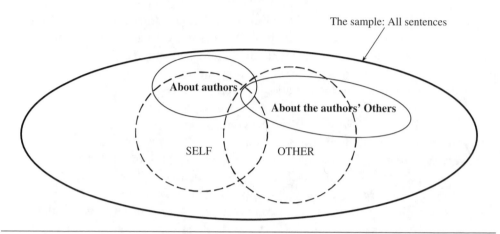

Figure 13.2   A Qualitative Illustration of the Semantic Validity of Two Categories

examples of sentences that this grammar will misidentify. Closer to content analysis, in the critique of his own contingency analysis, Osgood (1959, pp. 73–77) employs this strategy to discount exaggerated claims of what his analysis does. According to Osgood's contingency analysis, the following statement would be counted as an incident of association between *love* and *mother*:

1.   I love my mother.

But so would these statements:

2.   I loved my mother more than anyone else.

3.   Mother loved me.

4.   I don't love my mother.

5.   Have I always loved my mother?—Hell no!

6.   My beloved father hated mother.

Because *love* and *mother* co-occur in all six statements, contingency analysis would group them into the same equivalence class of *love-mother* co-occurrences. However, relative to statement 1, statement 2 shows contingency analysis to be insensitive to verbal qualifications of an expressed association—"more than anyone else" is not a frequency. Statement 3 shows this analysis to be unable to distinguish between active and passive constructions—that is, the target of love. Statement 4 shows it to be insensitive to negation, statement 5 shows it to be insensitive to irony, and statement 6 shows it to be insensitive to grammatical constructions. Osgood did not use these observations to argue against his method, of course; rather, he used them to clarify what it registers: statistical, not logical, associations among pairs of concepts, presumably in someone's mind. Here, even denying a relationship between two concepts would be considered evidence that they have something to do with each other.

A content analysis in a legal context may serve as a final example. In a libel case recorded at a Texas court as *Wood, et al. v. Andrews, et al.* (Dallas County, Cause No. 94–8888-C, 1997), the plaintiffs, 20 psychiatrists who worked for a mental health institution, hired a content analyst to establish objectively the libelous and defamatory nature of publicity they had received in the press. That publicity was attributed largely to one of the defendants, a lawyer who represented a number of former patients of the hospital where the plaintiffs worked (one of whom was a codefendant) who were suing that institution for patient abuse, malpractice, illegal profiteering, and insurance fraud. This content analyst retrieved all 52 newspaper articles published between 1993 and 1996 that contained references to that mental institution; 36 of these articles mentioned the lawyer defendant and 16 did not. She examined the 36 articles that mentioned the defendant and used for comparison the articles that did not. She then unitized all of the articles into 970 assertions, assigning each to one of 16 categories that emerged from her reading of the articles, focusing on kinds of bad publicity. She then drew her conclusions from a statistic of these categorizations.

In response, the defendant hired an expert to examine the content analyst's research and findings. The expert raised the issue of the semantic validity of the categories the analyst had used to make her point. Although she had conducted her analysis carefully, with categories traceable to the original assertions or their rephrases, her conclusions were irrelevant because her categories ignored the context that mattered in the case: the terms of the law, the legal definition of libel. Texas law defines libel in fairly specific terms. To be considered libelous, an assertion has to meet the following criteria:

i. Made with the intent to harm a person publicly or financially or in disregard of injurious consequences to another person

ii. Knowingly untrue

iii. Read and understood as stating facts

iv. Causing its readers to alter their speaking in ways that blacken a person's public image, impeaches that person's honesty, integrity, virtue, or reputation, and

v. Actually incurring financial injury to that person or expose that person to debilitating hatred, contempt, and ridicule.

In other words, assertions in the category of libel have to be (i) made with the intent to harm, (ii) known to be untrue, and (iii) read as stating facts. Evidence on criteria iv and v would presumably require observations or testimony. The content analyst's categories traced bad publicity about the plaintiffs to the defendant but failed to provide answers in the legally required categories. For example, accusations of insurance fraud, if true, are not libelous, regardless of how often they are mentioned. And assertions critical of the plaintiffs may not have been made with the intent to harm. In this context, a semantically valid content analysis would have to let the articles answer the questions in categories to which applicable law could apply—not how an average reader might interpret the newspaper articles. One could conclude that this analyst's categories had no semantic validity in the prescribed context.

Semantic validity acknowledges that recording units, when placed in one category, may differ in all kinds of ways, but not regarding the meanings that are relevant to the analysis, and units that turn up in different categories must differ in relevant meanings. The emphasis on relevant meanings is important, as text interpretations can be endless, whereas content analysts are concerned only with specific research questions. In the above examples, deviations from this ideal signaled that the procedures of an analysis needed to be altered, that the categories needed to be redefined, or that the findings should be discounted.

I will now state a simple measure of the semantic validity of categorizations and then show how it can also be applied in evaluations of the semantic validity of text searches. To begin, it is important to recognize that assigning the units of a sample to any one of several mutually exclusive categories amounts to partitioning that sample into mutually exclusive sets of units. The semantic validity of one method is established through the comparison of its partition with the partition obtained by another method that serves as validating evidence. Ideally, these partitions are identical, but in practice they rarely are. A minimal measure of the semantic validity of categorizations can be defined in these terms: Let

j denote one of a set of categories of analysis, 1, 2, 3, . . . ;

n be the size of the sample of textual units being categorized in two ways;

$A_1, A_2, A_3, \ldots A_j, \ldots$ be mutually exclusive sets of units distinguished by the method in question;

$E_1, E_2, E_3, \ldots E_j, \ldots$ be the validating evidence, the mutually exclusive sets of units distinguished by another method that is considered valid;

$\cap$ be the intersection of two sets, denoting the units common to both (AND in Boolean terms); and

be an operator that enumerates (provides a count of) the members of a set.

In these terms, when the two partitions are identical, all A_j and E_j contain the same units, $A_j = E_j = A_j \cap E_j$ for all categories j, then the measure should become unity, indicating that semantic validity is perfect. Deviations from this ideal should produce values less than unity. A measure that satisfies these requirements is

$$\text{Semantic Validity} = \Sigma\#(Aj{\cap}Ej)/n.$$

One can apply more sophisticated statistics, Cohen's (1960), for example, or a coefficient that would extend the measure to different metrics or allow overlapping sets, as in Figure 13.2. However, we are interested here only in the simplest approach to semantic validity.

Regarding the evaluation of the semantic validity of text searches, recall from Chapter 12 that searching a textual database for relevant units of text starts with the formulation of a suitable query. Formulating such a query involves considerable linguistic insight, largely because the population of texts within which a query searches for matching character strings is different from the population of meanings that are represented in the searched texts. A semantically valid query will identify all and only those units of text, or documents, that are relevant. A query may fail to identify documents that are relevant to a research question or may fail to exclude documents that are irrelevant to that question. Relevance, it should be kept in mind, is an attribution made by content analysts based on their understanding of the purpose of a research project. Search results, in contrast, stem from the matching of character strings with a given query.

In the technical literature on information retrieval, which concerns largely whether particular queries fail to retrieve documents that do contain the desired character strings or retrieve documents without matches, scholars have reported on the use of two measures for assessing the quality of search engines: precision and recall. *Precision* is the degree to which a search engine lists documents that match a query. *Recall* is the degree to which a search engine returns all the matching documents of a collection (Rijsbergen, 1979).

Technical failures can affect the semantic validity of text searches, but here we are concerned with comparing the results of an electronic text search (retrieved or not retrieved units of text) with the validating evidence obtained by human judgment (relevant or irrelevant units of text). In effect, these define two bipartitions of the textual universe, which can be represented numerically in the form of a fourfold table of frequencies:

Units of Text	Relevant	Irrelevant	
Retrieved	a Correct inclulsions	b Commissions	$a + b$
Not Retrieved	c Omissions	d Correct exclusions	$c + d$
	$a + c$	$b + d$	n

In this table, n is the size of the textual universe searched. Applying the above-stated semantic validity measure to this far simpler situation yields

$$\text{Semantic Validity} = (a + d)/n.$$

Two errors distract from the semantic validity of text searches. The first is the Error of Commission $= b/(a + b)$ [or 1–Precision], which is the proportion of the number b of irrelevant units of text that were mistakenly retrieved to the total number $(a + b)$ of retrieved units. In a search of articles containing self-references in the press, Bermejo (1997) found this error to be 16%, which is remarkably good. The other error is the

$$\text{Error of Omission} = c/(a + c) \text{ [or } 1\text{–Recall]},$$

which is the proportion of the number c of relevant units that the search failed to identify to the total number $(a + c)$ of relevant units in a textual universe. In a pilot study that involved retrieving articles on domestic violence from three newspapers, Wray and Hornik (1998) found errors of commission of 10%, 19%, and 29% and errors of omission of 12%, 20%, and 25%, although they cast their finding in terms of precision and recall. How the two measures reduce the semantic validity of text searches can be seen in this equation:

$$\text{Semantic Validity} = 1\text{–}(a + b)/n \text{ Error of Commission}$$
$$-(a + c)/n \text{ Error of Omission.}$$

In typical text searches, these two errors are rarely of equal significance, however. When a search result contains the answer to a question directly—that is, without further analysis—both errors weigh equally and the single measure of semantic validity is appropriate. But when a search aims at identifying documents for further examination, errors of commission merely create more work for coders, who usually do not have any problem eliminating irrelevant documents after reading, whereas errors of omission deprive content analysts of relevant data that could lead to different conclusions—hence the need to account for these errors separately.

An epistemological problem in assessing the semantic validity of text searches is that cells c and d are typically unknown. In fact, one cannot measure errors of omission unless one finds a way to examine or at least to estimate the number of unretrieved documents and the proportion of correct exclusions. For limited textual databases, the size n of the available textual universe may well be known, at least by approximation. Unfortunately, the size n of very large databases may be too large to yield meaningful calculations. However, such limitations do not apply to the more common semantic validations of content analysis categories for which samples tend to be finite and manageable in size.

13.2.3 Structural Validity

Structural validity is at issue when content analysts argue over whether the analytical constructs they have adopted accurately represent the known uses of available texts, the stable meanings, language habits, signifying practices, and behaviors in the chosen context. Thus structural validity assesses the backing (see Chapter 2, section 2.4) of an analyst's abductive inferences primarily from categorized text and secondarily in processes of categorizations, provided the latter involves coders that serve as a backing for inferences or interpretations implicit in the coding/recording process. This evidence may consist of unquestionable incidences of the stable relationships between potentially available texts and the targets of content analysis and valid theories about them. When a content analysis is designed de novo, and thus has no history of successes or failures, structural validation is the only way to lend credibility to its inferences.

The work of historians is most clearly of this kind. Although it is said that history never repeats itself, it may well repeat certain patterns that can be accounted for through generalizations, especially about human/social nature. For historians to rely on such patterns, they must be conceived as relatively permanent within a particular historical context. Dibble (1963), who analyzed arguments by historians in support of and against inferences about the factual nature of events drawn from historical documents, distinguished four kinds of evidence or generalizations for the structural validity of historical accounts. One kind of evidence concerns the roles and practices of the social institutions that create the records to be validated, using their own codes of conduct and preserving certain documents and not others. These are sociological generalizations about what Dibble calls "social bookkeeping" practices. A second kind concerns the characteristics of witnesses who describe what they experienced or report on what they heard. These are psychological generalizations about the working of memory, the influence of interests, and the influence of emotional or ideological involvement with the events in question. A third kind of evidence concerns how the structure of narratives relates to the narrated events. These are linguistic or literary generalizations about how texts are organized and what they mean to readers at that time. Finally, there are physical generalizations of how documents tend to travel, who accesses or reproduces them, how they reach their destinations, how they are filtered or filed, and how they fade or drop out of circulation. Dibble suggests that historians use such generalizations to validate or invalidate their inferences. They exemplify what content analysts do as well, perhaps a bit more systematically.

The inferences that Leites, Bernaut, and Garthoff (1951) made from speeches delivered on the occasion of Stalin's birthday, discussed in Chapter 9, serve as another particularly transparent example of structural validation in an essentially unique situation. Once the researchers' analytical construct was in place, the inferences from available speeches followed. The validity of their construct was established by experienced Sovietologists who argued by references to generalizations about how political discourse functioned in the Soviet Union, especially how politburo members close to Stalin would have to avoid showing interpersonal closeness. With the structural validity of their construct demonstrated, the results of its application were accepted on this ground—and later proved to be correct.

Osgood, Saporta, and Nunnally (1956) fashioned their evaluative assertion analysis according to then-prevailing theories of affective cognition, cognitive dissonance theory in particular, which had been substantiated in numerous controlled experiments with subjects. This was the only validating evidence used in this case, and through it the researchers sought to establish that the computations built into their analytical procedure structurally corresponded to what was known about individual cognition. Evaluative assertion analysis has been extended—for example, by Cuilenburg, Kleinnijenhuis, and De Ridder (1986) and Kleinnijenhuis, De Ridder, and Rietberg (1997)—based on the structural validity provided earlier and only occasionally reexamined.

13.2.4   Functional Validity

Functional validity is the degree to which analytical constructs are vindicated in use rather than in structure. A content analysis is vindicated by reference to its history of use, particularly by its absence of significant failures. *Usefulness* and *success* may mean many things, of course, and these concepts make sense only in the presence of alternative methods competing with each other in the same empirical contexts. To vindicate a content analysis, one must demonstrate that its analytical constructs, which account for the analyst's proceeding from available texts to the answers to given research questions, are useful over time and in many empirical situations. Whereas evidence for structural validity is based on a correspondence between what one knows about a context and how that knowledge is built into the analytical procedure, functional validity is grounded in whether or not or how well it works.

Functional validity has long been recognized, although it has been known by different names. Janis (1943/1965) suggested that because meanings unobservably mediate between texts (or "signs," as he preferred to call them) and observable behaviors, one can establish the validity of semantically oriented content analyses only indirectly, by "inferring validity from [their] productivity" (p. 65). He noted, "A content analysis procedure is productive insofar as the results it yields are found to correlate with other variables" (p. 70). In effect, Janis argued that because there is no validating evidence for how audience members understand given messages, accounting for references, attributions, assertions, and speculating about probable effects are justifiable only when the "categories . . . occur as variables in many true empirical propositions" (p. 65). He essentially bypassed answering the question of how or why an analysis produces the results it does as long as they connect with other phenomena that are considered interesting.

An example might be the use of neuronal network theory in the computation of word co-occurrences by the software system CatPac (Woelfel, 1993, 1997). The designers of this system incorporated several ideas into its operation: that concepts are represented by single words, that the textual proximity of pairs of words and the frequency of their co-occurrences affect the way they are stored/recalled in an author's or reader's brain, that the strength of their pairwise relationships is dynamically adjusted with use, that recent co-occurrences overshadow earlier ones, and so on. These propositions, individually convincing, could be regarded as validating the procedure structurally, and its proponents claim as much when they call CatPac a system that performs a "semantic network" analysis. However, the computations that yield results are so complex, and so little is known about how the human brain develops concepts, that the connection between how people conceptualize and how the computational procedure gets to its results remains obscure.

However, CatPac has been used extensively and applied to a variety of data by researchers interested in mass communication, marketing, politics, bibliographic citations, and many more areas. Improvements have been introduced over time. Occasional lacks of face validity caused the developers to make a variety of adjustments, such as excluding function words and stemming, lemmatizing the vocabulary to reduce grammatical variations considered meaningless in the context of the system's use. CatPac applications naturally migrated into areas that seemed most promising, particularly where the results correlated with other phenomena of interest or aided practical decisions. It found niches in which it proved itself of practical value, useful, and successful. Does CatPac really compute semantic networks? Not the way linguists and researchers in the artificial intelligence community conceptualize them. Does it replicate what neurons do in the brain? Surely not structurally. However, the very fact that it finds users and uses in competition with other computational techniques can be regarded as vindicating evidence, demonstrating its functional validity.

Correlative Validity   13.2.5

It is an epistemological fact (but a fact not always recognized in the literature of psychological testing) that correlations between test results and other variables relate measures of phenomena to each other, not phenomena. Correlations cannot bridge the epistemological gap between measures and the phenomena they claim to measure. Correlations do not predict, either—as I shall demonstrate below. They merely weigh the extent to which one measure can substitute for another. If the measures in a battery of measures are correlated with each other, those that correlate perfectly are substitutable without question, and those that correlate less than perfectly are substitutable to the degree of their correlation. The basic idea of correlational validity is that validity travels along high correlations. Validity always comes from somewhere—one or more trusted variables whose validity is established prior to or outside of efforts to establish correlational validity. If the results of a content analysis of crime reports in newspapers and the results of public opinion polls about perceived crime correlate higher with each other than either of the two variables with official crime statistics, as found by Zucker (1978), then content analysis and public opinion polling might well be substitutable for each other, but neither can replace crime statistics. If none of these variables can be trusted to begin with, validity cannot be an issue. Figure 13.3 depicts the general idea of correlational validity schematically.

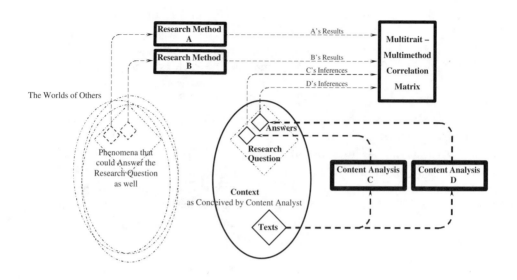

Figure 13.3   Correlative Validation

Campbell and Fiske (1959) develop the idea of validation by correlation statistics into a full-fledged methodology. Taking Popper's idea of falsification to heart, they argue that correlative validity of a new method requires not only high correlation with established measures of the trait it intends to measure but also low or zero correlation with established measures of traits it intends to distinguish. They call the former *convergent validity* and the latter *discriminant validity*. It follows that a research result can fail to be correlatively valid in two ways: by low correlations with measures that are known to measure the phenomena of interest and by high correlations with measures that are known to measure distinctly different phenomena or phenomena independent of the one intended to be measured.

To show that a measure possesses both convergent and discriminant validity, one must compute a battery of correlation coefficients between measures of a number of traits, each obtained by several independent methods. These are tabulated in what Campbell and Fiske call a multitrait-multimethod matrix (see also Alwin, 1974). A detailed discussion of this method is beyond the scope of this chapter, but Table 13.1 provides an example of such a matrix (for more on this method, see Krippendorff, 1980b). It compares three computer implementations of Osgood's main semantic differential scales of affective meaning, evaluative (E), potency (P), and activity (A) (see Chapter 7, section 7.4.4), by three researchers, Holsti (H), Osgood (O), and Saris (S) (see Saris-Gallhofer & Morton, 1978).

In this table, all correlations with themselves are listed on the main diagonal. These are unities, of course, and uninformative as such. Convergent validity would be demonstrated by high correlations, ideally unities, in the diagonals of

Table 13.1   Multitrait-Multimethod Matrix for Three Content Analyses

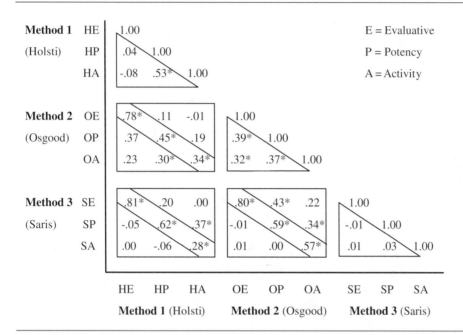

		HE	HP	HA	OE	OP	OA	SE	SP	SA
Method 1	HE	1.00						E = Evaluative		
(Holsti)	HP	.04	1.00					P = Potency		
	HA	-.08	.53*	1.00				A = Activity		
Method 2	OE	.78*	.11	-.01	1.00					
(Osgood)	OP	.37	.45*	.19	.39*	1.00				
	OA	.23	.30*	.34*	.32*	.37*	1.00			
Method 3	SE	.81*	.20	.00	.80*	.43*	.22	1.00		
(Saris)	SP	-.05	.62*	.37*	-.01	.59*	.34*	-.01	1.00	
	SA	.00	-.06	.28*	.01	.00	.57*	.01	.03	1.00

| HE   HP   HA | OE   OP   OA | SE   SP   SA |
| **Method 1** (Holsti) | **Method 2** (Osgood) | **Method 3** (Saris) |

the three heteromethod blocks. In these submatrices, they are all significant, as indicated by asterisks, but they differ regarding the affects being compared. The measures of the evaluative dimension correlate highest with each other, followed by the measures of potency; the measures of the activity dimension are lowest in all three instances. This is consistent with the findings of other research, suggesting that judgments of good and bad—heroes and villains, successes and failures, beauty and ugliness—yield better scales, turn out to account for more variance in semantic differential studies than the other two, and are also more reliable in content analyses generally. Discriminant validity is indicated when the off-diagonal correlations in the heteromethod blocks are lower than the correlations in their diagonals, ideally zero. Here they are lower, but still far from the ideal. In fact, the surprisingly significant correlations between OA and HP, OA and SP, and OP and SE suggest that the three dimensions of affective meanings are not clearly differentiated across these methods. However, the culprit in this lack of discrimination is found in the three monomethod triangles. Within Osgood's method, all three dimensions correlate significantly—that is, it does not discriminate too well among the three kinds of meanings. In Holsti's method, it is the correlation between the activity and potency dimensions that signals a lack of discrimination, whereas in Saris's method, off-diagonal correlations are near the ideal of zero, independent of each other, and show high discriminant validity.

This discussion is not intended to generalize about the three methods. They may differ for a variety of reasons (see Saris-Gallhofer & Morton, 1978). My only aim here is to show how convergent and discriminant validity can play out in correlative validations.

Another example is the validation of an index of argument quality by Cappella, Price, and Nir (2002). These researchers developed their index in the course of a study of online deliberations during the U.S. presidential elections in the year 2000. It counts the number of arguments that participants in this study could give in support of their own positions and, what is perhaps more interesting, the number of arguments that these participants could imagine others would have against their positions. Cappella et al. wisely refrain from claiming to measure opinion quality, as a single dimension would probably fail a semantic validity test. The name they give their measure reflects more closely what it actually measures, "argument repertoire." To test its convergent validity, they show that it correlates highly with numerous variables that could be construed as assessing aspects of a common construct, including political knowledge, political interest, flexibility (subjects' willingness to participate in various discussion groups), and mass-media exposure. They note that

> those with the capacity to write out reasons for their opinions and to identify relevant reasons for opposed opinions also express interest in politics, are more accurate in their factual political knowledge, and use the print and broadcast media as sources of their political news. Even their personal communication is more political and diverse. Coupled with . . . data . . . indicating higher argument repertoire for those with more education and more commitment to their ideology and party, [we] have good evidence of convergent validity. (pp. 83–84).

Cappella et al. do not show discriminant validity, however, and it is therefore not so clear what their measure distinguishes. It may well embrace general communication and social skills as well as intelligence, which would be far beyond the intention to define a measure that adds to the vocabulary of public opinion researchers.

13.2.6   Predictive Validity

Predictions extend available knowledge to as yet unobserved domains. The predicted phenomena may have existed somewhere in the past (e.g., historical events, characteristics of late authors, antecedent conditions of received communications), may be concurrent with the texts being analyzed (e.g., attitudes, psychopathologies, individual aptitudes, the extent to which someone is plagued by problems, the makeup of cultural climates), or may occur in near or distant futures (e.g., the consequences of persuasive messages, the success of future employees, the continuations of trends). I am suggesting two defining criteria for predictive validity. The first emphasizes the nature of evidence as in the *Standards* (American Educational Research Association et al., 1999): For correlational validity, validating evidence must be concurrent, whereas for predictive validity it need not be and in fact typically is not. The second defining criterion requires predictions to be specific, to select a set of observations that is smaller than the set of all conceivable ones—just as any answer to a research question must exclude some of the logically possible answers. Eventually, predictions are validated when the validating evidence stays within the set of predicted observations.

To draw a clear line between correlational and predictive validity, I return to Cappella et al.'s (2002) argument repertoire measure. These researchers found high correlations of argument repertoire not only with variables that belong to the same construct (as noted above), but also with variables that they conceptualized as caused by what argument repertoire measures: participation. They observed two kinds of participation: willingness to attend group deliberations about political topics and willingness to get involved in substantive exchanges while attending (p. 89). Both correlated highly with argument repertoire. Because all data of this study were concurrent and these variables correlated, the validity thereby established is correlational, even if one could argue, and hence conceptualize, that participation is an effect and not a cause.

However, conceptions of causality aside, once researchers state findings so as to be selective among conceivable alternatives and open to the consideration of evidence concerning these alternatives, predictive validation can take place. In fact, when Cappella et al. report that those with greater argument repertoires are more willing to participate in political deliberations, they make rather specific predictions that could be checked against future data. Establishing the validity of their predictions would require agreement with subsequent observations—not correlations, but observations concerning whether and how often people with high argument repertoires do indeed participate in one or both ways.

A classic example of predictive validation is George's (1959a) attempt to evaluate the Federal Communications Commission's predictions made from German domestic propaganda during World War II. All of the FCC analysts' inferences were available in the form of reports they had written. After the war, George was able to match the inferences, one by one, with documents that had then become available. He judged each of the inferences for which validating evidence was available as correct, nearly so, or wrong. He demonstrated that the FCC analysts' predictions were accurate to a degree better than chance. George's research (which was not as simple as this brief description makes it seem) suggests how analysts can bring subsequent evidence to bear on predictions.

To recap: Predictions cannot be validated by correlation. A watch that runs slow correlates highly with standard time but is incorrect nevertheless. Unless one knows the bias of the watch, one cannot tell the correct time with it. The infamous body counts disseminated by the U.S. government through the mass media during the Vietnam War may have correlated highly with military activity, but after a while nobody could trust the exaggerated numbers. To predict the author of an unsigned document, it is not enough to show that signed documents show a correlation between word choices and the identities of authors; the unsigned document must be traced to one author, ideally excluding all others.

Predictions of past, present, or future happenings from texts must also avow exclusions, happenings that are not expected. If a content analysis said yes to all possible answers to a research question, it would be as worthless as if it said no to all of them. The more selective a content analysis is, the more information it provides. Subsequent observations validate predictions when they occur within the set of observations that had been predicted, not outside that set (always or at least to a degree better than chance).

To quantify predictive validity, the measures that are appropriate are the same as those used to assess semantic validity. Both concern valid representations—in the case of semantic validity, of the meanings, referents, or uses of texts; and in the case of predictive validity, of whether the answers to research questions are borne out in fact. The appropriate measure of predictive validity is not correlation but agreement.

Figure 13.4, which is an overlay of Figure 2.1, locates the validation efforts discussed in this chapter within the components of content analysis (as discussed in Chapter 4).

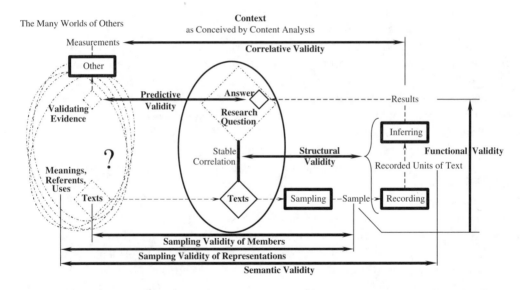

Figure 13.4   Comparisons in Different Kinds of Validity

CHAPTER **14**

A Practical Guide

This final chapter discusses three starting points for content analyses. For each, it recommends procedural steps, raises issues that might come up during the research, notes the junctures at which content analysts need to make decisions, and suggests what they need to take into consideration in making those decisions. It gives an overview of the entire content analysis process, from reconceptualizing the problem that content analysts are called on to solve to reporting their results, providing ample references to related material in the foregoing chapters.

In the preceding chapters, I have introduced the concepts involved in content analysis one by one and have suggested solutions to conceptual and methodological problems that content analysts need to address. In this chapter, I rearticulate these concepts with practice in mind, so that readers who have particular research problems that content analysis might solve will get an idea of what they can or need to do and why.

Like most social research, content analysis involves four kinds of activities:

- Designing an analysis

- Writing a research proposal

- Applying the research design

- Narrating the results

These activities are neither mutually exclusive nor entirely sequential. Surely, all inquiries start with some conceptualization of the research process, but as content analysis requires a great deal of preparatory effort, the design phase may well become part of a research proposal. Researchers who have their own resources, including students working on their theses, may not need to write formal research proposals, but they are nevertheless well-advised to have such proposals in mind. Often, the relationship between the design of a content analysis and the application of that design is circular. A seemingly perfect design may reveal flaws in its application that bring the researcher back to the drawing board to sample more data, reconceptualize the data language, improve the coding instructions, and even radically change the approach taken initially. This is the hermeneutic circle in scientific inquiry.

14.1   DESIGNING AN ANALYSIS

A design proposes something that would not come into being without guided efforts—here, a procedure for moving from potentially available observations, texts, sounds, and images to the narrated answers to a research question (see Figure 4.2). A research design consists of the detailed specifications that guide the handling of data and make the research reproducible and critically examinable at a later point in time. Aside from getting involved in available text, the development of a research design is the most intellectually challenging part of a content analysis. In the course of designing a study, analysts clarify their research interests, learn to respect their own readings as different from those of others, explore the questions they would like to see answered, delve into available literature for insights about the contexts of their analysis, and play with analytical possibilities—until step-by-step specifications emerge that promise to bring the analysis to a worthwhile conclusion (see Chapter 4).

Researchers may enter content analysis from different starting points. The possible starting points may not be equally desirable, but circumstances for research rarely are. Below, I discuss content analyses in terms of three points of entry:

- *Text-driven* content analyses are motivated by the availability of texts rich enough to stimulate the analysts' interests in them. As the research questions emerge, as analysts are becoming involved with such texts, text-driven analyses are also called "fishing expeditions."

- *Problem-driven* content analyses are motivated by epistemic questions about currently inaccessible phenomena, events, or processes that the analysts believe texts are able to answer. Analysts start from research questions and proceed to find analytical paths from the choice of suitable texts to their answers.

- *Method-driven* content analyses are motivated by the analysts' desire to apply known analytical procedures to areas previously explored by other means.

Text-Driven Analyses   14.1.1

A text-driven analysis starts with a body of text, as noted above: an interesting set of personal letters, a collection of taped interviews, the diary of a famous person, a compilation of comic books, transcripts of naturally occurring conversations, conference proceedings (a collection of presented papers), a significant period of publications (newspapers, professional journals, movies), election campaign speeches, news accounts of a particular crime, notes made during anthropological fieldwork, a collection of family photographs, advertisements in magazines published in different countries, reports to the shareholders of a corporation, library listings of a particular institution, articles mentioning a particular drug, telephone books, and so on.

Without an explicit research question in mind, researchers typically start by familiarizing themselves with the chosen body of texts. They may begin with "housekeeping" chores—cataloging the texts, unitizing the body of text into "packages" that can be handled more or less independent of each other. When the researchers have a sense of how many texts there are, they may explore apparent intertextualities: quotes, references, overlaps, rearticulations, elaborations, sequential orderings. They may also note how the texts reproduce, respond to, or elaborate on each other. Intertextualities form dependency networks among texts, which in turn suggest possible paths for reading the given body of texts—for example, along lines of narrative coherences, genres, or temporal sequences, or according to how various sources respond to each other. Constructions of intertextualities amount to ways of reading, but—to be clear—these always are an analyst's readings.

Next comes a reading of texts for the purpose of summarizing what these texts collectively mean to the analyst, what they denote, connote, or suggest, or how they are or could be used as a whole. If the body of texts is so large that a single individual cannot keep track of all the needed details while reading, content analysts may take advantage of a variety of computer aids, such as QSR's NVivo and N6, or examine word frequencies and KWIC lists with software such as Concordance, VBPro, WordStat, or TextQuest. Even the search functions of ordinary word processing programs, such as WordPerfect and Word, may be used for simple content analyses. ATLAS.ti is especially well suited to the creation of networks of texts. The advantage of such analytical aids lies in the assurances they can provide that text explorations are systematic, effectively countering the natural tendency of humans to read and recall selectively. This approach is called *interpretive* or *qualitative,* as opposed to *quantitative* (see Chapter 4, section 4.1.2), and *interactive-hermeneutic* with reference to computer aids (see Chapter 12, section 12.6).

Even when aided by qualitative text analysis software, it is important to note, such text explorations are essentially limited to a single analyst's conceptions and ability to read. Such software is convenient, but it does not make the process more objective.

When the volume of texts exceeds individual abilities as well, when teamwork becomes essential, the problems of coordinating the work of several analysts begin to dominate the research effort. It then becomes important that the analysts working on a project agree on the terms of the analysis; in addition, as differences in their individual readings will inevitably surface, the analysts need to render these readings in comparable categories. This will bring the analysis in line with the procedures described in Chapter 4—whether the analysis is called qualitative or quantitative. I continue this thread below, in section 14.1.2.

Problems of coordination among content analysts on a large project also challenge the analysts to overcome the temptation to take their own readings as the only ones that count, which often coincides with the belief that content is contained in text, an inherent quality of text, and that everyone ought to know what *it* is (see Chapter 2). Obviously, texts can be read variously and mean different things to different people. Recognizing this leads analysts to listen, while reading texts, to the voices of other readers—the texts' writers, audiences, and users—to understand what the texts mean to them, how language is implicated in their interpretation, the roles the texts do or could play in the lives of their users, and whose voice is represented, who listens, who responds, and who is silenced in these texts. Unless they consider alternative readings, content analysts are limited to analyzing their own understanding and nothing outside it. By reading with alternative voices in mind (see Krippendorff, in press-c), analysts begin to expand their horizons, to get a feeling for the context they need to construct to make room for diverse people associated with the texts and for the institutions that govern the texts' antecedent conditions, concurrent interpretations, and practical consequences. As this context becomes conceptually clear, so do the questions that analysts feel they could answer. Figure 4.3, which depicts this text-driven entry to content analysis, suggests that such questions arise not only from the virtual voices of other readers or users, but also from what the authors of pertinent literature on the context say.

Qualitative content analysts typically stop at their own interpretations of texts, however, and the recommendation I have just made is intended to undermine the very notion that texts can drive an analysis. Contrary to what lawyers are fond of saying, documents never speak for themselves—interpretations are always made by intelligent readers. And texts inevitably have several meanings. Although the seeming objectivity of computer searches tends to hide this fact, the queries that inform such searches are always formulated by the very analysts who also interpret the search results. When analysts acknowledge their own conceptual contributions and, by implication, the possibility of diverse readings, especially when they have to train coders to comply with written recording/coding instructions, their analyses can no longer be conceived as text driven. This brings us to the next, perhaps more preferable, way of entering a content analysis.

14.1.2   Problem-Driven Analyses

A problem-driven analysis derives from epistemic questions, from a desire to know something currently inaccessible and the belief that a systematic reading of potentially available texts could provide answers. Content analysts who start at this point tend to be involved in real-world problems: psychoanalysts seeking to diagnose the pathology of a patient; lawyers trying to generate evidence that will support or refute an accusation of plagiarism; historians hoping to clarify how a historical event unfolded; literary or forensic scholars aspiring to know who wrote an unsigned work; educators attempting to predict the readability of textbooks; mass-media researchers intending to substantiate claims of undesirable effects on civic society of TV election coverage; propaganda analysts looking for military intelligence hidden in enemy domestic broadcasts; rhetoricians desiring to measure how much civic knowledge candidates for political office bring to a debate. All of these are epistemic problems, problems of not knowing something deemed significant. Content analysts must convert such problems into research questions, which they then attempt to answer through a purposive examination of texts. In Chapter 3, I discuss the different kinds of inferences that analysts may draw from texts; here, the focus is on the steps that analysts may want to take to get to those inferences:

- Formulating research questions

- Ascertaining stable correlations

- Locating relevant texts

- Defining units of analysis

- Sampling the texts

- Developing categories and recording instructions

- Selecting an analytical procedure

- Adopting standards

- Allocating resources

14.1.2.1 Formulating Research Questions

Formulating research questions is by far the most important conceptual task that analysts face, for it is the key to a successful research design. As noted in Chapter 2, the research questions posed in content analysis have the following characteristics:

- They concern currently unobserved phenomena in the problematized context of available texts.

- They entail several possible answers.

- They provide for at least two ways of selecting from among these answers—if not in practice, then at least in principle.

The first of these defining features rearticulates the aim of content analysis: to make abductive inferences from texts to phenomena outside those texts. In Chapter 2 (section 2.4), I discuss how abduction is distinguished from induction (moving from particulars to generalizations) and deduction (moving from generalizations to particulars) as a form of reasoning that moves from particular texts, through context-sensitive explanations of these texts, to particular answers to research questions (i.e., from particulars to particulars). Such answers need to solve a problem in the widest possible sense, from solving an important mystery to informing a decision to act.

The second characteristic above demands of a research question that it entail several conceivable answers—neither an open field in which anything can happen nor a single answer that the analyst intends to prove.

The third feature suggests that it would not be sufficient simply to answer a research question, even for good reasons. The researcher should think of at least one other way to answer that question, independent of what a content analysis of the sampled texts will show, which could validate the answer, at least in principle: additional observations, correlations with measures already known to be valid, even observations of improved success in acting on the information the content analysis provided (see Chapter 13). A content analysis should be validatable in principle, and this entails an alternative method or independent evidence.

Novices in content analysis need to understand that not all questions qualify as research questions. For example, a question concerning whether a computer program is suitable for analyzing a body of text is a question about the properties of the software relative to available texts—it does not address anything in the context of the analyzed texts. The question of whether one can measure a desired quality of texts does not qualify either, because it concerns an analyst's ability and is answerable by that analyst's doing it. It has nothing to do with the chosen context of analysis. Nor are questions concerning how often an author uses a certain expression appropriate research questions. Counting is an operation performed on a body of text. Its result says nothing other than that someone has counted something. This argument applies to all computational abstractions: type/token ratios, vocabulary sizes, and various correlations within a text. Unfortunately, the history of content analysis is full of examples of researchers who have merely declared counts to be indices of phenomena, usually of social or political significance, without spelling out how their claims could be validated. For example, a count of the number of violent acts on television means nothing unless one has at least a hunch that high numbers of such acts are bad for something one wants to preserve. More pernicious are pseudoquestions that exclude alternative answers. In the 1930s, many journalists quantified categories of content as a way of "objectifying" preconceived public concerns. Content analysts must not confuse proving one's point in a public debate with pursuing a research question that has several answers.

In effect, the third definitional feature of research questions calls for their answers to be validatable in principle (see Chapters 2 and 13)—in principle because many content analytic situations preclude validation in practice. For example, history always happened in the past. It no longer is observable, although it arguably was at one time. The traces of historical events that do survive are nothing more than indirect indicators of the events themselves. Texts are no exception. Inferences about historical events are best correlated with other traces left behind. To find relevant traces, assess their trustworthiness, and relate them to appropriate dimensions of a content analysis, analysts require considerable insight into the context of the analysis. Psychotherapeutic diagnosis provides a different example. No therapist can enter a patient's mind, so the first definitional feature of research questions is satisfied. The American Psychiatric Association's *Diagnostic and Statistical Manual of Mental Disorders* (2000) lists all legitimate mental disorders for therapists to choose from. One may disagree with this list, but it does satisfy the second feature. The diagnosis, an informed selection among known mental disorders, might be confirmed by other therapists, validated by independent tests, or vindicated by a successful treatment. Similarly, the answer to the question of whether an author committed plagiarism or not may not be known for sure without witnesses or admission by the accused. The latter could validate or invalidate the conclusion derived from a systematic comparison of two texts. Some of the more traditional questions that content analysts have answered concerned what different audiences could learn from exposure to particular mass-media messages and the political leanings of newspaper editors. To validate inferences from these kinds of media messages, content analysts have compared their results with survey results, with information from interviews with experts, and with focus group data—all sources of validation on which social scientists rely heavily. Content analysts should be specific about what could validate or invalidate their results, even if no (in)validation effort is ever undertaken, because in doing so they tie content analysis to a multiply confirmable reality.

Well-formulated research questions not only guide a research design, they also constitute one-third of a content analyst's world construction, the framework within which the analysis is to be undertaken. Research questions concern the uncertain or variable part of that world (see Figure 2.1). The analysts' next two steps involve the stable parts of their world.

14.1.2.2 Ascertaining Stable Correlations (With the Research Questions)

Content analysis answers research questions by analyzing texts, which are understood quite generally to include images, sound, Web sites, symbolic events, even numerical data, provided they mean something in the chosen context. The abductive inferences that content analysis entails presuppose some knowledge on the analysts' part of how the research questions relate to available texts. This knowledge need not be, and typically is not, exclusively linguistic or semantic. Content analysts are rarely interested in what is said literally, by dictionary definition or according to a standard reader, if such a person exists. Content analysts are as interested in what is not said as they are in what is said—that is, they are interested in what texts reveal about phenomena not spoken of, such as ideological commitments or ethnic prejudices that are manifest in influences, consequences, and uses that may well go unrecognized by individual readers. Inferences of the latter kinds tend to rely on statistical knowledge and call for the use of complex analytical instruments. In Chapter 2, I describe these connections as stable correlations, stable or enduring because only if they can be assumed to remain invariant, at least during the analysis, can they justify the inferences that a content analysis is asked to make. Questions whose answers are not correlated with anything observable, readable, or accomplishable with texts cannot be answered.

Traditionally, content analysts have focused on *linguistic references, expressions* of attitudes, and *evaluations*. These assume a one-to-one correlation between textual units and the phenomena referred to, expressed, articulated, or, in a naive sense, "contained" in them. More recently, content analysts have relied on texts as *statistical correlates* of the phenomena of interest, using the wear and tear shown by library books to assess the popularity of certain topics, for example, or relying on the correlation between expressed public concerns and voting. Typically, such correlates stem from other methods of inquiry—such as public opinion research, media effects studies, perception experiments, and theories of cultural cognition—that often are concerned with frequencies, contingencies, and variances. Texts may be seen also as *by-products* of the phenomena of interest, such as when researchers use mass-media coverage to infer how the mass-media industry is organized; as *causes,* such as when researchers attempt to infer audience perceptions or media-induced anxieties; as *consequences,* such as when researchers analyze medical records to determine the population characteristics of patients; or as *instrumental,* such as when researchers take texts as evidence of manipulation efforts by the texts' producers, as in political or public health campaigns. Webb, Campbell, Schwartz, and Sechrest (1966) add to this list of possible connections *physical traces* that the phenomena of interest leave behind and *actuarial records* that institutions maintain for reasons other than analysts' interest in them. Dibble (1963) recognized the latter as well, and George (1959a) has reported the use of complex sociopolitical networks of stable correlations to answer research questions (see Chapter 9 and Figure 9.2). Artificial intelligence models account for still other stabilities in the world of content analysts, enabling them to obtain answers from sparse textual evidence.

The analysts' task at this step of a research project is to ascertain a reliable network of these correlations, correlations that researchers can rely on to be stable and general (invariant over time and in various situations), certain (able to determine or be determined), and selective (able to narrow the set of possible answers to a research question). Content analysts may utilize all kinds of sources for this knowledge. Past empirical research about text-context relationships is one such source. In Chapter 4 (section 4.2), I suggest several designs for the generation of empirical knowledge in preparation for a content analysis. Available theories and models of how the phenomena of interest are communicated within a social system can also serve as sources of needed evidence. Chapter 9 gives examples of analytical constructs that are as simple as the aforementioned one-to-one correlations and as complex as a model of how a government controls public opinion through its publications. Causality is not the only path, as suggested by the above list of correlations, nor do correlations need to be direct. Content analysts often lament the absence of general theories and the naive simplicity of theories that claim universality. Indeed, literature on the contexts of particular texts, another important source of knowledge of prevailing stabilities, often includes situation-specific descriptions, temporally limited "mini-theories," and highly qualified propositions, all of which could well support a content analyst's efforts. These if-then propositions may be derived from normal readings, known stereotypical reactions, widely used folk sayings, metaphors, colloquialisms, and so on. The hope is that such a network of propositions contains a path that connects available texts to the needed answers. A well-substantiated path is all that content analysts need to create.

In assuming such a stable network of correlations, analysts may need to keep track of the conditions under which these stabilities are warranted and when they become unreliable. For example, correlations that have been found to hold for undergraduate subjects may not be generalizable to other populations, or at least not without qualifications. In crisis situations, organizational rules may break down or be replaced by others. The meanings of verbal expressions may change over time and/or become variable from one social situation to another, or from one culture to another. Some content analysts are tempted to assume linguistic universality or to assume that correlations once found do not change under conditions other than those studied (see Figure 2.1), but assuming such correlations to be stable when they are not can seriously mislead content analysts.

Obviously, knowledge of the needed correlations is informed by how a context is defined. Political scientists look for correlations that differ from those that psychiatrists are able to consider. Sociologists and communication researchers approach content analyses with different constraints in mind, and the worlds that they respectively construct for given texts may well be incommensurate with one another.

A network of stable correlations constitutes the second third of the content analyst's world construction (see Figure 4.2). Its purpose is to channel, almost in an information theoretical sense, the diversity encountered in texts to the possible answers to a research question. The analysts' next step is one that is often mentioned as the starting point for content analysis: locating relevant texts.

14.1.2.3 Locating Relevant Texts

In content analysis, texts inform analysts' questions and so must be sampled from populations of texts that can be informative in this sense. A text is relevant if there is evidence for or an assumption of stable correlations between that text and answers to the research question. By backtracking along the path of the intended inferences, moving from the phenomena of interest along the stable correlations to potentially available texts, content analysts can justify the relevance of a population of texts to given research questions.

As noted above, traditionally content analysts have made their analytical efforts easy by assuming one-to-one relationships between textual units and the phenomena of interest, what they are assumed to refer to, express, or "contain." With this assumption, selecting (including reading and counting) texts virtually substitutes for selecting (including observing and enumerating) the phenomena addressed by the research questions. This hides the usually complex roles that texts play in social situations. For example, to infer variations in achievement motives over various periods of a culture, McClelland (1958) searched for messages in which achievements were *created, negotiated,* or *celebrated.* This led him not only to popular literature, biographies, and expressions in art, but also to images on Greek vases and postage stamps. Content analysts have a long history of analyzing the newspapers read by political elites in various countries to infer the politics of the citizens of those countries. This choice is grounded in the assumption that political agendas are set and public debates are spearheaded by certain leading newspapers, so-called prestige papers, rather than by local ones, which are more likely to reproduce what the prestige papers print and are, hence, less informative. To reveal an author's suspected racial or ethnic prejudices, content analysts may have to sample from the writings of that author not intended for publication, such as personal diaries or texts written specifically for the author's racial or ethnic in-group. When a source of texts has a stake in the outcome of the analysis, the content analysts need to consider what that source knows about how it might be analyzed and/or read and focus instead on textual characteristics that the source does not easily control or cannot control. This rules out instrumental aspects of communication.

Although the logic of such choices is pretty clear, it is not easy to be more specific about how content analysts go about deciding on the informativeness of the texts they propose to analyze. Reading a small sample is good start. Examining headlines or abstracts for clues to the relevance of texts is a common practice. Pursuing citation networks to the key publications is a strategy familiar to many scholars. Alleged expertise could also lead analysts to suitable populations, provided such attributions can be trusted. The reputation of a publication is another criterion for locating relevant texts. Often, however, content analysts have to be satisfied with what is made available to them. Propaganda analysts during wartime and analysts working for institutes that monitor international agreements have to start with what they can intercept. Scholarship on literary figures is limited to what is written by and about them and their times. Conversation analysts can record only with permission, which excludes many privileged conversations (and can introduce unwanted biases).

The Internet as well as large, full-text electronic databases and digital libraries have vastly expanded the availability of content analyzable texts. Browsers, text search engines, and computer-aided text analysis tools (see Chapter 12, section 12.4) can locate relevant texts in stages. Starting perhaps with vague hunches about what is relevant, text analysts may begin a search with queries that cast a deliberately wide net over all conceivable texts just to get a sense of how much is there. Making good use of abduction, analysts typically develop increasingly detailed explanations of the body of texts they have so far scanned, become clearer about how available text may be correlated with the research question, and iteratively narrow the search. During such explorations, content analysts develop conceptions of the available texts and how to analyze them while simultaneously reducing the sample of texts to a manageable size. Search engines typically are severely limited in what they can identify (see Chapter 12, section 12.4). There almost always remains a considerable gap between what they retrieve and what is relevant (see the discussion of semantic validity in Chapter 13, section 13.2.2). Nevertheless, techniques for sampling from electronic databases, Web pages, and on-line exchanges are improving, promising content analysts an increasingly rich source of textual data.

Given well-formulated research questions, and having a good sense of the network of correlations operating in the chosen context, available texts fix the otherwise wide-open variations that content analysis has to address. The analysts' decision on the population of texts to be analyzed completes the construction of the world in which the content analysis can proceed (see Chapter 2). We now turn to the components of content analysis (see Figure 4.2).

14.1.2.4 Defining Units of Analysis

One way to make a content analysis of a large volume of text manageable is to break it into smaller units and deal with each separately. In Chapter 5, three units of analysis are distinguished according to the functions they serve within the analytical process: *sampling units* are mutually exclusive units of text that are selectively included in an analysis (see Chapter 6); *recording units* are also mutually exclusive, either equal to or contained in the sampling units, but separately described, coded, or recorded in the terms of a data language; and *context units* set limits on the amount of text to be consulted in determining what a recording unit means (see Chapter 7). Chapter 5 also mentions *units of enumeration*, which usually coincide with recording units, sometimes in the form of numerical measurements: column inches, type sizes, ratios of different kinds of words, and scales.

In text searches by computer, units can be defined by proximity operators (see Chapter 12, section 12.4): a delineated stretch of text, a document, an article, or a paragraph that contains a match with the query. Search results may serve as sampling units or as recording units. It is conceivable that text searches will provide the answers to analysts' research questions, but this would be rare.

The definitions of units of analysis have important implications. When the units are mutually exclusive, counting them leads to comparable frequencies; when they overlap, it does not. Separating units also severs all relations among them, omitting information that resides between neighboring words or phrases. For example, taking single words as units disregards their roles in sentences, so that their syntactical meanings are lost; units of sentences omit the roles that sentences play in paragraphs, thought sequences, the points made in longer arguments, and so on. Thus unitizing a text is justifiable only if the relationships between units do not inform the research question. The above-mentioned context units are intended to preserve at least some of the information that surrounds the recording units. Generally, if units are too small (such as words or short expressions), semantic validity may suffer and the content analysis tends to become shallow. If units are too large (e.g., whole documents, Web pages, books, TV shows), the content analysis becomes unreliable (see Chapter 11, section 11.1).

14.1.2.5 Sampling the Texts

If the population of relevant texts is too large, content analysts may select representative samples of these texts. A heuristic approach to sampling is to start with any arguably unbiased sample of text, analyze it for how well it answers the research questions, and, if it fails to meet acceptable standards, continue to sample until the questions are either answered with reasonable certainty or proceeding becomes hopeless. The latter may signal the need for a redesign of the content analysis.

Chapter 6 suggests suitable sampling strategies. However, because texts are about phenomena outside or surrounding the texts, sampling in content analysis differs from sampling in other contexts—for example, sampling of individuals for public opinion surveys. In content analysis, researchers need to sample texts with two populations in mind: the "population" phenomena that correlate and hence lead to answers to a research question and the population of texts that represents these phenomena. In sampling the texts for a content analysis, researchers must give these phenomena a fair chance of contributing to the answer to the research question.

Chapter 6 also addresses the problem of texts that come into analysts' hands for reasons unrelated to the research questions (see the discussion of text-driven analyses above, in section 14.1.1). If texts are made available rather than purposefully sampled, their representativeness cannot be assured. They may be biased on account of their sources' selectivity. For example, historical documents survive for a variety of reasons that are usually unrelated to why they are of interest, politicians have good reason to hide embarrassing information from public view, and television news is not about what happens in the world but rather represents what the mass-media institutions deem newsworthy and can fit into available programming space. When the population of available texts is small, content analysts may not have the luxury of sampling and so face the problem of rectifying the sampling biases inherent in these texts.

14.1.2.6 Developing Categories and Recording Instructions

As I have noted above, when the volume of text exceeds a single researcher's analytical capabilities and analysts must therefore work in teams, or, even more important, when their results are to satisfy scientific standards and need to be replicable elsewhere, the analysts involved need to work not only together but also alike, or else their results will not be comparable. The coordination this requires is accomplished through the formulation of clear instructions for coders (see Chapter 7) to describe the same textual units in the same analytical terms, a data language (see Chapter 8). To ensure replicability, such instructions may include the following:

- A list of the qualifications that coders (observers, interpreters, judges) need for the task

- Descriptions of training procedures and instructional materials used to calibrate coders' conceptions

- Operational definitions of the recording and context units, and rules on how to distinguish them

- Operational definitions of the syntax (form) and semantics (meanings) of the data language (the categories or analytical terms) that coders are to apply in describing, translating, or categorizing each textual unit (Ideally, these definitions inform the cognitive operations that coders employ in reading and recording the texts.)

- Copies of the form(s) to be used in creating records and entering data for processing: spreadsheets, examples of completed questionnaires, and tabulations

Typically, before these instructions are applied by several coders and to a large body of text, the analysts need to pretest them on a small sample of texts and then modify and retest them until they satisfy reasonable reliability standards (see Chapter 11).

There are several well-known strategies for developing suitable categories and recording instructions. Unfortunately, many content analysts use categories that are uniquely tailored to available texts, in effect starting each content analysis from scratch, almost in the spirit of text-driven approaches. Although this strategy eases the coding task and increases reliability, it creates content analyses whose results are not comparable with each other, and therefore rarely advance theory. Although ingenuity is always welcome, content analysts who rely on conceptualizations that have proven successful elsewhere have a better chance of drawing on and contributing to existing knowledge.

A second strategy that many analysts use is to rely on the recording instructions of published content analyses with similar aims. I have mentioned various systems of categories in this volume (see Chapters 7 and 8), and readers can find other examples in the works of authors such as Berelson (1952), Holsti (1969), Weber (1990), Gottschalk (1995), Roberts (1997), Riffe, Lacy, and Fico (1998), and Neuendorf (2002). In addition, there are the categories built into computer programs, especially dictionary approaches (see Chapter 12, section 12.5.1).

Some content analyses rely on only a few variables, whereas others define very many. Some require only a page of instructions; the instructions for others fill whole books (e.g., Dollard & Auld, 1959; Smith, 1992b). There is no need to invent a new scheme if existing ones have proven to be productive.

A third strategy is to draw from available literature on or theories of the context of the analysis. If the descriptive accounts or theories about this context can be operationalized into categories for coding texts, then analysts can gain immediate access to what the literature suggests the stable correlations are. This is the path that Osgood, Saporta, and Nunnally (1956) took repeatedly, for example, in developing evaluative assertion analysis. This analysis operationalized theories of cognitive balance, which led to such theoretical concepts as "attitude objects," "connectors," and "common meaning terms." Where theories are unavailable, content analysis categories may be found in official classifications or taxonomies. If analysts need to describe occupational categories, it would make sense for them to consult official Federal Trade Commission listings or sociological studies of occupational status and prestige. For psychoanalytic research, the American Psychiatric Association's *Diagnostic and Statistical Manual of Mental Disorders* (2000) is indispensable. As these categories are widely used, content analyses that use them can tap into empirical findings that are cast in these terms. Along the same lines, if a content analysis is to provide variables for testing particular hypotheses about participation in political deliberation, then the analysts might take their categories from previous research in this area, as Cappella, Price, and Nir (2002) did, relying for their argument repertoire index on Kuhn's (1991) work on practical reasoning in everyday life. By deriving categories from established theories of the contexts of their analyses, researchers can avoid simplistic formulations and tap into a wealth of available conceptualizations.

In addition to being reliable, the categories of a data language should be tested, where possible, for their semantic validity. This is especially important for computer dictionaries, which, while always perfectly reliable, may tag or transform text in incomprehensible ways. In Chapter 12 (section 12.5.1), I describe an approach to the development of categories suitable for computer processing that may serve as a model for utilizing computer aids of the coding/dictionary variety.

14.1.2.7 Selecting an Analytical Procedure

The best analytical procedures parallel what is going on in the context of the available texts. Figure 9.1 depicts the inferential component of content analysis as a procedural model of the presumed stable text-context correlations. Evaluative assertion analysis (see Chapter 9, section 9.2.3), for example, models the transfer of attitudes from common meaning terms to objects and from one attitude object to another. It operationalizes a set of psychological propositions, amounting to a rather particular analytical construct. This analysis is appropriate only where attitudes are the target of research questions and the context conforms to how the process is theorized. Semantic network analysis (see Chapter 12, section 12.5.3) has a very different structure. It is an outgrowth of computational theories of cognition and is appropriate where these theories are proven valid.

The catalog of well-formulated analytical procedures from which analysts can choose is not very large. In making an informed choice from among several canned computer programs, assembling an analytical procedure from available components, or constructing one from scratch, content analysts are advised to do three things: (a) be clear about the network of stable correlations in their own world construction (analytical context), and (b) find out how texts are treated, processed, or transformed in the analytical procedures available, in order to (c) select the procedure whose operations provide the best model of the network of stable correlations and are therefore most likely to yield valid answers to the research questions.

Selecting among analytical procedures is not easy. Analysts should be aware that promoters of text analysis software tend to overstate their claims about what their software can do—promising that it can extract concepts from text when all it does is calculate statistically interesting word co-occurrences. For example, on closer examination, claims that a software package mines content, models text, or develops and tests theories automatically often boil down to disappointingly simple procedures that are far removed from what the impressive names suggest. Similarly, theorists often generalize the analytical powers of their own projects beyond available evidence. And, what is even more disheartening, most canned computer programs seal the assumptions built into them against outside inspection. These are some of the difficulties that analysts face in trying to make informed choices.

14.1.2.8 Adopting Standards

Given that the answers to content analysis research questions are inferences from texts about not-yet-observed phenomena, these answers are always of hypothetical validity. Standards serve to limit the uncertainty associated with such answers. This uncertainty is a function of three elements:

- The nature of the context of the texts being analyzed

- The extent of the analysts' knowledge of the text-context correlations

- The care with which the analysis is conducted

The nature of the context is not really under the analysts' control. Some contexts are highly structured, whereas others are chaotic or probabilistic. In some, the connections between texts and the answers to research questions are linear and direct; in others, those connections are statistical and vague, if not deliberately ambiguous. This limits the certainty of the inferences that analysts can make.

Knowledge of these correlations is another matter. No content analysis can be justified without some knowledge of this kind. But complete ignorance rarely exists. Content analysts are competent readers, at least in their own language and expertise, and do not let pass what seems incomprehensible to them. Beyond the ever-present face and social validity, content analysts may test for sampling, semantic, structural, and functional validity (see Chapter 13) and argue for the validity of their findings from the strengths of these tests, weaving information from appropriate literature and their own practical experiences into their rhetoric. In arguing for the validity of content analysis results, both proponents and critics rely on scientific standards of plausible reasoning. Such standards, although permeating discussions of scientific accomplishments, may not be quantifiable, attesting to the rhetorical nature of scientific research.

The third source of uncertainty, carelessness in conducting an analysis, shows up in at least two ways: as unreliability at the front end of an analysis, where it is measured with the help of suitable reliability coefficients (see Chapter 11), and in the way an analysis is designed to proceed to its result, also called internal validity (see Chapter 12). The recording/coding phase of content analysis is especially vulnerable to disagreements among coders, which show up in reliability tests.

But how high should standards be set? Obviously, when the results of a content analysis affect the life or death of a defendant in a court of law, when major business decisions are based on them, for example, or when whole populations during wartime are affected, standards need to be significantly higher than for scholarly work where the most that is at stake is the content analyst's reputation (see Chapter 11). The attainment of higher standards, although always desirable, tends to be more costly. It may require more careful preparatory investigations (see Chapter 4, section 4.2), a larger body of data (see Chapter 6), more sophisticated techniques of analysis, and so on. Content analysts may not wish to undertake projects whose standards are beyond their reach, both in terms of the needed resources and in terms of their responsibilities for analytical failures.

Standards for sampling, semantic, structural, and functional validity should be related to the level of validity demanded of the results. To decide on such standards, researchers may want to work backward from how certain, general, or selective the results need to be to how often-unavoidable imperfections can affect them.

The relationship between reliability—a function of the agreement between two or more analytical processes, coders, or devices (see Chapter 11)—and validity (see Chapter 13) is quite transparent. High reliability is a prerequisite of high validity but cannot guarantee it. Even perfect reliability, as achieved by any computer, cannot guarantee validity. In Chapter 11 (see section 11.4.4), I present standards that are applicable for Krippendorff's reliability coefficient alpha. The evaluation of the design of a content analysis, internal validity, is more qualitative in nature.

14.1.2.9 Allocating Resources

Content analysts have much to organize: analytical procedures, personnel, and scarce resources. Some activities may be reserved for the principal investigator, whereas others may be delegated to assistants, requiring training and instructions, or to professional research companies. Some must be executed in sequence—for example, the sampling of texts will have to take place before their coding, and coding must be done before analysis—and others may be done in parallel. Some take up short moments of time (e.g., running a computer program); others may be tedious (e.g., the reading and manual coding of text, most preparatory work, and the cleaning of dirty data). Limited resources—whether in qualified personnel, analytical devices, or funds—can impose organizational constraints on a project as well. Unless a content analysis is small and exploratory, analysts have to develop ways to organize their work.

There are numerous tools available to help analysts organize the processes of research. Most of these tools analyze the interconnected activities in a research project as a network. In such a network, arrows represent activities that one person or group can perform. By associating times and costs with each arrow, researchers can calculate needed resources, see potential bottlenecks, assign people to parallel or sequential activities, and estimate minimum and maximum amounts of time to completion.

Among the planning tools that content analysts may find useful are flowcharts such as those used in computer programming, the Program Evaluation and Review Technique (PERT), the Critical Path Method (CPM), and Gnatt charts (interested readers can find information on all of these on the Internet). These methods enable researchers to find the least expensive or the fastest paths to achieving research results and match available skills and resources with possible ways of organizing the analytical work.

Method-Driven Analyses   14.1.3

Method-driven analyses are suspect when they are motivated by what Abraham Kaplan (1964, p. 28) calls the "Law of the Instrument": When a child discovers how to use a hammer, everything seems to be in need of hammering. Analogously, when researchers get hooked on one analytical technique, when they become experts in its use, they may well end up applying that technique to everything in sight—and not without pleasure. Technologies have this attraction, and content analysts, especially those employing computer-aided text analysis software, are not immune. Typically, mastering any reasonably complex analytical technique requires analysts to invest so much of their time that they find it increasingly difficult to shift gears, even to see alternatives outside their expertise. Instead of starting from real-life problems, content analysts can be tempted by this technological expertise to look for areas of research where their preferred methods are arguably applicable. This raises the possibility that the insights gained from method-driven analyses are more reflective of what particular methods can produce than of how the objects of inquiry operate.

On the positive side, when researchers conduct method-driven content analysis, especially with validity concerns in mind, they simultaneously expand their method's areas of application while encountering its limitations. For example, the use of CatPac, a software package that fuses two ideas—the self-organization of neuronal networks and the movement of diverse social objects within abstract spaces (Woelfel & Fink, 1980)—migrated from tracking advertising and public relations campaigns to optimizing mass-media messages to analyzing communication, bibliographic, and vocabulary networks in social settings (Barnett & Doerfel, 1997). CatPac is now known largely as a clustering program for qualitative data, for texts in particular. In the path it took to arrive at this point, the software encountered failures and critics but also demonstrated successes and gained proponents. It found its niche.

Method-driven content analyses face fewer design issues than do problem-driven analyses, largely because once a method is chosen, analytical options are limited. For example, in CatPac, recording units are unalterably defined as character strings, usually single words. Instead of ascertaining their meanings, CatPac applies an algorithm directly to these words. It clusters words using information about their co-occurrences within specified stretches of text. The clusters resulting from such an analysis are interpreted as representing conceptions in the minds of speakers, in the culture of an organization, or in the public at large. Proponents of CatPac consider this automatic mapping to be the software's most important virtue, whereas critics miss the use of human intelligence. Once a method is chosen, the research questions that can be answered are usually fixed. In CatPac, they concern the clustering of textual units, interpreted as concepts, as moving over time, and thought to be manifest in the sources of the analyzed texts.

In the design of method-driven content analyses, usually only five preparatory steps remain for analysts to accomplish:

- Locating and sampling relevant texts

- Ascertaining stable correlations

- Preparing texts in method-specific and context-sensitive ways

- Adopting standards

- Allocating resources

Locating and sampling relevant texts in method-driven analyses is less an issue of finding texts that correlate with the answers to a research question than one of locating texts that are easily processed by the chosen method.

Regarding the second step above, method-driven content analysts are less inclined to explore correlations in a context for the directions an analysis could be taking than they are to ascertain whether the correlations surrounding the texts are compatible with the assumptions built into the chosen method. To continue the example above, CatPac assumes one-to-one relationships between single words or phrases and concepts in the minds of speakers. CatPac users are advised to examine literature or other sources of knowledge to determine whether its assumptions are warranted, whether the social phenomena of interest warrant this one-to-one relationship, and, more important, whether co-occurrences in texts are valid determinants of their meanings.

The preparation of texts in method-driven analyses resembles the previously described development of recording instruments, but not necessarily for use by coders. In CatPac, for example, analysts prepare a text by removing words deemed irrelevant, largely function words, and eliminating mere grammatical variations through stemming or lemmatization. Other text analysis software packages distinguish between go-words and stop-words, apply dictionaries that assign tags to words or phrases by which they are subsequently recognized, or parse sentences into components (see Chapter 12). Less automated analytical techniques, such as contingency analysis, require extensive manual editing of text. Justifications for these text transformations rely heavily on the analysts' judgments of what is relevant and what is not. Semantic validity is one applicable standard, reliability for manual editing is another, and computability by the method is a final and, in this approach, often primary criterion.

The adoption of standards in method-driven analyses essentially follows the arguments presented above, although some may not apply. For example, in computer analyses, reliability is not an issue. However, because computers are unable to comprehend texts the way humans do, semantic, structural, and functional validities are all the more important.

Finally, researchers must allocate their resources whether they are conducting problem- or method-driven analyses.

Method-driven content analysts tend to justify their methods by vindication (see Chapter 13). A method of analysis is vindicated when it consistently produces interpretable results. When a method crosses the limits of its usefulness, it produces obscure and uninterpretable results. CatPac has had such experiences. Unfortunately, many researchers are hesitant to report their failures, even though content analysts can learn more about the limits of some methods from failures than they can from successes.

WRITING A RESEARCH PROPOSAL   14.2

A research proposal puts forth the plan of a content analysis for consideration by a sponsor, dissertation committee, or teacher—someone who is able to grant permission, provide resources, or command time for the researchers to engage in the proposed inquiry. As such, a proposal has both a rhetorical function and a contractual function.

14.2.1   Rhetorical Function

The rhetorical function of the research proposal is to convince the sponsor(s) of two things:

- That the proposed research is worthwhile or beneficial
- That the researchers are capable of delivering what they propose

In academic research, scholars tend to accomplish the first of these by citing relevant literature to demonstrate a gap in knowledge or in method that the proposed research can be expected to narrow. Ideally, this gap is of social significance, widespread, and instrumental to other advances, not just of personal interest to the researchers. However, all funding agencies have their own missions, which are manifest in their histories of funding certain research projects and not others, just as scholars in positions to approve research proposals have their theoretical concerns and epistemological commitments. For a proposal to succeed, it needs to address these. In applied research, clients tend to seek information with practical implications. To be successful, proposals should demonstrate that the benefits of the research outweigh its costs.

Often, researchers face competing expectations when they set out to write a research proposal; such expectations may take the form of conflicting criteria from different departments of a funding agency, differing perspectives on the part of various members of a dissertation committee, or hidden agendas being pursued by decision makers. In such a case, the researchers' best strategy is to write a proposal that enrolls all decision makers into the project, giving each a reason to support it. In dissertation research, this sometimes means that a student needs to write one chapter for each committee member. A commercial research proposal may want to show how each stakeholder in the proposed research could benefit from its results, or at least not be disadvantaged by them, and perhaps even how all stakeholders could be brought together on account of the research.

Past accomplishments are clearly the best recommendations of researchers' abilities. Sponsors examine proposals for researchers' academic degrees and lists of their publications as well as reviews of the analysts' previous research, especially those written by reputable critics, and letters of support from respected authorities. Researchers without relevant previous research to show may compensate for this deficiency by providing compelling literature reviews in which they demonstrate familiarity with both the issues involved and how other researchers have solved or failed to solve similar research problems.

The research proposal does not merely discuss issues, however. It also needs to spell out the steps that the researchers intend to take and explain why. Indeed, probably the most convincing demonstration of the researchers' ability is a detailed research plan that evaluators can critically examine for its likely success. The proposal should also report on any preparatory work the researchers have completed that points to the challenging problems of the proposed research. In content analysis, this often means that the researchers should present evidence of the reliability of the proposed recording instructions and the capability of the analytical or computational techniques they intend to use, as well as explain how the texts to be sampled are relevant to the research question.

Contractual Function   14.2.2

A research proposal, once approved, entails the expectation that the sponsor or funding agency will provide what it has agreed to make available—financial resources, organizational help, or legal support—and that the researchers will deliver what they have proposed. The approval of a proposal creates contractual obligations whether the proposed research is intended to qualify an individual for an academic degree, to contribute theoretical insights, or to provide intelligence.

One of the characteristics of scientific research is that its results cannot be guaranteed before the research is completed. Just as researchers who propose to test a hypothesis must consider evidence in favor of that hypothesis and against it, so must content analysts who propose to answer a certain research question keep its possible answers open for the analysis to decide among them. Nature does what it does, and texts do not always yield what sponsors like to see and analysts hope to show.

In fact, lack of "cooperation" of texts often stimulates new insights and opens unanticipated turns, which brings us to the second peculiarity of scientific research: serendipity. A research proposal must outline at least one path to answering the research questions but at the same time preserve the analysts' ability to deviate from that path when unanticipated shortcuts become apparent, when new methods turn up, or when unforeseen findings surface—provided the research objective stays within expectations and scientific standards are not compromised.

The inability to guarantee particular results and serendipity in the conduct of research can be anathema to funding agencies that have vested interests in preferred outcomes. Proposal writers may need to address this peculiarity of research and convince the sponsors that all legitimate research questions have alternative answers, or formulate their research questions so that the sponsors see virtue in every possible answer.

Outline for a Research Proposal   14.2.3

A typical proposal for a content analysis includes all of the following parts:

■ *A statement of the general epistemic or methodological issue* that the proposed analysis will address: what that issue is and why and to whom it is significant

■ *A review of available literature on the context* in which this issue resides, showing the kinds of questions that have been asked and answered, the kinds of research methods previously applied, and what has worked and what has not, including the analysts' own research or experiences, if relevant

■ *A formulation of the specific research questions* to be answered by the proposed research, which should be embedded in an account of the framework adopted, and the *world of the analysis* that makes sense of these questions and points to a *body of text* by which the analysts expect to answer these questions (see Chapter 2)

■ *A description of the procedure to be followed,* including accounts of any preparatory research already undertaken or to be carried out, the hypotheses to be tested (see Chapter 4, section 4.2) as well as how and why they are to be tested, the proposed analytical steps (Figure 4.2), and the standards adopted for each. This description should cover the following:

The *units of analysis* (see Chapter 5) proposed, defined, and distinguished, and what they respectively contain and omit from the body of text

The *sampling strategies* (see Chapter 6) to be used, where the population of relevant texts is located, how easily available it is, criteria for adequate sample sizes, methods for correcting self-sampling biases, and the sampling validity to be achieved (see Chapter 13, section 13.2.1)

The *recording/coding categories* and *data language* (see Chapters 7 and 8) to be used, whether in the form of available computer dictionaries or search queries (see Chapter 12) or to be derived from theories, literature, or the texts themselves (see Chapter 4, section 4.1.2, and Chapter 12, section 12.6 for the latter); what these categories preserve or omit; semantic validity to be achieved (see Chapter 13, section 13.2.2); the reliability to be guaranteed (see Chapter 11); and the results of any pretests of the recording instructions

The computational (statistical or algebraic) *techniques for reducing* or summarizing the body of recorded text and the justifications for these techniques relative to what is known about the context of the texts

The *inferential procedures* that the analysts will ultimately use to answer research questions from texts (see Chapter 9): the analytical constructs that underlie these and any evidence for their structural and functional validity (see Chapter 13, sections 13.2.3 and 13.2.4), available computer programs to be used, and evidence of their previously established correlative or predictive validities, if any (see sections 13.2.5 and 13.2.6)

How and to whom the research results are to be made available: the *narrative forms* in which the answers to the research questions will be presented, using numerical arrays, graphic illustrations, or data files, for example, planned publications and presentations to conferences, or reports to sponsors; the *kinds of conclusions* drawn from the results, whether they are expected to advance theoretical knowledge, make recommendations for actions, or settle an issue; and a *critical assessment* of the uncertainties that are likely to remain associated with the larger issues that the results are to address

- *An account of the specific time periods and resources needed* to complete the proposed analysis (the costs of personnel, equipment, and outside services) presented in the form of a timeline of the phases of research showing the milestones to be achieved and the resources needed at each phase

- *A list of references to cited literature* that conforms to whatever style manual the sponsor of the proposal accepts and includes entries only for available publications

- *Appendixes* containing material pertinent to the proposal but not central to the potential sponsor's understanding of what is being proposed, such as examples of the kinds of texts to be analyzed, lists of texts to be sampled, the proposed categories of the analysis, its data language and/or recording instructions if already available, preliminary reliabilities achieved so far, specifications of the software to be utilized, preliminary analytical results, and testimony by experts supporting the proposed research

APPLYING THE RESEARCH DESIGN   14.3

Ideally, the work involved in carrying out a well-designed content analysis becomes routine. With all intellectual and methodological problems solved during the design phase, the analysis could be turned over to a research organization. In practice, however, problems are bound to emerge: Needed texts may turn out to be unavailable, scarcely relevant, or biased by the incorrigible self-sampling practices of their sources, and software may turn out not to work as expected. However, the most frequent disruptions stem from the inability to meet accepted standards of reliability (see Chapter 11) and validity (see Chapter 13). As solutions to such emerging problems cannot be specified in advance, short of discontinuing a content analysis altogether, researchers may have to go back and modify the defective parts of a research design (see Figure 4.2), keeping the overall research objective in mind. It is not unusual for a content analysis to need several iterations of locating unreliabilities, correcting their causes, and repeating these steps until applicable standards are satisfied. This is especially true in the development of coding/recording instructions. In addition to unreliabilities, new empirical findings and literature about the context of the analyzed texts can prompt reconstructions of the world the analysis was presupposing.

14.4   NARRATING THE RESULTS

Research proposals are written to convince sponsors, but research reports typically are addressed to other readers. Also, research reports usually go far beyond the mere statement of findings of fact. Such reports account for how analysts have accomplished what they set out to do; describe to which literature, judgments, or decisions the research results contribute; and raise questions for further exploration. In highly institutionalized settings—such as laboratories or public opinion polling organizations—where research questions are codified, researchers are well-known, and analytical procedures are well established, research reports may be limited to information about where the analyses deviated from the typical. Generally, a research report should offer details sufficient to convince at least three kinds of addressees of the importance of the results:

- The sponsor, agency, or client who approved and/or supported the research

- The content analysts' peers in the scientific community

- The public at large

These addressees may have conflicting agendas, which may have to be attended to separately.

Sponsors are interested, first, in whether the analysts fulfilled their contractual obligations. A research report needs to demonstrate that they have, and, where applicable, should also justify where and why the analysts deviated from the proposal. Second, funding agencies are keenly aware of the publicity they gain from having supported worthwhile research and often look for the social validity or political significance of the results. Political or commercial clients might be more interested in the benefits they can reap from the research, whereas academics may look for the knowledge advanced by the results. A research report may need to address these concerns. Third is the issue of empirical validity: Can the analysts' claimed results be trusted? Nonscientific users may be inclined to accept content analysis results on account of the analysts' scientific credentials or the reputations of the institutions where the analysts work. Users in the legal and scientific communities, in contrast, may approach a research report more critically, looking for and needing to find relevant details and evidence in support of findings.

For members of the scientific community, the ability to reproduce research results elsewhere is the most widely used standard. As the burden of proof is laid on the researchers, the research report must provide convincing evidence that the results can be reproduced. Measures of the reliability of the potentially unreliable components of an analysis—recording/coding, for example—can provide the needed assurances. Many scholarly journals require evidence for the reliability and statistical adequacy of research findings. But reliabilities merely put an upper limit on the validity of research results, as discussed above.

Because the answers that content analyses give are obtained through abductive inferences, analysts need to establish the validity of their inferences by making compelling arguments, which includes retracing the analytical steps they have taken and justifying each step in terms of whether it models or represents what is known about the context of the texts. Analysts can use sampling, semantic, structural, and functional validities (see Chapter 13) to support such arguments, especially when their results seem counterintuitive. However, content analysts should expect that even plausible research results may be received with a healthy dose of suspicion. The face validity they perceive may not be clear to all those who are touched by the research findings, and the analysts may need to go the extra mile to provide conclusive arguments for their inferences, even if the validity of their findings may seem obvious within their community of peers.

When research results are published, they enter the conversations of diverse readers. To convince these readers, analysts may want to create compelling narratives that explain what the research accomplished and the impacts the findings will have on the readers' lives, using concepts, comparisons, or metaphors that are meaningful in the readers' own worlds and not misleading.

Outline for a Research Report   14.4.1

Generally, a research report should contain the following parts (many of which are also found in the research proposal; see section 14.2.3, above):

- A *summary or abstract* of the research for decision makers who have little time to concern themselves with details (This part of the report often decides how readers regard the remainder.)

- A table of contents

- A statement of the epistemic or methodological issues that informed the analysis

- A *review of the literature* on the context in which these issues reside

- An *account of the framework adopted* for the content analysis, including the research questions addressed (with an explanation of the sponsor's or analysts' interest in these questions), the texts analyzed to answer the questions, and the context chosen to justify the analysis (see Chapter 2)

- A *description of the research design* actually followed, including the preparatory research undertaken (see Chapter 4), any complications encountered in the process, and how emerging problems were solved, with specific information in the following areas to enable critical evaluation of the process:

  The *body of texts* sampled: what it consists of, what motivated the analysts to choose it, by which strategy it was selected (see Chapter 6), and how the analysts dealt with biases (see Chapter 13, section 13.2.1)

The *data language* used (see Chapter 8): the system of descriptive categories and measurements the analysts employed to bridge the gap between raw texts and the computational techniques applied

The *units of analysis* (see Chapter 5): their operational definitions, how they were used in the process, and what they preserved and ignored from the texts

The *recording/coding process:* whether built into computer dictionaries or search queries (see Chapter 12) or enacted by human coders (see Chapter 7), the reliability (see Chapter 11) and, where evaluated, the semantic validity (see Chapter 13, section 13.2.2) of each variable

The *computational* (statistical or algebraic) *techniques employed to summarize, simplify, or reduce* the volume of records obtained from the body of texts

The *inferential techniques* (computer programs [see Chapter 12] or other analytical procedures [see Chapter 9]) utilized to answer the research questions and, where available, evidence of structural validity (see Chapter 13, section 13.2.3) or functional validity (section 13.2.4)

The *research results (the answers to the research questions):* in the form of data files, summaries, propositions of a factual nature, recommendations for actions, or judgments (suitably qualified by estimates of their validity), all crafted in a compelling narrative that the anticipated readers of the report can easily understand

A *self-critical appraisal:* of the analysis (Did it really yield something new?), of the time and resources spent (Was it worth the effort?), of the methods used in relation to other methods (Could there have been more appropriate techniques?), of the computational procedures used (Did they accomplish what was expected of them?), and of the meta-accomplishments of the analysis (Did it raise new questions for further explorations?)

■ *Additional matter*

A *list of references to cited literature*

Appendixes containing materials that enable interested readers to read beyond the report, such as the recording instructions, computer dictionaries used, reliabilities obtained, and tables of numerical findings, even data that could be used by other researchers (Scientific research is open, and data may need to be made available for reanalysis elsewhere.)

Acknowledgments of contributors to the research effort (All research projects proceed in networks of interpersonal relations. Because assistants, coders, consultants, advisers, librarians, and teachers do not expect to be acknowledged in official research reports, it is a gesture of generosity when researchers name those who have been involved.)

References

Abell, Peter. (1987). *The syntax of social life: The theory and method of comparative narratives*. New York: Oxford University Press.

Abell, Peter. (1993). Some aspects of narrative method. *Journal of Mathematical Sociology, 18*, 93–134.

Abelson, Robert P. (1963). Computer simulation of hot cognition. In Silvan S. Tomkins & Samuel Messick (Eds.), *Computer simulation of personality* (pp. 277–298). New York: John Wiley.

Abelson, Robert P. (1968). Simulation of social behavior. In Gardner Lindzey & Elliot Aronson (Eds.), *The handbook of social psychology* (pp. 274–356). Reading, MA: Addison-Wesley.

Abelson, Robert P., & Rosenberg, Milton J. (1958). Symbolic psychologic: A model of attitude cognition. *Behavioral Science, 3*, 1–13.

Adorno, Theodor W. (1960). Television and the patterns of mass culture. In Bernard Rosenberg & David M. White (Eds.), *Mass culture* (pp. 474–488). New York: Free Press.

Albig, William. (1938). The content of radio programs 1925–1935. *Social Forces, 16*, 338–349.

Albrecht, Milton C. (1956). Does literature reflect common values? *American Sociological Review, 21*, 722–729.

Alexa, Melina. (1997). *Computer-assisted text analysis methodology in the social sciences* (Arbeitsbericht 7). Mannheim: Zentrum für Umfragen, Methoden und Analysen.

Alexa, Melina, & Züll, Cornelia. (1999). *A review of software for text analysis* (Nachrichten 5). Mannheim: Zentrum für Umfragen, Methoden und Analysen.

Allen, Liska E. (1963). Automation: Substitute and supplement in legal practice. *American Behavioral Scientist, 7*, 39–44.

Allport, Gordon W. (1942). *The use of personal documents in psychological science*. New York: Social Science Research Council.

Allport, Gordon W. (Ed.). (1965). *Letters from Jenny*. New York: Harcourt Brace Jovanovich.

Allport, Gordon W., & Faden, Janet M. (1940). The psychology of newspapers: Five tentative laws. *Public Opinion Quarterly, 4*, 687–703.

Altheide, David L. (1987). Ethnographic content analysis. *Qualitative Sociology, 10*, 65–77.

Alwin, Duane F. (1974). Approaches to the interpretation of relationships in the multitrait-multimethod matrix. In Herbert L. Costner (Ed.), *Sociological methodology 1973–1974* (pp. 79–105). San Francisco: Jossey-Bass.

American Educational Research Association, American Psychological Association, and National Council on Measurement in Education. (1985). *Standards for educational and psychological testing*. Washington, DC: American Psychological Association.

American Educational Research Association, American Psychological Association, and National Council on Measurement in Education. (1999). *Standards for educational and psychological testing.* Washington, DC: American Psychological Association.

American Psychiatric Association. (2000). *Diagnostic and statistical manual of mental disorders* (4th ed., rev.). Washington, DC: Author.

American Psychological Association. (1954). Technical recommendations for psychological tests and diagnostic techniques. *Psychological Bulletin, 51*(Suppl. 2), 200–254.

Andsager, Julie L., & Powers, Angela. (1999). Social or economic concerns: How news and women's magazines framed breast cancer in the 1990s. *Journalism & Mass Communication Quarterly, 76,* 531–550.

Armstrong, Robert P. (1959). Content analysis in folkloristics. In Ithiel de Sola Pool (Ed.), *Trends in content analysis* (pp. 151–170). Urbana: University of Illinois Press.

Arnheim, Rudolf, & Bayne, Martha C. (1941). Foreign language broadcasts over local American stations. In Paul F. Lazarsfeld & Frank N. Stanton (Eds.), *Radio research 1941* (pp. 3–64). New York: Duell, Sloan & Pearce.

Aron, Betty. (1950). The Thematic Apperception Test in the study of prejudiced and unprejudiced individuals. In Theodor W. Adorno, Else Frenkel-Brunswick, Daniel J. Levinson, & R. Nevitt Sanford, *The authoritarian personality.* New York: Harper.

Ash, Philip. (1948). The periodical press and the Taft-Hartley Act. *Public Opinion Quarterly, 12,* 266–271.

Asheim, Lester. (1950). From book to film. In Bernard Berelson and Morris Janowitz (Eds.), *Reader in public opinion and communication* (pp. 299–306). New York: Free Press.

Atkinson, J. Maxwell, & Heritage, John. (Eds.). (1984). *Structures of social action: Studies in conversation analysis.* Cambridge: Cambridge University Press.

Averill, James R. (1985). The social construction of emotions with special reference to love. In Kenneth J. Gergen & Keith E. Davis (Eds.), *The social construction of the person* (pp. 89–107). New York: Springer-Verlag.

Baldwin, Alfred L. (1942). Personal structure analysis: A statistical method for investigating the single personality. *Journal of Abnormal and Social Psychology, 37,* 163–183.

Bales, Robert F. (1950). *Interaction process analysis.* Reading, MA: Addison-Wesley.

Barcus, Francis E. (1959). *Communications content: Analysis of the research 1900–1958: A content analysis of content analysis.* Unpublished doctoral dissertation, University of Illinois.

Barnett, George A., & Doerfel, Marya L. (1997, May). *A semantic network analysis of the International Communication Association.* Paper presented at the 47th Annual Meeting of the International Communication Association, Montreal.

Barton, Allen H. (1968). Bringing society back in: Survey research and macro-methodology. *American Behavioral Scientist, 12*(2), 1–9.

Bateson, Gregory. (1972). *Steps to an ecology of mind.* New York: Ballantine.

Bauer, Christian, & Scharl, Arno. (2000). Quantitative evaluation of Web site content and structure. *Internet Research, 10,* 31–41.

Baxter, Leslie A., & Montgomery, Barbara M. (1996). *Relating: Dialogues and dialectics.* New York: Guilford.

Becker, Howard P. (1930). Distribution of space in the *American Journal of Sociology,* 1895–1927. *American Journal of Sociology, 36,* 461–466.

Becker, Howard P. (1932). Space apportioned forty-eight topics in the *American Journal of Sociology*, 1895–1930. *American Journal of Sociology, 38,* 71–78.

Bengston, David N., & Xu, Zhi. (1995). *Changing national forest values: A content analysis* (Research Paper NC-323). St. Paul, MN: U.S. Department of Agriculture, Forest Service, North Carolina Forest Experimentation Station.

Bennett, Edward M., Alpert, R., & Goldstein, A. C. (1954). Communications through limited response questioning. *Public Opinion Quarterly, 18,* 303–308.

Benoit, William L., Blaney, Joseph R., & Pier, P. M. (1998). *Campaign '96: A functional analysis of acclaiming, attacking, and defending.* Westport, CT: Praeger.

Berelson, Bernard. (1949). What "missing the newspaper" means. In Paul F. Lazarsfeld & Frank N. Stanton (Eds.), *Communications research 1948–1949.* New York: Harper Brothers.

Berelson, Bernard. (1952). *Content analysis in communications research.* New York: Free Press.

Berelson, Bernard, & Lazarsfeld, Paul F. (1948). *The analysis of communication content.* Chicago: University of Chicago Press.

Berelson, Bernard, & Salter, Peter J. (1946). Majority and minority Americans: An analysis of magazine fiction. *Public Opinion Quarterly, 10,* 168–190.

Berelson, Bernard, & Steiner, George A. (1964). *Human behavior: An inventory of scientific findings.* New York: Harcourt Brace Jovanovich.

Berger, Peter L., & Luckmann, Thomas. (1966). *The social construction of reality: A treatise in the sociology of knowledge.* Harmondsworth: Penguin.

Berkman, Dave. (1963). Advertising in *Ebony* and *Life*: Negro aspirations vs. reality. *Journalism Quarterly, 40,* 53–64.

Bermejo, Fernando. (1997). *Press self-presentation: Self-reference and reflexivity in newspapers.* Unpublished master's thesis, University of Pennsylvania, Annenberg School for Communication.

Bernard, H. Russell, & Ryan, Gery W. (1998). Text analysis, qualitative and quantitative methods. In H. Russell Bernard (Ed.), *Handbook of methods in cultural anthropology* (pp. 595–646). Walnut Creek, CA: AltaMira.

Best, Michael L. (1997). Models for interacting populations of memes: Competition and niche behavior. *Journal of Memetics—Evolutionary Models of Information Transmission, 1,* 80–96.

Best, Michael L. (1998). Corporal ecologies and population fitness on the Net. *Journal of Artificial Life, 3,* 261–287.

Bishop, Stephanie. (1998). *Driving dangerously in the Prozac nation—Road rage: The making of a modern malady.* Unpublished manuscript, University of Pennsylvania, Annenberg School for Communication.

Blalock, Herbert M. (1964). *Causal inferences in non-experimental research.* Chapel Hill: University of North Carolina Press.

Bloch, Daniel A., & Kraemer, Helena Chmura. (1989). 2 × 2 kappa coefficients: Measures of agreement or association. *Biometrics, 45,* 269–287.

Bonfantini, Massimo, & Proni, Giampaolo. (1988). To guess or not to guess? In Umberto Eco & Thomas A. Sebeok (Eds.), *The sign of three: Dupin, Holmes, Peirce* (pp. 119–134). Bloomington: Indiana University Press.

Boot, N. (1980). Homography and lemmatization in Dutch texts. *ALLC Bulletin, 8,* 175–189.

Boulding, Kenneth E. (1978). *Ecodynamics.* Beverly Hills, CA: Sage.

Brennan, Robert L., & Prediger, Dale J. (1981). Coefficient kappa: Some uses, misuses, and alternatives. *Educational and Psychological Measurement, 41,* 687–699.

Broder, David P. (1940). The adjective-verb quotient: A contribution to the psychology of language. *Psychological Record, 3,* 310–343.

Broom, Leonard, & Reece, Shirley. (1955). Political and racial interest: A study in content analysis. *Public Opinion Quarterly, 19,* 5–19.

Brouwer, Marten, Clark, Cedric C., Gerbner, George, & Krippendorff, Klaus. (1969). The television world of violence. In Robert K. Baker & Sandra J. Ball (Eds.), *Mass media and violence* (Vol. 9, pp. 311–339, 519–591). Washington, DC: Government Printing Office.

Bruner, Jerome S., & Allport, Gordon W. (1940). Fifty years of change in American psychology. *Psychological Bulletin, 37,* 757–776.

Budd, Richard W. (1964). Attention score: A device for measuring news "play." *Journalism Quarterly, 41,* 259–262.

Budge, Ian, Robertson, David, & Hearl, Derek. (1987). *Ideology, strategy and party change: Spatial analyses of post-war election programmes in 19 democracies.* Cambridge: Cambridge University Press.

Cahnman, Werner J. (1948). A note on marriage announcements in the *New York Times. American Sociological Review, 13,* 96–97.

Campbell, Donald T. (1957). Factors relevant to the validity of experiments in social settings. *Psychological Bulletin, 54,* 297–311.

Campbell, Donald T., & Fiske, Donald W. (1959). Convergent and discriminant validation by the multitrait-multimethod matrix. *Psychological Bulletin, 56,* 81–105.

Cappella, Joseph N., Price, Vincent, & Nir, Lilach. (2002). Argument repertoire as a reliable and valid measure of opinion quality: Electronic dialogue during campaign 2000. *Political Communication, 19,* 73–93.

Cappella, Joseph N., Turow, Joseph, & Jamieson, Kathleen Hall. (1996). *Call-in political talk radio: Background, content, audiences, portrayal in mainstream media* (Report series no. 5). Philadelphia: University of Pennsylvania, Annenberg Public Policy Center.

Carletta, Jean, Isard, Amy, Isard, Steven, Kowtko, Jacqueline C., Doherty-Sneddon, Gwyneth, & Anderson, Anne H. (1997). The reliability of a dialogue structure coding scheme. *Computational Linguistics, 23,* 13–31.

Carley, Kathleen M. (1997). Network text analysis: The network positions of concepts. In Carl W. Roberts (Ed.), *Text analysis for the social sciences: Methods for drawing statistical inferences from texts and transcripts* (pp. 79–100). Mahwah, NJ: Lawrence Erlbaum.

Carmines, Edward G., & Zeller, Richard A. (1979). *Reliability and validity assessment.* Beverly Hills, CA: Sage.

Cartwright, Dorwin P. (1953). Analysis of qualitative material. In Leon Festinger & Daniel Katz (Eds.), *Research methods in the behavioral sciences* (pp. 421–470). New York: Holt, Rinehart & Winston.

Chomsky, Noam. (1959). Review of B. F. Skinner *Verbal Behavior*. *Language, 35,* 26–58.

Cohen, Bernard C. (1957). *The political process and foreign policy: The making of the Japanese peace settlement.* Princeton, NJ: Princeton University Press.

Cohen, Jacob. (1960). A coefficient of agreement for nominal scales. *Educational and Psychological Measurement, 20,* 37–46.

Content analysis: A new evidentiary technique. (1948). *University of Chicago Law Review, 15,* 910–925.

Corsaro, William, & Heise, David R. (1990). Event structure models from ethnographic data. In Clifford Clogg (Ed.), *Sociological methodology, 1990* (pp. 1–57). Oxford: Basil Blackwell.

Council on Interracial Books for Children. (1977). *Stereotypes, distortions and omissions in U.S. history textbooks.* New York: Racism and Sexism Resource Center for Educators.

Craig, Robert T. (1981). Generalization of Scott's index of intercoder agreement. *Public Opinion Quarterly, 45,* 260–264.

Cronbach, Lee J. (1951). Coefficient alpha and the internal structure of tests. *Psychometrika, 16,* 297–334.

Cuilenburg, Jan J. van. (1991). Inhoudsanalyse en computer. In Roel Popping & Jules L. Peschcar (Eds.), *Goed Geïnformeerd* (pp. 71–82). Houten, Netherlands: Bohn Stafleu Van Loghum.

Cuilenburg, Jan J. van, Kleinnijenhuis, Jan, & De Ridder, Jan A. (1986). A theory of evaluative discourse: Toward a graph theory of journalistic texts. *European Journal of Communication, 1,* 65–96.

Cuilenburg, Jan J. van, Kleinnijenhuis, Jan, & De Ridder, Jan A. (1988). Artificial intelligence and content analysis: Problems of and strategies for computer text analysis. *Quality and Quantity, 22,* 65–97.

Dale, Edgar. (1937). The need for the study of newsreels. *Public Opinion Quarterly, 1,* 122–125.

D'Andrade, Roy. (1991). The identification of schemas in naturalistic data. In Mardi J. Horowitz (Ed.), *Person schemas and maladaptive interpersonal patterns* (pp. 279–301). Chicago: University of Chicago Press.

D'Andrade, Roy. (1995). *The development of cognitive anthropology.* Cambridge: Cambridge University Press.

Danielson, Wayne A., Lasorsa, Dominic L., & Im, Dal S. (1992). Journalists and novelists: A study of diverging styles. *Journalism Quarterly, 69,* 436–446.

Danowski, James A. (1982). A network-based content analysis methodology for computer-mediated communication: An illustration with a computer bulletin board. In Michael Burgoon (Ed.), *Communication yearbook 6* (pp. 904–925). Beverly Hills, CA: Sage.

Danowski, James A. (1993). Network analysis of message content. In William D. Richards, Jr., & George A. Barnett (Eds.), *Progress in communication sciences* (Vol. 4, pp. 197–221). Norwood, NJ: Ablex.

Darnton, Robert. (1999, June 12). No computer can hold the past. *New York Times,* p. A15.

Dawkins, Richard. (1976). *The selfish gene.* New York: Oxford University Press.

Dawkins, Richard. (1982). *The extended phenotype: The long reach of the gene.* San Francisco: W. H. Freeman.

Deerwester, Scott C., Dumais, Susan T., Furnas, George W., Landauer, Thomas K., & Harshman, Richard A. (1990). Indexing by latent semantic analysis. *Journal of the American Society for Information Science, 41,* 391–407.

Denzin, Norman K., & Lincoln, Yvonna S. (2000). Introduction: The discipline and practice of qualitative research. In Norman K. Denzin & Yvonna S. Lincoln (Eds.), *Handbook of qualitative research* (2nd ed., pp. 1–28). Thousand Oaks, CA: Sage.

DeWeese, L. Carroll, III. (1977). Computer content analysis of "day-old" newspapers: A feasibility study. *Public Opinion Quarterly, 41,* 91–94.

Dibble, Vernon K. (1963). Four types of inferences from documents to events. *History and Theory, 3,* 203–221.

Diefenbach, Donald L. (2001). Historical foundation of computer-assisted content analysis. In Mark D. West (Ed.), *Theory, method, and practice in computer content analysis* (pp. 13–41). Westport, CT: Ablex.

Dollard, John, & Auld, Frank, Jr. (1959). *Scoring human motives: A manual.* New Haven, CT: Yale University Press.

Dollard, John, & Mowrer, O. Hobart. (1947). A method of measuring tension in written documents. *Journal of Abnormal and Social Psychology, 42,* 3–32.

Doreian, Patrick. (Ed.). (1993). Narrative methods [Special issue]. *Journal of Mathematical Sociology, 18*(1–2).

Dovring, Karin. (1954–1955). Quantitative semantics in 18th century Sweden. *Public Opinion Quarterly, 18,* 389–394.

Dumais, Susan T. (1992). LSI meets TREC: A status report. In Donna K. Harman (Ed.), *The First Text REtrieval Conference (TREC-1)* (NIST Special Publication 500–207). Washington, DC: U.S. Department of Commerce, National Institute of Standards and Technology.

Dumais, Susan T. (1993). Latent semantic indexing (LSI) and TREC-2. In Donna K. Harman (Ed.), *The Second Text REtrieval Conference (TREC-2)* (NIST Special Publication 500–215). Washington, DC: U.S. Department of Commerce, National Institute of Standards and Technology.

Dunphy, Dexter C. (1966). The construction of categories for content analysis dictionaries. In Philip J. Stone, Dexter C. Dunphy, Marshall S. Smith, & Daniel M. Ogilvie, *The General Inquirer: A computer approach to content analysis* (pp. 134–168). Cambridge: MIT Press.

Durig, Alex. (1995). The event frame. *Research Studies in Symbolic Interactionism, 7,* 243–266.

Dziurzynski, Patricia S. (1977). *Development of a content analytic instrument for advertising appeals used in prime time television commercials.* Unpublished master's thesis, University of Pennsylvania.

Eco, Umberto. (1994). *The limits of interpretation.* Bloomington: Indiana University Press.

Eigen, Manfred J., McCaskill, John, & Schuster, Peter. (1988). Molecular quasi-species. *Journal of Physical Chemistry, 92,* 6881–6891.

Ekman, Paul, & Friesen, Wallace V. (1968). Nonverbal behavior in psychotherapy research. In John Shlien (Ed.), *Research in psychotherapy* (Vol. 3, pp. 179–216). Washington, DC: American Psychological Association.

Ekman, Paul, Friesen, Wallace V., & Taussig, Thomas G. (1969). Vid-R and SCAN: Tools and methods for the automated analysis of visual records. In George Gerbner, Ole R. Holsti, Klaus Krippendorff, William J. Paisley, & Philip J. Stone (Eds.), *The analysis of communication content: Developments in scientific theories and computer techniques* (pp. 297–312). New York: John Wiley.

Ellison, John W. (1965). Computers and the testaments. In *Proceedings, Conference on Computers for the Humanities* (pp. 64–74). New Haven, CT: Yale University Press.

Evans, William. (2002). Computer environments for content analysis: Reconceptualizing the roles of humans and computers. In Orville Vernon Burton (Ed.), *Computing in the social sciences and humanities* (pp. 67–83). Urbana: University of Illinois Press.

Fan, David P. (1988). *Predictions of public opinion from the mass media: Computer content analysis and mathematical modeling.* New York: Greenwood.

Fan, David P. (1997). *Predictions of 62 time trends of public opinions and behaviors from persuasive information.* Unpublished manuscript, University of Minnesota, St. Paul.

Fan, David P., & Cook, R. Dennis. (1997). *Predictions of the Michigan Index of Consumer Sentiment from the press.* Unpublished manuscript, University of Minnesota, St. Paul.

Feigl, Herbert. (1952). Validation and vindication: An analysis of the nature and the limits of ethical arguments. In Wilfried Sellars & John Hospers (Eds.), *Readings in ethical theory* (pp. 667–680). New York: Appleton-Century-Crofts.

Fellbaum, Christiane. (Ed.). (1998). *WordNet: An electronic lexical database.* Cambridge: MIT Press.

Fenton, Frances. (1910). The influence of newspaper presentations on the growth of crime and other anti-social activity. *American Journal of Sociology, 16,* 342–371, 538–564.

Fleck, Ludwik. (1979). *Genesis and development of a scientific fact.* Chicago: University of Illinois Press. (Original work published 1935)

Fleiss, Joseph L. (1971). Measuring nominal scale agreement among many raters. *Psychological Bulletin, 76,* 378–382.

Fleiss, Joseph L. (1981). *Statistical methods for rates and proportions.* New York: John Wiley.

Flesch, Rudolph. (1948). A new readability yardstick. *Journal of Applied Psychology, 32,* 221–233.

Flesch, Rudolph. (1951). *How to test readability.* New York: Harper & Row.

Flesch, Rudolph. (1974). *The art of readable writing* (Rev. ed.). New York: Harper & Row.

Foltz, Peter W. (1990). Using latent semantic indexing for information filtering. In Proceedings of the 5th Conference on Office Information Systems [Special issue]. *ACM SIGOIS Bulletin, 11*(2–3).

Ford, Sarah, Fallowfield, Leslie, & Lewis, Shon. (1996). Doctor-patient interactions in oncology. *Social Science & Medicine, 42,* 1511–1519.

Foster, Charles R. (1938). *Editorial treatment of education in the American press.* Cambridge, MA: Harvard University Press.

Freeman, Steven F. (2001). *Patterns of executive attention in U.S. auto industry letters to shareholders 1963–1987.* Unpublished manuscript, University of Pennsylvania, Wharton School.

Furnas, George W., Deerwester, Scott C., Dumais, Susan T., Landauer, Thomas K., Harshman, Richard A., Streeter, Lynn A., & Lochbaum, Karen E. (1988).

Information retrieval using a singular value decomposition model of latent semantic structure. In Yves Chiaramella (Ed.), *Proceedings of the 11th International ACM SIGIR Conference on Research and Development in Information Retrieval* (pp. 465–480). New York: Association for Computing Machinery.

Garfield, Eugene. (1979). *Citation indexing: Its theory and application to science, technology and humanities.* New York: John Wiley.

Geller, A., Kaplan, D., & Lasswell, Harold D. (1942). An experimental comparison of four ways of coding editorial content. *Journalism Quarterly, 19,* 362–370.

George, Alexander L. (1959a). *Propaganda analysis: A study of inferences made from Nazi propaganda in World War II.* Evanston, IL: Row, Peterson.

George, Alexander L. (1959b). Quantitative and qualitative approaches to content analysis. In Ithiel de Sola Pool (Ed.), *Trends in content analysis* (pp. 7–32). Urbana: University of Illinois Press.

Gerbner, George. (1958). The social role of the confession magazine. *Social Problems, 6,* 29–40.

Gerbner, George. (1964). Ideological perspectives and political tendencies in news reporting. *Journalism Quarterly, 41,* 495–508.

Gerbner, George. (1966). An institutional approach to mass communications research. In Lee Thayer (Ed.), *Communication: Theory and research* (pp. 429–445). Springfield, IL: Charles C Thomas.

Gerbner, George. (1969). Toward "cultural indicators": The analysis of mass mediated public message systems. In George Gerbner, Ole R. Holsti, Klaus Krippendorff, William J. Paisley, & Philip J. Stone (Eds.), *The analysis of communication content: Developments in scientific theories and computer techniques* (pp. 123–132). New York: John Wiley.

Gerbner, George. (1985). Mass media discourse: Message system analysis as a component of cultural indicators. In Teun A. Van Dijk (Ed.), *Discourse and communications: New approaches to the analyses of mass media discourse and communication* (pp. 13–25). Berlin: Walter de Gruyter.

Gerbner, George, Gross, Larry, Morgan, Michael, & Signorielli, Nancy. (1994). *Television violence profile no. 16: The turning point: From research to action.* Philadelphia: University of Pennsylvania, Annenberg School for Communication.

Gerbner, George, Gross, Larry, Morgan, Michael, & Signorielli, Nancy. (1995). Growing up with television: The cultivation perspective. In Jennings Bryant & Dolf Zillmann (Eds.), *Media effects: Advances in theory and research.* Mahwah, NJ: Lawrence Erlbaum.

Gerbner, George, Gross, Larry, Signorielli, Nancy, Morgan, Michael, & Jackson-Beeck, Marilyn. (1979). *Violence profile no. 10: Trends in network television drama and viewer conceptions of social reality, 1967–1978.* Philadelphia: University of Pennsylvania, Annenberg School of Communications.

Gerbner, George, Holsti, Ole R., Krippendorff, Klaus, Paisley, William J., & Stone, Philip J. (Eds.). (1969). *The analysis of communication content: Developments in scientific theories and computer techniques.* New York: John Wiley.

Gerbner, George, & Marvanyi, George. (1977). The many worlds of the world's press. *Journal of Communication, 27*(1), 52–75.

Gergen, Kenneth J. (1985). Social constructionist inquiry: Context and implications. In Kenneth J. Gergen & Keith E. Davis (Eds.), *The social construction of the person* (pp. 3–18). New York: Springer-Verlag.

Gergen, Kenneth J. (1991). *The saturated self: Dilemmas of identity in contemporary life.* New York: Basic Books.

Gieber, Walter. (1964). News is what newspapermen make it. In Lewis A. Dexter & David M. White (Eds.), *People, society, and mass communication* (pp. 173–182). New York: Free Press.

Goodenough, Ward H. (1972). Componential analysis. In James P. Spradley (Ed.), *Culture and cognition* (pp. 327–343). San Francisco: Chandler.

Goodwin, Charles. (1977). *Some aspects of the interaction of speaker and hearer in the construction of the turn at talk in natural conversation.* Unpublished doctoral dissertation, University of Pennsylvania, Annenberg School of Communications.

Goodwin, Charles. (1981). *Conversational organization: Interaction between speakers and hearers.* New York: Academic Press.

Gottschalk, Louis A. (1995). *Content analysis of verbal behavior: New findings and clinical applications.* Hillsdale, NJ: Lawrence Erlbaum.

Gottschalk, Louis A., & Bechtel, Robert J. (1982). The measurement of anxiety through the computer analysis of verbal samples. *Comprehensive Psychiatry, 23,* 364–369.

Graham, Todd, & Witschge, Tamara. (2003). In search of online deliberations: Towards a new method for examining the quality of online discussions. *Communications, 28,* 173–204.

Groth, Otto. (1948). *Die Geschichte der deutschen Zeitungswissenschaft, Probleme und Methoden.* Munich: Konrad Weinmayer.

Guetzkow, Harold. (1956). Unitizing and categorizing problems in coding qualitative data. *Journal of Clinical Psychology, 6,* 47–58.

Hackett, Robert, & Zhao, Yaezhi. (1994). Challenging the master narratives: Peace protest and opinion/editorial discourse in the U.S. during the Gulf War. *Discourse & Society, 5,* 509–511.

Hansen, Anders. (1995). Using information technology to analyze newspaper content. In Raymond M. Lee (Ed.), *Information technology for the social scientist* (pp. 147–168). London: UCL.

Harary, Frank, Norman, Robert Z., & Cartwright, Dorwin P. (1965). *Structural models: An introduction to the theory of directed graphs.* New York: John Wiley.

Harris, Karen L. (1996). Content analysis in negotiation research: A review and guide. *Behavioral Research Methods, Instruments, & Computers, 28,* 458–467.

Hart, Roderick P. (1985). Systematic analysis of political discourse: The developments of diction. In Keith R. Sanders, Lynda Lee Kaid, & Dan Nimmo (Eds.), *Political communication yearbook 1984* (pp. 97–134). Carbondale: Southern Illinois University Press.

Harwood, Jake, & Giles, Howard. (1992). Don't make me laugh: Age representations in a humorous context. *Discourse & Society, 3,* 403–436.

Hatch, David L., & Hatch, Mary. (1947). Criteria of social status as derived from marriage announcements in the *New York Times. American Sociological Review, 12,* 396–403.

Hawk, Lee. (1997). "Listenability" of network newscasts: The change over sixteen years. *Feedback: Broadcast Education Association, 38*(2), 18–21.

Hays, David C. (1960). *Automatic content analysis.* Santa Monica, CA: Rand Corporation.

Hays, David C. (1969). Linguistic foundations for a theory of content analysis. In George Gerbner, Ole R. Holsti, Klaus Krippendorff, William J. Paisley, & Philip J. Stone (Eds.), *The analysis of communication content: Developments in scientific theories and computer techniques* (pp. 57–67). New York: John Wiley.

Heise, David R. (1995). *Specifying event content in narratives.* Unpublished manuscript, Indiana University. Retrieved from http://php.indiana.edu/~heise/eventcontent.html

Herdan, Gustav. (1960). *Type-token mathematics: A textbook of mathematical linguistics.* The Hague: Mouton.

Herma, Hans, Kriss, Ernst, & Shor, Joseph. (1943). Freud's theory of the dream in American textbooks. *Journal of Abnormal and Social Psychology, 38,* 319–334.

Hillman, James. (1995). *Kinds of power: A guide to its intelligent uses.* New York: Doubleday.

Holley, W., & Guilford, J. P. (1964). A note on the G-index of agreement. *Educational and Psychological Measurement, 24,* 749–754.

Holsti, Ole R. (1962). *The belief system and national images: John Foster Dulles and the Soviet Union.* Unpublished doctoral dissertation, Stanford University.

Holsti, Ole R. (1969). *Content analysis for the social sciences and humanities.* Reading, MA: Addison-Wesley.

Holsti, Ole R., Brody, Richard A., & North, Robert C. (1965). Measuring affect and action in international reaction models: Empirical materials from the 1962 Cuban crisis. *Peace Research Society Papers, 2,* 170–190.

Hopper, Robert, Koch, Susan, & Mandelbaum, Jennifer. (1986). Conversation analysis methods. In Donald G. Ellis & William A. Donahue (Eds.), *Contemporary issues in language and discourse processes* (pp. 169–186). Hillsdale, NJ: Lawrence Erlbaum.

Houle, Paul. (2002). [Contribution to a discussion of neural network content analysis programs on CONTENT@sphinx.gsu.edu], March 30.

Hubert, Lawrence. (1977). Kappa revisited. *Psychological Bulletin, 84,* 289–297.

Iker, Howard P. (1974). Select: A computer program to identify associationally rich words for content analysis: I. Statistical results. *Computers and the Humanities, 8,* 313–319.

Iker, Howard P. (1975). *Words system manual.* Rochester, NY: Computer Printout.

Iker, Howard P., & Harway, Norman I. (1969). A computer system approach toward the recognition and analysis of content. In George Gerbner, Ole R. Holsti, Klaus Krippendorff, William J. Paisley, & Philip J. Stone (Eds.), *The analysis of communication content: Developments in scientific theories and computer techniques* (pp. 381–405). New York: John Wiley.

Innis, Harold A. (1951). *The bias of communication.* Toronto: University of Toronto Press.

Institute for Propaganda Analysis. (1937). How to detect propaganda. *Propaganda Analysis, 1,* 5–8.

Jamieson, Kathleen Hall. (1984). *Packaging the presidency: A history and criticism of presidential campaign advertising.* New York: Oxford University Press.

Jamieson, Kathleen Hall. (1998). *A preliminary report on so-called "negative" ads and campaigning, October 7, 1998.* Philadelphia: University of Pennsylvania, Annenberg School for Communication.

Janda, Kenneth. (1969). A microfilm and computer system for analyzing comparative politics literature. In George Gerbner, Ole R. Holsti, Klaus Krippendorff, William J. Paisley, & Philip J. Stone (Eds.), *The analysis of communication content: Developments in scientific theories and computer techniques* (pp. 407–435). New York: John Wiley.

Janis, Irving L. (1965). The problem of validating content analysis. In Harold D. Lasswell, Nathan Leites, & Associates (Eds.), *Language of politics: Studies in quantitative semantics* (pp. 55–82). Cambridge: MIT Press. (Original work published 1943)

Janis, Irving L., & Fadner, Raymond H. (1965). The coefficient of imbalance. In Harold D. Lasswell, Nathan Leites, & Associates (Eds.), *Language of politics: Studies in quantitative semantics* (pp. 153–169). Cambridge: MIT Press. (Original work published 1943)

Janson, Svante, & Vegelius, Jan. (1979). On generalizations of the G index and the phi coefficient to nominal scales. *Multivariate Behavioral Research, 14,* 255–269.

Jefferson, Gail. (1978). Sequential aspects of storytelling in conversation. In Jim Schenkein (Ed.), *Studies in the organization of conversational interaction* (pp. 219–248). New York: Free Press.

Johnson-Laird, Philip N., Herrmann, Douglas J., & Chaffin, Roger. (1984). Only connections: A critique of semantic networks. *Psychological Bulletin, 96,* 292–315.

Josephson, John R., & Josephson, Susan G. (1994). Introduction. In John R. Josephson & Susan G. Josephson (Eds.), *Abductive inference: Computation, philosophy, technology.* New York: Cambridge University Press.

Kaplan, Abraham. (1964). *The conduct of inquiry: Methodology for behavioral science.* San Francisco: Chandler.

Kaplan, Abraham, & Goldsen, Joseph M. (1965). The reliability of content analysis categories. In Harold D. Lasswell, Nathan Leites, & Associates (Eds.), *Language of politics: Studies in quantitative semantics* (pp. 83–112). Cambridge: MIT Press.

Katz, Elihu, Gurevitch, Michael, Danet, Brenda, & Peled, Tsiyona. (1969). Petitions and prayers: A content analysis of persuasive appeals. *Social Forces, 47,* 447–463.

Katz, Elihu, Gurevitch, Michael, Peled, Tsiyona, & Danet, Brenda. (1969). Exchanges with clients: A diagnostic approach to organizations and professions. *Human Relations, 22,* 309–324.

Katz, Jonathan N. (1995). *The invention of heterosexuality.* New York: Dutton.

Kelly, Edward F., & Stone, Philip J. (1975). *Computer recognition of English word senses.* Amsterdam: North-Holland.

Kenski, Kate (with Jamieson, Kathleen Hall, & Romer, Dan). (1999). *Public smarter than press, pundits, or academics about so-called "negative" ads and campaigning* [Survey, October 6]. Philadelphia: University of Pennsylvania, Annenberg Public Policy Center.

Kim, Joohan, & Gamson, William A. (1999, May). *Computer assisted frame analysis (CAFA) of abortion issues: A pilot study.* Paper presented at the 49th Annual Meeting of the International Communication Association, San Francisco.

Klausner, Samuel Z. (1968). *Two centuries of child-rearing manuals* [Technical report to the Joint Commission on Mental Health of Children]. Philadelphia: University of Pennsylvania, Department of Sociology.

Klein, Malcolm W., & Maccoby, Nathan. (1954). Newspaper objectivity in the 1952 campaign. *Journalism Quarterly, 31,* 285–296.

Kleinnijenhuis, Jan. (1990, June). *Applications of graph theory to cognitive communication research.* Paper presented at the 40th Annual Meeting of the International Communication Association, Dublin.

Kleinnijenhuis, Jan, De Ridder, Jan A., & Rietberg, Edwald M. (1997). Reasoning in economic discourse: An application of the network approach to the Dutch press. In Carl W. Roberts (Ed.), *Text analysis for the social sciences: Methods for drawing statistical inferences from texts and transcripts* (pp. 191–207). Mahwah, NJ: Lawrence Erlbaum.

Klir, Jiri, & Valach, Miroslav. (1965). Language as a means of communication between man and machine. In Jiri Klir & Miroslav Valach, *Cybernetic modeling* (pp. 315–373). Princeton, NJ: D. Van Nostrand.

Kolbe, Richard H., & Burnett, Melissa S. (1991). Content-analysis research: An examination of applications with directives for improving research reliability and objectivity. *Journal of Consumer Research, 18,* 243–250.

Kracauer, Siegfried. (1947). *From Caligari to Hitler: A psychological history of German film.* London: Dennis Dobson.

Kracauer, Siegfried. (1952–1953). The challenge of quantitative content analysis. *Public Opinion Quarterly, 16,* 631–642.

Krendel, Ezra S. (1970). A case study of citizen complaints as social indicators. *IEEE Transactions on Systems Science and Cybernetics, 6,* 267–272.

Krippendorff, Klaus. (1967). *An examination of content analysis: A proposal for a general framework and an information calculus for message analytic situations.* Unpublished doctoral dissertation, University of Illinois, Urbana.

Krippendorff, Klaus. (1969a). Models of messages: Three prototypes. In George Gerbner, Ole R. Holsti, Klaus Krippendorff, William J. Paisley, & Philip J. Stone (Eds.), *The analysis of communication content: Developments in scientific theories and computer techniques* (pp. 69–106). New York: John Wiley.

Krippendorff, Klaus. (1969b). Theories and analytical constructs: Introduction. In George Gerbner, Ole R. Holsti, Klaus Krippendorff, William J. Paisley, & Philip J. Stone (Eds.), *The analysis of communication content: Developments in scientific theories and computer techniques* (pp. 3–16). New York: John Wiley.

Krippendorff, Klaus. (1970a). Bivariate agreement coefficients for reliability data. In Edgar F. Borgatta & George W. Bohrnstedt (Eds.), *Sociological methodology 1970* (pp. 139–150). San Francisco: Jossey-Bass.

Krippendorff, Klaus. (1970b). Estimating the reliability, systematic error and random error of interval data. *Educational and Psychological Measurement, 30,* 61–70.

Krippendorff, Klaus. (1970c). The expression of value in political documents. *Journalism Quarterly, 47,* 510–518.

Krippendorff, Klaus. (1970d). On generating data in communication research. *Journal of Communication, 20*(3), 241–269.

Krippendorff, Klaus. (1971). Reliability of recording instructions: Multivariate agreement for nominal data. *Behavioral Science, 16,* 222–235.

Krippendorff, Klaus. (1978). Reliability of binary attribute data. *Biometrics, 34,* 142–144.

Krippendorff, Klaus. (1980a). Clustering. In Peter R. Monge & Joseph N. Cappella (Eds.), *Multivariate techniques in communication research* (pp. 259–308). New York: Academic Press.

Krippendorff, Klaus. (1980b). *Content analysis: An introduction to its methodology.* Beverly Hills, CA: Sage.

Krippendorff, Klaus. (1986). *Information theory: Structural models for qualitative data.* Beverly Hills, CA: Sage.

Krippendorff, Klaus. (1987). Association, agreement and equity. *Quality and Quantity, 21,* 109–123.

Krippendorff, Klaus. (1991). Reconstructing (some) communication research methods. In Frederick Steier (Ed.), *Research and reflexivity* (pp. 115–142). Newbury Park, CA: Sage.

Krippendorff, Klaus. (1992, May). *Recent developments in reliability analysis.* Paper presented at the 42nd Annual Meeting of the International Communication Association, Miami, FL.

Krippendorff, Klaus. (1993). The past of communication's hoped-for future. *Journal of Communication, 43*(3), 34–44.

Krippendorff, Klaus. (1995a). On the Reliability of Unitizing Continuous Data. Chapter 2, pages 47–76 in Peter V. Marsden (Ed.). *Sociological Methodology, 1995,* Vol. 25. Cambridge, MA: Blackwell.

Krippendorff, Klaus. (1995b). Undoing power. *Critical Studies in Mass Communication, 12,* 101–132.

Krippendorff, Klaus. (1999, June). *Writing: Monologue, dialogue, and ecological narrative.* Paper presented at the 4th National Writing Across the Curriculum Conference, Ithaca, NY.

Krippendorff, Klaus. (in press-a). Measuring the reliability of qualitative text analysis data. *Quality and Quantity.*

Krippendorff, Klaus. (in press-b). Reliability in content analysis: Alternative recommendations. *Human Communication Research.*

Krippendorff, Klaus. (in press-c). The social reality of meaning. *American Journal of SEMIOTICS, 19*(1).

Krippendorff, Klaus, & Eleey, Michael. (1986). Monitoring the symbolic environment of organizations. *Public Relations Review, 12*(1), 13–36.

Kuder, G. F., & Richardson, M. W. (1937). The theory of the estimation of test reliability. *Psychometrika 2*(3), 151–160.

Kuhn, Deanna. (1991). *The skills of argument.* New York: Cambridge University Press.

Labov, William. (1972). *Sociolinguistic patterns.* Philadelphia: University of Pennsylvania Press.

Laffal, Julius. (1993). *A concept dictionary of English.* Essex, CT: Galley.

Landis, H. H., & Burtt, Harold E. (1924). A study of conversations. *Journal of Comparative Psychology, 4,* 81–89.

Landis, J. Richard, & Koch, Gary H. (1977). An application of hierarchical kappa-type statistics in the assessment of majority agreement among multiple observers. *Biometrics, 33,* 363–374.

Lashner, Marilyn A. (1990). Content analysis: A method for analyzing communications. *The Expert and the Law, 10*(1), 2–5.

Lasswell, Harold D. (1927). *Propaganda technique in the world war.* New York: Knopf.

Lasswell, Harold D. (1938). A provisional classification of symbol data. *Psychiatry, 1,* 197–204.

Lasswell, Harold D. (1941). The World Attention Survey: An exploration of the possibilities of studying attention being given to the United States by newspapers abroad. *Public Opinion Quarterly, 5,* 456–462.

Lasswell, Harold D. (1960). The structure and function of communication in society. In Wilbur Schramm (Ed.), *Mass communications* (pp. 117–130). Urbana: University of Illinois Press.

Lasswell, Harold D. (1963). *Politics: Who gets what, when, how.* New York: Meridian.

Lasswell, Harold D. (1965a). Detection: Propaganda detection and the courts. In Harold D. Lasswell, Nathan Leites, & Associates (Eds.), *Language of politics: Studies in quantitative semantics* (pp. 173–232). Cambridge: MIT Press.

Lasswell, Harold D. (1965b). Why be quantitative? In Harold D. Lasswell, Nathan Leites, & Associates (Eds.), *Language of politics: Studies in quantitative semantics* (pp. 40–52). Cambridge: MIT Press. (Original work published 1949)

Lasswell, Harold D., & Kaplan, Abraham. (1950). *Power and society: A framework for political inquiry.* New Haven, CT: Yale University Press.

Lasswell, Harold D., Leites, Nathan, & Associates. (Eds.). (1965). *Language of politics: Studies in quantitative semantics.* Cambridge: MIT Press.

Lasswell, Harold D., Lerner, Daniel, & Pool, Ithiel de Sola. (1952). *The comparative study of symbols.* Stanford, CA: Stanford University Press.

Latour, Bruno, & Woolgar, Steve. (1986). *Laboratory life: The construction of scientific facts.* Princeton, NJ: Princeton University Press.

Lazarsfeld, Paul F., Berelson, Bernard, & Gaudet, Hazel. (1948). *The people's choice: How the voter makes up his mind in a presidential campaign.* New York: Columbia University Press.

Lee, Chin-Chuan, Chan, Joseph Man, Pan, Zhongdang, & So, Clement Y. K. (2002). *Global media spectacle: News war over Hong Kong.* Albany: State University of New York Press.

Leites, Nathan, Bernaut, Elsa, & Garthoff, Raymond L. (1951). Politburo images of Stalin. *World Politics, 3,* 317–339.

Leites, Nathan, & Pool, Ithiel de Sola. (1942). *Communist propaganda in reaction to frustration* (Document No. 27). Washington DC: Library of Congress, Experimental Division for Study of Wartime Communications.

Lindsay, Robert K. (1963). Inferential memory as the basis of machines which understand natural language. In Edward A. Feigenbaum & Julian Feldman (Eds.), *Computers and thought* (pp. 217–233). New York: McGraw-Hill.

Lippmann, Walter. (1922). *Public opinion.* New York: Macmillan.

Löbl, Eugen. (1903). *Kultur und Presse.* Leipzig, Germany: Duncker & Humblot.

Loeventhal, Leo. (1944). Biographies in popular magazines. In Paul F. Lazarsfeld & Frank N. Stanton (Eds.), *Radio research 1942–1943* (pp. 507–548). New York: Duell, Sloan & Pearce.

Lombard, Matthew, Snyder-Duch, Jennifer, & Bracken, Cheryl Campanella. (2002). Content analysis in mass communication research: An assessment and reporting of intercoder reliability. *Human Communication Research, 28,* 587–604.

Lorr, Maurice, & McNair, Douglas M. (1966). Methods relating to evaluation of therapeutic outcome. In Louis A. Gottschalk & Arthur H. Auerbach (Eds.), *Methods of research in psychotherapy* (pp. 573–594). Englewood Cliffs, NJ: Prentice Hall.

Lynch, Kevin. (1965). *The image of the city.* Cambridge: MIT Press.

Maccoby, Nathan, Sabghir, F. O., & Cushing, B. (1950). A method for the analysis of news coverage of industry. *Public Opinion Quarterly, 14,* 753–758.

Mahl, George F. (1959). Exploring emotional states by content analysis. In Ithiel de Sola Pool (Ed.), *Trends in content analysis* (pp. 89–130). Urbana: University of Illinois Press.

Mann, Mary B. (1944). Studies in language behavior: III. The quantitative differentiation of samples of written language. *Psychological Monographs, 56*(2), 41–47.

Markov, Andrei A. (1913). Essai d'une recherche statistique sur le texte du roman *"Eugene Onegin"* illustrant la liaison des epreuves en chaine (Russian). *Bulletin de L'Académie Impériale des Sciences de St. Pétersbourg 6*(7), 153–162.

Martin, Helen. (1936). Nationalism and children's literature. *Library Quarterly, 6,* 405–418.

Martindale, Colin. (1990). *The clockwork muse: The predictability of artistic change.* New York: Basic Books.

Maruyama, Margoroh. (1963). The second cybernetics: Deviation-amplifying mutual causal processes. *American Scientist, 51,* 164–179.

Mathews, Byron C. (1910). A study of a New York daily. *Independent, 68,* 82–86.

Maxwell, A. E. (1970). Comparing the classification of subjects by two independent judges. *British Journal of Psychiatry, 116,* 651–655.

McClelland, David C. (1958). The use of measures of human motivation in the study of society. In John W. Atkinson (Ed.), *Motives in fantasy, action and society* (pp. 518–552). Princeton, NJ: D. Van Nostrand.

McClelland, David C., Atkinson, John W., Clark, Russell A., & Lowell, Edgar L. (1992). A scoring manual for the achievement motive. In Charles P. Smith (Ed.), *Motivation and personality: Handbook of thematic content analysis* (pp. 153–178). Cambridge: Cambridge University Press.

McCombs, Maxwell, & Shaw, Donald L. (1972). The agenda-setting function of mass media. *Public Opinion Quarterly, 36,* 176–187.

McCombs, Maxwell, Shaw, Donald L., & Weaver, David. (1997). *Communication and democracy: Exploring the intellectual frontiers in agenda-setting theory.* Mahwah, NJ: Lawrence Erlbaum.

McDiarmid, John. (1937). Presidential inaugural addresses: A study in verbal symbols. *Public Opinion Quarterly, 1,* 79–82.

McKnight, Katherine S., & Walberg, Herbert J. (1994). Neural network analysis of student essays. *Journal of Research and Development in Education, 32,* 26–31.

McTavish, Donald D., Litkowski, Kenneth C., & Schrader, Susan. (1997). A computer content analysis approach to measuring social distance in residential organizations for older people. *Social Science Computer Review, 15,* 170–180.

McTavish, Donald D., & Pirro, Ellen B. (1990). Contextual content analysis. *Quality and Quantity, 24,* 245–265.

Merrill, John C. (1962). The image of the United States in ten Mexican dailies. *Journalism Quarterly, 39,* 203–209.

Merritt, Richard L. (1966). *Symbols of American community, 1735–1775.* New Haven, CT: Yale University Press.

Merten, Klaus. (1991). *Inhaltsanalyse: Eine Einführung in Theorie, Methode und Praxis.* Opladen, Germany: Westdeutscher Verlag.

Miles, Josephine. (1951). The continuity of English poetic language. In *University of California publications in English* (pp. 517–535). Berkeley: University of California Press.

Miller, George A. (1951). *Language and communication.* New York: McGraw-Hill.

Miller, George A., Beckwith, Richard, Fellbaum, Christiane, Gross, Derek, Miller, Katherine J., & Tengi, Randee I. (1993). *Five papers on WordNet* (CSL Report 43). Princeton, NJ: Princeton University, Cognitive Science Laboratory.

Miller, Kevin J., Fullmer, Steven L., & Walls, Richard T. (1996). A dozen years of mainstreaming literature: A content analysis. *Exceptionality, 6*(2), 99–109.

Monge, Peter R., & Eisenberg, Erik M. (1987). Emergent communication networks. In Fredric M. Jablin, Linda L. Putnam, Karlene H. Roberts, & Lyman W. Porter (Eds.), *Handbook of organizational and management communication* (pp. 204–242). Newbury Park, CA: Sage.

Montgomery, Michael. (1989). *Protocol for using LAGS CodeMap and LagsMap microcomputer programs: CodeMap for a lexical item.* Retrieved July 3, 2003, from http://hyde.park.uga.edu/lags/protocol.txt

Morton, Andrew Q. (1963, November 3). A computer challenges the church. *Observer.*

Morton, Andrew Q., & Levinson, Michael. (1966). Some indications of authorship in green prose. In Jacob Leed (Ed.), *The computer and literary style* (pp. 141–179). Kent, OH: Kent State University Press.

Mosteller, Frederick, & Wallace, David L. (1963). Inference in an authorship problem. *Journal of the American Statistical Association, 58,* 275–309.

Mosteller, Frederick, & Wallace, David L. (1964). *Inference and disputed authorship: The Federalist.* Reading, MA: Addison-Wesley.

Murray, Edward J., Auld, Frank, Jr., & White, Alice M. (1954). A psychotherapy case showing progress but no decrease in the discomfort-relief quotient. *Journal of Consulting Psychology, 18,* 349–353.

Murray, Henry A. (1943). *Thematic Apperception Test manual.* Cambridge, MA: Harvard University Press.

Nacos, Brigitte L., Shapiro, Robert Y., Young, John T., Fan, David P., Kjellstrand, Torsten, & McCaa, Craig. (1991). Content analysis of news reports: Comparing human coding and a computer-assisted method. *Communication, 12,* 111–128.

Namenwirth, J. Zvi. (1973). Wheels of time and the interdependence of value change in America. *Journal of Interdisciplinary History, 3,* 649–683.

Namenwirth, J. Zvi, & Weber, Robert P. (1987). *Dynamics of culture*. Boston: Allen & Unwin.

Neuendorf, Kimberly A. (2002). *The content analysis guidebook*. Thousand Oaks, CA: Sage.

Newell, Allen, & Simon, Herbert A. (1956). The logic theory machine. *IRE-Transactions on Information Theory 2*(3), 61–79.

Newell, Allen, & Simon, Herbert A. (1963). General Problem Solver: A program that simulates human thought. In Edward A. Feigenbaum & Julian Feldman (Eds.), *Computers and thought* (pp. 279–293). New York: McGraw-Hill.

Nixon, Raymond B., & Jones, Robert L. (1956). The content of non-competitive newspapers. *Journalism Quarterly, 33,* 299–314.

North, Robert C., Holsti, Ole R., Zaninovich, M. George, & Zinnes, Dina A. (1963). *Content analysis: A handbook with applications for the study of international crisis*. Evanston, IL: Northwestern University Press.

Ogden, Charles Kay. (1937). *Basic English and grammatical reform*. Cambridge: Orthological Institute.

Osgood, Charles E. (1959). The representation model and relevant research methods. In Ithiel de Sola Pool (Ed.), *Trends in content analysis* (pp. 33–88). Urbana: University of Illinois Press.

Osgood, Charles E. (1974a). Probing subjective culture: Part 1. Cross-linguistic toolmaking. *Journal of Communication, 24*(1), 21–35.

Osgood, Charles E. (1974b). Probing subjective culture: Part 2. Cross-cultural tool using. *Journal of Communication, 24*(2), 82–100.

Osgood, Charles E., Saporta, Sol, & Nunnally, Jum C. (1956). Evaluative assertion analysis. *Litera, 3,* 47–102.

Osgood, Charles E., Suci, George J., & Tannenbaum, Percy H. (1957). *The measurement of meaning*. Urbana: University of Illinois Press.

O'Sullivan, Thomas C., Jr. (1961). *Factor analysis concepts identified in theoretical writings: An experiment design*. Lexington, MA: Itek Laboratories.

Paisley, William J. (1964). Identifying the unknown communicator in painting, literature and music: The significance of minor encoding habits. *Journal of Communication, 14*(4), 219–237.

Palmquist, Michael E., Carley, Kathleen M., & Dale, Thomas A. (1997). Applications of computer-aided text analysis: Analyzing literary and nonliterary texts. In Carl W. Roberts (Ed.), *Text analysis for the social sciences: Methods for drawing statistical inferences from texts and transcripts* (pp. 171–189). Mahwah, NJ: Lawrence Erlbaum.

Parsons, Talcott. (1951). *The social system*. New York: Free Press.

Parsons, Talcott, & Bales, Robert F. (1953). The dimensions of action-space. In Talcott Parsons, Robert F. Bales, & Edward A. Shills (Eds.), *Working papers in the theory of action* (pp. 63–109). New York: Free Press.

Patterson, Brian R., Neupauer, Nichola C., Burant, Patricia A., Koehn, Steven C., & Reed, April T. (1996). A preliminary examination of conversation analytic techniques: Rates of inter-transcriber reliability. *Western Journal of Communication, 60,* 76–91.

Pearson, Karl, et al. (1901). Mathematical contributions to the theory of evolution: IX. On the principle of homotyposis and its relation to heredity, to variability of the individual, and to that of race. Part I: Homotyposis in the vegetable kingdom. *Philosophical Transactions of the Royal Society, 197*(Series A), 285–379.

Pederson, Lee, McDaniel, Susan Leas, Adams, Carol, & Liao, Caisheng. (Eds.). (1989). *Linguistic atlas of the Gulf states: Vol. 3. Technical index.* Athens: University of Georgia Press.

Péladeau, Normand. (1996). *SimStat for Windows: User's guide.* Montreal: Provalis Research.

Péladeau, Normand. (2003, September 2). [Personal communication.]

Pennebaker, James W. (1997). Writing about emotional experiences as a therapeutic process. *Psychological Science, 8,* 162–166.

Pennebaker, James W., Francis, Martha E., & Booth, Roger J. (2001). *Linguistic Inquiry and Word Count (LIWC)* (2nd ed., PDF manual). Mahwah, NJ: Lawrence Erlbaum.

Pennebaker, James W., & Stone, Lori D. (2001, May). *LIWC 2001.* Contribution to a CATA workshop presented at the 51st Annual Meeting of the International Communication Association, Washington, DC.

Pennings, Paul, & Keman, Hans. (2002). Towards a new methodology of estimating party policy positions. *Quality and Quantity, 36,* 55–79.

Perreault, William D., & Leigh, Lawrence E. (1989). Reliability of nominal data based on qualitative judgements. *Journal of Marketing Research, 26,* 135–148.

Pescosolido, Bernice A., Grauerholz, Elisabeth, & Milkie, Melissa A. (1996). Culture and conflict: The portrayal of blacks in U.S. children's picture books through the mid- and late twentieth century. *American Sociological Review, 62,* 443–464.

Peter, Jochen, & Lauf, Edmund. (2002). Reliability in cross-national content analysis. *Journalism & Mass Communication Quarterly, 79,* 815–832.

Phillips, David P. (1978). Airplane accident fatalities increase just after newspaper stories about murder and suicide. *Science, 201,* 748–749.

Piault, Collette. (1965). A methodological investigation of content analysis using electronic computers for data processing. In Dell Hymes (Ed.), *The use of computers in anthropology* (pp. 273–293). The Hague: Mouton.

Pierce, Bessie L. (1930). *Civic attitudes in American school textbooks.* Chicago: University of Chicago Press.

Ploughman, Penelope. (1995). The American print news media "construction" of five natural disasters. *Disasters, 19,* 308–326.

Pocklington, Richard, & Best, Michael L. (1997). Cultural evolution and units of selection in replicating text. *Journal of Theoretical Biology, 188,* 79–87.

Pool, Ithiel de Sola. (1951). *Symbols of internationalism.* Stanford, CA: Stanford University Press.

Pool, Ithiel de Sola. (1952a). *The prestige papers: A survey of their editorials.* Stanford, CA: Stanford University Press.

Pool, Ithiel de Sola. (1952b). *Symbols of democracy.* Stanford, CA: Stanford University Press.

Pool, Ithiel de Sola. (Ed.). (1959a). *Trends in content analysis.* Urbana: University of Illinois Press.

Pool, Ithiel de Sola. (1959b). Trends in content analysis today: A summary. In Ithiel de Sola Pool (Ed.), *Trends in content analysis* (pp. 189–233). Urbana: University of Illinois Press.

Pool, Ithiel de Sola, Abelson, Robert P., & Popkin, Samuel L. (1964). *Candidates, issues and strategies: A computer simulation of the 1960 presidential election.* Cambridge: MIT Press.

Popping, Roel. (1988). On agreement indices for nominal data. In William E. Saris & Irmtraut N. Gallhofer (Eds.), *Sociometric research: Data collection and scaling* (Vol. 1, pp. 90–105). New York: St. Martin's.

Popping, Roel. (1997). Computer programs for the analysis of texts and transcripts. In Carl W. Roberts (Ed.), *Text analysis for the social sciences: Methods for drawing statistical inferences from texts and transcripts* (pp. 209–221). Mahwah, NJ: Lawrence Erlbaum.

Popping, Roel. (2000). *Computer-assisted text analysis.* London: Sage.

Posen, Solomon. (1997). The portrayal of the doctor in non-medical literature: The impaired doctor. *Medical Journal of Australia, 166,* 48–51.

Potter, W. James, & Levine-Donnerstein, Deborah. (1999). Rethinking reliability and reliability in content analysis. *Journal of Applied Communication Research, 27,* 258–284.

Potter, W. James, & Vaughan, Misha. (1997). Antisocial behaviors in television entertainment: Trends and profiles. *Communication Research Reports, 14*(1), 116–124.

Quillian, M. Ross. (1968). Semantic memory. In Marvin L. Minsky (Ed.), *Semantic information processing* (pp. 216–270). Cambridge: MIT Press.

Rainoff, T. J. (1929). Wave-like fluctuations of creative productivity in the development of West-European physics in the eighteenth and nineteenth centuries. *Isis, 12,* 287–307.

Rapoport, Anatol. (1969). A system-theoretic view of content analysis. In George Gerbner, Ole R. Holsti, Klaus Krippendorff, William J. Paisley, & Philip J. Stone (Eds.), *The analysis of communication content: Developments in scientific theories and computer techniques* (pp. 17–38). New York: John Wiley.

Reynolds, Henry T. (1977). *Analysis of nominal data.* Beverly Hills, CA: Sage.

Rice, Ronald E. (1990). Hierarchies and clusters in communication and library and information science journals, 1978–1987. In Christine Borgman (Ed.), *Scholarly communication and bibliometrics* (pp. 138–153). Newbury Park, CA: Sage.

Rice, Ronald E., Borman, Christine L., & Reeves, Bryan. (1988). Citation networks of communication journals, 1977–1985. *Human Communication Research, 15,* 256–283.

Rice, Ronald E., & Richards, William D., Jr. (1985). An overview of network analysis methods and programs. In Brenda Dervin & Melvin J. Voigt (Eds.), *Progress in communication sciences* (Vol. 6, pp. 105-165). Norwood, NJ: Ablex.

Richards, William D., Jr., & Rice, Ronald E. (1981). NEGOPY network analysis program. *Social Networks, 3,* 215–223.

Riffe, Daniel, & Freitag, Alan. (1996). *Twenty-five years of content analyses in* Journalism & Mass Communication Quarterly. Paper presented at the annual meeting of the Association for Education in Journalism and Mass Communication, Anaheim, CA.

Riffe, Daniel, Lacy, Stephen, & Fico, Frederick G. (1998). *Analyzing media messages: Using quantitative content analysis in research*. Mahwah, NJ: Lawrence Erlbaum.

Rijsbergen, Cornelis J. (1979). *Information retrieval*. London: Butterworth.

Roberts, Carl W. (1989). Other than counting words: A linguistic approach to content analysis. *Social Forces, 68,* 147–177.

Roberts, Carl W. (Ed.). (1997). *Text analysis for the social sciences: Methods for drawing statistical inferences from texts and transcripts*. Mahwah, NJ: Lawrence Erlbaum.

Rogers, Everett M., & Kincaid, D. Lawrence. (1981). *Communication networks: Toward a new paradigm for research*. New York: Free Press.

Rogers, Everett M., & Shoemaker, Floyd F. (1971). *Communication of innovations*. New York: Free Press.

Romme, A. Georges L. (1995). Boolean comparative analysis of qualitative data. *Quality and Quantity, 29,* 317–329.

Rosenberg, Stanley D., Schnurr, Paula P., & Oxman, Thomas E. (1990). Content analysis: A comparison of manual and computerized systems. *Journal of Personality Assessment, 54,* 298–310.

Ruesch, Jürgen, & Bateson, Gregory. (1951). *Communication: The social matrix of psychiatry*. New York: W. W. Norton.

Sacks, Harvey. (1974). An analysis of the course of a joke's telling in conversation. In Joel Sherzer & Richard Bauman (Eds.), *Explorations in the ethnography of speaking* (pp. 337–353). London: Cambridge University Press.

Salgado, Jesus F., & Moscoso, Silvia. (1996). Meta-analysis of interrater reliability of job performance ratings in validity studies of personnel selection. *Perceptual and Motor Skills, 83,* 1195–1201.

Salmond, Ann. (1982). Theoretical landscapes. In David Parkin (Ed.), *Semantic anthropology* (pp. 65–87). New York: Academic Press.

Samarel, Nelda, Fawcett, Jacqueline, Krippendorff, Klaus, Piacentino, Jayne C., Eliasof, Barbara, Hughes, Phyllis, et al. (1998). Women's perceptions of group support and adaptation to breast cancer. *Journal of Advanced Nursing, 28,* 1259–1268.

Saris-Gallhofer, Irmtraut N., & Morton, E. L. (1978). A validity study of Holsti's content analysis procedure. *Quality and Quantity, 12,* 131–145.

Schank, Roger C., & Abelson, Robert P. (1977). *Scripts, plans, goals and understanding: An inquiry into human knowledge structures*. Hillsdale, NJ: Lawrence Erlbaum.

Schnurr, Paula P., Rosenberg, Stanley D., & Oxman, Thomas E. (1992). Comparison of TAT and free speech techniques for eliciting source materials in computerized content analysis. *Journal of Personality Assessment, 58,* 311–325.

Schnurr, Paula P., Rosenberg, Stanley D., & Oxman, Thomas E. (1993). Issues in the comparison of techniques for eliciting source material in computerized content analysis. *Journal of Personality Assessment, 61,* 337–342.

Schrodt, Philip A., Davis, Shannon G., & Weddle, Judith L. (1994). KEDS: A program for the machine coding of event data. *Social Science Computer Review, 12,* 561–588.

Schutz, William C. (1958). On categorizing qualitative data in content analysis. *Public Opinion Quarterly, 22,* 503–515.

Scott, William A. (1955). Reliability of content analysis: The case of nominal scale coding. *Public Opinion Quarterly, 19,* 321–325.

Searle, John. (1969). *Speech acts: An essay in the philosophy of language*. Cambridge: Cambridge University Press.

Sebeok, Thomas A., & Orzack, Louis H. (1953). The structure and content of Cheremis charms. *Anthropos, 48*, 369–388.

Sebeok, Thomas A., & Zeps, Valdis J. (1958). An analysis of structured content with application of electronic computer research in psycholinguistics. *Language and Speech, 1*, 181–193.

Sedelow, Sally Y. (1967). *Stylistic analysis*. Santa Monica, CA: SDC.

Sedelow, Sally Y. (1989). *The interlingual thesaurus model for global technical communication: Research results*. (ERIC Document Reproduction Service No. ED324936).

Sedelow, Sally Y., & Sedelow, Walter A., Jr. (1986). Thesaural knowledge representation. In *Advances in lexicology: Proceedings of the Second Annual Conference of the UW Centre for the New Oxford English Dictionary* (pp. 29–43). Waterloo, ON: UW Centre for the New Oxford English Dictionary.

Sedelow, Sally Y., & Sedelow, Walter A., Jr. (1966). A preface to computational stylistics. In Jacob Leed (Ed.), *The computer and literary style*. Kent, OH: Kent State University Press.

Selltiz, Claire, Jahoda, Marie, Deutsch, Morton, & Cook, Stuart W. (1964). *Research methods in social relations*. New York: Holt, Rinehart & Winston.

Shanas, Ethel. (1945). *The American Journal of Sociology* through fifty years. *American Journal of Sociology, 50*, 522–533.

Shannon, Claude E., & Weaver, Warren. (1949). *The mathematical theory of communication*. Urbana: University of Illinois Press.

Shapiro, Gilbert. (1997). The future of coders: Human judgments in a world of sophisticated software. In Carl W. Roberts (Ed.), *Text analysis for the social sciences: Methods for drawing statistical inferences from texts and transcripts* (pp. 225–238). Mahwah, NJ: Lawrence Erlbaum.

Shapiro, Gilbert, & Markoff, John. (1997). A matter of definition. In Carl W. Roberts (Ed.), *Text analysis for the social sciences: Methods for drawing statistical inferences from texts and transcripts* (pp. 9–31). Mahwah, NJ: Lawrence Erlbaum.

Shneidman, Edwin S. (1963). The logic of politics. In Leon Arons & Mark A. May (Eds.), *Television and human behavior* (pp. 178–199). Englewood Cliffs, NJ: Prentice Hall.

Shneidman, Edwin S. (1966). *The logics of communication: A manual for analysis*. China Lake, CA: U.S. Naval Ordnance Test Station.

Shneidman, Edwin S. (1969). Logical content analysis: An exploration of styles of concludifying. In George Gerbner, Ole R. Holsti, Klaus Krippendorff, William J. Paisley, & Philip J. Stone (Eds.), *The analysis of communication content: Developments in scientific theories and computer techniques* (pp. 261–279). New York: John Wiley.

Shuman, Ronald B. (1937). Identification elements of advertising slogans. *Southwestern Social Science Quarterly, 17*, 342–352.

Siegel, Sydney, & Castellan, N. John. (1988). *Nonparametric statistics for the behavioral sciences* (2nd ed.). Boston: McGraw-Hill.

Simon, Herbert A. (1957). *Models of man*. New York: John Wiley.

Simonton, Dean K. (1994). Computer content analysis of melodic structure: Classical composers and their compositions. *Psychology of Music, 22*, 31–43.

Simpson, George E. (1934). *The Negro in the Philadelphia press*. Unpublished doctoral dissertation, University of Pennsylvania.

Singer, J. David. (1964). Soviet and American foreign policy attitudes: A content analysis of elite articulations. *Journal of Conflict Resolution, 8*, 424–485.

Skalski, Paul D. (2002). Message archives. In Kimberly A. Neuendorf, *The content analysis guidebook* (pp. 215–218). Thousand Oaks, CA: Sage.

Smith, Charles P. (1992a). Introduction: Inferences from verbal material. In Charles P. Smith (Ed.), *Motivation and personality: Handbook of thematic content analysis*. (pp. 1–17). Cambridge: Cambridge University Press.

Smith, Charles P. (Ed.). (1992b). *Motivation and personality: Handbook of thematic content analysis*. Cambridge: Cambridge University Press.

Smythe, Dallas W. (1954). Some observations on communications theory. *Audio-Visual Communication Review, 2*, 248–260.

So, Clement Y. K. (1988). Citation patterns of core communication journals. *Human Communication Research, 15*, 236–255.

So, Clement Y. K. (1995). *Mapping the intellectual landscape of communication studies: An evaluation of its disciplinary status*. Unpublished doctoral dissertation, University of Pennsylvania, Annenberg School for Communication.

Speed, Gilmer J. (1893). Do newspapers now give the news? *Forum, 15*, 705–711.

Spiegelman, Marvin, Terwilliger, Charles, & Fearing, Franklin. (1953a). The content of comics: Goals and means to goals of comic strip characters. *Journal of Social Psychology, 37*, 189–203.

Spiegelman, Marvin, Terwilliger, Charles, & Fearing, Franklin. (1953b). The reliability of agreement in content analysis. *Journal of Social Psychology, 37*, 175–187.

Stempel, Guido H., III. (1952). Sample size for classifying subject matter in dailies: Research in brief. *Journalism Quarterly, 29*, 333–334.

Stempel, Guido H., III. (1961). The prestige press covers the 1960 presidential campaign. *Journalism Quarterly, 38*, 157–170.

Stevens, Stanley S. (1946). On the theory of scales of measurement. *Science, 103*, 677–680.

Stone, Philip J. (1975). Report on the Workshop on Content Analysis in the Social Sciences, Pisa, 1974. *Social Science Information, 14*, 107–111.

Stone, Philip J., & Hunt, Earl B. (1963). A computer approach to content analysis using the General Inquirer system. In E. C. Johnson (Ed.), *American Federation of Information Processing Societies, conference proceedings* (pp. 241–256). Baltimore: American Federation of Information Processing Societies.

Stone, Philip J., Dunphy, Dexter C., Smith, Marshall S., & Ogilvie, Daniel M. (1966). *The General Inquirer: A computer approach to content analysis*. Cambridge: MIT Press.

Street, Arthur T. (1909, July 25). The truth about newspapers. *Chicago Tribune*.

Strodthoff, Glenn G., Hawkins, Robert P., & Schoenfeld, A. Clay. (1985). Media roles in a social movement: A model of ideology diffusion. *Journal of Communication, 35*(2), 134–153.

Sullivan, Dan. (2001). *Document warehousing and text mining*. New York: John Wiley.

Szykiersky, Dorit, & Raviv, Amiram. (1995). The image of the psychotherapist in literature. *American Journal of Psychotherapy, 49*, 405–415.

Tannenbaum, Percy H., & Greenberg, Bradley S. (1961). *J. Q.* references: A study of professional change. *Journalism Quarterly, 38,* 203–207.

Taylor, Wilson L. (1953). "Cloze procedure": A new tool for measuring readability. *Journalism Quarterly, 30,* 415–433.

ten Have, Paul. (1999). *Doing conversation analysis: A practical guide.* Thousand Oaks, CA: Sage.

Tenney, Alvan A. (1912). The scientific analysis of the press. *Independent, 73,* 895–898.

Tesch, Renata. (1990). *Qualitative research: Analysis types and software tools.* Bristol, PA: Falmer.

Thome, Helmut, & Rahlf, Thomas. (1996). Dubious cycles: A mathematical critique of the Namenwirth/Weber thesis on cultural change with an introduction into filter design methods. *Quality and Quantity, 30,* 427–448.

Thompson, Stith. (1932). *Motif-index of folk literature: A classification of narrative elements in folk-tales, ballads, myths, fables, mediaeval romances, exempla, fabliaux, jest-books, and local legends.* Bloomington: Indiana University Studies.

Tijssen, Robert J. W., & Van Raan, Anthony F. J. (1994). Mapping changes in science and technology: Bibliometric co-occurrences analysis of the R&D literature. *Evaluation Review, 18,* 98–115.

Toulmin, Stephen E. (1958). *The uses of argument.* Cambridge: Cambridge University Press.

Treichler, Paula A. (1988). Aids, homophobia, and biomedical discourse: An epidemic of signification. In Douglas Crimp (Ed.), *Aids, cultural analysis, cultural activism* (pp. 31–70). Cambridge: MIT Press.

Truzzi, Marcello. (1988). Sherlock Holmes, applied social psychologist. In Umberto Eco & Thomas A. Sebeok (Eds.), *The sign of three: Dupin, Holmes, Peirce* (pp. 55–80). Bloomington: Indiana University Press.

Tuggle, C. A. (1997). Differences in television sports reporting of men's and women's athletics: ESPN *SportsCenter* and CNN *Sports Tonight. Journal of Broadcasting & Electronic Media, 41,* 14–24.

Tukey, John W. (1980). Methodological comments focused on opportunities. In Peter R. Monge & Joseph N. Cappella (Eds.), *Multivariate techniques in human communication research* (pp. 489–528). New York: Academic Press.

Turow, Joseph. (1989). *Playing doctor: Television, storytelling, and medical power.* New York: Oxford University Press.

Valente, Thames W. (1993). Diffusion of innovations and policy decision-making. *Journal of Communication, 43*(1), 30–45.

Van Dijk, Teun A. (1977). *Text and context: Explorations in the semantics and pragmatics of discourse.* New York: Longman.

Van Dijk, Teun A. (1991). *Racism and the press.* New York: Routledge.

Van Dijk, Teun A. (1993). Principles of critical discourse analysis. *Discourse & Society, 4,* 249–283.

Wallace, Anthony F. C. (1961). *Culture and personality.* New York: Random House.

Walworth, Arthur. (1938). *School histories at war: A study of the treatment of our wars in the secondary school history books of the United States and in those of its former enemies.* Cambridge, MA: Harvard University Press.

Waples, Douglas, & Berelson, Bernard. (1941). *What the voters were told: An essay in content analysis.* Unpublished manuscript, University of Chicago, Graduate Library School.

Watzlawick, Paul, Beavin, Janet H., & Jackson, Don D. (1967). *Pragmatics of human communication: A study of interaction patterns, pathologies, and paradoxes.* New York: W. W. Norton.

Weaver, Donald H., Buddenbaum, Judith M., & Fair, Jo Ellen. (1985). Press freedom, media, and development, 1950–1979: A study of 134 nations. *Journal of Communication, 35*(2), 104–117.

Webb, Eugene J., Campbell, Donald T., Schwartz, Richard D., & Sechrest, Lee. (1966). *Unobtrusive measures: Nonreactive research in the social sciences.* Chicago: Rand McNally.

Weber, Max. (1911). "Geschäftsbericht" in Verhandlungen des Ersten Deutschen Soziologietages Vom 19.-22. Oktober 1910 in Frankfurt A. M. In *Schrift der Deutschen Gesellschaft für Soziologie* (pp. 39–62).

Weber, Robert P. (1984). Computer-generated content analysis: A short primer. *Qualitative Sociology, 7,* 126–174.

Weber, Robert P. (1990). *Basic content analysis* (2nd ed.). Newbury Park, CA: Sage.

Weick, Karl E. (1968). Systematic observational methods. In Gardner Lindzey & Elliot Aronson (Eds.), *The handbook of social psychology* (pp. 357–451). Reading, MA: Addison-Wesley.

Weitzman, Eben A., & Miles, Matthew B. (1995). *Computer programs for qualitative data analysis: A software sourcebook.* Thousand Oaks, CA: Sage.

Wellman, Barry, & Berkowitz, Stephen D. (Eds.). (1988). *Social structures: A network approach.* Cambridge: Cambridge University Press.

Wells, Robert A., & King, Erika G. (1994). Prestige newspaper coverage of foreign affairs in the 1990 congressional campaign. *Journalism Quarterly, 71,* 652–664.

White, David M. (1964). The "gatekeeper": A case study in selection of news. In Lewis A. Dexter & David M. White (Eds.), *People, society and mass communication* (pp. 160–172). New York: Free Press.

White, Paul W. (1924, May 31). Quarter century survey of press content shows demand for facts. *Editor and Publisher, 57.*

White, Ralph K. (1947). *Black Boy:* A value analysis. *Journal of Abnormal and Social Psychology, 42,* 440–461.

Wilcox, Dennis F. (1900). The American newspaper: A study in social psychology. *Annals of American Academy of Political and Social Science, 16,* 56–92.

Willey, Malcolm M. (1926). *The country newspaper: A study of socialization and newspaper content.* Chapel Hill: University of North Carolina Press.

Winograd, Terry, & Flores, Fernando. (1986). *Understanding computers and cognition: A new foundation for design.* Norwood, NJ: Ablex.

Woelfel, Joseph. (1993). Artificial neural networks for policy research. *Journal of Communication, 43*(1), 63–80.

Woelfel, Joseph. (1997). Attitudes as nonhierarchical clusters in neural networks. In George A. Barnett & Franklin J. Boster (Eds.), *Progress in communication sciences* (Vol. 13, pp. 213–227). Norwood, NJ: Ablex.

Woelfel, Joseph, & Fink, Edward L. (1980). *The measurement of communication processes: Galileo theory and method.* New York: Academic Press.

Wonsek, Pamela. (1992). College basketball on television: A study of racism in the media. *Media, Culture, and Society, 14,* 449–461.

Woodward, Julian L. (1934). Quantitative newspaper analysis as a technique of opinion research. *Social Forces, 12,* 526–537.

Wray, Ricardo, & Hornik, Robert C. (1998, July). *Validation of on-line searches of media coverage: An evaluation approach.* Paper presented at the 48th Annual Meeting of the International Communication Association, Jerusalem.

Wright, Charles E. (1964). Functional analysis and mass communication. In Lewis A. Dexter & David M. White (Eds.), *People, society, and mass communication* (pp. 91–109). New York: Free Press.

Yule, George U. (1944). *The statistical study of literary vocabulary.* London: Cambridge University Press.

Zeldow, Peter B., & McAdams, Dan P. (1993). On the comparison of TAT and free speech techniques in personality assessment. *Journal of Personality Assessment, 60,* 181–185.

Zillmann, Dolf. (1964). *Konzept der Semantischen Aspektanalyse.* Unpublished manuscript, Institut für Kommunikationsforschung, Zurich. (Mimeo)

Zipf, George Kingsley. (1935). *The psycho-biology of language: An introduction to dynamic philology.* Boston: Houghton Mifflin.

Zucker, Harold G. (1978). The variable nature of news media influence. In Brent D. Ruben (Ed.), *Communication yearbook 2* (pp. 225–240). New Brunswick, NJ: Transaction.

Züll, Cornelia, Weber, Robert P., & Mohler, Peter. (1989). *Computer-assisted text analysis for the social sciences: The General Inquirer III.* Mannheim: Zentrum für Umfragen, Methoden und Analysen.

Zwick, Rebecca. (1988). Another look at interrater agreement. *Psychological Bulletin, 103,* 347–387.

Index

Abductive inference, 32, 36-38, 85, 171, 320, 331, 344
Abelson, R. P., 293
Accurate representation standard, 193-194
Adorno, T. W., 72
Advertising, 28, 52, 71
Agency, 70
Agreement for coding, 221-250, 221 (figure)
    See also Alpha agreement, Agreement measures, Reliability
Agreement for unitizing, 220, 220 (figure). 251-256
    See also Guetzkow, 251, Holsti, 251, Osgood, 251
Albig, W., 104
Alexa, M., 262, 306
Alife software, 300-301
Allen, L. E., 65, 293
Allport, G. W., 7, 11, 27, 52, 64, 116
Alpert, R., 245, 248
Alpha agreement
    binary data, two observers, 223-227
    coincidence matrices, 219, 224-226, 228-230, 231
    contingency matrices, 226, 244, 246-247
    definition of, 222
    distribution, 237, 238 (figure)
    errors and, 222-223
    insufficient variation in data, 236-237
    interpretations of, 223, 226-227, 229, 232, 249
    limits of variation, 222
    metric differences, 232-236
    multiple nominal categories/observers, missing values, 230-232
    multiple nominal categories, two observers, 227-230
    multiple values/observers/metrics, 232-236
    sampling considerations, 238-241, 240 (table)
    standards, data reliability and, 241-243
    statistical properties of, 236-243
    statistical significance, 237-238
    unitizing reliability, calculation of, 251-256
    See also Agreement measures; Disagreement; Krippendorff's alpha; Reliability
Alpha coefficients
    Cronbach's alpha, 222, 249
    Krippendorff's alpha, 221-222, 251-252
Altheide, D. L., 16
American Reference Library, 274-275
Analysis design logic, 81-83, 82 (figure)
    abductively inferring, 85
    components of, 83-87, 86 (figure)
    data reduction, tabulations and statistics, 84
    different phenomena, same body of texts compared, 94, 95 (figure)
    discriminant function in, 91-93, 92 (figure)
    Hypothesis testing, 95-96
    inferring and analytical constructs, 85
    iterative loops in, 85-86
    narrating answers to research questions, 85
    observations/text-derived inferences, relations between, 95-96, 96 (figure)
    operationalizing expert knowledge, 90, 90 (figure)
    qualitative approaches in, 87-89, 89 (figure)
    quantification and, 87
    recording/coding and instructions for, 84-86
    sampling and sampling plans, 82, 84
    similar phenomena, different bodies of texts sompared, 93, 94 (figure)
    testing analytical constructs, 91, 91 (figure)

textual context and, 86-87
unitizing and unitizing schemes, 82-83
See also Recording/coding process;
    Research design; Sampling; Units
    of analysis
Analyst coordination, 249, 342
Analytical constructs, 34-35
    appropriateness of, 186-187
    certainty, sources of, 173-179
    computer-aided analysis and, 35
    confidence levels, 186
    context, 33-36
    context features, model of,
        172-173, 172 (figure)
    conversations/interactions and, 183
    direct indicators, 180-181
    discriminant function as, 174
    embodied practices and, 179
    established theories and, 176-179
    expert knowledge/experience and,
        175-176
    extrapolations, 180
    if-then statements, 35, 171
    indices/symptoms, 180-182
    institutional processes, 183-185,
        184 (figure)
    knowledge of uses of text in context,
        35-36, 175
    re-presentations and, 182-183
    standards, as, 180
    success/failure, previous experiences
        of, 173-174
    targets, variance of, 185-186
    testing, as a hypothesis, 91, 91
        (figure), 171-172
    types of, 179-185
    uncertainty, sources of, 185-186
    validity of, 319-320, 330-333
Analytical/representational techniques,
    191-192
    absolute vs. relative
        frequencies, 192
    associations and, 196, 206,
        207 (figure)
    attribution analysis, 202-205
    clustering and, 208-210, 209 (figure)
    contingency analysis, 205-208, 207
        (figure)
    co-occurrences, 195
    correlations, 196, 197 (figure),
        198-199
    cross-tabulations, 194-196,
        195 (table)

curve-fitting technique, 198-200,
    199 (figure)
factor analysis, 200
Fourier analysis, 199
multidimensional scaling, 200-201,
    201 (figure)
multivariate techniques, 196, 197-199,
    198 (figure)
profiles, 204-205, 205 (figure)
regression analysis, 197-198
semantic network analysis, 203,
    204 (figure)
structural equations and, 198
tabulations, 192-194,
    193-194 (figures)
See also Functional validity;
    Interpretive standards; Structural
    validity
Anderson, A. H., 135, 136
Andsager, J. L., 201
Annenberg School of
    Communications, 13
Anthropology, 12, 154, 180
Applications. *See* Content analysis
    applications; Research design
AQUAD software, 304, 305
Argumentation, xvii, 38, 336, 337
Aristotelian logic, xvii, xviii, 165
Armstrong, R. P., 108
Arnheim, R., 42
Artificial intelligence, xx, 65, 92, 289,
    291, 293
Ash, P., 55
Asheim, L., 52
Assertions analysis, 45
Associations, 196, 206, 207 (figure)
    word-association databases, 28
    See also Statistical association
        approaches
Associative memory, 14
Atkinson, J. W., 107, 108
ATLAS.ti software, 15, 304, 305,
    306, 341
Attitude measures, 7, 28, 177-178
Attribution analysis, 45, 76, 94, 202-205
Audience interpretation, 9-10
Auld, F., Jr., 61
Auto-categorization, 261
Auto-correlative functions, 180

Baldwin, A. L., 11, 181, 289
Bales, R. F., 11, 13, 51, 199, 287
Barnett, G. A., 297

Bateson, G., 67, 76
Bayne, M. C., 42
Bengston, D. N., 287
Bennett, E. M., 245, 248
Berelson, B., xxi, 5, 8, 9, 11, 19, 20, 23,
    28, 42, 45, 56, 62, 93, 103, 177,
    182, 193, 351
Berger, P. L., 69, 70
Bermejo, F., 277
Bernaut, E., 175, 176, 331
Best, M. L., 300, 301
Bias, 7
    English-language bias, 14
    inferences and, 10
    institutionalized messages and, 72
    reaction errors and, 40-41
    sampling plan and, 113, 321, 323
    systematic sampling and, 115
    varying probability sampling and, 116
    See also Interpretive standards
Bishop, S., 277
Bloch, D. A., 239, 241
Boolean accounts, 269-272, 277
Boolean logic, xvii, 277-279, 278 (figure)
Boolean operators, 154, 269, 270,
    270 (figure), 279
Bootstrapped distribution, 237,
    238 (figure)
Boulding, K. E., 49
Bracken, C. C., 244, 245
Brennan, R. L., 247
Broadcasts:
    analytical constructs about, 184-185,
        184 (figure)
    audience interpretation of, 9-10
    preparatory propaganda and, 9
    publicity efforts, inferences about,
        28-29
    See also Mass media; Television
        programming
Broder, D. P., 59
Brody, R. A., 51, 183
Brouwer, M., 195
Bruner, J. S., 116
Buddenbaum, J. M., 198
Burnett, M. S., 244
Burtt, H. E., 42

Campbell, D. T., 40, 315, 334, 346
Cappella, J. N., 104, 336, 337, 352
Carletta, J., 135, 136
Carley, K. M., 203, 204, 296, 297, 298
Carmines, E. G., 245

Cartesian analysis, 305
Castellan, N. J., 250
CATA. See Computer-aided text analysis
    (CATA)
Categorizations, 69-70, 126, 263-264,
    305-306, 324
CatPac software, 207, 290, 291, 332,
    333, 356-357
Causal explanations, 198, 293
Causal feedback loops, 163
Certainty, 173
    embodied practices and, 179
    established theories and, 176-179
    expert knowledge/experience and,
        175-176
    success/failure, previous experiences
        of, 173-174
    See also Uncertainty
CETA software, 283, 306
Chains-of-symbols theory, 4
Chance standard, 194, 196, 197, 206
Channels of communication, xviii, xx
Character strings, 262-263
    Boolean accounts, 269-272,
        270 (figure)
    CATA software and, 264, 265
    concordances, 266
    content analysis and, 263
    distributional indices, 265
    filters and, 265
    frequency accounts, 265
    go-words/stop-words, 265
    grammatical markers, 265
    KWIC lists, 266, 267 (figure)
    lemmatization, 265
    mapping texts, 267-268,
        268 (figure)
    prefixes/suffixes, 265
    readability measures, 265
    spell-checkers, 264-265
    stemming process, 265
    syntactical categories and, 263-264
    word co-occurrences, 268-269
    word frequencies, 264
    word list typology, 264
Chomsky, N., 59
Circular causal feedback loops, 163
Citation indexing, 118, 310
Clark, C. C., 195
Clark, R. A., 107, 108
Cloze procedure, 4
Clustering, 117, 208-210, 209 (figure), 291
Code-A-Text software, 310

CodeMap software, 267
Coding. *See* Computational content
    analyses; Recording/coding process
Coder
    background, 128-129
    Reliability, and, 217-219
    training, 129-131
Coefficient of imbalance, 7, 55-56,
    177-178
Cognitive dissonance theory, 331-332
Cognitive Science Laboratory (Princeton
    University), 279
Cognitive structure, 11
    social cognition, 65
    world views, cognitive models
        and, 139
Cohen, J., 246, 247, 248, 328
Cohen's kappa, 246-249
Coherence, 310
Coincidence matrices, 219, 224-226,
    228-230, 231
Collaboration:
    conversation, 16-17
    coordination of observers, 249
    research efforts, xx-xxi
Collective associative memory, 14
Communication, xiv
    channels of, xviii, xx
    computation, digital data and, xix
    differences in, 51-53
    electronic media and, xx
    expert objectivity and, xx
    history of, xviii-xx
    information transmission, xvii, xviii, 4
    mass communication research, 59, 71
    mathematical theory of, 4
    messages and, xviii
    networks of, 293
    nonverbal communication, 13
    patterns in, 51
    relational space, awareness of, xix
    routine forms of, 70
    self-understanding and, xvii
    social problems and, xix
    systems theory and, xix
    See also Content analysis; Language;
        Mass media
Comparisons. *See* Memetic approaches
Computational content analyses, 281
    coding/dictionary approaches,
        283-289
    computer-aided text entry
        features, 283

meaning and, 309
memetic approaches, 298-303
pre-editing tasks, 282-283
semantic network approaches,
    292-297, 295 (table), 298 (figure)
statistical association approaches,
    289-292
Computation, xix, 15, 35
Computer-aided Evaluative Text Analysis
    (CETA) software, 283, 306
Computer-aided text analysis (CATA),
    xiv, xxi, 12-13, 19, 203, 257-258
    analytical capabilities, 258-261
    analytical constructs and, 35
    character strings, accounts of, 262-272
    common platforms and, 308-309
    computational content analyses and,
        281-303
    content analysis packages and, 13-14
    digital texts and, 15
    future expansions of, 307-312
    human-based analysis and, 14-15, 23,
        85, 207-208, 214
    indices, 181-182
    intelligent browsers, 307-308
    interactive-hermeneutic explorations
        and, 303-307
    intertextualities, utilization of,
        309-310
    literal data processing, 13
    meaning, computational theories
        of, 309
    qualitative analysis and, 15
    reliability and, 214
    software for, 13, 14-15, 261-262, 264
    syntax of data languages and, 152
    text searches, 272-281, 278 (figure)
    user-friendliness, natural interfaces
        and, 310-312
    word processing software and, 14, 15,
        263, 284
    See also Software
Computer development, xvii-xviii
    computation, digital data and, xix
    data glut and, xxi
    electronic communication and, xx
Computer-mediated communication, 73
Conceivable worlds, 64
Concept analysis, xiv, 62-63
Concept dictionaries, 279
Concordances, 266
Concordance software, 264, 266, 341
Confidence, 186, 211, 219, 243

Consensus, 217, 250
Constructivism. *See* Social constructivist analysis
Container metaphor, xviii, xx, 20, 63, 74
Content
  context, and, 10, 24, 33-34
  container metaphor and, xviii, xx, 20, 63
  emerging in analysis, 19, 21-25
  inherent in text, 19-20
  manifest/latent content, xvii, 19-20
  property of source, 19-21
  See also Meaning
Content analysis, xiii-xiv
  anthropology and, 12
  attitude measures, 7
  audience interpretation, 9-10
  collaborative research in, xx-xxi
  communication, conceptualization of, xviii-xx
  computer-aided analysis, xxi, 12-15
  container metaphor and, xviii, xx, 20, 63
  contexts, 10
  data volumes, xx
  definition of, xvii, 18-21
  direct observation, 10
  electronic information/media systems, xx, xxi, 6
  empirically-grounded nature of, xvii-xviii
  explanatory capacity of, xix-xx
  general applications of, 11-12
  historical development of, 3, 17
  human-based analysis, 14-15
  inferences/predictions and, 10
  methodology of, xx-xxi
  propaganda analysis, 8-11
  psychology and, 11-12
  qualitative approaches to, 15-17, 87-89, 89 (figure)
  quantitative analysis and, 5-6, 7-8, 10-11
  shared meaning, 9, 23
  See also Analysis design logic; Analytical constructs
Content analysis applications, 44
  case examples, applications, 26-29
  conversations, 66-68
  empirical domains of, 46
  extrapolation, 47-53
  functions, 45, 46

  indices/symptoms, extratextual phenomena and, 58-62
  institutional processes, 68-74
  language uses and, 75
  linguistically constituted facts and, 75-77
  linguistic re-presentations, 62-66
  reading metaphor, 74-75
  research technique classification, 44-45
  standards, 54-58
  utility of, 45-46
  See also Recording/coding process; Research design; Sampling; Units of analysis
Content analysis concepts, 18
  analytical constructs, 34-36
  content analysis, definition of, 18-21
  context-sensitivity, 41-42
  contexts and validity, 33-34, 39-40
  data sample size, 42-43
  encoding/decoding paradigm, inferences and, 20-21
  epistemological elaborations, 21-25
  ethnographic content analysis, 21
  evidence validation, 39-40
  framework for, 29-30, 30 (figure)
  manifest content, 20, 25
  messages, container metaphor for, 20, 63, 74
  quantitative vs. qualitative methods, 19-20
  reading-rearticulation process, 30-31
  reliability/validity, 18, 212-214
  research questions, formulation of, 31-33, 285, 343-345
  systematicity, 19
  textual material, characteristics of, 19, 22-25, 30-31
  unobtrusiveness of method, 40-41
  unstructuredness of data, 41
  See also Analysis design logic; Analytical constructs; Inferences
Content Analysis Resources (University of Alabama), 262
Contexts, xiii, 10, 24, 25, 33-36
  analytical constructs, 34-35
  contributing conditions and, 34
  conversational practice and, 34
  correlation networks, 33, 34
  explication of, 34
  quantitative findings, 28
  semantic validity and, 323-324

sensitivity to, 41-42
textual significance and, 33
Contingencies, 12
Contingency analysis, 4, 205-208, 207
    (figure), 290, 326
Contingency matrices, 224-225
Conversational analysis, xviii, xix,
    65-66, 310
    analysis of, 16-17, 34, 66-68
    analytical constructs and, 183
    coding process, conversational moves
        and, 135, 136 (figure)
    contexts and, 34
    conversational moves, 138
    focus group conversations, 11
    natural settings and, 67
    pathologies of communication, 68
    power relationships in, 68
    propositional content, interactional
        role and, 66-67
    texts, transcripts, 75
    validity of analyses, 67-68, 313
Co-occurrences, 12, 94
    contingency analysis, 182,
        205-208, 326
    cross-tabulation and, 195-196
    indices/symptoms and, 181-182
    text searches and, 279
    word tables, 268-269, 291-292
Cook, S. W., 320
Coordinator software, 310
Corpus Linguistics, 274
Correlation coefficients, 196,
    197 (figure), 198-199
Correlation networks, 33, 34-35
Council on Interracial Books for
    Children, 57, 108
Craig, R. T., 250
Critical discourse analysis, 65
Critical Path Method (CPM), 355
Cronbach's alpha, 222, 249
Cross-tabulations, 194-196,
    195 (table), 272
Cuilenburg, J. J. van, 283
Cultural indicators, 11
Curve-fitting technique, 198-200,
    199 (figure)
Cushing, B., 116

Dale, E., 104
Dale, T. A., 203, 204
Danet, B., 108
Danielson, W. A., 58

Danowski, J. A., 291, 292
Darnton, R., 277
Data, xviii
    data defined, 81
    data making, 83, 89
    data mining, 207, 291
    literal data processing, 13
    reduction techniques, 243
    verbal corpuses, 49
    See also Record-keeping; Semantics of
        data, Texts
Data consortia, 15
Data languages, 126, 127, 150
    categories of variables, 153-167
    coder training and, 129-130
    constants in, 153-154
    definition of, 153-155
    exhaustiveness of sets of values, 132
    extensional lists in, 134
    function of, 150-152
    grammar of, 153-154
    information, requirement of
        24-25, 151
    logic in, 153-155
    mathematical operations and, 169,
        170 (table)
    metrics of values, 165-170
    nominal variables, 161
    mutual exclusiveness of values, 132
    ordering, 161-165
    semantics of, 151
    syntax of, 151-152, 153
    values of variables, 153-167
    variables, 155-161
    See also Analytical constructs;
        Semantics of data
Data mining, 207, 291
Datum defined, 81
Davis, S. G., 283
Dawkins, R., 299
Deductive inferences, 36
Democracy, xix, 6, 52
    propaganda and, 8
    public opinion research and, 77
Dendrograms, 209 (figure), 210
Denzin, N. K., 89
De Ridder, J. A., 283, 294, 295, 297
Designations analysis, 45
Design. See Analysis design logic;
    Research design
Deutsch, M., 320
Deviance, 57, 70
DeWeese, L. C., III, 15, 258

Dibble, V. K., 54, 331, 346
Dictionaries, 182, 183, 279
   CATA dictionaries, 284-287
   computational content analyses
      and, 283-289
   construction of, 287-288
   customizable dictionaries,
      285-286, 287
   discourse-specific dictionary, 182, 183
   functional validity of, 289
   lemmatization and, 284
   rhetorical quality categories, 286
   self-other distinction, 325, 326 (figure)
   semantic validity of, 288-289
   spelling checker as, 264-265
   stemming process as. 265, 211, 333
   word processing programs, 284
   See also Computational content
      analyses
Diction software, 260, 283, 285-286
Diefenbach, D. L., 14
Difference function δ_{ck}^2, 232-235
   interval metric, 234
   nominal metric and, 233
   ordinal metric and, 233-234
   ratio metric, 234-235
   unitizing for, 252-253, 253 (figure)
Difference studies, 51-53
Digital text, xix, 15, 43
Direct indicators, 180-181, 182
Direct observation, 10, 11, 31-32
   contexts, 33-36
   See also Indices/symptoms, Validity
Disagreement:
   deviations from a standard, 216
   inter-observer, 215
   intra-observer, 215
   observed/expected, 222, 223, 225,
      250, 253-256
   stability, 216
   systematic, 222-223
   See also Agreement; Alpha agreement,
      Reliability
Discomfort-relief quotient, 61
Discourse analysis, 16, 65
Discourse-specific dictionary, 182, 183
Discriminant function, 91-93,
   92 (figure), 174
Dissonance theory, 177-178
Distributional indices, 265
Documents:
   historical documents, 12, 26-27,
      331, 345

institutional records, 54, 331, 346
   personal documents, 11, 27, 63
Doerfel, M. L., 297
Doherty-Sneddon, G., 135, 136
Dollard, J., 61
Dominant cultures, 65
Dovring, K., 4
Doyle, A. C., 38
dtSearch software, 264, 304
Dunphy, D. C., 13, 25, 46, 325
Dynamic interdependency model, 51
Dziurzynski, P. S., 210

Eco, U., 37
Educational Resources Information
   Center (ERIC), 43, 274
Eisenberg, E. M., 297
Ekman, P., 104, 269
Electronic media, xx, 6, 15
   full-text databases, 43, 259, 274-275
   lexical databases, 279
   text archives, 275-276
   See also Internet; Text searches
Eleey, M., 28
Ellison, J. W., 62
Emic analysis, 21
Empirical inquiry, xvii-xviii, 32
Encoding/decoding paradigm, 20-21,
   24, 46
Entropy measures, 265
Equal attention standard, 65
ERIC, 43, 274
Ethnographic content analysis,
   16, 21
Ethnographic practices, 12, 25, 32
   data sample size, 42
   meanings, decisions on, 324
   reaction errors and, 40-41
Etic analysis, 21
Etymologies, 298-299
European Consortium for Political
   Research, 50
Evaluation standards, 55
   accuracy assessment, 56-57
   coefficient of imbalance and, 55-56
   newspaper reporting, 55
   semantic validity, text searches, 329
Evaluative assertion analysis, 177-178,
   331-332
Event Structure Analysis (ESA), 283,
   294, 306
Evidence validation, 39-40, 318-321,
   319 (figure)

Exhaustiveness, 132
Experimental Division for the Study of Wartime Communications, 8
Experimental psychology, 7, 11
Expert knowledge, xx, 90, 90 (figure), 175-176, 182, 218
Ex post facto validation, 39
Extrapolation, 47
  analytical constructs for, 180
  difference, 51-53
  patterns, 50-51
  systems, 47-49
  textual dynamics and, 53
  trends, 49-50
Extratextual phenomena, 58-62

Factoids, 297
Factor analysis, 199-200
Facts, 75
  attributions, 76
  institutional realities, 77
  public behaviors, 76-77
  social relationships, 76
Faden, J. M., 7, 52
Fadner, R. H., 7, 55, 56
Fair, J. E., 198
Fairness standard, 65
Fan, D. P., 14, 301, 302, 303
Fearing, F., 250
Federal Communications Commission (FCC), 9, 54, 57, 92, 141, 184, 337
Feedback, 31, 163
Feigl, H., 320
Fico, F. G., 20, 123, 244, 313, 314, 351
Fiske, D. W., 334
Fleiss, J. L., 242
Flesch, R., 58, 61, 265
Focus groups, 11, 27
Folktales, 12, 50, 63, 108, 269, 347
Foreign Broadcast Intelligence Service, 8-9
Forensics, 310
Foster, C. R., 42
Fourier analysis, 199
Freeman, S. F., 193
Freitag, A., 244
Frequencies of co-occurrences, 195-196
Frequencies of mentions, 60-62, 181, 182
  distributional indices, 265
  See also Character strings
Friesen, W. V., 104, 269
FT Profile, 43
Functional validity, 319, 332-333

Gamson, W. A., 284
Garfield, E., 51, 310
Garthoff, R. L., 175, 176, 331
Gatekeeping, 322
Geller, A., 101
Gender, 69, 133
Gendered institutions, 69
General Inquirer software, 13, 104, 264, 284-285, 287, 325
Generalizations:
  analytical constructs and, 176
  cluster sampling and, 117
  hypotheses development, 31-32
  index development, 61-62
  psychological research and, 27
  statistical generalization, 25, 32
  See also Analytical constructs
George, A. L., 9, 10, 39, 141, 173, 180, 182, 184, 337
Gerbner, G., 11, 13, 20, 23, 43, 51, 52, 58, 64, 65, 115, 187, 192, 193, 195, 300
German Sociological Society, 4
Go words, 265, 285
Goebbels, J., 9, 41, 104, 182
Goldsen, J. M., 211
Goldstein, A. C., 245, 248
Goodwin, C., 17
Gottschalk, L. A., 351
Graham, T., 167
Grammar, 48, 69, 76, 104
  counter-examples of, 325-326
  data languages, 153-154
  grammatical markers, 265
  stemming process, 265, 311, 333
  transformational grammars, 154, 155
Graph theory, 293
Gross, L., 43, 58, 115, 187, 192, 193, 300
Groth, O., 118
Groupings, 167-168, 168 (figure)
Groups. See Focus groups; Small group behavior
Guetzkow, H., 251
Gurevitch, M., 108

Habitualization, 69-70
Hacker concept, 203, 297, 298 (figure)
Hart, R. P., 285
Harvard Psychosociological Dictionary, 287
Hatch, D. L., 115
Hatch, M., 115
Hawk, L., 58

Hawkins, R. P., 193, 194
Hays, D. C., 13, 63, 65
Heise, D. R., 283, 294
Herma, H., 158, 159
Hermeneutics, 25, 32
    See also Interactive-hermeneutic research
Historical documents, 12, 26-27, 331, 345
Holmes, S., 38
Holsti, O. R., 13, 20, 21, 46, 51, 100,
    108, 183, 245, 251, 335, 351
Homonyms, 278-279
Houle, P., 92
Hubert, L., 250
Human-based analysis, 14-15, 23,
    207-208, 214
    consensus decisions and, 217
    individual inconsistencies and, 215, 216
    See also Computer-aided text analysis
        (CATA); Reliability
Hunt, E. B., 174
Hyperdimensional analogue to language
    (HAL), 291
HyperRESEARCH software, 304
Hypotheses, 31-32
    testing, simulation of, 137-139
    See also Analytical constructs

Identification standards, 54-55
Ideological vision, 16
If-then statements, 35, 171, 347
Iker, H. P., 290
Im, D. S., 58
Images, xiii, xviii
Imbalance coefficient of, 7, 55-56, 177-178
Indicative functions, 181
Indices/symptoms, 58
    accidental/irrelevant variables and, 181
    analytical constructs and, 180-182
    content analysis, extra-textual
        phenomenon and, 58-59
    direct indicators, 182
    discomfort-relief quotient, 61
    empirical validity of, 59-60
    frequencies of mentions, 60-62
    generalizability and, 61-62
    indirect indicators, 182-184
    mass communication research and, 59
    observer-dependent nature of, 58
    quantification and, 60-62
    readability, 58, 61, 181
    semantic satiation and, 62
Inductive inferences, 36
Inferences, xvii, 9, 10, 36-38
    abductive nature of, 36-38

argumentation theory and, 38
commercial applications and, 28-29
contexts, 25, 28, 33-36
deductive inferences, 36
definition of, 36
encoding/decoding paradigm and,
    20-21, 24
historical documents, 26-27
inductive inferences, 36
latent meanings, 141-142
limitations on, 24-25
networks of, 38
open-ended interviews, coding process
    and, 27
propaganda analysis, 26, 184-185
psychological research practice
    and, 27
research questions and, 31-33,
    353-345
social norms and, 28
texts, physicality of, 23
verbal records, analysis of, 11
word-association databases and, 28
    See also Analytical constructs; Content
        analysis applications; Content
        analysis concepts; Extrapolation,
        Indices/symptoms
Information in data
    administrative, 144-145
    coding and, 149
    organization of records,145-146
    requisite amount, 151
    substantive, 136-149
    Information mining, 261, 291
Information retrieval, 13, 155, 272, 329
Information society, xiii-xiv, xvii
Information theory, 4, 69
    cloze procedure, 4
    data languages and, 24-25, 151
    entropy measure, 265
    symbol chains, 4
    text temperature, 265
Information transmission, xvii, xviii, 5
    data languages, in, 151
    rumor transmission, 7, 118
    textual interpretation and, 24-25
    See also Propaganda analysis
Innis, H. A., 72
Institute for Propaganda Analysis, 8
Institutional processes, 68-69
    agency and, 70
    analytical constructs and, 183-185,
        184 (figure)
    communication, roles of, 73-74

communication, routine forms of, 70
deviance and, 70
economic explanations for, 71
gender, grammatical category of, 69
habitualization and, 69, 70
legal explanations for, 71
media of communication and, 72-73
political explanations for, 71
reciprocal categorizations and, 69-70
reinforcement principle and, 72, 73
rules of conduct, 71
technical-structural explanations for, 71-72
texts within, 72, 74
textual rearticulations, institutional network of, 300
See also Organizational communication research
Institutional realities, 77
Institutional standards, 57-58
Intelligent browsers, 307-308
Interaction process analysis, 11-12, 51, 63
analytical constructs and, 183
conversation analysis, 16-17
reality and, 16
themes in, 13
See also Conversational practices
Interactive-hermeneutic research, 303
automatic coding, 305
coding/conceptual schemes, sharing of, 306-307
computer aids and, 303-307
display of text, 304-305
hierarchical/non-hierarchical categorization and, 305-306
interoperability and, 306
manual coding and, 305
memoing/commenting, linking and, 306
representational theory of meaning and, 307
text entering, 304
unitizing,84, 251
Interactivity, xix, 14
Intercoder reliability, 215
Interdependency model, xix, 51
International Communication Association (ICA), 297
International exchanges, 63
Internet, xix, 15, 43, 119, 348
electronic text archives, 275-276

intelligent browsers, 307-308
search engines and, 273-274
software information, 262, 267
Interpersonal communication. See Conversational analysis
Interpretation, 9-10, 14, 88
contexts, 24, 33-36
hypothesis testing, simulation of, 137-139
interviewing, simulation of, 139-141
multiple, 88
open-ended reading and, 32
reliability and, 212
See also Interpretive standards
Interpretive standards
accurate representation, 193-194
balance, 7, 55-56, 177-178
bias, 192
chance cooccurances, 194, 196, 197, 206
equal attention, 64-65
linearity, 196
stable pattern, 193
uniform distribution, 192
Intertextuality, 63-64, 118, 309-310
Interval metric, 168-169, 234
Interval scales, 162
Interviews, 11, 27, 63, 139-141
Invalidation, 33
Isard, A., 135, 136
Isard, S., 135, 136

Jackson-Beeck, M., 43, 58, 187, 192, 193
Jahod, M., 320
Jamieson, K. H., 16, 58, 104
Janda, K., 269
Janis, I. L., 7, 25, 39, 44, 54, 55, 56, 126, 332
Joke-telling, 17
Josephson, J. R., 37
Josephson, S. G., 37
Journalism, xiii, xiv, xxi, 5
attitude measures and, 7
evaluative studies of, 55-56
surveillance function of, 74
truthful reporting in, 57
See also Content analysis; Newspapers; Propaganda analysis
Judgment standards, 57-58

Kansas Events Data System (KEDS) software, 283, 306
Kaplan, A., 163, 164, 211, 355

Kaplan, D., 101
Katz, E., 108
Kenski, K., 276
Keyword-in-context (KWIC) analysis, 14, 94, 203, 266, 267 (figure), 304, 311, 325, 341
Kim, J., 284
King, E. G., 120
Kinship terminology, 12, 48, 293
Kjellstrand, R., 14
Klausner, S. Z., 140
Kleinnijenhuis, J., 283, 294, 295, 297
Knowledge:
　actionable knowledge structures, 293
　expert knowledge, 175-176, 182
　noosphere of, 49
　operationalization of, 90, 90 (figure)
　See also Semantic network analysis
Koch, G. H., 250
Kolbe, R. H., 244
Kowtko, J. C., 135, 136
Kracauer, S., 10
Kraemer, H. C., 239, 241
Krendel, E. S., 58
Krippendorff, K., 13, 20, 25, 28, 29, 53, 71, 152, 182, 195, 221, 248, 250, 251, 254, 261, 265, 287, 307, 309, 320, 325, 341
Krippendorff's alpha, 256, 354
Kriss, E., 158, 159
KWIC (keyword-in-context) analysis, 14, 94, 203, 266, 267 (figure), 304, 311, 325, 341

Labov, W., 50
Lacy, S., 20, 123, 244, 313, 314, 351
Laffal, J., 279, 288
Landis, H. H., 42
Landis, J. R., 250
Language:
　analytical constructs and, 35
　conscious use of, xvii
　grammar in, 48, 69, 76
　logical expression, rhetorical theory and, xvii-xviii
　natural language processing, artificial intelligence and, 293
　public usage of, 76-77
　readability index, 58, 61
　reality and, 16
　re-presentations, 62-66
　semantic network analysis, 65
　semantic satiation and, 62

system of, 48
text search language, 279-281
See also Communication; Data languages; Facts; Symbols
Lasorsa, D. L., 58
Lasswell, H. D., 7, 8, 11, 49, 60, 73, 74, 101, 103, 104, 120, 139, 152, 163, 164, 287, 293, 300
Latent content, xvii, 19-20
Latent semantic indexing (LSI), 291
Lazarsfeld, P. F., xxi, 5, 8, 28, 42, 45
Legal system, xiv, 54-55, 327-328
Leigh, L. E., 245
Leites, N., 45, 175, 176, 331
Lemmatization, 265, 284, 311, 333
Levine-Donnerstein, D., 316, 317
Levinson, M., 62
Lexical databases, 279
LexisNexis, 43, 274, 275, 277, 279-280
Lincoln, Y. S., 89
Lindsay, R. K., 293
Linearity standard, 196
Linguistic Inquiry and Word Count (LIWC), 285, 286-287, 289, 306, 308
Linnean classification, 165, 168
Löbl, E., 4
Loeventhal, L., 49
Logical expression, xvii-xviii
Logic theory machine, 65
Lombard, M., 244, 245
Lorr, M., 130
Lowell, E. L., 107, 108
Luckmann, T., 69, 70
Lynch, K., 64

Maccoby, N., 116
Mahl, G. F., 67, 133, 135
Manifest content, xvii, 9, 19-20, 25, 323
Mapping, 64, 65, 267-268, 268 (figure)
Markoff, J., 20
Markov, A., 4
Marvanyi, G., 64, 65
Mass communication research, 59, 71
Mass media, xiv, xix, 4
　accurate representation standard of, 193-194
　analytical constructs and, 35
　audiences of, 23
　messages, production imprint on, 20
　message systems analysis and, 52-53
　new perspectives on, 11
　picture theory of content, 28

public opinion dynamics and, 301-303
social collapse and, 6
validation of analysis, 39-40
See also Broadcasts; Newspapers;
    Propaganda analysis; Television
    programming
Mathematical theory of communication, 4
McAdams, D. P., 14
McCaa, C., 14
McClelland, D. C., 107, 108, 348
McDiarmid, J., 7
McNair, D. M., 130
Meaning, xviii
    audience interpretation and, 9-10
    classical representational theory of, 307
    computational theories of, 309
    context sensitivity and, 41-42
    message context and, 10, 33-34
    text, meaning of, 22-26, 309
    word meanings, charting of, 14
    See also Inferences; Statistical
        association approaches; Texts
Measurement theory, 126, 211
MECA software, 296, 306
Media technology, xviii, xix
    electronic media, xx
    one-way communication
        technology, 73
    See also Electronic media
Megaputer Intelligence Web site, 291
Memetic approaches, 298-299
    newsgroups study, textual ecology,
        300-301
    public opinion dynamics,
        epidemiological model and,
        301-303
    text comparisons and, 299-300
Merrill, J. C., 56
Merritt, R. L., 213
Merten, K., 25
Messages, xviii
    audience interpretation, 9-10
    contextual factors and, 10
    electronic media and, xx
    expert objectivity and, xx
    institutionalization of, 72
    mass media and, xix, 20
    political symbols and, 7
    rhetorical analysis, 16
    See also Texts
Message systems analysis, 52-53
Method-driven analyses, 355-357
Metrics, 160-161, 165, 170 (table)

decision trees, 167
groupings, 167-168, 168 (figure)
interval, interval scale, 168-169, 234
nominal, nominal scale, 233
operational properties of, 170,
    170 (table)
ordinal, ordinal scale, 166-168,
    233-234
ratio, ratio scale, 169, 234-235
See also Data languages; Ordering
Miles, M. B., 262
Military intelligence, 8-9
Miller, G. A., 14, 126
Minnesota Contextual Content Analysis
    (MCCA), 285
Mohler, P., 287
Monge, P. R., 297
Morgan, M., 43, 58, 115, 187, 192,
    193, 300
Morton, A. Q., 62
Moscoso, S., 245
Mosteller, F., 61, 181
Mowrer, O. H., 61
Multidimensional scaling (MDS),
    200-201, 201 (figure)
Multitrait-multimethod matrix, 334-335,
    335 (table)
Multivariate techniques, 196, 197-199,
    198 (figure)
Murray, E. J., 61
Mutual exclusivity, 132
Myths. *See* Folktales

Nacos, B. L., 14
Namenwirth, J. Zvi, 50, 163, 198,
    199, 200
Narrative networks, 63-65, 76
National Archives and Records
    Administration, 274
Nationalism, 7
Nazi Germany, 9, 41, 139, 141
NEGOPY software, 291
Negotiation, 16
NetNews, 300
Networks, xix, xx
    citation networks, 51, 297, 310
    correlations, networks of, 33, 34-35
    inferential networks, 38
    intertextuality and, 118
    narrative networks, 63-65, 76
    social networks, 118
    socio-conceptual networks, 296-297,
        298 (figure)

See also Semantic network analysis
Neuendorf, K. A., 245, 351
Neuronal network model, 35, 207, 290-291, 292, 332-333
New School for Social Research, 8
Newspapers, 3-4
   attitude measures and, 7
   cluster sampling and, 117
   editorial sequences, 63
   mass media developments and, 6
   publicity, inferences about, 28-29
   quantitative analysis of, 5-6, 7-8
   relevance sampling and, 120
   reporting evaluation, 55
   rumor transmission, 7
   self-referencing, 277
   varying probability sampling and, 116
   See also Mass media; Propaganda analysis
Newtonian systems, 48
Nir, L., 336, 337, 352
Nominal metric, 233
Nominal variables, 161
Nonverbal communications, 13, 67, 105
Norms, 28
   See also Standards
North, R. C., 51, 183
NUD*IST software, 304, 305, 306
Nunnally, J. C., 106, 177, 178, 294, 297, 331, 352
NVivo software, 15, 304, 305, 306, 341

Objectivity, xx, 5
   attitude measures and, 7
   quantitative data and, 10-11
   text analysis software and, 341
   universal meaning and, 324
Observation. *See* Direct observation
Observer coordination, 249, 342
Ogden, C. K., 293
Ogilvie, D. M., 13, 25, 46, 325
Open-ended interviews, 11, 27
Ordering of values, 160, 161-162, 161 (table)
   chains, 162, 162 (figure)
   cubes, 163-164, 164 (figure)
   recursions, 162-163, 163 (figure)
   trees, 164-165, 165 (figure), 167-168
   See also Data languages; Metrics
Ordinal metric, 162, 166-168, 233-234
Organizational communication research, 53, 57-58
   conversation analysis and, 68

semantic network analysis and, 297
   See also Institutional processes
Orzack, L. H., 50
Osgood, C. E., 4, 51, 91, 104, 106, 136, 177, 178, 182, 199, 206, 207, 245, 251, 287, 290, 294, 297, 326, 331, 335, 352
O'Sullivan, T. C., Jr., 134
Oxford Text Archive, 274
Oxman, T. E., 14

Paisley, W. J., 13, 181
Paley, W. B., 267
Palmquist, M. E., 203, 204
Parallel communication, xix
Parallel-forms reliability, 215
Parson, T., 74, 199
Patterns, 50-51
   deviation from, 70
   qualitative analysis of, 53
   reciprocal categorizations and, 69-70
Pearson, K., 250
Pearson's product-moment coefficient, 244
Peirce, C. S., 58
Péladeau, N., 285
Peled, T., 108
Pennebaker, J. W., 289
Perreault, W. D., 245
Personal documents, 11, 27, 63
Personal structure analysis, 11, 290
Persuasion theory, 73
Persuasive argumentation. *See* Argumentation
Phillips, D. P., 91
Piault, C., 154
Picture theory of content, 28
Pierce, B. L., 42
Plagiarism, 204-205, 205 (figure), 299
Plumb Design Visual Thesaurus, 279
Point-to-point communication, xix
Polar adjective scales, 162
Political analysis, xiv, 4, 6
   analytical construct development, 184-185, 184 (figure)
   differences, 52
   expert knowledge and, 175-176
   public messages, nationalism and, 7
   quantitative indicators and, 10
   representational data, 7, 16
   semantic validity and, 324-325
   trends, 50

world revolution, evidence for, 11
   See also Propaganda analysis
Political intelligence, 8-9
PoliTxts archive, 275
Polls, 6-7
Pool, I. S., 12, 43, 45, 52, 62, 182
Popping, R., 221, 262
Popular heroes, 49
Potter, W. J., 316, 317
Power relationships, 68, 69, 70
Powers, A., 201
Pragmatical content analysis, 44-45
Prediction, xvii, 10, 321, 336-338
Prediger, D. J., 247
Prefixes, 265
Prejudice. *See* Bias
Preparatory propaganda, 9
Price, V., 336, 337, 352
Printed matter, xviii, 3-4
   See also Newspapers; Written texts
Probability theory, 4
   relevance sampling and, 119
   varying probability sampling and, 116
Problem-driven analyses, 342-343
   analytical procedure, selection of,
      352-353
   categories/recording instructions,
      development of, 350-352
   correlation network stability and,
      345-347
   relevant texts and, 347-349
   research questions, formulation of,
      343-345
   resource allocation and, 355
   sampling texts and, 350
   standards, adoption of, 353-354
   units of analysis, definition of,
      349-350
Profiles, 204-205, 205 (figure)
Profit motivation, 5
Program Evaluation and Review
   Technique (PERT), 355
Project Gutenberg, 274
Propaganda analysis, 8
   analytical construct and, 184-185,
      184 (figure)
   audience interpretation and, 9-10
   case example of, 26
   communication systems models and, 10
   ideological vision and, 16
   indirect indicators, 182-184
   military/political intelligence and, 8-9,
      139, 141

predictive validity and, 337
preparatory propaganda, 9
quantitative data and, 10-11
   See also Content analysis
Proposals. *See* Research proposals
Proximity operators, 279
Psychoanalytical theory, 7
Psycho-logic, xviii, 177-178, 293
Psychology, xviii, 7
   association psychology, 289-290
   content analysis, applications of, 11-12
   psychological testing, 314-315
   research activities, 27
   thematic apperception test (TAT)
      stories, 11, 14
Public behaviors, 76-77
Public Broadcasting Service (PBS), 28-29
Public mind, 65
Public opinion, xiv, 5, 6
   content analysis, substitute for, xx, 35
   mass media coverage and, 35
   mass media data and, 301-303
   political reality and, 77
   text analysis and, 75
   text re-articulations/comparisons and,
      299-300, 301-303
   varying probability sampling and, 116
   See also Propaganda analysis

Qualitative analysis, 10, 15-16, 19-20
   characteristics of, 17
   computer-aided analysis, 15
   content analysis and, 87-89,
      89 (figure)
   conversation analysis, 16-17
   discourse analysis, 16
   ethnographic content analysis, 16, 21
   hypotheses testing, 138-139
   narrative networks and, 64-65
   patterns, 53
   rhetorical analysis, 16
   social constructivist analysis, 16
Quantitative analysis, xiii, 10-11, 19
   attitude measures and, 7
   contextual significance and, 28
   historical practice of, 4
   indices and, 60-62
   interval metric, 168-169
   newspaper analysis, 5-6, 7-8
   political information and, 10

RADIR study, 52
Rahlf, T., 50

Rand Corporation, 13
Rapoport, A., 49, 58, 59, 300
Ratio metric, 169, 234-235
Ratio scales, 162
Rationality, xvii-xviii
Reaction errors, 40-41
Readability index, 58, 61, 181, 265
Reading metaphor, 74-75
Reality, 16, 25, 56
    conceivable worlds and, 64
    critical discourse analysis and, 65
    institutional realities, 77
    See also Facts
Reciprocal categorizations, 69-70
Recording/coding process, 84-85, 703
    coder qualifications for, 127-129
    coder training, 129-131
    content, familiarity with, 128
    data language definition and, 129-130
    function of, 125-127
    instructions for, 127, 131
    mechanical measurements and, 126
    record-keeping in, 143-149,
        143 (figure)
    replicability and, 128-129, 130-131
    self-applied instructions and, 131
    units of analysis in, 99-101
    See also Semantics of data
Record-keeping, 143, 143 (figure)
    administrative information and,
        144-145
    instructions for, 148-149
    multi-level data, organization of,
        145-146
    recording instruments/techniques,
        errors and, 146-148
Regression analysis, 197-198
Regressive Imagery Dictionary (RID),
    285, 286
Reitberg, E. M., 283
Relational text analysis, 261, 293, 294
Relationships, 76
    conversational practice and, xviii,
        67, 68
    interpersonal communication,
        relational space and, xix
    intertextualities, 309-310
    model development, 35
    public behaviors and, 76-77
Reliability, 18, 20, 211-212
    accuracy, 215-216
    coding instructions, interpretations of,
        217-218

coding process and, 220-221,
    221 (figure)
computer-aided analysis and, 214
consensus and, 217
conversation analyses and, 67
decision schemes and, 135
disagreements, 215, 216
expert knowledge and, 218
perfect reliability, 218, 222, 252
reproducibility, 212, 215, 216-217
semantic differential scales and, 137
split-half technique, 216
stability, 215, 216, 218
standards for, 241-243
types of, 214-216, 215 (table)
unitizing process and, 110, 219-220,
    220 (figure)
validity and, 212-213, 214 (figure)
See also Agreement; Alpha agreement;
    Disagreement
Reliability coefficients:
    Bennett et al.'s S, 245-246, 248
    Cohen's kappa, 246-249
    correlation and, 244-245, 249, 250
    Cronbach's alpha, 222, 249
    expected percent agreement, 245-246
    Krippendorff's alpha, 221-222,
        251-252
    observed/expected agreement, 229,
        245-246
    Pearson's product-moment
        coefficient, 244
    percent agreement, 245, 245-246, 248
    reliability concerns and, 248-249
    Scott's pi, 245-246, 247, 248,
        249, 250
    Spearman's rank correlation
        coefficient rho, 250
    See also Alpha agreement;
        Disagreement; Reliability
Reliability data, 219-221
    canonical form of, 219
    defined, 219
    generating, 216-219
    test-retest conditions and, 215
    sample sizes required, 239-241,
        240 (table)
    split-half technique, 216
    standards for, 241-243
    test-standard conditions, 215-216
    test-test conditions and, 215, 217
    types of, 214-216, 215 (table)
Religious texts, 3-4

See also Propaganda analysis
Replicability, 212, 215, 216-217, 351
Representational techniques. *See*
  Analytical/representational
  techniques; Sampling
Re-presentation, xiii, 7, 16, 56
  analytical constructs and, 182-183
  cognitive processes, simulations of, 65
  conceivable worlds and, 64
  conversation analysis, 65-66
  critical discourse analysis and, 65
  mapping, 64, 65
  narratives, conceptual structures and,
    62-63
  qualitative research on, 64-65
  sequenced narrative networks and, 63,
    64-65
  written texts, intertextuality and,
    63-64
Reproducibility, 212, 215,
    216-217, 351
Research design, 340
  analytical procedure, selection of,
    352-353
  application of, 361
  categories/recording instructions,
    development of, 350-352
  correlation network stability and,
    345-347
  interpretive process and, 342
  method-driven analyses, 355-357
  problem-driven analyses, 342-355
  question formulation, 343-345
  relevant texts and, 347-349
  replicability and, 351
  resource allocation and, 355
  sampling texts, 350
  standards, adoption of, 353-354
  text-driven analyses, 341-342
  units of analysis, definition of,
    349-350
Research proposals, 357
  contractual function of, 359
  outline for, 359-361
  rhetorical function of, 358-359
Research questions, 31-33, 285, 343-345
Research reports, 362
  addressees of, 362-363
  outline for, 363-364
Reuters wire service, 275
Revolution and the Development of
  International Relations (RADIR)
  study, 52

Rhetorical analysis, 16
Rhetorical tradition, xvii-xviii, 4
Rietberg, E. M., 294, 295, 297
Riffe, D., 20, 123, 244, 313, 314, 351
Roberts, C. W., 106, 351
Rosenberg, M. J., 293
Rosenberg, S. D., 14
Rumor transmission, 7, 118

Sabghir, F. O., 116
Sacks, H., 16
Salgado, J. F., 245
Salter, P. J., 56, 193
Sampling, 84, 111
  census, 120
  cluster sampling, 116-117
  confidence levels and, 186
  content analysis and, 112-113
  convenience sampling, 120-121
  enumerated populations of texts
    and, 114
  experiments in, 122-124
  informativeness, equality/inequality in,
    113-114, 116
  purposive sampling, 119
  random sampling, 114
  relevance sampling, 118-120
  representation theory and, 113
  sample size, 121-124, 186
  snowball sampling, 117-118
  split-half technique and, 124, 216
  statistical sampling theory and, 112,
    113, 117, 121-122, 122 (figure)
  stratified sampling, 115-116
  systematic sampling, 115
  techniques in, 113-121
  units, sampling units, 98-99, 112
  validity of, 319, 321-323
  varying probability sampling, 116
Saporta, S., 106, 177, 178, 294, 297,
    331, 352
Saris-Gallhofer, I. N., 335
Scales of measurement, 136-137,
    157, 162
  See also Data Languages, Metrics
Schank, R. C., 293
Schnurr, P. P., 14
Schoenfeld, A. C., 193, 194
Schrodt, P. A., 283
Schutz, W. C., 135
Schwartz, R. D., 40, 346
Scientific methods, xiii, 5, 20
  hypothesis development, 31-32

See also Research design
Scott's pi, 245-246, 247, 248, 249, 250
Scott, W. A., 245, 248
Search engines, 273
Searle, J., 157
Sebeok, T. A., 13, 50, 269
Sechrest, L., 40, 346
Sedelow, S. Y., 14, 267, 283
Self-interest, 31
Self-other distinction, 325, 326 (figure)
Self-reflexivity, xvii, 65
Selltiz, C., 320
Semantical content analysis, 45
Semantic aspect scale, 162
Semantic differential scales, 51, 136-137,
    157, 169, 287
Semantic network analysis, 65, 203,
    204 (figure), 292-293
  actor-action-target network, 293
  artificial intelligence research and, 293
  event structure analysis and, 294
  kinship relationships and, 293
  organizational networks, 297
  predicate-type analysis, 294-296,
      295 (table)
  relational memory and, 293
  relational texts in, 294
  socio-conceptual networks and,
      296-297, 298 (figure)
Semantics of data, 132
  decision schemes, 135, 136 (figure)
  exhaustiveness and, 132
  extensional lists and, 133-135
  hypothesis testing, simulation of,
      137-139
  idio-logic and, 142
  inferential reasoning, latent meanings
      and, 141-142
  interviewing, simulation of,
      139-141
  magnitudes/scales and, 136-137
  mutual exclusivity and, 132
  single vs. multiple-word category
      designations, 133
  verbal designations and, 132-133
  See also Data languages;
      Record-keeping
Semio software, 290
Semiotics, 25
Shanas, E., 49
Shannon, C. E., 4, 69
Shapiro, G., 20
Shapiro, R. Y., 14

Shared coding/conceptual schemes,
    306-307
Shared meaning, 9, 23
Sherlock Holmes, 66
Shneidman, E. S., 142
Shor, J., 158, 159
Shuman, R. B., 42
Siegel, S., 250
Signorielli, N., 43, 58, 115, 187, 192,
    193, 300
Sign-vehicle analysis, 45, 54, 126, 323
Simonton, D. K., 53
Simulation, 13
  cognitive processes, 65
  hypothesis testing, 137-139
  interviews, 139-141
  suicide note, 174
Simultaneity, xix
Singer, J. D., 129
Skalski, P. D., 275
Small group behavior, 11-12, 51
Smith, C. P., 107
Smith, M. S., 13, 25, 46, 325
Smythe, D. W., 10
Snyder-Dutch, J., 244, 245
So, C. Y. K., 64, 265
Social cognition, 65
Social constructivist analysis, 16, 48
Social deviance, 57, 70
Social grammars, 76
Social science research, xiii
  computer systems and, xx
  content analysis and, 7-8
  digital data, computation and, xix
  interval metrics and, 169
  social deviance and, 57
  social networks, 118, 293
  surveys/polls, 6-7
  unobtrusive techniques and, 40-41
Social Science Research Council
    Committee on Linguistics and
    Psychology, 12
Social structures, xix, xx
  collective associative memory, 14
  dominant cultures, 65
  linguistically constituted realities and,
      76-77
  newspapers, influence of, 5
  norms, content analysis and, 28
Social systems, 48, 74, 118
Social weather metaphors, 5-6
Socio-conceptual networks, 296-297,
    298 (figure)

Sociological systems theory, 74
Software, 13
    human readers and, 207-208
    interactive-hermeneutic analysis
        software, 15
    text analysis software, 14, 261-262
    word processing software, 14-15
    world model of, 183
    See also Computer-aided text analysis
        (CATA)
Spearman's rank correlation coefficient
    rho, 250
Speech act theory, 310
Speech disturbances, 133, 135
Speed, G. J., 49
Speier, H., 8
Spell-checkers, 264-265
Spiegelman, M., 250
Split-half technique, 124, 216
Stability, 193, 215, 345-347
Standardization, 13, 15
Standards, 54
    adopting standards, 353-354
    analytical constructs and, 180
    evaluations, 55-57
    identifications, 54-55
    institutional, 57-58
    judgments, 57-58
    truth, 57, 216
    types of, 179-185
    See also Interpretive standards;
        Reliability standards; Validity
Statistical association approaches,
    289-292
Statistical generalization, 25, 32
Statistical properties of alpha, 236
    confidence interval, 238
    distribution, bootstrapped, 237,
        238 (figure)
    insufficient variation, 236-237
    sampling considerations,
        238-241, 240 (table)
    statistical significance, 237-238,
        238 (figure)
Statistical sampling theory, 112-113, 117,
    121-122, 122 (figure)
Steiner, G. A., 177
Stemming process, 265, 311, 333
Stempel, G. H., III, 116, 122
Stereotypes, 297
Stone, L. D., 289
Stone, P. J., 13, 25, 46, 174, 325
Stop words, 265, 285, 291

Structural validity, 319, 330-331
Strodthoff, G. G., 193, 194
Suci, G. J., 136
Suffixes, 265
Sullivan, D., 291
Support vector machines (SVMs), 92, 291
Survey research, 6-7
Symbols, xiii, xvii, 297
    chains-of-symbols theory, 4
    political symbols, 7, 11
    See also Communication; Language
Symptoms. See Indices/symptoms
Synonyms, 278, 279
Syntactical categories, 263-264
Syntactical distinctions, 104-105,
    109-110
Syntax of data languages, 151-153
Systematicity, 19
Systems, xix, 10
    autonomous systems, 50, 52
    behavior of, auto-correlation and, 180
    complex analytical constructions
        and, 53
    components of, 47-48
    message systems, 52-53
    Newtonian system, 48
    social systems, 74
    theory of, 48-49
    verbal corpuses and, 49, 53
    See also Extrapolation

Tabulations, 192-194, 193-194 (figure),
    197 (figure)
    See also Cross-tabulations
Taft-Harley Labor Act, 55
Tagged text, 325, 352
Tannenbaum, P. H., 136
Taussig, T. G., 269
Teamwork. *See* Collaboration
Technology. *See* Computer-aided text
        analysis; Computer-mediated
        communication; Electronic media;
        Media technology
Television programming:
    accurate representation standard and,
        193-194
    reality shows, 56-57
    stratified sampling of, 115-116
    violence indices and, 52, 58, 60,
        187, 344
    See also Broadcasts; Mass media
Tenney, A. A., 5, 48, 300
Term weighting, 281

Terwilliger, C., 250
Tesch, R., 262
Test-retest conditions, 215
TestSmart software, 290, 308
Test-standard conditions, 215-216
Test-test conditions, 215, 217
Text Analysis Info Web site, 262
TextAnalyst software, 290, 291
TextArc Web site, 267
Text-driven analysis, 341-342
TextPack software, 14, 285
Text preparation. *See* Computational
    content analyses
TextQuest software, 306, 308, 341
Texts, xiii-xiv, xvii, xviii
    computer systems and, xx, 12-15, 43
    definition of, 19
    familiarity with, 175
    full-text databases, 43
    inferences and, 23, 25
    information, limiting factor of, 24-25
    interpretation, 24
    intertextuality and, 63-64, 118,
        309-310
    latent content, xvii, 19-20
    manifest content, 9, 20, 25, 323
    meanings, 22-25
    multiple meanings in, 22-23
    populations of, 114
    reader-independent qualities and, 22
    reading-rearticulation process and,
        30-31
    religious texts, 3-4
    shared meaning in, 23
    uses of, 35-36
    See also Re-presentation, Contents
Text searches, 272-273
    Boolean logic and, 277-279,
        278 (figure)
    fuzzy search, 281
    Internet searches, 273-275
    lexical databases, 279
    proximity operators of queries in, 105
    purposes of, 276-277
    query formulation guidelines, 277-279
    reference sources for, 279
    results, levels of, 273
    search engines and, 273
    semantic validity and, 276, 277
    specialized languages and, 279-280
    term weighting, 281
    textual databases, 274-275
TextSmart software, 306, 310

Thematic apperception test (TAT) stories,
    11, 14
Theme identification, 261
Thome, H., 50
Thompson, S., 108
Tijssen, R. J. W., 291
Toulmin, S. E., 38, 171
Tracking methods, xiv
Trees, 164-165, 165 (figure), 167-168
Trends, 49-50, 53
Truth standard, 57, 216
Tukey, J. W., 152
Turn-taking, 17, 34
Turow, J., 104
Type/token ratio, 344

Uncertainty, 40, 185
    confidence levels and, 186
    construct appropriateness and,
        186-187
    sources of, 353-354
    targets, variance of, 185-186
    See also Certainty
Understanding. *See* Interactive-
    hermeneutic research
Uniform distribution standard of, 192
Units of analysis, 83, 97-98
    analytical functions of, 103
    categorical distinctions of,
        105-106
    coding units, 99-101
    context units, 101-103
    enumeration units, 102-103
    natural units, 104-105, 109
    physical distinctions of, 103-104
    productivity, efficiency/reliability and,
        109-110
    propositional distinctions of, 106-107
    recording units, 99-101
    sampling units, 98-99
    syntactical distinctions in,
        104-105
    thematic distinctions, 107-109
    unitizing, 98, 220, 220 (figure).
        251-256
    See also Alpha coefficient; Sampling
Unobtrusiveness, xiii, 40-41, 44
Usenet, 300
Uses and gratifications approach, 177

Validity, 18, 19, 25, 313
    concurrent validity, 316
    construct validity, 315

content analysis and, 316-318,
    338 (figure)
content validity, 315
convergent validity, 334-335
conversations analyses and,
    67-68
correlative validity, 320-321, 333-336,
    334 (figure), 335 (table)
criterion-related/instrumental
    validity, 315
discriminant validity, 334, 335
empirical validity, 315
evidence validation, 39-40,
    318-321, 319 (figure)
ex post facto validation, 39
face validity, 313-314
functional validity, 320, 332-333
indices and, 59-60
invalidation, 33
obstacles to, 316-318
predictive validity, 321, 336-338
reliability and, 212-213,
    214 (figure)
research questions and, 32-33
sampling validity, 319, 321-323
semantic validity, 319, 323-330,
    326 (figure)
social validity, 314-315
structural validity, 320, 330-332
tests of, 212
Value categories, 163-164, 287
Value studies, 11, 50
Values of variables, 153, 155-156
Van Dijk, T. A., 16
Van Raan, A. F. J., 291
Variables, 155-156
    accidental/irrelevant variables, 181
    composite index of, 243
    data languages, recording process and,
        157-160, 159 (figure)
    implicit/explicit definition of, 156-157
    metrics, 160-161, 166-170
    nominal variables, 161
    open-ended vs. limited variables, 156
    ordering of values in, 160, 161-165
    scales of measurement of, 157, 162
    values of, 153, 155-156
    See also Data languages
Varying probability sampling, 116
VBPro software, 264, 285, 341
Venn diagrams, 270, 278
Verbal corpuses, 49, 53
Verbal discourse, xviii, 11

Verbastat software, 310
Violence profiles, 11
Virage software, 269

Wallace, D. L., 61, 181
Weaver, D. H., 198
Weaver, W., 69
Webb, E. J., 40, 346
Weber, M., 4
Weber, R. P., 50, 163, 198,
    200, 203, 266, 287, 351
Weddle, J. L., 283
Weitzman, E. A., 262
Wells, R. A., 120
White, A. M., 61
White, R. K., 11
Willey, M. M., 6
Windows-like software, 311
WinMAX software, 304, 305
Witnesses, 331
Witschge, T., 167
Woelfel, J., 207, 290, 291
Wood, et al. v. Andrews, et al,
    327-328
Woodward, J. L., 6
Word-association databases, 28
Word co-occurrences,
    268-269
Word counts. See Character strings; Text
    searches
Word-distance matrix, 291-292
Word frequencies, 264, 265, 311, 341
Wordlink software, 291-292
WordNet software, 14, 279, 288
Word processing software, 14, 15, 263,
    284, 341
WORDS software, 290
WordStat software, 264, 266, 285, 286,
    287, 292, 306, 308, 341
Workshop on Content Analysis in the
    Social Sciences, 13
World Attention Survey, 7, 11,
    104, 120
Wright, C. E., 74
Written texts, xviii, 11
    computer text analysis and,
        12-13, 15
    conversation analysis and, 75
    narrative networks, 63-64
    reality and, 16
    See also Newspapers; Printed matter

Xu, Z., 287

Yellow journalism, 5, 6
Young, J. T., 14
Yule, G. U., 61, 181

Zeldow, P. B., 14
Zeller, R. A., 245
Zeps, V. J., 13, 269

Zillman, D., 137, 162
Zipf's law, 264
Zucker, H. G., 95, 333
Züll, C., 262, 287, 306
Zwick, R., 247
ZyLAB software, 264, 304

About the Author

Klaus Krippendorff (Ph.D., communication, University of Illinois, Urbana, 1967) is Professor of Communication and Gregory Bateson Term Professor for Cybernetics, Language, and Culture at the University of Pennsylvania's Annenberg School for Communication. In addition to having published numerous articles in journals of communication, sociological methodology, cybernetics, and system theory, he is the author of *Information Theory: Structural Models for Qualitative Data* and *A Dictionary of Cybernetics,* editor of *Communication and Control in Society,* and coeditor of *The Analysis of Communication Content: Developments in Scientific Theories and Computer Techniques.* Aside from supporting various initiatives to develop content analysis techniques and continuing his work on reliability measurement, he is currently involved in four exciting projects: With epistemology in mind, he inquires into how language brings forth reality; as a critical scholar, he explores conditions of entrapment and possibilities of liberation; as a second-order cybernetician, he works with recursive conceptions of self and others in conversations—public and organizational; and as a designer, he attempts to move the meaning and human use of technological artifacts into the center of design considerations, causing a redesign of design.

The first edition of *Content Analysis,* published in 1980, has taught a generation of social scientists about the methodology of content analysis. This second edition represents a substantial revision of that volume, taking into account input from Dr. Krippendorff's students and colleagues as well as experiences gained in the pursuit of practical projects. It is expanded to include recent developments, especially in computer-aided text analysis, and continues the first edition's careful and critical examination of how texts and images can support inferences about phenomena not yet observed.